CONT

SHERRY BOECKH has mor[...] ing on travel for CBC Tele[...] for Canada's major newspa[...]

GEORGE BRYANT was for many years the travel editor of the *Toronto Star,* Canada's largest newspaper. Since 1949 he has covered places and events in every province and territory in Canada.

ASHOK CHANDWANI, with many years' experience as a senior writer and editor at Montreal daily newspapers, was the travel editor at *The Gazette* and is now senior editor. He also reviews restaurants and writes an occasional cooking column for the newspaper.

JEAN DANARD, a long-time author of travel articles for Canada's *Financial Post,* is now a freelance writer in Ontario.

NAN DROSDICK, a newspaper and magazine writer, editor, and photographer for more than 20 years, has covered Atlantic Canada since 1979.

CHARMAINE GAUDET, who was born on Prince Edward Island and now lives in Nova Scotia, has for 15 years written about her native province for magazines in the U.S. and Canada.

MAURA GIULIANI has spent the last 13 years in the Ottawa area working as a freelance writer and editor.

JOHN GODDARD is the author of *Last Stand of the Lubicon Cree,* a land-rights saga set in northern Alberta. He has travelled throughout the Canadian North as a reporter and photographer for the Canadian Press news agency, and is currently at work on a new book, *Cargo Cult,* chronicling a recent trip through Indonesia.

JOSEPH HOARE, a fifth-generation Canadian, has been a staff researcher and food editor at *Toronto Life* since 1978.

LAWRENCE JACKSON visited Newfoundland on a summer research job in 1971, and hasn't been able to tear himself away. He has published articles in most major Canadian magazines, and is currently a science writer with the Federal Department of Fisheries and Oceans.

MARY KELLY, a communications consultant in Montreal, is the author of a guide to the city as well as a contributor to several guidebooks about the province of Quebec.

HAZEL LOWE was the associate travel editor of *The Gazette* and travel editor at *The Montreal Star* and Southam News, a Canada-wide feature service. Based in Montreal, she is now a freelance writer.

GARRY MARCHANT, the winner of many international travel writing awards, writes travel articles for the *Asian Wall Street Journal Weekly,* as well as magazines in North America, Asia, and Europe.

MARNIE MITCHELL, a Vancouver native, has worked in tourism both in British Columbia and abroad. She specializes in travel writing, contributing to Canadian and international publications.

LEE SCHACTER, who has lived in Manitoba all her life, has written for the *Winnipeg Free Press* as well as various magazines.

DAVID E. SCOTT, a native of Quebec, was the travel editor of the *London Free Press* in Ontario for 15 years. Since then he has written *The Ontario Getaway Guidebook, A Taste of Ontario Country Inns,* and *Ontario for Free*.

DAVID STARRE, a communications consultant and part-time freelance travel writer and photographer, has written about Saskatchewan for many years.

COLLEEN WHITNEY THOMPSON, a freelance travel writer and native of New Brunswick, is the author of *New Brunswick Inside Out,* a recipient of the American Express Award for travel writing on Canada, and the travel columnist for the *Saint John Telegraph Journal*.

STEVE VEALE lives in Toronto and is a freelance contributor of travel articles to various newspapers and magazines. He is a member of the Society of American Travel Writers.

ROBERTA WALKER spent more than a decade exploring every corner of Alberta, during which time she founded *Real Travel,* a magazine for adventurous travellers. She now works as a broadcaster for the Canadian Broadcasting Corporation.

THE BERLITZ
TRAVELLERS GUIDES

THE BERLITZ TRAVELLERS GUIDE TO CANADA

Sixth Edition

ALAN TUCKER
General Editor

BERLITZ PUBLISHING COMPANY, INC.
New York, New York

BERLITZ PUBLISHING COMPANY LTD.
Oxford, England

THE BERLITZ TRAVELLERS GUIDE
TO CANADA
Sixth Edition

Published by Berlitz Publishing Company, Inc.
257 Park Avenue South, New York, New York 10010, U.S.A.

Distributed in the United States by
the Macmillan Publishing Group

Distributed elsewhere by Berlitz Publishing Company Ltd.
Berlitz House, Peterley Road, Horspath, Oxford OX4 2TX, England

ISBN 2-8315-1711-7
ISSN 1057-4778

Designed by Beth Tondreau Design
Cover design by Dan Miller Design
Cover photograph by Lanny Nagler
Maps by Bette Duke
Illustrations by Bill Russell
Copyedited by Patricia Fogarty
Edited by Mitchell Nauffts

Printed in the United States of America
1 3 5 7 9 10 8 6 4 2

THIS GUIDEBOOK

The Berlitz Travellers Guides are designed for experienced travellers in search of exceptional information that will enhance the enjoyment of the trips they take.

Where, for example, are the interesting, out-of-the-way, fun, charming, or romantic places to stay? The hotels described by our expert writers are some of the special places, in all price ranges except for the very lowest—not just the run-of-the-mill, heavily marketed places in advertised airline and travel-wholesaler packages.

We are *highly* selective in our choices of accommodations, concentrating on what our insider contributors think are the most interesting or rewarding places, and why. Readers who want to review exhaustive lists of hotel and resort choices as well, and who feel they need detailed descriptions of each property, can supplement the *Berlitz Travellers Guide* with tourism industry publications or one of the many directory-type guidebooks on the market.

We indicate the approximate price level of each accommodation in our description of it (no indication means it is moderate in local, relative terms), and at the end of every chapter we supply more detailed hotel rates as well as contact information so that you can get precise, up-to-the-minute rates and make reservations.

The Berlitz Travellers Guide to Canada highlights the more rewarding parts of the country so that you can quickly and efficiently home in on a good itinerary.

Of course, this guidebook does far more than just help you choose a hotel and plan your trip. *The Berlitz Travellers Guide to Canada* is designed for use *in* Canada. Our writers, each of whom is an experienced travel journalist who either lives in or regularly tours the city or region of Canada he or she covers, tell you what you really need to know, what you can't find out so easily on your own. They identify and describe the truly out-of-the-ordinary restaurants, shops, activities, and sights, and tell you the best way to "do" your destination.

Our writers are highly selective. They bring out the significance of the places they *do* cover, capturing the personality and the underlying cultural and historical resonances of a city or region—making clear its special appeal.

The Berlitz Travellers Guide to Canada is full of reliable information. We would like to know if you think we've left out some very special place. Although we make every effort to provide the most current information available about every destination described in this book, it is possible too that changes have occurred before you arrive. If you do have an experience that is contrary to what you were led to expect by our description, we would like to hear from you about it.

A guidebook is no substitute for common sense when you are travelling. Always pack the clothing, footwear, and other items appropriate for the destination, and make the necessary accommodation for such variables as altitude, weather, and local rules and customs. Of course, once on the scene you should avoid situations that are in your own judgment potentially hazardous, even if they have to do with something mentioned in a guidebook. Half the fun of travelling is exploring, but explore with care.

ALAN TUCKER
General Editor
Berlitz Travellers Guides

Root Publishing Company
350 West Hubbard Street
Suite 440
Chicago, Illinois 60610

CONTENTS

MAPS

THE
BERLITZ
TRAVELLERS
GUIDE
TO
CANADA

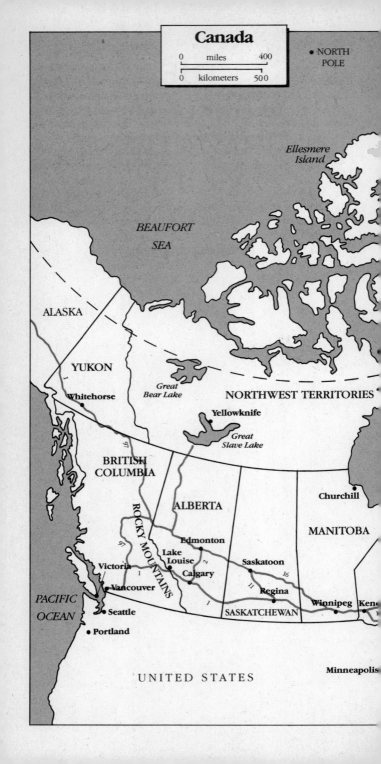

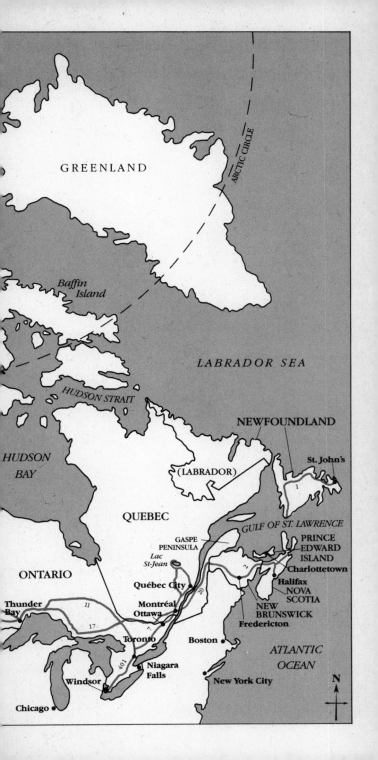

OVERVIEW

By George Bryant

George Bryant, for many years the travel editor of the Toronto Star, *Canada's largest newspaper, has been a reporter, columnist, correspondent, and editor since 1949. He has travelled more than one million miles for the* Star, *covering places and events in every province and territory of Canada, as well as other countries around the world.*

Canada has delights to please any visitor, including sophisticated cities with downtown cores alive with people and remarkably free of crime.

It has historic forts, a European settlement that predates Columbus by 500 years, and a province that offers not only a Continental flavor but the only walled city north of Mexico.

It has sports palaces, ski runs that reach the clouds, and fine hotels—not to mention more than 25 million inhabitants, the vast majority of whom exhibit a small-town friendliness even on the subways of the largest cities.

But when all that is said, the major lure of Canada remains the wonders of its endless outdoors, the magnificent prospects to be found from ocean to ocean, the mountains, waterfalls and fjords, glaciers, lakes, beaches, rock-bound coasts, and wildlife.

And that outdoors does seem endless, as visitors soon discover, because the land is not just huge, it's immense, sprawling nearly 5,000 miles across the top of the North American continent and encompassing all the land, water, and ice between Buffalo, New York, and the North Pole.

That's a mind-boggling 3,851,809 square miles, and it offers one problem along with a lot of bonuses: You have to know what you want to do and see as well as where to find it.

As to the bonuses, size is not an attraction in itself, but at these dimensions it does provide room for infinite variety. Canada can offer just about anything short of hula skirts and coral reefs a traveller could want—from a simulated journey through space to a walk on a glacier or close-up encounters with migrating polar bears.

A visitor can run television cameras or count radioactive ants at Toronto's Ontario Science Centre, stand behind the thundering curtain of water that is Niagara Falls, watch mountain rams battle at the edge of Alberta's Icefield Parkway, take afternoon tea in Victoria's Empress Hotel, experience the unforgettable dawn beauty of Lake Louise in the Canadian Rockies, explore the narrow alleys and superb restaurants of Quebec City's walled acres, go whale watching in the Gulf of St. Lawrence, or admire the genius of Alexander Graham Bell at a museum near his summer home in Baddeck, Nova Scotia.

And that's just barely scratching the surface. You can also visit the spot in Newfoundland where Vikings built a settlement long before William conquered England, or another place, near Wood Mountain, Saskatchewan, where 4,000 Sioux under Chief Sitting Bull, fresh from their annihilation of General George Armstrong Custer and his men, settled peacefully into camp at the behest of a few North West Mounted Police officers.

After that you can ski the longest runs in North America at Whistler/Blackcomb in British Columbia, look out over Lake Ontario from the deck of Toronto's CN Tower (the tallest free-standing building in the world), shop the miles of underground malls beneath Montreal's streets, and then head for Cape Breton to explore the magnificently restored Fortress of Louisbourg (which cost more to rebuild than France's Louis XV spent on it in the first place, although he grumbled at the time that he was paying so much he awoke every morning expecting to see its towers rising over the western horizon).

And still that is a mere beginning, just a sampling. There are ten provinces standing shoulder to shoulder just above the U.S. border, and north of them two vast regions: the Yukon and the Northwest Territories. (The latter comprises fully a third of the country, although it is now in the process of being divided in two, with the eastern two-thirds of the region, called Nunavut, about to become a new territory governed by its 18,000 Inuit—once called Eskimo—inhabitants.) Every one of them has its own attractions, man-made as well as natural.

As a result there is no one tourist route that everybody follows, no London or Paris where most visitors land. Rather, there are several major gateways: Montreal, Toronto, or Vancouver on the main tourist routes, particularly for visitors from overseas; St. John's (Newfoundland), Saint John (New Brunswick), Halifax, Quebec City, Ottawa, Winnipeg, Edmonton, or Calgary on the secondary routes. The one you use will depend on which Canada you want to visit. (We'll help you with that choice a bit further on.)

Then there are the scores of highway crossing points along the U.S.–Canada border from Maine to Washington, including a busy bridge at Niagara Falls, and ferries and passenger ships on both sides of the continent. So there's no lack of entry points or transport once you've made your decision to visit.

Canadians are friendly, if a little reserved and a bit shy, a sober inheritance from the Scottish Presbyterians who flocked to the land when the Highland clearances took place in the last century. They're fun-loving enough but not as exuberant as citizens south of the border or, indeed, in the province of Quebec, where the tongue is French and the residents add a Gallic flair and color to everything they do.

That reserve sometimes makes English-speaking Canadians slow in proffering help or advice, but if asked they'll overwhelm you with information and/or aid. And mostly—except for Newfoundland's Irish Outport lilt and a bit of a burr in the Ottawa Valley—in the same accent, a neutral sort of North American English with the Scottish heritage coming through on words such as "out" and "about," which have an "oot" and "aboot" sound to English-speaking visitors, particularly those from the United States.

Why so few regional accents? Because the railway moved west with settlers in the last century and there was constant passenger traffic back and forth between the new settlements and the old. The result: No isolated pockets of residents to develop regional speech patterns.

Though these English-speaking Canadians may look and sound much like Americans, they are different. They shared a common history with their neighbors to the south up to the American Revolution, but then everything turned upside down, as a look at any Canadian history book will reveal. U.S. Revolutionary heroes are villains or traitors (Benedict Arnold was one who came to his senses), and the War of 1812 was a naked attempt by the U.S. to swallow the infant colony to the north—all of which gives Canadians a somewhat different perspective on the world.

In the East, from the Maritimes (Prince Edward Island, Nova Scotia, and New Brunswick) through to Ontario, the

United Empire Loyalists (the Canadian name for the Tory landowners, doctors, lawyers, businessmen, and farmers who fled the American Revolution) are revered as founding fathers, with annual celebrations to honor their memory. U.S. visitors are welcomed, of course.

In the West there was one short war of rebellion against the Crown but no cowboy-and-Indian shootouts, no gun-slingers or gunfights at the O.K. Corral. It was a West that wasn't so wild, a West where several thousand Sioux would peacefully obey one Mountie who spoke for the Queen.

The measure of this West lies in a little graveyard near the old headquarters of the North West Mounted Police at Fort Walsh, in southern Saskatchewan. In this northern Boot Hill there are more than a dozen gravestones, but only one records the death of a Mountie by violence. Constable Marmaduke Graeburn, age 19, whose very name proclaims that this was not Dodge City or Tombstone, was mysteriously shot from ambush on November 17, 1879. All the others died of natural causes.

So Canadians retain more of the British heritage than their continental neighbors, in speech, in folklore, in atti-tude, even in humor. Quebec is an exception, of course, and Canadians in Newfoundland, which was a British colony until 1949, have that Irish lilt in their speech and ways.

Canada for Travellers

Newfoundland

Newfoundland is the most easterly province and a good place to start a quick cross-country rundown of major sights and points of interest. It is a place of cliffs, pounding seas, fisher-men, wilderness parks, and little ports with such ingenuous names as Joe Batt's Arm, Bumble Bee Bight, Witless Bay, Heart's Content, Sap's Arm, and Dating Cove; a place where the speech, the shanties, and the songs have a wonderfully vital humor—if you can decipher the accent. As well it's the place where the Vikings landed 1,000 years ago and planted a colony, recording the event in their sagas. They were later driven away by hostile Indians, but the remains of their settle-ment—six low, sodded burrows, a smithy, cooking pits, and, of course, a sauna—have been found at L'Anse-aux-Meadows at the north end of the island. The spot, low-lying by a gray sea, is now a World Heritage Site; the Vikings' Spartan way of life can be studied, without envy, at a re-created village nearby.

Nova Scotia

Southwest of the island, across Cabot Strait, lies Nova Scotia, where it's a good idea to leave extra time for the Fortress of Louisbourg and the Bell Museum. At the former, costumed attendants whisk you back to 1774, a hard year to leave; at the latter, there are so many examples of Alexander Graham Bell's genius, in fact or photograph, that a day can pass like a dream.

Drive the Cabot Trail, too, while you're on Cape Breton, and try the Lighthouse Route heading south from Halifax along a coast that's furrowed and rocky. Don't forget Peggy's Cove, a postcard-perfect bay that's now one of the most photographed spots on earth—but still worth a look.

New Brunswick and Prince Edward Island

Tories fleeing the Revolution helped build Nova Scotia— one year three-quarters of all the Harvard graduates in the world wintered there—but it's across the Bay of Fundy to the northwest in New Brunswick that United Empire Loyalist Days are celebrated in a big way, with costumes, speeches, parades, and re-created military units of the time.

The Loyalists weren't the only ones to find refuge in New Brunswick. So, too, did the Acadians, settlers of French heritage who had been expelled from Nova Scotia by the British. Although many made their way south to become the Cajuns of Louisiana, others sank new roots along the Bay of Chaleur in what is now New Brunswick. There, just a few hundred miles from their original homes, they flourished as fishermen and farmers—a heritage visitors to this region of sand dunes and ceaseless winds, of stories and songs delivered in French accents, will soon discover.

Prince Edward Island, just north of New Brunswick across Northumberland Strait, is Canada's smallest province, a summertime playground known for its lobsters and wide, warm-water beaches, and also the onetime home of Lucy Maud Montgomery, author of *Anne of Green Gables.*

Quebec City and Montreal

Northwest across the Gulf of St. Lawrence lies Quebec City, where the city within the walls dates back to 1608 and Le Château Frontenac Hotel towers like a turreted castle above the St. Lawrence River. If you can't stay at the Château, visit it for its magnificent view and be sure to wander the Old Town, with its fine restaurants, strolling minstrels, and joie de vivre. There's nothing artificial about the Gallic flavor in the province. Despite more than two centuries of political union with English Canadians, French culture in Quebec is vibrant and strong, so much so, in fact, that debates about separating from the rest of Canada are an ongoing feature of life here. But for visitors, the French fact simply adds a Latin flavor to everything you do.

West of the city the resorts of the **Laurentians**, those old round-topped mountains, are full of song and après-ski parties in winter and nature lovers in summer. And in Montreal, a city second only to Paris in French speakers, there's an underground city to roam, a rapids to run, some of the world's best food, and a major-league baseball team, the Expos, to cheer. Or boo.

Ottawa, Ontario, and Toronto
Canada's capital, Ottawa, at the juncture of the Ottawa River and the Rideau Canal, has a small-town feel, a Parliament to observe, museums to visit, and in winter a canal skating rink that stretches for miles.

In Ontario, there's Niagara Falls—where there *is* some schlock, but mostly majesty—and one of the world's unique trains, the Polar Bear Express (a misleading name—it shows riders nary a bear), which travels from Cochrane north through the wilderness to Indian country at Moosonee and Moose Factory on James Bay. Another train trip known for its scenery runs from Sault Ste. Marie through the north woods to Agawa Canyon, north of Lake Huron and well away from the works of man.

Toronto, like Montreal, has superb restaurants and a major-league baseball team, the Blue Jays, who play under a SkyDome that rolls open on sunny days. Visit in summer and Toronto's Ontario Place offers a complex of theaters, pubs, and entertainment built out over the waters of Lake Ontario; ferries chug off to the parks on the Toronto islands, and the Harbourfront beckons with folk singers, poets, dancers, and shows of every sort.

Manitoba and Saskatchewan
To the west is Manitoba, where you can take a train that really does offer glimpses of polar bears. Operated by VIA Rail, the national passenger service, it runs from Winnipeg to Churchill, where the great white giants lumber out onto the pack ice of Hudson Bay every autumn. Farther west is Saskatchewan, a place of wheat and endless sky, of Fort Walsh and Wood Mountain Post and the Sioux encampment, and of the battlefields of the short-lived North West Rebellion.

Alberta

West again is Alberta, where two of the continent's most magnificent wilderness parks, Banff and Jasper, are connected by the Icefields Parkway, 230 km (143 miles) of breathtaking beauty.

Icefields Parkway snakes through the main range of the Rockies, with mountains, glaciers, and waterfalls on every side. Each turn of the wheel brings new vistas, changing always as the light changes, so that no scene is ever the same from minute to minute. And, since it runs through national parks, on any trip visitors may see bear, elk, wolf, moose, deer, or mountain sheep (males often use its level pavement as jousting fields).

There are campsites, lodges, and resorts in and around the parks, and the Château Lake Louise, in Banff, is a good place to stay overnight—if only to see the lake, backed by Victoria Glacier, in the mist of a summer dawn. Then drive the parkway, staying overnight in Jasper and stopping on the return trip to walk on the Athabasca Glacier, part of the enormous Columbia Icefield that parallels the road, the largest sheet of glacial ice in North America south of the Arctic.

This is a province, too, of badlands and dinosaur bones, and is a good place to learn about horses or try trail riding at spots like the Homeplace Ranch in Priddis, nestled among the foothills of the Rockies.

British Columbia and Vancouver

You can take a train from Jasper to Vancouver and roll through the passes as the mountains turn dark against a sunset sky, then rise at dawn to see the bulk of the coastal ranges in British Columbia—a memorable experience. B.C. is striking not just for the drama of a mountain dawn but for its far-flung delights: range after range of snow-capped peaks, wild rivers and timbered valleys, rugged coasts and green islands. Few visit British Columbia and fail to fall under its spell.

Vancouver, between the mountains and the sea, boasts one of the world's most beautiful settings, while the provincial capital, **Victoria**, on Vancouver Island, is the most British of North American cities, in climate, gardens, accent, and attitude. Most visitors stroll Vancouver's Stanley Park and ride the ferries to the Gulf Islands; tour Victoria's outstanding Provincial Museum with its evocative sounds and smells; admire the bright blooms of Butchart Gardens; and take Victorian tea in the Empress Hotel lobby, where time seems to stand still.

North of Victoria is Pacific Rim Park, where waves from

the Pacific beat on a long, lonely shore and the Trans-Canada Highway ends in an appropriately wild setting.

North again along the mainland coast behind the barrier islands lies the Inside Passage, a spectacular stretch of fjords and glaciers. In the interior are ghost towns and mining camps, relics of the days when gold rather than scenery was the lure.

The Yukon and Northwest Territories

It was the lure, too, on the Trail of '98, when the world flocked to the Yukon Territory "clean mad for that muck called gold." This and more can be learned in Whitehorse and Dawson, where you can pan for nuggets, hear the poems of Robert Service read, and watch the modern version of his dance-hall girls kick up their heels again.

There's a road to the Arctic Ocean now, the Dempster Highway, which runs from the Yukon through the Northwest Territories to Tuktoyaktuk, an Inuit settlement on the Beaufort Sea. But most visitors to the Territories, which for the moment encompass all of northern Canada east of the Yukon, fly in to remote lakes or camps for fishing or nature studies. Or they visit Wood Buffalo Park, which straddles the border of Alberta and the Territories far to the south of Tuktoyaktuk.

These are only a few of the pleasures to be discovered in Canada. Details on them as well as hundreds of others can be found in the following chapters.

USEFUL FACTS

When to Go

Unless they choose to ski the Rockies of Alberta or the Laurentians in Quebec, most visitors prefer the warm weather between May and Canadian Thanksgiving, the second weekend of October. Summer weather can range from a muggy 90° F (about 30° C) in Toronto to a dry prairie heat of 80° F (about 25° C). It is also the season when sandy beaches bloom in the mild Maritimes and the sun shines for about 20 hours a day in the briefly balmy Northwest Territories.

Winter temperatures, on the other hand, often descend to a chilly 15° F (about −10° C) in windy Montreal or a mind-numbing −20° F (about −30° C) in northern Saskatchewan. Best to plan a summer visit.

Entry Documents and Provisions

This is the easiest border crossing a U.S. citizen can make; not even a passport is required (though it doesn't hurt to have one). All that's needed is some proof of citizenship, such as a birth certificate or Social Security card. And with a few standard questions (place of birth, current residence, purpose of visit, length of stay) you'll be sent on your way. Visitors from the United Kingdom or any of its dependent territories (from Hong Kong to the Turks and Caicos islands) do not need visas to enter Canada, though they should have valid passports. (The same applies if you are arriving from Australia.)

Hunters may bring "long guns" (defined as hunting rifles or shotguns) into the country without a gun permit, although they must have a valid hunting license.

Motorists entering Canada should render all radar-detecting devices inoperative and note that some provinces (e.g., Ontario) do not allow studded tires; other provinces permit them only in winter.

Household pets may be imported from the U.S. and parts of Europe (some restrictions apply for certain countries; check with Customs in advance), provided each animal has a veterinarian's certificate of vaccination against rabies. More exotic animals, such as birds from South America, are subject to quarantine or may even be refused an entry permit. Again, check in advance with Customs.

Getting There

By Plane. Canada is a huge country, second only to Russia in landmass, although the plethora of flights to its major air terminals and the daily connections provided by its intracity carriers (there are hourly flights between Toronto and Ottawa, for example) somehow make it seem manageable. International terminals with flights from both the U.S. and Europe arriving daily are found in the following major cities: Vancouver, Calgary, Edmonton, Winnipeg, Toronto, Montreal, and Halifax.

Canadian carriers servicing the international market include Air Canada, the government-operated airline, and the ever-growing Canadian Airlines International, which purchased the country's third major airline, Wardair, a few years back.

The major airline carriers offer additional service from Europe during the busy months; most have daily (often nonstop) flights from various terminals in the U.K. and Europe. There are countless charter flights connecting the two continents as well. For instance, Air Canada has daily flights (direct and nonstop) from Heathrow, while Canadian Airlines provides similar service from Gatwick. British Airways flies daily from Heathrow, while Lufthansa Airlines flies out of its main hub in Frankfurt and the Dutch KLM uses Schipol Airport in Amsterdam. These flights all arrive in Toronto and Montreal; connections to other parts of the country are made through those two Canadian entry points.

For those who wish to visit Vancouver from Down Under, Qantas and Canadian share the route, with Qantas taking travellers to Honolulu and Canadian picking up the service from there. Lufthansa flies direct to Toronto from Australia, making the mandatory stop at Frankfurt.

As for flying to Canada from the United States, there is no lack of available carriers and scheduled flights. For example, with the combination of carriers (including Air Canada, American, and Continental) using both La Guardia and Newark airports in the New York City area, there are dozens of daily flights to Toronto and Montreal. Flight time to either city is about an hour, enough time to sip an airline libation and orient yourself by reading a Canadian newspaper. Direct Chicago–Toronto service is provided by Air Canada, United, and American from O'Hare; American flies to Toronto from Dallas/Fort Worth; and Air Canada, United, American, and USAir fly nonstop from the West Coast. Nonstop service from the West Coast to Vancouver is offered by Air Canada, Canadian, United, and Delta, with connecting flights to the western cities of Calgary and Edmonton.

Travel from the United States to various parts of Canada may require some changes and advance booking plans; for instance, there is no direct service from New York to Vancouver or Miami to Vancouver. Such trips necessitate changes in major gateway cities such as Toronto or Chicago. When you decide what part of the country you want to visit, check with your favorite airline as to its routes and schedules.

By Car. Again, this is the easiest border crossing for an American citizen (see Entry Documents and Provisions), especially along busy corridors such as Detroit–Windsor or Niagara Falls, U.S.A. and Canada, where citizens of both nationalities make daily crossings for their jobs, an afternoon of shopping, or perhaps an evening meal in a foreign country.

Normally, a verbal declaration of citizenship, place of residence, and proposed length of stay is all that's required to drive across the U.S.–Canada border. The question-and-answer session may take less than a minute, but the wait—especially with all the camper-trailers and mobile homes on the road during the summer vacation season—can be well over an hour at the more popular entry points.

Motorists on the East Coast can enter the **Maritime provinces** only through two border points on the Maine–New

Brunswick border: via Highway 95 from Houlton or via Highway 3 from Calais. From New Brunswick, on the other side of the border, you can follow the Trans-Canada Highway into Nova Scotia and onto Cape Breton Island, although to reach Prince Edward Island or Newfoundland you'll have to take a car ferry. Check with local tourist information offices for schedules and prices (see below).

On the West Coast, you can reach **Victoria**, on Vancouver Island, by ferry (passengers only) daily from Seattle. Following the approximately 2½-hour ferry ride along the coast, all passengers pass through the standard customs check prior to leaving the ship. Ferries (passengers and vehicles) also run daily between Victoria and Port Angeles, Washington.

A slower but less expensive option (U.S. $28, one way) is the "shuttle bus" from the Seattle–Tacoma airport to downtown Vancouver, with stops in downtown Seattle, the Bellingham airport, the international border, and Vancouver International Airport along the way. Allow 3 to 4 hours for the trip.

Road signs and speed limits are posted in kilometers instead of miles. (One hundred kilometers is approximately 62 miles; 300 km is a mere 186 miles. Gasoline and oil are measured in liters; one U.S. gallon is 3.78 liters.)

Seat belts for drivers and passengers are compulsory in most provinces (except Alberta, Prince Edward Island, the Yukon, and the Northwest Territories), as is proof of automobile liability insurance. (Note: Visiting motorists are advised to obtain a Canadian Non-Resident Inter-Provincial Motor Vehicle Liability Card, available through U.S. insurance companies.) The Canadian Automobile Association (CAA) will provide full service to any AAA member as well as members of any other affiliated automobile group.

A final caution: Most Montreal drivers seem to have taken the New York cab drivers' training course.

Car Rentals

It is a relatively simple matter to arrange a car rental in Canada; a visitor must produce identification (listing permanent address) and a valid driver's license (or international license), and usually must be over 25 years of age.

Rates are comparable to those advertised in the U.S., with most companies offering special weekend rates or weekly discounts; you can leave the vehicle at a corresponding office in another province, although there'll probably be a drop-off charge applied to your bill. Rental agencies can be found in major cities and airports, with the big-name firms—Avis, Budget, Hertz—all operating in Canada.

You can also request information from Tilden Inter-Rent, the largest Canadian-owned agency (its U.S. affiliate is National Inter-Rent): Tilden Inter-Rent, P.O. Box 114, Toronto, Ontario L5P 1A2; Tel: (416) 676-2647; in the U.S. and Canada, Tel: (800) 227-7368.

Getting Around

By Plane. Airplanes are used almost like taxicabs by most professional people in Canada; hourly flights between major political and business centers within the Toronto–Ottawa–Montreal–Quebec City power corridor are the rule rather than the exception. In addition, Air Canada and Canadian Airlines International offer daily flights linking the country's major cities.

Because Canada is so vast, there are numerous regional "feeder" airline companies connecting urban centers to the far reaches of individual provinces. A good many are affiliated with Air Canada or Canadian. When in doubt, contact either carrier for a list of options and up-to-date information on these smaller regional airlines.

By Rail. Crossing the country from Halifax to Vancouver takes about four days (with an overnight in Montreal) and costs approximately CDN $500. From Toronto to Vancouver it's a mere $425. These are base prices, of course, and a sleeper or roomette (well advised for this long trip) will cost more. Prices will vary depending on advance purchase, age (i.e., youth, regular, senior citizen), family or group rates, and so on.

With the termination of passenger service by both the CP and CN (Canadian Pacific and Canadian National, respectively), VIA Rail is now the only passenger line in Canada. As with air service, however, there are regional feeder rail lines that will take you off the beaten path and into the far reaches of every province (except for the Yukon and Northwest Territories, which do not have rail service). A coast-to-coast rail adventure on VIA, usually booked solid all summer, will include amenities from white-glove, four-fork dining (reservations must be booked in advance) to fast-food snack bars, parlor cars, smoking lounges, drawing rooms, and private roomettes.

VIA will also provide "on and off" privileges for those who wish to get off the train and spend a day or two in various spots along the line—say, an overnight in Edmonton combined with a day or two exploring the wilderness glories of Jasper National Park. If you want to experience the vastness of Canada this is one of the most cost-effective and pleasurable ways of stretching your travel dollar. For complete information on prices and rail timetables, check with a travel agent or your local railroad (i.e., Amtrak, British Rail, etc.), or write directly to VIA Rail Canada, 2 Place Ville Marie, Lobby Level, Montreal, Quebec H3B 2G6; Tel: (800) 561-3949 or (514) 871-6000.

Telephones

A local telephone call can last a minute or an hour; the rate will be the same. Only long-distance connections are subject to per-minute charges. You can dial direct to any point in the U.S., Europe, or most areas of the world. And if they are not on strike, the operators of Bell Canada will be happy to assist with difficult overseas connections.

To call Canada from the U.S., just dial the long distance "1," then the area code and telephone number. From overseas, dial the overseas operator code, then the country code, "1," area code, and number. (See the Accommodations Reference list at the end of each chapter for local area codes.)

Local Time

Canada uses time zones similar to those in the United States, but claims six different regions from coast to coast as opposed to the three used by its neighbor to the south; when it is noon in Vancouver (or Los Angeles), it is, respectively, 1:00 P.M. in Calgary; 2:00 P.M. in Winnipeg; 3:00 P.M. in Montreal and Toronto; 4:00 P.M. in Halifax—and 4:30 P.M. in Newfoundland (one of the mysteries of the time zone system). Unfortunately, the time zones don't follow neat provincial boundaries. With the aforementioned exception of Newfoundland, the Maritimes—Labrador, Prince Edward Island, Nova Scotia, and New Brunswick—are on Atlantic standard time, 1 hour ahead of the eastern standard time of New York and Toronto (and so only 4 hours behind Greenwich mean time).

Most of Canada uses daylight saving time (DST) from the end of April to the end of October, gaining an hour of summer's sun.

Electric Current

The same electrical system is used in Canada as in the United States: 110 volts, 60 amps AC. There is no need for adapters or converters for any electrical appliance brought into the country from the U.S.

Currency and Taxes

The Canadian dollar, including the relatively new $1 coin known affectionately as the "loonie" (so named after the

loon imprinted on it), is the legal tender. American money is
accepted in many areas and by many establishments, but it is
best to convert your U.S. dollars in order to get the full rate
of exchange, which fluctuates daily. In the past few years the
U.S. dollar has been valued somewhere between 10 and 20
percent higher than its Canadian counterpart. As of May 1989
the Canadian Mint ceased printing the green $1 bills.

Many provincial governments claim a percentage of the
price of an item, restaurant bill, or hotel room, although the
amount varies from province to province; for instance, in
Ontario this sales tax is 8 percent, whereas Alberta doesn't
collect one at all.

In its infinite wisdom, the ruling Conservative government now levies a 7 percent federal tax. Officially called the
GST, or Goods and Services Tax, it is tacked onto everything
from fast-food meals to hotel bills, from chewing gum to
prescription drugs. This means that in a province such as
Ontario residents and visitors alike will pay 15 percent on
top of the advertised price.

In certain circumstances (e.g., for hotel bills), foreign
visitors may reclaim the GST portion of their expenses after
returning home. To do so, keep all your receipts and be sure
to pick up the Visitors GST Claim Form when leaving the
country (available at any border crossing).

Business Hours

The general business day in Canada parallels the standard
nine-to-five, Monday-through-Friday routine of the United
States. Banks are open from 10:00 A.M. to 3:00 P.M., although
some branches of major banks and various trust companies
have been extending their hours on both ends in an effort to
attract customers.

Most department stores and shopping malls are open
until 6:00 P.M., with extended hours—usually until 10:00
P.M.—on Thursdays and Fridays; convenience outlets and
drugstores are often open until 11:00 P.M., with many in
major centers (as well as some supermarkets) open around
the clock.

For years Canada maintained its famous "blue laws,"
which shut everything down for the Sabbath. After frequent
constitutional challenges and widespread ignoring of the
laws in populated tourist areas, however, the legal taboos on
Sunday shopping were finally relaxed in the spring of 1992.

Holidays

Certain holidays are celebrated by the entire country (i.e.,
Christmas, New Year's), while some occasions (such as St-

Jean-Baptiste Day in Quebec) affect only an individual province. If travelling in the fall season, remember that Canada sets aside the second weekend in October (with the Monday as the official holiday) for its annual Thanksgiving turkey feast.

The following holidays are observed throughout the country (banks, schools, government buildings, and most shops will likely be closed): New Year's Day; Good Friday; Easter Monday; Victoria Day (a "movable" holiday to mark Queen Victoria's birthday, always celebrated on the Monday preceding May 25, to make a three-day weekend); Canada Day, the Canadian equivalent of Independence Day (always July 1); Labour Day (the first Monday of September); Thanksgiving (the second Monday of October); Remembrance Day (November 11; based initially on the armistice of 1918—signed on the eleventh day of the eleventh month at 11:00 A.M.—it now commemorates the sacrifices made in both world wars as well as Korea); Christmas; and Boxing Day (December 26; shopping sales usually take place on December 27).

Provincial holidays include British Columbia Day, which falls on the first Monday of August. Manitoba, New Brunswick, the Northwest Territories, and Ontario all celebrate a similar Civic Holiday, which also falls on the first Monday of August. Quebec has its separate St-Jean-Baptiste festivities every June 24, while both the Yukon and Newfoundland romp through a Discovery Day celebration: the third Monday of August for the Yukon and the second to last Monday in June for the Atlantic island province.

Further Information

Tourist offices for the individual provinces and territories can provide specific information regarding each region— the sights and sites, various types of accommodations and dining establishments, tourism literature—as well as answer your practical questions.

British Columbia: Tourism B.C.
   Parliament Buildings
   Victoria, B.C. V8V 1X4
   Tel: (604) 685-0032 or (800) 663-6000 from the U.S. and elsewhere in Canada; Fax: (604) 660-3383

Alberta: Alberta Tourism
   City Centre, 10155 102 Street
   Edmonton, Alberta T5J 4L6
   Tel: (403) 427-4321 or (800) 661-8888 from the U.S. and elsewhere in Canada; Fax: (403) 427-0867

Saskatchewan: Tourism Saskatchewan
1919 Saskatchewan Drive
Regina, Saskatchewan S4P 3V7
Tel: (306) 787-2300 or (800) 667-7191 from the U.S. and
elsewhere in Canada; Fax: (306) 787-2909

Manitoba: Travel Manitoba
Department 20, 7th floor
155 Carlton Street
Winnipeg, Manitoba R3C 3H8
Tel: (204) 945-3777 or (800) 665-0040 from the U.S. and
elsewhere in Canada; Fax: (204) 945-2302

Ontario: Ontario Travel
Queen's Park
Toronto, Ontario M7A 2R9
Tel: (416) 314-0944 or (800) ONTARIO from the U.S. and
elsewhere in Canada; Fax: (416) 314-7372

Quebec: Tourisme Québec
P.O. Box 20000
Quebec City, Quebec G1K 7X2
Tel: (514) 873-2015 or (800) 363-7777 from the U.S. (ex-
cept Alaska) and elsewhere in Canada

Nova Scotia: Department of Tourism and Culture
P.O. Box 456
Halifax, Nova Scotia B3J 2R5
Tel: (902) 424-5000 or (800) 341-6096 from the U.S., (800)
565-0000 from elsewhere in Canada

New Brunswick: Tourism New Brunswick
Box 12345
Fredericton, New Brunswick E3B 5C3
Tel: (506) 453-2444 or (800) 561-0123 from the U.S. and
elsewhere in Canada; Fax: (506) 453-5370

Prince Edward Island: Department of Tourism, Parks and
Recreation
Visitors Services Division
P.O. Box 940
Charlottetown, P.E.I. C1A 7M5
Tel: (902) 368-4444 or (800) 565-0267 from the U.S. and
elsewhere in Canada

Newfoundland and Labrador: Department of Tourism and
Culture
P.O. Box 2730
St. John's, Newfoundland A1B 4K2
Tel: (709) 729-2830 or (800) 563-6353 from the U.S. and
elsewhere in Canada; Fax: (709) 729-0474

Yukon: Tourism Yukon
P.O. Box 2703

Whitehorse, Yukon Y1A 2C6
Tel: (403) 667-5340; Fax: (403) 667-2634
Northwest Territories: Northwest Territories Tourism
P.O. Box 1320
Yellowknife, N.W.T. X1A 2L9
Tel: (403) 873-7200 or (800) 661-0788 from the U.S. and
elsewhere in Canada; Fax: (403) 920-2756

—*Steve Veale*

BIBLIOGRAPHY

One of the best sources of travel books in Canada is Open
Air Books & Maps, 25 Toronto Street, Toronto, Ont. M5C 2R1;
Tel: (416) 363-0719.

General

DAVID J. BERCUSON AND J. L. GRANATSTEIN, *Collins Dictionary
of Canadian History, 1867 to the Present.* Among other
items, it gives some background leading to the Canada-U.S.
Free Trade Agreement.

PIERRE BERTON, *The National Dream* (covering 1871–1881)
and *The Last Spike* (1881–1885). A two-volume history of the
planning and building of the transcontinental railways and
the people and adventures involved.

MICHAEL BLISS, *Years of Change: 1967–1985.* A provocative
review of recent Canadian history, with questions for discus-
sion. Includes the Constitution Act of 1982. Century of Canada series.

HUGH BRODY, *The Living Arctic.* An experienced northern
anthropologist talks about the Inuit and their dependence
on the land.

STEPHEN BROOK, *Maple Leaf Rag: Travels Across Canada.*
British writer Brook is seldom off base in this light and often
humorous look at the Canadian countryside and the people
who live there.

CRAIG BROWN, ED., *Illustrated History of Canada.* Six historians and geographers tell how Canada and its people developed.

BILL COO, *Scenic Rail Guide to Western Canada* and *Scenic
Rail Guide to Central & Atlantic Canada.* Mile-by-mile
guides to 12,600 miles of track and road from a 30-year rail
veteran.

ROBERTSON DAVIES, *The Lyre of Orpheus*. Third in a trilogy (*The Rebel Angels, What's Bred in the Bone*) in which Davies, a distinguished writer, essayist, and dramatist, depicts some of the geography of Canadian society over the past century.

OLIVE PATRICIA DICKASON, *Canada's First Nations*. A comprehensive, detailed account of Canada's aboriginal people, from prehistoric times to the present. It includes an excellent bibliography and index, as well as 100 pages of notes—in other words, everything you ever wanted to know about the subject and then some.

RICHARD GWYN, *The Northern Magus*. The best of the many biographies about Pierre Elliott Trudeau.

PETER GZOWSKI, *The New Morningside Papers*. Highlights from and comments on Gzowski's weekday-morning national radio program revealing the lives and loves of everyday Canadians.

————, *The Latest Morningside Papers*. The third in the series, featuring nostalgic, vividly written letters from listeners past and present.

J. RUSSELL HARPER, *Painting in Canada: A History*. A survey of major artists only, starting with Abbé Pommier in 1663 and ending in the 1980s.

COLE HARRIS, ED., AND GEOFFREY MATTHEWS, CARTOGRAPHER, *Historical Atlas of Canada*. The story of Canada from the ice sheets of 18,000 B.C. to the 18th century, told in graphs, pictures, maps, and essays.

DONALD KERR AND DERYCK HOLDSWORTH, EDS., *Historical Atlas of Canada, Vol. III*. Canadian history from 1891 to 1961, in words and pictures. Volume II, on the 19th century, is still to come.

A. R. M. LOWER, *Colony to Nation: A History of Canada*. An easy-to-read survey through the end of World War II. Lower explains why things happened, with minimal attention to dates and details.

KENNETH MCNAUGHT, *The Penguin History of Canada*. A general history of Canada, revised and updated in 1988.

ANDREW MALCOLM, *The Canadians*. An American who lived in Canada analyzes the differences between the two cultures.

ALBERT AND THERA MORITZ, *Oxford Illustrated Literary Guide to Canada*. Biographies of contemporary writers.

PETER NEWMAN, *The Canadian Establishment* and *The Acquisitors*. The old-boy network and uses and abuses of power by the people who, in the author's opinion, run the country.

PETER NEWMAN, ED., *Debrett's Illustrated Guide to the Canadian Establishment*. Portraits in text and photographs of the country's trendsetters in business and the arts; includes 21 dynasties and more than 600 individuals.

PENNY PETRONE, ED., *First People, First Voices*. A collection of aboriginal writing—speeches, letters, diaries, prayers, songs, and stories—from the 1630s to the 1980s.

Quick Canadian Facts. A pocket encyclopedia with answers to 1,000 questions.

The West
MARK ABLEY, *Beyond Forget: Rediscovering the Prairies*. A wonderful mixture of travelogue, oral history, politics, and environmental study.

DORIS ANDERSEN, *Evergreen Islands*. History of the islands between the north end of Vancouver Island and the mainland.

LAURA BEATRICE BERTON, *I Married the Klondike*. A Toronto schoolteacher's life in the Yukon, 1907–1932.

PIERRE BERTON, *Klondike: The Last Great Gold Rush*. Gripping history, rich in human details, of the 1897–1898 Klondike frenzy.

————, *The Promised Land: Settling the West, 1896–1914*. History written in Berton's usual provocative and dramatic style.

JAMES R. BUTLER AND ROLAND R. MAW, *Fishing: Canada's Mountain Parks*. Where and what to fish. One in a series on outdoor pleasures by Lone Pine Publishing.

MARJORIE WILKINS CAMPBELL, *The Saskatchewan*. History of the area drained by the great river that rises in the Rockies and empties into Manitoba's Lake Winnipeg.

BEN GADD, *Handbook of the Canadian Rockies*. Covers geology, history, recreation, plants, animals, even butterflies in encyclopedic detail.

RENIE GROSS, *Dinosaur Country*. Text and many illustrations on the Alberta Badlands, where dinosaurs used to roam.

RICK KUNELIUS, *Animals of the Rockies*. A 71-page pamphlet with text and illustrations.

CHAUNCEY LOOMIS, *Weird and Tragic Shores*. One of the best books on the search for the Northwest Passage.

ERNIE LYALL, *An Arctic Man*. Lyall recounts his 65 years practicing the Inuit way of life.

J. W. GRANT MACEWAN, *West to the Sea*. A history of western Canada from prehistoric man to postwar industry.

BRUCE OBEE, *The Gulf Islands*. A guide to, more than a history of, the better-known islands off the south end of Vancouver Island.

GREY OWL, *Men of the Last Frontier* (1931) and *Tales of an Empty Cabin* (1936). The real name of this Englishman was Archie Belaney. As Grey Owl he adopted Indian customs, worked as a trapper in northern Saskatchewan, and wrote about his Indian friends and animal companions, becoming one of Canada's first conservationists in the process.

ARCHIE SATTERFIELD, *Chilkoot Pass*. A history of the mountain pass made famous by the Klondike goldseekers.

ROBERT SERVICE, *Songs of a Sourdough* and *The Best of Robert Service*. Includes Service's best-known Klondike poem, "The Cremation of Sam McGee."

Ontario

ERIC ARTHUR, *Toronto: No Mean City*. A guide to Toronto's architectural history and architects.

MARGARET ATWOOD, *Cat's Eye*. Mainly set in Toronto, a nostalgic yet incisive look at the maturing of a woman artist. Atwood at her best.

JAMES BARRY, *Georgian Bay*. A narrative-style history with plenty of anecdotes.

ROBERT BOTHWELL, *A Short History of Ontario*. As the title says, a quick read.

BARBARANNE BOYER, *Muskoka's Grand Hotels*. Text and illustrations on dozens of past and present properties.

WILLIAM S. FOX, *The Bruce Beckons: Story of Lake Huron's Great Peninsula*. Interweaving fact and folklore, the author tells why the little-known Bruce is such a special place.

EDWIN C. GUILLET, *Early Life in Upper Canada*. Telling details bring the past vividly to life.

MARJORIE HARRIS, *Toronto: City of Neighborhoods*. A very readable account of the hows and whys of Toronto's ethnicity.

GARY HORNER, *Bicycle Guide to Western Ontario* and a much smaller *Bicycle Guide to Eastern Ontario*. The author, who seems to have biked much of the southern portion of this huge province, offers mapped routes and local highlights, as well as tips on health, safety, and what to wear.

JOANNE KATES, *Exploring Algonquin Park*. This updated version of a 1983 guide is filled with an habitué's knowledge of the 100-year-old park's flora and fauna as well as its canoe and backpacking routes. Kates, whose parents have operated a nearby children's camp since 1934, also offers many level-headed suggestions about how to maintain the pristine nature of this wilderness treasure.

ROBERT LEGGET, *Rideau Waterway*. The definitive history of, and guide to, this Ontario canal system, with photos.

JACK MINER, *Wild Goose Jack*. An autobiography by the naturalist who turned his Kingsville, Ontario, farm into a renowned sanctuary for wild geese and ducks.

SUSANNA MOODIE, *Roughing It in the Bush*. Life in Upper Canada (Ontario), circa 1830–1850, as described by an English gentlewoman.

SHELLEY J. PEAVEN, *Exploring Manitoulin*. Stretching more than 100 miles along the north shore of Lake Huron, Manitoulin is the world's largest freshwater island and still a relatively undiscovered tourist destination. The author outlines five auto tours of the island and includes much interesting information about its settlement, architecture, and the legends of its aboriginal people, who comprise about half the population. This is also a handy guide for bicyclists.

Quebec

GORDON DONALDSON, *Battle for a Continent: Quebec 1759*. A lively account of the British conquest.

DAVID FENNARIO, *Balconville*. A powerful play—half-English, half-French—about life in a contemporary blue-collar Montreal neighborhood.

WILLIAM KIRBY, *The Golden Dog*. A romance by the 19th-century writer set in old Quebec, 1748–1777.

ROGER LEMELIN (translated by Mary Finch), *The Plouffe Family*. The story of a large, lovable French-Canadian family that later became a popular TV series.

RENE LEVESQUE, *Memoirs of René Lévesque*. The autobiography of the late *premier ministre,* who brought separatism to the fore in Quebec.

HUGH MACLENNAN, *Two Solitudes*. The first popular novel to examine the gulf between the French and English in Montreal. A Canadian classic.

MIA AND KLAUS (with commentary by Hugh MacLennan), *Quebec*. An imaginative photographic record of the land and its four seasons.

DESMOND MORTON, *Sieges of Quebec: 1759–60*. The background, strategies, and personal conflicts that resulted in France's loss of Quebec City—and thus New France—to the English.

HILDA NEATBY, *Quebec: The Revolutionary Age, 1760–1791*. The historical roots of the unrest in modern Quebec. One installment in the 18-volume Canadian Centenary series.

Atlantic Provinces

DAVID BELL, *Early Loyalists of Saint John*. A good look at Loyalist-era life as the New Brunswick city flourished.

WILL R. BIRD, *Off Trail in Nova Scotia*. Anecdotes, local characters, and lore off the beaten track.

F. W. P. BOLGER, ED., *Canada's Smallest Province*. A definitive history, if somewhat academic in style, of Prince Edward Island.

WILLIAM C. BORRETT, *Historic Halifax: Tales in the Old Town Clock*. A compilation of radio broadcasts about events and people from the city's first 200 years.

JERRY DENNIS, *The Best Bicycle Tours of Eastern Canada*. The author outlines 12 tours, two in each of the six eastern provinces, and includes maps, a little history, provincial traffic laws, and tips on food, lodging, and staying healthy.

HAROLD HORWOOD, *Dancing on the Shore: A Celebration of Life at Annapolis Basin*. An amateur naturalist looks at the animal life of Nova Scotia.

DON MACGILLVRAY AND BRIAN TENNYSON, EDS., *Cape Breton Historical Essays*. Insightful and feisty comment, with maps, on the high and low points in the history of this very Scottish extremity of Nova Scotia.

NEIL MACKINNON, *This Unfriendly Soil: The Loyalist Experience in Nova Scotia*. The heartbreaks and adjustments that had to be made.

W. S. MACNUTT, *New Brunswick: A History, 1784–1867*. A good general history of the province from the Loyalist era to Confederation.

PETER L. MCCREATH AND JOHN G. LEEFE, *History of Early Nova Scotia*. How the province figured in New World and European history, from the Edict of Nantes in 1598 (which granted the French people freedom of worship) to 1782.

LUCY MAUD MONTGOMERY, *Anne of Green Gables*. Set on Prince Edward Island, this children's classic has become a staple of world literature.

CLAIRE MOWAT, *The Outport People*. A warm fictional memoir of life in a small Newfoundland fishing village where the only access is by sea.

FARLEY MOWAT, *The New · Founde · Land*. A noted environmentalist who writes with passion, the author paints a vivid—not always pleasant—picture of this island province: its landscape, history, wildlife, and wondrous people. Mowat in top form.

PETER NEARY AND PATRICK O'FLAHERTY, EDS., *By Great Waters: A Newfoundland and Labrador Anthology*. Selections, many told as narratives, that portray the province's boisterous history and culture from A.D. 1003 to the present.

IRENE L. ROGERS, *Charlottetown: The Life in Its Buildings*. A history of Prince Edward Island's capital city and its architecture.

STUART TRUEMAN, *An Intimate History of New Brunswick*. Stories about the Acadians and other ethnic groups who comprise the population of this friendly province.

Food and Accommodation

MARGARET ROSS CHANDLER, *Great Little Country Inns of Southern Ontario*. A selective list of 53 inns, starting in Bayfield on Lake Huron and ending at Gananoque on the St. Lawrence River.

EDITIONS ULYSSE, *The Best Bed & Breakfasts in Quebec*. A bilingual paperback published by a company known for its French and English guides.

MARVIN FREMES, *Historic Inns of Ontario*. Each inn has been visited by the author.

ANNE HARDY, *Where to Eat in Canada*. A straightforward guide for lovers of good food.

LAKE OF BAYS PUBLICATIONS, *Muskoka Dining Guide and Favourite Recipes*. This small Natural Heritage paperback provides some Muskoka history as background before suggesting where to dine.

GERDA PANTEL, *Canadian Bed & Breakfast Guide*. With 1,000 entries.

DAVID E. SCOTT, *A Taste of Ontario Country Inns.* A province-wide guide to country inns, with the chef's favorite recipe from each.

PATRICIA WILSON, *A Treasury of Canadian Bed & Breakfast* and *The Ontario Bed & Breakfast Book, with a Quebec supplement.*

—*Jean Danard*

NOVA SCOTIA

By Nan Drosdick

Nan Drosdick is an award-winning travel writer whose work appears in major Canadian and U.S. publications. She is a member of the Society of American Travel Writers and the American Society of Journalists & Authors.

Forming the angled southeastern rim of Atlantic Canada, Nova Scotia seems more island than peninsula, so much so that the province has dubbed itself "Canada's ocean playground."

The province, whose name translates as "New Scotland," juts far out into the North Atlantic, its 4,625-mile coastline washed by the Atlantic, the Gulf of St. Lawrence, Northumberland Strait, and the Bay of Fundy. (To visualize its shape, think of a mammoth lobster 347 miles from end to end, with its tail formed by the southwestern coastal curve at Yarmouth and its claws at the opposite end formed by the islands of Cape Breton.)

About two-thirds the size of Scotland, Nova Scotia is large, spanning 21,100 square miles, and so spread out that it defies convenient categorization. As a result, it has not one but many regional focal points. The common denominator is that all are bounded by the ocean and located some distance from one another, though the province's almost 6,000 miles of roads and expressways do an excellent job linking everything together. Each regional focal point doubles as a gateway by which visitors enter and leave that particular part of the province.

Halifax is the central focus on the Atlantic coast, and the gateway for international visitors arriving by air. Along the

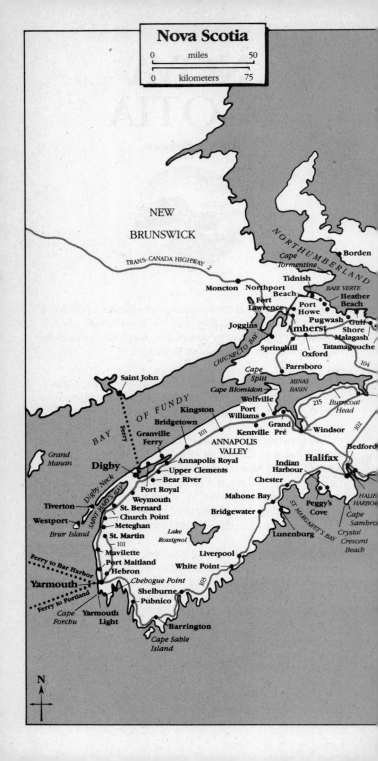

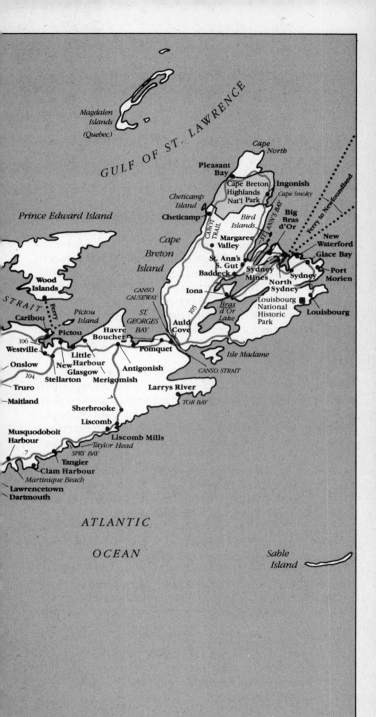

Bay of Fundy, Yarmouth and Digby are gateways for visitors arriving from Maine or New Brunswick by ferry. Northumberland Strait's gateways are Amherst (by highway from New Brunswick) and Pictou (with its ferry connections to nearby Prince Edward Island). Cape Breton has the Gulf of St. Lawrence along one coast and the Atlantic on the other, and is linked by ferry to Newfoundland, at North Sydney. The province's interior is mostly undeveloped; towns and attractions are mainly clustered on the coasts.

Some visitors come to Nova Scotia to trace ancestral roots. Festivals are another strong lure, and include everything from province-wide lobster suppers, to regattas and military muster at Halifax's Citadel, to ethnic shows like the annual Festival of the Tartans at New Glasgow and the once-every-four-years Gathering of the Clans, held alternately between Scotland and Nova Scotia (and next scheduled for the province in 1995). The strongest draw of all, however, is Nova Scotia's idyllic seacoasts, ribboned with roads and dotted with picture-book villages, and altogether perfect for exploring. The province is the best known in Atlantic Canada for beaches, seafood dining, local wines, the arts scene, and crafts shopping.

Summer is Nova Scotia's peak tourist season, with the most sun in Cape Breton's Sydney during July and in Halifax and Yarmouth during August. Expect temperatures to peak in the high 60s°–70s° F (low to mid-20s° C)—and be sure to bring a few woolies, as a sudden dip can send the temperature into the 50s° F. Bring a raincoat, too, because summer showers may be brief but drenching. During late summer, the same hurricanes that ravage the Caribbean can blow themselves out weak as pussycats with a day or two of rain on the final leg through Atlantic Canada. Overall, the province has nice weather with a bit of whimsy.

Once, Nova Scotians reclaimed their province for themselves after Labour Day—but no more. Bus tours have discovered the spectacular fall foliage, and visitors revel in the cool, clear days. Late spring remains the undiscovered, uncrowded season, with the seaports often banked in thick fog until noon and temperatures comparable to the slightly cooler autumn days.

MAJOR INTEREST

Small, tranquil, unspoiled towns
British, Loyalist, French, Acadian, and especially
    Scottish heritages

Beaches
Seacoast scenery and dining

Halifax
Harborfront for sightseeing, shopping, dining,
   nightlife
Historic Properties' restored period buildings
Maritime Museum of the Atlantic
Halifax Citadel National Historic Park

Elsewhere along the Atlantic
Peggy's Cove
Sherbrooke Village

Bay of Fundy Coast
The Evangeline Trail
Scenic beauty of the Annapolis Valley
Royal Historic Gardens in Annapolis Royal
Port Royal National Historic Site

Northumberland Strait Coast
Joggins Fossil Cliffs, upper Chignecto Bay
Pictou Scots heritage

Cape Breton
Fortress of Louisbourg
Alexander Graham Bell Museum
Cabot Trail, Cape Breton Highlands National Park

THE ATLANTIC SEACOAST

Nova Scotia has its Atlantic seacoast in mind when it claims
the province has "so much to sea." It is a great stretch of
fringing seacoast, 400 miles from Yarmouth in the southwest
to the Strait of Canso in the northeast, a series of low cliffs
alternating with beaches, deep bays, dunes, and marshes—
and marked all along with lighthouses. (**Sable Island**, an
uninhabited and desolate sandspit dotted with wrecked
ships and lighthouses, lies some 180 miles southeast of
Halifax.)

   The Atlantic seacoast is a paradox, both the most developed
and least developed part of the provincial coastline. The
capital city of Halifax lies at its midpoint on a densely devel-

oped peninsula, with the city's affluence overflowing to the southwest and the select Mahone Bay settlements. The coast northeast of Halifax, on the other hand, is a slice of the province as it once was, good roads notwithstanding. There's a dual mood along the Atlantic, a sense of Canada at its spit-and-polished best but with a coastline nonetheless reminiscent of old England before piers lined its shores.

HALIFAX

Halifax is the focal point of the Atlantic coast. The province is served by major expressways, three of which converge in the metropolitan area. Locals understand how one highway feeds into another with number changes, but it may be confusing to visitors, so study the roads first on a map. Highway 103 links Halifax to Yarmouth (which faces Portland, Maine) on the south shore, while meandering Highway 7's two lanes run along the eastern shore. Highway 101 cuts across the province in the direction of Minas Basin, and then follows the Annapolis River and St. Mary's Bay southwest to Yarmouth. Highway 102 heads in a northeasterly direction, connecting with Highway 104 (the Trans-Canada) in the vicinity of Truro. From there it heads west, north, and west again to Amherst near the New Brunswick border or northeast to Pictou on Northumberland Strait. By all means, take alternate coastal roads when possible, as they're far more scenic and reveal more of the local flavor.

For much of the 17th-century French and English skirmishing for control of the North American continent was centered around Port Royal, founded by the French in 1605 on a finger of land washed by the Annapolis River and the Bay of Fundy. Burned by the British in 1613, the fort was rebuilt by the French, who then encouraged farmers to settle along the upper Fundy coastline. By 1632, some 45 Acadian villages had been established in the area. Continual harassment by the British, however, forced the French to relocate their principal garrison across the Annapolis River to what is now Annapolis Royal by 1705.

The British, who seized Port Royal in 1710 and renamed it Fort Anne, were awarded mainland Nova Scotia in 1713 by the Treaty of Utrecht, and immediately set about creating Nova Scotia's first capital at Annapolis Royal. Overwhelmed by England's military superiority, France abandoned the Acadian settlements along the Fundy and retreated to the timbered wilderness of Ile Royale (Cape Breton), where it set about establishing a presence on the Atlantic coast at

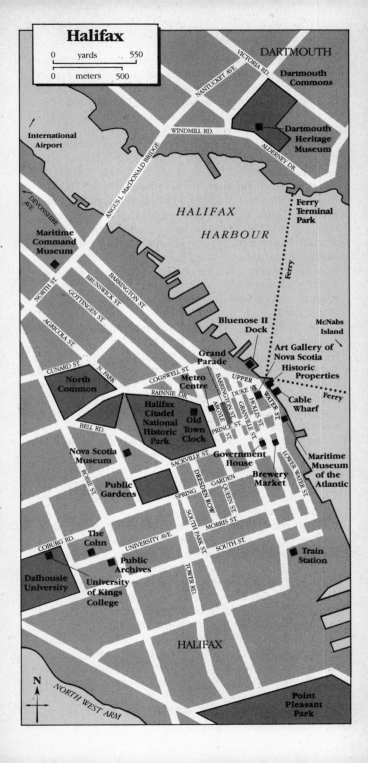

Louisbourg. The English responded to the French presence on Cape Breton by establishing Halifax in 1749. In a further effort to counterbalance French Roman Catholicism in the New World, the Crown began to settle German and Swiss Protestants and some French Huguenots in the area of Lunenburg, on the coast southwest of Halifax.

For all intents and purposes, French colonial ambitions in the New World were quashed by the establishment of Halifax. The French had been at work on the Fortress of Louisbourg for more than 20 years when, in 1745, 4,000 New England militiamen and the Royal Navy seized it. Like a phoenix, Louisbourg rose again—only to be crushed again, this time in 1758 after a two-month siege. Meanwhile, the Acadian Deportation Act of 1755 resulted in thousands of Acadians who refused to take loyalty oaths being ousted from their farms and sent packing—initially to England's colonies on the eastern seaboard, and later, by their own volition, to Louisiana, to various Caribbean islands, or to France itself.

The ruthless deportation solved nothing. By 1764 the exodus of Acadian refugees was so great that ships carrying them were often refused landing rights at foreign ports. In the face of this hostility, many Acadians chose to return—not to Halifax or the upper Fundy, by that time settled by pro-British immigrants, but rather to the rocky, inhospitable coastline between Digby and Yarmouth as well as the remote hinterlands of Cape Breton.

Unrest along the eastern seaboard in succeeding decades and then the American Revolution fueled Loyalist immigration to other Crown lands; in 1783 ships from New York brought pro-British settlers to Shelburne on the south shore, whose population soon swelled to 16,000. The future composition of the province was set.

For its part, Halifax has always been a city propelled by strong-willed people. **Government House** owes its splendid design to Royal Governor John Wentworth, a Loyalist and luxury-loving former New Hampshire governor who in 1800 demanded and got a residence to equal his ambitious plans for the city. And to this day no one has forgotten King George III's illustrious son Prince Edward, who flaunted local propriety with his French mistress, Julie St. Laurent. Generous Governor Wentworth loaned the lovers his Hemloch Ravine estate on Bedford Basin (northwest of the city), and the couple lived there from 1794 to 1800. Once back in London the prince married a proper German princess, who gave birth to Victoria in 1819. Julie St. Laurent returned to France to live out her life in seclusion.

Halifax has always been a sentimental city as well, and its people treasure its landmark, the oversize **Old Town Clock**, a gift from Prince Edward. The splendid **Halifax Public Gardens** are a tribute to his daughter, Queen Victoria; the ornate red-roofed bandstand was built to mark the Queen's Golden Jubilee. And as Queen Victoria esteemed the Scots, so has Halifax, modeling its Dalhousie University after the University of Edinburgh.

Founded for Crown defense with a ring of formidable forts, the city never fired a gun in anger, and today the forts are all parks, many—like Halifax Citadel—of national historic significance. Her Majesty's Royal Navy (after 1910 the Royal Canadian Navy) has been based here for centuries, Halifax Harbour being Atlantic Canada's major port. Her Majesty's Canadian Dockyard, where sloops and brigantines have given way to aircraft carriers, hydrofoils, submarines, destroyers, and supply-ship convoys, is part of the harbor complex.

Halifax's past also includes privateers, who harried the towns of the eastern seaboard during the American Revolution and unloaded their booty into warehouses along Water Street, and later were blockade runners during the United States Civil War—on the South's side. As well, the Cunard steamship empire started along the waterfront here. In the 1970s, when the harborfront was more dilapidated than functional and some Haligonians thought the heart of the city was aged beyond repair, an infusion of research, historical restoration, and new construction backed by federal and provincial investment brought back all that the centuries had hidden. Halifax is, as a result, both old and new.

A bon vivant sense of tradition is bound up in Halifax, making it a city of casual propriety whose pace seems both leisurely and measured. Halifax is, most of all, a city that exists to be enjoyed, with Atlantic Canada's most abundantly available music, theater, performing arts, and art. It is also known for its sociability and willingness to find any good reason to create an event. Its greatest is the annual **Nova Scotia Tattoo**, a celebration of the province's military history. For a week in late June/early July, military bands, pipe bands, choirs, and various other ensembles attract upward of 50,000 spectators to the Metro Centre.

Halifax is worth a visit of three to five days, more if excursions are planned. Like the rest of the province, it works Monday to Friday, parties Friday and Saturday, and closes up tight as a drum on Sunday. Also like the rest of the province, it shares Canada's unspoken feeling that nothing of any great accomplishment happens in summer, when it resigns itself quite graciously to welcoming visitors. Early autumn's balmy foliage months (through October) are becoming an extension of the traditional tourist season.

Exploring the City

THE HARBORFRONT

Contained on its own peninsula, the city is easy to handle on foot, spreading out to the north, south, and east from the Old Town Clock, the city landmark on the Citadel grounds overlooking the harborfront. The harborfront is *the* reason to visit Halifax. The main summertime happenings (like the Cable Wharf outdoor concerts and the ubiquitous street performers) cluster along promenades on Water Street and adjacent side streets, as well as up the steep hill leading to the Halifax Citadel and nearby sights.

The re-created harborfront stretches along eight city blocks of the angled seven-mile-long peninsula. The setting is both picturesque and a Haligonian domain, as locals by the thousands use the ferry terminal for Dartmouth, a ten-minute trip across the harbor to the north. From the harborfront Halifax overlooks her sister city across a fast-moving array of oceangoing vessels, small sailing craft, and usually several oil rigs parked improbably in the middle of the harbor.

Options for getting out on the water can be found along the wharves from the *Bluenose II* to the Maritime Museum at the foot of Sackville Street, and run to all manner of Nova Scotian craft, including a paddle-wheeler and deep-sea-fishing charters. The ferry from Cable Wharf to **McNabs Island**, with its historic defense batteries, walking trails, and a beach at the entrance to Halifax Harbour, costs about $8 round trip.

In similar fashion sightseeing operations are lined up one after another on the harborfront, from Historic Properties, a national historic site on the corner of Duke and Upper Water streets, to **Brewery Market**, a cavernous space on Lower Water Street where Alexander Keith's brewery made and bottled India Pale Ale from the early 1800s to 1971; today it's a complex of shops, bars, and restaurants, with a farmers' market on Saturday mornings in the central courtyard.

Historic Properties

Historic Properties, which starts near the **Privateers' Warehouse** shopping and dining complex and extends up the hillside to Granville Street, is the core of the harborfront area. In all, it is an enclave of ten restored buildings—

colorful, scrubbed, stone-and-shingled structures that are remarkably well kept, considering the crowds. The nearby **Art Gallery of Nova Scotia**, on the corner of Hollis and George streets, has changing exhibits of top-notch provincial painters, sculptors, and artisans ranging from the traditional to the avant-garde.

Maritime Museum of the Atlantic

Having seen the harbor, you'll want to visit the Maritime Museum of the Atlantic, on Water Street between Prince and Sackville streets. Some of the province's most interesting seafaring craft, as well as Queen Victoria's royal barge, are displayed on the exhibit hall's main floor. The only star missing is *Bluenose,* whose image graces the Canadian dime. Launched in 1921, the Lunenburg-built schooner sank off Haiti in 1946; its replica, *Bluenose II,* does summer duty as a harbor sightseeing schooner and is berthed next to the waterfront Halifax Sheraton. In *Bluenose*'s place is a smaller sloop from East Chester, one of a dozen such originals providing a close-up look at the craftsmanship that produced some of the world's fastest schooners and sloops.

UP THE HILLSIDE

Halifax is at its commercial best along the hillside area stretching from the harborfront up to the Old Town Clock: Sightseeing vans, taxis, rickshaws, and a double-decker bus wheel along Water Street and the nearby side streets, offering a number of ways to see the city. A brisk jaunt up the steep hillside, usually on George Street, is the way Haligonians do it, stopping midway at **Grand Parade**, the city's historic parade square, where more often than not in summer street musicians, magicians, and madcap performers mingle with lunching office workers, shoppers, strollers, and tourists.

Halifax Citadel National Historic Park

The Citadel area above the harborfront is worth a full day. The Citadel itself is an island of grass whose interior fortress is the site of summer tours and military drills. The Victorian-style Public Gardens lie adjacent. The **Nova Scotia Museum**, a block north of the Gardens, devotes its lower floor to natural-history exhibits.

While the domain below the Citadel belongs to the harborfront, the area beyond it, where the peninsula flattens out, is residential. The southern portion is where the rich folks live. It's also the home of several of Halifax's universities, among them Dalhousie. The cream of provincial performing

arts appears at the **Cohn,** Dalhousie's cultural center, though
it shares the spotlight with the Metro Centre in front of the
Old Town Clock. Working-class neighborhoods rim the ship-
yards farther to the north. **The Maritime Command Museum,**
ensconced off Gottingen Street, offers a stunning display of
naval memorabilia and ship portraits in an old mansion.

NIGHTLIFE AND DINING IN HALIFAX

Nightlife is dense in the hillside area, although not as steamy
with crowds as it was several years ago, when pub crawling
was the way to go. Young professionals and the college
crowd still flock to **Bistro Too** on South Park for weekend
jazz, and to **Brandy's** on Market Street, with its ever-present
record spinner. They also favor **My Apartment** and the
adjacent **Lawrence of Oregano,** which share live bands and
the same block on Argyle Street. A slightly older crowd
seems to prefer the spots on Water Street: **O'Carroll's,** with
folk music in the lounge; the **Clipper Bar & Grill** at the
Clipper Cay restaurant, with regional performers; and **Privateers' Warehouse,** with a pub on the Lower Deck and jazz,
rock, and blues on the Middle Deck. The **Harbourfront Bar**
at the Halifax Sheraton is the place to see and be seen,
especially on Friday nights, while the **Flamingo Café** at the
Maritime Centre on Barrington Street is the venue for live
blues, rock, Afro-pop bands, and incredible reggae.

The hillside below the Citadel is also where you'll find the
city's best restaurants, which makes it especially convenient
for those who like to combine dinner with dancing and a
nightcap. Lobster may be what visitors want most when dining
in the province, and it's on every menu, but more sophisticated fare can also be found. Seafood is plentiful—fried,
broiled, sauced, or in a Wellington pastry—and the same goes
for meat dishes, with an emphasis on beef. Halifax is a wine-
drinking city, doting on imports, but varieties of local Grand
Pré and Jost whites and reds are abundant too. The downside
to this scene is space, as most of these restaurants in historic
buildings are picturesque but small; in season you'll have to
be content with any table, reservations notwithstanding.

Along Historic Properties' harborfront, the major contend-
ers, each worth serious consideration, are the **Upper Deck
Waterfront Fishery & Grill** (Tel: 902/422-1289), with a surprisingly creative and consistently good Continental-style
menu featuring seafood, lamb, and steaks; **Salty's** (Tel: 902/
423-6818), at the harbor's edge, with exquisite views and a
balanced menu of seafood, pasta, and tender cuts of red
meat; and **O'Carroll's** (Tel: 902/423-4405), on the inland side

of Water Street, with enduring classics such as steak and sauced seafood.

On the hillside, **Ryan Duffy's** (Tel: 902/421-1116), upstairs at the corner of Spring Garden and Dresden Row, offers steak, seafood, and a celebrated Caesar salad. The **Five Fishermen Restaurant** (Tel: 902/422-4421), in historic quarters on Argyle Street, has emerged as a contender with its offerings of scallops, shrimp, and lobster. The **Silver Spoon** and its fine reputation for desserts are firmly entrenched on Granville Street, where its straightforward entrées and outrageously fine flans and cheesecake remain unchallenged. Expect to spend $20 to $40 per person, not including wine, for the city's finest dining. Reservations are always recommended; Tel: (902) 429-6617.

A ride on the ferry to Halifax's sister city opens up more possibilities, including **La Perla Dining Room** (Tel: 902/469-3241), serving local quail and pheasant northern Italian–style directly across the street from Dartmouth's ferry terminal.

SHOPPING IN HALIFAX

You'll find a wide range of galleries and shops in Halifax. Surprisingly, Haligonians see their gorgeous provincial craft goods as exports for tourists and themselves wear high-priced imports from Korea and elsewhere, so check labels if you want local products. You'll find genuine provincial crafts at **Jennifer's of Nova Scotia**, 5635 Spring Garden Road, where shelves overflow with homespuns and knits. Other worthwhile crafts and clothing buys can be found at **Suttles and Seawinds**, in the Halifax Sheraton at 1919 Upper Water Street.

Celtic Traditions, 1533 Barrington Street, has an unusually fine assortment of provincial crafts in the Scottish vein, including pewter and pottery by Fiona Irwin. The Art Gallery of Nova Scotia's **Gallery Shop**, on the corner of Hollis and George streets, showcases the finest in often avant-garde crafts and jewelry by the province's most established and highly regarded artists and artisans. For ship portraits and seascapes of value, check out **Zwicker's Gallery** on Doyle Street (off Spring Garden Road). To catch up on literary pursuits, try the **Book Room**, 1664 Granville Street, a favorite haunt of well-read Haligonians; the **Pair of Trindles Bookshop** at Historic Properties stocks only Canadian authors and publications. Finally, for tartans ad infinitum, **Plaid Place**, 1903 Barrington Street, stocks tartans imported from Scotland as well as the provincial tartan woven in Yarmouth, either by the yard or in apparel.

STAYING IN HALIFAX

The view is what's important here, with a convenient location running a close second. The horseshoe-shaped ▶ **Halifax Sheraton**, one of two truly deluxe hotels in the province, abuts both the harborfront and Historic Properties. Rooms overlooking the busy harbor offer the most spectacular views in Atlantic Canada, with prices to match. Interior rooms, on the other hand, though less expensive, also have far less interesting views. Regardless of their location, all rooms are large and decorated in soothing pastels.

The ▶ **Canadian Pacific Chateau Halifax**, across a maze of busy one-way streets from the Sheraton, has been a Halifax landmark for more than two decades. The hotel's starkly contemporary exterior hides a formal lobby in which Oriental rugs, lustrous mahogany paneling, and gleaming marble floors are much in evidence. Guest rooms show a simple affinity for dark-wood furnishings and tasteful decor. Thanks to energetic management, the hotel has worn well over the years, with improvements to its facilities the rule rather than the exception. For all its merits, the Chateau Halifax lacks the cheek-to-jowl proximity to the harborfront area of the Sheraton, and so you can expect to pay a few dollars less than you would at the latter. If you ask for a harbor-facing room on the seventh floor, however, you'll probably never know the difference.

The otherwise highly commendable ▶ **Delta Barrington** turns its back on the harborfront area altogether, sacrificing stimulating views for good value for your money. The Barrington offers a scaled-down version of the Chateau Halifax's Old English motif without cheating on the deeply cushioned chairs and sofas, the brass accents, and the polished-wood decor. And as in other Halifax hotels, the dining room offers adequate food accompanied by prompt, polite service. Perhaps its greatest asset is its location across the street from the city's Grand Parade pocket park, as centrally located on the hillside as a visitor can be.

The ▶ **Cambridge Suites Hotel**, a member of the popular chain, is situated farther up the hill on Brunswick Street opposite the Halifax Citadel. Everything about this place is crisply modern, from its uncluttered exterior to the roomy suites within. The moderately priced suites come in three basic configurations, and are equipped with small refrigerators, microwaves, and coffee makers. There's also a small dining room off the lobby and a spa facility with a whirlpool, sauna, and exercise room.

THE HALIFAX METROPOLITAN AREA

The metropolitan Halifax–Dartmouth area, with almost 400,000 inhabitants, presents a marked contrast to the self-contained harborfront and Citadel area, covering as it does a 25-mile radius of harbors and inlets, lakes and rivers, seacoast and open ocean. The metro area comprises Halifax (the center) and the bedroom communities of Dartmouth (its Heritage Museum and Black Cultural Centre, both with genealogical records, are interesting), Bedford, and the Sackvilles.

PEGGY'S COVE

This protected seacoast village on St. Margaret's Bay, 40 minutes southwest of Halifax over winding two-lane roads, is also in metro's domain. Signs for the **Lighthouse Route** (a designated sightseeing drive) point the way from Halifax. The famous fishing village, with its own lighthouse perched above acres of granite boulders deposited by Ice Age glaciers, is one of Canada's most photogenic, and photographed, spots. The 100-foot-long monument to Canadian fisherfolk that William deGarthe carved on the face of a granite outcropping in the village's midst is today a provincial park (two deGarthe murals are in nearby St. John's Anglican Church).

Still, while the boulder-wrapped cove can be blissfully peaceful, it's more usually packed with visitors and tour buses. Somehow there's room for everyone, as visitors scramble across boulders or cluster around the lighthouse. If crowds bother you, plan to arrive before the buses pull in around 9:00 A.M. or wait until they clear out around 4:00 P.M. And don't forget to wear rubber-soled shoes: The rocky surfaces can get slippery, and visitors have been known to tumble into the drink.

The **Sou'wester Restaurant**, Peggy Cove's only public dining room, is handy for a quick snack. It's just as easy, however, to continue on to **Candleriggs'** dining room and craft shop in Indian Harbour, a five-minute drive to the north via Highway 333. Along the way you'll see several off-road signs advertising lobster suppers—and lunches, too— that are worth following up if plain but hearty seafood is what you had in mind. Otherwise, plan to be in Halifax for dinner.

HEMLOCK RAVINE AND THE
CITY OF LAKES

Back in Halifax, you can follow the Bedford Highway (Highway 2) along Bedford Basin to Hemlock Ravine, the former haunt of Prince Edward and Julie St. Laurent, and now a city park. Remnants of the former estate include the round **Music House**—separated from the rest of the estate by the highway and closed to the public—a heart-shaped pool, and miles of walking paths shaded by hemlocks, some 100 feet tall (parking lots are signposted inside the park).

On the other side of Halifax Harbour, **Dartmouth** describes itself as the City of Lakes. There are more than a dozen small lakes in the region, most of them gifts of the retreating ice at the close of the last ice age some 10,000 years ago. Locals are partial to **Grand Lake** (also known as Shubenacadie Grand Lake or just Shubenacadie Lake, an extension of the Shubenacadie River). Outdoor enthusiasts will find two provincial parks on Grand Lake's eastern shore: **Laurie Provincial Park** offers a pleasant countryside setting and a range of activities, including boating, swimming, picnicking, hiking, and camping. **Oakfield Provincial Park**, to the north, offers more of the same, *sans* campsites, in a less congested setting. Both are only a 20-minute drive from downtown Halifax. To get to Grand Lake, take the MacKay Bridge over The Narrows to Highway 111, get off at exit 4 and follow Highway 118 north through pretty woodlands to Highway 102 (exit 5), then make a quick right onto Route 2 heading north. Laurie Park is ten minutes north of the exit, Oakfield a few minutes beyond that.

Here and throughout the province Nova Scotia's provincial parks provide picnic tables, drinking water, and toilets; if the park has a beach there will also be changing rooms, all open from late May to early October. Most of the provincial parks are unsupervised and without lifeguards, however, except where seaside tides are strong.

ELSEWHERE ON THE ATLANTIC COAST

East of Dartmouth, the surf angles just right for surfing and sail-boarding; several outfits in Halifax rent equipment. **Crystal Crescent Beach**, 29 km (18 miles) due south of Halifax at Cape Sambro, is a favorite with local surfers, as are the **Lawrencetown**, **Martinique**, and **Clam Harbour** beaches to the east.

Otherwise, departing Halifax—whether to head south-west via the expressway (Highway 103) or scenic Light-house Route, or northeast on the **Marine Drive** along the eastern shore—calls for an immediate directional choice. Beaches are found along both routes; the sea is cold, but warms in pools between sandbars, and the many salt marshes make for good bird-watching.

The South Shore

Museums

On the south shore, Haligonians commute as far as the Chester–Mahone Bay–Lunenburg triangle. Facing the Atlan-tic across sheltered harbors and coves, these are three of the province's most charming upscale enclaves, with a good range of select shops and restaurants to be found among them. As far as museums go, the pièce de résistance is Lunenburg's **Fisheries Museum of the Atlantic**, on the water-front, which documents the trials and triumphs of centuries of seafaring. Like other provincial museums, it's open daily from mid-May to mid-October, 9:30 A.M. to 5:30 P.M. The **DesBrisay Museum** in Bridgewater (the area's expressway gateway) is another delightful attraction, with displays on early Lunenburg County's Micmac Indian and German settle-ments; outside, tables under the trees are ideal for picnick-ing. From mid-May to the end of September the museum is open 9:00 A.M. to 5:00 P.M., Monday through Saturday, and 1:00 to 5:00 P.M. on Sundays.

Fine Dining and Inns

In the **Mahone Bay** area, if it looks good, it is—high prices notwithstanding. Northwest of Chester in Marriots Cove, the **Galley Seafood Restaurant** (Tel: 902-275-4700) offers a menu nicely balanced between seafood and cuts of meat, all served in a dimly lit dining room overlooking sailboats and yachts. In Chester itself, the stately Georgian-style **Captain's House** (Tel: (902/275-3501) on Central Street also overlooks the water, and continues to offer consistently good food from an English-style menu despite its transition from inn to restau-rant to inn with public dining rooms.

Lunenburg's outstanding restaurant can be found in the Victorian-style ▶ **Bluenose Lodge** (Tel: 902/634-8851), on the corner of Falkland Avenue and Dufferin Street. You won't be treated to views of the harbor from its first-floor dining room, but the traditional maritime fare is expertly prepared and presented, and guest rooms on the floors above are more than pleasant. The ▶ **Compass Rose Inn** (Tel: 902/634-8509) on busy King Street is smaller but just as picturesque, with four period guest rooms and two licensed dining rooms.

Shopping and Other Activities

Shop wares are even more plentiful here than in Halifax. **Suttles and Seawinds**, featuring designer calicos superbly fashioned into women's and children's apparel, is based at 466 Main Street in Mahone Bay. Provincial arts and crafts are found at **Chester's Warp and Woof** on Water Street, which is also the place for exquisitely crafted hooked rugs from Cheticamp on Cape Breton.

Nothing else along the south shore can equal this trio of towns for creature comforts and pleasure. If and when town interests pale, head for the 70-room ▶ **Oak Island Inn & Marina** (exit 9 off Highway 103, midway between Chester and Mahone Bay) to sign up for a fishing charter; or, if you prefer, visit one of the many beaches along this stretch of coastline—the best is at **Sand Hills Beach Provincial Park**, south of Barrington in Villagedale, an almost three-hour drive from Lunenburg via the Lighthouse Route.

The Marine Drive

The northeast route from Halifax is quite different from its south shore counterpart. Settlements along the coast here are sparse and rustic. **W. J. Krauch**, a major exporter of smoked fish based in Tangier, about 80 km (50 miles) east of Dartmouth, also retails Danish-style salted eel, salmon, and mackerel; if it's not too busy, visitors can tour the smokehouse.

Another 80 km (50 miles) farther on, about 2½ hours east of Halifax, the remote ▶ **Liscomb Lodge** stretches along the Liscomb River in Liscomb Mills. The rustic but toney trappings here include a main lodge with a spacious dining room overlooking river rapids, a newish hotel, and nicely furnished chalets, some with fireplaces. The resort is a favorite stop for tour buses, which means it's sometimes crowded cheek-to-jowl at lunch, but Atlantic Canadians like it during quieter times for honeymoons—the outlying chalets are especially secluded and romantic.

Sherbrooke

Farther north along Highway 7 lie new and old Sherbrooke. The modern village is a four-corners settlement, best known for **Bright House**, with its airy dining quarters and a back bakery esconced in a historic setting along the highway.

Sherbrooke Village, one of Nova Scotia's regional museums, has 30 remarkably preserved buildings reclaimed from the mid-1800s, a time when the village prospered from gold mining and lumbering. Today the village's water-powered sawmill, re-created from memory by a local Micmac Indian craftsman, is worth a look. A bit farther upstream, the St. Mary's River is noted for its excellent salmon fishing.

Beaches

What remote Marine Drive lacks in development it more than makes up for with long, scenic beaches; **Martinique Beach**, two miles of fine sand, is south of the village of Musquodoboit Harbor, an hour east of Halifax. Other popular stretches of sand include **Taylors Head**, another hour beyond Martinique; and **Tor Bay**, which is south of Larrys River about two and a half hours northeast of Taylors Head.

THE BAY OF FUNDY COAST

The Bay of Fundy— one of the world's natural wonders—and its coast are the province's leading attractions after Halifax.

The Fundy and its Nova Scotia seacoast, facing New Brunswick across the bay, coexist like the proverbial lion and lamb. About 100 billion gallons of seawater rush into the funnel-shaped estuary twice a day. Tides at **Yarmouth**, at the southwestern end of the province, rise 12 feet. At **Burncoat Head** on Minas Basin, near Windsor, where the estuary narrows, tides can run as high as 54 feet. All along the Fundy's upper reaches the enormous surge spills over into rivers, led by the tidal bore—the advance wave sometimes up to three feet high. Six hours later the tide pulls back, laying bare red, glistening mud flats and stranding boats that will be buoyant again in a few hours.

Yet another reason to explore the region is its abundance of festivals. Among the better-known ones, **Digby's Scallop Days** runs for four days in August, while the **Festival Acadien de Clare**, with its Evangeline pageant, animates Church Point and Meteghan for six days in July.

As is the case in much of the province, the Fundy shore's road system hugs the coast at the expense of the sparsely settled interior. The exceptions are two old stagecoach routes: Highway 101, which traces the curve of the shoreline from Yarmouth to Windsor, a five-hour drive, before swinging southeastward through the interior in the direction of Halifax; and Highway 102, which heads north across the interior from Halifax, ending at Truro, the southern terminus of the Trans-Canada, Highway 104. The more picturesque secondary roads along the Minas Basin coast are less travelled and provide unforgettable glimpses of the tempestuous tides. (Be careful walking the Minas Basin bay floor, however, as tides pour in at eight to ten feet per hour.)

YARMOUTH

Yarmouth is southwestern Nova Scotia's principal city and the province's largest port west of Halifax. It is also Nova Scotia's closest link to United States ports in Maine, with the ferry crossings from Bar Harbor and Portland taking 6½ and 11 hours, respectively.

Entering the province in Yarmouth, the visitor faces an immediate choice. One route out of town (Highway 101) heads northeast along the Bay of Fundy to Digby (two hours by car) before entering the lush Annapolis Valley. The other choice is Highway 103, which loops around the southern end of the province and continues along the south shore past White Point, Lunenburg, Mahone Bay, and Chester to Halifax in five hours (see the Atlantic Coast section above). Tantalizing choices notwithstanding, a third option is to stop in Yarmouth before moving on. This port city has enough attractions to occupy a full day of your time, and more if its subtle, easygoing pace appeals to you.

The **Yarmouth County Museum and Archives**, housed in an old granite church at 22 Collins Street, is one of the best reasons to visit Yarmouth. The main floor's magnificent collection of ship portraits is one of Canada's largest, and includes barques, schooners, and brigantines from the period when Yarmouth was Canada's second-largest port of registry in tonnage. The museum also offers a well-stocked research library as well as the kind of local memorabilia that makes such a place interesting, all of it skillfully documented and presented. From June 1 to October 15 it's open from 9:00 A.M. to 5:00 P.M., Monday through Saturday, and from 1:00 to 5:00 P.M. on Sundays; winter hours are 2:00 to 5:00 P.M., Tuesday through Saturday, or by appointment with the curator.

Local historian James Farish described Yarmouth as "solid,

substantial, nothing luxurious"—still a fitting description, although such adjectives don't hint at the stylish houses and commercial buildings along Main Street. For visitors the town's layout is uncomplicated: Main Street runs north and south along the harborfront, with cross streets intersecting it. The ferry terminal is at the end of Forest Street. Collins Street has the county museum. The Arts Centre on Parade Street has summer events, so check the playbill. From June to October there's a Saturday morning farmers' market on Hawthorne Street. The city's **Seafest**, in mid- to late July, revolves around boat races, theater, and seafood.

The **Yarmouth Wool Shoppe**, 352 Main Street, near the ferry, is the place to buy Nova Scotian tartan—by the yard or as kilts and such. The local bar scene unfolds until 11:00 P.M. at the **Clipper Ship** on Main Street, with a large selection of beers, live music, and dancing. Upscale drinkers may prefer **Haley's Lounge**, in the Rodd Grand Hotel on Main Street, where the sentimental harmonies of the 1950s and 1960s are featured most nights.

STAYING AND DINING IN YARMOUTH

If watching ferries arrive and depart sounds appealing, try the ▶ **Rodd Colony Harbour Inn**, 6 Forest Street, with 24 of its 65 rooms overlooking the ferry terminal; rooms with the view of the harbor are always in demand, so be sure to book ahead. The two front rooms—one with twin four-posters and the other with a queen-size four-poster—at the ▶ **Murray Manor Guest House**, directly across the street at the corner of Forest and Main, also have views of the waterfront, and the tariff includes a hearty breakfast.

If you can do without a waterfront view, Yarmouth has a number of other lodging options. The high-rise ▶ **Rodd Grand Hotel** has nicely appointed rooms overlooking the north end of the Main Street shopping area, a dining room, an indoor pool, and a whirlpool. There is, in addition, a spate of motels lining the major access roads into town. Among the best are the ▶ **Best Western Mermaid Motel**, 545 Main Street, with a heated outdoor pool as well as a pub and lounge; and the ▶ **Journey's End Motel**, inland at 96 Starrs Road near the shopping mall, with clean, basic units and the lowest rates in town.

The best dining in the area is found about 8 km (5 miles) north of the city at Hebron's **Manor Inn** (Tel: 902/742-2487), which sets a fine table in period surroundings. **Harris' Seafood**, along Route 1 in the direction of Hebron, is popular with locals, its plain exterior notwithstanding.

Bicycle Rentals

Thanks to the flat lay of the land, the Yarmouth area is sublime biking terrain. Bikes can be rented for $12 a day from either **Bailey's** or the **Rodd Grand Hotel** outlet, both on Main Street.

One of the best biking routes follows Main Street west before turning left onto Cape Forchu, a peninsula ending at Yarmouth Light, about 12 km (7½ miles) south of town. Along here is where you'll find the picture-postcard view of Yarmouth, so bring your camera. Cape Forchu was sighted and named by Champlain as he sailed the Bay of Fundy before establishing a French presence at Port Royal in 1605. The area may also be the site of Leif Eriksson's Vinland; a large inscribed runic stone, now on exhibit at the Yarmouth County Museum in town, was found in the area in 1812. The equally charming, though slightly shorter route heading south from Yarmouth to Chebogue Point is lined with pink and purple lupines in summer and affords glimpses of long-legged willets wading along the coast from May to August.

East of Yarmouth

Shelburne, with its stock of Loyalist-period buildings and an excellent harbor, is a two-hour-plus drive on backcountry coastal roads, passing interesting Acadian settlements in **the Pubnicos** on the way. Be sure to stop at West Pubnico's **Lighthouse de Pombcoup**, on Route 335, the first crafts shop in Nova Scotia's oldest Acadian area created expressly for outsiders. The area's interesting history is on display at West Pubnico's **Musée Acadien**. The museum is open June 15 to Labour Day, 8:30 A.M. to 4:30 P.M., Mondays and Saturdays; 8:30 A.M. to 6:30 P.M., Tuesday through Friday; and noon to 4:00 P.M. on Sundays. If an Acadian lunch sounds appetizing, your next stop should be the low-profile **Red Cap Restaurant** in the same village, where the rappie pie brims with chicken chunks and the grated potatoes are as translucent as pearls.

Cape Sable Island, where the well-known Cape Islander fishing craft has been made by Atkinson Boatbuilders since the early 1900s, lies a half hour south of the Pubnicos via Route 3 and a short causeway from the mainland; visitors are welcome to poke around the shipyard as long as they observe safety precautions. The **Archelaus Smith Museum** in nearby Centreville houses displays relating to the lobster fishing and shipbuilding industries on which the island's residents depend. The museum is open mid-June to late September.

For dining, return to the mainland and Barrington Passage, at the junction of Routes 3 and 330, where the large but cozy **Old School House Restaurant** wins plaudits for its natural foods and fruit salads, hearty fish chowder and charbroiled halibut or haddock, fresh breads and homemade desserts.

Nearby **Barrington**'s Meeting House, dating from 1765, is the oldest Nonconformist house of worship in Canada; its woollen mill gives visitors an up-close look at early Industrial Age textile technology. Both are open during the summer season only. The **Seal Island Lighthouse Museum** in Barrington is a replica of the light on the nearby small island of the same name, and affords visitors panoramic views from the top of the tower; open June 15 to September 30, 9:30 A.M. to 5:30 P.M., Monday through Saturday, and from 1:00 to 5:00 P.M. on Sundays.

The French Shore

Port Royal, a French fur-trading post established by Samuel de Champlain in 1605, was Canada's first permanent European settlement. By the start of Queen Anne's War in 1702, France had relocated the settlement across the Annapolis River to what is now Annapolis Royal, northeast of present-day Digby. The Peace of Utrecht (1715), which ended the War of the Spanish Succession (and by extension Queen Anne's War), awarded French Acadia to the British, who renamed it Nova Scotia. Abandoned by its French founders, Annapolis Royal became the capital of the new Crown colony, and remained so until 1749, when Halifax assumed that role.

What followed stands as one of the more conspicuous blots on England's long and mostly glorious history. French Acadian farm families living along the upper Fundy coast, many of them resident in the area for more than a century, professed their neutrality, but George II demanded unqualified oaths of allegiance, with the result that most of Nova Scotia's 8,000 Acadians were eventually deported in the expulsion of 1755. British subjects, first New England Planters, then, during the American Revolution, Loyalists lured by the promise of free land, settled along the coast around Yarmouth and from Weymouth north to Windsor—most often on the productive land formerly worked by the Acadians.

Those Acadians who managed to return after the expulsion were left with parts of the rocky seacoast known as the **French Shore**, the municipality of Clare, consisting of 18 villages scattered along the lower reaches of St. Mary's Bay southwest of Digby. Even today it is a region distinct from the rest of the province, as evidenced by the provincial highway, which, posted with speed-limit warnings between St. Martin and St. Bernard, becomes a 25-mile-long stretch of two-lane Acadian road. The houses along this rural corridor are large and austere, sometimes gabled, in contrast to Quebec's brightly painted mansard-roofed houses.

Today Acadians are fishermen and mink and fox ranchers, rather than the tillers of the soil they were in the years before the expulsion. **Meteghan**, where visitors can buy fresh lobster and scallops from boats docked at its busy wharves, is the busiest French Shore port. Restaurants hereabouts—particularly **La Râpure Acadienne** (Tel: 902/769-2172) and, on the campus of the Université Ste-Anne, **Le Casse-Croûte** (Tel: 902/769-2001), both in nearby Church Point—serve the province's most authentic deep-dish rappie pie, an Acadian potato dish filled with meat or chicken. South of Church Point near Cape St. Mary itself, the normally frigid waters of the Bay of Fundy warm up enough to allow swimming in the tidal flats off **Mavilette Beach**.

All along the narrow roads of the region imposing churches attest to the Roman Catholicism of its inhabitants. Church Point's St. Mary's Church has a 185-foot-high steeple anchored with 40 tons of ballast to keep it from toppling in the fierce Fundy winds.

Of course, the sea looms large in the region's past. During the Great Age of Sail in the 1800s, the coast from Yarmouth to Maitland was thick with crowded ports and busy ship-yards. More than a century later, during the U.S. experiment with Prohibition, St. Mary's Bay became a favorite haven for East Coast rumrunners.

Weymouth

Northeast along the coast in the direction of Digby, Wey-mouth, on the northern edge of the French Shore, has a different kind of history. Once a bitter territorial bone of contention between Loyalists from New Jersey, who carved the town from the forests, and Acadians intent on resettling after the 1755 expulsion had driven them from the region, Weymouth today is a low-profile study in reconciliation. Its northern end is centered around the former St. Thomas Anglican Church, where the local historical society now serves English-inspired afternoon teas and pastries on sum-mer Thursdays. Elsewhere, the town's commercial beat is dominated by Acadian names. One such enterprise is the comfortable ▶ **Goodwin Hotel**, the French Shore's sole hotel among a plethora of motels. This century-old inn has a dozen plain but immaculate guest rooms upstairs, pleasant downstairs parlors backed by a family-style dining room, and, outside, wide porches for lazing. Better still, the Goodwin's owner-chefs, the Comeaus (she from New Brunswick and he of the ubiquitous French Shore Comeau clan), create some of the heartiest down-home cooking in the Maritimes. Be sure to try the roasted chicken with sweetly spiced stuffing, and the lighter-than-air lemon pie.

DIGBY

Digby, the province's smallest gateway town and one of the approximately 150 coastal towns that, aside from Halifax, together form Nova Scotia's premier sightseeing region, is the terminus for the two-and-a-half hour ferry ride from Saint John, New Brunswick, across the Bay of Fundy. Stretching almost 170 miles from Yarmouth to Windsor, the coast is shadowed by Highway 101, otherwise known as the **Evangeline Trail**, after Longfellow's poem, which eloquently depicts the expulsion of the Acadians in 1755. What happened afterward, however, is what makes the contemporary route so interesting. Returning Acadians (many, including those who became Louisiana Cajuns, didn't return) settled along the previously mentioned French Shore southwest of Digby, while Loyalists fleeing the American Revolution homed in on Digby, Annapolis Royal, and elsewhere along the coast northeast of Digby. The resulting differences in architecture and lifestyle are striking, and owe their existence to the fact that Acadians and Anglos coexisted through the years with very little cultural interaction.

Today this coastal route resembles a long main street, with Digby conveniently situated at its midpoint. Although the little seaport can be used as a day-tripping base for swings up and down the coast, it works equally well to drive through Digby, stay overnight farther up the Annapolis Valley, and return to town for a day. Digby's ▶ **Pines Resort Hotel**, on the shore road leading to the ferry terminal, is a reason to stay longer. Unquestionably the province's most splendid resort estate, the Norman-style mansion and adjacent chalets are outshone only by their setting on the prow of a hill overlooking the town and Annapolis Basin. The golf course (open to the public) rolls with the terrain and hiking trails cut across the hillsides. The Pines' cuisine is French under chef Bernard Meyer's direction, while the overall ambience is Canadian at its toney best. In short, this is a retreat untarnished by commercialism or the harsher realities of the outside world.

What Digby is known for, aside from its famed scallop fleet, is the **Admiral Digby Museum**, on the harbor at 95 Montague Row, a place brimming with local historical tidbits. To get a more cohesive picture of the port's past, walk the harborfront and *then* browse through the exhibits housed in this restored mid-18th-century structure. Open June 22 to September 30, 9:00 A.M. to 5:00 P.M. daily.

The town hugs the southwestern corner of the broad Annapolis Basin and was founded by Admiral Robert Digby, a British naval officer who in 1783 led a convoy of 1,000 Loyalists, some of whom brought doors, windows, and other valuables from their New York and New England homes, up the tempestuous Fundy to settle in the area. These days, thanks to a downtown renovation project that has resulted in new lighting, ornamental brickwork, and planters overflowing with flowers in summer, it looks better every year. A sightseer's walk follows Montague Row along the harbor to Fishermen's Wharf, where the scallop fleet, one of the largest inshore fleets in the world, is docked. Their catch is Digby's fame, and can be found for sale at the wharf's **Royal Fundy Market** or succulently prepared at small restaurants.

Stores line Water Street, which is intersected at points by passageways once used to haul fish up from the beach or hay in the other direction. The **Thistle Down Inn** on Montague Row rents bikes for $10 a day.

DINING IN DIGBY

Like all seaports, Digby has a rousing bar scene, although it's quieter since Porky's Pub on the outskirts of town closed. **Club 98**, at 34 Water Street, has been revamped with live weekend entertainment and a disk jockey on weeknights. The club is also now the lounge of the refurbished **Fundy Restaurant** (reservations recommended; Tel: 902/245-4950), where diners can feast on Digby's raison d'être—tender, oversize scallops pan- or deep-fried. Haddock fillets are another local specialty. Both will prove even more appetizing at a table on the newish patio or in the enclosed solarium that overlooks the harbor and the scallop draggers at anchor. The other dinner and evening choice worth considering is the restaurant at the **Pines Resort Hotel**, just outside town in the direction of the ferry, where the menu favors pricey Continental cuisine, Château Latour heads a mostly French wine list, and the entertainment revolves around organ music, dancing, and Singapore slings. Again, reservations recommended; Tel: (902) 245-2511.

THE ANNAPOLIS VALLEY AND THE FUNDY COAST

What lies along the Fundy is, simply put, a major cut above most North American sightseeing regions, stretched-out distances notwithstanding. Thirty minutes southwest of Digby on the narrow **Digby Neck Peninsula**, also known as Digby Gut, whale-watching excursions depart from Westport, on **Brier Island**, during the summer months. The coast's best-known attraction, however, is the glacier-scoured corridor extending northeast from Digby to Windsor, much of it backed by the high, protective ridges known as the North and South Mountains. The result is the exquisite **Annapolis Valley**, where fruit orchards grow rooted in rich alluvial soil, warmed by sunshine and nourished by moisture from the sea.

The Annapolis Royal Area

Annapolis Royal, 40 minutes northeast of Digby via Route 1 (the Evangeline Trail), is worth a stop for its **Royal Historic Gardens** (open mid-May to mid-October, 8:00 A.M. to dusk), as well as Fort Anne, where England's decisive victory over the French turned the tide in their early-18th-century struggles for New World dominance. The town itself lies northeast across the Annapolis River from Port Royal, established by Champlain in 1605 and generally credited as the country's first permanent European settlement. The ten-minute drive from Annapolis Royal takes you through Granville Ferry, a postcard-pretty village and the location of the **Market House Gallery**, on the corner of Granville Street and Letney Lane, which stocks avant-garde pottery, raku, and glassware made by local craftspeople. **Port Royal National Historic Site**, another five minutes from Granville Ferry, features a re-creation of Port Royal Habitation, the Norman-style fort based on plans drawn up by Champlain.

Upper Clements Family Vacation Park, the area's newest attraction, is in the town of the same name, some ten minutes southwest of Annapolis Royal. Although the park was conceived as a tourist attraction to boost the region's economy, it nonetheless gets across an educational message, using its themes to explain Nova Scotia's legends and history, as well as providing a showcase for local craftspeople and artisans.

Annapolis Royal To Windsor

The heart of the Annapolis Valley is the 50-mile corridor that stretches northeast of Annapolis Royal up to Windsor. All along here you'll find pretty towns and the nearby drama of the Fundy tides. Although you can drive to Windsor from Annapolis Royal in about two hours, plan on at least double that, as you will almost surely be lulled by the peaceful prosperity of **Bridgetown**, **Kentville**, and **Wolfville**. The influence of the Planters and Loyalists who settled the area is strong, and an aura of affluence persists to this day. It is more lovely and fragrant still during the **Apple Blossom Festival** in late May, when Kentville becomes the center of parades and concerts. Bridgetown, on Route 1 some 24 km (15 miles) northeast of Granville Ferry, is the location of the **Gallery at Saratoga**, Carleton Corner and Highway 201, which exhibits the paintings of Kenneth Tolmie, including a number of rural scenes from his regionally acclaimed Bridgetown series. Open year-round, 2:00 to 5:00 P.M., or by appointment (Tel: 902/665-4508).

The civilized sensibilities on display in these towns may cause you to forget the fierce Fundy, just minutes from their tree-shaded main streets. Which is understandable—during the almost two-hour drive from Digby to Wolfville you will not catch sight of the great bay once. The Fundy at its fiercest rushes in and out of Minas Basin, one of two arms created by Cape Chignecto at the bay's upper end. **Cape Blomidon**, which may have gotten its name from sailors who called it "Blow Me Down Cape," extends northward into Minas Basin at its narrowest point, creating a bottleneck that results in some of the highest tides in the world. An expedition to the peninsula can easily fill a day, and should include the 13-km (8-mile) trail to the cliffs at **Cape Split**, with spectacular views of the surging tides below.

Windsor to Parrsboro

From the cape you can see **Parrsboro**, on the basin's north shore, basking in the fame brought by *National Geographic*'s periodic visits to the nearby site of the world's largest fossil find. The Fundy erodes the seacoast in the Parrsboro area, exposing an abundance of semiprecious gemstones; the village's tourist office sponsors summer rock-hound trips for agate and amethyst.

As close as Parrsboro may appear to be from Cape Blomidon, you'll have to skirt the eastern end of Minas Basin, a five-hour drive, to get there. **Truro** makes an excellent intermediate stop. As the town is more industrial than touristy, however, it's possible to stay on the outskirts without missing anything. The ▶ **Best Western Glengarry**, a better-than-average motel, lies just off Highway 102 on Willow Street. Another option is the relatively new two-story ▶ **Journey's End Motel**, on Meadow Drive off exit 15, which offers clean, spacious rooms at modest rates.

By all means take the coastal **Glooscap Trail** (Route 215) from Windsor to Truro, allowing a half day for the leisurely trip. The road wends past Burncoat Head, where the world's highest tides peak at 54 feet. Farther on in **Maitland**, where Canada's largest full-rigged wooden ship was launched in 1874, Lawrence House (open daily in season) showcases memorabilia relating to William D. Lawrence, the ship's builder, as well as the local shipbuilding industry. All along the route the sea seems to boil twice a day; in places it is so fierce, in fact, that it pushes tidal bores into certain rivers at high tide. This is a time to watch the sea, but not to wade.

Unfortunately, good dining spots in the area are in short supply, with Parrsboro's red-roofed **Stowaway Restaurant** on Lower Main Street one of the few worthwhile stops. Meals—try the baked flounder with lobster sauce and homemade fruit pies—are filling and reasonably priced, and made all the more appealing by views of the surging tides; Tel: (902) 254-3371.

STAYING AND DINING
ON THE FUNDY COAST

The Fundy region boasts a number of interesting towns in which to stay, with accommodations ranging from stylish historic farmhouses like the ▶ **Auberge Sieur de Monts** in Granville Ferry outside Annapolis Royal, to Victorian-style manor houses such as the ▶ **Bread & Roses Country Inn**, the ▶ **Queen Anne Inn**, and ▶ **Hillsdale House** in Annapolis Royal. Rates are moderate, seldom more than $85 per night.

There are pockets of significant historical interest here as well. In the latter half of the 18th century, England encouraged disaffected farmers from the newly created New England states—the New England Planters as they're known in Nova Scotia—to settle in the Annapolis Valley on land vacated by French Acadians. The ▶ **Planters' Barracks** in Port Williams, a restored garrison house in which British soldiers were billeted when it was known as Fort Hughes, was built in 1778 to protect Loyalist farmers who had resettled in the area after the tumultuous deportation of the Acadians. Restored to its former elegance in the early 1980s and reopened as an inn in 1984, the eclectic Georgian-style manor house has six suites and an array of antiques that changes as the innkeepers acquire new provincial pieces. Use of the tennis court and bikes are included in the room rate.

Of more recent vintage, Betsy Harwood, former co-owner of Halifax's Fat Frank's restaurant, has expanded into inn-keeping with the ▶ **Tattingstone Inn** in Wolfville, a stately 19th-century structure with adjacent carriage house and cottage. Many of its expensive rooms are furnished with canopy beds and equipped with fireplaces, and its lush setting is enhanced by Harwood's dining room, which serves the finest in provincial fare; try the peppered Atlantic salmon and, for dessert, sauced chocolate pâté. Guests can work off the extra calories in a number of ways: The inn has a heated pool, steam room, and tennis court on the premises.

The carriage trade dotes on this part of Nova Scotia, so rich in rolling landscapes, historic country inns, and impressive old houses, many doubling as restaurants of merit. Even the modern ▶ **Best Western Aurora Inn**, a better-than-average motel on Kingston's Main Street, a two-hour drive northeast of Digby, has a classy air about it. Heaping portions of beef tournedos, as well as sautéed scallops or the Sunday brunch with quiches and hot and cold meats, are drawing cards with locals and visitors alike.

That may explain why there are so few restaurants per se in the area, as almost every inn has a cozy public dining room. Worth a stop strictly on the merits of its restaurant is **Newman's** (Tel: 902/532-5502) in Annapolis Royal, where the sautéed scallops with garlic are especially good; after November's black-bear hunting season bear dishes are also available while they last.

The ▶ **Old Orchard Inn**, an oversize motel in Wolfville, deserves special mention (although it's not easily found: Leave Highway 101 at exit 11, drive through the underpass, and look for the big sign on your right). Its dining room, with sweeping views of Cape Blomidon and the Minas Basin, is tonier than many restaurants in Halifax, and its service and presentation are among the best in the province. Seafood and lobster reign in the main dining room, and the desserts are positively sinful. Reservations advised; Tel: (902) 542-5751.

THE NORTHUMBERLAND STRAIT COAST

From Baie Verte at the New Brunswick border to the Strait of Canso—the narrow strip of water separating mainland Nova Scotia from Cape Breton—the warm waters of Northumberland Strait wash an angled seacoast scalloped with bays and more than 40 beaches. Windsurfing, sailing, swimming, and clamming are just some of the activities available to visitors.

Haligonians know this coast as the north shore and have been using it as a summertime escape for generations. From Amherst, founded more than 200 years ago as the French and Indian Wars wound down, to Pictou, birthplace of New Scotland—and today the gateways to New Brunswick and Prince Edward Island, respectively—it is a region where a simpler, easygoing way of life is colored by a nostalgia for days gone by.

THE SUNRISE TRAIL

The region's coastal sightseeing route is called the Sunrise Trail—well marked with road signs of the sun rising above rippling waters—and follows the strait on two-lane back-country roads through a hundred four-corner villages that seem to have been bypassed by time. From Amherst, the route's meanderings follow Route 6 along the coast to Pictou, then become part of the Trans-Canada Highway spur (Highway 106) between Pictou and New Glasgow. From there it follows Route 245 to Malignant Cove, continues around Cape George as Route 337, and becomes the Trans-Canada (Highway 104) again in Antigonish.

The Trans-Canada enters the province from New Brunswick at Amherst and runs inland south of the Sunrise Trail to Truro, at the eastern end of the Bay of Fundy, before continuing east to New Glasgow and Antigonish. Use the Trans-Canada for making time, and save the Sunrise Trail, which lopes along the coast for 200-plus miles in a far more enjoyable, leisurely way, for sightseeing.

The province's official road map is the only guide you'll need for this region. The large tourist information centers at entry points in Amherst and Pictou, as well as in Antigonish, stock free descriptive literature; towns like Springhill, Tatamagouche, and Truro also have summertime tourist bureaus stocked with regional information.

In these parts, local folks celebrate the summer season for themselves, while at the same time properly welcoming visitors as guests at lobster suppers, festivals, and church socials. A large percentage of the population traces their ancestry to Britain—the legacy of one of the Crown's most successful efforts to transform French Acadia into Anglo Nova Scotia. After the 1755 expulsion, Loyalist New Englanders settled Amherst, Onslow Township, and Merigomish, while Scottish immigration spread through Pictou and Antigonish counties.

Work-hungry immigrants and the discovery of Pictou County's 48-foot-thick coal seam at Stellarton meshed during Canada's industrial revolution. The country's first successful steel ingots were poured in Trenton, near Pictou. Riches opened architecture's door, particularly in Pictou, where 20 early-19th-century buildings are now designated historic landmarks.

Some heavy industry remains, but the frenzied development of the 19th century has given way to more serene scenes: fields of strawberries and blueberries, greenhouses filled with roses at **Oxford**, and the once-fledgling **Jost Vineyards**, which now produce award-winning wines (tours offered Monday through Saturday at 3:00 P.M., summer only) on the Malagash Peninsula. There have been decades of partiality for golf at the semi-private Amherst Golf and Country Club (which welcomes visitors), and a strong reverence for the area's Scottish heritage, now marked memorably at St. Francis Xavier University in Antigonish, where the **Hall of the Clans** reading room in the Angus L. MacDonald library is adorned with the handcarved crests of the area's founding patriarchs; in summer, the library is open daily from 8:30 A.M. to 4:30 P.M.

Beaches and Lobster Pounds

Northumberland Strait in summer is a comfortably warm 70° to 75° F (20° to 24° C), its many sandbar fingers perfect for dips and lazy floating. Among the nicest spots are **Northport Beach**, northeast of Amherst; **Gulf Shore Provincial Park**, three miles north of Pugwash; and **Rushton's Beach**, protected by the headlands of Tatamagouche Bay. (Red-sand beaches are picturesque, but the iron oxide stains. If you prefer white-sand beaches, they extend eastward from the Antigonish area; those from the New Brunswick border to Antigonish are strictly the iron-oxide type.)

Lobster fanciers will relish the sight of pounds (holding tanks) brimming with fresh lobster at the head of the strait's seaport wharves; Northport Beach has a nearby lobster pound, and **Port Howe**, west of Pugwash, has a whole string of pounds filled with the day's catch. Here and everywhere along the province's coasts, lobster harvesting is strictly limited according to the season; for example, western Northumberland Strait's time of bounty is May and June. Not to worry. Seaport fish stores *always* stock the delicacy, and lobster is on every provincial menu. The strait's eastern end is the realm of big-time game fish; a 678-pound bluefin tuna took the hook at Auld Cove on St. George's Bay in 1979. Charters operate out of **Havre Boucher**, northeast of Auld Cove.

AMHERST

It's a matter of minutes from Amherst, in the northwestern corner of the province, to New Brunswick via the Trans-Canada Highway, which loops around town. Amherst itself is a long seven-hour drive from Digby, almost nine hours from Yarmouth, and four hours from Halifax. All of which helps explain why Amherst is a story unto itself, and definitely worth a stopover of several hours, or better yet, a leisurely day spent exploring the entire area.

The **Cumberland County Museum**, a top-notch regional museum at 150 Church Street, tells the story best. Amherst was founded in 1760 and named for the British major-general who had won the province for the English Crown by defeating the French two years earlier at Louisbourg, on Cape Breton. It is now a county shire town, the second-largest settlement in the Northumberland Strait region, and boasts some of the province's best Victorian Canadiana along its main streets.

In its early heyday the region contributed four Fathers of Confederation, one of whom was Senator Robert Dickey; his white 1831 Victorian manor house today houses the museum. Amherst was so affluent in Dickey's day that conspicuous consumption became the art of understatement. The senator's modest mansion, set amid a spacious hilltop lawn, began as Grove Cottage, resplendent with almost two dozen windows punctuating its façade and fireplace chimneys across the rear roof line.

Exhibits here trace the cultivation of the diked Tantramar Marshes, first by French Acadians, then by Yorkshire immigrants after 1772. Textile and shoe manufacturing during the 19th century made Amherst rich, and the resultant wealth accounts for the stately mansions lining Victoria and its cross streets, as well as the many impressive red-sandstone commercial buildings. The museum is open daily in season, Tuesday through Saturday the rest of the year; Tel: (902) 667-2561.

Today Amherst seems drenched in quiet. Whatever's happening can be found along the northern rim of Victoria Street, which crosses the Trans-Canada Highway. Any noise there usually originates from **King Pin Beverage** on Gerard Avenue, where a draft-beer crowd packs the place late Friday and Saturday nights to listen to live music. Farther up Victoria, **Touch of Country** stocks provincial crafts, Grohmann knives from Pictou, Dominion chairs and tables made in Bass River, and Baderno cookware from Prince Edward Island; strictly local buys can be found at the Thursday market fair in the parking lot behind **Bird's Restaurant** and **Cecil's Bakery**, the favorite local chow combination. Cecil's redesigned rear section includes a patio for outdoor dining.

For lodgings, the Amherst area offers half a dozen motels designed for visitors driving through from New Brunswick. These include the ► **Auberge Wandlyn Inn** off Highway 104 (exit 3) in town, or the ► **Fundy Winds Family Motel** at the Fort Lawrence crossing (Highway 104, exit 1A); either will do for an overnight stay.

Around Amherst

Outside town, two-lane roads wander across tidy farmland; many of the farms have pick-your-own berry fields and produce stands in season. The Amherst area and Cumberland County are known for summer blueberries, with the season coming to a climax with culinary festivals and advertised church socials for a week in August.

Three-hundred-million-year-old fossil trees are embedded in the cliffs at **Joggins**, on the eastern shore of upper Chignecto Bay, southwest of Amherst. Tides churn up the beaches beneath the cliffs, exposing pieces of amethyst; looking is legal, taking what's attached to bedrock isn't. Closer to town, Victoria Street leads across the Trans-Canada Highway into the **Amherst Point Migratory Bird Sanctuary**, where more than 200 species make themselves at home among the 1,225 acres of the Tantramar Marshes (with trails). Bucolic **Heather Beach**, 40 km (25 miles) to the northeast on Northumberland Strait's shallow Gulf Stream–warmed waters, is a perfect spot for swimming, clamming, and, in May and June, buying lobster fresh off the boats.

PICTOU

Pictou—not only old, but of great provincial significance—
is three hours east of Amherst via the Sunrise Trail and 15
minutes north of New Glasgow (or 10 minutes from Caribou, the terminus for ferries to Prince Edward Island).

Nova Scotia's beloved Scottish heritage originated here in
1773 with the landing of Highlanders aboard the *Hector*—
an event that is still revered. Sanctity brings its own rewards:
Aside from some industrial development, garish commercialism has bypassed the town. Pictou merits an overnight stop,
and longer if you want to explore.

The oldest part of town, along the harbor, is a pretty place
with an unusual assortment of architectural styles; there's
Scottish stone domestic from the early settlement years, Second Empire (a rare style in Nova Scotia), Victorian, and
Canadian eclectic. The oldest structure here is the 1806
McCulloch House, overlooking the harbor, and today a component of the Nova Scotia Museum complex. Open May 15 to
October 15, 9:30 A.M. to 5:30 P.M., Monday through Saturday,
and 1:30 to 5:30 P.M. on Sundays.

Pictou's pulse is found along Water Street, a diminutive
slice of the Old World, and one so enchanting that it has been
earmarked for federal and provincial restoration funds. The
first project on the agenda is the re-creation of the three-
masted, black-hulled *Hector*. But it's the thoroughly modern
DeCoste Entertainment Centre (Tel: 902/485-8848 for upcoming events) that's the draw these days, with a full slate of
national and regional theater, dance, and music offered in one
of the province's best concert halls.

STAYING AND DINING IN PICTOU

For formal (and expensive) dining in an 1810 stone house,
try the **Consulate Inn & Restaurant** (once the American
consulate) at the corner of Water and Willow streets. The
restaurant, which serves lunch and dinner, is open June
through September; Tel: (902) 485-4554 for reservations.

A few years ago, the ▶ **Braeside Inn** (formerly the Hotel
L'Auberge), on Front Street overlooking the water, was revamped, in part rebuilt, and completely redecorated by new
owners. The new look enhanced the dining room, which has
splendid harborfront views and a decor featuring soft raspberry and green tones. The owners also added an atrium-style
greenhouse and created an eclectic, still-evolving menu,
strong on Continental cuisine, with salmon imported from
New Brunswick and duckling from Quebec as its major din-

ner entrées. As an inn the Braeside is resplendent, with a
Chinese-decor lobby, middle-floor guest rooms featuring wal-
nut furnishings, and a top floor done in early American.
Originally conceived as a gathering place for artists, the
Braeside quickly outgrew its original clientele and now attracts guests and diners from as far as Halifax; Tel: (902) 485-
5046 for dinner reservations.

Lots of local color and culinary goodies characterize the
four-day **Pictou Lobster Carnival**, held in early July. Tributes
to the area's Scottish heritage fill five days in July at nearby
New Glasgow's **Festival of the Tartans**. In Antigonish, to the
east of Pictou near the coast, the **Antigonish Highland
Games** are staged over nine days from early to mid-July, at
which time there are absolutely no vacancies anywhere in
the area.

When all else fails, try the ► **Best Western Claymore Inn**,
an inexpensive and better-than-average motel in Antigonish,
just a short distance from the site of the games; you'll need
to make arrangements beforehand, however.

Around Pictou

Pictou's shoreline is for relaxing, maybe windsurfing at
Little Harbour, and certainly for enjoying the resort trappings at the ► **Pictou Lodge Resort**, a venerable property
on Braeshore Road, north of town, where a relaxed luncheon is served on the screened porch for locals and visitors
in the know. For reservations, Tel: (902) 485-4322.

Nearby Wharf Road leads to **Pictou Island**, nice for a
picnic lunch and solitary island hikes. Carefree Cruises operates out of **Caribou Wharf** (north of Pictou) from June to
October; a fishing charter with gear for 10 people runs $60
an hour when the fiberglass *Special K* is not otherwise
running morning Pictou Harbour tours ($10) or afternoon
Pictou Island tours ($15).

On the way to Cape Breton, the **Pictou County Historical
Museum**, 86 Temperance Street in New Glasgow, is well
worth a stop, particularly if you're a railroad buff—the
Samson, one of Canada's earliest steam locomotives, is on
exhibit nearby. The museum is open June through August,
9:30 A.M. to 5:00 P.M. daily. Farther east, almost on Cape
Breton itself, **Pomquet Beach** is carpeted with dunes (unusual for this area) and laced with boardwalks leading down
to the water. Although you'll want to stay on the walks, as
poison ivy flourishes hereabouts, the beach is sandy and the
water fine for swimming.

CAPE BRETON ISLAND

For many visitors, Cape Breton is the definitive Nova Scotia. The island rises from sea level at the Canso Strait and tops out in the Cape Breton Highlands, a wild and almost inaccessible tableland plateau laced with hiking trails and rimmed by the **Cabot Trail**, the spectacular auto sightseeing route. Along the island's western coastline Acadian villages face the Gulf of Saint Lawrence, plied in summer by **whale-watching charter boats** out of Cheticamp. Just inland, anglers from all over the world congregate to fish for Atlantic salmon in the **Margarees** area. The Atlantic coast boasts the offshore **Bird Islands**, with their gray seals, puffins, and seabird colonies reached by cruises from Big Bras d'Or.

Cape Breton has a distinctness about it that owes much to **Bras d'Or**, an inland sea as deep as 900 feet in some places, its fjordlike coastline dotted with marinas. The western portion of the island, home to scattered Scottish and Acadian settlements, is Cape Breton's scenic half. **Sydney**, situated on the smaller eastern portion of the island, is Cape Breton's industrial center and was the island's capital when it was a colony independent of Nova Scotia. Alexander Graham Bell, who was born in Scotland and made his fortune in the United States with the invention of the telephone, spent summers on Cape Breton at **Baddeck** on Bras d'Or, where his descendants still summer. Visited together, the double island is one of North America's most interesting vacation retreats.

Midsummer is festival season on Cape Breton. **Gaelic Mod** at Gaelic College runs for a week in early August, and revolves around Scottish piping, drumming, and Highland dancing. Glace Bay's **Festival on the Bay** spans the last half of July, and more grassroots doings can be found at New Waterford's **Coal Dust Days** in mid-July. **Action Week** in early August is Sydney's summer festival.

Aside from Sydney, Cape Breton lacks a central focus, so allow extra time to see it. The island's routes tend to run southwest to northeast; sightseeing is best done by selecting the destination and any peripheral sights along the way, planning your itinerary with the aid of a map, and using the Trans-Canada Highway whenever possible. (As Highway 104, the Trans-Canada ends in Auld Cove on the mainland, and resumes on the other side of the Canso Causeway as Highway 105. Its eastern terminus is North Sydney, 248 km/154 miles northeast of Canso.)

From Cabot to Coal

Cape Breton is most closely associated with Scottish Highlanders, the province's largest cultural base. In reality, however, it is a thorough mix of different peoples, starting with
the Micmac Indians, who today account for 2,000 of the
island's 175,000 inhabitants.

England's claim to North America was based on John
Cabot's sighting of Cape Breton in 1497. Not that it mattered.
By the early 16th century Portuguese fishermen were regular
visitors to the Ingonish area. The French made some inroads
on the islands during the 17th century, establishing a Jesuit
mission at Englishtown in 1629 and a small fishing village at
St. Ann's. The enterprising Nicholas Denys, a French explorer
and merchant, is credited with founding Cape Breton's first
permanent settlement at St. Peter's, but a fire in 1669 put an
end to that enterprise.

Cape Breton remained a French colonial backwater
throughout the 17th century, as the French and English concentrated their energies on gaining control of the mainland's
Port Royal area, settled by Champlain in 1605. By 1719, 200
French farming families had settled in the Sydney area, with
others laying claim to Isle Madame, off the southern end of
the island, and a year later (the same year that construction on
Louisbourg Fortress was begun) French miners were digging
coal at Glace Bay.

The first Anglo infusion came, as usual, with Loyalists
fleeing the American Revolution and settling Sydney. The
next to arrive were a party of Scots, who arrived in Sydney
Harbor aboard *Northern Friends* in 1802; by the 1850s there
were 50,000 Scots on Cape Breton. Not all stayed; Rev.
Norman MacLeod and his flock from South Gut St. Ann's
went on to Australia in 1851, for example. The mix became
even more cosmopolitan during the latter part of the 19th
century, as the local coal and steel industries lured Greeks,
Chinese, West Indians, Eastern Europeans, Lebanese, Syri-
ans, and Italians (from Boston and Italy)—all told, a total of
23 ethnic groups.

Cape Breton's earliest lures had been fur trading and
fishing. The coal frenzy, in contrast, gave rise to the illusion
of neverending riches and delusive dreams—illusions finally dispelled during the post–World War II steel slump
and, later, as oil replaced coal as an energy source.

For today's visitors, the scenic beauty of both the interior
and the coast has a powerful impact, yet Cape Bretoners are
the real lure. They are courteous in a most civil way, never
intruding but very willing to assist if needed.

SYDNEY

Sydney, Cape Breton's largest city and the third largest in the province, is a five-hour drive from Pictou or seven-plus hours from Halifax. The Trans-Canada is the quickest over-land route into the area (although flying in from Halifax is even quicker and easier). The expressway slices through central Cape Breton, hugging the western shore of Bras d'Or, the inland sea, before ending at North Sydney's ferry terminal (where you can make connections to Newfound-land). Sydney lies farther south and east via the express-way's continuation (Highway 162) around Sydney's Atlantic harbor.

The city is best known as Nova Scotia's steel town; it is also the main commercial hub for coal towns like Glace Bay and Sydney Mines. In fact, it is coal rather than steel that un-dergirds so much of Sydney's history. As early as 1719 French settlers and troops were digging coal from Port Morien cliffs to fuel the **Fortress of Louisbourg**, New France's premier settlement in this part of Canada, and today only a half hour southeast of Sydney on the coast.

France's commitment to Louisbourg was not without its irony. By the early 1700s England had chased the French out of the Port Royal area and onto Ile Royale, as Cape Breton was then known. Instead of choosing the area around Port Morien, however, where a settlement placed atop the cliffs could watch for enemy attacks, or Sydney harbor, even more spacious than England's jewel of a military harbor at Halifax, the French chose Louisbourg, with its uncomplicated harbor embraced by a flat plain hard by the open Atlantic.

While it was still under construction, a volunteer army in the service of the British Crown swooped down on the garrison in 1745 and forced it to surrender after a 49-day siege. Three years later a peace treaty returned Louisbourg to the French, who saw it fall to the British a second and final time in 1758. France's claims to Atlantic Canada were finished—as much a casualty of 150 years of struggle for New World dominance as of its military commanders' appre-ciation for the beauty of a place rather than its strategic value.

So that it would never rise as a threat to the Crown again, British forces had demolished Louisbourg by 1760. The Crown's plan to strengthen its hand in Atlantic Canada un-folded 24 years later when Loyalists fleeing the American Revolution founded Sydney. With Sydney as its capital, Cape

Breton became a Crown colony in 1785, and in 1820 the island was annexed by Nova Scotia.

A century and a half later, as metropolitan Sydney's economy floundered due to diminished steel and coal demand, the federal government re-educated many of the area's unemployed miners and steelworkers in the ways of 18th-century construction and then looked on approvingly as they rebuilt a portion of the old fortress town. This time Louisbourg's purpose was, and still is, to bolster Cape Breton's economy through tourism. Today it is a magnificent re-creation of a walled town, with 50 perfectly duplicated buildings, costumed guides, and a strong atmosphere of authenticity.

The Louisbourg **Craft Workshops**, initially government funded and now self-sufficient, specialize in the design, production, and marketing of a fine line of distinctive Cape Breton crafts and wares.

Not surprisingly, Cape Breton's former status as a French colony and the ensuing struggles for dominance between England and France help explain Cape Bretoners' sense that their home is a place apart. As the region's major commercial hub, this is particularly true of Sydney, notwithstanding its location off to one side of the island. As a base for day trips, Sydney offers visitors tantalizing proximity to Cape Breton's grandeur as well as many interesting attractions.

Exploring Sydney

Sydney stretches along the harbor's eastern side, with its historic residential North End occupying a narrow peninsula. Piers in the area are now used by cruise ships from June to October. Industrial Sydney is situated farther northwest along the harborfront and is known as Whitney Pier. The 19th-century influx of immigrants from around the world settled near the area's coke oven, and the ethnic churches here—Polish, African Orthodox, and Ukrainian—are now historic properties.

The Sydney that visitors will want to see stretches from the North End along Esplanade (the location of its old whipping post), which eventually becomes Kings Road. The blocks up from Esplanade are full of interest. Crafts, a vital part of the recovering economy, have found a sizable niche in the upper floors of the **Lyceum**, 255 George Street, once Sydney's performing-arts center. (The Cape Breton Centre for Heritage and Science uses the first floor for exhibits.) Concerts and so forth have moved over to the **Centre 200** on George Street, which becomes the focus of Action Week festivities in early August. A parking lot on George Street is also home to a thriving farmers' market on Sunday mornings in summer—a good place to browse for more crafts as well as fresh produce and baked goods. **Island Crafts** on Charlotte Street, which runs parallel to Esplanade, is another interesting stop. The shop is the local outlet for 300 craftspeople, whose wares, while not cheap, are unusual, with an emphasis on Cape Breton specialties such as weavings and knitted clothing.

STAYING IN SYDNEY

The city's hotels and motels (a third of Cape Breton's lodgings) are located along the harborfront, making lodgings easy to find and size up. Most are your basic motor inn charging moderate to expensive rates. Even so, they're usually filled with tour groups, which means you'll want to make reservations in advance.

The best for years has been the three-story ▶ **Holiday Inn Sydney** on Kings Road; the corner mini-suites offer expansive harbor views. The ▶ **Delta Sydney Hotel**, on Esplanade, is a worthy competitor, as *all* of its rooms overlook the water. The ▶ **Wandlyn Cape Bretoner Motel**, farther out on Kings Road, is set back from the street, and offers pleasant, if basic, amenities, while the ▶ **Cambridge Suites Hotel**, well situated on Esplanade near the Delta Sydney, is the city's newest addition and offers such extras as a sauna, exercise room, and a rooftop spa pool.

DINING AND NIGHTLIFE IN SYDNEY

You'll find a number of fine restaurants in the neighborhood around Esplanade; unfortunately, as there are not nearly enough to meet the demand, most are usually crowded. **Arthur's** (Tel: 902/539-6750), in the Holiday Inn Sydney on Kings Road, and the Delta Sydney's **Des Barres** restaurant (Tel: 902/567-7015), on the Esplanade, are upscale places for straightforward meat and seafood entrées; during the summer reservations are advised. **Joe's Warehouse & Food Emporium** (Tel: 902/539-6686), inland on Charlotte Street, lures casual diners (no jackets or ties) with lavish portions of prime rib and New York strip steak. For no-frills seafood and meat entrées, try **Jaspers Family Restaurant** (Tel: 902/539-7109) at George and Dorchester streets, one of three Jaspers dining rooms in town offering similar fare.

Some of the province's liveliest nightlife is found along Charlotte Street and its cross streets. Among the most animated is **Smooth Herman's** (downstairs from Joe's Warehouse), where younger locals and professional types imbibe beer and the latest alcoholic concoctions to the sound of live bands. The over-30 crowd seems to prefer **Ivory's** in Keddy's Motel on Kings Road.

The Island Outside Sydney

The Miners' Museum in **Glace Bay**, on the Atlantic, offers a mine tour and a re-created village where you can sit down to a hearty, inexpensive meal.

Getting to know Cape Breton through its people is an important part of any visit, and there's no better way to do it than staying a night or two at one of Cape Breton's Bed & Breakfast homes. A particularly nice one is ► **The Manse** in Louisbourg, where Cape Bretoner Dorothy Brooks has converted the former manse of the Presbyterian (now United) Church into a welcoming bed and breakfast with a long front porch and upstairs guest rooms. About 60 homes on the island, from historic gems to more modest establishments, belong to the association, with most pricing their overnight accommodations at about $45. All serve full breakfasts, often with homemade baked goods. For a list of member establishments, contact the Tourism Distribution Centre, P.O. Box 1448, Sydney, Nova Scotia B1P 6R7; Tel: (800) 565-9464 or (902) 539-4359. Reservations can also be made directly at each lodging.

BADDECK

Baddeck, the largest community on Bras d'Or, lies 70 km (43 miles) west of Sydney on the Trans-Canada Highway; at its wharf and marinas you can rent a canoe or sailboat for enjoying the lake's pleasures. Baddeck's main street runs off the Trans-Canada along the lake, with its attractions lined up one after another. **Alexander Graham Bell National Historic Park**, the resort's best-known attraction, sits on a hilltop on Shore Road. Bell's eclectic interests, from communications to medicine, are reflected in the three splendidly conceived exhibit halls here, worth two to three hours of your time. There's also a splendid view of Baddeck and Bras d'Or from the complex's rooftop gardens; ask one of the staff to point out Beinn Bhreagh, the Bell estate (it's still owned by the family), nestled on a hillside overlooking the lake.

Staying and Dining in the Area

Baddeck boasts Cape Breton's best assortment of dining places. Lobster is always on menus—try the ► **Inverary Inn Resort** (ask for a table on the back porch overlooking Bras d'Or; Tel: 902/295-3500), the **Telegraph House**'s Victorian-style dining room (Tel: 902/295-9988), or the plain lobster fixings at **Baddeck Lobster Suppers** (from 4:00 to 9:00 P.M. in the former Legion Hall). The town has lodgings galore, mostly motels, as it is on the Cabot Trail bus circuit. Many cuts above the ordinary are the above-mentioned Inverary Inn, with a lakeside motel and cottages behind the main lodge, and ▶ **MacNeil House**, a restored 19th-century mansion offering Jacuzzi- and fireplace-equipped suites on the grounds of the Silver Dart Lodge motel.

Iona's **Nova Scotia Highland Village**, south of Baddeck via the Trans-Canada and winding Route 223—plan on an hour to cover a distance that's only 16 km (10 miles) as the crow flies—is another worthwhile stop, its historic buildings an example of early Scottish settlement hereabouts. The 43-acre site is open to the public mid-June to mid-September, Monday through Saturday from 9:00 A.M. to 5:00 P.M., and Sundays from 11:00 A.M. to 6:00 P.M. The adjacent ▶ **Highland Heights Inn** is a neat-as-a-pin motel with a window-walled restaurant overlooking the lakeshore.

The Cabot Trail

The Cabot Trail is what Cape Breton is all about—180 miles of some of North America's most beautiful scenery, with more than a few scary ascents and descents. The highway, like Cape Breton Highlands National Park, which is bordered by the Cabot Trail on three sides, is open year-round. With no stops the drive takes about six hours; mid-June through September, when the weather is mostly clear and shops and restaurants are open, are the best months.

There are several ways to experience this scenic treasure. As quickly as possible is one way—and the way most of the lumbering sightseeing buses from U.S. and Canadian cities do it. Much better is the easy-does-it approach, poking through seaports and exploring side roads with stops at marked overlooks. The best mile-by-mile description is found in the province's travel guide, free from Nova Scotia Tourism, P.O. Box 456, Halifax, Nova Scotia B3J 2R5. (This guide also gives detailed descriptions of other scenic drives in Nova Scotia, and is an invaluable source of history and practical information.) The parts of the trail bordering the national park are detailed in literature available from Cape Breton Highlands National Park, Ingonish Beach, Nova Scotia B0C 1L0; Tel: (902) 285-2535. The information center at the Port Hastings end of the Canso Causeway also stocks Cabot Trail brochures. Another good local source is the Cape Breton Tourism Association, P.O. Box 1448, 20 Keltic

Drive, Sydney River, Nova Scotia B1S 1P5; Tel: (800) 565-9464 or (902) 539-9876.

Driving the Cabot Trail works best if you size it up first on a map. Like other provincial sightseeing routes, it is marked with signs (but no route number), in this case a mountain peak looming over the sea. Drivers uncomfortable with twisting roads and narrow shoulders will want to drive the route in a clockwise direction, starting and ending in Baddeck. That way you'll be on the inside lane, with the many steep drop-offs to the surf below one lane safely removed. The seaport of **Pleasant Bay**, with the stone picnic shelter known as the Lone Sheiling, marks the route's halfway point and is located at the national park's northwestern corner on the Gulf of St. Lawrence.

The Margarees

Of course, you'll encounter some memorable spots along the way. Heading in a clockwise direction from the Baddeck area, you come upon the lush glens of the Margarees some 45 minutes northwest of Hunters Mountain—a circular route off the Cabot Trail takes you into the valley and the village of Margaree Valley. The rustic but very adequate ▶ **Normaway Inn** resort lodge at the end of a tree-lined lane here wins raves for its home-cooked meals. (If you decide to spend the night ask for one of the nine lodge rooms rather than a cabin; the lodge is nicer.) In town, the **Salmon Museum** is devoted to the art of salmon fishing and local fishing lore.

Cheticamp

Back on the Cabot Trail, Cheticamp, an Acadian seaport on the Gulf of St. Lawrence, is another 45 minutes north. Interesting stops here include the small **Acadian Museum** on Main Street (open mid-May to mid-October, 9:00 A.M. to 6:00 P.M. daily), with a crafts shop and Acadian-style food served on the premises; and the **Dr. Elizabeth LeFort Gallery & Museum**, in the building known as Les Trois Pignons, which, in addition to serving as a genealogical and cultural center, also houses 20 examples of Elizabeth LeFort's hooked tapestries (some of which hang in halls of state around the world).

Cape Breton Highlands National Park

The entrance to the park lies three miles beyond Cheticamp; its tourist center (May to October) has plenty of literature on hand, and its bookstore is well stocked with volumes about the province and Atlantic Canada (the park's other center at Ingonish Beach has similar offerings).

The heart-stopping ups and downs of the Cabot Trail begin here and continue across the park's northern border to the Atlantic and then south on the winding seacoast route to the Ingonish Ferry area. The highway tops French Mountain at 1,492 feet above sea level, dips to 1,222 feet at MacKenzie Mountain, and then takes you through a series of 10- to 12-percent grade switchbacks. The biggest thrill comes at **Cape Smokey**, just outside the park boundaries at Ingonish Ferry, where the road descends 1,200 feet in two miles of swooping switchbacks. Mountain majesties aside, there are a number of interesting places along the way: A park with picnic tables and a small beach marks **Cabot's Landing**, 10 km (6 miles) north of the trail at Cape North, while **Neil Harbour**, on the Atlantic at the park's northeastern corner, has fresh fish and lobster for sale on its wharf.

The ▶ **Keltic Lodge** in **Ingonish Beach**, a manorial lodging set on a fingerlike peninsula, is your best bet for a meal. Overnight accommodations here include 32 rooms in the main lodge, 40 rooms in the newer White Birch Inn, and 26 two- and four-bedroom cottages. The Keltic Lodge's fine facilities range from a heated outdoor pool, tennis courts, and the nearby Highlands Golf Links (18 holes; open to the public from June to mid-October) to skiing (the ski season runs from January to March). Ingonish Beach, as the name implies, also has a couple of swimming beaches—one on the Atlantic, another on a lake.

The St. Ann's Area

A final pocket of interest lies near the end of the Cabot Trail around **St. Ann's Bay** and **St. Ann's Harbour**. North Shore's Plaster Park overlooks the bay and has sinkhole ponds. Below Indian Brook the road divides, with Route 312 joining the Trans-Canada in the direction of Sydney. The trail road heads inland past St. Ann's Harbour to South Gut St. Ann's, where it joins up again with the Trans-Canada.

Plan an hour for the **Nova Scotia Gaelic College** in South Gut St. Ann's—more if the spirit of the place moves you. North America's only Gaelic college offers six-week summer language classes, as well as facilities for Highland dancing, piping, and weaving. Its Celtic Arts Centre sells clan tartans by the yard in addition to the Nova Scotian tartan in kilts and apparel, while the college's Great Hall of the Clans makes much of local Scottish ancestries with a variety of exhibits. Open mid-May to mid-October, 8:30 A.M. to 4:30 P.M. daily (8:30 A.M. to 8:30 P.M. in July and August).

From Gaelic College it's about 20 minutes on the Trans-Canada to Baddeck. Driving the entire Cabot Trail calls for a long, long day—it makes more sense to break up the drive with an overnight stay or perhaps several leisurely days, taking advantage of the Keltic Lodge's creature comforts. The Normaway Inn (see above) is another option; the latter is also an outfitter for Atlantic salmon fly-fishing on the Margaree River. June to September is open season, and a non-resident fishing license is easy to obtain.

GETTING AROUND

Halifax

By Air. Halifax International, a spacious easy-in, easy-out complex some 40 km (25 miles) northeast of the city, serves as the hub for provincial, domestic, and several international flights daily.

The main airlines serving Halifax are Air Canada and its regional affiliated airline Air Nova, and Canadian Airlines International, whose affiliated airline is Air Atlantic. Ticket counters for the four Canadian airlines are separate at the Halifax airport (as well as at the Yarmouth and Sydney airports), but the relationships are worth noting, as reservations may be made through the larger airlines for their smaller affiliates. Arriving in Halifax are Air Canada/Air Nova's nonstop flights from Montreal, Ottawa, and Toronto, and international flights from Boston, Newark, London, and Glasgow. Canadian Airlines International also offers domestic and international service, and flies nonstop from Toronto, Ottawa, and Montreal. Other carriers serving the province are Air St. Pierre from St. Pierre, the French island off Newfoundland, and KLM Royal Dutch Airlines from Amsterdam. Several regional charter airlines serve the province as well.

Car rental desks, including Avis (which also has offices in Yarmouth and Sydney), Budget, Hertz, Tilden, and Thrifty, can be found near the baggage pickup area. Cars are parked beyond the terminal, so take along a luggage cart. A shuttle to Halifax/Dartmouth hotels ($12, one way) meets incoming flights. Taxis are lined up outside, and the fare into town is about $34; a seat in a limousine can be had for $40.

By Car and Bus. From September to May, and aside from rush hours, driving in Halifax is no problem. Parking, on the other hand, is extremely difficult, though most major hotels provide parking for their guests. The local bus runs everywhere. Acadian Lines provides service to points throughout the province from the bus terminal on Almon and Robie streets, while smaller lines like Zinck's service Sherbrook and the eastern shore.

By Rail. VIA Rail, near the waterfront, offers service to some provincial gateways. Cuts have been discussed recently, but for now the trains still chug along their appointed rounds, with stops in Amherst, Springhill, and Truro before pulling into Halifax; service east of these points has been discontinued.

Yarmouth

Plan ahead: 200,000 people arrive annually in Yarmouth on ferries arriving from Maine ports. Reservations during the summer months are essential.

By Sea. Prince of Fundy Cruises' *Scotia Prince* makes the 11-hour crossing to and from Portland, Maine, daily from early May through October, with departures from Yarmouth at 10:00 A.M. and from Portland at 9:00 P.M. The one-way fare is $75 per person, and $98 per vehicle; if you want a cabin, it will cost an extra $32 to $95. The foregoing prices are in U.S. dollars, and the cruise line expects payment in U.S. currency—the provincial information center near the ferry terminal will convert currency, as will banks in Yarmouth. Contact Prince of Fundy Cruises, Box 4216, Portland, Maine 04101; Tel: (207) 775-5616 locally; (800) 482-0955 in Maine; (800) 341-7540 from elsewhere in the U.S. and Canada; and (902) 742-6460 for the Yarmouth terminal.

Marine Atlantic's *Bluenose* operates year-round, with daily six-hour crossings to and from Bar Harbor, Maine, mid-June to mid-September, and two or three times a week the rest of the year. One-way passage is $48 per person, and $60 per vehicle. Marine Atlantic can be contacted at Box 250, Purves Street, North Sydney, Nova Scotia B2A 3M3; Tel: (902) 794-5700. In the United States contact Marine Atlantic in care of the Terminal Supervisor, 121 Eden Street, Bar Harbor, Maine 04609; Tel: (800) 341-7981.

Visitors in the know make advance reservations as far ahead as possible. In both Yarmouth and Digby (to New Brunswick), Marine Atlantic tickets have to be picked up an hour before sailing—and two hours beforehand in North Sydney (to Newfoundland)—or the reservations are canceled automatically.

By Air. Air Nova flies to Yarmouth from Halifax, and also offers nonstop flights from Boston. If Cape Breton is on your itinerary, you might want to consider flying from Yarmouth via Halifax to Sydney, as the trip takes about 13 hours by car.

In Town. Public transit in the Yarmouth area is excellent, with local buses stopping everywhere. Taxis and shuttles to the Rodd Grand Hotel wait outside the ferry terminal. Avis and Budget rental cars are also available at the ferry terminal, as well as at the airport. Acadian Lines, offering daily bus service to Digby and elsewhere, can be found at the old railroad station on Main Street.

Digby

The *Princess of Acadia* is another Marine Atlantic ferry—see the Yarmouth Getting Around section above for details on addresses, phone numbers, and reservations. The 2½-hour crossing on the sometimes turbulent Bay of Fundy to Saint John, New Brunswick, is made year-round and costs $20 per person, $45 per vehicle. From Digby, the ferry sails at 5:00 A.M., 1:00 P.M., and 8:15 P.M.; Saint John departures are at 12:30 A.M., 9:30 A.M., and 4:45 P.M. There are fewer departures on Sundays.

At the Digby ferry terminal there are wall phones to call a taxi, The Pines' shuttle service, and Avis. The local airport, 8 km (5 miles) from Digby, offers a limited number of connecting flights, mainly charter flights to **Grand Manan** (see the New Brunswick chapter) in the Bay of Fundy. Acadian Lines provides daily bus service to most towns along the coast.

Amherst

Nova Scotia's only land connection to mainland Canada is through New Brunswick via Amherst. The major crossing is at Fort Lawrence, five minutes northwest of town; from there the route leads to Moncton, New Brunswick, on the Trans-Canada Highway. Fort Lawrence's information complex stocks literature about Nova Scotia in general, with an emphasis on the Amherst area; a kilt-clad piper plays the bagpipes on the half hour, daily, from May through August, adding a nice touch. The second border crossing in the area is at Tidnish, 24 km (15 miles) northeast of Amherst via Route 366, which leads to Cape Tormentine, New Brunswick, and the ferry connection to Borden, Prince Edward Island.

By Bus. Acadian Lines serves a variety of provincial towns, and also connects with New Brunswick's SMT bus line in Moncton, which in turn services the Cape Tormentine ferry terminal and connects with Greyhound from the United States and Voyageur from Montreal. Local bus service links Springhill, Oxford, and Parrsboro. Otherwise, there is no local service, so be prepared to walk or take taxis.

Rent-A-Wreck (better than the name implies) and Budget have offices in Amherst. Daily rail service from Amherst to provincial points via Truro, and to Moncton in New Brunswick, is also available.

Pictou

Northumberland Ferries connects Caribou, 15 minutes north
of Pictou, with Wood Islands, Prince Edward Island, across
Northumberland Strait. The service operates May to mid-
December, with 19 departures daily (6:00 A.M. to 9:50 P.M.)
from each ferry gateway during the peak summer season. Car
waiting lines can be horrendous, but tend to ease up after 6:00
P.M. and before 10:00 A.M. The round-trip cost for the 1¼-hour
crossing is $8 per person, and $26 per vehicle. Contact
Northumberland Ferries at the Caribou or Wood Islands
terminals for details; Tel: (800) 565-0201 in Nova Scotia and
Prince Edward Island, or (902) 566-3838 locally. The ferry
company can also be contacted at Box 634, 94 Water Street,
Charlottetown, Prince Edward Island C1A 7L3.

Pictou slipped off the well-worn tourist track decades ago,
which makes it an especially nice spot to visit but a tough
one to get around in: Wheels are a must. Pictou County
Transit connects the town with New Glasgow, 20 minutes to
the southeast, as well as other area villages. If you want to
get to Halifax or other provincial points, take the Pictou
County bus to New Glasgow, with its more extensive bus
connections. Avis has offices in New Glasgow and Stellarton;
Budget, Tilden, and Rent-A-Wreck have offices in the area as
well.

Sydney

By Air. Frequent Halifax–Sydney service is offered by Air
Nova and Air Atlantic. Once on the ground there are no
hotel shuttles, but Avis and other car-rental agencies have
desks at the airport, and taxis (15 minutes to town) are
available. Acadian Lines, on Terminal Road, has frequent bus
departures to various destinations throughout the province.

In Town. In Sydney itself, the local bus company covers
the town and also services Glace Bay and the North Sydney
area. For sightseeing, ask at your hotel for touring company
phone numbers. Briands Cab does the Cabot Trail in taxis;
the fare for each of three passengers is $55.

By Sea. Ferry service to Newfoundland is based in North
Sydney, with Marine Atlantic handling the service—specifics
are detailed in the Yarmouth Getting Around section above.
The ferry terminal is located on the north side of Sydney
Harbour; access is via the Trans-Canada Highway, which
moves fast along here, so watch for the signs.

Marine Atlantic has been retiring old ferries and adding
new ships, resulting in staggered schedules from North
Sydney and Port-aux-Basques and Argentia in Newfoundland. Because departure times vary widely, it's wise to check

the exact times beforehand with Marine Atlantic if either of these provincial gateways is on your itinerary.

Between North Sydney and Port-aux-Basques, service is daily year-round, with additional departures July through September. The old crossing time of 7 hours has been cut to 5 hours on the new *Caribou* and the even newer *Joseph and Clara Smallwood.* The cost is $16 per person, and $50 per vehicle.

The North Sydney-to-Argentia crossing has been trimmed from 19 hours to approximately 14 hours, with the above-mentioned *Smallwood* assigned to the crossing since the *Ambrose Shea* was retired. The ferry leaves North Sydney at 7:00 A.M. on Tuesdays and Fridays; from Argentia it departs at 9:00 A.M. on Wednesdays and Saturdays. The daylight crossings cut down on the use of cabins; if you do request a cabin, expect to pay $95 to $100 on a daytime crossing, and $120 to $125 on a nighttime crossing. The basic charge is $45 per person, and $100 per vehicle, with service offered from mid-June to early September.

Further Information

The province's government-run museums are open mid-May to mid-October. Privately owned museums are not as predictable, with their hours, aside from the summer months, varying from museum to museum. To order a copy of the province's informative and up-to-date travel guide, contact Nova Scotia Tourism and Culture, P.O. Box 456, Halifax, Nova Scotia B3J 2R5. Check In, the provincial reservations service, can book overnight accommodations at a 5-percent discount off regular rates; participating establishments are indicated in the Nova Scotia travel guide (see above) by a check mark. For further information, or to make reservations, contact Check In, Suite 515, 1800 Argyle Street, Halifax, Nova Scotia B3J 3N8. Tel: (902) 425-5781; Fax: (902) 425-6924; in the U.S. and Canada, Tel: (800) 565-0000.

ACCOMMODATIONS REFERENCE

The rates given below are projections *for peak seasons during the 1994 calendar year; at other times of the year they* may *be considerably less. Unless otherwise indicated, rates are based on double rooms, double occupancy; provincial and federal taxes are included in all rates. As rates are subject to change, always double-check before booking.*

▶ **Auberge Sieur de Monts**. P.O. Box 2055, R.R. 2, **Granville Ferry**, N.S. B0S 1K0. Tel: (902) 532-5852. $53 (inn and cottage; breakfast included).

▶ **Auberge Wandlyn Inn.** P.O. Box 275, Highway 104/ Victoria Street, **Amherst**, N.S. B4H 3Z2. Tel: (902) 667-3331; Fax: (902) 667-0475; in the U.S., Tel: (800) 561-0006; in eastern Canada, (800) 561-0000. $100–$112.

▶ **Best Western Aurora Inn.** P.O. Box 609, 338 Main Street, **Kingston**, N.S. B0P 1R0. Tel: (902) 765-3306; Fax: (902) 765-8228; in the U.S. and Canada, Tel: (800) 528-1234. $85–$92.

▶ **Best Western Claymore Inn.** P.O. Box 1720, Church Street, **Antigonish**, N.S. B2G 2M5. Tel: (902) 863-1050; Fax: (902) 863-1238; in the U.S. and Canada, Tel: (800) 528-1234. $60–$98.

▶ **Best Western Glengarry.** 150 Willow Street, **Truro**, N.S. B2N 4Z6. Tel: (902) 893-4311; Fax: (902) 893-1759; in the U.S. and Canada, Tel: (800) 528-1234. $106–$112.

▶ **Best Western Mermaid Motel.** 545 Main Street, **Yarmouth**, N.S. B5A 1J6. Tel: (902) 742-7821; in the U.S. and Canada, Tel: (800) 528-1234. $105.

▶ **Bluenose Lodge.** P.O. Box 399, Falkland Avenue and Dufferin Street, **Lunenburg**, N.S. B0J 2C0. Tel: (902) 634-8851. $77.

▶ **Braeside Inn.** P.O. Box 1810, 80 Front Street, **Pictou**, N.S. B0K 1H0. Tel: (902) 485-5046. $53–$117.

▶ **Bread & Roses Country Inn.** P.O. Box 177, 82 Victoria Street, **Annapolis Royal**, N.S. B0S 1A0. Tel: (902) 532-5727. $83–$94.

▶ **Cambridge Suites Hotel.** 1583 Brunswick Street, **Halifax**, N.S. B3J 3P5. Tel: (902) 420-0555; Fax: (902) 420-9379; in Canada, Tel: (800) 565-1263. $112–$160.

▶ **Cambridge Suites Hotel.** 380 Esplanade, **Sydney**, N.S. B1P 1B1. Tel: (902) 562-6500; Fax: (902) 564-6011; in Canada, Tel: (800) 565-9466. $93–$115 (includes Continental breakfast).

▶ **Canadian Pacific Chateau Halifax.** 1990 Barrington Street, **Halifax**, N.S. B3J 1P2. Tel: (902) 425-6700; Fax: (902) 425-6214; in the U.S. and Canada, Tel: (800) 828-7447. $170–$193.

▶ **Compass Rose Inn.** P.O. Box 1267, 15 King Street, **Lunenburg**, N.S. B0J 2C0. Tel: (902) 634-8509. $65–$77.

▶ **Delta Barrington.** 1875 Barrington Street, **Halifax**, N.S. B3J 3L6. Tel: (902) 429-7410; Fax: (902) 420-6524; in the U.S., Tel: (800) 877-1133; in Canada, (800) 268-1133. $200.

▶ **Delta Sydney Hotel.** 300 Esplanade, **Sydney**, N.S. B1P 1A7. Tel: (902) 562-7500; Fax: (902) 562-3023. $93.

▶ **Fundy Winds Family Motel.** P.O. Box 1136, exit 1A off Highway 104, **Amherst**, N.S. B4H 3Y6. Tel: (902) 667-3881. $45.

▶ **Goodwin Hotel.** P.O. Box 15, Highway 1, **Weymouth**, N.S. B0W 3T0. Tel: (902) 837-5120. $50.

▶ **Halifax Sheraton.** 1919 Upper Water Street, **Halifax**, N.S. B3J 3J5. Tel: (902) 421-1700; Fax: (902) 422-5805; in the U.S. and Canada, Tel: (800) 325-3535. $174–$209.

▶ **Highland Heights Inn.** P.O. Box 19, **Iona**, N.S. B0A 1L0. Tel: (902) 725-2360; Fax: (902) 725-2800. $80.

▶ **Hillsdale House.** P.O. Box 148, 519 St. George Street, **Annapolis Royal**, N.S. B0S 1A0. Tel: (902) 532-2345. $71–$94.

▶ **Holiday Inn Sydney.** 480 Kings Road, **Sydney**, N.S. B1S 1A8. Tel: (902) 539-6750; Fax: (902) 539-2773; in the U.S. and Canada, Tel: (800) HOLIDAY. $119.

▶ **Inverary Inn Resort.** P.O. Box 190, Shore Road, **Baddeck**, N.S. B0E 1B0. Tel: (902) 295-3500; Fax: (902) 295-3527. $105–$188.

▶ **Journey's End Motel.** 12 Meadow Drive, **Truro**, N.S. B2N 5V4. Tel: (902) 893-0330; Fax: (902) 897-0176; in the U.S. and Canada, Tel: (800) 668-4200. $83.

▶ **Journey's End Motel.** 96 Starrs Road, **Yarmouth**, N.S. B5A 2T5. Tel: (902) 742-1119; Fax: (902) 742-1114; in the U.S. and Canada, (800) 668-4200. $73.

▶ **Keltic Lodge.** P.O. Box 70, Middle Head Peninsula, **Ingonish Beach**, N.S. B0C 1L0. Tel: (902) 285-2880; Fax: (902) 285-2859. $283–$300 (includes breakfast and dinner).

▶ **Liscomb Lodge.** Route 7, **Liscomb Mills**, N.S. B0J 2A0. Tel: (902) 779-2307; Fax: (902) 779-2700. $112 (main lodge); $122 (chalets).

▶ **MacNeil House.** P.O. Box 399, c/o Silver Dart Lodge, Shore Road, **Baddeck**, N.S. B0E 1B0. Tel: (902) 295-2340; Fax: (902) 295-2484. $207.

▶ **The Manse.** Strathcona Street, **Louisbourg**, N.S. B0A 1M0. Tel: (902) 733-3155. $45.

▶ **Murray Manor Guest House.** 225 Main Street, **Yarmouth**, N.S. B5A 1C6. Tel: (902) 742-9625. $61.

▶ **Normaway Inn.** P.O. Box 121, Egypt Road, **Margaree Valley**, N.S. B0E 2C0. Tel: (902) 248-2987; Fax: (902) 248-2600; in the U.S. and Canada, Tel: (800) 565-9463. $188–$234 per night (includes breakfast and dinner); $1,218–$1,500 per week (includes breakfast and dinner).

▶ **Oak Island Inn & Marina.** P.O. Box 6, **Western Shore**, N.S. B0J 3M0. Tel: (902) 627-2600; Fax: (902) 627-2020; in the U.S. and Canada, Tel: (800) 565-5075. $70–$93.

▶ **Old Orchard Inn.** P.O. Box 1090, **Wolfville**, N.S. B0P 1X0. Tel: (902) 542-5751; Fax: (902) 542-2276. $70–$98.

▶ **Pictou Lodge Resort.** P.O. Box 1539, Braeshore Road, **Pictou**, N.S. B0K 1H0. Tel: (902) 485-4322; Fax: (902) 485-4945. $116–$148; $189 (cabin).

► **Pines Resort Hotel.** P.O. Box 70, Shore Road, **Digby**, N.S. B0V 1A0. Tel: (902) 245-2511; Fax: (902) 245-6133. $126–$190; $231–$242 (includes breakfast and dinner).

► **Planters' Barracks.** Starrs Point Road, R.R. 1, **Port Williams**, N.S. B0P 1T0. Tel: (902) 542-7879; Fax: (902) 542-4442. $65–$100.

► **Queen Anne Inn.** P.O. Box 218, 494 Upper St. George Street, **Annapolis Royal**, N.S. B0S 1A0. Tel: (902) 532-7850. $59–$94.

► **Rodd Colony Harbour Inn.** 6 Forest Street, **Yarmouth**, N.S. B5A 3K7. Tel: (902) 742-9194; Fax: (902) 742-6291; in the U.S. and Canada, Tel: (800) 565-9077. $93.

► **Rodd Grand Hotel.** P.O. Box 220, 417 Main Street, **Yarmouth**, N.S. B5A 4B2. Tel: (902) 742-2446; Fax: (902) 742-4645; in the U.S. and Canada, Tel: (800) 565-7633. $105–$123.

► **Tattingstone Inn.** 434 Main Street, **Wolfville**, N.S. B0P 1X0. Tel: (902) 542-7696; Fax: (902) 542-4427. $92–$140.

► **Wandlyn Cape Bretoner Motel.** 560 Kings Road, **Sydney**, N.S. B1S 1B8. Tel: (902) 539-8101; Fax: (902) 539-1734; in the U.S., Tel: (800) 561-0006; in eastern Canada, (800) 561-0000. $90.

NEW BRUNSWICK

By Colleen Whitney Thompson

Colleen Whitney Thompson, a freelance travel writer and native of New Brunswick, is the author of New Brunswick Inside Out, *a recipient of the American Express Award for travel writing on Canada, and the travel columnist for the* Saint John Telegraph Journal.

If there were a miniaturized version of Canada, New Brunswick might well be it. With a 35 percent French-Acadian population concentrated mostly in the northeastern section and the rest generally of British descent, New Brunswick is an amalgamation of two cultures that sometimes blend, and often differ completely.

Jacques Cartier explored its shores in 1534. Seventy years later Samuel de Champlain sailed into Saint John harbor on the feast day of Saint John the Baptist, hence its name. Other explorers named the coastland area Utopia, one saying "the country is as pleasing as the good cheer."

Already settled by scattered handfuls of Acadians who defied England's order to leave (Acadia was the name for the area when it was largely a French colony—before the British expelled the French inhabitants in the mid-1700s), New Brunswick became overwhelmingly Loyalist after the American Revolution as American refugees who remained loyal to the king arrived by the thousands. At that time the province was named in tribute to the reigning British monarch, George III, of the house of Brunswick, and its capital city called Fredericton after his second son, Frederick. Nevertheless, Acadians continued to cling to the province's northern shores, their heritage, in many ways, unchanged.

The coffeepot-shaped province is tucked into Quebec along its northern border and joined to Maine the length of its western border; a narrow neck of land to the southeast connects it to Nova Scotia. Three-quarters of the province glories in a rugged seacoast that combines 700 miles of warm, sandy beaches with majestic headlands beneath which the highest tides in the world occur. Scattered off the Fundy coast to the south and facing Nova Scotia are escapist islands of incredible serenity.

Cities such as Saint John and Fredericton, steeped in a British heritage, offer nostalgic glimpses of the country's Loyalist past, good restaurants, theater, professional sports, and modern accommodations.

In towns such as Caraquet on the **Acadian Peninsula**, which juts into the Gulf of St. Lawrence, and Bouctouche on the Northumberland Strait coast to the south of the penin-sula, French is the language most often heard, and fishing the common industry. At a historical Acadian village near Caraquet the past comes to life, modern motels and historic inns tempt overnighters, craggy beaches afford warm-water swimming, and fresh lobster right off the boats is a summer-time tradition.

The rugged and relatively uninhabited forest lands of the interior rise to high mountains and spread out for a hundred miles on either side of scenic highways. Jade-green canoeing streams, home of trout, bass, and Atlantic silver salmon, meander through woodlands rich in wildlife. Some of these rivers, including the fabled **Miramichi**, wind on through the heartland to the coast at Newcastle, south of the Acadian Peninsula, an area noted for the "come all ye" ballads of lumbermen. Lovely old towns dotted with the sturdy homes of early lumber barons line the route; the hospitality of the region is sincere.

The mighty **Saint John River** cuts a blue path diagonally across the province from its northwest corner to Saint John on the south shore, providing exceptionally scenic driving throughout its valley. A number of cities and small historic towns hug its shores. **Kings Landing**, a re-created river-landing village west of Fredericton, provides an authentic look at the Loyalist past. Elsewhere, marinas offer well-appointed havens for yachts and small craft, and car ferries crisscross the river.

New Brunswick craftspeople are responsible for the resur-gence of old-time crafts such as weaving and glassblowing in the Maritime provinces, and outlets are plentiful. Pewter items, including jewelry, are of the highest quality, especially those of **Aitkin's Pewter** in Fredericton. Potters such as Tom

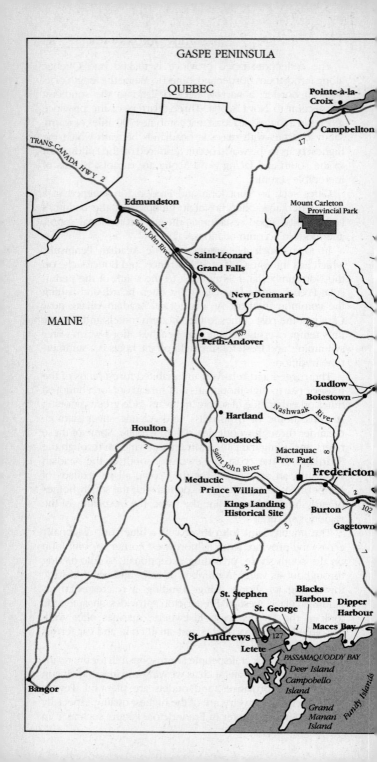

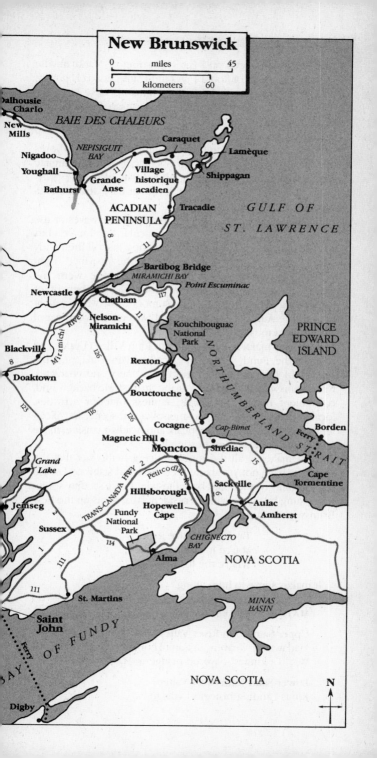

Smith of St. Andrews and Peter Powning of Markhamville (near the junction of Route 1 and the Trans-Canada Highway, halfway between Saint John and Moncton) have been accorded the status of artist rather than artisan. Weavers such as **Madawaska Weavers** in Saint-Léonard and **Loomcrofters** in Gagetown sometimes outfit royalty.

For warm-water swimming, the sandbar-protected shores of Northumberland Strait from Shediac to **Kouchibouguac National Park** are outstanding. Above that, along the province's northern border, are the excellent **Baie des Chaleurs** beaches.

Hardier souls brave the cool **Fundy Coast** waves at the bottom of the province, where spectacular tide-carved cliffs and rocks adorn no less inviting beaches. Just off the Fundy Isles, in the southwestern corner of the province, right whales (so-named by whalers because these were the whales they were looking for) frolic for the benefit of sightseeing expeditions. (The best months for whale watching are late August, September, and November, when warm clothing is a must.)

With four major areas—the Saint John Valley (Upper and Lower), the Fundy Coast, the Acadian Peninsula, and the Miramichi region—each distinct in scenery and character, New Brunswick is ideal for touring. Its historic background, convenient network of roads, endless outdoor activities, local festivals, surprisingly cosmopolitan art scene, and excellent examples of local, European, and Acadian cuisine, make it both enjoyable and interesting.

What makes it all the more enticing is the fact that the residents have not yet abandoned their old-fashioned sense of hospitality or their laid-back lifestyle. There's a ditty sometimes sung by the province's residents that sums up the New Brunswick attitude.

> Take it easy, take it easy,
> You're in the maritimes,
> Where the livin' is slow. . . .

It makes sense to hum along.

MAJOR INTEREST

Upper Saint John River Valley
Madawaska Weavers in Saint-Léonard
World's longest covered bridge in Hartland

Lower Saint John River Valley
Kings Landing historical village

Fredericton
Beaverbrook Art Gallery
Legislative Building Library (rare copy of Domesday
   Book and Audubon prints)
Christ Church Cathedral
Changing of the Guard, Officer's Square
River Jubilee celebrations
Boyce Farmers' Market

Historic village of Gagetown
Loyalist-era architecture of Kingston and Belleisle
   peninsulas

The Fundy Coast
18th-century town of St. Andrews-by-the-Sea
Whale-watching cruises out of Grand Manan and
   Deer Island
Roosevelt home on Campobello Island

Saint John
Shops, restaurants, historic buildings at Market Slip
   Loyalist Landing Place
Historical walks
Old City Market
Loyalist Days celebration
International Gathering of the Irish
Reversing Falls Rapids

Scenic St. Martins area
Fundy National Park
Rocks and caves at Hopewell Cape
University of Moncton Acadian Museum and Art
   Gallery
Moncton's Tidal Bore and Magnetic Hill

The Acadian Peninsula
Beaches, park, and lobster festival in Shediac
Kouchibouguac National Park and beaches
Blessing of the Fleet at Caraquet
Village Historique Acadien
Fishing charters out of Dalhousie

The Miramichi
Fishing
Atlantic Salmon Museum in Doaktown
Irish festival in Chatham

Food in New Brunswick

An edible fern called the fiddlehead is a particularly favorite spring food in New Brunswick. It's available frozen year-round, and some restaurants feature it with fresh Atlantic salmon. Dulse, a dried purple seaweed, is another popular snack favored by the locals.

Fish and shellfish, although readily available on the coast, are not always prepared with finesse, except for lobster, which is usually boiled to perfection. Deep frying is, alas, the usual method, but steaming, poaching, and broiling are catching on. Lobster season varies from one area of the province to the next. Along the Bay of Fundy it runs from March 31 to June 29; in Chignecto Bay from March 1 to July 31; along Northumberland Strait from August 10 to October 15; and in the Baie des Chaleurs from May 1 to June 30. Thanks to holding pounds (ponds), however, fresh lobster is always available.

Local lamb and pork can be delicious, and Acadian specialties such as chicken *fricot* (a stew), *poutine rapé* (a potato ball with a core of pork), and a delicious dessert pastry, *poutine à trou,* are served throughout the Acadian area.

SAINT JOHN RIVER VALLEY

The Saint John River flows a scenic 250-mile course through the province, occasionally forming the border between Maine and New Brunswick, meandering through rolling farm-lands, rushing over a high ledge to create a dazzling waterfall, and brushing against a number of historic towns and three major cities along its winding route. Water slides and zoos, an exceptional art gallery, a lovely capital city, plenty of crafts outlets, and free river ferries make this route exceptionally rewarding.

Madawaska

The extreme upper section of the Saint John River Valley, from Edmunston to Grand Falls, is French in character and noted for its regional specialties as well as the independent nature of its people. Because of this spirit, it's often called the Republic of Madawaska. **Edmundston**, located in the heart of Madawaska County, is its undisputed capital. It's a happy little city with a noisy festival, the Foire Brayonne, held during the first week of August and, year-round, a reputation for good dining—try the **Praga** (Tel: 506/735-

5567), on Victoria Street, or the surprisingly fine cuisine at
La Terrasse (Tel: 506/739-7321), in the Howard Johnson's
hotel downtown on Rice Street. **Seafood Paradise** (Tel: 506/
739-7822), a steak-and-seafood place at 174 Victoria Street,
has lobster year-round.

Saint-Léonard to New Denmark

In Saint-Léonard, 42 km (26 miles) to the south via the
Trans-Canada Highway (Highway 2), which here follows the
west bank of the Saint John River, the studios of the renowned **Madawaska Weavers**, on Main Street, are worth a
stop for skirts, scarves, ties, or place mats. Farther south in
Grand Falls a park and footpath follow along the magnificent
gorge created by the river as it surges through a rocky
channel. For a taste of Danish food and aquavit, follow Route
108 southeast some 15 km (9 miles) to the 100-year-old
community of New Denmark and the **Valhalla Restaurant**
(Tel: 506/553-6614), on Foley Brook Road. An interesting
small museum in town traces the history of the community,
from its founding by Danish immigrants a century ago to the
present. Open daily, mid-June to Labour Day.

New Denmark to Woodstock

Heading south out of town, a pretty country drive along
Routes 108, 393, and 109 brings you into Perth-Andover, on
the east bank of the river, where the locally famous **York's
Dining Room** (Tel: 506/273-2847) serves up gargantuan
quantities of old-fashioned New Brunswick country cooking.
Open May through mid-October.

In **Hartland**, another 55 km (34 miles) to the south via
Route 105 or the Trans Canada (which you pick up in
Florenceville), the longest covered bridge in the world is
visible as you drive along the highway. Built in 1899, the
wooden structure is 1,282 feet long and spans the Saint John
River. As you continue south on the Trans-Canada you'll
come to **Heino and Monika's Restaurant** (Tel: 506/328-6622)
in the ▶ **John Gyles Motor Inn**, west of the sleepy town of
Woodstock. The restaurant serves deliciously authentic German food, while the motel offers spanking clean rooms and
views of the valley.

Lower Saint John River Valley

Kings Landing Historical Site

One of the province's major attractions is also a great way to
forget about highway driving for a while. Cars are not

allowed in Kings Landing, a re-created river-landing village of the late 1700s located 35 km (22 miles) west of Fredericton. At this showcase of early Loyalist-era living a costumed staff works the fields and tends the hearths of old homes as wagons rumble along dirt roads, taking foot-weary visitors to the far end of the village or the **Kings Head Inn**, where traditional meals are served and cold beer and cider are offered in the old Tap Room. On the Trans-Canada (Highway 2), 5 km (3 miles) east of Kings Landing, the ▶ **Chickadee Lodge Bed & Breakfast** offers rustic fishing lodge–type accommodations with all the modern conveniences.

Travellers looking for more luxurious accommodations will find them 10 km (6 miles) east of Kings Landing at the ▶ **Kingsclear Hotel and Resort**, just below the Mactaquac Dam on Route 6. The resort offers airy, lodge-like public areas, attractive rooms with river views, and a few two-bedroom cottages. An excellent dining room (the chef is French-trained) with special Sunday buffets, a welcoming bar, an indoor pool, and unique meeting rooms (one a replica of a tribal council chamber) are part of the complex. Guests can even angle for salmon in a deep river pool right in front of the hotel.

Mactaquac Provincial Park

The main entrance to Mactaquac Provincial Park, on the north bank of the Saint John River, is 20 minutes from Kings Landing via the Trans-Canada, Route 274 (across the Mactaquac Dam), and Route 105. In addition to a beach and excellent camping facilities, the park has a championship 18-hole golf course open to the public ($24 weekdays, $28 on weekends).

From Mactaquac Park, it's only 12 km (7½ miles) to Fredericton, on the south bank of the river.

Fredericton

Fredericton's 44,000 residents like to boast that it's the loveliest of Canada's Atlantic cities—a claim that is usually not disputed. Part of the capital's charm is its setting on the banks of the broad Saint John River, where lush green hillsides and drooping willows provide an Old English tranquillity.

Fredericton's British heritage is further emphasized by the graceful spire of Christ Church Cathedral rising above the feathery blanket of maples and elms that, along with tidy homes and Victorian mansions, line its neatly laid out streets.

The British established a military base here in 1785, Loyalists founded the University of New Brunswick (then Kings College) the same year, and when the cathedral foundation was laid in 1845 Queen Victoria made Fredericton a city.

A gracious and social place from the beginning, Fredericton's upper-crust young people, immortalized in prints by 19th-century artists, were known as "the fashionables." Even today, Governor's levees and Beaux-Arts balls, cruises and sculling on the river, band concerts in the park and a profusion of old-time craft activities keep part of Fredericton's spirit firmly anchored in a bygone era. But bustling shopping malls now compete with the traditional **Queen Street** shops by the river, while glass office buildings and modern bridges have replaced old iron structures, causing some pockets of the past to disappear along with them.

It's a walking city, with much of its history in the downtown area and "up the hill" at the University of New Brunswick. A quick lesson on its past can be pleasantly learned by taking a free walking tour with a costumed guide, available at City Hall during the summer.

AROUND IN FREDERICTON

There's an odd cornucopia of treasures among Fredericton's downtown attractions. At the **Beaverbrook Art Gallery** on lower Queen Street, one whole wall is hung with Salvador Dalí's *Santiago el Grande*, considered one of his finest works. The collection here includes works by the likes of Gainsborough, Sir Joshua Reynolds, and J. M. W. Turner, a Gobelins tapestry, and an excellent representation of Canadian and American regional artists. The **Legislative Building Library**, across the street, displays a rare copy of the 1087 Domesday Book, the first census ever taken (at the instigation of William the Conqueror). Also on view are 435 hand-colored copper engravings by John James Audubon. A block to the west, **Christ Church Cathedral**'s stained glass is best seen from inside, where you'll also find another of those Fredericton surprises: the original model for London's Big Ben. In late May the cathedral, which dates to 1845, hosts a colorful **Festival of the Arts**, complete with crafts and musical entertainment.

The **York Sunbury Historical Museum**, on Officer's Square, would like to be known for its native artifacts and accurately restored rooms of the Loyalist and Acadian periods. But it's the stuffed body of a mammoth 42-pound frog, said to have been caught in a nearby lake, that is cherished by residents and remains a top drawing card. The museum is part of the original restored British Military Compound, which encompasses two blocks and includes a guardhouse and officers' and enlisted men's quarters, all open to the public. Every day but Sunday during the summer a band of red-coated soldiers is piped into the compound for the **changing-of-the-guard ceremony**.

The streets near Officer's Square offer their share of fine crafts shops, including **Aitkin's Pewter** at 81 Regent Street and **Shades of Light** at 288 Regent. There's a gift shop with exceptional items, local and imported, in the **Sheraton Inn Fredericton**, 255 Woodstock Road, as well. The work of acclaimed local artists can be purchased at outlets such as **Gallery 78**, 796 Queen Street (across from the Beaverbrook Art Gallery), while **Mulhouse Crafts**, across the river in Lower St. Mary's, is the place for traditional country crafts and top-quality British goods.

Other worthwhile stops include small galleries like the **National Exhibition Centre**, on the corner of Queen and Carleton streets (a 20-minute walk south of Officer's Square), an excellent small gallery filled with heritage displays, exceptional hobby and craft products, and the works of local artists, many of them charmingly lighthearted and whimsical. There's also the University of New Brunswick, one of the oldest educational institutions in North America, where the building that housed the first astronomical observatory in North America is still extant.

About three times a year regional craftspeople and artists hold mammoth markets in the city. Times and locations vary, but the best known—with everything from blown and stained glass to woven goods, metalwork, and handcrafted furniture—is always held over the Labour Day weekend (the first weekend in September) at nearby Mactaquac Park.

Harness racing made its debut in Fredericton in 1863, and drivers and sulkies still zip around the **Fredericton Raceway**, five blocks south and west of the Queen Street area off Smythe Street. (Curling is the residents' game in winter.) Racing sculls set out from the **Aquatic Center**, on the riverbank west of the Westmoreland Street Bridge, and at the beginning of July everything centers around the water for the **River Jubilee** celebrations.

No visit to Fredericton is complete without a stop at the **Boyce Farmers' Market**, which happens every Saturday from 6:00 A.M. to noon on George Street, two blocks south of Officer's Square. Although local products are supposed to be the draw, it's as a gathering place for residents, visitors, politicians, artists, musicians, writers, actors, and any VIP who happens to be in town that the market is best known.

STAYING AND DINING
IN FREDERICTON

The ▶ **Lord Beaverbrook Hotel**, situated on Queen Street next to the Beaverbrook Art Gallery, is one of the two hotels in town (although there are plenty of motels, including a large Howard Johnson's). Rooms are adequate and modern, if not exactly deluxe, and the Beaverbrook is handy for sightseeing and shopping downtown, as well as close to government offices. Its **River Room** is a happy-hour haunt until 8:00 P.M., when the ear-splitting music begins and the clientele changes, while the **Top Deck** bar is a popular outdoor gathering spot in the summer. Steaks are the ticket in the hotel's **Maverick Room**, and there's also a heated pool and children's water-play area in the complex.

Hugging the banks of the Saint John River, about a ten-minute walk from downtown, the two-year-old ▶ **Sheraton Inn Fredericton** is a welcome addition to the city's hotel scene. Most of its 223 well-appointed rooms (the Sheraton also has a number of suites) have sunset views overlooking the river, and the hotel's state-of-the-art facilities include a beautiful lobby, heated indoor and outdoor pools, and **Bruno's** (Tel: 506/457-7000), an informal café serving daily breakfast and lunch buffets. All of which helps explain its popularity with both business travellers and tourists; you'll want to book in advance to guarantee yourself a room.

The better restaurants tend to be scattered around town. **Mei's**, 73 Carlton Street, serves Szechuan cuisine spiced to your taste. Reserve in summer; Tel: (506) 454-2177. For sweet Cantonese, try the **Pink Pearl**, 343 Queen Street, which is locally famous for its crispy wontons and inexpensive week-end dinner buffets (6:00 to 9:00 P.M.); Tel: (506) 450-8997. Excellent Greek pitas and souvlaki are the specialties at **Panos Donair**, a pleasant little lunchroom (open till 10:00 P.M.) with an inexpensive menu and liquor license at 1111 Regent Street. For good pub food and a convivial atmosphere to go along with it, try the **Lunar Rogue Pub** (Tel: 506/450-2065), 625 King Street, or the **Hilltop Pub** (Tel: 506/458-9057), 152 Prospect Street.

South of Fredericton

South of Fredericton heading toward Saint John, Route 102 is far prettier and more interesting than the straight-through Highway 7. **Goan's On—The Muffin Shop**, in an old general store in the small town of Burton, is an excep-tional stop for tea or lunch, while **Old Orchard Crafts**, about 5 km (3 miles) west of Burton, offers an extensive selection of locally produced handicrafts.

Gagetown

In Gagetown, a sleepy town on the Saint John River (the city once dreamed of becoming the province's capital), nothing much has changed in generations. On Front Street facing the river there's a general store (with ice cream) at **Colpitts Marina**, a popular destination for yachtspeople from up and down the East Coast (especially on summer weekends); the marina is also the place to rent sailboats and houseboats.

Elsewhere in town, the Queen's County Museum (open 10:00 A.M. to 5:00 P.M., June to September), on Front Street, was once the gracious home of one of the so-called Fathers of Confederation. A 200-year-old blockhouse nearby now houses **Loomcrofters**, noted designers and weavers of tartans and plaids. **Flo Grieg's** pottery studio, located in an old store on Front Street, and **Claremont Crafts**, whose artists create enamelware and batik items in a distinctive old home on Tilley Road, are also good stops here.

The ▶ **Steamers Stop Inn** on Front Street is one of the province's most enchanting old-fashioned hostelries. Each room is decorated in a specific turn-of-the-century style, and the charming dining room (Tel: 506/488-2903) is a pleasant spot in which to linger. There's also a crafts shop featuring the work of local artisans on the premises. ▶ **Loaves and Calico Country Inn**, an excellent lunchroom on the corner of Mill and Tilley roads, also has overnight accommodations.

Grand Lake to the Belleisle Peninsula

The Saint John River in this region is broad and varied, with car-ferry crossings along the alternate routes to Saint John itself providing access to historic peninsulas and beautiful pastoral scenery. From Gagetown, Fredericton, or Saint John, for example, boaters can sail or motor into **Grand Lake**, with its much-indented shoreline. Motorists can take the ferry from Gagetown (on Route 102) to Lower Jemseg, where a left turn on the river road takes you to **Jemseg** and its Saturday-morning farmers' market. And from Jemseg, it's just a short drive west along the river via the Trans-Canada (Highway 2) to the swimming beaches of **Grand Lake Provincial Park**.

Heading back into Lower Jemseg, a left turn puts you onto Route 715, which follows the western shore of scenic **Washademoak Lake** around the Kingston Peninsula. At Cambridge-Narrows you can cross over to the beautiful **Belleisle Peninsula**, following Route 710 south to the small town of Hatfield Point. The surrounding area is dotted with tidy country homes, small farms, mossy churchyards, and numerous bed and breakfasts. Typical of these are the ▶ **Cambridge-Narrows B&B** and the ▶ **Long Island Home B&B**, both small and homey, and both overlooking the water with access to beach swimming. (Cambridge-Narrows also has a number of quiet, pretty campsites.)

From here, any one of a handful of country roads (consult a map) leads to Gondola Point on **Kennebecasis Bay**, where yet another ferry crossing puts you within shouting distance of Highway 1 (well signed) and Saint John. (See the Fundy Coast section next for more on Saint John.)

THE FUNDY COAST

One of the most popular areas of New Brunswick for visitors is the Fundy coast, a region known for its small islands and tiny fishing villages, wave-battered rocks drenched with awesomely high tides, and large national park, as well as the cosmopolitan but historic old city of Saint John.

Passamaquoddy Bay and the Islands

St. Andrews-by-the-Sea

Just east of the U.S.–Canadian border, and south of Highway 1 via Route 127, the lovely old town of St. Andrews-by-the-Sea spreads its mellow homes and streets back from the shores of Passamaquoddy Bay. More than half the buildings here were erected before 1900, 14 of them in the 1700s. The best way to explore the town is by foot or rented bicycle. Bicycles can be rented at the venerable old ▶ **Algonquin Hotel**, 184 Adolphus Street, where kilted bellhops speed your luggage to large, modernized rooms and dining on the wide verandah is de rigueur; tennis and golf are also available.

The shops along Water Street are full of British woollens, china, handicrafts, antiques, and the works of well-known local artists. A lobster roll or a bowl of chowder at the **Lighthouse Restaurant** (open mid-May to mid-October; Tel: 506/529-3082), 1 Patrick Street, is a Fundy tradition, as is dinner at the atmospheric old ▶ **Best Western Shiretown Inn** (Tel: 506/529-8877) on Water Street, or the elegant little **L'Europe**, around the corner at 48 King Street (reservations required; Tel: 506/529-3818).

Another enjoyable way to experience St. Andrews is to stay at the beautiful Victorian ▶ **Rossmount Inn**, just north of town off Route 127, where the decor includes elegant antiques and scenic views. For a homier look and feel, try the ▶ **Pippincott Bed & Breakfast**, in town at 208 Prince of Wales Street, where the tastefully decorated rooms sport a variety of special touches and afternoon tea is a welcome break from the summertime crowds. If you're planning to stay at either place in season, be sure to book well in advance.

While in town, visit the **Huntsman Marine Laboratory and Aquarium** on Joe's Point Road, a few minutes' drive from the downtown area. The **Algonquin Golf Course**, said to be one of the most beautiful in Canada, runs along Passamaquoddy Bay and is open to the public; greens fees are a very reasonable $28 for 18 holes, $16 for nine.

Deer and Campobello Islands

The free ferry (passengers and their vehicles) to **Deer Island**, a small landfall ringed by serene harbors and dotted with tiny villages, departs from Letete, south of St. George on the east shore of Passamaquoddy Bay. (From St. Andrews, follow Highway 1 to St. George and the well-marked turn for Route 43; Letete is a 15-minute drive on the latter.) Friendly fishermen on the island will point out Old Sow Whirlpool, offshore at Deer Point, and direct you to the best lobster outlets. Three cozy guest rooms are available in the village of Lambert's Cove at ▶ **West Isles World**, a bed and breakfast that offers accommodations with private baths in a separate apartment. The very hospitable Cline family can also provide whale-, bird-, and seal-watching cruises.

Campobello Island is reached by private ferry ($2 per passenger, $11 for your vehicle) from Deer Island or by bridge from the Maine town of Lubec. There's a pretty seaside golf course here open to the public ($15 for nine holes; $22 all day), but the big attraction is the **Roosevelt Summer Home**, unchanged since FDR's last visit. The movie *Sunrise at Campobello* was filmed on the island, and Greer Garson, its star, stayed in historic ▶ **Owen House**, a lovely bed-and-breakfast inn with fireplaces in the bedrooms.

Grand Manan Island

Girded by cliffs and topped by lighthouses at either end, Grand Manan Island is a two-hour ferry ride from the mainland village of Blacks Harbour, located off Highway 1 on Route 776. The ferry ride alone ($8 per person, $24 per vehicle) is worth the trip, with the occasional seal following in the ferry's wake, whales sometimes spotted on the horizon, and sea lions grumping from the rocks. On the island itself, the old ▶ **Marathon Inn**, on a hill above the ferry landing, offers eight old-fashioned but comfortable rooms in its main building along with 20 newly renovated rooms in an annex. The smaller—but no less atmospheric— ▶ **Compass Rose B&B**, just up the road (open May to October only), is a friendly, well-run inn that also serves wonderful chowder and afternoon tea. At both places, reservations confirmed in advance are recommended during July, August, and September (when whale-watching is usually excellent).

Whale-watching expeditions leave from the Marathon, where bicycles also can be rented. The cottage of noted American writer Willa Cather, who spent her summers at Whale Cove, draws curious visitors and admiring fans from around the world despite the fact it's closed to the public. Elsewhere nature trails crisscross the island, although a car is needed for excursions to Dark Harbour, where dulse is harvested and photographers gather each evening for spectacular sunsets. Once darkness descends, the islanders say the sound of a phantom rower is often heard. He's believed to be the ghost of one of Captain Morgan's men, doomed to guard the old pirate's treasure forever. Old legends are believable here.

Blacks Harbour to Saint John

Back on the mainland, follow Route 778 east past Beaver Harbour to Highway 1. Continue east for 26 km (16 miles) to the village of Lepreau, where Route 790 south leads to small fishing villages like **Dipper Harbour**, which offers magnificent sunsets. **Eastern Outdoors** (Tel: 506/634-1530) here rents sea kayaks ($35 per day for a single, $55 for a double) to adventurous visitors who'd like to explore the shoreline from a different perspective. The boats are transported to the shoreline by the outfitter, with all necessary gear included in the price of the package. Areas that can be explored include Passamaquoddy Bay and the Fundy Isles, the Dipper Harbour area, the lower Saint John River Valley, and the St. Martins area west of Saint John (see below). For further information on these and other tours, send for the *Outdoor Adventure Guide* published by the Department of Economic Development and Tourism, P.O. Box 6000, Fredericton, New Brunswick E3B 5H1.

In **Maces Bay**, a couple of miles to the west, you can sit on the wharf and watch the boats chug in while enjoying a fresh lobster roll from the **Fundy Haven** restaurant across the road. From Maces Bay, it's only 32 km (20 miles) via Route 790 and Highway 1 to Saint John.

Saint John

As far as North American cities go, Saint John is ancient. Champlain sailed into its harbor in 1604, and 30 years later French colonist Charles de la Tour established a permanent settlement here. Ousted by the English in 1703, the Acadian population was replaced by colonists from New England and, in 1783, masses of Loyalists who fled the United States after the American Revolution. In 1785 Saint John became Canada's first incorporated city. It has the oldest police force in the country (established in 1826, even before the British bobbies) and the oldest city market charter in North America.

It's also noted for its native sons. Movie moguls and stars such as Louis B. Mayer (who used to ride on the back of his father's junk wagon), Walter Pidgeon (who began here as a baritone singer), and Donald Sutherland (of *M*A*S*H* fame) played childhood games (although not all at the same time) among the ancient stones of Loyalist Burying Grounds. Benedict Arnold ran a business near the harbor, and Harry Houdini and Ethel Barrymore graced the stage at the ornate Old Capital Theatre—which today, like everything else in Saint John, is being restored.

The harbor is Saint John's focal point and the site of its most historic event, the landing of the Loyalists in 1783. On that day 3,000 refugees from the American Revolution landed on the rocky banks, quickly followed by thousands more who wished to live "under the King." Aided by the Micmac and Maliseet Indians of the area, who showed them how to survive the harsh winters, the newcomers soon created a thriving port city noted for the elegant lifestyles of its gentry. Much of that gracious era survives to this day.

AROUND IN SAINT JOHN

Saint John sprawls up from its ice-free harbor, with redbricked and lantern-lined **King Street** its main thoroughfare from the restored Market Slip and Market Square on the waterfront to King Square and the **Loyalist Burying Grounds** in the center of town. Shops, historic sites, excellent restaurants, and some fine hotels are spread out in every direction, with walking the best way to explore the area; walking-tour maps are available through the tourist offices at City Hall and Sydney Street, or at the Tugboat Information Center at Market Slip. In addition, costumed guides lead historical walks from Barbour's General Store at Market Slip.

The historic core of the city is concentrated near the harbor. At 120 Union Street, **Old Loyalist House**, a gracious 1817 home that remained in the same family for five generations, reflects the well-to-do Loyalist way of life. The late-19th-century **Old City Market**, two blocks up from the harbor, with entrances on Charlotte and Germain streets, extends for a full block. Under its arched roof, built with hand-hewn timbers by early ship carpenters, vendors display red lobster, yellow wheels of cheese, barrels of purple dulse (the dried seaweed residents eat like potato chips), preserves, maple syrup, flowers, and crafts. A couple of snack bars cater to light appetites (the best hot dogs in town are sold here), and outdoor cafés offer lunch in the sun.

Antiques stores and craft shops such as the **Windrush Galleries**, where Inuit and Indian arts are featured, line Prince William Street and its offshoot lanes. Saint John's **Jewish Historical Museum**, 29 Wellington Row, is also well worth a visit.

Market Slip, at the foot of King Street, is the ideal place to take the city's pulse and explore its past. You'll find a group of small historic buildings set up as museums here, and plenty of shops, restaurants, and promenades in the restored complex of old warehouses now known as **Market Square**. Devouring seafood under the outside umbrellas at **Grannan's** (Tel: 506/634-1555) is a favorite local pastime during the summer months. This is also where the festivities marking **Loyalist Days** begin in late July, and the folk dancing of cultural groups from across Canada is presented during August's **Festival by the Sea**. Saint John also has a strong Irish heritage, which is celebrated enthusiastically during the last week of July with the **International Gathering of the Irish** festivities.

A skywalk leads from Market Square to the extensive facilities of the Aquatic Center, Saint John's legacy from the 1985 Canada Games. The complex ($3.50 for adults) boasts a number of Olympic-size lap pools, a children's pool, an exercise pool, a water slide, weight and training rooms, a sauna, and a snack bar.

Two of the city's major attractions are a bit far for walking but only a short trip by taxi. The **New Brunswick Museum**, 277 Douglas Avenue (opened in 1842 as the first public museum in Canada), deserves an hour or two for an overview of the province's past and present. The collection includes native artifacts, early shipbuilding relics, Loyalist rooms, and a modern-art gallery.

A bit farther on, the **Reversing Falls Rapids** puts on a show twice every 24 hours when the strong Fundy tide (40 or more feet) tries to push up the Saint John River. Because the river is so powerful, the tides are turned around and the result is a series of boiling whirlpools and angry, rippling rapids. There is one drawback. If the pulp mill across the river is emitting fumes that day, you may want to skip the sight. Luckily the odor doesn't seem to permeate downtown Saint John.

STAYING AND DINING IN SAINT JOHN

The Market Square complex is the location of the Hilton chain's smallest hotel, the ▶ **Saint John Hilton**, with most rooms decorated in Loyalist style (pine furniture, homespun drapes and upholstery, period prints) and many providing an excellent view of the town or harbor. Both the Hilton and the ultramodern ▶ **Delta Brunswick Inn** offer plenty of parking. The Delta, which overlooks restored King Street (with its entrance on the same), is connected to the **Brunswick Square** shopping complex, a two-tiered center filled with chic boutiques, antiques markets, and occasional amateur theater. Rooms in the hotel are large and beige, with well-stocked minibars and fluffy towels. And while the hotel's overall ambience is more businesslike than the cosier Hilton, it's just as comfortable.

There are, in addition, some good restaurants in the area. The chef's light hand at **Incredible Edibles**, 42 Princess Street, makes for pleasant terrace dining in a historic building; Tel: (506) 633-7554. Traditional dining is excellent in the Delta Brunswick's **Shucker's Seafood Restaurant** (Tel: 506/648-1981) or the Hilton's more elegant, Loyalist-style **Turn of the Tide** (Tel: 506/693-8484). Exceptional French cuisine can be found at **La Belle Vie** (Tel: 506/635-1155), in a renovated historic mansion on Lancaster Avenue.

East from Saint John

St. Martins

The cozy little town of St. Martins, a nearly perfect example of a Fundy fishing village, is about 32 km (20 miles) east of Saint John via Route 111. Stately old homes with widow's walks back up to lush green forest. Two covered bridges, two long wharves—where lobster boats are usually tied up—and a Fundy lighthouse set against the sea add to the scene. The high Fundy tides have scoured rocks into mushroom-like shapes and polished a hole right through one of the red cliffs that guards the sheltered harbor and crescent-shaped beach. St. Martins is a find and should be savored; the best way to do that is to stay at the ▶ **Quaco Inn**, where some rooms face the sea and the four-course dinner is by reservation only (Tel: 506/833-4772). Just down the road, the ▶ **St. Martins Country**

Inn is another fine old building, with 13 guest rooms done up in period decor and a widow's walk providing lovely views of the sea. Both places are busy during the summer months, but rooms are often available on short notice. While arriving without a reservation is okay if you like to live dangerously, it makes more sense to book ahead.

Fundy National Park

Continuing along the coast: Magnificent Fundy National Park stretches along the shore and pushes into game-filled woodlands. A golf course (open to the public; $8 for nine holes, $22 all day) runs along a rocky ridge overlooking the bay, with deer appearing in the fairways in such numbers at twilight that they sometimes seem more like overgrown rabbits. Driving at night here can be hazardous if speed-limit signs aren't heeded, as the area also abounds in moose that often take exception to anyone but themselves on the wooded roads.

The ▶ **Fundy Park Chalets** and the ▶ **Caledonia Highlands Inn and Chalets**, both within the park, offer modern, comfortable accommodations (good for families) in a secluded area where wildlife often wanders near at dusk. The park also offers a good restaurant and activities such as hiking, canoeing, fishing, swimming (in a heated pool), and beachcombing.

Look for terrific sticky buns, lobster, and crafts in the park gate village of **Alma**. About 50 km (31 miles) farther on at **Hopewell Cape** it's possible to walk among giant rock sculptures and explore tide-scoured caves in the cliff face.

Moncton

Moncton, the second city of the Fundy area, was founded by Acadians and Pennsylvania Dutch and Germans who came here to farm and build ships. Situated inland close to the mouth of the Petitcodiac River, approximately 152 km (94 miles) northeast of Saint John, it's known to many as the gateway to Acadia, and much of its population is bilingual. Once an important railway center, its rail role has dwindled in recent years, although you'll still see mementoes of the age of steam in Centennial Park (where an old locomotive is enshrined), as well as in the Moncton Museum.

The **Acadian Museum**, on the campus of the University of Moncton (New Brunswick's only French-language university), has a large collection of artifacts, but Moncton's main claim to fame has always been two phenomena of nature, the

Tidal Bore and the Magnetic Hill. Some say they are highly overrated, others consider them fascinating.

The **Tidal Bore** happens twice every 24 hours, when the fierce Fundy tides are funneled into the narrow mouth of the Petitcodiac River, creating a low tidal wave that covers red mud riverbanks in the wink of an eye and a wide river out of what was a trickle seconds before. The best place to see it is Bore View Park on Main Street, where you can also pick up a tide table at the information center.

Magnetic Hill, just off the Trans-Canada Highway (Highway 2) at Mountain Road, seems to be an uphill grade when, in fact, it is actually a downhill slope. Startled motorists, who sometimes turn off the ignition and put the car in neutral, find themselves coasting "uphill" at an ever-increasing rate. There is also a large water-theme park, called **Magic Mountain**, at the hill.

Moncton's best and most expensive hotel, the ▶ **Hotel Beauséjour**, is centrally located, decorated with Acadian charm, and has a good restaurant known for its Continental dishes. For excellent seafood try **Fisherman's Paradise, Dieppe** (Tel: 506/859-4388), 375 Dieppe Boulevard (off Champlain Street), or the noted **Cy's** (Tel: 506/857-0032), 170 East Main Street (near Bore Park).

The shopping in Moncton is some of the best in the province, with the red-brick courtyards of the downtown area particularly attractive in summer, when hanging baskets adorn lampposts and benches and cafés become prime people-watching spots. **Rubin's**, in the Champlain Mall off Main Street, is a good stop for designer women's wear. **Suttles and Seawinds**, 827 Main Street, sells a variety of maritime handicrafts. **Gifts Galore**, 569 Main Street, is another good choice for handicrafts.

Sackville and the Tantramar Marshes

The town of Sackville, about 56 km (35 miles) southeast of Moncton via the Trans-Canada, is known for its English atmosphere, the lovely campus of Mount Allison University (home to the excellent **Owens Art Gallery**), and the ▶ **Marshlands Inn**, an antiques-filled mansion with a dignified dining room partial to local products (including homemade ice cream and locally grown berries).

The weathered barns, golden grasses, and wonderful light of the nearby **Tantramar Marshes** have always attracted artists to the area, and their workshops (bring your purse or wallet) are plentiful. Amateur historians will be fascinated by the ingenious, centuries-old system of dams and dikes, called *aboiteaux,* that is responsible for the biological diversity of these rich grasslands, while bird-watchers will delight in the opportunities to view rare waterfowl. Guided tours of the marshes are offered in summer; for details, contact the Tourist Information Centre in Aulac (Highway 2, less than a mile from the Nova Scotia border).

THE ACADIAN PENINSULA

The Acadian area in northeastern New Brunswick includes sandy shores warmed by the Gulf Stream, several cities, a major national park, and scores of fishing communities where, in some ways, life has changed little in generations. The curious history of the region enfolds the traveller in a friendly French environment that recalls France itself.

In 1755 the British victors of the French and English wars for possession of the continent and its lucrative fur trade expelled French settlers from parts of the maritime region. Scattering in many directions, including Louisiana (where they are known as Cajuns), the so-called Acadians attempted to build new lives. Small bands of them refused to leave the land where they had lived for generations, however, and hid in the woods and remote coastal areas of New Brunswick, biding their time until the British relented and once more allowed them to build permanent residences.

The Acadians had the good sense to settle along the temperate shores of Northumberland Strait and the **Baie des Chaleurs**, where the waters are warmer due to the wash of the Gulf Stream and the mainland is protected from storms blowing in off the Gulf of St. Lawrence by both Prince Edward Island and the Gaspé Peninsula of Quebec.

Today, nowhere is the Acadian legacy in New Brunswick more pronounced than on the Acadian Peninsula, that part of the northeast shore extending from Point Escuminac north and west to Bathurst. Here, meadows sweet with wild strawberries and wildflowers stretch inland from the coast and ethereal mists hang over lonely peat bogs and marshlands reclaimed from the sea. By the sea itself, long, lively wharves, colorful with lobster traps and buoys, embrace sturdy little lobster boats, while lighthouses and church spires soar against incomparable summer skies. Old customs, such as the Blessing of the Fleet, where the local priest blesses the outgoing boats, are still observed and Sunday Mass fills churches to overflowing.

Traditional crafts such as rug hooking, quilting, and wooden ship building are still part of everyday life on the Acadian Peninsula, and although the modern world has long

since arrived, there is a certain Acadian joie de vivre that
bubbles up in singalongs, bonfires, and lobster parties on
the beach or simply over a good meal in a restaurant.
Although French is the first language of the area, English is
common enough so that an Anglophone at one table can
easily understand the conversation at the next as it switches
back and forth from French to English in an unconscious
blending of the languages.

Shediac

In Shediac, northeast of Moncton, shallow water captured
between sandbars is often warmed by the sun to bathtub
temperature, and lobster suppers are a feature of everyday
life. Some of the best are served at **Fisherman's Paradise** (mid-
April to mid-September; Tel: 506/532-6811), on Main Street,
and **Paturel's** (where there's also a fresh lobster outlet; May to
mid-September; Tel: 506/532-4774), 5 km (3 miles) east of
town on Route 133 in the direction of Cap-Bimet. ► **Chez
Françoise** (May 1 to December 31; Tel: 506/532-4233), a fine
old mansion turned inn on Shediac's Main Street, boasts an
excellent dining room where cut glass sparkles, antique furniture glows, and tiled fireplaces warm summer evenings.
Parades, lobster feeds, sports competitions, and pageants are
part and parcel of the mid-July **Shediac Lobster Festival**.

Shediac to Point Escuminac

As you drive north and west along Highway 11, the signs
change from English to French and little roadside restaurants advertise their "homard," "coque frit," and "pomme
frit" (lobster, fried clams, and french fries). Shore routes
such as 134, 175, and 505 pass through timeless fishing
villages and small seaside towns like **Cocagne**, where an
international hydroplane regatta is held in early August, and
Bouctouche (buck-TOOSH), with miles of deserted sandy
beaches.

Just beyond Bouctouche, the ► **Bouctouche Bay Inn**
sprawls along the shore, offering comfortable accommodations, good seafood, and German specialty desserts (German cheesecake, German strawberry cake). **Richibucto**, up
the coast via Route 134, holds a scallop festival July 3–10,
while Route 117 through **Kouchibouguac National Park**
(kooch-ee-boo-QUACK) takes you past sensational warm-
water beaches and miles of sand dunes. You can take the
short side road (6 km/3½ miles) off Route 117 to **Point
Escuminac**, where a typical Acadian fishing wharf juts out
from a long sandy beach and a wooden sculpture, silhou-

etted against the sea, honors the more than 50 village
fishermen who perished in a sudden storm in 1959.

Shippagan and Caraquet

In **Shippagan**, at the tip of the Acadian Peninsula some 188 km
(117 miles) north of Point Escuminac, a marine museum
provides a close-up look at sea creatures. Although the nearby
Lamèque area, where the major industry involves peat bogs,
may seem an unlikely place for a Baroque music festival,
every July international choirs, ensembles, and famous con-
ductors gather in the innovatively decorated church in the
town of Ste-Cécile here.

The prosperous fishing town of **Caraquet** sits on rocky
cliffs overlooking lovely beaches and the Baie des Chaleurs.
Each year during the annual **Acadian Festival de Caraquet**
(on the weekend closest to August 15) there's a Blessing of
the Fleet ceremony before the flag-bedecked boats head out
to set their traps. At the busy wharf a market sells fresh fish
and shellfish.

One of the best restaurants in Caraquet is in the old
▶ **Hotel Paulin**, 143 Boulevard St. Pierre West. The tiny
dining room is noted for its careful preparation, and with
notice an authentic Acadian feast can be arranged by owner
Gerard Paulin. Once a restaurant for railroad passengers, the
Paulin retains a bit of the feeling of that era. It also has small,
uniquely decorated guest rooms, although some share a
bathroom down the hall. Tel: (506) 727-9981. For those who
find the rooms at the Paulin a little too quaint, the modern
motel-style ▶ **Auberge de la Baie**, 139 Boulevard St. Pierre
West, is a comfortable alternative.

Village Historique Acadien

Five kilometers (3 miles) west of Caraquet on Highway 11, the
re-created Village historique acadien provides a look at Acadian history in the decades after the expulsion. Horses
whinny, wagon wheels creak, bells toll from the chapel, and
the smells of fresh wood shavings, salt cod, and baking bread
waft from various buildings. The happy little village has
spawned a resurgence of pride in the area's cultural legacy,
and is well worth a visit for anyone curious about the Acadians
and their history.

Bathurst to Campbellton

Bathurst, a busy pulp-mill town at the head of Nepisiguit Bay,
66 km (41 miles) west of Caraquet, used to greet you with the
overpowering fragrance of sulfur. But a state-of-the-art filter-
ing system installed by the mill seems to have eliminated the

problem. **Youghall Beach,** north of town, is a favorite spot for swimming, and there are several good motels in the area, among them the ▶ **Atlantic Host Inn** on Highway 11 (here called Boulevard Vanier), a large motel with a pool, a good dining room, a bar, and pleasant rooms.

Still, come dinnertime, most people who travel in this area head for the small town of Nigadoo, 20 km (12 miles) north of Bathurst via Route 134, where **La Fine Grobe** turns out gourmet meals in a rustic lodge hung with paintings for sale. The menu includes interesting local specialties such as rabbit in creamy mustard sauce as well as plenty of seafood. Reservations advised; Tel: (506) 783-3138.

Deep-sea-fishing charters and scenic cruises aboard the *Chaleur Phantom* are available in the small town of **Dalhousie,** located 94 km (58 miles) northwest of Bathurst via Highway 11. You'll find the *Phantom* at the ferry wharf at the bottom of Renfrew Street; Tel: (506) 684-4722.

There's an English cast to **Campbellton,** another 28 km (17 miles) to the west, which holds its Salmon Festival in late June. Just across the bridge in Quebec, a museum contains artifacts recovered from the Restigouche River that date back to 1760 and the Battle of the Restigouche, which marked the end of the wars between the English and French. The ▶ **Aylesford Inn Bed and Breakfast** (Tel: 506/759-7672), 8 MacMillan Avenue in Campbellton, combines excellent dining (guests only) with pretty rooms and views, while the ▶ **Bonaventure Lodge** (May 1 to October 31; Tel: 506/237-2134) in the village of New Mills, southeast of Campbellton, offers German specialties and good seafood along with seaside accommodations.

MIRAMICHI AREA

The centrally located Miramichi (mirry-ma-SHEE) region was settled by Scots, Irish, and English, and today is a mecca for sportsmen who come to hunt and fish at outfitters' camps. Country roads wind past streams and rivers where avid anglers fly cast in hip-deep water and canoes glide over the surface. Legends, great men, folklore, folk festivals, and heritage museums are all part and parcel of a Miramichi visit.

Boiestown to Blackville

It's hard to say where the Miramichi starts. Its natives begin to refer to it as soon as they leave Fredericton heading north along the scenic Nashwaak River on Highway 8. At **Boies-**

town, where you hit the main branch of the Miramichi River, the feel of the region begins to seep in. Giant statues of woodsmen stand by the road, and a Woodmen's Museum provides an excellent look at the area's background.

All your sportfishing needs can be arranged at ▶ **Pond's Chalet Resort** in Ludlow, 6 km (3½ miles) northeast of Boiestown, where the accommodations run to rustic log cabins or a main lodge overlooking the heavily fished Miramichi. The lodge's main dining room (Tel: 506/369-2612) is open to the public, and is full of interesting mementoes of the area and its logging past. **Doaktown**, another 20 km (12 miles) farther east, and **Blackville**, 35 km (22 miles) beyond Doaktown, are to sportfishing what the Rockies are to downhill skiing. In Doaktown, local conservationists were instrumental in establishing the **Atlantic Salmon Museum**, after that silvery fighting fish was driven to the brink of extinction by destructive commercial fishing practices.

Newcastle

Newcastle, at the mouth of the Miramichi River, some 51 km (32 miles) northeast of Blackville, is another pulp-mill town, but its past claim to fame has been its association with the Cunard empire. At one time the Cunards employed almost everyone in the area, either in cutting trees for their ships or in the shipyards themselves. When the steam engine came along the industry declined, but the homes of wealthy lumbermen and shipbuilders still grace the streets of Newcastle and nearby **Chatham**.

Newcastle is also where Max Aitkin, who became British peer Lord Beaverbrook, grew up. His family home, the **Old Manse**, is now a well-stocked library devoted to local history. Beaverbrook's ashes rest in the base of his statue in the town square, a parcel of land he gave to the city.

The ▶ **Wharf Inn**, on Jane Street, has 70 comfortable rooms, six of them with kitchen facilities, as well as a restaurant and indoor pool. Across the river in Nelson-Miramichi, the ▶ **Governor's Mansion Inn**, formerly the home of one of New Brunswick's lieutenant governors, is a very special bed and breakfast characterized by lumber-baron elegance. The steaks and seafood at the **Portage** (Tel: 506/773-6447) in Chatham, also across the river from Newcastle, are touted throughout the area.

In early August Newcastle hosts a folk-song festival open to all comers. Its performers are usually old-timers who sing the "come all ye" ballads of the original settlers. But it seems to be the Irish who made the most lasting impression here; not only do the inhabitants speak with a touch of brogue, but Chatham hosts the biggest Irish festival in Canada (in mid-July).

The **Miramichi Natural History Museum** (open daily, 10:00 A.M. to 8:00 P.M., May to September) in Chatham and the **MacDonald Farm Historic Park** (9:30 A.M. to 4:30 P.M. daily, summer only) in Bartibog Bridge (the latter approximately 13 km/8 miles north of Chatham via Highway 11) are devoted to the history of the area. The ledgers of Cunard and the old stones of the MacDonald farm whisper of a time when life was rich, even opulent, in a bounteous land.

GETTING AROUND

July and August, when the temperature here can climb to 90° F (30° C), constitute the peak tourist season. It's wise to book accommodations in advance if you're planning a visit during either month. June and September are excellent months for touring, with all but empty roads, fine days, and cooler nights. Brilliant foliage begins to appear in late September and lasts through mid-October. Casual clothing is the rule, although some of the better restaurants expect more formal attire.

New Brunswick's provincial and national parks offer groomed trails for cross-country skiing, as do many communities and small hotels. Downhill skiing is available at several locations around the province, with winter ski weekends at Edmundston's **Mount Farlagne** an especially popular activity. Most communities have indoor skating rinks; hockey is a provincial craze, and minor league teams operate in Moncton and Fredericton. Curling is also a common winter pastime, with rinks in all major cities and most small communities.

Road conditions are generally good throughout the winter months, with bare pavement the norm except in midwinter (late December, January, early February). Winter temperatures can dip well below zero, but central heating keeps all accommodations cozy (although some smaller inns and motels close during the winter months). Most campgrounds and tourist attractions close for the winter, although **Kings Landing** does serve old-fashioned candlelit dinners in November and December. (Reservations advised; Tel: 506/363-5090.)

New Brunswick's highway system is good and continually being upgraded, with facilities plentiful along major tourist routes. The only map you'll need is the free one available at tourist information centers. The Department of Economic Development and Tourism, P.O. Box 6000, Fredericton, N.B., E3B 5H1 (Tel: 800/561-0123 in the U.S. and Canada), has plenty of other helpful information.

The major entry points into the province are St. Stephen,

Houlton, and Edmundston on the U.S.–Canada border; Cape
Tormentine opposite Prince Edward Island; and Aulac, on
the provincial border with Nova Scotia. A Marine Atlantic
ferry operates year-round between Digby, Nova Scotia, and
Saint John. The approximately 3-hour trip costs $20 per
person, $45 per vehicle, one-way. For departure times and
reservations in the U.S., Tel: (800) 341-7981; in Canada
(except Newfoundland), Tel: (902) 742-6800; in Newfoundland, Tel: (709) 772-7701.

Canadian Airlines International and Air Canada service the
province through the airports at Saint John, Fredericton, and
Moncton. Air Atlantic, a subsidiary of Canadian, offers daily
flights to and from the country's major Atlantic cities, as well
as Boston, Montreal, and Ottawa. Air Nova, a subsidiary of Air
Canada, offers daily service to the Atlantic provinces, as well
as Montreal, Toronto, and Ottawa.

The SMT bus line connects with major bus lines throughout Canada and the United States. VIA Rail connects with
Amtrak; for VIA Rail information and/or reservations, Tel:
(800) 561-3949 in the U.S. and most of Canada; within the
Maritimes, Tel: (800) 561-3952.

ACCOMMODATIONS REFERENCE

The rates given below are projections *for peak seasons
during the 1994 calendar year; at other times of the year
they may be considerably less. Unless otherwise indicated,
rates are based on double rooms, double occupancy; provincial and federal taxes are included in all rates. As rates are
subject to change, always double-check before booking.*

▶ **Algonquin Hotel.** 184 Adolphus Street, **St. Andrews**, N.B.
E0G 2X0. Tel: (506) 529-8823; Fax: (506) 529-4194; in the
U.S. and Canada, Tel: (800) 563-4299. $120–$243.

▶ **Atlantic Host Inn.** P.O. Box 910, Boulevard Vanier,
Bathurst, N.B. E2A 4H7. Tel: (506) 548-3335; Fax: (506) 548-
9769. $64–$83.

▶ **Auberge de la Baie.** P.O. Box 516, 139 Boulevard St.
Pierre West, **Caraquet**, N.B. E0B 1K0. Tel: (506) 727-3485;
Fax: (506) 727-3634. $76.

▶ **Aylesford Inn Bed and Breakfast.** 8 MacMillan Avenue,
Campbellton, N.B. E3N 1E9. Tel: (506) 759-7672. $53–$59
(includes breakfast).

▶ **Best Western Shiretown Inn.** P.O. Box 145, 218 Water
Street, **St. Andrews**, N.B. E0G 2X0. Tel: (506) 529-8877; Fax:
(506) 529-3044; in the U.S. and Canada, Tel: (800) 528-1234.
$53–$78.

▶ **Bonaventure Lodge.** P.O. Box 8, Site 13, Route 11, **New Mills**, N.B. E0B 1M0. Tel: (506) 237-2134. $57–$68.

▶ **Bouctouche Bay Inn.** P.O. Box 445, **Bouctouche**, N.B. E0A 1G0. Tel: (506) 743-2726; Fax: (506) 743-2387. $71–$83.

▶ **Caledonia Highlands Inn and Chalets.** P.O. Box 99, Fundy National Park, **Alma**, N.B. E0A 1B0. Tel: (506) 887-2930. $71.

▶ **Cambridge-Narrows B&B.** R.R. 1, **Codys**, N.B. E0E 1E0. Tel: (506) 488-2000 or 3426; Fax: (506) 488-2000. $40.

▶ **Chez Françoise.** P.O. Box 715, 93 Main Street, **Shediac**, N.B. E0A 3G0. Tel: (506) 532-4233 or 2975. $53–$71.

▶ **Chickadee Lodge Bed & Breakfast.** Highway 2, **Prince William**, N.B. E0H 1S0. Tel: (506) 363-2759. $54.

▶ **Compass Rose B&B.** Route 776, North Head, **Grand Manan**, N.B. E0G 2M0. Tel: (506) 662-8570. $65.

▶ **Delta Brunswick Inn.** 39 King Street, **Saint John**, N.B. E2L 4W3. Tel: (506) 648-1981; Fax: (506) 658-0914; in the U.S. and Canada, Tel: (800) 268-1133. $93–$117.

▶ **Fundy Park Chalets.** P.O. Box 72, **Alma**, N.B. E0A 1B0. Tel: (506) 887-2808. $73.

▶ **Governor's Mansion Inn.** **Nelson–Miramichi**, N.B. E0C 1T0. Tel: (506) 622-3036. $35.

▶ **Hotel Beauséjour.** P.O. Box 906, 750 Main Street, **Moncton**, N.B. E1C 1E6. Tel: (506) 854-4344; Fax: (506) 858-0957; in the U.S., Tel: (800) 828-7447; in Canada, (800) 268-9411. $105–$120.

▶ **Hotel Paulin.** 143 Boulevard St. Pierre West, **Caraquet**, N.B. E0B 1K0. Tel: (506) 727-9981. $52 (shared bath); $77 (bath *en suite*).

▶ **John Gyles Motor Inn.** R.R. 1, **Woodstock**, N.B. E0J 2B0. Tel: (506) 328-6622. $56.

▶ **Kingsclear Hotel and Resort.** R.R. 6, **Fredericton**, N.B. E3B 4X7. Tel: (506) 363-5111; Fax: (506) 363-3000; in the U.S. and Canada, Tel: (800) 561-5111. $77–$130 (rooms); $177 (cottages).

▶ **Loaves and Calico Country Inn.** P.O. Box 175, **Gagetown**, N.B. E0G 1V0. Tel: (506) 488-3018. $42.

▶ **Long Island Home B&B.** R.R. 2, Wickham, **Hatfield Point**, N.B. E0G 2A0. Tel: (506) 425-2444. $35.

▶ **Lord Beaverbrook Hotel.** 659 Queen Street, **Fredericton**, N.B. E3B 5A6. Tel: (506) 455-3371; Fax: (506) 455-1441; in the U.S. and Canada, Tel: (800) 561-7666. $85.

▶ **Marathon Inn.** North Head, **Grand Manan**, N.B. E0G 2M0. Tel: (506) 662-8488. $81–$105; $58 (shared bath).

▶ **Marshlands Inn.** P.O. Box 1440, 59 Bridge Street, **Sackville**, N.B. E0A 3C0. Tel: (506) 536-0170; Fax: (506) 536-0721. $85–$101.

▶ **Owen House**. P.O. Box 16, Welshpool, **Campobello**, N.B. E0G 3H0. Tel: (506) 752-2977. $72 (private bath and breakfast).

▶ **Pippincott Bed & Breakfast**. P.O. Box 318, 208 Prince of Wales Street, **St. Andrews**, N.B. E0G 2X0. Tel: (506) 529-3445. $60–$80.

▶ **Pond's Chalet Resort**. Keith Pond, Porter Cove Road, **Ludlow**, N.B. E0B 1N0. Tel: (506) 369-2612; Fax: (506) 369-2293. $71; $95 (suite).

▶ **Quaco Inn**. St. Martins, N.B. E0G 2Z0. Tel: (506) 833-4772; Fax: (506) 833-2531. $65–$92.

▶ **Rossmount Inn**. R.R. 2, **St. Andrews**, N.B. E0G 2X0. Tel: (506) 529-3351; Fax: (506) 529-1920. $112.

▶ **Saint John Hilton**. One Market Square, **Saint John**, N.B. E2L 4Z6. Tel: (506) 693-8484; Fax: (506) 657-6610; in the U.S. and Canada, Tel: (800) 445-8667. $105–$183.

▶ **St. Martins Country Inn**. R.R. 1, **St. Martins**, N.B. E0G 2Z0. Tel: (506) 833-4534; Fax: (506) 833-4725. $67–$95.

▶ **Sheraton Inn Fredericton**. 225 Woodstock Road, **Fredericton**, N.B. E3B 2H8. Tel: (506) 457-7000; Fax: (506) 457-4000; in the U.S. and Canada, Tel: (800) 325-3535. $93–$132.

▶ **Steamers Stop Inn**. P.O. Box 155, Front Street, **Village of Gagetown**, N.B. E0G 1V0. Tel: (506) 488-2903; Fax: (506) 488-1116. $53–$65 (shared bath); $77 (private bath).

▶ **West Isles World Bed and Breakfast**. Lambert's Cove, **Deer Island**, N.B. E0G 2J0. Tel: (506) 747-2946. $60 (three-night minimum).

▶ **Wharf Inn**. P.O. Box 474, Jane Street, **Newcastle**, N.B. E1V 3M6. Tel: (506) 622-0302; Fax: (506) 622-0354; in the U.S. and Canada, Tel: (800) 561-2111. $71–$88.

PRINCE EDWARD ISLAND

By Charmaine Gaudet

Charmaine Gaudet, a native Prince Edward Islander, regularly contributes articles on travel, food, and lifestyle to magazines in the United States and Canada, and has written guidebooks to cities in New Brunswick as well as to Prince Edward Island.

Prince Edward Island is a crescent carved out of brick-red sandstone—gently rolling, carpeted in green fields, and edged in wide, powdery beaches. The island, which stretches above the northern coast of New Brunswick and, to the east, Nova Scotia, has charmed visitors since ancient times. As early as 2,000 years ago, mainland Micmac Indians revered it as the sacred summer residence of the Great Spirit. Abegweit, they called it, meaning "cradled on the waves," and they crossed Northumberland Strait each summer to fish here, eventually making it their year-round home. French explorer Jacques Cartier, the first known European visitor, was similarly smitten and, upon seeing the island in 1534, immediately declared it "the fairest land 'tis possible to see."

These days, the island's tranquil countryside wears the patchwork pattern of farmland and the snug neatness of rural villages, with a smattering of pretty fishing ports. In addition to its scenic charm, Prince Edward Island has some of eastern Canada's best warm-water beaches, a vibrant summer musical-theater festival, the storybook Anne of Green

Gables farmhouse in Cavendish, world-famous tuna fishing, excellent golf courses, and an abundance of unpretentious restaurants specializing in fresh seafood. Canada's smallest province is a mecca for modern-day tourists, who each summer swell the island's permanent population of 123,000 to almost half a million. At the same time, the island's essentially rural character—evident in the deep green carpet of potato fields, the ever-present drone of tractors, and the sight of grazing milk cows—spares it from most of the usual commercialism found in popular tourist destinations.

The compact island—140 miles long and from 4 to 40 miles across—boasts an intricate network of paved roads. Major attractions tend to be focused within a 25-mile radius of **Charlottetown** (population 15,000), P.E.I.'s capital and only city. The popular north-shore beaches of **Prince Edward Island National Park**, which is also the site of the Green Gables farmhouse, are just 12 miles north of the city. The south shore's less spectacular beaches attract islanders and knowledgeable visitors to warmer swimming waters only a few minutes from Charlottetown.

In recent years the quality and quantity of the island's handicrafts have made them a legitimate attraction in themselves. While you will no doubt run across the usual selection of crocheted baby booties and salt-glazed honey pots, many island craft shops carry outstanding work, both traditional and contemporary. The best of island crafts include handmade quilts, braided rugs, pottery, wooden furniture, toys, hand-knit sweaters, and stained glass.

Avoid the common mistake of trying to "do" Prince Edward Island in a day. Instead, plan on three to five days—time enough to relax on the beaches, take in a stage performance at the **Charlottetown Summer Festival**, have a "feed" of lobster, browse through the numerous craft and antiques shops, and explore at a leisurely pace in tune with the laid-back island way of life.

As for the best time to visit, try to schedule your Prince Edward Island holiday in summer or early fall. Daytime temperatures in the summer average a pleasant 73° F (22.5° C) and constant light sea breezes temper even the hottest days. Evenings, by contrast, can be sweater-cool. In summer, the water around the island, particularly along the south shore, is as warm as any on the eastern seaboard north of Florida. September is generally temperate as well, and the tourist traffic dies down considerably after Canadian Labour Day. By mid-September to early October most attractions, gift shops, and seasonal accommodations are closed.

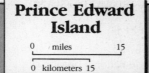

Prince Edward Island

0   miles   15

0   kilometers   15

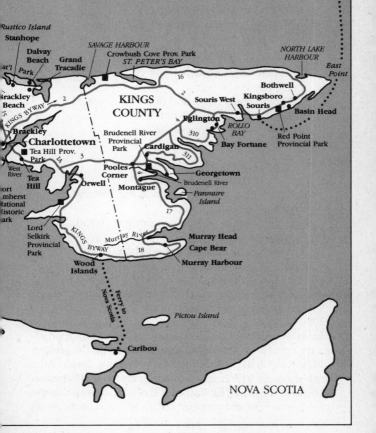

*GULF OF
ST. LAWRENCE*

Ferry to Magdalen Islands

Rustico Island
Stanhope

**Dalvay
Beach**
**Grand
Tracadie**

at'l
Park

SAVAGE HARBOUR
Crowbush Cove Prov. Park
ST. PETER'S BAY

*NORTH LAKE
HARBOUR*

*East
Point*

**rackley
Beach**

2

16

2   **Souris West**

Bothwell
Kingsboro
Souris

Basin Head

15

KINGS BYWAY

**KINGS
COUNTY**

4   **Eglington**

*ROLLO
BAY*

Red Point
Provincial Park

Brackley
Charlottetown
Tea Hill Prov.
Park

2

Brudenell River
Provincial Park

310

Cardigan

311

Bay Fortune

*West
River*

1A
3

**Pooles
Corner**

Georgetown

Brudenell River

**ort
mherst
ational
istoric
ark**

**Tea
Hill**

Orwell

Montague

*Panmure
Island*

Lord
Selkirk
Provincial
Park

KINGS BYWAY

Murray River

17

18

Murray Head
Cape Bear
Murray Harbour

**Wood
Islands**

Ferry to
Nova Scotia

Pictou Island

Caribou

NOVA SCOTIA

MAJOR INTEREST

Charlottetown
Province House national historic site
Charlottetown Summer Festival
St. Dunstan's Basilica
St. Paul's Anglican Church
Old Charlottetown's shops, cafés, and waterfront

Elsewhere in Queens County
Prince Edward Island National Park
Green Gables Farmhouse and Golf Course
Lucy Maud Montgomery's birthplace in New
    London
Anne of Green Gables Museum at Silver Bush, in
    Park Corner
Traditional lobster suppers
Victoria-by-the-Sea scenic fishing village
Tea Hill Provincial Park beaches
Orwell Corner historic village

Kings County
Village of Murray River
Panmure Island beaches
Brudenell River Provincial Park
Scenic Bay Fortune area
Red Point, Basin Head, and Bothwell beaches
Tuna-fishing charters at North Lake
Crowbush Cove Provincial Park beach

Prince County
Town of Summerside
Acadian Museum at Miscouche
Traditional Acadian handicrafts at the Abrams
    Village Handcraft Co-op
Mill River Provincial Park's resort, golf course, camp-
    ing, water sports
Indian arts and crafts on Lennox Island
Village of Tyne Valley
Malpeque area and Cabot Provincial Park beach
Re-created shipyard and restored shipbuilder's home
    at Green Park Provincial Park

Prince Edward Island is divided into three counties of approximately equal area. **Queens County** draws by far the greatest
number of visitors, and includes Charlottetown, much of the
north-shore resort area, and coastal scenery typified by beautiful beaches, bays, and fishing ports. Queens County is also the
most commercialized area, particularly around Cavendish on

the north shore, where tourist operators have capitalized on Green Gables and the national park as a premise for innumerable attractions, from children's theme parks to a string of souvenir shops and fast-food stands.

While the easternmost county, **Kings County**, has fewer commercial tourist attractions, its bay-notched coast offers scenery as pretty and beaches as powdery as those in Queens County. It also boasts a port known as the "Tuna-Fishing Capital of the World," and an outstanding 18-hole golf course at Brudenell River.

Windswept sandstone cliffs, remote beaches, and a rich sense of history endow **Prince County**, comprising the western third of the island, with a timeless quality. The south shore is home to Acadians, many of whom still speak the ancient French dialect brought over by their 18th-century ancestors. A hundred years ago the area spawned shipbuilding empires, now recalled by a re-created shipyard at Green Park. Prince County also offers one of eastern Canada's best golf courses, at Mill River.

QUEENS COUNTY
Charlottetown

You can easily explore downtown Charlottetown on foot, combining sightseeing and shopping with a walking tour. Hook up with **City of Charlottetown Historic Walking Tours** (Tel: 902/566-5548) for a guided stroll through the old city (July and August only) or pick up a copy of *Walks in Charlotte Town,* available at local bookstores, or *A Walking Tour of the Charlottetown Waterfront,* a newly published guide available at Visitor Information Centres.

Situated on an inlet of Northumberland Strait and named for Queen Charlotte, wife of George III, Charlottetown has been the capital of Prince Edward Island since 1763, the year the island was ceded to Britain.

The center of historic Charlottetown is dominated by the 1964 **Confederation Centre of the Arts**, a massive, modern, and arguably inappropriate concrete structure plunked down amid brick and wooden 19th-century storefronts. The center was built as a national memorial to the birth of Canadian nationhood, which was set in motion at the Charlottetown Conference a hundred years earlier. Today it houses an 1,100-seat theater, an art gallery, a library, and a gift shop filled with an eclectic collection of Canadian crafts.

Next door, **Province House**, the site of the conference, still houses the Prince Edward Island legislature. Visitors are welcome to tour much of the Georgian-style building, including the restored Confederation Chamber. Province House is open daily from June 1 to mid-October, and weekdays the rest of the year.

From May 1 to September 30 the **Charlottetown Summer Festival** kindles excitement in this normally quiet city. Tourists flock to see *Anne of Green Gables* (Canada's longest-running musical), as well as the alternating performances that have given the festival a deserved reputation as the country's major musical-theater showcase. (You'll want to reserve tickets in advance; Tel: 902/566-1267, or 800/565-0278 within the Atlantic provinces.) The Mackenzie Theatre across the street provides an intimate atmosphere for plays and revues more suited to the small stage.

Nearby on Great George Street, **St. Dunstan's Basilica** is a flamboyant Gothic-style edifice with 200-foot spires and a magnificent interior featuring Gothic Revival fan vaulting, intricate marble detailing, a stunning German rose window, and stained glass windows by contemporary island artist Henry Purdy. **St. Paul's Anglican Church**, next to the Confederation Centre, was designed by the island's foremost 19th-century architect, William Critchlow Harris, whose brother, portrait painter Robert Harris, is best known for his *Fathers of the Confederation,* lost in the 1916 fire that destroyed the Parliament buildings in Ottawa. Together, the brothers are largely responsible for **All Souls Chapel**, the intimate chapel hugging the western wall of St. Peter's Cathedral on Rochford Street, with William designing the building itself and Robert contributing the 18 paintings adorning its interior.

Victoria Park, a 40-acre pine-studded greenbelt, overlooks Charlottetown Harbour. The park's seaside walk leads past the elegant residence of the province's lieutenant governor and the six-gun battery remaining from Fort Edward, built in 1805 to defend the harbor mouth. **Beaconsfield**, the handsome yellow Victorian mansion near the park entrance, houses the offices of the Prince Edward Island Museum and Heritage Foundation, the Centre for Genealogical Research, and a bookstore with a large selection of books on the history of the island.

Harness racing is Prince Edward Island's favorite sport, with islanders in droves heading for the **Charlottetown Driving Park** in mid-August for the annual Gold Cup and Saucer Race—the biggest racing event of the season. The annual evening event is preceded by a late-morning parade of floats, marching bands, and clowns through downtown Charlottetown.

STAYING IN CHARLOTTETOWN

Accommodations are plentiful downtown. ▶ **The Prince Edward**, on Queen Street, has all the amenities you'd expect of the city's most luxurious, and expensive, hotel. In addition, every evening except Sunday the hotel offers a traditional Scottish-Irish cabaret as well as a dinner-theater package. Tickets are $15 per person for the cabaret, $37 for the dinner show. Reservations recommended for groups; Tel: (902) 566-2222.

Recently restored to its former elegance, ▶ **The Charlottetown—A Rodd Classic Hotel**, on the corner of Kent and Pownal streets, is slightly less expensive than the Prince Edward but offers the same package of modern amenities. The landmark hotel is also home to The Feast, a lively dinner-theater show featuring an island-style buffet. The show is staged nightly, Tuesday through Sunday, and costs about $27 per person. Reservations advised; Tel: (902) 894-7371.

The ▶ **Elmwood Heritage Inn** on North River Road, the ▶ **Duchess of Kent Inn** at 218 Kent Street, the ▶ **Great George Inn** at 455 University Avenue, and the ▶ **Dundee Arms Inn** at 200 Pownal Street all offer plenty of Victorian charm and antiques-filled guest rooms. For those preferring motel-style accommodations, Charlottetown has several clean, comfortable choices, among them the ▶ **Best Western MacLauchlan's Motor Inn** on Grafton Street and the ▶ **Inn on the Hill**, on the corner of University Avenue and Euston Street, downtown; the ▶ **Kirkwood Motor Hotel**, several blocks from the downtown area on University Avenue; and the ▶ **Rodd Confederation Inn** and ▶ **Rodd Royalty Inn and Conference Center**, both on the outskirts of the city at the junction of Route 2 and the Trans-Canada Highway (Highway 1). During July and August, the peak tourist season on the island, it's a good idea to book accommodations at least a week or two in advance, particularly at inns and bed-and-breakfast establishments.

DINING AND SHOPPING IN CHARLOTTETOWN

There are a number of good dining options in Charlottetown. Downtown, the **Claddagh Room** (Tel: 902/892-9661), 131 Sydney Street; the **Peakes Quay Restaurant & Lounge** (Tel: 902/368-1330), 1A Great George Street; the **Marina Dining Room** (Tel: 902/892-2461), 238 Grafton Street; and the **Garden of the Gulf** (Tel: 902/566-2222), in the Prince Edward Hotel on Queen Street, all specialize in superbly prepared seafood. The Garden of the Gulf's surf-and-turf buffet ($18.95; daily from 5:30 to 9:00 P.M.) includes a dazzling array of entrées and homemade fresh berry pies.

Lobsterman's Landing (Tel: 902/368-2888), on the Prince Street Wharf, lives up to its name, offering lobster—in the shell, in salads, in chowder—as well as other seafood. For steak lovers, the menu also lists a basic New York strip. Or you can opt for pizza and people watching at **Pat's Rose and Grey Room** (Tel: 902/892-2222), a former drugstore lined with knickknacks on Richmond Street, across from the Confederation Centre stage door. Pat's is a busy after-theater spot, naturally, as is the nearby **Off Broadway Café** (Tel: 902/566-4620), 125 Sydney Street.

The island has a sizable Lebanese population (Joseph Ghiz, Prince Edward Island's premier, is of Lebanese descent), with Lebanese-owned businesses particularly common in Charlottetown. The steak sandwich on Lebanese bread is a favorite with regulars at **Cedar's Eatery** (Tel: 902/892-7377), 81 University Avenue, while nearby **Papa Joe's** (Tel: 902/566-5070), at 345 University, serves up a tempting Lebanese combination plate. For what is probably the best selection of authentic Lebanese dishes, however, you'll have to stop in at **Shady's Restaurant** (Tel: 902/628-1919), on St. Peter's Road in the Sherwood Shopping Centre, about a five-minute drive from downtown.

Back downtown, the **Confederation Court Mall** defines the city's core with a square block of shops offering such specialties as Maritime-made pine furniture, local and imported woollen knits, and high-quality Paderno stainless-steel cookware (there's a value-priced Paderno factory outlet here).

A few short blocks to the south, the 19th-century architecture, crafts shops, and food emporiums of the **Old Charlottetown** waterfront invite exploring for an hour or two. The most recent addition to the waterfront area is **Peakes Wharf**, named after shipbuilder James Peake, the island's most prominent 19th-century businessman. The complex includes numerous restaurants, an old-fashioned general store and warehouse, as well as another Paderno factory outlet.

The North Shore

Brackley Beach, 18 km (11 miles) north of Charlottetown via Route 15, is one of five gateways to Prince Edward Island National Park. (The other four are at Stanhope and Dalvay to the east and Cavendish and North Rustico to the west.) At the **Dunes Studio Gallery**, a modern glass-and-wood building set against a backdrop of national park sand dunes and Brackley Bay, one-of-a-kind sculptural and functional ceramics vie for attention with hand-blown glass, stained glass hangings, painted-silk clothing and banners, and exquisite hand-knit sweaters.

The neighboring ▶ **Shaw's Hotel and Cottages** has two claims to fame: Established in 1860, it is the island's oldest family-operated summer resort (open June 1 to October 1), and there are few island restaurants that serve better home cooking. The hotel's dining room (Tel: 902/672-2022) is open daily, but in July and August the Sunday buffet—an opulent array of fresh fish and shellfish, hot meats, salads, and home-made breads and desserts—is the star attraction.

Shaw's is also the home of **North Shore Windsurfing**, where for $15 an hour you can rent sailboards, small sail-boats, canoes, and rowboats. (Thanks to its steady breezes and gentle, sandy shoreline, P.E.I. is one of the best and most popular windsurfing spots in eastern Canada.)

Prince Edward Island National Park

A large chunk of that shoreline is protected as Prince Edward Island National Park, a ribbon of white-sand beaches stretching some 40 km (25 miles) along the island's north shore. Because most people flock to the Cavendish and Brackley beaches, those at Rustico Island and Dalvay are relatively uncrowded and perfect for long, solitary walks.

▶ **Dalvay-by-the-Sea**, at the eastern end of the national park, was built in 1896 as a summer home by onetime Standard Oil president Alexander MacDonald. Today the sprawling mansion is a comfortable lodge and resort operated by the park from mid-June to mid-September. The dining room (Tel: 902/672-2048), which is open to the public, specializes in fresh seafood, including perfectly poached salmon, and homegrown vegetables.

The nearby **Stanhope Golf and Country Club**, featuring one of the island's longest and most challenging golf courses, is also open to the public. Ranging along beautiful Covehead Bay, the 18-hole, par-72 course is open for play from early May through the end of October, with greens fees running about $20 a round, depending on the month. For tee times, Tel: (902) 672-2842.

▶ **Stanhope by the Sea**, on Route 25, has welcomed over-night guests since 1817. The new owners have attractively renovated the hotel's original 35 rooms, while adding an additional 24 rooms in the main building along with a number of cottages. As its name implies, the hotel is a stone's throw from the ocean—or, more specifically, the sheltered waters of Covehead Bay. Its dining room (Tel: 902/ 672-2047), which is open for breakfast and dinner and specializes in fresh seafood, offers beautiful views of the bay and the headland beyond, the latter belonging to Prince Edward Island National Park. Open June 15 to Labour Day.

The Rusticos

The village of **South Rustico**, just west of Brackley Beach, has several points of interest. From town, take Route 243 north to a small collection of Victorian buildings clustered around **Saint Augustine's Church** (1838). The **Farmer's Bank Museum** occupies the first floor of what once was Canada's smallest chartered bank, as well as its first people's, or cooperative, bank, established in 1861. (The museum is open late June to early September, Monday through Saturday from 9:30 A.M. to 5:00 P.M., and Sundays from 1:00 to 5:00 P.M.) The lovely ▶ **Barachois Inn** here, a restored Victorian home with six guest rooms, offers lots of historic charm and a great view of Rustico Bay.

From South Rustico, take a quick jaunt along the pretty Hunter River via Routes 258 and 224 to the village of New Glasgow and the **P.E.I. Preserve Company**. Located in the former village dairy, P.E.I. Preserve makes delicious liqueur-spiked preserves from island fruit, as well as specialty mustards, vinegars, and honey—all of it handsomely displayed and offered for sale in a sunny bakeshop/tearoom where fresh pastries, tea, and coffee are served.

Back on Route 6, which here is part of the Blue Heron Drive, the fishing villages of **Rusticoville** and **North Rustico** are legendary for their scenic charms. ▶ **The Breakers by the Sea**, a relatively new resort complex located 8 km (5 miles) east of Cavendish, has fully equipped two-bedroom cottages with large private decks and propane barbecues on eight acres overlooking North Rustico Harbour and the Gulf of St. Lawrence. Guests also have the option of staying in one- or two-bedroom suites complete with microwaves and Jacuzzis. Open mid-May to the end of October.

Anne of Green Gables

The simple white **Green Gables Farmhouse** near the **Cavendish** entrance to Prince Edward National Park draws visitors from around the world, thanks to a red-haired freckle-faced orphan and the book that made her and her island-born author-creator an overnight sensation. The orphan Anne Shirley, whom Mark Twain called "the dearest and most loveable child in fiction since the immortal Alice," made her debut in the 1908 novel *Anne of Green Gables,* written by

Cavendish native Lucy Maud Montgomery. In the interim, the novel has been translated into 16 languages and inspired worldwide stage and screen productions, including the Charlottetown festival musical and two recent award-winning TV movies aired in Canada and the United States. The 18-hole **Green Gables Golf Course** overlooking the house and its surrounding nature walks is both challenging and beautiful, and is open to the public. Greens fees are $24 in July and August, and $22 in May, June, September, and October. For tee times, Tel: (902) 963-2488.

Modern-day Cavendish, the hub of the island's tourist trade, bears little resemblance to the sleepy farming community of Avonlea, its fictional counterpart described in Montgomery's novels. However, Montgomery's pristine island is more recognizable elsewhere on the north shore: along the powdery beaches, below the steep, red bluffs of Orby Head, in pretty ports such as North Rustico Harbour and New London, and in meadows knee-deep in wildflowers—all places where the author loved to roam.

The **Cavendish Boardwalk**, a collection of gift shops, is a good place for souvenirs and beachwear. While here, drop in at **Cow's Homemade Ice Cream**, a small island chain of ice cream parlors that also specializes in bovine-inspired clothing and novelties.

If you decide to make Cavendish your base you'll find many good accommodations offering convenient access to beaches, great ocean views, lots of recreational facilities, and close proximity to other attractions. The best include: the ▶ **Kindred Spirits Country Inn and Cottages**, situated on spacious grounds right next to the Green Gables house and golf course; and the ▶ **Island Wild Cottages** and ▶ **Sundance Cottages**, both on Route 6, a short walk from the heart of the village.

Or you can continue west on Route 6 past the village of Stanley Bridge and south on Route 238 to Found Mills, where **Gepetto's Workshop** (open daily from early June through late September) is filled with beautiful handcrafted wooden marionettes, puppets, toys, and games.

At the intersection of Routes 6 and 8 in the village of **New London**, the tiny white cottage where Montgomery was born in 1874 is now a museum chock-full of Montgomery memorabilia, including the author's wedding dress and original editions of her books. (Open daily June 1 to mid-October.) A bit farther north on the **Blue Heron Drive** (Route 20), **Silver Bush**, the Park Corner farmhouse home of her favorite cousins, also has been converted into a museum (open daily June 1 to mid-October). Overlooking the real "Lake of Shining Waters," which figures prominently in the Anne books, Silver Bush is still owned by relatives of the author.

Lobster Feeds

This is Lobster Supper country, and several area community halls and restaurants serve up the most traditional of Prince Edward Island feasts—or "feeds," as the locals say: typically, boiled lobster in the half shell, preceded by clam chowder and served with heaping portions of potato salad, coleslaw, homemade pickles, and fresh-baked rolls, bread, pies, cakes, and strawberry shortcake. Reliably good are the **St. Ann's Church Suppers** (Tel: 902/964-2385) in Hope River, the **New London Lions Club Lobster Suppers** (902/886-2599), the **New Glasgow Lobster Suppers** (Tel: 902/964-2870), and the lobster suppers served at the **Fisherman's Wharf Restaurant** (Tel: 902/963-2669) in North Rustico and the **Fiddles 'n Vittles Restaurant** (Tel: 902/963-3003) in Bayview.

Woodleigh Replicas

Woodleigh Replicas, on Route 234 east of Burlington, lends a distinctly foreign flavor to Prince Edward Island. Dunvegan Castle, the Tower of London, St. Paul's Cathedral, and nearly 20 other famous architectural landmarks of the British Isles are accurately detailed in large-scale models. Begun 40 years ago by a retired World War I colonel who wanted to transplant some part of his ancestral homeland to Prince Edward Island, Woodleigh has become one of the island's most-visited attractions.

For lunch stop at the nearby **Kitchen Witch Tea Room** (Tel: 902/886-2294) on Route 234, in Long River. Located in an old schoolhouse, this cozy little restaurant specializes in hearty sandwiches, soups, and pies, and also offers a nice selection of teas and coffees.

Cabot Beach Provincial Park

Back on Route 20: Continue south and west to Malpeque, where signs point the way to Cabot Beach Provincial Park. In addition to its landscaped picnic and playground areas, the park boasts one of the island's most beautiful white-sand beaches, and is usually much less crowded than the national park.

The South Shore

Victoria-by-the-Sea

Located off Highway 1, 40 km (25 miles) southwest of Charlottetown, this storybook village is tucked just inside the boundary of Queens County. The tiny fishing port has some good antiques and handicraft shops, live summer theater in the historic **Victoria Playhouse**, and a tearoom (in the blue converted harness shop across from the playhouse) that serves a real high tea and mouth-watering desserts. Another sweet attraction in the village is **Island Chocolates**, which makes and sells confections made with pure Belgian chocolate, as well as tasty baked items and picnic baskets to order. The newish **Landmark Café** (Tel: 902/658-2286) in town offers a light menu featuring seafood and pasta dishes, salads, and homemade breads and desserts.

Prince Edward Island's rivers are winding, lazy streams banked by cultivated fields; the Clyde and West rivers, with their rural valleys, are typical. The hilltops of **Strathgartney Provincial Park** provide a nice overview of the area, which you can explore at your leisure by following secondary routes (9 and 19A) through pretty communities such as St. Catherines, Long Creek, and New Dominion.

Fort Amherst National Historic Site

For another scenic detour, leave Highway 1 at Clyde River, follow Routes 247, 9, and 19A to Canoe Cove, then take Route 19 (part of the Blue Heron Drive) east along the coast to Rocky Point and Fort Amherst (open daily June 16 to Labour Day, 10:00 A.M. to 6:00 P.M.). Situated at the narrow mouth of Charlottetown Harbour, the park occupies the former site of Port-La-Joye, the first capital of the island under the French regime of the early 1700s. The British built Fort Amherst in 1758, and today an interpretive center and rolling lawns covering the collapsed earthworks are all that remain.

From New Dominion, Route 19 leads across the beautiful West River to Meadow Bank and one of the island's oldest rural restaurants, **McCrady's Green Acres** (Tel: 902/566-4938), which is locally famous for its home-style cooking. The **Bonnie Brae** (Tel: 902/566-2241), on Highway 1 in the nearby bedroom community of Cornwall, a few miles west of Charlottetown, offers a varied menu that includes such traditional island favorites as lobster, fish, and roast beef, as well as schnitzels and other German-Swiss specialties (the owner-chefs are Swiss). The all-you-can-eat lobster buffet offered every evening is outstanding, as are the feather-light European desserts. The **Island Market Village** on the North River causeway is an eclectic collection of gift shops selling everything from handknit sweaters to carved wooden decoys. You'll also find a Cow's Homemade Ice Cream parlor, go-carts, and paddle boats here.

Smooth red sand and warmer water characterize the beaches of the south shore. While less spectacular than those to the north, the south shore beaches often offer better swimming and fewer crowds. **Tea Hill Provincial Park**, east of Charlottetown at the base of scenic Tea Hill, is one of the best, in addition to being a prime clam-digging spot.

Orwell Corner Historic Village

A visit to Orwell Corner, located a short jog off Highway 1 on Route 210, will have you thinking you've stepped back into the 19th century. Operated by the P.E.I. Museum and Heritage Foundation, the re-created rural crossroads village is a working farm community. Every Wednesday night through the summer, Orwell Corner holds weekly *ceilidhs,* programs of Scottish musical entertainment (usually with fiddle music and step dancing). It's also the site of two popular annual events: the strawberry social in mid-July—an old-fashioned strawberries-and-ice-cream affair with games, historic costumes, and old-time foot-stompin' music—and, in late August, the **Scottish Festival and Highland Games**, featuring kilt-clad Highland pipe bands and dancers, storytellers, and traditional athletic competitions like the caber toss (not unlike heaving a telephone pole), hammer throw, and putting the stone.

Nearby **Lord Selkirk Provincial Park** is the scene of a similar Highland games celebration in early August. The park overlooks the cove where in 1803 three ships landed with 800 Highlanders from the Isle of Skye, constituting the island's largest Scottish migration.

KINGS COUNTY

The bay-notched shoreline of eastern Prince Edward Island is a sightseer's delight. You'll find some of the best scenery here off the beaten track; the road to Cape Bear and Murray Head, for example, offers a view from high bluffs that is well worth the short side trip.

Murray River, just west of the picturesque port of Murray Harbour, was once a shipbuilding center. Today the cozy village is a center for crafts. One of the most interesting shops is **Shumate's Toy Factory**, where the proprietor, a Santa Claus look-alike, makes old-fashioned handmade wooden pull-cars, animals, and other toys. Murray River is also home to **Terrace Heights** (Tel: 902/962-2465), which in a relatively short period of time has established itself as one of the island's best restaurants. Fresh seafood is a specialty, and everything is homemade, including the bread and sumptuous desserts.

From Murray River, the **Kings Byway Drive** (Route 17) leads eastward to Route 347 and the long, narrow isthmus connecting **Panmure Island** to the mainland. Protected as **Panmure Island Provincial Park**, the narrow neck of land is edged in powdery beaches, making it a popular spot in summer. The lighthouse here is one of the island's most photographed spots.

Montague

The pretty town of Montague, on Highway 4 at the mouth of the Montague River, has an interesting museum housed in its former post office. Open Monday through Saturday from mid-June to mid-September, the **Garden of the Gulf Museum** tells the story of the British settlers who arrived in the area in 1765. Nearby, seal-watching charters (daily from mid-May through mid-October) leave from the Montague marina. **Cruise Manada** offers two-hour afternoon excursions ($13.50 per person) up the beautiful Montague and Brudenell rivers. Highlights include a guided tour of a harbor seal colony, native seabird sightings, and a look at a working mussel farm. The same outfit offers sunset cruises daily ($25), with Champagne and steamed mussels. For information and reservations (required for all evening cruises), Tel: (902) 838-3444.

In town on Main Street (Route 17), the **Lobster Shanty North** (Tel: 902/838-2463) is a popular spot for seafood, including Prince Edward Island's favorite crustacean. At the adjacent ▶ **Lobster Shanty North Motel and Cottages** visitors will find comfortable lodgings conveniently located to nearby beaches and a variety of outdoor activities.

Brudenell River Provincial Park

The Kings Byway Visitor Information Centre at Pooles Corner contains a wealth of information on the history, sights, and attractions of eastern Prince Edward Island. While here, have lunch in the dining room of the ▶ **Whim Inn** (Tel: 902/838-3838), where the food is plain but good. Nearby, beautiful 1,400-acre Brudenell River Provincial Park boasts an outstanding par-72 championship golf course. Offering a variety of open and narrow fairways, tricky water holes, and scenic river views, the course is considered one of eastern Canada's finest. Greens fees range from $19 to $24, depending on the time of year. For tee times, Tel: (902) 652-2342 (June 15–September 15) or 652-2356 (off-season). The park's self-guided wildflower walk through the forest is another pleasant way to stretch your legs.

A short causeway takes you to tiny **Brudenell Island** and the early 18th-century burial ground of the area's first Scottish settlers. The island looks across the river mouth to Brudenell Point, where a simple cairn marks the site of a 16th-century Acadian fishing settlement. The ▶ **Rodd Brudenell River Resort**, overlooking the golf course, offers simple but comfortable accommodations in 50 chalet-style cabins and housekeeping units. During peak tourist season (July and August), it's a good idea to book ahead. The Kings Playhouse, in neighboring **Georgetown**, stages live summer theater.

The Bay Fortune Area

From Georgetown, backtrack on Highway 3 and then follow Routes 311 (via Route 321) and 310 along the coast to scenic **Eglington** and **Bay Fortune**. Beach access, good swimming, row boating, and clam digging make the ▶ **End of the Rainbow Cottages**, on Howe Point Road just off Route 310 in Eglington, a good choice for an overnight stay. The three housekeeping cottages (including one built in 1836) come complete with sundecks and gas barbecues. Or surround yourself with a little bygone romance at the ▶ **Inn at Bay Fortune**, on Route 310 itself. The inn, which overlooks the beautiful harbor, was once the summer home of a colorful colony of playwrights and actors. Its 11 guest rooms all have bathrooms *en suite,* and most also have a fireplace sitting area. Reservations during the peak summer season are suggested at both places.

The beauty of P.E.I.'s **Bay Fortune** area, the charm of its riverside cottages a pleasing contrast to the brooding spruce forest, makes it a popular summer resort. It is also steeped in legend. Pirate treasure is said to be buried along the sandstone banks of **Abells Cape** (reached via a dirt road off Route 310), which itself is rumored to be haunted by the ghost of Edward Abell, a bullying landlord who was murdered in the early 19th century by a desperate tenant.

Perched on the beach in the community of Souris West farther up the coast, the **Platter House** (Tel: 902/687-2764) is an informal, cafeteria-style eatery where, not surprisingly, the huge seafood platter is probably your best bet. The Victorian-style ▶ **Matthew House Inn** overlooks the harbor in nearby Souris. With a cozy library and parlor, an abundance of period art and furniture, and amenities such as bicycle rentals on the premises, Matthew House is another accommodation that will remind you of a bygone era.

MAGDALEN ISLANDS

Swimming, bicycling, windsurfing, seafood, and scenery draw thousands of visitors to "the Maggies" (Iles-de-la-Madeleine) every summer. The 62-mile-long hook-shaped archipelago belongs to Quebec, and is five hours by sea from **Souris**, where a car ferry makes twice-daily crossings to and from the islands. (Car-ferry rates are $29 per person, and an additional $55 per vehicle. Reservations recommended in summer. For information, Tel: 902/687-2181; for reservations, Tel: 418/986-3278.) Most of the archipelago's 14,000 inhabitants live on the largest islands: Cap-aux-Meules, Havre-aux-Maisons, Havre-Aubert, Grosse Ile, and Ile de l'Est, which are connected by paved roads stretched over long sandspits. The remainder live on tiny Ile d'Entrée, which is connected by ferry (twice daily) to Havre-Aubert.

If you want to visit the Magdalens, set aside at least four days, as the better part of two days will be spent travelling. The islands offer many good accommodations, with the best being the ▶ **Château Madelinot**, ▶ **Motel Boudreau**, ▶ **Auberge Madeli**, and ▶ **Motel Bellevue** on Cap-aux-Meules, and the ▶ **Motel Thériault** on Havre-aux-Maisons. All offer good restaurants and are close to beaches. The 101-room Château Madelinot, the islands' largest accommodation, offers week-long packages that include use of the hotel's health club.

While French is the language spoken by most islanders, service in hotels, motels, and restaurants is bilingual. Bus tours of the islands and car rentals can be arranged at the airport. For reservations and additional information, call Quebec Tourism at (800) 363-7777 or the Magdalen Islands tourist bureau at (418) 986-2245; Fax: (418) 986-2327. (For more on the Magdalens, see also the Quebec Province chapter.)

Beaches and Fishing

Beautiful beaches are a trademark of eastern Prince Edward Island; three of the best can be found at **Red Point Provincial Park** (the beach is a five-minute walk from the park), Basin Head, and Bothwell. **Basin Head** and **Bothwell** are part of a sand dune system that stretches 20 km (12 miles) to East Point. The **Basin Head Fisheries Museum** (open mid-June to Labour Day, 9:00 A.M. to 5:00 P.M. daily), right next to Basin Head beach, gives visitors a look at re-created boat and tackle sheds, a canning factory, a fish-box factory, and a smokehouse. The museum also hosts a giant seafood barbecue as part of its annual Harvest of the Sea celebration in early August.

The ▶ **Singing Sands Sea Breeze Motel** restaurant (Tel:

902/357-2371), on Route 16 near the entrance to Basin Head, serves good, simple fare on the order of club sandwiches, hamburgers, and pan-fried fish. Rooms in the motel are plain but clean, and offer a beautiful view of the dunes and ocean.

The waters around Prince Edward Island are among the world's best tuna-fishing grounds. You can charter a tuna boat from several ports, including North Rustico in Queens County; and North Lake Harbour, 16 km (10 miles) west of East Point, and Red Head Harbour, farther west on St. Peter's Bay, both in Kings County. Indeed, charters out of **North Lake Harbour**, which bills itself as the "Tuna Fishing Capital of the World," have hooked several record-breaking bluefin. Cor's Deep Sea Fishing (Tel: 902/357-2603), Robertson's Tuna & Deep Sea Fishing (Tel: 902/357-2029), and North Lake Tuna Charters (Tel: 902/357-2055) are the main operations in town, and should be booked at least a day in advance. The boats leave around 9:00 A.M. and return by 6:00 P.M.—unless there's a feisty bluefin hooked on the end of the line, in which case a fisherman might do battle many hours longer. Charter rates run around $300 to $400, which can be divided among as many as four anglers.

From North Lake Harbour, follow Route 16 west along the coast some 40 km (25 miles) to the pretty community of **St. Peter's**, at the head of St. Peter's Bay. The first settlement here was established by shipwrecked French sailors during the 18th century and soon grew into one of the island's chief fishing ports. It was named for the first European to permanently settle on the island—Comte St. Pierre, who in 1720 obtained a land grant elsewhere on the island and established the French capital of Port-La-Joye, across the harbor from present-day Charlottetown.

Route 350, off Highway 2 heading west, leads to **Crowbush Cove Provincial Park**, which has a variety of recreation facilities in addition to a beautiful white-sand beach.

PRINCE COUNTY
The South Shore

The **Lady Slipper Drive Visitor Information Centre**, located just east of Summerside in Wilmot, about 56 km (35 miles) west of Charlottetown via Highway 1, has information on places of interest in and around western Prince Edward Island. In **Summerside** itself, the island's second-largest town, you can visit the **International Fox Hall of Fame and Museum**, downtown on Fitzroy Street (open May to September, Monday through Saturday, 8:00 A.M. to 4:00 P.M.). The museum chronicles the island's fox-farming industry, which experienced its heyday between 1915 and 1920, when a pair of silver foxes went for as much as $35,000. The town's waterfront area also boasts a newish shopping complex called **Spinaker's Landing**, as well as the **Eptek National Exhibition Centre and P.E.I. Sports Hall of Fame**.

The ▶ **Silver Fox Inn**, downtown on Granville Street, offers plenty of historic charm in one of the town's loveliest 19th-century houses. The house, with six guest rooms, is furnished with handsome antiques throughout, and while the inn doesn't have a dining room, it does serve a Continental breakfast. Also downtown, but on Harbour Drive overlooking the waterfront, the ▶ **Loyalist Country Inn** tempts travellers with an array of popular amenities, including an indoor pool and sauna, tennis courts, a licensed dining room and lounge, and ten rooms with *en suite* whirlpool tubs. (Two of the inn's rooms are designed with physically challenged travellers in mind.) The ▶ **Arbor Inn**, located on the eastern outskirts of town and past winner of the Prince County Hospitality Award, offers luxuriously appointed rooms with amenities such as waterbeds, Jacuzzis, and stereos. The ▶ **Best Western Linkletter Inn** (with one of the better dining rooms in town) on Market Street and the ▶ **Quality Inn** on Water Street both offer comfortable accommodations within easy walking distance of the downtown area. Nearby **Linkletter Provincial Park** has a very good red-sand beach but tends to get crowded on weekends.

The Acadian Shore

Miscouche, on Highway 2 west of Summerside, is the gateway to the Acadian Shore, which extends west and north as far as St-Chrysostome on Egmont Bay, an area where most of the Prince Edward Islanders of French descent are concentrated. Acadia, as students of the colonial period know, was a territory made up of present-day Prince Edward Island, New Brunswick, Nova Scotia, southeastern Quebec, and eastern Maine. From the early 1600s to the early 1700s France and England battled over this vast territory, until it finally passed into English possession for good in 1713. Through the first half of the 18th century tensions between the two nations intensified, and between 1755 and 1763 the English exiled some 10,000 of the area's French-speaking settlers to France or the then-French colony of Louisiana—where their modern-day descendants are known as Cajuns.

Some of Prince Edward Island's Acadians escaped into the woods, while others fled to the mainland and returned later. Today many of their descendants on the island's Acadian Shore still speak a variation of their forefathers' Old French, which predates the modern French language as established in the 17th century by the French Academy. The recently expanded **Acadian Museum of P.E.I.** (open year-round) in Miscouche has a number of exhibits devoted to this fascinating albeit tragic history, as well as a collection of Acadian artifacts dating to the early 1700s.

Though the Acadian Pioneer Village in Mont-Carmel, southwest of Miscouche via the **Lady Slipper Drive** (Route 11), is a somewhat generic collection of re-created historic buildings, its **Etoile de Mer** restaurant (Tel: 902/854-2227) specializes in authentic Acadian food; try the chicken *fricot,* a hearty chicken stew, or *râpure,* a crusty casserole made with grated potatoes, pork, and molasses. The **Abram Village Handcraft Co-op**, located in the village of the same name at the junction of Routes 124 and 165, is the best place to shop for braided and hooked rugs, quilts, woven wear, wooden toys, and other traditional Acadian crafts.

Situated at the northwestern corner of Egmont Bay (follow the Lady Slipper Drive around the bay), the ▶ **West Point Lighthouse** (1875) has been converted into an inn with nine antiques-furnished double rooms, including two rooms with whirlpool tubs and first-day complimentary breakfast. The lighthouse overlooks the white-sand beach of **Cedar Dunes Provincial Park**, and contains displays and items from the days when it was a working light. There's also a small dining room downstairs that serves seafood chowder and home-baked goods.

North Shore

From West Point, continue north along Route 14 to Campbellton, then east via Route 145 to Bloomfield Corner, and finally right onto Highway 2 for a short distance to **MacAusland's Woolen Mill**. The old-fashioned mill washes, cards, spins, dyes, and weaves raw wool into handsome, durable blankets that, because they're made of 100 percent virgin wool, last a lifetime. Reasonably priced, MacAusland's blankets are among the best buys on the island. The mill also stocks a good selection of woollen yarns manufactured on the premises.

Mill River Provincial Park

Route 136, which you can pick up about a mile east of MacAusland's, leads to Mill River Provincial Park and its golf course, considered by many to be the island's finest. Greens fees run about $20 from mid-June to mid-September, and drop to $16 in the off-season. Tee times should be made 48 hours in advance by calling (902) 859-2238.

The 1,200-acre provincial park is also the location of the ▶ **Rodd Mill River Resort**, which offers its pampered guests large, comfortable rooms (with suites also available); tennis and squash courts; two indoor pools; saunas and whirlpools; a giant water slide; canoe, bicycle, and windsurfing rentals; and boat tours of the beautiful Mill River.

The **Lennox Island Micmac Indian Reservation**, about 40 km (25 miles) east of the Mill River resort, has an arts and crafts shop that carries the traditional woven baskets of the Micmac tribe, as well as jewelry, ceremonial masks, and many one-of-a-kind items by a variety of Native American artists and artisans. To get to the reservation, follow Highway 2 to Portage, turn left onto Route 12, and continue on Route 163 over the Lennox Island causeway.

In the center of nearby **Tyne Valley**, a village of Victorian gingerbread homes, **Shoreline Sweaters & Tyne Valley Studio** carries a good selection of woollen sweaters (including the lobster patterns that have become the shop's signature) in addition to handlooms and fine crafts. In early August the town's annual four-day Oyster Festival celebrates the region's famous bivalve with oyster-shucking competitions and suppers.

Succulent Malpeque oysters are prized around the world for their superior flavor, and take their name from **Malpeque Bay**, where they were first harvested. Today Malpeque oysters are cultivated in sheltered coves scattered around the island's long coastline and as a result are readily available in most restaurants.

Green Park Provincial Park

From Tyne Valley, Route 12 leads to Green Park Provincial Park, the former estate of one of the island's wealthiest shipbuilders. Prince Edward Island was an important shipbuilding center in the 19th century, and the restored Green Park house symbolizes as well as anything the enormous fortunes amassed here during the "Golden Age of Sail." An interpretive center (open June 15 to Labour Day, 9:00 A.M. to 5:00 P.M.), beautifully landscaped grounds, and a smooth red-sand beach are added incentives to spend some time visiting this pretty provincial park. In mid-August the park plays host to an annual old-fashioned Blueberry Social, continuing a tradition first begun by the estate's former owner.

GETTING AROUND

By Sea. The ferry ride across Northumberland Strait is a highlight for thousands of tourists visiting Prince Edward Island. Marine Atlantic operates year-round car-ferry service between Cape Tormentine, New Brunswick, and Borden, Prince Edward Island, with hourly crossings in summer from 6:30 A.M. to 8:30 P.M. (and less frequently after 8:30). Northumberland Ferries operates a second car ferry service from late April to mid-December between Caribou, Nova Scotia, and Wood Islands, Prince Edward Island, with hourly summer crossings. The ferry takes 45 minutes from New Brunswick (about $6 per person round trip, and $16 for your car) and 90 minutes from Nova Scotia ($7.50 per person round trip, and $24.50 for your car). Neither outfit accepts reservations, which results in long lines and two- to three-hour waits during the summer months. Plan on arriving at the terminals early in the day or in the evening, when traffic is lightest.

By Air. Charlottetown's airport is serviced by five airlines—Air Canada, Air Nova, Canadian Airlines International, Air Atlantic, and Inter-Canadian—with direct daily flights to and from Halifax, Toronto, Ottawa, and Montreal. At present there are no direct flights into Charlottetown from the U.S. or U.K.

On the Island. Prince Edward Island has a very good highway system, with paved roads leading to all major population centers, attractions, and points of interest. The official Prince Edward Island Visitors Map, available free at any visitor information center, is the only map you'll need. One note of caution: While traffic generally moves at a steady pace and at the speed limit, watch for slow-moving tractors, harvesters, and other farm vehicles, particularly on secondary roads.

There are three coastal sightseeing routes around the province: the 190-km (118-mile) **Blue Heron Drive** (named for the migratory water birds that visit the island by the thousands each summer) in central Prince Edward Island; the 375-km (233-mile) **Kings Byway** in the east; and the 288-km (179-mile) **Lady Slipper Drive** (named for the wild Lady Slipper orchid, the island's floral emblem) in the west. All three scenic drives lead to, or near, major attractions, and are marked clearly and frequently with roadside symbols. The drives are also color-coded on the Prince Edward Island Visitors Map.

ACCOMMODATIONS REFERENCE

The rates given below are projections *for peak seasons during the 1994 calendar year; at other times of the year they may be considerably less. Unless otherwise indicated, rates are based on double rooms, double occupancy; provincial and federal taxes are included in all rates. As rates are subject to change, always double-check before booking.*

▶ **Arbor Inn.** 380 MacEwan Road, **Summerside**, P.E.I. C1N 4X8. Tel: (902) 436-6847. $38–$93.

▶ **Auberge Madeli.** P.O. Box 427, rue Principale, **Cap-aux-Meules**, Que. G0B 1B0. Tel: (418) 986-2211; Fax: (418) 986-2886. $80.

▶ **Barachois Inn.** Route 243, **South Rustico**, P.O. Box 1022, Charlottetown, P.E.I. C1A 7M4. Tel: (902) 963-2194. $111.

▶ **Best Western Linkletter Inn.** 311 Market Street, **Summerside**, P.E.I. C1N 1K8. Tel: (902) 436-2157; Fax: (902) 436-4499. $83–$104.

▶ **Best Western MacLauchlan's Motor Inn.** 238 Grafton Street, **Charlottetown**, P.E.I. C1A 1L5. Tel: (902) 892-2461; Fax: (902) 566-2979. $120–$132.

▶ **The Breakers by the Sea.** Route 6, **Rusticoville**, P.E.I. C0A 1N0. Tel: (902) 963-2555. $120.

▶ **The Charlottetown—A Rodd Classic Hotel.** P.O. Box 159, **Charlottetown**, P.E.I. C1A 7K4. Tel: (902) 894-7371; Fax: (902) 368-2178; in the U.S. and Canada, Tel: (800) 565-RODD. $110.

▶ **Château Madelinot.** P.O. Box 265, Highway 199, **Cap-aux-Meules**, Que. G0B 1B0. Tel: (418) 986-3695; Fax: (418) 986-6437. $110.

▶ **Dalvay-by-the-Sea.** P.O. Box 8, **York**, P.E.I. C0A 1P0. Tel: (902) 672-2048; in winter, Tel: (902) 672-3315. $195–$310 (includes breakfast and dinner).

▶ **Duchess of Kent Inn.** 218 Kent Street, **Charlottetown**, P.E.I. C1A 1P2. Tel: (902) 566-5826. $56–$70.

▶ **Dundee Arms Inn.** 200 Pownal Street, **Charlottetown**, P.E.I. C1A 3W8. Tel: (902) 892-2496; Fax: (902) 368-8532. $99–$111 (motel); $111–$158 (inn).

▶ **Elmwood Heritage Inn.** P.O. Box 3128, North River Road, **Charlottetown**, P.E.I. C1A 7N8. Tel: (902) 368-3310. $99–$146 (includes breakfast).

▶ **End of the Rainbow Cottages.** Howe Point Road off

Route 310, **Eglington**, R.R. 4, Souris, P.E.I. C0A 2B0. Tel: (902) 687-3502. $70–$88.

► **Great George Inn**. 455 University Avenue, **Charlottetown**, P.E.I. C1A 4N8. Tel: (902) 892-4206; Fax: (902) 368-3806. $146 (includes Continental breakfast).

► **Inn at Bay Fortune**. Highway 310, **Bay Fortune**, R.R. 4, Souris, P.E.I. C0A 2B0; in winter, 266 Foote Road, South Glastonbury, CT 06073. Tel: (902) 687-3745; in winter, (203) 633-4930. $129–$187 (includes full breakfast).

► **Inn on the Hill**. 150 Euston Street, **Charlottetown**, P.E.I. C1A 1W5. Tel: (902) 894-8572; Fax: (902) 368-3556. $129; $142–$177 (suites).

► **Island Wild Cottages**. Route 6, **Cavendish**, R.R. 2, Hunter River, P.E.I. C0A 1N0. Tel: (902) 963-2193. $128–$164.

► **Kindred Spirits Country Inn and Cottages**. Highway 6, **Cavendish**, P.E.I. C0A 1N0. Tel and Fax: (902) 963-2434. $59–$135 (inn); $85–$181 (cottages).

► **Kirkwood Motor Hotel**. 455 University Avenue, **Charlottetown**, P.E.I. C1A 4N8. Tel: (902) 892-4206; Fax: (902) 368-3806. $98.

► **Lobster Shanty North Motel and Cottages**. P.O. Box 158, Route 17, **Montague**, P.E.I. C0A 1R0. Tel: (902) 838-2463; Fax: (902) 838-4272. $69 (motel or cottage).

► **Loyalist Country Inn**. 195 Harbour Drive, **Summerside**, P.E.I. C1N 5R1. Tel: (902) 436-3333; Fax: (902) 436-4304. $109–$122; $158 (honeymoon suites).

► **Matthew House Inn**. P.O. Box 151, 15 Breakwater Street, **Souris**, P.E.I. C0A 2B0. Tel or Fax: (902) 687-3461. $99–$164 (includes breakfast).

► **Motel Bellevue**. P.O. Box 188, 40 rue Principale, **Cap-aux-Meules**, Que. G0B 1B0. Tel: (418) 986-4477. $100.

► **Motel Boudreau**. P.O. Box 685, 280 rue Principale, **Cap-aux-Meules**, Que. G0B 1B0. Tel: (418) 986-2391. $82–$94.

► **Motel Thériault**. P.O. Box 207, Dune du Sud, **Havre-aux-Maisons**, Que. G0B 1K0. Tel: (418) 969-2955. $60–$70.

► **The Prince Edward**. 18 Queen Street, **Charlottetown**, P.E.I. C1A 8B9. Tel: (902) 566-2222; Fax: (902) 566-1745. $160–$206.

► **Quality Inn**. 618 Water Street East, **Summerside**, P.E.I. C1N 2V5. Tel: (902) 436-2295; Fax: (902) 436-6277. $77–$102.

► **Rodd Brudenell River Resort**. P.O. Box 67, **Cardigan**, P.E.I. C0A 1G0; November–April, P.O. Box 432, Charlottetown, P.E.I. C1A 7K7. Tel: (902) 652-2332; Fax: (902) 652-2886; in the U.S. and Canada, Tel: (800) 565-RODD. $123 (hotel); $92–$115 (cottages).

► **Rodd Confederation Inn**. P.O. Box 651, Route 1, **Char-**

lottetown, P.E.I. C1A 7L3. Tel: (902) 892-2481; Fax: (902) 368-3247; in the U.S. and Canada, Tel: (800) 565-RODD. $80–$92; $102–$110 (suites); $110 (apartments).

► **Rodd Mill River Resort**. P.O. Box 399, **O'Leary**, P.E.I. C0B 1V0. Tel: (902) 859-3555; Fax: (902) 859-2486; in the U.S. and Canada, Tel: (800) 565-RODD. $116.

► **Rodd Royalty Inn and Conference Center**. P.O. Box 2499, junction of Routes 1 and 2 West, **Charlottetown**, P.E.I. C1A 8C2. Tel: (902) 894-8566; Fax: (902) 892-8488; in the U.S. and Canada, Tel: (800) 565-RODD. $94–$108 (hotel); $83 (motel).

► **Shaw's Hotel and Cottages**. Route 15, **Brackley Beach**, P.E.I. C1E 1Z3. Tel: (902) 672-2022; Fax: (902) 672-3000. $199–$252 (hotel; includes breakfast and dinner); $210–$280 (cottages; includes breakfast and dinner).

► **Silver Fox Inn**. 61 Granville Street, **Summerside**, P.E.I. C1N 2Z3. Tel: (902) 436-4033. $64–$74.

► **Singing Sands Sea Breeze Motel**. Route 16, **Kingsboro**, P.E.I. C0A 2B0; in winter, P.O. Box 1097, Station Q, Toronto, Ont. M4T 2P1. Tel: (902) 357-2371; in winter, (416) 488-3538. $47–$64.

► **Stanhope by the Sea**. P.O. Box 9, Route 25, **Little York**, P.E.I. C0A 1P0. Tel: (902) 672-2047. $99 (inn); $111 (new inn); $848 per week (cottages).

► **Sundance Cottages**. Route 6, **Cavendish**, R.R. 1, Hunter River, P.E.I. C0A 1N0. Tel: (902) 963-2149; in the U.S. and Canada, Tel: (800) 565-2149. $121–$187.

► **West Point Lighthouse**. R.R. 2, **O'Leary**, P.E.I. C0B 1V0. Tel: (902) 859-3605. $82 (inland view); $94 (sea view); $129 (tower room).

► **Whim Inn**. Junction of Routes 3 and 4, **Pooles Corner**, P.E.I. C0A 1G0. Tel: (902) 838-3838; Fax: (902) 838-5116. $55–$60 (motel); $70 (housekeeping units).

NEWFOUND-LAND

AND LABRADOR

By Lawrence Jackson and Margaret M. Kearney

Lawrence Jackson visited Newfoundland on a summer re-search job in 1971, and hasn't been able to tear himself away. He has published articles in most major Canadian magazines, and is currently a science writer with the Federal Department of Fisheries and Oceans. Margaret M. Kearney, a freelance writer and broadcaster based in St. John's, was formerly employed by the Newfoundland Department of Tourism.

Newfoundland (new-fun-LAND) is a place apart from the melting pot of the Canadian mainland—less North American than European, a blend of England and Ireland as they were in the last century. Newfoundlanders, who joined the Canadian union only in 1949 (Labrador having been ceded to the Dominion of Newfoundland in 1927), still think of themselves as a separate nation with their own traditions and customs. They call their island "the Rock," an affectionate term that conveys both the meagerness of its soil as well as their own wry sense of humor.

Roots run deep here. Indian and Eskimo hunters roamed western Newfoundland and southern Labrador for almost 8,000 years. At the tip of the Great Northern Peninsula, the Norse dropped in briefly almost 500 years before Columbus "discovered" North America. The early days of European contact echo most resoundingly on the eastern edge of Newfoundland, in the remnants of colonial wars and in the Old World architecture of St. John's.

History lives, too, in the accents, vocabulary, and grammar that are so distinctive to the province. The men who wrote *The Dictionary of Newfoundland English* spent 25 years tracking down unique words and expressions, many long since extinct in other parts of the English-speaking world, and some invented locally to reflect unusual aspects of the Newfoundland experience.

Newfoundlanders don't ask where you come from; they ask where you belong. Indeed, one of the subtler satisfactions of visiting the province is to rediscover a sense of belonging most North Americans have lost. In the smaller communities, especially, you will glimpse an earlier, quieter time, a time when people knew their neighbors, children grew up amid grandparents, and the evening entertainment was Uncle Charlie with a yarn and Jessie with a song.

Much of this has changed, though chiefly in its intensity. For all the penetration of soap operas, rock videos, and junk food, Newfoundland and Labrador retain the most vivid and durable folk culture in North America.

Visitors to the province can tour the oldest European settlement in North America, dine on pan-fried cod tongues and seal-flipper pie, see performances of unique folk theater and music, or jig fish from a trap boat. You can also take a ferry from Fortune, on the island's Burin Peninsula, to the French islands of St. Pierre and Miquelon—the last vestige of France's once-vast North American empire.

The chief attraction of the province, however, is splendid scenery and abundant wilderness. Some of the best of it, like the awesome **Torngat Mountains** of northern Labrador, is scarcely more accessible than the High Arctic, while other wild and lovely regions can be reached by car or on foot. In the southern portions of the **Avalon Peninsula**, in fact, you may have to stop your car to let caribou clop across the pavement. And this just a few hours' drive from St. John's, the capital city.

For sportfishermen, Newfoundland and Labrador are spattered with lakes and streaked with rivers—all filled with trout and many bearing salmon—offering endless scope for angling.

Then too, the province is just catching on to "adventure travel," with whales and icebergs its most popular attractions. Newfoundland waters are home to 17 species of whales, dolphins, and porpoises, and the most common, the humpback, frequently puts on quite a show. (In the outport communities, try to contain your enthusiasm for icebergs and whales. Residents will understand your excitement but they cannot share it. Whales and icebergs are often a tor-

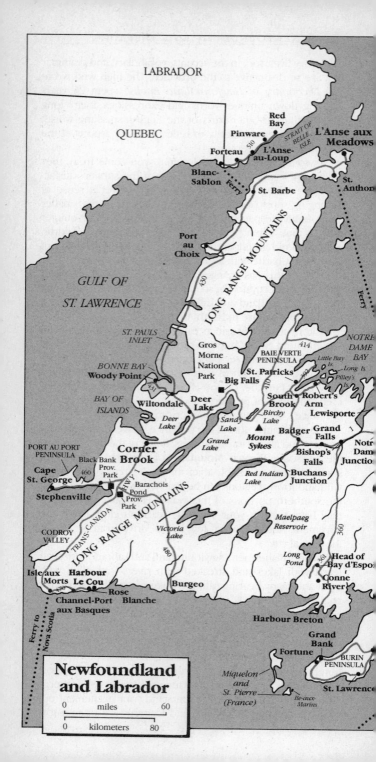

Newfoundland and Labrador

| 0 | miles | 60 |

| 0 | kilometers | 80 |

LABRADOR

QUEBEC

Red Bay

Pinware

Forteau 510

Blanc-Sablon

L'Anse-au-Loup

STRAIT OF BELLE ISLE

L'Anse aux Meadows

Ferry

St. Barbe

St. Anthony

Port au Choix

GULF OF ST. LAWRENCE

LONG RANGE MOUNTAINS

430

Ferry

ST. PAULS INLET

Gros Morne National Park

BAIE VERTE PENINSULA

414

NOTRE DAME BAY

Little Bay

Long Is.

Pilley's Is.

BONNE BAY

Woody Point

431

Big Falls

410

St. Patricks

492

Robert's Arm

BAY OF ISLANDS

Wiltondale

Deer Lake

Deer Lake

Sandy Lake

South Brook

Birchy Lake

Lewisporte

Grand Lake

Mount Sykes

Badger

Grand Falls

PORT AU PORT PENINSULA

Corner Brook

Black Bank Prov. Park

460

HWY 1

Barachois Pond Prov. Park

Red Indian Lake

Bishop's Falls

Buchans Junction

Notre Dame Junction

Cape St. George

Stephenville

TRANS-CANADA

CODROY VALLEY

Victoria Lake

Maelpaeg Reservoir

360

LONG RANGE MOUNTAINS

480

Long Pond

361

Head of Bay d'Espoir

Isle aux Morts

Harbour Le Cou

Rose Blanche

Burgeo

Conne River

Channel-Port aux Basques

Harbour Breton

Ferry to Nova Scotia

Grand Bank

Fortune

BURIN PENINSULA

Miquelon and St. Pierre (France)

Ile-aux-Marins

St. Lawrence

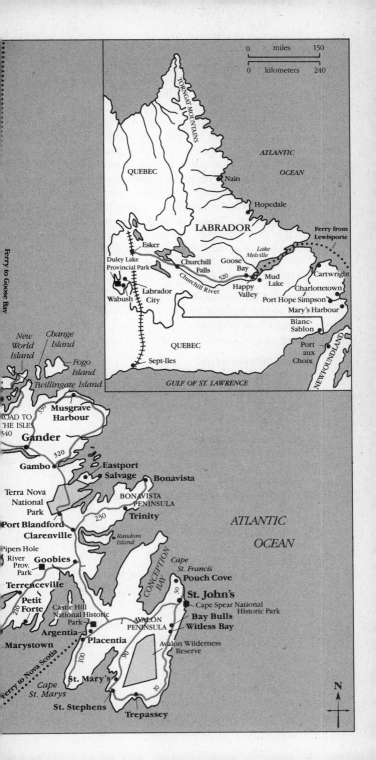

ment to fishermen, tangling and tearing their gear.) Other outdoor attractions include sea kayaking, white-water canoeing, mountain climbing, wildlife photography, snowmobiling, and cross-country skiing.

Except for hunters seeking moose or woodland caribou (of which Newfoundland has the most accessible herds on the continent), the best time to visit is July and August, when you stand at least a reasonable chance of sunshine and the summer festivals are in progress. Earlier than that, even in June, there may be week-long fog and bone-chilling rainstorms. September is sunny but cool, a good time for motoring and sightseeing, though the arts and folk festivals are over by the end of August and most of the major tourist attractions close after the Labour Day weekend.

MAJOR INTEREST

Western Newfoundland
Gros Morne National Park
Port au Choix prehistoric site
L'Anse aux Meadows Norse settlement site

Central Newfoundland
Historic settlements of the Notre Dame Bay area
Road to the Isles for scenery, seafood, and icebergs
South coast's isolated fishing villages
Superb freshwater fishing

Eastern Newfoundland
Terra Nova National Park
Historic village of Trinity for whale-watching excursions
Southern Newfoundland Seamen's Museum in Grand Bank

French Islands of St. Pierre and Miquelon
Island tours
Dining
Historic fishing settlement of Ile-aux-Marins
Relaxed rural atmosphere

Avalon Peninsula
Seabird colonies at Witless Bay and Cape St. Mary's
Early French fortifications at Placentia

St. John's
Signal Hill
19th-century architecture
Picturesque Quidi Vidi village
Cape Spear National Historic Park

Time now to state a few assumptions and offer some advice. Our coverage of the province assumes that you'll arrive by ferry from Nova Scotia, in summer, and will explore New-foundland by car or RV. Most visitors do. If the wilderness of Labrador entices you, the choices are altogether different, and so we discuss them later. (See the Getting Around section at the end of the chapter.)

In summer, the ferries from Nova Scotia serve both ends of Newfoundland's south coast, arriving in and departing from **Channel-Port aux Basques** to the southwest and **Argentia** to the southeast. The Trans-Canada Highway (Highway 1) connects the two; a good strategy if you have at least a week (and have made ferry reservations ahead of time) is to arrive on one ferry and depart on the other, seeing as much of the island in between as time allows.

Visitors arriving in the province for a shorter stay, say three to five days, will be better off concentrating on a specific region, leaving the rest for another visit. To organize the province into manageable chunks we've adopted the same regional designations used in the *Newfoundland and Labrador Travel Guide,* published by the provincial government. You can order a copy along with the official provincial highway map by calling (800) 563-6353 or (709) 729-2830. Study the guide with the map in hand; you'll need both to weigh your choices.

Now for the regions:

- **Western Newfoundland** is a mountainous and highly scenic region running from the island's southwest corner to the tip of its Great Northern Peninsula. Highway and ferry connections also tie the region to the southern corner of Labrador. The major attractions here are **Gros Morne National Park**, a stunning sea- and mountainscape, and two sites of historic significance: the early Basque whaling station at **Red Bay**, in southern Labrador, and the restored Norse settlement at **L'Anse aux Meadows**.
- **Central Newfoundland** includes the largest block of wilderness on the island, itself flanked by the isolated and sparsely settled south coast and the equally scenic but more accessible **Notre Dame Bay** area on the island's north coast. The latter is noted for its charming villages, most of them totally dependent on the inshore fishery.
- **Eastern Newfoundland** includes **Terra Nova National Park** and two peninsulas with long and colorful ties to the sea. The villages on the **Bonavista**

Peninsula, on the island's northeast coast, typify the inshore fishery, with its reliance on stationary nets set to intercept migrating fish. The larger communities on the **Burin Peninsula** trace their roots to the more aggressive Grand Banks fishery, in which schooners and, more recently, large trawlers range much farther afield.

Eastern Newfoundland also offers the connection to the islands of **St. Pierre** and **Miquelon**, the last outpost of France in the New World. Although the islands' inhabitants buy their crusty loaves and wine with francs, competitive sports, intermarriage, and a brisk trade in smuggled liquor and tobacco bind them to their Newfoundland neighbors.

- In terms of European settlement, the **Avalon Peninsula** is by far the oldest part of the province, with history among its chief attractions. It's also Newfoundland's most settled region, and since lively human contact is another attraction, the Avalon has much to offer visitors.

- **Labrador**, as its residents insist, is a world apart. This huge mainland portion of the province is still largely wilderness, difficult to reach and worth the effort. The world's largest caribou herd, world-record brook trout, some of the oldest bedrock on earth, the highest mountains east of the Rockies, and cultural diversity and traditions all its own are among the superlative attractions of the region.

Now for some advice:

Huge problems in the fisheries are going to mean a dislocation of the outport economy for at least the next several years. The closing of the northern cod fishery has put about 20,000 people out of work and is shaking the foundations of roughly two-thirds of the rural communities in the province. The impact on visitors is hard to predict. When the fisheries were thriving, tourism had little to offer many communities, as it didn't mesh easily with the real business of outport Newfoundland: landing and processing fish. Tourists were welcome in these communities, but incidental. As a result, the facilities and amenities necessary to reap benefits from tourism were slow to develop.

With the crisis a fact of life, tourists will probably be more welcome than ever. Still, the mood in many of these communities may be gloomy or anxious, and facilities may get run-down as money gets tight. But Newfoundlanders are used to hardship. Most will retain their resilience and good humor. Clinging to a rock, you tough out the hard times and take your pleasure where you can.

Visitors will likely notice that many local people litter their province shamelessly. This may be the flip side of one of the area's major charms: the durability of old habits and customs. Not long ago, nearly everything people used was biodegradable. Unfortunately, habits haven't caught up with excessive packaging and planned obsolescence. There are few beaches, trails, or back roads where you won't see pop cans, chip bags, or even discarded appliances and derelict cars.

So complain. Express your amazement and dismay. Littering is the chief blotch on an otherwise admirable regional character; while attitudes are changing, they can't change fast enough.

A final word of advice: Get off the Trans-Canada Highway whenever you can. The highway was finished in 1965, which means the real character of Newfoundland evolved in villages whose only link to the world and to each other was the sea. Keep those roots in mind and hit the coast where you can.

The other imperative when visiting Newfoundland is to slow down; the scenery isn't going anywhere. Leave some slack in your itinerary and watch for chances to mingle with local residents. The glory of Newfoundland is its people, some of whom will need a little time to assess you before they warm up. Hang around the wharf. Ask directions and advice. If your photos have people in them, try to make friends before snapping the shot. And cultivate the old-timers. They've seen things that will astound you, and most of them love to talk.

NEWFOUNDLAND

WESTERN NEWFOUNDLAND

This is both the oldest and newest part of the province. Although the earliest archaeological sites are found in the area, permanent settlement of it by Europeans was delayed until the late 19th century. In the resolution of colonial squabbles between England and France, the French were allowed to fish but not to settle on Newfoundland's west coast. In turn, French control of the fishery delayed the natural expansion of settlement.

So while the traces of human activity in the area are early indeed, the communities you'll encounter today are relatively young by Newfoundland standards. There is a rawness here that you won't find in the older settlements of the Avalon Peninsula and the northeast coast. While history abounds, most of it is the history of earlier inhabitants.

The dominant geologic feature of the region is the **Long Range Mountains**, an extension of the great Appalachian chain, which run the full length of Newfoundland's west coast, crowding the local population onto a narrow coastal plain. Striking fjords cut into the range in the Bay of Islands and Gros Morne National Park.

Channel-Port aux Basques

Visitors to the region disembark from the ferry at Channel-Port aux Basques (the "Channel" is usually dropped in conversation), at the southwesternmost tip of the island. The surrounding area attracted French, Portuguese, and Basque fishermen as early as the 16th century. Fishing is still important here, and anyone who sits down to chat with the locals will hear some interesting yarns. Most economic activity these days, however, centers around the Marine Atlantic ferries. Before you set out on the Trans-Canada Highway heading north, consider detouring east on Route 470 to villages like **Rose Blanche**, **Harbour le Cou**, and **Isle aux Morts**—the last so named because of the many ships that pranged in the treacherous waters offshore. If you have the time, stop along the way to prowl the rocky shore, or hike inland over the mossy heath so typical of coastal Newfoundland.

Newfoundland is defined by its major bays: It is the junction of land and sea, not the land itself, that shapes the lives and character of its people. For a visitor arriving at Port aux Basques, the first of these large bays is **St. Georges Bay**, around the shores of which two distinct cultural groups have settled: the Micmac Indians and Acadian French. (While most of Newfoundland was peopled by folks moving westward along the coasts from the Avalon Peninsula, these two groups moved into the area from Cape Breton, across the Cabot Strait.) If you've arrived after a spell of warm weather, you also may be able to enjoy a swim in salt water—a rare treat in Newfoundland, where the water temperature usually is more suited to polar bears. **Black Bank Provincial Park**, a long expanse of sandy beach off Route 460 on St. Georges Bay, offers fine bathing in good weather.

Side Trips off the Trans-Canada

Most visitors, eager to reach Gros Morne National Park, push on to Corner Brook without pausing for long in this area. Two interesting detours await those with more time. One takes you west on Route 460 to the Acadian communities of the **Port au Port Peninsula**; the other follows Route 480 some 156 km (97 miles) east and south to Burgeo, on the island's south coast.

If you arrive on the Port au Port Peninsula during the month of July, be sure to stop in **Stephenville** and ask about the Stephenville Theatre Festival, which offers fine drama; for information, Tel: (709) 643-4982. Stephenville itself, like Gander to the east, benefited from the construction of a large United States air base during World War II. More recently it has been designated Canada's first International Free Trade Zone (which only means no provincial sales tax is collected within the city limits). In the community of **Cape St. George**, about 60 km (37 miles) farther west via Route 460, the folk festival known as "Une Longue Veillee" celebrates the French heritage of the area, usually over the first weekend in August; for further information, Tel: (709) 644-2050.

The trip to **Burgeo** via Route 480 begins near **Barachois Pond Provincial Park**, at the foot of the Long Range Mountains. The highway, though not yet fully paved, takes you through some of the wildest portions of Newfoundland's interior to a fishing port first settled in the 18th century.

CORNER BROOK

If you decide to pass on the side trip to Burgeo and continue instead up Highway 1 to Corner Brook (population 25,000), you'll find yourself surrounded by some of the most striking scenery in the province. The **Bay of Islands**, whose waters were charted by Captain James Cook in 1764, pokes three long arms into the foot of the Long Range Mountains here. (A monument to Cook, at the head of the bay, is one of the most popular attractions in town, especially at sunset.) The town itself is built on Humber Arm, the most southerly of the three and the outlet for the Humber River, one of the province's major salmon streams. As the commercial and transportation hub of the region, Corner Brook offers a nice mix of urban comforts and rural pleasures, including an Arts and Culture Centre with a fine collection of work by local artists on University Drive; a shortish 18-hole golf course (Tel: 709/634-

5550 for tee times); and a wide range of accommodations. Try the stylish ▶ **Glynmill Inn** on Cobb Lane or the ▶ **Holiday Inn Downtown** at 48 West Street. Corner Brook also has a variety of bed-and-breakfast establishments. One of these, ▶ **Brake's Hospitality Home**, offers Newfoundland-style meals and a library stocked with books on the province.

If you're here in mid-July be sure to catch the town's annual **Hangashore Festival** in Prince Edward Park, with its emphasis on modern versions of traditional Newfoundland music, much of it brought to the New World from Europe centuries ago; for further information contact Harry Tibbo at (709) 634-8309.

A curiosity of another sort at 12 Farnell's Lane is the **Sticks and Stone House**, a monument to the whimsy of a man who spent 25 years decorating the interior of his home with tiny stones and popsicle sticks, pop can lids, and the radiator grills from old cars. This sort of folk art flourishes in Newfoundland. As you drive through small towns and coastal communities keep an eye out for "yard art"—bizarre decorations, whirligigs, and the like. (You won't need to watch for that other regional eccentricity: vivid and unlikely combinations of house paint. They'll leap out at you as you drive.)

Northeast of Corner Brook, Highway 1 follows the scenic Humber Valley past **Marble Mountain**, a fine downhill ski area with one of the longest seasons in eastern Canada (December to April), and then along the shores of Deer Lake to the town of the same name.

Although it began as a logging community in the 1890s, **Deer Lake**'s main business today is transportation. Its airport serves Corner Brook and the surrounding area, and the town's location at the junction of Highway 1 and Route 430 makes it an important hub of tourist and commercial traffic.

GROS MORNE NATIONAL PARK

Gros Morne, which was designated a UNESCO World Heritage Site in 1988, is the most popular tourist destination in the province and offers some of the most striking scenery in eastern Canada. Lakes, deep fjords, and Gros Morne itself—a 2,000-foot-high plateau (the second-highest point in Newfoundland)—dominate the landscape. (It's a day-long trek for sturdy hikers to the top of Gros Morne and back.) The park affords visitors the opportunity to camp, fish, hike, and boat, and park authorities have put a lot of thought and effort into trails, interpretive displays, and other facilities. The park's majestic scenery and spectacular sunsets are a boon for photographers, and amateur botanists are delighted by the many species of rare wildflowers—among them the showy lady's slipper and the yellow cymbidium—found within its boundaries.

You reach Gros Morne from Deer Lake via Route 430, also known as the **Viking Trail**. (The park boundary is approximately 35 km/22 miles from the junction of Highway 1 and Route 430.) In Wiltondale, Route 431, a scenic secondary road, heads west toward South Arm, one of the park's great fjords, following its southern shore 30 km (19 miles) to **Woody Point**, a pretty little village at the edge of **Bonne Bay**. While you're in the area, take the short detour west to Trout River, a fishing village just outside the park's boundaries. Here Route 431 will take you over a high, eerie tableland, as desolate and striking as anything this side of Baffin Island, in the high Arctic. A 20-minute ferry ride from Woody Point (in operation mid-June to mid-September) takes you across Bonne Bay to **Rocky Harbour**, where you can rejoin the Viking Trail.

Another delightful excursion is a boat tour of **Western Brook Pond**. The pond is reached via an easy hike from the highway near Sally's Cove, about 40 km (25 miles) north of Rocky Harbour. The deep gorge at the end of the pond, slashed out of the base of the Long Range Mountains, is among the most dramatic sights in Newfoundland. Information on departure times and rates for the excursion is available at the entrance to the park.

Accommodations in Gros Morne are scarce, unless you're camping. The community of **Cow Head**, north of St. Paul's Inlet, has two bed and breakfasts and a 22-unit motel with a dining room. For accommodations south of the park, you have to backtrack to Deer Lake or Daniel's Harbour, which between them offer a handful of motels.

The Great Northern Peninsula

North of the park, Route 430 hugs the coast, passing through one small village after another, each with its own character and identity. To the east, outstanding salmon streams with names like Portland Creek, River of Ponds, and Castors River tumble down from the Long Range Mountains on their way to the ocean. The scenery, especially views of the icy blue Gulf of St. Lawrence, is striking. The chief attractions from Gros Morne to the tip of the Great Northern Peninsula, however, are historic—and prehistoric.

At **Port aux Chois** (port-a-shwa), 80 km (50 miles) north of Gros Morne, there's a national historic park with artifacts from three prehistoric cultures. Workers excavating a basement in 1967 stumbled upon the extensive remains left behind by the Maritime Archaic people, the first human inhabitants of the region, remains that included three cemeteries, parts of nearly 100 skeletons, and a wealth of artifacts so well preserved that this site alone has provided much of what we know of that ancient New World culture.

In time the Maritime Archaic population was displaced by southward-migrating Dorset Eskimos, who in turn were displaced by Beothuk Indians. It was the Beothuks' fate to come into contact with the island's European settlers in the 18th and 19th centuries. As whites settled the coast, the Beothuks were cut off from marine resources crucial to their survival, until eventually they were driven back into a hinterland that couldn't support them year-round. The fine interpretive center here examines this long and still-elusive past.

THE LABRADOR STRAITS

Some 72 km (45 miles) north of Port aux Choix, visitors can make a fascinating detour to an area known as the Labrador Straits. During the summer a ferry leaves twice daily from **St. Barbe**, crossing the narrow Strait of Belle Isle to **Blanc-Sablon** on the Quebec–Labrador border.

The **Strait of Belle Isle** funnels migrating whales, seals, and schools of fish between the Labrador Sea and the Gulf of St. Lawrence. The abundance of marine life in the strait has drawn people to its shores for at least 8,000 years. Today visitors can glimpse a few chapters of that long history at **L'Anse-Amour**, an ancient Indian burial site about 30 km (19 miles) northeast of Blanc-Sablon via Route 510, a paved road, and at **Red Bay**, another 75 km (47 miles) beyond that via the same route. At Red Bay, marine archaeologists have recovered from the frigid waters just offshore remains of an ambitious Basque whaling and sealing operation dating to the early 16th century. According to archaeologists, as many as 20 ships would spend the season at Red Bay, making it the first industrial site in the New World.

More contemporary pleasures hereabouts include the **Bakeapple Festival**, named for a berry that grows profusely in the area and ripens in mid-August. Although the festival is a joint effort of the various communities in the region, Forteau is the focus of it. There are, in addition, two famous salmon rivers in the area: the Forteau and Pinware, both at their best in July. Anglers on the Forteau favor the ► **Labrador Salmon Lodge**; the ► **Pinware River Lodge**, in the village of the same name, is convenient to the Pinware River.

As is often true of fishing lodges, these are expensive options for the general traveller, and are usually booked months in advance besides. Non-anglers will find a few bed and breakfasts, cabins, and housekeeping units scattered among the communities of L'Anse au Clair, Forteau, L'Anse au Loup, and West St. Modeste, with the largest of these the ▶ **Northern Light Inn** in L'Anse au Clair, about 8 km (5 miles) east of the Quebec–Labrador border.

Know, too, that spots on the ferry are at a premium in the summer, and advance reservations essential; you can make them at the entrance to Gros Morne National Park, or directly through either of the lodges mentioned above. (See the Accommodations Reference list at the end of the chapter for booking information.) And whatever you do, don't forget to pack the insect repellent: Labrador's reputation for black flies and mosquitoes is well-deserved.

ST. ANTHONY AND L'ANSE AUX MEADOWS

Back in Newfoundland, St. Anthony, famous as the headquarters of the Grenfell Mission, is approximately 136 km (84 miles) northeast of St. Barbe via Route 430. The mission was founded nearly a century ago by Dr. Wilfred Grenfell, a British doctor who spent his life raising funds to serve the isolated villages of northern Newfoundland and coastal Labrador. In addition to hospitals and nursing stations, Grenfell helped establish a fishermen's cooperative and a crafts industry that still delights souvenir-hunting visitors. (Here, as well as in other towns in northern Newfoundland and southern Labrador, watch especially for embroidered parkas and superbly made sealskin boots.) Two other attractions of interest are Grenfell House, the doctor's home, and the **Jordi Bonet Murals**, a ceramic panel depicting the lives of the area's people and the work of the Grenfell Mission among them. The murals are in the rotunda of the Charles Curtis Memorial Hospital.

The ▶ **Vinland Motel**, near the junction of Routes 430 and 436, and the ▶ **Saint Anthony Motel**, in town, are comfortable motor inns. The former has 27 rooms and 10 housekeeping units, with prices in the $85 range; the latter has 22 rooms and tends to be a few dollars less. Or you can head on to the ▶ **Valhalla Lodge**, on Route 436 in Griquet near L'Anse aux Meadows, before visiting that famous Norse site the next day.

The most charming accommodation in the area, however, is the ▶ **Tickle Inn** at Cape Onion, where a fourth-generation descendant of the area's first recorded settler has restored the house built by his ancestor and turned it into a charming guest home with four rooms and remarkable food. The inn is located well out of town on Route 437, about 20 km (12 miles) of gravel road branching off Route 436; open June to September only.

L'Anse aux Meadows National Historic Park
On the coast due north of St. Anthony, this world-renowned park protects a well-restored settlement dating from A.D. 1005 to 1025—the oldest European settlement yet discovered in North America, as well as the only fully authenticated Norse site south or west of Greenland. The site, which was rediscovered in 1960 after some fine sleuthing by a Norwegian couple, is believed to have been founded by Icelandic settlers under Thorfinn Karlsefini following close on the heels of the famous Leif Ericsson, who may have voyaged even farther south. Declared a UNESCO World Heritage Site in 1978, today L'Anse aux Meadows comprises a small Norse farm complex and a smithy where bog iron was smelted nearly a thousand years ago.

CENTRAL NEWFOUNDLAND

Central Newfoundland was the home of the **Beothuk Indians**, who succumbed to hardship, disease, and persecution in the early 19th century. Their passing, in spite of late and clumsy efforts to save them, is one of the most poignant episodes in Newfoundland's history.

The Beothuk occupied the watershed that dominates the island's interior. Today, as in their day, it is trout, salmon, caribou, and black bear country, a vast wilderness of boggy spruce and birch forest sloping northeastward toward Notre Dame Bay. From the west, motorists enter the region via the Trans-Canada Highway (Highway 1), heading northeast from Deer Lake. The highway skirts the shore of **Sandy Lake**, crossing the route favored by caribou migrating between the Great Northern Peninsula and the central interior. It was near here, in 1878, that moose were first introduced to Newfoundland—and, ironically, given the subsequent explosion of the moose population, where the last known Newfoundland wolf was shot.

Baie Verte Peninsula

Soon eastbound travellers face the first of what will be many tantalizing detours. Route 410 heads north down the spine of the Baie Verte Peninsula, dead-ending after 85 km (53 miles) in the fishing village of Fleur de Lys. Secondary roads off Route 410 spread like roots to lesser headlands. Few join up, all are scenic, and the sheer number of them makes for hard choices.

If you decide to explore the peninsula, be sure to visit the **Baie Verte Miner's Museum**, in the town of Baie Verte, which documents the long history of copper and asbestos mining in the area. In the Fleur de Lys area, the Dorset Eskimo people left a record of their presence almost 1,000 years ago, including bowls and lamps carved out of soapstone quarried from a nearby cliff face.

OUTPORT COMMUNITIES

Successive Newfoundland governments have despaired of bringing hospitals, schools, pavement, and similar services to people in hundreds of scattered villages, some as small as two or three families. Residents of isolated islands, especially, were encouraged to move to centers more easily serviced. But where the fishing was good and family roots ran deep, many people hung on, waiting for the ferries and causeways that might eventually link them with the rest of the province.

Today the more remote communities make for interesting out-of-the-way destinations. And remember, if people stare, it's not because they're unfriendly; instead, it's usually because they're trying to determine if you're the offspring of someone who has moved away.

Among such interesting outport communities in the Notre Dame Bay area, east of the Baie Verte Peninsula, are **Little Bay Islands**, reached by ferry from St. Patrick's on Route 392, and **Pilley's Island** and **Long Island**, reached by road, causeway, and ferry from the community of Robert's Arm on Route 380.

THE EXPLOITS AREA

The Trans-Canada takes a long jog south at **South Brook**, situated at the head of Halls Bay. When you get to **Badger**, at the junction of Highway 1 and Route 370, consider backtracking on Route 370 into the heart of Beothuk country. The last known survivors of the race, Mary March and Shanawdithit, were captured north of Badger in 1823. Route 370, which pushes 60 km (37 miles) into the island's heavily forested interior, skirts the north end of beautiful **Red Indian Lake** before dead-ending in the tiny hamlet of Buchans. The surrounding wilderness is an angler's paradise. **Mary March Provincial Park**, 3 km (2 miles) west of Buchans Junction on the shore of Red Indian Lake, occupies the site of a Beothuk winter camp. Motorists can refuel and stock up on groceries in Buchans Junction, and there's a small hospitality home in Buchans itself.

Grand Falls–Windsor

Returning to Highway 1, turn east toward Grand Falls–Windsor, the site of Newfoundland's first paper mill and today the largest community between Gander and Corner Brook. It's an attractive modern town, and remains one of the largest suppliers of newsprint in the world. Don't miss the **Mary March Regional Museum** (open daily year-round) here, which depicts the lives of the Beothuks and the early settlers who displaced them. Another noteworthy sight is the Atlantic Salmon Interpretation Centre, occupying a spot on the Exploits River where a fishway allows salmon to bypass the falls for which the town is named. Anglers eager to try their luck will find plenty of good salmon and trout streams nearby. The 102-room ▶ **Mount Peyton Hotel** (with an additional 32 motel-style rooms and 16 efficiency units) is the biggest and most comfortable accommodation in the area.

Bishop's Falls, a short distance to the east, is a major crossroads. From here, Route 350 heads north to the Bay of Exploits and then on to the logging and fishing communities of the Notre Dame Bay area. Route 360, on the other hand, heads due south across the unpopulated interior of Newfoundland to a very different shore.

The South Coast

Newfoundland's splendid but isolated south coast stretches from Port aux Basques at the southwestern tip of the island eastward to Terrenceville at the head of Fortune Bay. Where the northeast coast of Newfoundland is swept by drifting pack ice in the spring and frigid currents year-round, the south coast is largely ice-free. This, and access to major fishing grounds not far offshore, gives the region a winter fishery—a prospect unthinkable anywhere else in the province.

Route 360 heading south from Bishop's Falls crosses the broadest expanse of wilderness in Newfoundland, a region of spruce forest, high rocky hills, and countless streams and ponds. About 150 km (93 miles) south of Bishop's Falls, Route

361 branches off toward **Head of Bay d'Espoir**, the site of Newfoundland's first major hydroelectric development. (The name means Bay of Hope, but locals pronounce it "Bay Despair.") Nearby is **Conne River**, a Micmac Indian community. Although there are motels and tourist cabins in Bay d'Espoir, the region is off the main tourist route and lacking in most amenities.

Farther south, Route 360 divides again where it hits the **Connaigne Peninsula**, branching out to serve the many fishing communities in the region. The largest of these is **Harbour Breton**, the end of the road figuratively as well as literally. Secondary roads on either side of the peninsula lead to small villages huddled on the area's many bays and inlets.

Visitors with the luxury of time can visit this remote coast by boat—a prospect that has become easier in recent years thanks to the M.V. *Marine Courier* and M.V. *Marine Runner,* Marine Atlantic packets that now provide year-round passenger service to the region. You can catch whichever one happens to be in service (usually the smaller, faster *Marine Courier* during the summer season) roughly every other day in either Port aux Basques or Terrenceville. As schedules are subject to change, however, it's best to contact Marine Atlantic for up-to-date information; in Port aux Basques, Tel: (709) 695-7081; in the U.S., Tel: (800) 341-7981. Ports of call include fishing villages where roads are nonexistent and outport life remains tied to the rhythms of nature and the sea. And though it can be foggy for days at a time, if you're lucky enough to catch a clear day you'll discover the south coast's essential charm: It is one of the very few places left in North America where you can voyage into the past.

THE ROAD TO THE ISLES

After a surfeit of one-way choices, motorists are likely to relish the smorgasbord of options they'll face back on the Trans-Canada at Notre Dame Junction. Route 340, the famous Road to the Isles, weaves along the southeast shore of **Notre Dame Bay**. The surrounding region, a maze of lovely islands knit together by a network of causeways and ferries, is unusually well served by hotels, motels, and guest homes. In Newfoundland, the density of place-names on a map is often a clue to a region's prosperity, past or present. In the Notre Dame area, the place-names obscure the details on the highway map, hinting at a long and productive history.

Lewisporte, about 15 km (9 miles) from the junction of the Trans-Canada and Route 340, is a busy regional hub and the terminal for Marine Atlantic freighters and ferries serving northern Newfoundland and Labrador. (Labrador service is usually booked months in advance; see the Getting Around section at the end of the chapter for Marine Atlantic booking information).

Twillingate and New World Island

From Lewisporte, Route 341/340 and its many branches head northeast to the communities of Twillingate and New World Island. Although the surrounding area was first settled in the 18th century, modern roads were unknown until 25 years ago. As a result, the layout and character of these villages evolved in the absence of the automobile—a fact that's beautifully evident. Almost all are organically fitted to the contours of bedrock and harbor, as true to their setting as old trees are to theirs. And in most, you'll find a general store that sells just about everything needed for day-to-day living, not to mention the many practical items that have long since disappeared from city stores.

In Twillingate itself you can buy lobster fresh from the pot or gather blue mussels from beds right beside the road. The **Twillingate Museum** (open June to mid-September) is housed in a fine old church home, and opens a window onto 18th-century life in the region. The Fish, Fun and Folk Festival, held over the last weekend in July, highlights West Country English dance, recitation, and music.

On both New World and Twillingate islands you're also in the track of icebergs carried south by the Labrador Current. In good years dozens of the great ice islands are often visible from the shore at once. The compressed ice in the bergs can be thousands of years old, and is frequently colored sky blue or jade green, with spires that may thrust upwards hundreds of feet into the air.

For accommodations in the area, try the small ► **Anchor Inn Motel** or one of the two bed and breakfasts in town. There are also bed and breakfasts in nearby **Summerford**, **Virgin Arm**, and **Boyd's Cove**, as well as a campground in the provincial park at **Dildo Run**. (The tourist information booth in Notre Dame Junction also has brochures from the many comfortable lodgings in the area.)

Change Islands and Fogo Island

Don't leave the area without considering a visit to Change Islands and Fogo Island, both reached by ferry from the village of Farewell on Route 335. Change Islands hasn't changed much. It's still a community of well-kept clapboard houses and tiny gardens, small boats slipping out to sea, and small boys and old-timers gathering on wharves. The

▶ **Seven Oaks Island Inn & Cottages** here offers eight rooms (six with bathrooms *en suite*) and meals in a restored historic home, along with three two-bedroom housekeeping cottages; the owners can also arrange boat charters to view whales and icebergs.

Fogo Island, a little farther out, has been settled since the 1700s. The island remained isolated until recently, however, so that people cleave to many age-old customs as well as a vaguely Elizabethan dialect. These same residents, who live in communities with names like **Seldom, Barr'd Islands**, and **Joe Batt's Arm** (named for a deserter from Captain James Cook's expedition to this island-dotted coast), dug their heels in when government began promoting resettlement in the 1960s. Defying the pressure to move eventually revitalized their fishing-based economy with a cooperative that's still active.

GANDER

Gander, at the junction of Highway 1 and Route 330, has had a long association with aviation. It achieved special prominence early in World War II, as the Germans were shooting down British planes faster than they could be built. North American factories soon stepped up production to fill the breach. Because these North American–built fighters and bombers lacked the range to fly to Europe, the Allies quickly built a circuit of airfields on the fringes of the North Atlantic. Gander, which had been carved out of the forest in the early days of commercial aviation to provide a large airport close to Europe, was made the headquarters of Ferry Command and became a major conduit for aircraft bound for Britain.

As commercial aviation flourished after the war, Gander grew into its current role as a refueling stop for trans-Atlantic flights. Today it's a thriving, cosmopolitan town of 15,000, amply served by reasonable hotels and restaurants. Two good choices are the 106-room ▶ **Albatross Motel**, with its own dining room and cocktail lounge, and the ▶ **Hotel Gander**, with 148 rooms and five suites as well as an indoor pool. If Gander's role in international aviation interests you, don't miss the exhibits at the **Gander International Airport,** or the four historic aircraft (Hudson bomber, Voodoo, Canso water bomber, and Beech 18) on display downtown.

THE GANDER LOOP

Route 330/320, which circles the coast north and east of Gander, is also known as the Gander Loop. Not far from town, you can stop to admire the magnificent groves of white birch at **Jonathan's Pond Provincial Park.**

In Gander Bay, Route 330 turns northeast to service the fishing communities on a long historic shore. In **Musgrave Harbour,** about 65 km (40 miles) northeast of Gander Bay, a fishermen's museum is housed in a former store built by the messianic Sir William Coaker, who began to organize a powerful fishermen's union in the winter of 1908–1909. Farther east, a cluster of villages occupies the approach to **Bonavista Bay.** Each has a proud history and many have small museums. Although there are few organized tourist services in the region, enterprising visitors can negotiate with local fishermen for a day on the water or with their sons for guided hikes into trout ponds in the hills.

The Gander Loop ends at **Gambo,** the birthplace of Joey Smallwood, the energetic politician who led Newfoundland into the Canadian confederation and then served as the province's premier for 23 years.

EASTERN NEWFOUNDLAND

This region comprises two extremely different peninsulas as well as Terra Nova park, Newfoundland's first national park. The **Bonavista Peninsula,** which is accessed via Route 230 and its secondary roads off the Trans-Canada Highway, extends northeastward into the chilly waters of the Labrador Current, with its cargo of icebergs, pack ice, and the occasional polar bear marooned on a drifting floe. The peninsula is deeply cut by a number of bays, with no one part of it far from the sea. The **Burin Peninsula,** to the southwest, juts out from the south coast like a huge boot kicking at the French islands of St. Pierre and Miquelon (for which see below).

Approaching from the west on Highway 1, consider detouring on Route 310 to the **Eastport** area, about 20 km (12 miles) east of Glovertown and the Trans-Canada Highway. With its fine beach, theme park, and numerous cottages and efficiency units, this is holiday country for Newfoundlanders and visitors spilling over from the national park. If you have children, and can adjust to the notion of western trail rides in a maritime province, you may want to visit the **Splash 'n Putt Resort,** which has horses, miniature golf, and a water slide.

For a more authentic attraction, drive another 10 km (6 miles) east to **Salvage,** the oldest community in the region and a charming place indeed. Or take the ferry over to **St. Brendan's Island,** named for the Irish monk who is thought to have sailed to Newfoundland before the Norse. (St. Brendan's is another community that refused to resettle.) The ferry leaves from Burnside, 8 km (5 miles) north of Eastport via a gravel road.

Another worthwhile diversion hereabouts is offered by **Ocean Watch Tours**, which takes visitors out to view whales and icebergs on its vessel the *Northern Fulmar*. The crew is extremely well informed about whales and their environment, and can add an extra dimension to any beachcombing you do during the rest of your stay in the province. For further information, contact Mark or Fraser Carpenter at (709) 677-2327.

TERRA NOVA NATIONAL PARK

Less spectacular than Gros Morne, Terra Nova's charms are nevertheless considerable. Visitors can get an idea of its scenic diversity as they follow the Trans-Canada around and through the park's fjord-like inlets and thick forests. The sheltered waters of **Newman Sound** offer fine canoeing, and the 18-hole golf course at Twin Rivers, near the southern entrance to the park, is superbly scenic. The park has interpretive exhibits at two reception centers, and offers a variety of films and live performances at two outdoor theaters near the **Malady Head** and **Newman Sound** campgrounds, both of which are sign-posted on the highway.

The Bonavista Peninsula

At **Port Blandford**, also near the southern entrance to the park, Route 233 heads east to some of the oldest settlements in the province. The highway is unpaved at first, but soon turns to pavement in Lethbridge, where it becomes Route 230. Two provincial parks east of Lethbridge, **Rattle Falls** and **Jiggin' Head**, offer hiking trails amid terrific scenery.

Local accents in the area still echo the West Country dialects of Devon and Cornwall, the area from which John Cabot recruited a crew for his voyage of discovery in 1497. Nova Scotians have another version, but Newfoundlanders insist that the first land Cabot saw was Cape Bonavista.

Bonavista itself is a lovely town with several historic attractions. The **Bonavista Museum** has a large collection of church records and artifacts administered by an enthusiastic curator; the **Mockbeggar Property** is a complex of traditional buildings; and the **Cape Bonavista Lighthouse**, staffed by guides in period costume, has been restored to its late-19th-century condition. All three are open daily during the summer.

Elsewhere on the peninsula, Catalina and Port Union are situated in the heart of Coaker Country. Coaker organized exploited fishermen in the area into the powerful Fishermen's Protective Union. Although resistance from the Roman Catholic Church helped to confine the union to Newfoundland's largely Protestant northeast coast, it was able to boast a membership of some 20,000 by 1914. A museum in Catalina, housed in an old railway station, contains many relics of the period.

TRINITY

Trinity—located off Route 230 on Route 239—is one of the oldest European settlements in North America. In a province short of capital and overflowing with history, the government has recognized its special importance and devoted scarce funds to the restoration of many of its oldest buildings. The first vice-admiralty court in the New World was held here in 1615, but Trinity was an established commercial center long before that. It was also here, toward the end of the 18th century, that the smallpox vaccination was tried for the first time. The town has been in the fish business for more than 350 years, and has been building wooden boats for much of that.

Just walking around Trinity is delightful, but a visit to the town's interpretive center, with its maps, photographs, and illustrations, will make your visit much more meaningful. After such a stop, you can take your pick of historic sites, including a museum and archives, a restored blacksmith shop, a railway museum, and a restored merchant's home.

Trinity is also a noted spot for whale-watching, with pods of the great mammals cruising past its headlands throughout the summer months. **Ocean Contact** (Tel: 709/464-3269), one of Newfoundland's oldest continuously operating whale-watching outfits, was founded by Dr. Peter Beamish, who involves his customers in an ongoing research program that uses rhythmic acoustic signals to communicate with the whales.

Nearby **Port Rexton** and **Trouty** offer a variety of accommodations, from guest homes to motels, housekeeping units, and cabins. In Trinity itself, Beamish and his wife, Christine, offer total immersion in whale lore and research—including seminars and fascinating slide shows—at their 12-room ▶ **Village Inn**, an English-style hostelry chock full of traditional furniture. The Beamishes also can arrange boat charters, kayak rentals, and sightseeing tours of the region with knowledgeable guides.

RANDOM ISLAND AND CLARENVILLE

Random Island, one of the largest islands off the Newfoundland coast, almost fills the bay it occupies. Narrow inlets surround the island, and are sheltered by its bulk. It was from the shore of one of these, **Smith Sound**, that William Cormack set out with a Micmac guide in 1822 in an effort to locate the last of the Beothuks. He never found them, although he walked clear across Newfoundland in the process.

Clarenville, a busy commercial center on the Trans-Canada, can serve as a convenient base for visits to smaller communities. It has a variety of accommodations, including the ▶ **Holiday Inn Clarenville**, which offers the kind of comfortable and familiar lodgings travellers expect from that well-known chain.

The Burin Peninsula

The Burin Peninsula has been a major fishing center for more than 400 years. In the 16th century French, English, and Portuguese fished the nearby **Grand Banks**, sun-drying their catches on the shore. Although the technology has changed drastically, descendants of those early fishermen still patrol the Grand Banks: the French from St. Pierre; the Portuguese in trawlers sailing from Aveiro, Portugal; and the English by way of their descendants in Newfoundland and Nova Scotia.

Route 210, the highway to the Burin Peninsula, leaves the Trans-Canada at **Goobies**, hitting the head of Placentia Bay within a few miles of the junction. This is pleasant, hilly country, with good trout and salmon angling nearby; it also has become popular as second-home country for many Newfoundlanders. At **Piper's Hole River Provincial Park**, just west of Swift Current, an abandoned railway line offers a fine trail along the river through forests of birch and fir.

Beyond Swift Current, the road ascends to the mossy barrens so typical of Newfoundland's highlands and coastal areas. The terrain is scarcely different from large swaths of the Canadian Arctic, except that the mosses here are lusher.

Terrenceville

A branch of the highway heads toward Terrenceville as Route 210 nears the base of the peninsula. Terrenceville is the eastern terminus of Marine Atlantic's packet service to the south coast. (Port aux Basques is the other terminus.) From June to mid-September, two ocean-going launches serve 15 coastal communities, many with no other means of access. In good weather it's a marvelous way to visit these remote villages; in rough weather, on the other hand, it can be a landlubber's nightmare. The boats usually have room for last-minute passengers, however, so if you're interested, leave room in your itinerary and check the marine forecast before committing. Most of the passengers on this run will be local people, glad to talk and to help you understand what you see. For further information, contact Marine Atlantic at (709) 695-7081 or, in the U.S., (800) 341-7981.

Marystown

Marystown, 150 km (93 miles) southwest of the Trans-Canada, is the largest community on the peninsula and one of four Burin ports able to accommodate deep-sea trawlers. The 138-room ▶ **Motel Mortier** here offers comfortable, recently renovated accommodations and eight housekeeping units in a single building. You may want to spend a day or two exploring the many inshore fishing communities clustered between Marystown and the town of Burin, another trawler port not far away.

Grand Bank and Fortune

From Marystown, Route 210 and its secondary roads loop around the end of the peninsula. It's probably best to drive the route counterclockwise, which allows you to visit the fascinating **Southern Newfoundland Seaman's Museum** (open daily year-round) in the town of **Grand Bank** first.

Grand Bank is a fine old town, especially down toward the waterfront, where fortunes made in the fishery are reflected in its many handsome homes. In summer the town promotes a "Heritage Walk" that shows off its grander buildings. Visitors interested in this option should contact Sadie Parsons; Tel: (709) 832-1080. If you decide to spend the night, ▶ **Granny's Motor Inn**, on the highway, offers recently renovated rooms and a kitchen that excels in the preparation of fresh fish.

Fortune, a few miles to the south, is another deep-sea fishing port as well as the terminus for ferries to France—or that tiny New World corner of it known as St. Pierre and Miquelon (see below).

St. Lawrence and Placentia Bay

Circling the southern shore of the Burin you'll come to **St. Lawrence**, once the world's largest producer of fluorspar. It was also here, in February 1942, that two U.S. Navy vessels drove ashore on the nearby cliffs, resulting in the loss of

more than 200 men. The heroic efforts of the local population saved 182 others, and the U.S. government, as a gesture
of its appreciation, built a 22-bed hospital for the town.

Leaving the Burin Peninsula, you can backtrack on Route
210 to the Trans-Canada, or take the ferry shortcut across
Placentia Bay to the Avalon Peninsula. The ferry mainly
accommodates local traffic but may have room for the occasional tourist vehicle. Motorists who decide to take a chance
on there being space should watch for the turnoff off Route
210 to **Boat Harbour, Brookside,** and **Petit Forte,** a road not
numbered on most highway maps. The ferry leaves from
Petit Forte and stops in South East Bight and Little Paradise
before crossing to Argentia.

ST. PIERRE AND MIQUELON

Few visitors to Newfoundland realize that France—or at
least a tiny piece of it—lies just off the province's south
coast. St. Pierre and Miquelon, the largest islands in a small
archipelago comprising a dozen islets and countless rocks,
are situated some 12 miles off the tip of the Burin Peninsula
in the Gulf of St. Lawrence. Discovered by the Portuguese in
1520 and claimed for France by Jacques Cartier on his
second voyage to North America in 1536, the islands were
settled by Breton, Norman, and Basque fishing families in
the decades that followed. Over the next century ownership
of the islands passed back and forth between France and
Britain, until the Treaty of Paris returned them to France for
good in 1763.

At first a colony, then an overseas territory, the archipelago became a territorial collectivity, or *département,* of the
French Republic in 1976. Today almost 5,800 St. Pierrais (as
they call themselves) live on **St. Pierre,** ten square miles of
volcanic rock dotted with freshwater ponds, peat bogs,
muskeg, and clumps of stunted trees and scrub vegetation.
Miquelon, linked to the island of **Langlade** (shown on most
maps as Little Miquelon) by a sandy isthmus, supports a
population of fewer than 700 people on its 90 square miles.
There are, in addition, a few summer homes on tiny **Ile-aux-
Marins** (Mariner's Island), located off the mouth of St.
Pierre's harbor.

Useful Facts

While Canadians and Americans planning to visit the islands do not need passports or visas, customs officials will ask to see adequate identification (e.g., driver's license, birth certificate). On your return to Canada you'll have to pass through Canadian Customs and Immigration, and will be subect to Canada's duty-free importation limits. A free brochure listing duty-free items is available at the ferry office in **Fortune**, on Newfoundland's Burin Peninsula (see the Getting Around section at the end of the chapter for information on getting to the islands), as well as at Canadian customs offices and all Canadian airports from which international flights depart.

The French franc is the common currency, although Canadian and U.S. dollars are accepted everywhere. Shops are open Monday through Saturday from 9:00 A.M. to noon and from 1:30 to 6:00 P.M.—unless a cruise ship is in port, in which case most places stay open until the passengers head back to the boat. Alcohol and tobacco products, perfumes, designer clothing, and kitchenware are the chief bargains. From 6:00 to 11:00 P.M., as well as on Sundays, small shops called *depanneurs* sell food, wine, liquor, and cigarettes.

A pure Parisian French (unlike the French spoken in much of Quebec) is the lingua franca on St. Pierre and Miquelon. Most islanders know a little English, however, and those in the retail or tourism sectors are bilingual. Visitors should experience no difficulty doing business or getting around, as the local people pride themselves on their hospitality; if the person you stop on the street for directions doesn't understand English, chances are he will go out of his way to find someone who does.

As for the weather on St. Pierre and Miquelon, let's just say that winter comes early and stays late, usually through the middle of April. The rest of the year is often windy, damp, and foggy (especially in June and July), with considerable variations in temperature. The fickle weather is caused by the frigid Labrador Current. Visitors on tight schedules will be better off using the ferry service from Fortune, rather than relying on one of the small commuter airlines that service St. Pierre, as flights often are fogged out, or in.

If you plan to call ahead before your arrival, keep in mind that this is France: Phone calls to either island should include the prefix for the international operator, "011." Once you arrive on St. Pierre, don't forget to set your watch half an hour ahead of Newfoundland time, which is 90 minutes ahead of eastern standard time, the time in New York, Montreal, or Toronto.

The Local Economy

Although fishing and the servicing of fishing boats have always been the lifeblood of St. Pierre and Miquelon, rum-running and a crafty brand of piracy have also played major roles in the islands' history. In the 1920s, the United States' experiment with Prohibition all but shut down St. Pierre's fishery, as local fish-processing plants were used to warehouse the estimated 300,000 cases of Canadian and French spirits that passed through the tiny port each month. From St. Pierre a ragtag fleet would deliver the contraband to hidden coves dotting the East Coast from Maine to Maryland.

Officially, at any rate, those days have passed, with the economy of the islands now dependent on fishing, government, and tourism. But in private islanders will admit there's a fourth component to the local economy: smuggling liquor and tobacco into Canada through Newfoundland. Provided he or she acts like a tourist, an interested visitor can observe contraband-loaded boats mingling with the islands' small fishing fleet before making the run to the mainland. The boats, usually aluminum vessels called Clarenville boats—after the Newfoundland town where they're manufactured—are easy to spot. They look like local fishing craft, with one difference: the two large Yamaha outboard motors attached to the stern. The operations aren't more clandestine than they are simply because loading liquor and tobacco onto a boat isn't against the law in St. Pierre. It's Canada's laws that are broken when the contraband is off-loaded on Canadian soil and disappears into the night before steep import taxes and duties can be levied on it.

If a form of rumrunning still flourishes here, modern navigational aids and government-operated lighthouses have ended the profitable island trade known as "pirate farming." The technique was simple enough: Farmers on either side of the strait separating Miquelon and Langlade would tie lanterns to their cows and then turn them loose along the shoreline. Occasionally, an unwary skipper would mistake the lanterns for navigational beacons and pile his ship on the rocks between the two islands. The Miquelonnais would rescue the crew if they could, and then salvage everything of value from the wrecked ship. So many ships were wrecked between Miquelon and Langlade, it is said, that the wreckage acted as a trap for sand and other detritus, eventually forming the long isthmus that now joins the two islands.

ST. PIERRE

St. Pierre (the name of the island and its only town) is a singular place, its distinct French trappings complementing an Irish-style hospitality that's extended to visitors as they shop, enjoy exquisite cuisine in a fine restaurant, or sip a *digestif* in one of its very European cafés.

The town's small wood-frame houses, clustered together along narrow streets that radiate up sometimes steep hillsides from the harbor, come in a kaleidoscope of colors. Each tiny yard has a patch of bright flowers in summer and a small plot of carefully tended vegetables. Many houses have *tonbours,* distinctive enclosed porches added to the front or side, where they prevent snow and icy winds from blowing in every time someone enters or exits.

The commercial life of the town is pretty much confined to the waterfront near the Customs House on **Place Général de Gaulle**. Store windows in the neighborhood showcase bargains in French luxury goods and designer clothing. Scattered among the private homes are a handful of bakeries; grocery, fish and butcher shops; restaurants; and several discotheques. Signs tend to be small and discreet; the store with the best selection of wines and spirits, for example, is identified by a small sign bearing the words "Gerard Vallee," the owner's name. Customers are escorted to the basement, where they are left to rummage through several rooms stacked floor to ceiling with cases and part cases of wine and liquor.

Elsewhere, a four-story wall divides an entire paved block. The wall is used as a jai alai backboard, with players often seen practicing on one side of the wall while animated contests of *petoncle* or *boules* (a form of bowling) are waged on the other. Soccer and hockey also inflame passions here. St. Pierre fields two soccer teams, and Miquelon one, with the teams competing against each other; local hockey teams also compete against teams from Newfoundland.

Around the Island

There is no place in the town of St. Pierre that cannot be reached on foot in ten minutes. Visitors wanting a leisurely, bilingual overview of town can hop aboard **Le Petit Saint-Pierre**, a rubber-tired minitrain that makes a regular circuit of the downtown waterfront area during the summer months.

As you can't bring your car over on the ferry and rental cars aren't available on the island itself, your options for exploring St. Pierre's 20 miles of roads are limited to motor-bikes, bicycles, or a guided tour. Your hotel will be happy to make arrangements for you, or you can deal directly with Didier Dérout at 24 rue Maréchal Foch; Tel: (508) 41-38-39.

A tour of the town and island is available in a small motor coach ($6 for adults, $3 for children). The 90-minute loop includes three superb vantage points overlooking town, the harbor, and scenic Ile-aux-Marins. In town, the tour bus passes the major shops, the television and radio station, the 80-bed hospital, the residence of the governor (who is sent over from the mother country for a three-year stint), and the staff quarters for the 16 nattily uniformed, kepi-hatted gen-darmes (who, along with their families, are also sent over for three-year stints). Again, your hotel can make arrangements and advise you as to departure times.

The points of interest outside town include a colony of summer homes, trout-filled Lake Savoyard, an abandoned bootlegger's warehouse from the Prohibition era, and **Cutty Sark Villa**, the last of the island houses built entirely of wood salvaged from liquor crates. The tour also stops at the island's cemetery on the outskirts of town. Because St. Pierre has no topsoil to speak of, the St. Pierrais bury their dead in cement vaults above ground. "Each family goes in the same hole," the driver explains cheerily. "Sometimes they're stacked four or five deep."

STAYING ON ST. PIERRE

There are four hotels and six bed-and-breakfast operations on St. Pierre. The oldest and largest, with 46 rooms (23 in the main building and 23 newer rooms in an adjacent annex called the Hôtel St. Pierre), is the three-star ▶ **Hôtel Robert**, on Quai de la République overlooking the busy harbor. This is where Al Capone stayed when he visited St. Pierre in the 1920s—a fact that Jean-Pierre Andrieux, the hotel's owner, will be happy to share with you. Andrieux personally meets the ferry from Fortune, escorts guests to his hotels, and, over a complimentary drink, offers an introduction to the island's history, as well as tips on shopping and dining. Although his hotel doesn't have a dining room, a Continental breakfast (included in the cost of your room) is offered in the bar-lounge overlooking the harbor; the St. Pierre annex has a bar and full-service dining room. In both, Andrieux has assembled collections of island artifacts, including the Pan-ama hat given to Andrieux's father by Capone during his visit.

The other three-star property in town is the ▶ **Hôtel Ile-de-France**, 6 rue M. Georges Lefèvre, with 24 small but perfectly adequate rooms and a bar-lounge and restaurant. The rooms here do not overlook the harbor, and, as at the Hôtel Robert, they do not come with telephones or television (both of which are available in the lounge). Visitors planning to stay overnight at either place will want to make reservations well in advance of their arrival. (See the Accommodations Reference list at the end of the chapter for contact information.)

DINING ON ST. PIERRE

The Golden Arches haven't yet reached this far-flung corner of France, and it's likely to be a long time before they do. Food is taken seriously here, and runs the gamut from crispy golden croissants and exquisitely decorated pastries to the richest of entrées awash in calorific sauces, glazes, and gravies. Freshness is paramount, as evidenced by the abundance of fresh seafood, the crusty breads and rolls baked daily, and the right-from-the cow dairy products.

In one important respect, however, St. Pierre is no different than the mainland: As ownership and chefs change, so too does the quality and price of a meal. For now, the best French cuisine on the island is served at **La Ciboulette** (Tel: 508/41-21-00), on rue Marcel Bonin about four blocks from the Customs House on the waterfront. A small sign identifies this unassuming little place, whose two front rooms contain rectangular tables seating up to eight people each. Reservations are recommended, and guests are seated together as they arrive—a painless way to make new friends. Seafood prepared with a semi-nouvelle touch is the house specialty, and the wine list puts most liquor stores on the mainland to shame—as do the very reasonable prices. Expect to pay $32–$42 for dinner for two, before the grape. But don't expect lightning-fast service. Dining at La Ciboulette is a leisurely, civilized affair in the classic European manner, so allow two full hours for the four-course meal.

Simpler fare at half the price prevails at **Chez Dutin** (Tel: 508/41-24-92), two blocks up from the waterfront at 20 rue Amiral Muselier, where the Dutin family has operated a restaurant for 50 years. Six tables in the unadorned front rooms seat up to eight people each. Operating on two four-burner ranges in a small, spotless kitchen, Marianne Dutin herself prepares all the food and waits on the tables; her only help is a girl who removes and washes the dishes. The happy result is traditional French cuisine as if your mother had made it.

The newest culinary experience on the island is offered in the dining room of the ▶ **Hôtel St. Pierre**, where thick steaks served sizzling hot on stone platters make for a tasty change of pace from the seafood-heavy menus elsewhere in town.

Lighter fare is available at **Le Maringouin'fre** (Tel: 508/41-36-79), a crêperie-snack bar at 22 rue Général Leclerc, and at the café in the Hôtel Ile-de-France, 6 rue M. Georges Lefèvre.

MIQUELON

Although the 25-km (16-mile) tour of Miquelon really doesn't include enough points of interest to warrant a full day on the island, treated as a leisurely outing in the country it can be a pleasant and relaxing way to spend the better part of one. Full-day tours ($65 per adult) leaving at 8:00 A.M. and returning by 6:00 P.M. can be booked through your hotel in St. Pierre. Visitors who want to explore Miquelon at their own pace can make the crossing from St. Pierre on the *St-Eugene V;* the round-trip fare is $26, and once on Miquelon you can hire a driver at the dock. For $30 round trip, five days a week, you can also make the ten-minute flight from St. Pierre in an eight-passenger Cherokee airplane. In summer there are up to five return flights daily. For further information, contact Air St. Pierre, 9 rue Albert Briand; Tel: (508) 41-47-18.

Once on the island, visitors on the organized tour are led from the ferry dock to the community center for a slide show of island sights, and then on to a restaurant for a Continental breakfast. After breakfast and a tour of the village, the bus heads out to salt ponds and wild moors ending at rugged, wave-pounded cliffs. Stops are made at a quarantine station where Charolais cattle from France once had to pass muster before being allowed into Canada; a seal colony or two; a beach that's ankle-deep in mussels; and another spot where minke whales can be seen feeding on capelin (a sardine-like fish) close to shore.

At the north end of town the ten-unit ▶ **Motel Miquelon** should open for its second season in May 1994. The units are constructed of British Columbia cedar, and include four-piece bathrooms, a master bedroom, and a small kitchenette with two-burner stove and refrigerator. But the real attraction here is peace and quiet—and plenty of it. The motel is perched above Miquelon Bay, where guests can forage for mussels and clams or work on their surf-casting. And that pretty much exhausts your activity options. For additional information and/or reservations, contact the Tourist Bureau de Miquelon; Tel: (508) 41-61-87.

Ile-aux-Marins

For the better part of 200 years, this tiny island at the mouth of St. Pierre's harbor was home to 800 fishermen and their families. For much of that time, waterfront space on St. Pierre was claimed by the owners of large vessels. On Ile-aux-Marins local fishermen found space to moor their dories and dry their fish on the rocks. But as St. Pierre schooner owners began going bankrupt in the early years of the century, more and more space became available on the St. Pierre waterfront and one by one the residents of Ile-aux-Marins moved back to the bigger island; by 1963 Ile-aux-Marins had no year-round residents.

Many of those who moved from the tiny island maintained their homes there as summer cottages. Today the government is in the process of restoring Ile-aux-Marins as an historic village. Individuals who wish to build summer homes on the island may, provided they faithfully replicate one of its original buildings. Visitors can take the ten-minute boat ride from St. Pierre to the island and wander the settlement with a guide. More than a dozen buildings have been restored to period condition, including the church, a lighthouse, a fort, the town hall, and a number of private homes. Elsewhere, many marine and fishing-related artifacts have been gathered and are on display in a museum. For ferry departure times, contact the tourist office on rue du 11 Novembre; Tel: (508) 41-22-22.

—*David E. Scott*

THE AVALON PENINSULA

The Avalon Peninsula is joined to the rest of Newfoundland by a rib of bedrock separating Trinity Bay from Placentia Bay. Geologists have determined that the peninsula split from the main European landmass some 400 million years ago and slowly drifted westward on its underlying tectonic plate before attaching itself to Newfoundland. Hardy Basque fishermen were the first Europeans to exploit its rich offshore fisheries, and in the century after John Cabot "discovered" the island they were joined by the English, French, and Spanish. The Basques were squeezed out as the others crowded in, with the Spanish suffering the same fate as their

Basque neighbors after the English defeated the Grand Armada in 1588. The French hung on for a time, but they, too, all but disappeared after the English emerged as the victors of the French and Indian Wars two centuries later. Substantial immigration in the 19th century imparted a distinctly Irish cast to the peninsula's population, which it retains to this day.

As the piece of North America nearest Europe the Avalon keeps adding its name to the history books for the "earliest this" and the "smallest that." The first successful undersea cable came ashore here in 1886. Fifteen years later Marconi dispensed with such wires when he received the first trans-Atlantic radio message on St. John's Signal Hill. The first trans-Atlantic telephone cable reached Newfoundland in 1956. Several notable aerial crossings began or ended on the Avalon as well. Today adventurers exploiting the peninsula's proximity to Europe set out in a variety of outlandish craft, risking their lives for 15 minutes of glory as the first to cross the Atlantic in . . . whatever.

The Avalon is shaped like a crude capital H, with Conception Bay and St. Mary's Bay jutting in toward the peninsula's middle. As the oldest and most settled part of Newfoundland, it has villages occupying nearly every suitable cove and a well-developed highway system. Most roads follow the coast, always the scenic choice, giving visitors several options to most destinations. On the Avalon you rarely have to retrace your steps, though some places are so lovely you may want to.

Most visitors who get this far make St. John's their base, enjoying its range of dining and entertainment options after a day on the road. There are guest homes in many of the smaller communities, however, as well as motels in the larger ones; if you find a region you especially like, chances are good you'll be able to settle in comfortably for a few days.

ST. JOHN'S

St. John's claims to be the oldest city in North America (though Mexico City might dispute the claim). As a nearly perfect harbor conveniently situated close to the Grand Banks, it was heavily visited by Europeans almost from the moment it was discovered. Named by John Cabot, who sailed into its harbor on June 27, 1497, the feast day of St. John the Baptist, it was already a major commercial hub by the time Jacques Cartier, the discoverer of the St. Lawrence

River, sailed through the Narrows in 1534 in order to resupply and repair his ships. Over the next two centuries France and Britain fought for possession of the strategic harbor, until Britain retook St. John's for the last time in 1762. Major fires have destroyed much of the city on two occasions, but the older sections still look old indeed.

St. John's rewards a walker. A harbor full of freighters and fishing boats, hills as steep and scenic as those of San Francisco, colorful wooden row houses, grand mansions, an abundance of fine stone churches, a delightful network of paths along a modest river, and residents who nod and smile at strangers—these are just some of the things visitors have to look forward to. Details on a variety of walking tours can be obtained from the city's tourism office; Tel: (709) 576-8106.

Signal Hill National Historic Site

Signal Hill, the prominent bluff that guards the entrance to the harbor, offers a striking view of the city and its approaches. The hill was heavily fortified and frequently fought over during the colonial period. Now Canada's largest national historic park, Signal Hill's attractions include the Queen's Battery fortifications, dating to the last years of the 18th century (when an ascendant France under Napoleon was once again considered a threat to England's New World possessions), and the colorful Signal Hill Tattoo, a daily reenactment of colonial-era military exercises staged throughout July and August.

Cabot Tower, at the top of the hill, was built in 1897 to commemorate the 400th anniversary of Cabot's discovery of St. John's as well as the 60th year of Queen Victoria's reign. Today the tower houses displays celebrating Marconi's triumph here in 1901.

Around the Hill

Visitors who can should walk, rather than drive, down from the hill. One trail skirts impressive cliffs on its way to the **Battery**, a delightful corner of the city where a narrow street winds between houses clinging to the steep hillside overlooking the harbor entrance. (At one point the footpath has to cross an obliging family's front porch.) The other path from the top of Signal Hill takes you to **Quidi Vidi battery**, yet another fortification built during the colonial-era struggles for the city. The annual St. John's Regatta, North America's oldest sporting event, is held on nearby **Quidi Vidi** (kiddy-viddy) **Lake**. Held the first Wednesday of August, it dates back to 1826 (some say earlier) and features hard-fought rowing contests, bands, food booths, and games of

chance that vie for the attention and disposable income of
the 50,000-plus spectators. Regatta Day is a popular provincial holiday and draws visitors—including the Queen, the
governor general, and the Canadian prime minister on different occasions in the past—from near and far; you should
have confirmed reservations if a night or two in the St. John's
area at this time of year is on your itinerary.

The lake itself spills over a set of rapids into Quidi Vidi
harbor, the setting for one of the most charming and secluded villages in the province—a delightful surprise just
minutes from the heart of the city.

Downtown

Back downtown, **Commissariat House**, on King's Bridge
Road, dates to 1821, when it housed the assistant commis-
sary general of the city's British garrison. Today it stands as
an elegant example of Georgian-period architecture; guided
tours daily during the summer. A short walk east brings you
to **St. Thomas' Anglican Church** (1836), better known as the
"Old Garrison Church," the oldest ecclesiastical structure in
the city. St. John's two other historic churches are within easy
walking distance. Dating from the mid-19th century, the
Roman Catholic **Basilica of St. John the Baptist**, on Military
Road, commands a view of the harbor and boasts twin
towers topping out at 138 feet. The impressive **Anglican
Cathedral of St. John the Baptist** (1849), a short distance to
the south at Church Hill and Gower Street, is one of the
oldest and best examples of ecclesiastical neo-Gothic architecture in North America.

Murray Premises, a beautifully preserved and restored
mercantile complex at the south end of Water Street—itself
one of the oldest thoroughfares in North America—has
been the site of commercial activity since the 16th century,
when cargoes of fish and trayne oil were bought and sold on
the spot and then shipped to trading centers in Europe.
These days it houses a variety of restaurants, cafés, and shops
specializing in European imports. You'll also find a gallery of
the **Newfoundland Museum** here, the bulk of whose excellent collection of native artifacts and seafaring paraphernalia
is housed one block to the north on Duckworth Street. The
museum is open daily year-round.

Municipal Parks

Memorial University lies within the boundaries of **Pippy
Park**, 4,000 acres of hilly woodland and lakes. Visitors to the
park can keep their golf game sharp on a nine-hole course,
pitch a tent at a full-service campground, or stroll through

the **Memorial University Botanical Gardens** at Oxen Pond.
Created by an enthusiastic botanist, the gardens contain
examples of most of the island's indigenous flora, including
dozens of flowering species not found elsewhere in Atlantic
Canada. The gardens are open May through November;
closed Mondays and Tuesdays.

Bowring Park, located on Waterford Bridge Road in the
city's west end, is a good spot to feed the swans, admire the
many fine statues here, and have a picnic in bucolic surroundings.

STAYING AND DINING IN ST. JOHN'S

St. John's boasts a number of fine hotels, all conveniently
located downtown. Most of them are rarely full except when
there's a large convention in town. The newest is the
▶ **Radisson Plaza Hotel** on New Gower Street, at the western
end of the downtown area. Built to capitalize on an offshore
oil boom that has yet to materialize, the Radisson offers
luxurious rooms and suites, a swimming pool, a sauna,
exercise facilities, and **Newman's**, a fine dining room. The
▶ **Hotel Newfoundland**, its chief competitor, is located on
Cavendish Square, just a few blocks from the shops on
Duckworth Street. The Newfoundland is the first choice of
many repeat visitors to the city, and has its own widely
patronized dining room where, according to local legend,
cod au gratin was invented. Both hotels are pricey, with the
Radisson slightly less expensive.

Among the other options in town, the ▶ **STEL Battery
Hotel** occupies a choice location on Signal Hill Road overlooking the harbor—a panorama best appreciated from its
own well-respected dining room. Though not so loftily situated, the ▶ **Journey's End Hotel** also overlooks the waterfront, and offers clean, comfortable rooms and an excellent
location on Water Street, making it perhaps the best value
for your money.

Elsewhere in St. John's, a number of fine old homes have
been converted into bed and breakfasts. One of them,
▶ **Monroe House**, at 8A Forest Road, is the home of a former
prime minister, and features three large bedrooms, each
with its own bath. The ▶ **Kincora Hospitality Home**, at 36
Kings Bridge Road, is a fine restored Victorian home with
gorgeous antique furniture and five guest rooms with bathrooms and fireplaces *en suite*. A full gourmet breakfast and
off-street parking are included in the room rate. The ▶ **Prescott Inn**, 19 Military Road, offers spacious rooms with fireplaces, a library of books about Newfoundland and Labrador,
and much original art. ▶ **Compton House**, at 26 Waterford

Bridge Road, is a grand mansion slightly farther from downtown. For a bit more than the price of a regular suite guests can opt for one of the three whirlpool suites here, each with a queen-size bed, fireplace, and Jacuzzi *en suite*. ▶ **Victoria Station**, at 290 Duckworth Street, has one of the city's better restaurants on its ground floor. Most if its ten rooms have a fireplace and kitchen, and all have private baths.

Dining in St. John's has evolved light-years from the days when a "jigg's dinner"—corned beef boiled with cabbage, potatoes, carrots, turnips, and peas—was the dietary mainstay for many Newfoundlanders. Today the island's residents, especially in St. John's, are more cosmopolitan in their eating habits, and venturesome enough to support a number of fine restaurants. In town, excellent seafood and a good wine list make the **Stone House** (Tel: 709/753-2380), a few minutes' walk from the Hotel Newfoundland at 8 Kenna's Hill, one of the city's best restaurants. The extensive menu at **The Cellar** (Tel: 709/579-8900), at Baird's Cove off Water Street (directly across from the Courthouse), includes such specialties as blackened chicken, rack of lamb, and stir-fried scallops.

Of the many Chinese restaurants in St. John's, the **Magic Wok** (Tel: 709/753-6907), despite its somewhat seedy location at 402 Water Street and unpromising appearance, is consistently good.

Adventurous diners will want to try tender pan-fried cod tongues—a delicacy in such demand that some are even imported from Europe—and flipper pie. The latter is seal meat, but from the shoulder, not the flipper. It is dark and gamey, resembles sea duck, and is highly recommended. The best place to eat flipper pie is the **Woodstock Colonial Inn** (Tel: 709/722-6933), a 15-minute drive west of St. John's on Topsail Road (Highway 60).

One other local dish worth trying is fish and brewis, an old seaman's standard that consists of salt cod stir-fried with soaked hardtack and "scrunchins," fried bits of salt pork. Though it sounds like the dreadful concoction of a particularly sadistic English boarding school cook, it's surprisingly good.

SHOPPING AND NIGHTLIFE IN ST. JOHN'S

Many of St. John's most interesting downtown specialty shops are housed in gaily painted wood-frame buildings strung out along a mile-long stretch of Duckworth and Water streets. Lately, however, the impact of recession and a glut of suburban malls has hit the downtown area hard. You know—or hope—business and real estate prices have bottomed out when a fortune teller ("97% Accuracy Guaranteed") opens up in a choice location. But a few good stores still stock items of interest to visitors. **Word Play**, a fine bookstore at 221 Duckworth, has shelves of books on Newfoundland as well as a broad selection of volumes on art, history, and travel. **Nonia**, 286 Water Street, with a good selection of outport cottage-industry products, and the **Cod Jigger**, 250 Duckworth Street near the corner of Prescott, are your best bets for provincial handicrafts. The **Newfoundland and Labrador Crafts Development Association** can take much of the credit for the high and rising quality of crafts in the province. Their displays at Devon House, 59 Duckworth Street, are well worth a visit.

One fairly new and attractive craft product to watch for is engraved slabs of pyrophyllite, also known as soapstone. Newfoundland soapstone is a soft lemon-colored stone quarried from a site not far from the city. Local craftsmen have taken to etching wildlife portraits or scenery onto its polished surface. Done well, the effect is quite striking.

For a small city, St. John's is a lively spot, attracting many of the best musicians, actors, and comedians from around the province. Something in the culture has fostered a genius for satire. In the 19th century, Johnny Burke, "the Bard of Prescott Street," wrote songs satirizing city politics and sold them on the street. Today, Johnny Burke's heirs produce witty and often outrageous comedy, much of it performed at the remarkable institution known as the **LSPU Hall**, on Duckworth Street. Formerly, the headquarters of the Long Shoreman's Protective Union, the building has been taken over by the "arts crowd" and turned into one of the cultural nerve centers of the province. Concerts, exhibits, and quality dramatic productions are among its offerings, and musical groups also perform on a little outdoors stage at lunchtime throughout the summer. For traditional music of a high caliber, especially jigs, reels, and plaintive laments, watch for groups like Figgy Duff and the Irish Descendants, or solo performers such as Jim Payne, Pamela Morgan, Kelly Russell, and Anita Best. For the all-too-rare combination of hilarious comedy and good music, watch for Buddy Wasisname and the Other Fellers. Favorite blues and jazz artists from the province include Roger House, Jeff Dyer, and Dennis Parker.

Although St. John's tends to corner the best performers, many of these and other artists are busy on the province's summer festival circuit. In St. John's itself, **Bridgett's Pub** on Cookstown Road and **Erin's Pub** on Water Street are two establishments with track records for supporting local and regional artists. **Fred's Records**, 198 Duckworth Street, is the place to get advice on Newfoundland music or to buy the tapes of any local performer who catches your fancy.

DAY TRIPS FROM ST. JOHN'S
The Avalon has so many attractive communities, you're bound to happen upon a few that go unmentioned here.

Marine Drive
To start your tour of the greater St. John's area, follow Route 30, also known as Marine Drive (which begins in the city as Logy Bay Road), north. Allowing extra time to stop, get out of the car, and take photos, you'll need only a half day to explore a series of splendid coves and villages, several with gravel beaches backed by imposing cliffs. These are some of the oldest communities in Newfoundland, although here and elsewhere the exact dates are obscure, as settlement was banned throughout the 17th and 18th centuries. People settled anyway, and sometimes chose poor harbors in order to discourage visits from the authorities. **Pouch** (pronounced "pooch") **Cove**, the last community on this route, is one of these, and may have been occupied as early as 1611. The pavement ends here, but a rough gravel road traverses the short distance to **Cape St. Francis**, a rugged, scenic headland.

Cape Spear National Historic Park
Another worthwhile half-day trip starts in downtown St. John's and follows Route 11 up and over the Southside Hills to Cape Spear, the easternmost point in North America. If you get here early enough (about 4:20 A.M. on a high summer morning) you may be able to count yourself among the first people in North America to see the sun rise. (Visitors thinking about joining the dawn patrol should check the forecast the night before; Cape Spear is often fogged in.) When it's not too windy, the experience is often made more memorable by the sound of whales blowing in the sea below. Sound sleepers who come out later in the day can poke around the park's two lighthouses, one a modern concrete structure and the other, Newfoundland's oldest, a restored wooden building dating to 1835 (open mid-June through Labour Day).

On the way back from Cape Spear consider a side trip to **Petty Harbour**, one of the most attractive and progressive fishing communities in Newfoundland. You can reach it via Route 11, which branches off Route 10 halfway back to St. John's.

Witless Bay

The three islands of the **Witless Bay Islands Ecological Reserve** are located off the coast some 48 km (30 miles) south of St. John's (take Route 10 to Bay Bulls). Here, every July and August, thousands of petrels, murres, razorbilled auks, puffins, terns, and gulls nest and hatch their young in a spectacle that has to be seen (and heard) to be believed. Boat tours out of St. John's, Bay Bulls, and Witless Bay (see below) get visitors close without actually landing on the island sanctuaries. Allow half a day for a tour of the islands and the return trip to St. John's.

Whale-watching excursions (best in June, July, and August); boat tours of scenic **Conception Bay**; and excursions to the seabird colonies south of the city leave at various times throughout the day from St. John's harbor, as well as from the historic village of **Bay Bulls**, south of St. John's on Route 10. For information on these and other options, contact **Harbor Charters** (Tel: 709/726-5000) in St. John's, or **O'Brian's Bird Island Charters/Humpback Tours** (Tel: 709/753-4850) in Bay Bulls.

Touring the Avalon Peninsula

Avalon Wilderness Reserve

If, instead of returning to St. John's, you decide to continue south via Route 10 along the Avalon's "Southern Shore," you'll end up looping around the peninsula's unpopulated interior, much of which is protected as the Avalon Wilderness Reserve. The reserve is home to a herd of about 5,000 woodland caribou that roam back and forth over the protected barrenlands feeding on lichen and moss. In spring and summer, when the animals extend their range southward, the highway outside of **Trepassy** is one of the best places to see them. Although you need a permit to enter, the reserve also has one canoe route and numerous hiking trails; for permits and further information, contact the Parks Division, Dept. of Tourism & Culture, P.O. Box 8700, St. John's, Nfld. A1B 4J6; Tel: (709) 729-2424; Fax: (709) 729-1100.

Trepassy itself dates to the early 17th century, when it was the principal settlement of an ill-fated Welsh colony. Today it offers visitors a small regional museum, comfortable accommodations at the 12-unit ▶ **Trepassy Motel & Tourist Home**, and good fishing in area streams.

Trepassy to the Trans-Canada

In the village of St. Stephens, about 30 km (19 miles) west of Trepassy, Route 10 becomes Route 90 and swings north.

Frequented by Basque fishermen centuries ago, this area now attracts visitors to its two provincial parks, **Holyrood Pond** and **Point La Haye**, with overnight camping facilities at the former. Route 90 continues north through the community of St. **Mary's**, where the Irish heritage of its residents is still very much in evidence, and then heads inland until it hits the Salmonier Arm of St. Mary's Bay. From there the road veers to the northeast past the Salmonier River (one of the best salmon rivers on the peninsula) and **Salmonier Nature Park**, an enclosed 40-hectare reserve that's home to more than a dozen species of indigenous birds and animals. From early June through Labour Day the park is open Wednesday through Sunday, noon to 7:00 P.M.

From the park it's another 12 km (7 miles) to the Trans-Canada (Highway 1) and either St. John's, to the east, or the rest of the province to the west.

Cape St. Mary's

One of Newfoundland's most spectacular bird sanctuaries is found at Cape St. Mary's, at the very tip of the Avalon's southwest horn. From St. John's, 200 km (120 miles) to the northeast, motorists have a choice of routes: the Trans-Canada west to Route 100 and then south to the cape, or the Trans-Canada to Route 81 south, Route 91 west, and Route 100 south. The latter option, though longer and unpaved in spots, takes you by scenic **Cataracts Provincial Park**, with its two photogenic waterfalls.

Whatever your choice of routes, the sanctuary itself is a half-hour walk from the lighthouse where you'll have to park your car. From the middle of June to the middle of August, about 50,000 pairs of gannets (the second-largest gannet colony in North America) hatch and raise their young on a towering sea stack separated from bird-watchers and photographers by a 300-foot chasm. Murres nest among the gannets, and kittiwakes occupy the narrow ledges on the cliff below. While it's an unforgettable experience for even casual visitors, take note that the Cape St. Mary's area is wild and barren, with steep cliffs and gusty winds; caution should be exercised at all times when viewing or photographing the birds.

Placentia

Placentia, north of Cape St. Mary's and about a 90-minute drive west of St. John's off Route 100 (reached via the Trans-Canada), is the one place on the peninsula outside of St. John's that demands a visit. At one time the French capital of Newfoundland, Placentia was built on a bar between two river estuaries overlooked by fortified hills. The principal fortifications, which were built and bolstered during the 17th and 18th centuries by the French and then the English, have been excavated, restored, and protected as part of **Castle Hill National Historic Park**. In addition to the fortifications and gorgeous views of Placentia Bay, visitors will find an interpretive center with artifacts from the fort as well as what is perhaps the oldest gravestone on the island, that of the famous privateer Captain John Svigaricipi, who was buried in 1694. Trails link the various structures on the grounds, and there are a number of picnic tables for those who pack a lunch. The park is open daily year-round.

LABRADOR

Labrador, the huge mainland portion of the province, is larger than Newfoundland and the other Atlantic provinces combined. It's also difficult and costly to reach, although the rewards to wilderness and outdoors enthusiasts are great. In large part this is because Labrador's very remoteness has spared much of its wilderness from development while preserving many elements of its traditional culture.

For resourceful visitors, Labrador offers a blend of sights and experiences few other regions can match. Along its far north coast, eastern Canada's highest mountains rise from sea level to heights of more than 5,000 feet. Inland, the world's largest caribou herd roams the Labrador–Ungava Peninsula, and lakes and rivers too numerous to count offer Atlantic salmon and trophy-size brook trout. All along Labrador's bare and rugged coast, humpback whales cruise and porpoises gambol in the shadow of cliffs and icebergs, while nesting colonies of hundreds of thousands of seabirds fill the air with their clamor.

Despite its sparse population (roughly 35,000 spread over an area the size of Colorado), Labrador is more culturally diverse than Newfoundland, with a blend of native peoples, mixed-blood settlers, and fairly recent immigrants from the "South" drawn to its wilderness by large-scale construction projects. This diversity is one of the fascinations of the region, even if visitors often find themselves confusing the Innu (Indian) with the Inuit (Eskimo) people.

Not surprisingly, Labradorians display a fierce pride in

their history and culture. This pride is vividly reflected in the publication called *Them Days Magazine,* a unique and highly regarded oral history quarterly that has been put out by a small staff for nearly 20 years. Anyone who wants to understand Labrador and its people should pick up a copy.

Transportation links to and within Labrador are improving but still basic. The different types of networks do not mesh easily, which tends to chop the territory into regions with little but their remoteness in common. (The various travel options for visitors are more fully discussed in the Getting Around section below.)

One further note: While the vast majority of visitors arrive in the province in summer, some areas are actively promoting winter tourism. Labrador is one of them. For that matter, many Labradorians prefer winter, especially the late winter, when the sun is high and days start getting longer. In Labrador, this is the season of carnivals, snowmobile races, dog-team races, and cross-country ski touring.

THE COAST

Although the Labrador coast is a land of stern beauty, in summer the harshness eases and a visitor can enjoy its natural splendor. What he or she will find then is an Arctic landscape in a sub-Arctic latitude, with caribou, Arctic hare, gyrfalcons, and occasional polar bears to prove it. But black flies and mosquitoes can spoil it, so be sure to carry insect repellent and pray for a breeze.

Southern Labrador, an area sometimes called the Labrador Straits (for which see the Western Newfoundland section above), is the only part of the coast accessible by paved road.

Eastern Labrador, the area to the north of the Strait of Belle Isle, is a fascinating, little-known region where many people still migrate between their summer fishing stations on the coast and a handful of larger winter communities situated in the shelter of deep bays. Pack ice in the spring and stormy weather in the fall make for a short fishing season. As a result, the people who live here have always had to secure part of their livelihood from the game, fur, berries, and firewood that the wilderness provides. Many know their environment intimately and make superb guides. And though they are just as friendly as Newfoundlanders, it may take them a bit longer to warm up. If you linger among them, however, you're bound to make friends you won't forget.

Alas, tourist facilities are limited and there are no roads into the area or between communities. Scheduled bush plane service from Goose Bay and St. Anthony is one way in. Coastal boats are another. Those willing to improvise and take their chances on meals and accommodation can try to hire local fishermen to run them by boat from one village to the next. Visitors willing to travel in this fashion can set their own pace—as long as that pace is not too fast. Don't expect a tight schedule to mean much here. And be sure to plan every scheduled movement with the caution, "weather permitting."

There are small hotels in **Mary's Harbour**, **Port Hope Simpson**, **Charlottetown**, and **Cartwright**. Most area villages also have at least one house that commonly boards visitors. If you get to Mary's Harbour, try to find someone to take you to historic **Battle Harbour**. Once a major trading and service center for the area, Battle Harbour is now all but abandoned, although it is in the process of being restored.

Labrador Leisure Tours and Charters (Tel: 709/938-7254 after 6:00 P.M.), in Cartwright, offers excursions to a seabird sanctuary on the Gannet Islands, where you can see murres, puffins, razorbills, and terns. Humpback whales are common at times, and minke whales even more so. Icebergs are another regular feature of the early summer seascape along this coast.

Northern Labrador, the region north of Lake Melville, the long saltwater inlet that divides the territory, is the home of the majority of Labrador's Inuit, about half its Innu, and many of its more recent settlers. A region rich in fish and game, it has been the scene of cultural clashes ever since the Maritime Archaic people, who occupied the coast unchallenged for almost 4,000 years, succumbed to the first of a series of Eskimo migrations from the north. Since then, other peoples have drifted in, dominated the region for a time, then given way to still others from the north, south, and, eventually, Europe.

Today the people of northern Labrador are again dealing with radical change, and paying a high price in terms of cultural stress and dislocation. Unemployment in the region is high and alcohol abuse severe in some communities.

Yet northern Labrador offers sights and experiences unlike anyplace else. Many of them are hard to reach. The **Torngat Mountains**, far to the north of **Nain**, the region's northernmost community, are as high and wild as any adventurer could hope for. In recent years climbers and kayakers have discovered this spectacular country, even though it takes a chartered bush plane or fishing boat to get there. The same is true of the old mission buildings at **Hebron**, north of Nain, and now a national historic site.

For those travellers with less time and money to spend,

splendid wild country is accessible by boat from any of the region's coastal communities. **Tasiujatsoak Wilderness Camp** (Fax: 709/922-2823), operating out of Nain, offers canoeing, hiking, and whale- and seal-watching in the company of Inuit guides.

In the various communities themselves, local museums and crafts stores offer insights into the region's culture and history. There are small local museums in Nain and Hopedale, and crafts stores in each of the villages. Hopedale is also the site of old mission buildings, one of them the oldest wooden frame structure in eastern Canada. It, too, has been declared a national historic site and is undergoing restoration.

In recent years the quality of Inuit carvings available in Nain and other communities has improved markedly. Materials today include not only the traditional soapstone but a remarkable semiprecious stone known as **labradorite**, found in great abundance in the area. Labradorite flashes dazzling colors, most commonly peacock blue.

THE LAKE MELVILLE AREA

Despite its freshwater name, Lake Melville is a long tidewater fjord that penetrates into the heart of Labrador. As recently as 1942 there were only two small trappers' settlements at its western end. That same year, however, construction began on a massive military airfield, and the prospect of construction jobs at good wages drew struggling fishermen in from the coast. They and their families soon founded Happy Valley next to the air base, which itself became known as Goose Bay.

Today **Happy Village–Goose Bay** is the administrative and supply center for much of Labrador, as well as the unofficial capital of a vast wilderness region on the verge of being discovered by the outside world. A cultural highlight of the region, usually held in August, is the **Labrador Canoe Regatta**, featuring canoe races, music, and traditional foods. Ask also about the **Labrador Heritage Museum**, which has tools of the trapper's trade as well as relics of the infamous Hubbard Expedition, in which a brash young American outdoors writer ventured too far into the wilderness and ended up starving to death.

While you're here, try to arrange a boat trip across the Churchill River to **Mud Lake**, which despite its name is one of the most charming villages in all of Labrador. There are no roads in the community and thus no vehicles—except for snowmobiles, which dart everywhere in winter and lapse into welcome silence in summer. Mud Lake's tidy house are built along a narrow channel and connected only by footpaths, with Labrador's endless spruce forest as their backdrop.

There are three hotels and two bed and breakfasts in the Happy Valley–Goose Bay area. Among the former is the ▶ **Labrador Inn**, a full-service hotel with 73 rooms, a dining room, and a bar and lounge. Hotel prices are substantially higher than at similar establishments in Newfoundland, ranging from $65 to $100 a night for a double room.

Goose Bay Outfitters Ltd. (P.O. Box 171, Happy Valley, Labrador A0P 1E0; Tel: 709/896-2423 in summer) has lodges on various lakes and rivers in the region; Frank Phillips, the Director of Labrador Services (2 Hillcrest Road, Happy Valley, Labrador A0P 1E0; Tel: 709/896-0241), will also be happy to provide information on fishing camps, some of them located 200 to 300 miles north of Happy Valley–Goose Bay in an unimaginably vast wilderness area.

North West River and **Sheshatsheits** occupy opposite sides of a small river about 48 km (30 miles) northeast of Goose Bay. Sheshatsheits, an Innu community, was established some 40 years ago by people whose ancestors had roamed the Labrador interior for thousands of years, living chiefly off caribou. North West River, a much older community, is an early trappers' settlement and the former Labrador headquarters for the Grenfell Mission. Like Mud Lake, it was established before the invention of the automobile and so has the look of a place where most people walk. The town's residents are the mixed-blood descendants of English, French, and Scots traders and trappers and their native wives.

Be sure to check out the local crafts store while you're here, and don't miss the studio of **John Goudie**, a silversmith who creates wonderful silver rings and brooches inlaid with labradorite and walrus ivory. **Labrador Scenic** (Tel: 709/497-8326), an adventure tour company that operates out of North West River, offers day trips as well as longer canoe and wilderness trips into the empty reaches north of Lake Melville.

WESTERN LABRADOR

Both in scale and style, western Labrador is a world apart from the more traditional communities of central and coastal Labrador. In this region, technology on a huge scale rules the day.

Above all else, western Labrador is a land of superlatives. At **Churchill Falls**, the biggest river in the province has been diverted from its cascades and channeled into turbines to generate electricity for New York State. In **Labrador City** and **Wabush**, giant trucks haul ore from immense open-pit iron mines. All three communities began as company towns, created to house and serve employees. These days the mining communities, especially, are struggling to find alternatives to their vulnerable one-industry economies, although they are not without charms. **Duley Lake Provincial Park** west of Labrador City has camping sites, picnic areas, and a sandy beach (don't forget your wet suit). In **Grand Hermine Park** lucky visitors may catch glimpses of wild foxes and resting caribou.

For summer visitors, this is great canoe and sportfishing country as well. Western Labrador is a vast plateau that, from the air, seems to be at least 50 percent water; the lakes and streams in the region abound with brook trout, lake trout, pike, and landlocked salmon. **Drover's Labrador Adventures** (Tel: 709/944-6947), in Labrador City, offers canoe trips, forest hikes, caribou hunts, and spectacular fishing. **Labrador Adventure** (Tel: 709/925-3235), in Churchill Falls, offers four- and six-day tours that include river running in speed boats, touring the underground powerhouse at the hydro complex, and more great fishing.

There are two hotels in Labrador City, one in Wabush, and one in Churchill Falls. The ► **Lobstick Lodge & Motel**, the only other accommodation in the area, is located 378 km (234 miles) west of Goose Bay and 84 km (53 miles) east of Churchill Falls, and has 16 rooms usually filled with caribou hunters and sportfishermen.

GETTING AROUND

Newfoundland

Newfoundland is serviced by Air Canada and Canadian Airlines International and their subsidiaries, Air Nova and Air Atlantic, respectively, through airports at St. John's, Gander, Stephenville, Deer Lake, and St. Anthony. Although there's regularly scheduled service to St. John's from a number of larger cities in both Canada and the United States, the most convenient and frequent connection from the mainland is a direct Toronto–St. John's flight.

Visitors to Newfoundland with the luxury of time will quickly realize that the best way to see the island is by car or camper. Most major car-rental agencies (Avis, Budget, Hertz, Thrifty, Tilden) have desks at the airports mentioned above, as well as at the major ferry terminals.

Bus service on the island tends to be regional in nature.

Fleetline Bus Company Ltd. (Tel: 709/722-2608) serves the Conception Bay area from St. John's. At the other end of the island, Viking Express (Tel: 709/634-4710) offers regular service to the Great Northern Peninsula from its depot in Corner Brook. Most of the regional carriers offer connecting service to CN Roadcruiser Service's daily cross-island Trans-Canada runs. For information on the latter, Tel: (709) 737-5916.

For visitors with their own vehicles, Newfoundland is connected to the mainland by Marine Atlantic ferries operating between North Sydney, Nova Scotia, and Channel-Port aux Basques, at the southwestern tip of the island, or Argentia (summer only) on the west coast of the Avalon Peninsula (just an hour and a half by car from St. John's). Ferries (usually the M.V. *Caribou,* Canada's largest ferryboat) run twice *daily* (more frequently on Sundays and Mondays in summer) between North Sydney and Port aux Basques (a five-hour trip one way), and twice *weekly* between North Sydney and Argentia (a 12-hour run on the M.V. *Clara and Joseph Smallwood*). The Argentia run is usually booked a month in advance. In summer, a week or less is all the advance notice needed to book a spot on the ferry to Port aux Basques.

Marine Atlantic also offers ferry and passenger-ship service to many parts of Newfoundland that cannot be reached by car. For information, contact Marine Atlantic at (709) 695-7081; Fax: (709) 695-4209; in the U.S., Tel: (800) 341-7981.

Eastern Labrador

Although visitors can reach Labrador by air, sea, and land, the options are limited, especially to and along the coast.

Labrador's three major airports at Goose Bay, Churchill Falls, and Wabush are served by Canadian Airlines International as well as several small regional carriers, with scheduled service from St. John's, Halifax, and Montreal. Labrador Airways, operating out of Goose Bay, flies to smaller airstrips in the major coastal communities. A number of bush plane companies, using float-equipped aircraft, will fly you almost anywhere in the province.

Other travel options include various combinations of road, rail, ferry, and coastal boat, described by region below.

From central Newfoundland, the direct Lewisporte–Goose Bay run, which takes 34 hours one way, is an unforgettable sub-Arctic experience filled with icebergs, seals, whales, and—in calm, sunny weather—the famous northern mirages in which islands appear to be floating in the sky. The ferry, the M.V. *Sir Robert Bond,* operates twice-weekly from mid-June through mid-September. It is also heavily booked; reservations should be made through Marine Atlantic (Tel: 709/535-6876; in the U.S., 800/341-7981) as many months in advance as possible.

Coastal Boats. The moratorium on the northern cod fishery has opened up one of the best and most unusual travel bargains in Canada: touring the Labrador coast on a working freighter. The service is intended chiefly for coastal residents, who have few other means of getting around, as well as for Newfoundlanders who have fished off Labrador for generations. Before the moratorium, Marine Atlantic had to strictly limit tourist access to these vessels to keep from displacing the people for whom the service was intended. But the moratorium has cut passenger traffic heavily, and so tourists are now welcome.

Two vessels, the *Northern Ranger* and the *Taverner,* sail between Lewisporte and Nain, the northernmost community in Labrador. Along the way they cruise a glorious coastline and stop at tiny, unimaginably scenic fishing villages, dropping off everything from groceries to snowmobiles and furniture. The total round trip is generally 15 days, with one vessel leaving Lewisporte every eight days. The *Northern Ranger* is newer and more comfortable, but the *Taverner* has a gritty charm of its own. Genial crews, fascinating passengers, and a pronounced informality add to the satisfactions of this voyage. Marine Atlantic has plans to aggressively promote the service, so reservations are advised. Although the fare as of this writing was unsettled, travellers should expect something in the neighborhood of $700 one way.

Visitors often arrive in Labrador by one mode of transport and leave by another. For example, you can fly into Goose Bay via commercial jetliner, take the coastal boat to Nain and points north, and then take the ferry to Lewisporte in Newfoundland. A word of advice, however: On the freighter/passenger vessels, the northbound boats stop longer in each community, as most of the freight they carry originates in Lewisporte and is unloaded as the boat proceeds up the coast. Southbound, the boats may stop only long enough to pick up passengers and mail.

Central Labrador

The completion in 1992 of the 480-km (300-mile) road from Esker to Happy Valley–Goose Bay has at last given the latter community, at the western end of Lake Melville, a road connection (albeit primitive) into the interior. It also offers adventurous visitors who arrive by ferry in Goose Bay a surface route to central Labrador. Visitors contemplating this option should know that the road is at the farthest reaches of the provincial highway system. Long stretches of it are rough gravel, road conditions will vary with the weather, and services are scarce.

Western Labrador

Visitors to the region now have three choices: The **Quebec North Shore and Labrador Railway**, built to haul iron ore from Schefferville, Quebec, north of Esker and Churchill Falls, to Sept-Iles, Quebec, a tidewater port on the St. Lawrence, is obliged to carry cars and passengers as well, although not to make it easy for them. (It does not accept credit cards, for example.) The train leaves Sept-Iles on Mondays and Thursdays, and traverses some of the most spectacular scenery in eastern North America. Your vehicle follows on a freight train a day or two later, and is carried as far north as Labrador City, where you're reunited with it. The service is popular, but not enough so to make reservations necessary. For further information, Tel: (709) 944-8205.

A more recent and adventurous option is to drive the partially paved highway from Baie Comeau, Quebec, on the north shore of the St. Lawrence estuary, to Labrador City, a distance of 581 km (360 miles). If you decide to do it, be sure to carry plenty of cash and at least one spare tire, and ask about services along the road before you leave Baie Comeau. The country through which you'll pass is just being opened up, and the amenities of travel are virtually nonexistent.

The road from Baie Comeau is part of the long-awaited **Trans-Labrador Highway**, the western portion of which has just been connected to the Quebec highway system. Until recently, the only surface option to Churchill Falls was shipping your car to Labrador City (see above), and then driving on a well-maintained gravel road from there. Now, however, bridges on the western portion of the Trans-Labrador Highway have been completed, providing motorists a direct (albeit long and dusty) link between Labrador City and the Quebec road network.

St. Pierre and Miquelon

By Air. In summer, Air St. Pierre offers up to four flights a week from Halifax, Nova Scotia; three flights a week from Sydney, Nova Scotia; and two flights a week from Montreal's Mirabel Airport. Provincial Airways offers three flights a week from St. John's, Newfoundland.

By Boat. You can drive to Fortune, Newfoundland, on the Burin Peninsula, and make the crossing (passengers only, $47.95 for adults) to St. Pierre on either the 200-seat *St-*

Eugène V (leaving at 2:15 P.M. daily) or the 90-passenger *Arethusa* (leaving at 1:15 P.M. daily). The crossing takes 1 hour and 45 minutes on the *Arethusa,* and only 55 minutes on the *St-Eugène V,* which zips along at a bracing 32 knots per hour. For reservations on the *St-Eugène,* Tel: (709) 832-2006 or 0429; on the *Arethusa,* Tel: (709) 832-0429.

By Package Tour. SPM Tours Ltd. offers a variety of packages originating in St. John's. Packages include reduced rates at the luxury Radisson Hotel in St. John's, round-trip transportation from St. John's to Fortune, the ferry crossing to St. Pierre and back, and accommodations in St. Pierre. For further information and/or reservations, contact: SPM Tours Ltd., 38 Gear Street, St. John's, Nfld. A1C 2J5; Tel: (709) 722-3892.

By Cruise Ship. From mid-June to Labour Day, the 600-passenger M.V. *Gruziya* makes six-night, seven-day round-trip cruises to St. Pierre and Miquelon from Montreal. The ship docks in St. Pierre for only five hours, however, allowing passengers time enough for a quick tour of the island, and little else. Other points of interest on the voyage include the St. Lawrence and Sanguenay rivers; Charlottetown, P.E.I., Percé Rock and Gaspé on Quebec's Gaspé Peninsula; and Quebec City itself. Your travel agent has details. If interested, be sure to book early; this cruise is always booked months in advance.

ACCOMMODATIONS REFERENCE

The rates given below are projections for peak seasons during the 1994 calendar year; at other times of the year they may be considerably less. Unless otherwise indicated, rates are based on double rooms, double occupancy; provincial and federal taxes are included in all rates. As rates are subject to change, always double-check before booking.

▶ **Albatross Motel.** P.O. Box 450, Highway 1, **Gander**, Nfld. A1V 1W8. Tel: (709) 256-3956; Fax: (709) 651-2692; in Canada, Tel: (800) 563-4900. $95.

▶ **Anchor Inn Motel.** P.O. Box 550, **Twillingate**, Nfld. A0G 4M0. Tel: (709) 884-2776; Fax: (709) 884-2326. $66 (motel units); $84 (housekeeping units; $462 weekly).

▶ **Brake's Hospitality Home.** 25 Cooper's Road, **Corner Brook**, Nfld. A2H 3Y8. Tel: (709) 785-2077. $40 (includes breakfast).

▶ **Compton House.** 26 Waterford Bridge Road, **St. John's**, Nfld. A1E 1C6. Tel: (709) 739-5789. $82–$118 (includes breakfast).

▶ **Glynmill Inn.** P.O. Box 550, **Corner Brook**, Nfld. A2H

6E6. Tel: (709) 634-5181; Fax: (709) 634-5106; in Canada, Tel: (800) 563-4400. $70–$91.

▶ **Granny's Motor Inn.** P.O. Box 809, Highway Bypass, **Grand Bank**, Nfld. A0E 1W0. Tel: (709) 832-2180 or 2355; Fax: (709) 832-0009. $70.

▶ **Holiday Inn Clarenville.** P.O. Box 967, **Clarenville**, Nfld. A0E 1J0. Tel: (709) 466-7911; Fax: (709) 466-3854; in the U.S. and Canada, Tel: (800) HOLIDAY. $120.

▶ **Holiday Inn Downtown.** 48 West Street, **Corner Brook**, Nfld. A2H 2Z2. Tel: (709) 634-5381; Fax: (709) 634-1723; in the U.S. and Canada, Tel: (800) HOLIDAY. $106–$120.

▶ **Hotel Gander.** 100 Trans-Canada Highway, **Gander**, Nfld. A1V 1P5. Tel: (709) 256-3931; Fax: (709) 651-2641; in the Atlantic provinces, Tel: (800) 563-2988. $73–$85.

▶ **Hôtel Ile-de-France.** 6 rue Maître Georges Lefèvre, **St. Pierre et Miquelon**, France. Tel: (508) 41-31-62 (dial international operator first). $100.

▶ **Hotel Newfoundland.** P.O. Box 5637, Cavendish Square, **St. John's**, Nfld. A1C 5W8. Tel: (709) 726-4980; Fax: (709) 726-2025; in the U.S., Tel: (800) 828-7447; in Canada, Tel: (800) 268-9411. $156–$200.

▶ **Hôtel Robert.** Contact: SPM Tours Ltd., 38 Gear Street, **St. John's**, Nfld. A1C 2J5. Tel: (709) 722-3892; Fax: (709) 722-9243. $288 (two-night minimum; includes round-trip fare from Fortune, complimentary cocktail, and information session).

▶ **Hotel St. Pierre.** Contact: SPM Tours Ltd., 38 Gear Street, **St. John's**, Nfld. A1C 2J5. Tel: (709) 722-3892; Fax: (709) 722-9243. $310 (two-night minimum; includes round-trip fare from Fortune, Continental breakfast, complimentary cocktail, and information session).

▶ **Journey's End Hotel.** 2 Hill O'Chips, **St. John's**, Nfld. A1C 6B1. Tel: (709) 754-7788; Fax: (709) 754-5209; in the U.S. and Canada, Tel: (800) 668-4200. $114.

▶ **Kincora Hospitality Home.** 36 King Bridge Road, **St. John's**, Nfld. A1C 3K6. Tel: (709) 576-7415. $62–$77 (includes full breakfast).

▶ **Labrador Inn.** P.O. Box 58, Station C, **Goose Bay**, Labrador A0P 1C0. Tel: (709) 896-3351; Fax: (709) 896-3927; in Newfoundland, Tel: (800) 563-2763. $100.

▶ **Labrador Salmon Lodge.** P.O. Box 96, **Forteau**, Labrador A0K 2P0. Tel: (709) 931-2913. Rates available upon request.

▶ **Lobstick Lodge & Motel.** Contact: P.O. Box 86, **Churchill Falls**, Labrador A0R 1A0. Tel: (709) 925-3235. Rates available upon request.

▶ **Monroe House.** 8A Forest Road, **St. John's**, Nfld. A1C 2B9. Tel: (709) 754-0610. $77.

▶ **Motel Miquelon.** Contact: Tourist Bureau de Miquelon, 1 rue Antoine Soucy, **St. Pierre et Miquelon,** France. Tel: (508) 41-61-87 or (508) 41-63-10. $62.

▶ **Motel Mortier.** P.O. Box 487, **Marystown,** Nfld. A0E 2M0. Tel: (709) 279-1600; Fax: (709) 279-4088. $54–$90; $96 (housekeeping units).

▶ **Mount Peyton Hotel.** 214 Lincoln Road, **Grand Falls–Windsor,** Nfld. A2A 1P8. Tel: (709) 489-2252; Fax: (709) 489-6365; in Atlantic Canada, Tel: (800) 563-4894 (reservations only). $97 (hotel); $96 (efficiency); $86 (motel).

▶ **Northern Light Inn.** General Delivery, **L'Anse au Clair,** Labrador A0K 3K0. Tel: (709) 931-2332; Fax: (709) 931-2708. $70–$86.

▶ **Pinware River Lodge.** C/o Arthur Fowler, **L'Anse-au-Loupe,** Labrador A0K 3L0. Tel: (709) 925-5789. Or: 3 E. Huron Street, Chicago, IL 60611. Rates available upon request.

▶ **Prescott Inn.** 17–19 Military Road, **St. John's,** Nfld. A1C 2C3. Tel: (709) 753-6036. $75 (includes breakfast).

▶ **Radisson Plaza Hotel.** 120 New Gower Street, **St. John's,** Nfld. A1C 6K4. Tel: (709) 739-6404; Fax: (709) 570-1622; in the U.S. and Canada, Tel: (800) 333-3333. $156–$168.

▶ **Saint Anthony Motel.** P.O. Box 475, **St. Anthony,** Nfld. A0K 4S0. Tel: (709) 454-3200; Fax: (709) 454-2402. $65–$72.

▶ **Seven Oaks Island Inn & Cottages.** P.O. Box 57, **Change Islands,** Nfld A0G 1R0. Tel: (709) 621-3256 (in season); Tel: (709) 635-2247 (off season). $60–$78; $102 (housekeeping units).

▶ **STEL Battery Hotel.** 100 Signal Hill Road, **St. John's,** Nfld. A1A 1B3. Tel: (709) 576-0040; Fax: (709) 576-6943; in the U.S. and Canada, Tel: (800) 563-8181. $83–$119.

▶ **Tickle Inn.** P.O. Box 62, R.R. 1, **Cape Onion,** Nfld. A0K 4J0. Tel: (709) 452-4321 (in season); (709) 739-5503 (off season). $48.

▶ **Trepassy Motel & Tourist Home.** General Delivery, Route 10, **Trepassy,** Nfld. A0A 4B0. Tel: (709) 438-2934. $55.

▶ **Valhalla Lodge.** P.O. Box 10, **Gunners Cove,** Nfld. A0K 2X0. Tel: (709) 623-2018; Fax: (709) 623-2144. $50 (includes breakfast).

▶ **Victoria Station.** 290 Duckworth Street, **St. John's,** Nfld. A1C 1H3. Tel: (709) 722-1290; Fax: (709) 722-2483. $78–$102.

▶ **Village Inn.** P.O. Box 10, **Trinity,** Nfld. A0C 2S0. Tel: (709) 464-3269; Fax: (709) 464-3700. $60.

▶ **Vinland Motel.** P.O. Box 400, **St. Anthony,** Nfld. A0K 4S0. Tel: (709) 454-8843; Fax: (709) 454-8468. $85.

MONTRÉAL

By Mary Kelly

Mary Kelly, a communications consultant in Montréal, is the author of a guidebook to the city as well as a contributor to several books about the province of Québec.

Wedged between Mont-Royal and the St. Lawrence River, Montréal attracts nearly six million visitors annually with a vigorous mixture of French and English cultures, food and fashion, international film, jazz, and comedy festivals, and spirited conviviality. Two-thirds of Montréal's three million inhabitants claim French as their mother tongue; English-speaking Canadians and more than a hundred other ethnic minorities (*les autres* to Francophones) make up the other third. This unusual combination of sensibilities and speech makes the city unlike any other in North America.

Montréal is richly endowed with distinctive *quartiers:* Vieux-Montréal, where the city was born in 1642; the Golden Square Mile, cradle of Canada's 19th-century commercial aristocracy; Plateau Mont-Royal, traditional first address of the city's immigrants; and half a dozen other less-storied but equally interesting neighborhoods. Along with its neighborhoods, Québec's largest city abounds in many other singular attractions.

MAJOR INTEREST

Lachine Rapids
Dining and cafés, especially for French cuisine
Vieux-Montréal and the Vieux-Port
Shopping in the Underground City
Musée des beaux-arts de Montréal
Parc du Mont-Royal for nature and panoramic views

Parc Olympique (site of 1976 Summer Olympics)

Montréal Botanical Garden

Château Dufresne museum of decorative arts

Oratoire St-Joseph

Parc des Iles (site of Expo '67)

Annual events: International Fireworks Competition, World Film Festival, International Jazz Festival, Juste Pour Rire comedy festival

The Rapids

The most dramatic way to discover firsthand why Montréal was established where it was—on the south shore of an anvil-shaped island in the St. Lawrence River—is to sign up with **Lachine Rapids Tours** (Tel: 514/284-9607), a company that takes passengers nine miles upstream for jet boating among the angry whitecaps of the Lachine Rapids. With luck, the day will be sunny and warm, and Jack Kowalski, an ebullient Pennsylvanian and one of the company's owners, will be on board to provide an irreverent and amusing commentary, in English and French, on the city and its river.

The excursion is a reminder that Québec's largest metropolis is not only a river city like London, Paris, and Vienna but also one of the world's great island cities, comfortably seated in the first row of the second rank (to paraphrase Somerset Maugham) behind New York, Hong Kong, Singapore, and Venice.

Kowalski's aluminum-hulled vessel, named *Saute-Mouton* (Leapfrog), slips away from **Quai Victoria** in Montréal harbor and glides upstream on the swiftly flowing St. Lawrence. At first, its course is crowded with wharves, jetties, and islands, but soon the river bellies out to lake-size proportions.

Downstream at Québec City, the 750-mile-long St. Lawrence broadens into an estuary, a mighty, tide-tugged arm of the sea that beckoned Jacques Cartier in 1535 with its promise of a waterway to the Far East. From there the French explorer navigated the river inland to an island crowned by a wooded mountain and stepped in broad terraces. One of these was the site of a palisaded Iroquois village called Hochelaga. The hospitable Indians welcomed Cartier with dancing and a feast. Later they led him to the summit, which he named for the cardinal of the Medicis, who had been Bishop of Monreale in Sicily (Monreale became Mont-Royal in French). The navigator planted a wooden cross on the ridgetop and caught his first glimpse of the rapids to the west. Beyond, said the Iroquois, lay a freshwater sea. And beyond that, Cartier might have speculated, his mind dazzled by visions of pearls, spices, and silks, lay China.

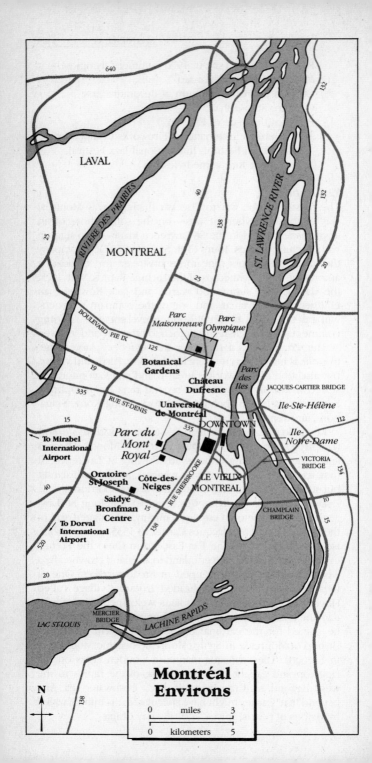

Montréal Environs

N

0 — miles — 3

0 — kilometers — 5

Alas, between the dream and the destination flashed dangerous white water—the rapids—and Cartier reluctantly turned back. He had unknowingly reached the head of deepwater navigation on the St. Lawrence, where journeys by oceangoing vessels had to be continued by rivercraft. At that terminus, the settlement of Montréal would rise a century later.

Back aboard the *Saute-Mouton,* the same impediment faced by Cartier looms into view. Passengers hunker down under slickers and sou'westers as the skipper regales all hands with tales of other daredevils who challenged the rapids: first, Etienne Brûlé, Canada's original *coureur de bois,* who lived among the Hurons, learned their language, and became a liaison between them and French fur traders; next, Cartier's successor, Samuel de Champlain, the "Father of New France"; and, much later still, during the age of Victorian tourism, the 18-year-old Prince of Wales (later Edward VII), who enjoyed a rollicking ride in 1860 on a steamboat piloted by a Kahnawake Indian in full traditional dress.

Within seconds the jet boat plunges into a maelstrom, bucking and churning in water that boils over sedan-sized boulders, only the first skirmish in a 30-minute battle as the boat slaloms back and forth through the rapids on a route designed to generate maximum thrills. The St. Lawrence regularly sweeps over the windshield in great sheets.

The half-hour return trip to Quai Victoria provides an opportunity to dry out and admire the Montréal skyline silhouetted against the green ridge of Mont-Royal, with the vast dome of the Oratoire St-Joseph peering over the upland's western shoulder. To the right, freighters ease through the St. Lambert Lock on the St. Lawrence Seaway (the modern 2,300-mile waterway that would have enabled Cartier to bypass the rapids).

The *Saute-Mouton* slips beneath Route 112's Victoria Bridge, the longest in the world at the time of its completion in 1859 and the first to span the St. Lawrence. The boat then eases past the Cubist modules of Moshe Safdie's Habitat apartment complex, stacked on the riverbank to the left like a child's building blocks. Habitat was built as an "experiment in urban living" for Expo '67, Montréal's vastly successful world's fair. The skeletal frame of Buckminster Fuller's geodesic dome, another vestige of the fair, peeks above the foliage of Ile-Ste-Hélène, one of a dozen islets strewn like stepping-stones along the length of the city's waterfront. Finally, the passengers are deposited back at Quai Victoria.

A Crossroads Between Continents

At first glance, Montréal seems foreign to the North American continent, a European city somehow run aground on alien shores. In the past decade or so, this aesthetic aspect (combined with an exceptionally favorable exchange rate) has made the metropolis a bustling backlot for American filmmakers looking for the streets of Rome or Paris only six hours from Hollywood. For any European visitor, strolling through Place Jacques-Cartier or Square Dorchester is an oddly familiar experience. Surely, the City Hall is a copy of the Hôtel de Ville in Paris, and the Cathédrale Marie-Reine-du-Monde a miniature of St. Peter's in Rome?

Yet to North Americans, there's no mistaking Montréal for any other city on the continent: raffish, risqué, carefree, a wide-open town. Certifiably French, foreign. An exotic place, romantic, sensual, its past filled with adventure and colorful characters.

It is, as well, a city of diversity and complexity, with a non-French ethnic population that's a mixture of English and a hundred other minorities. Greeks, Italians, Portuguese, and Jews each have a community 100,000-strong. There are Asians and Haitians too. Montréal is also cosmopolitan, fashionable, intellectual, a political hotbed, a university town, bohemian, a mecca for artists and nonconformists who gather here to slip the stifling bonds of provincialism. And it is a cultured city that supports fine arts museums, two symphonies, ballet companies, an opera company, and French and English theater. Not to mention the biennial Festival de Théâtre des Amériques, which takes over the city every other spring, and the now annual Festival International de Nouvelle Danse. Both have established international reputations for presenting superior avant-garde and over-the-edge theater and dance.

As in France, dining out in Montréal tends to be a ritual: The best meals are evening-long affairs with a late start, uncounted courses, unrestrained conversation, uninhibited conviviality. The city's café society, perhaps the largest on the continent, thrives on Bishop, Crescent, Laurier, St-Denis, St-Laurent (the Main), St-Paul, and half a dozen other lively thoroughfares. In summer, these cafés *en plein air*—more than 400 at last count—may be the quintessential Montréal social forum. Striped awnings are unrolled; bright umbrellas bloom above sidewalk tables. A jug of *sangría,* a carafe of wine, a mug of beer, and spirited companions combine with a comfortable setting for watching the world go by and savoring the precious days and evenings of the few warm

months. Montréal is indeed theatrical, extroverted, and gre-
garious.

Peaceful cooperation exists between the French and *les
autres,* except for the die-hard factions on either side. The
Parti Québécois of the late René Lévesque was a painful but
necessary instrument for asserting the primacy of French
language and culture in the province of its North American
birth. The last decade has seen the ascendancy of a well-
educated, bilingual Québécois business class that has displaced priests, politicians, lawyers, and bureaucrats as the
province's elite.

This new generation of Québécois has shattered longtime
Anglophone domination of the province, even elbowing
into *le haute monde.* A society-page roster of a recent Hunt
Club soirée at the Ritz (what could be more Anglo?) reads
like a *Who's Who* of Francophone high society, with a sprinkling of WASPs for old time's sake. Culturally and economically, the Québécois are confidently *maîtres chez nous.*

Montréal celebrated its 350th birthday in 1992, with the
city transformed into one big street party from May to
October. Several new projects were unveiled as well, including the Biodome eco-theme park; the redevelopment of the
Vieux-Port area—Canada's birthday present to the city—into
a waterfront park featuring landscaped gardens, bike paths,
and an open-air cinema; the restoration of the Champs de
Mars, one of the city's oldest civic squares; and the creation
of Place du 350e, the newest public square and outdoor
performance space in the downtown area. Despite the ongoing debate about constitutional reform and the looming
referendum on Québec's future in Canada, it's business as
usual in *la belle province.*

Vieux-Montréal

From Quai Victoria, the patinated spires and gleaming domes
in Vieux-Montréal (Old Montréal) present an essentially antique picture; the eye willingly overlooks the dissonant details
of modernity. At the district's eastern extremity a copper
statue of the Virgin Mary stands behind the tiny **Notre-Dame-
de-Bonsecours** chapel. Built in 1771, it is known as the sailors'
chapel and has a roofline cluttered with steeple and tower.
Beside the church shines the silver dome of **Bonsecours
Market,** Canada's Parliament from 1849 to 1852 and, for
decades following, Montréal's principal market. Restored to
its former glory as part of the city's 350th birthday celebrations, it is now an information center, exhibition hall, and

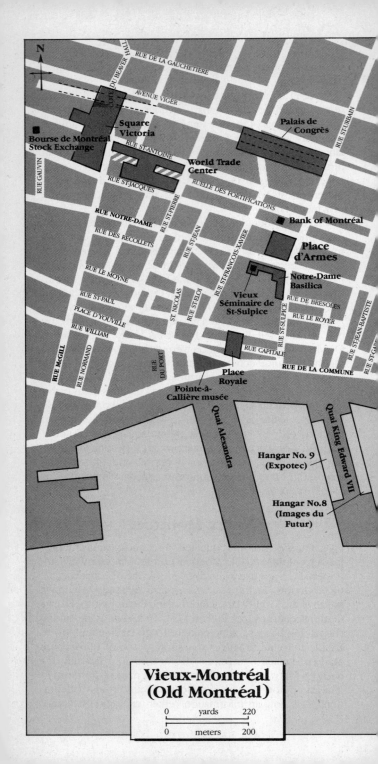

Vieux-Montréal
(Old Montréal)

| 0 | yards | 220 |
| 0 | meters | 200 |

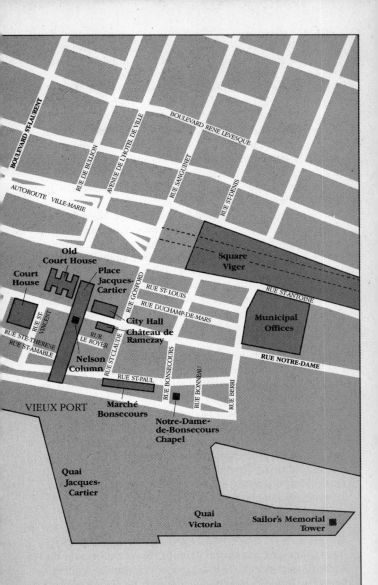

BOULEVARD ST-LAURENT

RUE DE BULLION

AVENUE DE L'HOTEL DE VILLE

BOULEVARD RENE LEVESQUE

RUE SANGUINET

RUE ST-DENIS

AUTOROUTE VILLE-MARIE

**Old
Court House**

**Court
House**

**Place
Jacques-
Cartier**

**Square
Viger**

RUE GOSFORD

RUE ST-LOUIS

RUE ST-ANTOINE

RUE DUCHAMP-DE-MARS

RUE STE-THERESE

RUE ST-VINCENT

RUE
LE ROYER

**City Hall
Château de
Ramezay**

**Municipal
Offices**

RUE NOTRE-DAME

RUE ST-AMABLE

**Nelson
Column**

RUE ST-CLAUDE

RUE ST-PAUL

RUE BONSECOURS

RUE BONNEAU

RUE BERRI

VIEUX PORT

**Marché
Bonsecours**

**Notre-Dame-
de-Bonsecours
Chapel**

**Quai
Jacques-
Cartier**

**Quai
Victoria**

**Sailor's Memorial
Tower**

ST. LAWRENCE RIVER

small-scale convention center available for public and private events.

On a slight elevation behind Bonsecours' classical façade rises the Second Empire roof of City Hall, where, on a second-floor balcony in 1967, Charles de Gaulle fanned the flames of separatism with his disruptive exhortation, *"Vive le Québec libre!"* Farther west, sunlight gleams off the white cupola of the former Palais de Justice. Still farther west, twin Gothic spires nicknamed Temperance and Perseverance soar above the nave of Notre-Dame Basilica, cynosure of the Roman Catholic faithful since 1829.

Behind these archaisms, the more familiar North American cityscape to the north and northwest reaffirms itself in concrete apartment buildings and office high rises, undistinguished except for the anodized elegance of the Bourse de Montréal (Stock Exchange Tower) and the cruciform mass of Place Ville-Marie. Then the eye looks deeper into the scene and alights on another of Montréal's unique views: Behind the downtown spires, Mont-Royal lifts a leafy crown bejeweled with a metal cross, the thematic antecedent of Place Ville-Marie.

But this view is fast changing: The expanded Palais des Congrès de Montréal convention center opened in 1991 and the World Trade Centre office-retail and hotel followed in 1992. The latter occupies several city blocks in Vieux-Montréal, including **rue St-Jacques**, formerly the "Wall Street" of Canada. Nearby are two other megascale commercial projects: a 51-story office tower project with a winter garden and year-round outdoor skating rink (à la New York's Rockefeller Center) nestled between Place Bonaventure and Place du Canada; and the "sculpted" 45-story IBM–Marathon building, facing the Sheraton Centre.

THE WATERFRONT

The waterfront area has also undergone critical development in the past half dozen years or so: critical because the harborside and rue de la Commune form the southern boundary of Vieux-Montréal— cradle of the city, its greatest tourist attraction, and, second only to Québec City's Place Royale, a repository of the nation's past. The 95-acre historic district extends west to rue McGill, east to rue Berri, and north to rue St-Antoine—roughly corresponding to the city's old perimeter walls.

(The Montréal street grid is actually oriented on a northeast–southwest axis, but no one in the city follows that. The convention is that rue Sherbrooke runs east–west, and boulevard St-Laurent (the Main) runs north–south. So, for example, Université de McGill is west of St-Laurent, and Vieux-Montréal and the river are at the southern end of town.)

New here is the **Pointe-à-Caillière musée d'archéologie et d'histoire de Montréal**, designed by local architect Dan Hanganu. Located near Place Royale (the site of the first European settlement in Montréal), the museum incorporates the city's first Catholic cemetery with portions of its original fortifications (dating to 1643). With its triangular structure recalling the shape of the 19th-century Royal Insurance Company building that formerly occupied the site, the museum is itself an artifact, combining physical elements of the city's early history with permanent and special exhibitions devoted to Montréal's role as a cultural and commercial crossroads. The museum is open Tuesday through Sunday, 10:00 A.M. to 5:00 P.M. (and until 8:00 P.M. during the summer).

Most of the surrounding architecture is Victorian, although there remain enough crooked alleys and cockeyed houses from earlier eras to proclaim the district's three and a half centuries of habitation. The old quarter is enclosed and intimate, the scale human. Around every corner a new scene presents itself—a confusion of ancient masonry and fire escapes, a carriageway leading to an enclosed courtyard, a curving row of century-old graystone buildings (no two of them alike), a blue sliver of the St. Lawrence glimpsed between dwellings.

Since the area's revival in the 1960s, scores of fieldstone dwellings and warehouses along the narrow streets have been scrubbed down and renovated; they are now occupied by shops, restaurants, clubs, businesses, studios, museums, and private homes. The venerable *quartier* has become a vibrant place in which to live, work, eat, and play.

There's little danger that Vieux-Montréal will turn into a touristy museum piece like New York City's South Street Seaport or Boston's Faneuil Hall–Quincy Market. Even when it was down at the heels, this was still a working neighborhood, with banks along rue St-Jacques, law offices and courthouses on rue Notre-Dame, and, along lesser thoroughfares, import-export companies, shipping firms, photography studios, book publishers, printers, nightclubs, restaurants, even a costume emporium.

The Piers

After its revival, Vieux-Montréal still found itself cut off from the river—its lifeline since the 17th century—by fenced dockyards, railroad tracks, and a phalanx of five grain elevators that seemed to crush the old city with their mass. Then, in the late 1970s, the bulk of the dockyard operations shifted several miles east. Down came the fences and the elevators. What remained were the railroad tracks, several hangars, and four empty piers as broad as aircraft-carrier decks: Alexandra, King Edward, Jacques-Cartier, and Victoria. The river had been "returned" to the city, and a great debate began: What to do with this wonderful new resource?

Fortunately, the city spurned the usual pressures to construct a megaproject and instead chose a modest, step-by-step plan that produced two grassy, landscaped expanses on either side of the tracks; grade crossings for pedestrians; cycling paths; and renovation of the 1922 Sailor's Memorial Tower at the head of Quai Victoria. New restaurant facilities and picnic areas, as well as a number of attractions unveiled during the 1992 birthday celebrations, have transformed it once again.

Today people drift down from Place Jacques-Cartier, the heart of Vieux-Montréal, to stroll around the piers, rent bicycles or pedal boats, play the giant S.O.S. Labyrinth maze game, or enjoy the free live performances and multicultural events of the Café-Théâtre du Vieux-Port. Clowns, jugglers, musicians, balloon sculptors, and food vendors add to the festive air as a once moribund part of town comes alive with activity. Concerts take place on summer nights beneath a big-top tent on Quai Jacques-Cartier; later in the evening the musical torch is passed to Québécois *chanteurs* performing on a beer-garden boat docked at the end of the pier.

A flea market occupies part of former Hangar No. 8, while the hangar's upper level is devoted to one of the Vieux-Port's two major annual summer exhibitions, **Images du Futur**. This international showcase highlights the latest technological advances in the visual arts: laser and video displays, computer graphics, holography, sound-and-light-wave sculptures, computer-synthesized soundscapes, and multisensory, multimedia installations.

Next door in Hangar No. 9 is **Expotec**, an equally popular exhibition presenting interactive displays about the latest scientific and technological developments of interest to the general public. Attracting some 300,000 people, the 1993 exhibition was devoted to ingenuity in action: everything from how things work to questions you've always wanted to ask. Also here is the seven-story-high, 70-foot-wide IMAX Super Cinema screen, which presents films year-round.

Those who want to see Canada at work can tour the Great Lakes freighter *Maplecliffe Hall,* which carries grain from

Thunder Bay to a deep-sea transfer terminal at Baie-Comeau on the north shore of the Gulf of St. Lawrence; from late June to early September business is slow, so the owners dock the *Maplecliffe* at the Vieux-Port and welcome visitors on board.

PLACE JACQUES-CARTIER

Until the 1960s, Place Jacques-Cartier, a cobbled rectangle sloping down from Montréal's ornate City Hall to rue de la Commune, was the city's busiest open-air market (the only reminders of this function are flower stands on a narrow median). Today the plaza justifiably remains the focal point of Vieux-Montréal. Place Jacques-Cartier can be magical, especially on a warm summer night, with the splashing Vauquelin fountain, the shadowy columns on the City Hall's floodlit façade, the sidewalk vendors and street musicians, the *calèches* drawn by stoic nags snuffling battered oat bags. The caricaturists and Titians of the tourist trade sketch furiously along tiny rue St-Amable, outdoor cafés democratically mix boisterous visitor and resident alike beneath their colorful awnings, and, beyond the Vieux-Port, cruise boats glittering with strings of lights beat against the dark current.

At the top of the square stands the controversial **Nelson Column**, erected in 1808 as the first commemorative anywhere in the world to honor the victor of the Battle of Trafalgar. Anglophones didn't like it because it faced away from the river; Francophones hated it because it honored a British admiral who had defeated the French. During the *séparatiste* 1970s it was a provocative and convenient target for sloganeers.

Château Ramezay

Just east of the square and opposite City Hall stands the Château Ramezay, one of a handful of structures in Montréal that date from the French regime. Now a museum furnished in 18th-century style, this robust fieldstone dwelling was built in 1705 for the eleventh governor of Montréal, Claude de Ramezay. The château was commandeered by the Continental Army in 1775 during the American occupation of the city. Among the invaders who were billeted here while trying to rally Canada to the Revolutionary cause were an old and tired Benjamin Franklin, Benedict Arnold, General Richard Montgomery, and John Carroll, a Marylander who became the first Roman Catholic bishop of the United States. It was Carroll's unenviable task to convince the staunchly Catholic *habitants* that their religion could accommodate both Rome and the new republic. He failed. (Many Americans do not know that the Continental Army invaded Canada and occupied Montréal during the War of Independence. Is this a testament to the two countries' generally friendly relations since 1812, which make such an infringement seem so unlikely, or is it indicative of Canada's traditionally obscure role in American affairs?)

The old quarter's most delightful thoroughfare is the east–west **rue St-Paul**, one of Montréal's original streets and the first to be lighted with oil lamps (in 1815). Now paved with bricks and brightened with Victorian lampposts, St-Paul's late-19th-century stone commercial buildings have been pleasingly reborn as airy, gracious restaurants, boutiques, craft shops, artists' lofts and studios, even specialty stores for flags and kites.

PLACE D'ARMES

Vieux-Montréal's other principal square, Place d'Armes, in the northwest part of the area, has a more serious demeanor than Place Jacques-Cartier, despite the tourist buses and *calèches* that congregate here. In its center a ten-foot-high statue of Paul de Chomedey, sieur de Maisonneuve, stands near the site where, in 1644, the city's founder and a tiny band of men successfully defended Montréal (then a missionary outpost called Ville-Marie) against an attack by 200 Iroquois warriors. A statue of one of the vanquished natives kneels at the base of the monument, which is crowded with other historical figures, including Jeanne Mance, who established Montréal's first hospital; Charles LeMoyne, whose sons founded New Orleans and Mobile, Alabama; and the vigilant mastiff Pilote, whose barking alerted the settlement to the impending danger of an Iroquois attack.

Notre-Dame Basilica

Notre-Dame Basilica, one of the largest examples of the Gothic Revival style in North America, dominates the south side of the square, its twin spires reaching a height just two and a half feet short of those of Notre-Dame in Paris. The history of the church, which was completed in 1829, is rife with anomalies. Montréal's Protestants and Jews contributed to its construction, and its architect, James O'Donnell, was not only Protestant and Irish but a New Yorker as well. His work on the church inspired his conversion, and after his death his body was entombed beneath the first pillar to the right of the altar, with an entire church as his eloquent epitaph.

The dazzling interior is gilt and soaring polychromatic blue, similar to Sainte Chapelle in Paris. Three rose windows in the roof contribute much-needed light to the vast nave, and 14 stained glass windows designed in Limoges present a historical frieze relating the founding of Montréal. The extraordinarily detailed altar and pulpit are ornamented with wooden statues of the prophets. In summer, the church hosts a popular series of chamber concerts by the Orchestre Symphonique de Montréal.

Vieux Séminaire de St-Sulpice

Adjacent to Notre-Dame behind a tall fieldstone wall and a wrought-iron gate is the Vieux Séminaire de St-Sulpice, constructed in 1685 and generally considered to be Montréal's oldest building. The appearance of the squat medieval-looking structure is lightened by a charming classical portal with Ionic pilasters and the lacy seminary clock, reputedly the oldest public timepiece in North America (1701).

For more than 300 years the seminary has served as a residence and headquarters for the Sulpicians, who bought the island of Montréal in 1668 from de Maisonneuve and La Société de Notre-Dame de Montréal for 130,000 livres (about $260,000). The Sulpicians administered the legal and religious life of the settlement, kept its records (still in the building's subterranean barrel vaults), and granted concessions to prospective landowners.

Bank of Montréal

Confronting Notre-Dame on Place d'Armes, physically and spiritually, is the nation's oldest bank, the Bank of Montréal, founded in 1817. Built in the 1840s and modeled after Rome's Pantheon, the bank's stately Neoclassical headquarters anchors rue St-Jacques, once the "Wall Street" of Canada. (Like its New York City counterpart, rue St-Jacques ran inside a rampart that fortified the city in its early days.) The elegant portico and Corinthian columns were little altered by a massive renovation and expansion of the building by the celebrated firm of McKim, Mead, & White at the turn of the century. Inside, however, wealth is apotheosized by a row of 40 brass-topped syenite columns and the magnificent 90-foot dome they added to the original structure. Throughout, bronze lamps, marble counters, and brass gates gleam with loving care and heavy use.

Surrounding the square are other temples of finance and insurance, the business legacy of Montréal's conservative Scottish-Canadian ruling class. An eight-story sandstone structure on the southeast corner, built in 1888 and vigorously gargoyled and grilled, is Montréal's first skyscraper.

Central Business District

To get from Vieux-Montréal to the central business district take rue McGill, at the western end of the *vieux quartier,* heading north. You'll pass **Square Victoria**, a windswept expanse overwhelmed by the Bourse de Montréal and the twin aluminum façades of the Bell-Banque Canadien Nationale complex. Here rue McGill becomes Côte du Beaver Hall, named after the 19th-century estate of fur trader Joseph Frobisher, which at the time was out in the country, beyond the city walls.

The twisting street climbs a modest escarpment and intersects a narrow east–west thoroughfare called de la Gauchetière. A few blocks east, Montréal's tiny **Chinatown**, home to about 300 residents, is squeezed between two massive public works projects, the Complexe Guy-Favreau to the north (home of federal offices in Montréal) and the Palais des Congrès (convention center) to the south. On Sundays, these narrow streets fill with life as Chinese families from more affluent addresses visit relatives and patronize the old neighborhood's restaurants, shops, and specialty stores.

Return to Côte du Beaver Hall and continue north to boulevard René Lévesque (formerly boulevard Dorchester), an east–west commercial canyon hemmed in by such landmarks as the Hydro-Québec Building, Place Félix Martin's twin granite and marble towers, the C-I-L House, Le Reine Elizabeth Hotel, Place Ville-Marie, and the IBM–Marathon building.

THE UNDERGROUND CITY

Montréal's celebrated underground city, **la ville souterraine**, began at **Place Ville-Marie** in the early 1960s when architect I. M. Pei and developer William Zeckendorf decided to build a shopping concourse beneath the trio of office towers Pei had designed. The all-weather arcade was such a hit that other developers plugged into the system and the underground network spread. (Part of the network is actually above ground—city officials prefer the term "weatherproof city"—but the underground designation has stuck.) Today it gives Montrealers ten miles of coatless access to seven hotels, ten shopping plazas, two train stations, a dozen commercial buildings, residential high-rises, 30 movie theaters, more than 1,400 shops, and hundreds of restaurants and bars. Some building clusters are within walking distance; other neighborhoods can be reached by taking the metro.

For example, west of the central business district the

Atwater metro station runs to the haute couture shops of **Westmount Square** (one of the last projects designed by Mies van der Rohe), well known as Anglophone turf in the old days, and **Place Alexis-Nihon**, with its myriad shops and inexpensive restaurants. In the heart of the central business district tunnels link the Bonaventure subway station with Canadian Pacific's Windsor Station (used for commuter trains), **Place du Canada**, Le Château Champlain, and **Place Bonaventure**. Place Bonaventure, in turn, is connected to Canadian National's Gare Centrale (Central Station), Le Reine Elizabeth Hotel, and Place Ville-Marie.

A few blocks east, north–south passages link the Palais des Congrès, the Complexe Guy-Favreau, and the **Complexe Desjardins**, the most impressive of the indoor arcades. Three office towers and the 601-room Hôtel Le Meridien (for which see Accommodations, below) are grouped around a multi-level galleria called **La Place**. Daylight streams through seven-story windows, fountains and islands of greenery defy winter, and enormous mobiles twist gently above shoppers bound for boutiques.

A tunnel under rue Ste-Catherine connects the Complexe Desjardins with the **Place des Arts**, the city's major cultural center, near the Université de McGill. Plays, ballets, operas, concerts, and films from the Montréal World Film Festival are presented at the complex's Jean Duceppe, Wilfred-Pelletier, Maisonneuve, and Café de la Place theaters. The newest kid on the Place des Arts block is the **Musée d'art contemporain de Montréal**, which opened in May 1992 and houses the country's largest collection of contemporary Canadian art. Located at the corner of Jeanne-Mance and Ste-Catherine streets facing the Complexe Desjardins, it was designed by architect Gabriel Charbonneau, who also designed the museum's original facilities in Cité du Havre, part of the old Expo '67 site. The museum's state-of-the-art facilities include the Cinquième Salle, a 350-seat theater adjacent to the main building, as well as a restaurant and boutique. The museum connects directly to the rest of the Place des Arts complex via the corridor between the metro and its rue Ste-Catherine entrance, and is open daily except Mondays, 11:00 A.M. to 6:00 P.M. (and until 9:00 P.M. on Wednesdays).

East of the central business district, the Berri-UQAM subway station tunnels beneath several office towers, the Voyageur bus terminal, and the Université du Québec à Montréal. Light streams into the seven-story **Les Atriums** here, a shopping mall with cascading waterfalls, reflecting pools, and a tropical garden below street level.

Facing Les Atriums to the east, the Terminus Autobus (bus

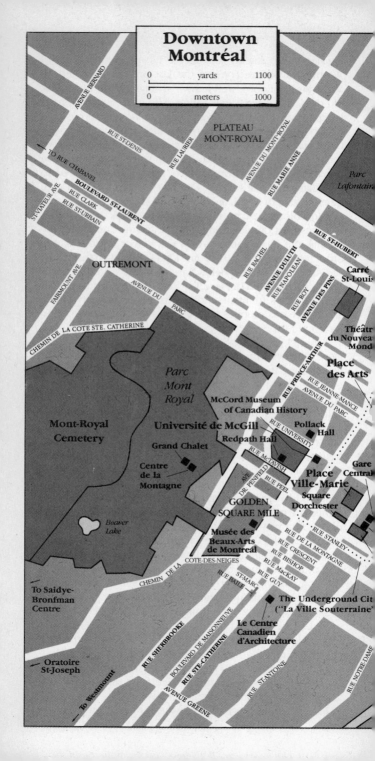

Downtown Montréal

| 0 | yards | 1100 |
| 0 | meters | 1000 |

AVENUE BERNARD

RUE ST-DENIS

RUE LAURIER

AVENUE DU MONT-ROYAL

RUE MARIE ANNE

PLATEAU MONT-ROYAL

TO RUE CHABANEL

BOULEVARD ST-LAURENT

ST-VIATEUR AVE.

RUE CLARK

RUE ST-URBAIN

Parc Lafontaine

RUE ST-HUBERT

RUE RACHEL

AVENUE DULUTH

RUE NAPOLEON

RUE ROY

AVENUE DES PINS

Carré St-Louis

FAIRMOUNT AVE.

OUTREMONT

AVENUE DU

PARC

CHEMIN DE LA COTE STE. CATHERINE

Théâtre du Nouveau Monde

Place des Arts

RUE PRINCE-ARTHUR

RUE JEANNE-MANCE

AVENUE DU PARC

Parc Mont Royal

McCord Museum of Canadian History

Mont-Royal Cemetery

Université de McGill

RUE UNIVERSITY

Pollack Hall

Grand Chalet

Redpath Hall

RUE McTAVISH

Centre de la Montagne

AVE. DR. PENFIELD

RUE PEEL

Place Ville-Marie

Gare Centrale

Square Dorchester

Beaver Lake

GOLDEN SQUARE MILE

Musée des Beaux-Arts de Montreal

RUE STANLEY

RUE DE LA MONTAGNE

RUE CRESCENT

RUE BISHOP

RUE MacKAY

RUE GUY

COTE-DES-NEIGES

CHEMIN DE LA

ST-MARC

RUE BAILE

To Saidye-Bronfman Centre

The Underground City ("La Ville Souterraine")

Le Centre Canadien d'Architecture

Oratoire St-Joseph

RUE SHERBROOKE

BOULEVARD DE MAISONNEUVE

RUE STE-CATHERINE

RUE ST-ANTOINE

RUE NOTRE-DAME

To Westmount

AVENUE GREENE

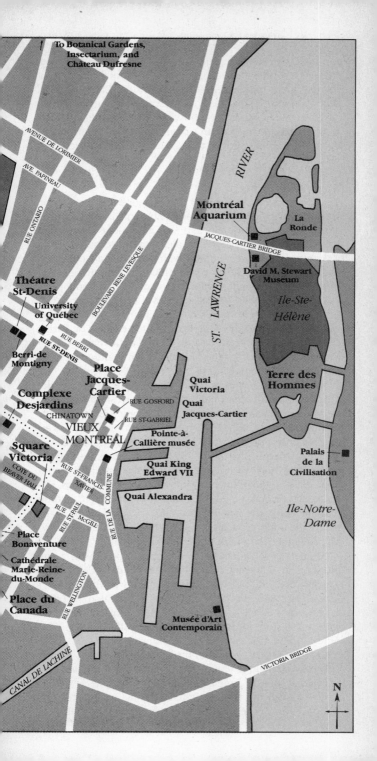

terminal) to the north, rue Berri to the west, and rue Ste-Catherine to the south is Berri Square, a former parking lot the city spent millions on to transform into **Place du 350ᵉ**. With its sloping lawns, placid waterways, sculptures by artist-architect Melvin Charney, and outdoor café, the square is now a pleasant oasis in an urban landscape dominated by concrete, and has proved to be a hit with Montrealers and visitors alike.

Recent Additions

The underground city gained three major complexes in the second half of the 1980s. One block north of Place Ville-Marie, at the corner of University and Ste-Catherine, is **Place Montréal Trust**. This gigantic complex has a five-story central atrium and courtyard complete with fountain—all topped off by huge skylights. The more than 100 trendy boutiques here offer virtually something for everyone in taste and price range, while the glass wall at street level alongside the McGill College Promenade makes an ideal people-watching spot. Popular eateries in the complex include **Le Notre de Paris**'s divine patisserie and chocolatier, as well as **Les Palmes** "Californian" courtyard restaurant, which offers outdoor terrace dining during the warmer months. Tel: (514) 499-9903.

Place Montréal Trust, which connects underground to the former Simpson department store on its western side, connects on its eastern side to the long-standing **Eaton** department store—one of the Big Three retailers doing business on Ste-Catherine since the turn of the century. **Le Centre Eaton**, which opened in the fall of 1990, incorporates the former Eaton store and warren-like Les Terrasses complex into a huge glass-and-marble emporium with some 250 shops. Designed by Peter Rose, also architect of Le Centre Canadien d'Architecture, the restyled complex continues to be a key part of the underground city, as is **La Baie**, just one block east. Their neighbor is a rather unusual one at that.

Set between Eaton and La Baie (each occupying a city block on Ste-Catherine) is **Les Promenades de la Cathédrale**, a major retail-and-office complex. Some say it symbolizes an "open marriage" between commerce and religion: Its office tower looms above the venerable Christ Church Cathedral, with a 150-store retail mall located directly beneath. The redevelopment of this Montréal landmark drew some criticism when it first opened in the fall of 1988, which in turn only served to pique Montrealers' penchant for the new and unusual; it soon became a favorite shopping spot, as well as a retreat from the bustle of Ste-Catherine commerce. The complex's most elegant addition, **Le Parchemin** (Tel: 514/

844-1619), opened to much gastronomic fanfare in the spring of 1989. Aside from being the first major French restaurant to open downtown in some years, it is notable for its unusual location—the 1876 Christ Church Cathedral rectory and parish house.

Les Cours Mont-Royal is the third—and most grandiose—of the newer complexes. The once-renowned Sheraton Mont-Royal Hotel, whose halcyon days are still fondly recalled by Montréal's elite, had fallen into disrepair and disrepute in recent years. In 1988 it was reborn as a luxury condominium, office, and retail complex. A beauty to behold—inside and out—with many of the hotel's original architectural highlights and treasures triumphantly restored, Les Cours Mont-Royal has become a mecca for Montrealers seeking refinement in their daily lives. Boutiques, restaurants, a magnificently chandeliered vaulted lobby, atriums, sweeping staircases, fountained courtyards featuring live entertainment and mini exhibitions, as well as a cinema with Egyptian decor, have gone a long way toward restoring this landmark structure to its former glory.

SQUARE DORCHESTER

Back at Place Ville-Marie, continue west along boulevard René Lévesque to the western end of the downtown office towers. Here, the thin frame of the Canadian Imperial Bank of Commerce building rises over Square Dorchester, for more than a century one of the loveliest spaces in the city. Square Dorchester, with Place du Canada to its south, is often considered the "center" of the center. It is also the locale for the Art Deco–inspired **Infotouriste headquarters** in the Dominion Square Building. Situated at street level on the north side of the Square, Infotouriste is run by the Greater Montréal Convention and Tourism Bureau and the Maison du Tourisme Québec and should be the initial pitstop for first-time visitors to the city.

Public squares are the finest legacy of the Victorian era in Montréal. Indeed, it would be difficult to imagine the city without these pocket-size oases, some gifts of philanthropists (Beaver Hall, Viger, Phillips), others vacant land that was miraculously preserved (St-Louis). Square Dorchester itself was expropriated from a Catholic cemetery, and around it was erected the largest collection of eclectic, notable buildings produced by Victorian architects anywhere in the city.

The **Cathédrale Marie-Reine-du-Monde**, at the southeast corner of the square, was started in 1870 by Bishop Ignace Bourget as a reminder to English Montréal that the Church of Rome still ruled in what was then Canada's largest city. A wonderful historical curiosity, the neo-Baroque confection is (perhaps fortunately) the world's only quarter-size replica of St. Peter's in Rome—and the very embodiment of cultural colonialism.

The former Windsor Hotel, gutted and reborn on the west side of the square as shops and offices, began life as luxurious accommodations for wealthy bourgeoisie nostalgic for the cosmopolitan Second Empire of Napoleon III ("salons frescoed and furnished in strictly Egyptian style," noted early promotional literature). The Dominion Square Building and the massive Sun Life Building are rich mixtures of classical, Renaissance, and Baroque elements: in sum, Beaux Arts. Although the square has lost some of its glamour and spatial balance, it remains one of the most harmonious environments in the city.

By 1910 **rue Ste-Catherine**, which runs parallel to and north of boulevard René Lévesque, was the city's main commercial thoroughfare. It is still a busy shopping area, set today between the central business district and the restaurants and nightclubs of rue Crescent. Montréal's large department stores—La Baie, Eaton, and Ogilvy—and an unbroken stretch of retail shops line the street. To the north is rue Sherbrooke, the southern boundary of the famous Golden Square Mile, and home to some of Montréal's most elegant boutiques.

The Golden Square Mile

The British conquest of New France in 1759 unleashed on Montréal a commercial class of shrewd, tough-minded Scotsmen, many of them refugees from the brutal Highland clearances. Within a generation the McTavishes, the McGills, and the Frasers dominated the city's fur trade, then its financial institutions, and finally its politics. These "Caesars of the Wilderness" built grand country estates north of the city, where they entertained on an imperial scale. (This tradition, along with the historic congeniality of the French population, may represent the twin streams that nourish Montréal's enduring reputation for lavish hospitality and joie de vivre.)

Industrialization brought sugar mills, breweries, factories, and railroads; the tireless Scots dominated those too. Ogilvies, Cantlies, McDougalls, Molsons, Macdonalds, Strathconas, McIntyres, Drummonds, and Rosses—famous names in the annals of Montréal—continued the relentless residential climb up Mont-Royal.

From the late 1800s to World War II, 70 percent of Canada's wealth was concentrated in the hands of some 25,000 residents of what was called the Golden Square Mile, bounded by Sherbrooke on the south, avenue des Pins (angling along the ridges of Mont-Royal) to the north, rue McTavish to the east, and chemin de la Côte-des-Neiges to the west. It was the cradle of Canada's commercial aristocracy, the men who built Canada: the wealthy merchants, founders of international steamship lines, bankers, railroad barons, all the kings of capitalism in an illustrious, audacious age.

Determined to proclaim their power and prosperity, they hired Stanford White from New York City, who, along with Montréal's own Maxwell brothers, designed Italianate palaces on the wooded slopes. Expensive automobiles, race horses, gardens, and greenhouses—all the external trappings of *nouveaux riches*—announced to the world that their day in the sun had arrived.

These prosperous Victorians exercised at the Montréal Amateur Athletic Association clubhouse on rue Peel, took high tea at the Ritz-Carlton, sent their towheaded scions to McGill (founded by fur trader James McGill just to the east of the Golden Square Mile), and soaked up culture at the Musée des beaux-arts de Montréal (also within the Golden Square Mile), whose galleries were hung with Rembrandts, Constables, and Renoirs from their own private collections.

Much of the glory has since crumbled beneath the wrecker's ball. More fortunate structures became alumni offices and faculty clubs for McGill; others were enlisted for diplomatic duty along avenue McGregor (now Docteur-Penfield) and avenue des Pins, Montréal's Consulate Row. Echoes of this gilded age reverberate in the art galleries and elegant shops along Sherbrooke that cater to a diminished carriage trade. Still, a brief look around the Golden Square Mile conveys some sense of the awesome concentration of power and wealth, unlike anything Canada had ever seen—or is likely to ever see again.

McCord Museum of Canadian History

Down on Sherbrooke, still occasionally referred to as Montréal's Fifth Avenue, the Ritz-Carlton Kempinski Hotel, gracious monarch of the street, has been the favorite watering hole of Square Milers since 1912. Holt Renfrew, one block west, supplied fur coats to four generations of British royalty. Some blocks east, facing the Roddick Gates of McGill, the McCord Museum and its famed Notman Photographic Archives underwent a $20-million renovation and expansion in

1992 to coincide with Montréal's 350th birthday. Hailed as one of the most successful restorations and renovations of an important Montréal building to date, the "new" McCord boasts an exhibition space worthy of its vast collection of Canadian artifacts. The museum is open daily except Mondays from 10:00 A.M.; admission is free on Thursday evenings from 6:00 to 9:00 P.M.

Musée des beaux-arts de Montréal

The McCord's cultural neighbor to the west, the Museum of Fine Arts, was designed by the Maxwell brothers. Canada's oldest art institution (dating from a distressingly recent 1860), it was moribund for years, seemingly irrelevant to much of the community. It finally closed in 1973 for a badly needed renovation and expansion, which doubled the museum's size with the addition of a modern wing. In 1984 the bronze front doors behind the Ionic portico were flung open, and Montréal responded. More recently, splashy major exhibits of works by Bouguereau, Picasso, Leonardo da Vinci, and Dalí have boosted attendance. Open Tuesday to Sunday, 11:00 A.M. to 6:00 P.M.; Wednesdays and Saturdays from 11:00 A.M. to 9:00 P.M.

Rue Crescent Area

The museum was so invigorated by its success that a second pavilion, designed by internationally renowned architect Moshe Safdie, opened to great fanfare in the fall of 1991. Today it dominates the south side of rue Sherbrooke, stretching from Crescent to Bishop, and extending almost halfway to de Maisonneuve, elevating the tone of Montréal's liveliest west-end street scene, which spills over onto the parallel streets of Bishop, de la Montagne, and MacKay. Fears that it would eviscerate one of North America's largest concentrations of Victorian homes, all splendidly renovated, have proven unfounded. The new pavilion incorporates the façade of the landmark New Sherbrooke Apartments, and the night along Crescent still belongs to music, laughter, and frivolous conversation.

The area is an Anglo counterpart to the clubs and bars along the predominantly Francophone St-Denis, east of the central business district. Young professionals congregate at the **Winston Churchill Pub** (known locally as "Winnie's"), one of the old favorites here. Other upwardly mobile types congregate at **Thursday's**, connected by a passageway— Montréal is a veritable rabbit warren of underground corridors—to a basement disco and the **Hôtel de la Mon-**

tagne, an upscale hostelry with a good restaurant, intimate bar, and splendid Art Nouveau lobby (see Accommodations, below, for more on the Hôtel de la Montagne). Rockers and the university crowd favor the **Hard Rock Café**, directly across the street.

Le Faubourg Ste-Catherine

Not far from Crescent—and not to be missed—is Le Faubourg Ste-Catherine. This lively market emporium has revitalized the neighborhood around Guy and Ste-Catherine streets, attracting throngs of sightseers and Montreal bon vivants since it opened in 1986. International cuisine of the finger-food type can be enjoyed on the spot or as take-out fare for picnic noshes. It also boasts a liquor store, flower stall, boutiques with handicraft and artisan wares from Québec and Central and South America, and a cinema.

Le Centre Canadien d'Architecture

Le Faubourg's toniest neighbor is the Canadian Centre for Architecture. Located at St-Marc on rue Baile, this museum is a veritable showcase of architecture past, present, and future. The magnificently restored Shaughnessy House mansion is its centerpiece, flanked on either side by two connecting wings designed by project architect Peter Rose. The Centre, the only museum in the world dedicated solely to architecture, houses one of the world's most important and extensive collections of prints, drawings, maquettes, models, and books relating to the subject. As well, the CCA has exhibition halls, a bookstore, and an auditorium for public use. There are regular tours of the museum and its grounds, which occupy the city block from rue Baile to boulevard René Lévesque Ouest and St-Marc to du Fort. Open Wednesdays and Fridays, 11:00 A.M. to 6:00 P.M.; Thursdays from 11:00 A.M. to 8:00 P.M.; and Saturdays and Sundays, 11:00 A.M. to 5:00 P.M.

Parc du Mont-Royal

For more than a century, Montréal's mountain, a swayback ridge whose twin summits rise 750 feet above the island, has been a place of refuge in the heart of the city, a reassuring presence, a retreat for recreation, seclusion, contemplation.

The upland's spiritual role was its earliest. In 1535, as already noted, Cartier named the mountain for a cardinal and planted a wooden cross on the summit. De Maisonneuve duplicated this pious act in 1643 as thanksgiving to God for sparing his year-old mission from a flood. This religious theme was continued in the 1850s, when farms on the mountain's north slope were turned into two cemeteries, one Catholic, one Protestant—"the most romantic and secluded burying grounds in the world," according to an 1856 guidebook. In 1924, to commemorate de Maisonneuve's long-vanished cross, the St. Jean-Baptiste Society raised a 100-foot iron cross illuminated by 150 lightbulbs— a homely beacon proclaiming Québec's Catholic roots for 50 miles on a clear night.

A brief secular intrusion occurred when wealthy landowners partitioned the mountain into private estates. With unusual foresight, the city stepped in to expropriate the land for a park—at least that half of the mountain not occupied by sprawling necropolises. In 1874 a similar astuteness guided the councillors in their choice of landscape architect: Frederick Law Olmsted, the celebrated genius behind Manhattan's Central Park and the Capitol grounds in Washington. Seventeen years of experience had instilled in Olmsted the conviction that a park should serve the subtle purpose of restoring city dwellers spiritually—a tenet in keeping with the mountain's early function.

Olmsted interfered with Mont-Royal's natural attributes as little as possible: "If it is to be cut up with roads and walks, spotted with shelters and streaked with staircases it is likely to lose whatever natural charm you first saw in it. Your mountain of less than a thousand feet is royal in name only by courtesy, and if you attempt to deal with it as if it had the impregnable majesty of an alpine monarch, you only make it ridiculous."

The park is still largely as Olmsted envisioned, an urban sanctuary untrammeled by zoos and amphitheaters, undiminished by muggers, oversize portable radios, or boardwalks, untainted by what Olmsted called "insipid picturesqueness." Thick stands of maple and oak, spruce and chestnut, floriated meadows and secluded glades are the haunts of squirrels fattened on baguette crumbs; woodchucks, red foxes, snowshoe hares, pheasants, broad-wing hawks, and herring gulls, up from the docks, are plentiful.

The animals share their leafy domain with joggers and cyclists, elderly strollers, and parents with babies. On summer Sundays especially, the mountain echoes with the conversation of picnicking families. Hikers leave on nature walks from the **Grand Chalet**, a seigneurial-style hall built in the center of the park in 1931 and a blatant compromise of Olmsted's original plan. More sedentary types buy snacks from a bustling concession stand inside the chalet and eat beneath the historic scenes and heraldic crests of Québec,

Canada, and England that decorate the walls. The royal blue of France highlights the heavy beams of the buttressed ceiling. A terrace in front of the chalet offers fine views of the city below; on clear days you can see the Green Mountains of Vermont.

At Beaver Lake, a 15-minute walk west of the chalet, junior yachtsmen sail their toy sloops and schooners while sunworshippers bronze on the sloping lawns. Here, in winter, downhill skiers grasp a short tow rope to take up a nearby incline's modest challenge, cross-country skiers set off along five miles of mountaintop trails, snowshoers galumph through the woods, and skaters pirouette on the frozen lake.

Plateau Mont-Royal

This old commercial and residential district stretches about 20 blocks north of rue Sherbrooke and about the same distance east of avenue du Parc, on the eastern side of Mont-Royal. The plateau is Montréal at its most intensely ethnic and urban: densely populated, extravagantly Victorian. Three main commercial thoroughfares—du Parc, St-Laurent, and St-Denis—run north to south through it. Lining the narrow side streets are brick- and limestone-faced duplexes and triplexes with distinctive balconies and spiraling exterior staircases, ornate trademarks of Montréal's architectural landscape.

The staircases, a feature imported from the rural Québec of the 1880s, saved space by eliminating interior stairs and doubled as fire escapes. (Considered unsafe, they were banned in new construction by a 1940s city ordinance, but existing ones were exempted.) Montréal's *balconville* is a counterpart to New York City's brownstone stoop, a refuge from summer heat, a perch from which to gab with neighbors, a sentry post for watching children at play on the sidewalks below.

These days **avenue du Parc** is the most ethnically diverse street in Montréal. When the area was first developed in the 1880s it was predominantly Jewish, and traditional Orthodox garb is still a frequent sight along the busy, scrabbling avenue. Subsequently, Greeks settled here, then Portuguese, and most recently Latin Americans from Guatemala, Nicaragua, and Mexico.

OUTREMONT

Like nearby St-Laurent, avenue du Parc is a microcosm of the city's diversity that becomes more gentrified the farther north you go. The avenue cuts through the area known as Outremont, the Francophone counterpart of toney Westmount. Roughly speaking, Outremont is considered to be the neighborhood bordered by avenue du Mont-Royal and Mont-Royal itself to the south and west, chemin de la côte Ste-Catherine and avenue Van Horne to the north, and abutting the Plateau Mont-Royal area to the east. The French elite, including Québec premier Robert Bourassa, live in this enclave, often in stately mansions on the lower reaches of Mont-Royal. Quiet tree-lined streets and many small public parks exist alongside chic boutiques and bistros. Shopping is big business here, and Laurier and Bernard avenues in particular cater to the carriage trade. The area is also increasingly the haunt of adventurous Anglophones, drawn by the promise of oh-so-French ambience, reliably fine food, and lively, informal café society. The ethnic hubbub of Plateau Mont-Royal is right next door, and the harmonious coexistence of the two neighborhoods is yet another example of the cosmopolitan nature of Montréal.

Rue St-Denis

This is Montréal's boulevard St-Michel, the *quartier Latin,* a Francophone student ghetto of bookstores, cafés, boutiques, restaurants, smoky jazz clubs, cinemas, and theaters. The action centers on the Montréal campus of the Université du Québec à Montréal, at Ste-Catherine and St-Denis, which has an enrollment of 12,800.

Every July the **Juste Pour Rire** (Just for Laughs) **Festival** turns St-Denis between Sherbrooke and boulevard René Lévesque into one big block party. Some performers give free shows at outdoor bandstands to thousands of comedy lovers, who mill about the sidewalks until late into the warm summer evenings, while members of the comedy elite (Bob Newhart, Sandra Bernhard, Milton Berle, Roseanne Barr Arnold, Martin Mull, Lily Tomlin, Andre-Phillipe Gagnon) perform at venues like the Théâtre St-Denis, one of the largest cinemas in North America when it was built in 1908. Now eleven years old, the festival has become big business, spawning HBO and CBC/Radio Canada specials and attracting the world's top talent scouts.

North of Sherbrooke, St-Denis loses much of its student character and becomes a wide avenue lined with graystone town houses, splashy boutiques, salons, and cafés. Crowned with trees and bordered on three sides by elegant Victorian houses inhabited by some of Québec's brightest cultural lights, Carré St-Louis, just north of Sherbrooke, is St-Denis's apogee and the loveliest residential square in the city. The turn-of-the-century graystone mansions almost vibrate with a profusion of ornamental details—arched porches, lacy balconies, frilly rooftop ironwork, turrets, dormer windows, bulging cornices—all conspiring to evoke the image of gracious Victorian city life. **Rue Prince-Arthur**, at the square's western end, is a pedestrian mall lined with dozens of inexpensive, bring-your-own-bottle restaurants, mostly Greek.

THE MAIN

Boulevard St-Laurent, popularly known as the Main, has long been a sociological isobar, a de facto demarcation between the English west end of the city and the French east end; in between lies a wide buffer zone of immigrants. Tradition has it that newcomers got off the boat at the docks in Vieux-Montréal and just walked north along the Main, a moniker that comes from the street's former name, rue Principale du Faubourg St-Laurent, or St. Lawrence Main Street.

The Lower Main, between René Lévesque and Sherbrooke, and along Ste-Catherine between Jeanne-Mance and St-Denis, is a mild-mannered Tenderloin of taverns, strip joints, porno theaters, and tattoo parlors. These are mixed with more reputable business landmarks such as Main Importing and the **Montréal Pool Room**, famed for its "steamies" (steamed hot dogs slathered with chopped onion, mustard, and coleslaw—former mayor Jean Drapeau's favorite junk food). At night the Tenderloin's bikers, hookers, and pushers are like snakes: They won't bother you if you don't bother them.

The Main and its side streets are most strongly associated with the Jewish immigrants who crowded into the neighborhood during the czarist pogroms of the 1880s. One reason for the continuing connection may be that their descendants enriched Canadian culture with a remarkable outpouring—musician Alexander Brott, artist Stanley Lewis, sociologist Lionel Tiger, and, most especially, such literary luminaries as poets Irving Layton, A. M. Klein, and Leonard Cohen (Westmounter by birth, Plateau Mont-Royal resident by choice).

Certainly the funniest voice from the streets belongs to Mordecai Richler, whose stinging satires—*Son of a Smaller Hero, The Apprenticeship of Duddy Kravitz, St. Urbain's Horseman, Joshua Then and Now*—have become indelibly linked with the Jewish quarter. Remnants of Duddy's world remain: Richler's boyhood home at 5257 St-Urbain; Wilensky's Light Lunch (established in 1931) on the corner of Clark and Fairmount; the rococo Rialto Cinema on Parc, where Duddy and his pals ogled the cupids and nymphs in diaphanous robes (painted on the ceiling in 1920 by Emmanuel Briffa); the Fairmount Bagel Factory on Fairmount, of course, and its arch-rival the Bagel Shop on St-Viateur. (Montréal bagels are lighter, thinner, and believed by residents to be far superior in taste to their more celebrated New York cousins.)

North of Sherbrooke, the Main has taken on a different character in recent years. Yes, the delis, luncheonettes, cheap but hearty restaurants, junk stores, wholesalers, and clothing stores that have proved a boon to many a bargain hunter or impoverished soul throughout the Main's history are still here. They have been joined, however, by fashionable boutiques featuring clothes, jewelry, and accessories by Québécois and avant-garde designers. And every day seems to herald the arrival of yet another bistro, café, bar, nightclub, bookstore, or gallery representing the latest wave of "immigrants" to the area—up-and-coming artists and entrepreneurial gentrifiers.

The Main north of Prince-Arthur, once solidly Jewish, is now an olio of Greek restaurants, Jewish tailors, Portuguese bakeries, German meat markets, and Hungarian social clubs. The Banque Laurentienne at avenue des Pins has window signs in French, English, Spanish, Portuguese, Italian, Greek, Ukrainian, and Hebrew. Farther north, side streets like Duluth, Rachel, Mont-Royal, and Laurier have also been gentrified with fern-hung *brocheteries,* bars, and boutiques. This has been wrought by *la petite bourgeoisie décapant*—the paint-stripping, middle-class progeny of immigrants who hoisted themselves into upscale neighborhoods after World War II (much to the dismay of longtime, low-income residents).

Still farther north on St-Laurent, up around rue Laurier, you'll find one of Montréal's hottest new neighborhoods. Here run-down storefronts have been stripped, sandblasted, and renovated beyond Duddy's recognition into industrial-chic clothing stores and nouvelle restaurants. The needle trade has been augmented (but not supplanted) by designer boutiques like Le Château, while bagels have yielded to sophisticated beaneries such as Berlin, Prego, Chez Better, and La Cucina.

Schwartz's

But the most influential institution on the Main (at the corner of rue Napoléon) remains the humble **Montreal Hebrew Delicatessen** (established in 1927), usually called Schwartz's after its original owners, Maurice and Reuben Schwartz. A single, narrow room with ancient waiters, Formica tables, and what may be the original decor, Schwartz's is famed far and wide for its Montréal smoked meat, the tender, aromatic result of a secret Romanian recipe.

Like Swann contemplating a *madeleine,* far-flung ex-Montrealers of all ethnic persuasions become misty-eyed just thinking about Schwartz's smoked-meat sandwiches, which seem to embody all their longings for and associations with the old hometown. Emotions intensified by the imagined injustice of their economic exile at the hands of the *séparatistes,* they sit over drinks at the roof bar of the Park Plaza Hotel in Toronto and similar watering holes in Calgary, Vancouver, and Miami, itemizing sentimental lists of what they've left behind: the Canadiens, the mountain, the bars along Crescent, the Ritz-Carlton's garden restaurant, the clubs of Vieux-Montréal, Montréal bagels, "and this little hole in the wall on the Main where you can get the best smoked meat in the world. . . ."

THE ARTS IN MONTREAL

Montréal's venues for the performing arts include the **Théâtre Saint-Denis** in the *quartier Latin,* scene of rock concerts year-round and comedy during the comedy festival in July. It is near the Université du Québec à Montréal. Concerts and recitals are also given at the Université de McGill's **Pollack Concert Hall** and **Redpath Hall**, and the Université de Montréal's **Salle Claude Champagne**.

The **Rialto Cinema** in the now very trendy Outremont area (about a 10-minute drive west of downtown) presents more avant-garde music, dance, and theater productions, as do the relatively new **Agora de la Danse** theater, **Strathearn Centre**, and **Théâtre La Chapelle** in the Plateau Mont-Royal area. The Saidye Bronfman Centre (see below)—a long-time performing and visual arts mecca for Montrealers—presents dance, music, film, theater, and spoken-word programs in English, French, and Yiddish. It is also the home of North America's only permanent Yiddish Theatre troupe, founded some 35 years ago by Dora Wasserman.

The **Centaur Theatre**, Montréal's only major English-language theater, is housed in the Neoclassical former stock-exchange building at 453 rue St-François-Xavier, in Vieux-Montréal. Also presented here are first-class Canadian and international theater classics by Montréal's newer English theater companies, including Bulldog Productions, Geordie Productions, Theatre 1774, the Black Theatre Workshop, and the Montréal Theatre Ensemble. The Université de McGill's recently refurbished 306-seat **Moyse Hall** and Concordia

University's **D.B. Clarke Theatre** are also used by the city's theater, dance, and music groups. The four major French-language theaters are the **Théâtre de Quat'Sous** on avenue des Pins, the **Théâtre du Nouveau Monde** on rue Ste-Catherine—just south of Place des Arts—the **Théâtre d'Aujourd-hui** on St-Denis above Sherbrooke, and the **Théâtre du Rideau Vert** on upper St-Denis.

Montréal, which is the home base for a number of troupes, is considered the dance capital of Canada. Among the best-known troupes are Ballets Classiques de Montréal, Les Grands Ballets Canadiens, Montréal Danse, LaLaLa Human Steps, Les Ballets Jazz de Montréal, Michael Montanaro Dance Company, Margie Gillis, and Tangente—the last a magnet for many of the city's more avant-garde choreographers. Most have established international reputations and can be seen at Place des Arts, Agora de la Danse, or any of the Maisons de la Culture performance spaces around town.

Every autumn the **Festival International de Nouvelle Danse** presents the hottest and most avant-garde dance troupes and soloists from the international scene. Be forewarned: Tickets for this event always go quickly—such is the caliber of the companies and the fanaticism of Montréal dance fans. For program information, Tel: (514) 287-1423; to order tickets, Tel: (514) 790-1245 or (800) 361-4595 (in Québec, eastern Ontario, and the United States).

OTHER ATTRACTIONS

Montréal Botanical Garden

Located in Parc Maisonneuve, but light-years away in spirit, the highly rated Montréal Botanical Garden is the third largest in the world (after those in Berlin and London). More than two million people a year admire the flowers and other plants that flourish in the ten interconnected greenhouses and 30 outdoor gardens here. The gardens' star attraction, however, is the largest bonsai collection outside Asia. Visitors enter the peaceful bonsai greenhouse through a moon gate, symbol of perfection and fertility. A more recent addition is a Japanese garden and pavilion, where the daily enactment of the Japanese tea brewing and drinking ritual is a highlight. Also not to be missed is the new **Dream Lake Friendship Garden**, conceived and built in the People's Republic of China as a birthday gift to the city. Striking for its beauty and atmosphere of quiet repose, the six-acre garden comprises 16 different landscapes linked by a sinuous path. Open daily, 9:00 A.M. to 4:30 P.M. (7:00 P.M. during the summer).

For a foreign encounter of another kind, take the free

shuttle bus to the nearby **Montréal Insectarium**, which houses more than 250,000 specimens—both live and dead—from 100 countries.

The latest addition to this peaceful enclave is the **Montréal Biodome**, a 10,000-square-foot "environmental" museum occupying the site of the former Olympic Vélodrome. Climate-controlled versions of four ecosystems—the tropical forest, the Laurentian forest, the St. Lawrence marine environment, and the polar world—are on display, along with their indigenous flora and fauna. Open daily, 9:00 A.M. to 6:00 P.M. (8:00 P.M. during the summer).

Le Château Dufresne

The Château Dufresne is one of the loveliest small museums in Canada. Housed in a restored Beaux Arts mansion just across from the Botanical Garden, this museum of the decorative arts features ground-floor period rooms (an Oriental smoking room, a cluttered dining room) furnished in Victorian and Edwardian styles, and presents regular exhibitions on international design trends and artifacts, contemporary and otherwise. Open Wednesday to Sunday, 11:00 A.M. to 5:00 P.M.

Oratoire St-Joseph

The world's largest shrine to Saint Joseph, Canada's patron saint, the Oratoire St-Joseph was the last architectural gasp of monolithic Catholicism in an increasingly secular society. Founded by a lay member of the Congregation of the Holy Cross named Brother André, the oratory evolved from a simple wooden chapel into an internationally known shrine that welcomes more than three million visitors a year—some pious, some merely curious, some racked by disease or deformity, all hoping for help by praying to Brother André and Saint Joseph. The former doorman, who died in 1931, was beatified in 1982 by Pope John Paul II.

The oratory and its grounds cover six acres of landscaped terraces at the western end of Mont-Royal in the Côte des Neiges area, near the Université de Montréal. At the head of a 99-step staircase—the central concrete steps are flanked by wooden ones for pilgrims ascending on their knees, a practice not so common as it was 20 or 30 years ago but still seen occasionally—stands the solid, low mass of the Crypt Church.

Looming above is an immense Renaissance-style basilica, begun in 1924 and not finished until 1967. Its great green copper-sheathed dome is second in size only to St. Peter's in Rome. The oratory is most impressive when a colorful light show illuminates the basilica and the carillon chimes, whose bells originally were intended for the Eiffel Tower. The shrine's observatory (some 850 feet above sea level) is the highest point in Montréal's landscape and is immediately recognizable from miles away.

PARC DES ILES

The city tried to maintain a permanent exhibition at the Expo '67 site on Ile-Notre-Dame and Ile-Ste-Hélène in the St. Lawrence River, but lack of funds and commitment led to the deterioration of the pavilions and a drop in attendance. With the birthday summer of 1992 looming, however, **Terre des Hommes** (Man and His World) was finally restored to something like its former glory. Renamed Parc des Iles, the $25-million renovation project saw the planting of 4,000 trees, the installation of new bike paths and walking trails, and the construction of entertainment and recreation facilities, including a huge natural amphitheater. Today ferries (one of them a converted school bus) shuttle an increasing number of visitors from Jacques-Cartier Quai in the Vieux-Port to the refurbished expo site. (Parc des Iles can also be reached via the Jacques Cartier Bridge, as well as by metro.)

On **Ile-Notre-Dame**, the Palais de la Civilisation, the French pavilion during Expo '67, is host to major art exhibitions (Gold of the Thracian Horsemen in 1987, the Cités-Cinés homages to Hollywood in 1989 and 1990, an exhibition of rare Roman and Italian art treasures in 1992). Concerts, both formal and impromptu, are staged in manicured floral gardens that were created for an international flower show in 1980. The Olympic rowing basin does duty in winter as a skating rink, and every June the Gilles Villeneuve Race Track hosts the Grand Prix Molson du Canada.

Ile-Ste-Hélène, which Champlain named for the patron saint of his 12-year-old bride, is home to **La Ronde amusement park**—Coney Island by the river (although a Coney Island with a face-lift). Nearby, L'Aquaparc's 20 water slides are great fun on a hot summer day, but only the truly brave attempt the near-vertical chute. The **Montréal Aquarium** is small, but don't overlook the 20,000-gallon coral-reef tank with its brilliantly colored tropical fish.

At the **David M. Stewart Museum**, students dressed in 18th-century uniforms representing members of the Fraser Highlanders and La Compagnie Franche de la Marine drill within the stone walls of an 1824 fort during the summer. But Canadiana is not all this museum has to offer (though it does have an impressive permanent collection). It is also the venue for exhibitions exploring the history and culture of

many of the world's great civilizations. Open daily except
Tuesdays, 10:00 A.M. to 5:00 P.M.

Saidye Bronfman Centre

Just two blocks west of Avenue Victoria and the Côte Ste-
Catherine metro station is the nationally renowned Saidye
Bronfman Centre, long recognized as a driving cultural
force within the Jewish community, in particular, and Montréal as a whole. Accessible by car (just one block east of
the Décarie Expressway, four blocks north of Queen Mary
Road), the Centre is open year-round, with many of its
activities free to the public. In particular, the Centre's gallery is recognized in national and international art circles
for the excellence of its contemporary art exhibitions. It is
also home to the Yiddish Theatre group. Check local newspapers for listings of upcoming events.

GETTING AROUND

By Air. Some 60 airlines serve Montréal's two main airports.
Dorval Airport, on the island west of downtown, handles
flights from North America (including other points in Canada); Mirabel Airport, about 65 km (40 miles) northwest of
the city, presently is used for charters and flights arriving
from other continents.

Major airlines with nonstop service to Dorval include Air
Canada and Canadian Airlines International from most cities
across Canada. From the United States, Air Canada flies
nonstop from Boston, New York, Fort Lauderdale, Miami,
Orlando, and Tampa, and direct from Los Angeles and San
Francisco via Toronto. Canadian Airlines International and
American Airlines fly from Chicago via Toronto. Delta Air-
lines flies nonstop from Boston, New York, Atlanta, and
Miami, and direct from Fort Lauderdale via New York or
Boston. USAir flies nonstop from Syracuse, Buffalo, Philadel-
phia, and Baltimore. And British Airways flies nonstop from
Detroit.

As for international flights into Mirabel, Air Canada flies
nonstop from London, Brussels, Paris, Nice, and Zurich, and
direct from Frankfurt and Vienna via Toronto, as well as from
Nice via London. British Airways flies nonstop from London.
Canadian Airlines International flies direct from London,
Manchester, Milan, and Munich via Toronto, and nonstop
from Paris and Rome. And Aer Lingus flies direct from
Dublin and Shannon via Boston or New York. Montréal-
bound Australian visitors are served by Canadian Airlines
International from Sydney via Toronto and by British Air-
ways from Sydney, Melbourne, and Perth via London.

A metered cab from Dorval to downtown costs about $23 (before tip); private limousines cost slightly more, depending on destination but regardless of the number of passengers. Cab fare from Mirabel is at least $56 (before tip).

A bus service called Autocar Connoisseur leaves every 30 minutes from Dorval for downtown Montréal, with stops at the Sheraton Centre, the Château Champlain, Le Grand Hôtel, and Le Reine Elizabeth Hotel. The final destination is the Voyageur bus terminal at Berri-UQAM, a metro station. The trip takes about 20 minutes and costs between $8.50 and $11.75, depending on your destination.

Autobus Aéro Plus service from Mirabel to the Gare Centrale behind Le Reine Elizabeth Hotel costs $12.50, one way. The trip takes about an hour, and includes a stop at the Voyageur bus terminal. Autobus Aéro Plus also runs a shuttle between the two airports, with the fare about $11.75, one way.

By Car/Bus. Visitors travelling by car from the west and east arrive in Montréal via Route 20 or Route 40 (via the Trans-Canada Highway). Three major expressways link Montréal with the United States: Interstate 87 in New York, and either 87 or 91 in Vermont. Buses from Québec City and the United States—Auger, Auger-Colonial, and Greyhound—arrive at the centrally located Voyageur terminal.

Car rentals are expensive, with occasional discounting on weekend rates. Most companies charge for mileage. For information and reservations, try: Avis Rent-a-Car (Tel: 514/866-7906 or 800/879-2847); Budget Rent-a-Car (Tel: 514/866-7675 or 800/268-8900); Hertz Rent-a-Car (Tel: 514/842-8537 or 800/654-3001); Thrifty Rent-a-Car (Tel: 514/845-5954 or 800/367-2277); or Tilden Inter-Rent (Tel: 514/878-2771 or 800/387-4747). The legal driving age in Canada is 16, although you must be 21 to rent a car. New York motorists visiting Québec should note that the state and provincial governments now have a reciprocal agreement on traffic violations. In other words, a traffic violation committed in Québec will be fined and penalized as if it had occurred in New York.

By Train. Both VIA Rail Canada and Amtrak from the United States arrive in downtown Montréal at the Gare Centrale, on the south side of Le Reine Elizabeth hotel across boulevard René Lévesque from Place Ville-Marie. The station is accessed from the metro via the Bonaventure station.

Public Transportation. Montréal's bus and subway systems are, for the most part, clean, safe, and efficient. There are five metro lines connecting 65 stations, each decorated differently with specially commissioned murals, ceramics, and stained glass. The metro runs from 5:30 A.M. to 1:00 A.M. (except for the Blue Line, which stops at 11:00 P.M.). The fare for both bus and subway is $1.75 for any length trip (exact change is required for buses). Passengers can transfer between bus and metro at no extra charge.

Calèches (open carriages) offer rides year-round from starting points at Square Dorchester and on Mont-Royal. *Calèches* can also be hailed in Vieux-Montréal around Place Jacques-Cartier and Place d'Armes, as well as on Bonsecours, Gosford, de la Commune, and Notre-Dame streets. The hourly cost is about $40.

Tour Operators. The major sightseeing bus-tour company is **Autocar Connoisseur-Gray Line** (Tel: 514/934-1222). **Héritage Montréal** (Tel: 514/875-2985), an architectural conservation group, and **Tours Diamant** (Tel: 514/744-3009) organize bus and walking tours through many neighborhoods. Copies of Héritage Montréal's "Steps in Time" brochures, listing 15 neighborhood walking tours (including Vieux-Montréal), are available from its office at 1181 rue de la Montagne. **Guidatour** (Tel: 514/844-4021) and the **Montréal Sightseeing Company** (Tel: 514/484-0104) provide licensed guides and escort services for traditional and specialized tours (individuals and groups) in several languages. **Visites de Montréal** (Tel: 514/933-6674) offers group sightseeing tours in and around the city, while **Step on Guides Inc.** (Tel: 514/935-5131), like the others in most respects, also offers walking tours of the Underground City. **Taxi LaSalle** (Tel: 514/277-2552) cab drivers are also registered guides for Montréal visits, with the length of tour and destination adjusted to individual itineraries. The cost is generally $28 an hour, with a maximum of four persons per cab.

Croisières du Port de Montréal (Tel: 514/842-3871 or 800/667-3131) offers a variety of tours of the St. Lawrence River from early May to mid-October. **Lachine Rapids Tours** (Tel: 514/284-9607) offers jet-boat excursions ($45 per person) through the Lachine Rapids. **Amphi Tour** (Tel: 514/386-1298) offers a unique experience: a guided tour of Vieux-Montréal and the Vieux-Port on land and water, courtesy of its "Kamada" amphibious bus. The one-hour tour ($18 per person) operates daily from May through October.

Last but not least, the glass-roofed, climate-controlled *Bateau-Mouche* (Tel: 514/849-9952), which docks at Quai Jacques-Cartier, offers one-and-a-half-hour tours of Ile-Ste-Hélène, Ile-Notre-Dame, and the restored Lachine Canal daily from May through October.

Seasonal Events

Montréal's seasonal events include the Benson & Hedges **International Fireworks Competition**, with spectacular shows presented by entrants from a dozen countries. Some six million people watch the kaleidoscopic productions, which usually take place from late May to mid-June. Also in June is the **Tour de l'Ile de Montréal** amateur cycling race. Now in its ninth year, the event attracts almost 45,000 cycling enthusiasts. Starting at the Parc Olympique, cyclists follow a course that takes them along most of the major streets on the island.

Beginning June 30, Montréal's **International Jazz Festival** takes over the city with two weeks of nonstop music. Last year's edition, the festival's 14th, featured more than 2,000 musicians from 20 different countries. For information on this year's festival, call the InfoJazz line at (514) 523-3378.

The world's largest comedy festival, the **Festival Juste Pour Rire**, follows right on the heels of the jazz festival for two weeks in late July. Featuring a mix of free outdoor events and paid indoor shows, in both English and French, the festival has gone over the one-million mark in attendance each of the last two years.

The **World Film Festival** in August, one of the best in North America, screens hundreds of international films at venues all over town. Attendance at this tremendously popular event now tops a quarter of a million. On a smaller scale but of critical and popular interest is the annual **Montréal International Festival of New Cinema and Video** in October, where, in the past, avant-garde works by the likes of Wim Wenders and Jim Jarmusch have been screened.

The fall offers annual music festivals to suit all tastes, beginning with the **International Rock Festival** in late September–early October, followed by the **Montréal New Music Festival** in mid-October, the latter a showcase for emerging local and international artists and bands. Late fall sees a gathering of international Francophone artists for the two-week **Francofolie Festival** of song at a variety of venues.

As far as weather is concerned, fall can come as early as mid-September, with alternately wet and cold days followed by brilliant sunshine, crisp, clear air, and cloudless blue skies. Montréal's mountain and the surrounding countryside offer the glories of whole areas seemingly consumed by fire, as the fall foliage turns to brilliant crimsons, flaming oranges, deep golds, rusts and purples—a spectacle no Montrealer ever tires of.

Winter can also come early, with the first snowfall and

freezing temperatures arriving as early as November. Though recent winters have seen something of a warming trend, don't be fooled: winter in Montréal is long, cold, and snowy, and can linger (in milder form) into early April. For outdoor enthusiasts, this is a boon—it's not unusual to see Montrealers heading up to the Laurentians for that last skiing trip on Easter weekend—but creatures of comfort need not despair: indoor activities abound, with the emphasis on arts and cultural events.

March heralds Québec's maple syrup season—coinciding with the spring thaw—an event that Montrealers and visitors can literally sink their teeth into. All around Montréal are *cabanes à sucre* serving up such traditional Québécois fare as maple-soaked beans, bacon, potatoes, bread, omelets, pancakes, deep-fried dumplings, sugar pie, and maple taffy rolled in snow. An excellent introduction to Québec culture and its legendary joie de vivre, maple-syrup festivities offer visitors an insider's glimpse of the traditions and bonhomie that forged French Québec's character and influenced so profoundly its English, Irish, and Scottish settlers.

The cultural scene truly takes off in mid-spring. Street musicians, artists, sidewalk cafés, outdoor festivals, parades, and sports competitions proliferate from Easter on, as the warmer weather brings out the people. For those not inclined to the festival scene, Montréal offers sightseeing, shopping, dining, and people-watching in abundance well into the night.

As for clothing, whatever the season, layered dressing is the best approach. In winter and summer, particularly, be prepared to add and shed layers as you go in or out of doors. Survival dictates a warm hat, scarf, gloves, and waterproof boots in winter; down jackets and fur coats are the preferred choice of many. Fall, spring, and even summer will likely require a sweater and light jacket or raincoat to cope with sudden temperature changes and the occasional rainfall. In winter expect temperatures of 14° F (−10° C) and below; in summer (late June and July especially), expect them to soar above 90° F (32° C). For weather forecasts, Tel: (514) 283-4006; for winter road conditions, Tel: (514) 873-4121.

ACCOMMODATIONS

Montréal underwent hotel construction booms prior to Expo '67 and the 1976 Summer Olympics. Several hotels that date from those memorable events have undergone much-needed face-lifts so as to keep up with the cutthroat competition in a crowded market. The last few years have also seen the addition of a number of new players, most notably the Hotel Inter-Continental Montréal, the sumptuous corner-stone of the new World Trade Centre complex, and the Hôtel Vogue, in the heart of the downtown area. Despite overcapacity, prices remain high, even with a reasonable Canadian dollar (worth about U.S. $0.80). Many large downtown hotels, including the Hôtel Méridien and L'Hôtel Shangrila, which rely on a Monday-through-Thursday business clientele, offer greatly reduced weekend rates to keep their rooms filled. Even the elegant Ritz-Carlton promotes weekend deals. Travellers may have to stay a minimum of two nights, but often such incentives as a welcoming cocktail, Continental breakfast, or a free city tour are included.

There is now a central reservations clearinghouse for hotels in the greater Montréal area. The same number can be called for information about sightseeing tours, sports and entertainment packages, and special events. Contact: Montréal Reservations Center, P.O. Box 707, Station C, Montréal, Québec H2L 4L6. Tel: (514) 864-0055; Fax: (514) 864-0077 or 0199; in the U.S. and Canada, Tel: (800) 567-8687.

The following accommodations in downtown Montréal have been selected for their location, amenities, and value for money. The rates given are *projections* for peak seasons during the 1994 calendar year and unless otherwise indicated are based on double rooms, double occupancy. As rates are subject to change, always double-check before booking. The area code in Montréal is 514.

▶ **Howard Johnson Plaza.** Less expensive than many of the big downtown luxury hotels, this establishment just east of the Université de McGill campus is popular with bus-tour groups. Completely renovated in 1988, the Plaza now boasts a spa with whirlpool, sauna, and exercise machines. The lobby has been spiffed up as well, as has the hotel's restaurant, with lots of brass and marble in evidence. Bay windows overlook Sherbrooke, and there's an outdoor terrace for summer dining.

475 rue Sherbrooke Ouest, Montréal, Québec H3A 2L9. Tel: 842-3961; Fax: 842-0945; in the U.S. and Canada, Tel: (800) 654-2000. $99.

▶ **Bonaventure Hilton International.** The Bonaventure boasts the most unusual location of the midtown luxury hotels: the top six floors of Place Bonaventure (west of Square Victoria and just south of the city's business center), a massive, six-acre complex housing retail shops, offices, and a vast exhibition hall. The hotel's 400 rooms are distributed around an inner courtyard and decorated in classic contemporary style. Guests can stroll through a rooftop Japanese garden and swim year-round in a heated outdoor pool, while similar attempts to create privacy and quiet seclusion have succeeded in blocking out all but the view of surrounding skyscrapers. In addition, the hotel's **Le Castillon** restaurant is widely acclaimed for its excellent French cuisine.

One Place Bonaventure, Montréal, Québec H5A 1E4. Tel: 878-2332; Fax: 878-1442; in the U.S. and Canada, Tel: (800) HILTONS. $139–$236.

▶ **Le Centre Sheraton Montréal**. Elegantly understated appointments and an excellent restaurant are the hallmarks of this expensive hotel, located one block west of Square Dorchester near the Gare Windsor. Many rooms come with sofa beds in addition to the usual amenities, and all are decorated in eye-catching color schemes. Executive suites are on the top five floors—the popular "hotel within a hotel" concept for pampered guests and celebrities. Elsewhere in the hotel, one end of the lobby is taken up by a plant-filled atrium, and Continental cuisine dominates the menu at **Le Boulevard**, where grilled hotstone meals and fish dishes are counted among the specialties and a muted Asian-style decor in green, salmon, and red adds to the soothing ambience.

1201 boulevard René Lévesque Ouest, Montréal, Québec H3B 2L7. Tel: 878-2000; Fax: 878-3958; in the U.S. and Canada, Tel: (800) 325-3535. $195–$230.

▶ **Le Château Champlain**. With arched windows that make it look like a giant cheese grater, this 36-story Canadian Pacific property is something of a departure from its stately CP Hotels siblings. (It's also located directly across the street from the parent corporation's historic sandstone headquarters.) Standard doubles come with the usual amenities, junior suites with a queen-size sofa bed in addition to a king-size bed. The popular **Bar Gauguin** on the 36th floor offers outstanding views of midtown and Mont-Royal (according to some, the window in the women's washroom has the best panorama of downtown and the mountain), while the hotel's Caf' Conc dinner show, featuring all the glam, gams, and glitter of a slightly risqué French song-and-dance revue à la Folies-Bergères, is popular with visitors and Montrealers alike.

1 place du Canada, Montréal, Québec H3B 4C9. Tel: 878-9000; Fax: 878-6761; in the U.S. and Canada, Tel: (800) 441-1414. $155–$250.

▶ **Holiday Inn Crowne Plaza**. Every city has a Holiday Inn and Montréal is no exception. (In fact, there are five in the metropolitan area.) The chain's flagship hotel in Montréal offers the creature comforts one has come to expect of

Holiday Inns from Alaska to the Far East. Recently renovated, the Crowne Plaza is a modest jewel, with two executive floors, an indoor pool, a health club, a café-restaurant, and two bars on the premises. Popular with convention groups, the hotel is next door to the Hôtel La Citadelle, just five minutes from the heart of downtown.

420 rue Sherbrooke Ouest, Montréal, Québec H3A 1B4. Tel: 842-6111; Fax: 842-9381; in the U.S. and Canada, Tel: (800) HOLIDAY. $150–$155.

▶ **Hôtel La Citadelle**. Recently purchased by the Hôtels Senneville chain, La Citadelle has been done over as a European-style hotel, heavy on the marble and burgundy-and-mauve decor. The staff is friendly and efficient, and the jazz piano lounge is as comfortable as a living room. Large double rooms, costing about 20 percent less than they would in midtown luxury hotels, are popular with business travellers. Ask for a north-facing room for wonderful views of Mont-Royal.

410 rue Sherbrooke Ouest, Montréal, Québec H3A 1B3. Tel: 844-8851; Fax: 844-0912; in the U.S. and Canada, Tel: (800) 465-6654. $145.

▶ **Hôtel Delta Montréal**. One of Montréal's newer hotels, the Delta is a best buy in an excellent midtown location east of McGill, near La Citadelle and the Howard Johnson Plaza. Most rooms have two double beds, color cable TV, and balconies. Other amenities include a business center, day-care services, and a health club with indoor and outdoor pools. Mesquite-grilled meat and fish are the house special-ties at **Le Bouquet**, one of the city's most attractive hotel dining rooms, and there is music most nights in the hotel's bar.

475 avenue President Kennedy, Montréal, Québec H3A 1J7. Tel: 286-1986; Fax: 284-4342; in the U.S., Tel: (800) 877-1133; in Canada, (800) 268-1133. $238.

▶ **Le Radisson-Gouverneurs Montréal**. The location is not promising: The serrated V-shaped building on the south side of Square Victoria is just north of expressway ramps and east of elevated train tracks. Still, after extensive renovations, the Radisson now offers glassy, if isolated, elegance, with win-dowed elevators, the city's only revolving rooftop restaurant, a pool, and an atrium lobby. The **Chez Antoine** bistro, decked out in Art Nouveau–style, is known for its grilled meat specialties. The hotel is adjacent to the Bourse de Montréal and within walking distance of Vieux-Montréal.

777 rue University, Montréal, Québec H3C 3Z7. Tel: 879-1370; Fax: 879-1761; in the U.S. and Canada, Tel: (800) 333-3333. $178.

▶ **Hôtel Château Versailles**. Montréal's most charming European-style hotel inspires Bermudian loyalty: Guests keep coming back and wouldn't think of staying anywhere else. To create their hotel, which is just west of the point where chemin de la Côte-des-Neiges descends into Sherbrooke and becomes rue Guy, French-born André Villeneuve and his Canadian wife, Marie-Louise, connected four graystone mansions built between 1911 and 1913, restored plaster moldings and fireplaces, and scoured the province for antique furnishings. The rooms are simple, clean, and functional, and a number overlook a courtyard garden. There is no bar, and only breakfast is served in the 12-table dining room, although afternoon tea is available from room service. A ten-minute walk away, though, are the boutiques, bars, and restaurants of Bishop, Crescent, and de la Montagne streets.

1659 rue Sherbrooke Ouest, Montréal, Québec H3H 1E3. Tel: 933-3611; Fax: 933-7102; in the U.S., Tel: (800) 361-3664; in Canada, (800) 361-7199. $119–$149.

▶ **Hôtel La Tour Versailles**. It seems there's no arguing with success. Now facing the Château Versailles on Sherbrooke is a newer version of that old favorite: Expansion of the original wouldn't have been possible without destroying its turn-of-the-century appeal. Also owned and operated by the Villeneuves, this former office tower has been converted into an intimate high-rise hotel where the staff excels in the professional service visitors have come to expect from a Villeneuve operation. Although charmingly decorated throughout, the corner suites are particularly pleasing. A bonus for both establishments is the luxuriously appointed ground-floor restaurant, **Les Champs Elysées**, where the food vies with the decor for honors and the service is always impeccable. A hit since it opened, the restaurant has become a little less formal and expensive since Chef Jalby took over from Christian Levesque.

1808 rue Sherbrooke Ouest, Montréal, Québec H3H 1E5. Tel: 933-3611; Fax: 933-7102; in the U.S., Tel: (800) 361-3664; in Canada, (800) 361-7199. $119–$149.

▶ **Hôtel Inter-Continental Montréal**. The newest hotel in Montréal offers the ne plus ultra in ambience, service, and surroundings, which is why, since it opened in late 1991, it has become the preferred home away from home for jet-setters and executive-class types who demand the best wherever they travel. The hotel is part of the landmark World Trade Centre in Vieux-Montréal and incorporates the 1888 Nordheimer Building into its layout. Every effort was made to successfully integrate the design of the new turreted hotel

tower with its historic counterpart. Granite and wood paneling are used throughout the interior and, in a novel touch, the
original vaults of the older building have been converted into
dining, bar, banquet, and reception facilities. The tower's 359
guest rooms and 22 suites feature state-of-the-art amenities
amid Victorian-inspired furnishings. Each guest room has a
minibar and refrigerator, dual-line phones with PC and fax
hookup, a large desk, and twice-daily maid service. The hotel
also features a health club with lap pool, sauna and steam
rooms, and gym facilities that open onto a landscaped roof
garden. For the business traveller, there's a fully equipped
Executive Business Centre with secretarial, translation, and
communications services, as well as an executive lounge.

360 rue St-Antoine Ouest, Montréal, Québec H2Y 3X4. Tel:
987-9900; Fax: 847-8730; in the U.S. and Canada, Tel: (800)
327-0200. $132–$195.

▶ **Hôtel de la Montagne**. One of Montréal's smaller hotels, the de la Montagne is favored by affluent business and
pleasure travellers in their thirties and forties who frequent
places like the Morgan in Manhattan. Owner Bernard Rague-
neau manages the lodgings, restaurants, bars, and disco-
theque. The foyer is nearly overwhelmed by a rococo-style
fountain, but the bar is intimate, with a jazz duo playing most
nights. Rooms are furnished in French Provincial style, and
amenities include a rooftop summer pool (with open-air
restaurant and bar), connection to the disco one flight down
from the lobby, and access to the back of one of rue Crescent's busiest singles bars by the same route.

1430 rue de la Montagne, Montréal, Québec H3G 1Z5. Tel:
288-5656; Fax: 288-9658; in the U.S. and Canada, Tel: (800)
361-6262. $132–$143; $216 (suite).

▶ **Hôtel Le Méridien Montréal**. A four-star luxury hotel in
an unusual location, Air France's Méridien anchors one
corner of the Complexe Desjardins, a multilevel glassed-in
plaza bounded by three office towers and the hotel itself.
Rooms are decorated in contemporary style, and come with
a sitting area, work table, and separate dressing area. The
hotel's **Café Fleuri** is one of the city's best, as are the
swimming pool, the sundeck, and the garden terrace. Although the Méridien is slightly removed from downtown, it
is convenient via all-weather corridors to Place des Arts,
Chinatown, and the convention center. And Vieux-Montréal
is only a short, above-ground walk away. The hotel is popular with movie people during the August film festival, and in
recent years has also become the official headquarters for
musicians and organizers of the Montréal International Jazz

Festival, with many concerts taking place on its outdoor terraces.

4 Complexe Desjardins, C.P. 130, Montréal, Québec H5B 1E5. Tel: 285-1450; Fax: 285-1243; in the U.S. and Canada, Tel: (800) 543-4300. $120–$210.

▶ **Hôtel Vogue.** Billed as "a grand hotel particulier"— defined by the French as a dwelling remarkable for its discreet, personalized, and exclusive services—the intimately scaled Hôtel Vogue arrived on the scene in the spring of 1991 offering elegantly appointed rooms furnished in Late Empire style, a gracious staff, and superb dining and entertaining facilities. All rooms and suites come with a king- or queen-size bed, down comforters and pillows, a whirlpool bath, fax machine, and electronic combination safe among their amenities. The Vogue's **Société Café**, already a favorite with Montréal's café society types, features Euro-Asian cuisine, while its **l'Opéra le Bar** is a popular spot for cocktails or informal get-togethers.

1425 rue de la Montagne, Montréal, Québec H3G 1Z3. Tel: 285-5555; Fax: 849-8903; in the U.S. and Canada (business hours only), Tel: (800) 465-6654. $160–$216.

▶ **L'Hôtel Ritz-Carlton-Kempinski.** As the grande dame of Montréal hotels, the Ritz has been dispensing Old World hospitality to silver-haired tycoons and svelte beauties since 1912. Guests have included Mary Pickford and Douglas Fairbanks, Edward VIII and Queen Marie of Romania, and Dick and Liz, who were married here in 1964—again. Designed by Beaux-Arts specialists Whitney Warren and Charles D. Wetmore, the Ritz encapsulates this starchy stretch of rue Sherbrooke: elegance and grace, wealth and power, understatement and tradition, and, occasionally, stuffy pretension. Jackets and ties are mandatory for men, even at the **Café de Paris** bar (maître d' John Dominique once denied entrance to a jeans-clad Mick Jagger), and its outdoor garden terrace with duck pond is a favorite power-breakfast and brunch spot in summer. When booking, ask for a room facing Mont-Royal.

1228 rue Sherbrooke Ouest, Montréal, Québec H3G 1H6. Tel: 842-4212; Fax: 842-4907; in the U.S., Tel: (800) 241-3333; in Canada, (800) 363-0366. $230–$245.

▶ **Hotel Lord Berri.** This no-frills establishment north of boulevard René Lévesque in the Latin *quartier* offers moderate prices and adequate rooms with simple furnishings. There is no bellhop or room service, only a café-bistro. Minibars and nonsmoking floors are also featured.

1199 rue Berri, Montréal, Québec H2L 4C6. Tel: 845-9236;

Fax: 849-9855; in the U.S. and Canada, Tel: (800) 363-0363. $99.

▶ **Le Quatre Saisons.** One of the best (the hotel has racked up several awards recently) of Montréal's modern hotels, Le Quatre Saisons is a favorite with international expense-account types. The large rooms in this 31-story tower on rue Sherbrooke, at the southern end of the Golden Square Mile, are attractively furnished with Georgian-style writing desks and decorated in colorful chintz. Facilities include a Gymtech health club and a year-round outdoor heated pool. The hotel also boasts two top-flight restaurants: **Le Cercle**, which serves Californian, Italian, and French cuisine, and has an outstanding wine cellar; and **Zen**, a clone of London's trendy Chinese restaurant of the same name.

1050 rue Sherbrooke Ouest, Montréal, Québec H3A 2R6. Tel: 284-1110; Fax: 845-3025; in the U.S., Tel: (800) 332-3442; in Canada, (800) 268-6282. $245–$295.

▶ **Le Reine Elizabeth.** Not too many years ago the city's largest midtown luxury hotel was little more than a monotonous concrete slab atop the Gare Centrale opposite Place Ville-Marie. Recent renovations have resulted in a much brighter and more welcoming lobby and rooms that are modern and spacious. Management also added an executive floor with the usual business-type amenities. Some of the old haunts, like the **Beaver Club**, the domain of chef Jean Cardeaux, a member of the Académie Culinaire de France, are still compelling as well. The restaurant, which is the only one in town to list cigars on its menu, is named for the 19th-century fraternity of fur-trade barons that counted New Yorker John Jacob Astor as an honorary member. There's also a popular bistro, **Le Montréalais**, in the hotel offering Continental cuisine. Tour groups and local conventions are mainstays of the Queen Elizabeth, which has a convenient downtown location with connections to the metro.

900 boulevard René Lévesque Ouest, Montréal, Québec H3B 4A5. Tel: 861-3511; Fax: 954-2256; in the U.S. and Canada, Tel: (800) 828-7447. $125.

▶ **L'Hôtel Shangrila Best Western.** With a central location on Sherbrooke near the McGill campus and excellent weekend rates, L'Hôtel Shangrila is a favorite of travellers more interested in comfort than luxury. Every floor of this refurbished hostelry has a distinct theme lifted from Asian folklore, with the Eastern motif even extending to the bell captain, who sports a six-piece blue Mongolian warrior's suit with silver bangles. The standard double comes with the usual amenities (double beds, color cable TV, minibar), and the hotel also has a Szechuan restaurant by the name of Dynasty de Ming as well as a coffee shop overlooking the corner of Peel and Sherbrooke for the convenience of its guests.

3407 rue Peel, Montréal, Québec H3A 1W7. Tel: 288-4141; Fax: 288-3021; in the U.S. and Canada, Tel: (800) 528-1234. $111; $199 (suite).

—Mary Kelly

DINING

Montréal loves to eat and party. There are more than 5,000 restaurants and dozens of cuisines to choose from—in fact, the city rivals New York as the gastronomic capital of the continent. We've selected just *some* of the good ones—or most interesting ones. In a predominantly French-speaking city, it is French cuisine that dominates. But Montrealers seem to be obsessed with Italian, Chinese, Japanese, and Indian cuisine as well. And, of course, there are the cuisines of the many other nations from which the city's residents hail.

Montrealers generally eat late, though not as late as people in Spain. Peak dining time is 8:00 P.M. Unless you have a reservation, try to arrive for dinner at 7:00 P.M. or 9:30 P.M. to ensure a table. At lunch, if you're not in at a popular spot by 12:15 don't bother arriving until 2:00 P.M. This is a city that has turned the two-hour lunch into an art form.

Montrealers also stay out late, regardless of the day of the week. Bars in the province of Québec can serve liquor up to 3:00 A.M., seven days a week. On most nights they don't close until 4:00 A.M.

Lunch is always a bargain. All restaurants offer three-course meals at low, prix-fixe rates. This means you can lunch at expensive restaurants for a quarter to half of what it might cost at night. And remember: Provincial law requires all restaurants to post their menus outside.

Liquor and wine are heavily taxed in Québec, and mark-ups are high in restaurants and bars. A premium cognac in a bar can cost $6 and up. A good bottle of wine is rarely below $25 in a restaurant, although you can find acceptable table wines for about $20. Federal and provincial taxes totaling 15 percent apply to all food and liquor sales. To that, you are expected to add at least 15 percent as a tip.

The telephone area code in Montréal is 514.

French and Continental

Bistro Bagatelle. This bistro at 4806 avenue du Parc (corner of Villeneuve Ouest) is notable for its reasonably priced, quasi-nouvelle French cuisine. There are always six to eight kinds of fresh fish on the menu, along with meat, poultry, and veal. Often you can find a fish consommé or a gratin of mussels with crayfish bisque sauce. When available, the fresh leg of lamb with garlic confit is terrific. Vegetables, served crisp but in very small quantities, are perfectly cooked. Closed Sundays. Tel: 273-4088.

Chez La Mère Michel. The French cuisine at this downtown spot (1209 rue Guy, just south of Ste-Catherine Ouest) is as memorable as the setting: a romantic old stone house with lots of stained glass. The cooks do impressive things with tournedos, sweetbreads, lamb, and seafood, and a covered terrace open year-round adds to your enjoyment of their skills. The service is courteous, and you'll want to have a drink in the bar downstairs, if only to admire its coziness. Closed Sundays. Tel: 934-0473.

Gargantua & Pantagruel. This reliable, bring-your-own-wine establishment occupies a charming four-story house at 3873 rue St-Denis in central Montréal. A huge basket of *crudités* at each table and a charcuterie buffet featuring seafood, sausages, and salads are included in the prix-fixe dinner for $17.95, with seafood casseroles, steak, and lamb among the entrées. A less-expensive, rotating prix-fixe dinner for $10.95 also includes the *crudités* and buffet. Tel: 843-6317.

Laloux. Another in a new generation of French bistros, this one, a block from carré St. Louis at the corner of avenue des Pins Est and rue Laval, is rather austere and less lively than its rivals. The cuisine has definite nouvelle touches, with a hint of California—ginger, sesame, and lemon are some of the innovative flavorings. Try the crab bisque or any of the fish dishes. Closed Sundays. Tel: 287-9127.

La Marée. You'll feel as if you've stepped into another century when you enter this romantic 18th-century graystone restaurant at 404 Place Jacques-Cartier in Vieux-Montréal. Specialties include fresh seafood, some with exquisite sauces. Try a pâté of turbot or fresh halibut in a lobster cream sauce. Tel: 861-9794 or 8126.

La Rapière. This venerable downtown institution has long been known for its hearty, bourgeois French cuisine. Old World service (spotless linen, heavy cutlery, warmed plates) complements such dishes as boudin noir (black or blood pudding), veal liver, and fresh fish. 1490 rue Stanley at de Maisonneuve. Closed Sundays. Tel: 844-8920.

Le Castillon. On the 17th floor of the massive Place Bonaventure complex and part of the downtown Hilton, this roof-garden restaurant comes complete with lush vegetation, flowing water, and ducklings. (The ducklings disappear in winter, though the garden stays.) Indoors, the decor is somewhat imperial, with plush chairs. Best bets here are the seasonal specials. Tel: 878-2332.

Le Cercle. Located in the Four Seasons downtown (1050 rue Sherbrooke Ouest), this is one of the better hotel restaurants in the city. Although menu prices tend to reflect its upscale location, the three-course prix-fixe dinner for $20 is a bargain. A la carte entrées, which are prepared with flair and an eye to colorful presentation, rely on fresh market ingredients and goodies like sun-dried tomatoes, olives, and dill tzatziki. Tel: 284-1110.

L'Express. Lines are the norm in front of this most popular of Montréal bistros, located at 3927 rue St-Denis, between Roy and Duluth. The ambience—noisy conversations, much flailing of arms—competes with reasonably priced bistro fare. Portions are hearty; try the soups or steak tartare. Call a day in advance for reservations; Tel: 845-5333.

Le St. Amable. Classic versions of kidneys, sweetbreads, and sole are served in this romantic and expensive Vieux-Montréal haunt (188 St-Amable, off Place Jacques-Cartier). Try to eat downstairs; it's ultra cozy and transports you back to a bygone era. Tel: 866-3471.

Les Continents. Another fine hotel restaurant, this one in Vieux-Montréal's Hotel Inter-Continental (360 rue St-Antoine Ouest). The menu here is international, innovative, and market-oriented, with wild mushrooms, sweetbreads, fresh fish, and black beans among the ingredients in the chef's inventive sauces and wrappings. Tel: 987-9900.

Les Halles. Located in the heart of the rue Crescent bar-and-boutique jungle downtown, this is one of the best French restaurants in Montréal. The ambience on the lower floor is pure upscale Parisian bistro. If you'd rather avoid the noise and bustle, you can book upstairs in the romantic dining room. The menu frequently offers specials and is always innovative. If you're up for a splurge, ask for a dinner planned by the chef. From the regular menu, try the quail mousse or tart of duck, veal, and foie gras flavored with truffle juices, rosemary, Port, and Cognac. Or order one of the fish dishes and, if you have a taste for them, calf sweetbreads. 1450 rue Crescent, between de Maisonneuve Ouest and Ste-Catherine Ouest. Tel: 844-2328.

Les Mignardises. Muted decor and an intriguing menu distinguish this highly nouvelle and very expensive French restaurant at 2037 rue St-Denis, between Sherbrooke and Ontario. You'll swoon over the lobster soup and marvel at the artistry of dishes such as salad of scallops and turbot in a pimento sauce. Tel: 842-1151.

Ritz Garden. During the summer, the perfect place for afternoon tea or a leisurely dinner is here at the luxurious Ritz-Carlton Hotel, 1228 rue Sherbrooke Ouest. Even though you'll pay for it, you won't regret the setting—ducklings on a pond, lush lawns, umbrellas, and so on. Splurge on caviar or lobster, sole or smoked salmon. Altogether, very decadent and memorable. Tel: 842-4212.

Seafood

Chez Delmo. Not much has changed over the last 26 years in this Vieux-Montréal fish restaurant. Two long, polished-wood oyster bars line the aisle leading to a modest dining room where longtime waitresses politely and competently serve an unchanging menu of fish and seafood.

In season, Chez Delmo has the best raw oysters in town, and it's usually more fun to sit at the long bars than in the simple dining room. Order the fresh fish of the day and skip any sauces that might be suggested with it unless you like them heavy and old-fashioned—the fish here is best grilled or sautéed. 211 rue Notre Dame Ouest, between rues St-Francis-Xavier and St-Pierre. Closed Sundays. Tel: 849-4061.

Etoile d'Océan. An unpretentious entrance at 101 rue Rachel Est (a couple of blocks east of boulevard St-Laurent) leads to a large, cozy dining room connected by a short passage at the back to a bar next door. Blue-and-white ceramic tiles with Moorish motifs, dark wood beams, a ceiling of red roof tiles, Algarve pottery, fishing nets, and lampshades made from seashells all conspire to transport you to Portugal.

Try the clams in coriander sauce, fried squid, or *carne Alentejano,* a traditional dish from the Alentejo province consisting of generous cubes of succulent fried pork tossed with clams in their shells and served in a tomato, garlic, and fresh coriander sauce. Tel: 844-4588.

Italian

Baci. Some of the best Italian food in Montréal is served in this ultramodern, multilevel restaurant downtown. There's a variety of seating choices, from the lush conservatory up front to the cozy, sunken dining rooms. Sauces for pasta are creative, and classical dishes like risotto are executed with finesse. The fish and veal dishes are also good. 2095 avenue McGill College, between Sherbrooke Ouest and avenue President Kennedy. Closed Sundays. Tel: 288-7901.

Bocca d'Oro. Superbly designed and decorated, this downtown Italian restaurant (1448 rue St-Mathieu, between de Maisonneuve Ouest and Ste-Catherine Ouest) also has an excellent kitchen. Its fresh-daily specials, announced by the waiters, are your best bet, although a plate of pasta with three different sauces never disappoints. Tel: 933-8414.

Café Modigliani. Paintings by the owner and discarded props from long-forgotten plays dominate the decor at this eclectic Italian hideaway on the Plateau Mont-Royal. Ledges along the front glass walls sport angled mirrors, birdcages, and cactuses. On weekends, jammed into a small corner, a piano player entertains diners with soft jazz. Stay an hour or ten, the owners won't mind. The cooking is home-style, with pastas and veal accompanied by predictable, unpretentious sauces, and the food is reasonably priced and satisfying. 1251 rue Gilford, between Mont-Royal Est and boulevard St-Joseph Est. Tel: 522-0422.

Il Gentile Rico. Located on the rejuvenated strip of boulevard St-Laurent between avenues Laurier and Bernard, this discreet little place tends to be overlooked. While the cooking isn't likely to win any awards, it does offer good value for the money. Factor in the friendly, prompt service, pleasant, unobtrusive decor, and comfortable seating, and it all adds up to a satisfying night on the town.

Cream, garlic, parsley, and easy-on-the-tomatoes seem to be the formula here, creating an effect that's perhaps more French than Italian in some dishes. Try the homemade spinach-and-ricotta cannelloni, served in a cream-rich, rib-sticking sauce of white wine, tomatoes, and parsley. The shrimp and veal dishes are also good. 5308 boulevard St-Laurent, between Fairmount and St-Viateur. Tel: 273-3472.

La Sila. One of the best Italian restaurants in town, La Sila is in the heart of the Latin Quarter at 2040 rue St-Denis, between Sherbrooke Est and Ontario Est. The veal and homemade pastas are excellent here—the secret is home-grown herbs used fresh. Cream, tomato, and basil are also used with great imagination. The scampi cardinale—ten plump devils sautéed with Cognac and served in a rich cream sauce—is worth the splurge. La Sila is the sort of place where they only turn the tables once a night, so reserve and plan on a long, leisurely dinner. Closed Sundays. Tel: 844-5083.

Pizzeria Napoletana. Known mostly for its superb pizzas, this crowded family-operated restaurant in the Little Italy district of the city also serves outstanding made-on-the-premises gnocchi, tortellini, cannelloni, and lasagna.

The fettucine and spaghetti are the dried, packaged kind but served to order and properly *al dente*. The home-style sauces used with the pizzas and pasta immerse you in the lusty pleasures of southern Italian cooking: ripe tomatoes, garlic, olive oil, onions, oregano, basil, and sharp peppers. Be prepared for lines at supper time, especially on weekends. And don't forget to bring your own wine. 189 rue Dante at the corner of rue de Gaspé; no credit cards, no reservations.

Trois Marie. Three motherly women run the kitchen at this Little Italy restaurant much the same way they would at home—with affection, authority, and an uncompromising attachment to routine.

Most of the goodies are served on a rotating weekly schedule. On Mondays you're guaranteed cotoletta (veal cutlet) Parmigiana or Milanese, roast beef, and spezzatino (veal). Thursdays, it's chicken cacciatore and tripe among five specials. Fridays bring sole, cod, and clam sauce, in keeping with the former Roman Catholic tradition of meatless Fridays. And so on.

The regular menu is short but includes such favorites as spaghetti bathed in olive oil and garlic; *slices* of the latter, singed a golden brown, decorate the top—no skimping on garlic here. 6934 rue Clark at the corner of rue Mozart; no credit cards. Tel: 277-9859.

Villa Orlando. Don't be put off by the suburban location of this restaurant—there are handsome rewards to be reaped at the end of the 20-minute drive or cab ride out to 3060 boulevard St-Joseph, in Lachine. (Call for directions.) The Calabrese chef is a wizard with pasta sauces, traditional as well as innovative, and his veal and fish dishes are made from market-fresh ingredients. Service is attentive and the atmosphere pleasant. Tel: 634-9219.

Hispanic

Fiesta Tapas. The menu of Spanish snack-size dishes here changes weekly, but there's generally a good assortment of fish, mushroom, potato, squid, quail, shrimp, and sausage dishes. Graze on a few to make a meal or gorge on the paella for two. In Vieux-Montréal at 479 rue St-Alexis (corner of Notre-Dame Ouest). Closed Sundays. Tel: 844-5700.

La Hacienda. Soft mariachi music, a terrace, tropical colors, and arches all add to the illusion you're in sunny Mexico when you dine at La Hacienda. It's the closest thing Montréal has to a true Mexican restaurant, as opposed to TexMex or CalMex or—dare we say it—CanMex. La Hacienda makes liberal use of (coriander) cilantro in dishes that feature fresh ingredients, and offers a good selection of meat and chicken dishes as well as several kinds of burritos and enchiladas. 1148 avenue Van Horne at rue L'Epée in central Montréal. Open for dinner only. Tel: 270-3043.

Pappacitos. The menu at Pappacitos is as straightforward as the trappings—self-service trays and disposable dishes—but there is a lot of love evident in the preparation of the popular Mexican food cooked here. Dollar for dollar this weekday (6:00 A.M. to 5:00 P.M.) breakfast and lunch restaurant in the Bell Canada building downtown offers superlative value and quality. And when they ask if you want a medium hot salsa or the "dangerous stuff" they're not kidding about the latter. 741 avenue Viger Ouest. No reservations.

Greek

Faros. Everything is tops at this Greek psarotaverna (fish tavern) off avenue du Parc—from the fresh fish to the pikilia. Don't miss the soft-shell crabs, if they have them; they're memorable, as is the grilled octopus. 362 rue Fairmount Ouest. Tel: 270-8437.

Milos. Quite simply the best (and most expensive) Greek psarotaverna in town. If you can, come for lunch; it's far less crowded then, and the service less harried. Whether you arrive for lunch or dinner, you'll face a perplexing choice of the freshest fish flown in from all corners of the world. It's prepared the traditional Greek-islands way—a whole fish grilled on charcoal, served boned, with a brushing of olive oil and oregano. For the big splurge, try the truly jumbo shrimp in garlic, or lobster. 5357 avenue du Parc, between Fairmount Ouest and St-Viateur Ouest. Tel: 272-3522.

Molivos. You'll find blue and white accents on everything from tablecloths to the walls at this cheerful, comfortable Greek fish restaurant at 4859 avenue du Parc (near boulevard St-Joseph Ouest). The Molivos menu is compact and simple. A selection of pikilia—hot or cold hors d'oeuvres that include tzatziki and tarama—is offered, as are octopus, squid, and shrimp. Or you can choose from a basket of fresh fish brought to your table. You can't go wrong—everything is good here, and the service is friendly and efficient. Tel: 271-5354.

Middle Eastern

Daou. Although it's one of the best Lebanese restaurants in the city, Daou has a staff that leaves a lot to be desired. If you can cope with indifference and confusion occasionally tempered by friendliness, you'll enjoy the home-style Middle Eastern dishes served in this simple, unpretentious north-end setting. These include kabobs and kibbehs; tabbouleh; baba ghannouj (babaganoush); falafel; and meat, spinach, and thyme pies. 519 Faillon Est, between rues St-Denis and Lajeunesses. Tel: 276-8310.

La Medina. The absence of the traditional belly dancer makes this rue St-Denis establishment an unusually peaceful Moroccan restaurant. Here the music mingles gently with the soothing sound of running water in a mini-fountain, setting the tone for a relaxed sampling of the restaurant's North African Arabic cuisine.

The restaurant is divided into two sections, one with conventional Western tables and chairs, the other with low Moroccan divans and sofas. Delicate brass and glass lamps cast a warm glow on walls adorned with Moroccan rugs. Antique guns and daggers are displayed in the front section, while the Moroccan section features a genuine desert chieftain's tent as an exotic canopy over the richly brocaded sofas.

The harira soup, a rich, filling creation made with chick peas, green lentils, and fresh coriander, is outstanding here. If you feel like splurging, order the couscous royale. It arrives in a deep Moroccan clay dish ringed with a thick layer of perfectly cooked couscous covering chunks of tender chicken and lamb, the whole topped with turnips, carrots, chick peas, and Merguez (sausages) and crowned with four skewers of grilled lamb and veal. 3464 rue St-Denis, just north of rue Sherbrooke Est. Call ahead to reserve if you want to sit in the Moroccan section. Tel: 282-0359.

Indian

Bukhara. You don't come to this expensive, upscale establishment in the heart of the downtown club district for the curries—they don't serve any. Instead, Bukhara serves up superb Indian cuisine from the country's erstwhile northwest frontier. All meats, poultry, and seafood are marinated and grilled in tandoors—huge clay ovens installed in a central glass cage. Vegetables are grilled here, as well, and excellent breads are prepared fresh as you watch. Specialties of the house include a marvelous whole leg of lamb, grilled pomfret (a delectable flatfish from the Indian Ocean), authentic butter chicken, and good black dal. 2100 rue Crescent. Tel: 289-9808.

Le Taj. Two chefs preside over glass-enclosed tandoors at this elegant downtown restaurant. Patrons can choose from a range of northern curries, kormas, and tandoori dishes, as well as a good selection of appetizers, and the fresh Indian breads are among the best in the city. So is the service. 2077 rue Stanley. Closed Sundays. Tel: 845-9015.

Star of India. This is the place to go if you crave London-style curries. The kitchen at this downtown fixture can be relied upon to produce vindaloos and hot Madras curries in varying degrees of spiciness. Tandoori chicken and other grilled meats are also available, and the vegetable curries are always fresh. 1806 rue Ste-Catherine Ouest. Tel: 932-8330.

Woodlands. This downtown restaurant is the city's best for southern Indian cuisine. The *masala dosas*—lacy, golden, lentil-rice crepes stuffed with spicy potatoes—are never less than outstanding, while other regional dishes such as *idlies* (steamed lentil-rice cakes), *vadai* (deep-fried lentil dough-nuts), and *upuma* (spicy semolina) are accompanied by complex sauces featuring fresh coconut, black mustard seeds, ginger, asafoetida, turmeric, and fresh coriander.

Woodlands also offers a full range of northern Indian tandoori dishes, breads, and curries, but their quality has yet to match that of the dishes from the south. Which doesn't mean you should ignore them—some of them, the chicken tikka in particular, are very good. 1241 rue Guy, just south of Ste-Catherine Ouest. Closed Sundays. Tel: 933-1553.

Yogi. This full-service restaurant and bar lurks behind the second-floor fast-food court of a renovated office complex downtown. Yogi's chef is expert with the tandoor, and his marinated grilled meats and freshly baked breads are among the city's best. Yogi also offers a substantial, all-you-can-eat buffet at lunch and dinner for under $10. La cour du Roi, 1231 Ste-Catherine Ouest. Tel: 982-9943.

Chinese, Korean, and Southeast Asian

Chao Phraya. Wade warily into the spicy delights at this Thai restaurant on trendy avenue Laurier in central Montréal—they can turn out to be fiery surprises. The fish, duck, pork, chicken, beef, and seafood dishes here wear the enticing flavors of lemon grass, fresh coriander, coconut milk, sweet basil, and those deadly "bird's eye" chilis, and the portions are generous. 50 avenue Laurier Ouest. Tel: 272-5339.

Chez Flamingo. On weekends, this downtown establish-ment offers a show that's true dinner theater: A smiling chef casually tosses a thick snake-like length of dough that magi-cally becomes two, then four, then a hundred or more strings of spaghetti. Draped over a wooden stick, the fresh noodles, or Fun Fe Fé, are whisked away to the kitchen as diners gawk, then applaud, and the lucky ones who ordered the noodles sit back and wait for their transformed return. On a recent visit, they arrived in a cloud of aromatic steam, having been sautéed in a spicy black-bean sauce with shreds of fresh ginger and strips of beef and peppers. Other treats on the menu include Ta-Ching's Masterpiece Chicken (Sizzle Service)—half a deep-fried doré smothered in special hot sauce and shrimp toast. 1809 rue Ste-Catherine Ouest. Tel: 937-7418.

Hong Kong. This no-frills Chinatown restaurant at 1023 boulevard St-Laurent offers good Cantonese cuisine at bargain prices. The service is swift, the bare tables adorned only with bottled sauces, and the seating cafeteria-style. The menu features a wide range of duck, pork, lobster, fish, chicken, beef, noodle, rice, or vegetable dishes. Some of the favorites include barbecued pork and duck on rice, lobster Cantonese-style or with fresh ginger and shallots, beef with fresh lotus root, watercress in oyster sauce, steamed jumbo shrimp, and Singapore noodles. Tel: 861-0251.

Joz. The Beijing-style wraplings filled with spiced, puréed pork or chicken are a specialty at this restaurant, which takes its name from the Chinese word for dumpling. Steamed or pan-fried, they make an exceptional first course off a menu remarkable for its MSG-free dishes. Another suggestion: golden half-moon-shaped slices of eggplant deftly plumped with puréed chicken. 5717 avenue Monkland, in the west end's N.D.G district. Tel: 481-4406.

Korea House. The lobby of a medical building in west-central Montréal is the hidden setting for a taste of Korea. Here you'll find every variety of steamed, boiled, grilled, fried, and marinated fish, seafood, beef, noodles, bean sprouts, vegetables, and rice. Everything is seasoned with palate-tickling combinations of ginger, sesame, mustard, soy, bean paste, garlic, and hot red peppers. The fish stew, in particular, contains a good dose of most of these ingredients along with delicious fresh salmon. Less spicy dishes include *kalbi,* marinated and grilled beef short ribs; and *bindaedeok,* golden mung-bean pancakes. Located a few blocks east of busy boulevard Décarie at 4950 Queen Mary Road. Tel: 733-7823.

L'Or Blanc. A sprawling, elegant Szechuan and Thai restaurant with very reasonable prices, L'Or Blanc is an especially good deal at lunchtime, when complete meals can be had for under $10. The service is as upscale as the decor, and the ingredients are always fresh—even the spring rolls are made on the premises. 1232 avenue Greene, between rues de Maisonneuve Ouest and Ste-Catherine Ouest. Tel: 932-1244.

L'Orchidée de Chine. With its Art Deco dining rooms spread over two levels, this establishment at 2017 rue Peel (on the corner of de Maisonneuve Ouest) qualifies as one of the classier Szechuan restaurants in town. (The waiters even dress black tie.) Noteworthy are the eggplant in garlic, the five-flavored boned pork spareribs, the squid sautéed with red bell peppers, the chicken with Szechuan pepper, and the

sautéed beef in a spicy garlic sauce. Call to reserve; closed
Sundays. Tel: 287-1878.

Muraille de Chine, Tong Por, and **Cathay.** Each of these
Chinatown restaurants has a battery of dim-sum chefs, and
each offers a bewildering variety of those delicious "heart's
delight" snacks daily between noon and 3:00 P.M. All three
also feature Great Hall of the People decor and seating to go
along with their impressive à la carte Cantonese lunch and
dinner menus. **Muraille de Chine** is at 1017 boulevard St-
Laurent (Tel: 875-8888); **Tong Por** is at 43 rue de la Gauchetière Est (Tel: 393-9975); and **Cathay** is at 73 rue de la
Gauchetière Ouest (Tel: 866-3131).

Phayathai. Phayathai, one of Montréal's best Thai restaurants, serves tasty fish, crab, squid, and meat dishes flavored with fresh coriander, lemon grass, basil, coconut
milk, and, where called for, fiery peppers. Try the mixed
seafood *po tak* soup—firm white fish, shrimp, and a crab
claw in a broth whose peppery lemon-grass and citrus-leaf
seasoning will leave your eyes watering and mouth on
afterburn. The same fire is present in the spicy sauce
covering the *pla lad plik* (a whole deep-fried fish) and
chili-fried crab claws. Milder dishes include the salads
with squid or beef, the mixed noodles, and the boneless
chicken in a sauce of coconut milk, green peas, fresh
bamboo shoots, and basil. Downtown at 1235 rue Guy,
just south of Ste-Catherine Ouest. Tel: 933-9949.

Japanese

Azuma. Try the whole fried fish at this East End restaurant
(901 Sherbrooke Est near rue St-André)—it's something
you won't find at the other Japanese restaurants in town.
The place is informal but generally crowded, so reservations are in order. Sushi, served at night only, is fresh and
somewhat cheaper than the competition's. Tel: 525-5262.

Jardin Sakura. A sprawling restaurant and sushi bar with a
good selection of fresh fish, a wide range of hot dishes, and
reasonable prices. The chefs here do interesting things with
eggplant, eel, and tuna. Downtown at 2114 rue de la
Montagne. Tel: 288-9122.

Osaka. An unpretentious family-run restaurant at 2137
Bleury, just south of Sherbrooke Ouest, Osaka has no sushi,
but the soups, sukiyaki, tempura, and teriyaki dishes are very
good. The ambience is casual, and the friendly staff will
cheerfully tailor a meal to your whims. Tel: 849-3438.

Tokyo Sukiyaki. Because of its location in a semi-industrial
neighborhood, the oldest and most consistently packed Japa-

nese restaurant in Montréal can be found only with the aid of a map. From the outside it looks little different from the garages and warehouses nearby. Inside, it's a warm and intimate sukiyaki house where all guests sit in raised tatami rooms after taking their shoes off. The rooms are built around streams and tiny bridges, which lend them an exotic air. Reservations are a must—the place is open only for dinner. Tokyo Sukiyaki offers a full range of standard Japanese dishes, including sukiyaki, shabu-shabu, and tempura. 7355 Mountain Sights, south of rue Jean-Talon Ouest. Tel: 737-7245.

Other

Alexandre. This chic downtown bar-restaurant at 1454 rue Peel serves food until 2:00 A.M. daily. Fronted by a summer terrace, the ground floor has a bar and a mostly French menu. Upstairs, you'll find an English pub-type atmosphere, complete with a variety of beers on tap and mostly British fare. Both floors also serve innovative Italian cuisine, with the very reasonable prices ranging between $5.75 and $19.75. Tel: 288-5105.

Bagel-Etc. Bagel-Etc., an all-night joint, re-creates the old diners of New York City and Montréal with lots of taped late-night jazz and a menu that has everything from caviar and Champagne to bagels and blintzes. You can also get half-decent Hungarian-style goulash, East European sausage and cabbage, schnitzels, herring, and smoked salmon, as well as a variety of elaborate burgers. 4320 boulevard St-Laurent, just south of rue Marie-Anne. Tel: 845-9462.

Café Mozart. The elegant, somewhat whimsical decor contributes to the delightful other-world ambience at this postcard-pretty Austro-Hungarian restaurant. Borscht, blini with caviar, and pork with gnocchi are only a few of the traditional dishes on the menu. And yes, the desserts are as rich and chocolaty as those served in Vienna and Budapest. Downtown at 2090 rue de la Montagne, north of de Maisonneuve Ouest. Tel: 849-1482.

Café Santropol. The sixties have yet to end for this eclectic café-restaurant on the Plateau Mont-Royal. The colors are only slightly short of Day-Glo and the mismatched banquettes, chairs, and tables come in assorted shapes, sizes, and shades. In summer the tree-shaded backyard offers more tables, wind chimes, a birdhouse, a pond with goldfish, and sometimes Chaucer—a canine neighbor from upstairs. Santropol's passion for color is evident in its gigantic sandwiches, which bear names like Sisters of Jeanne Mance and Yelapa Moon. Fresh grapefruit, orange, kiwi, watermelon, cantaloupe, cucumber, alfalfa sprouts, and red cabbage accompany thick slices of brown bread filled with lobster and cheese spreads, ham, or salamis. They also serve more than 50 kinds of tea and excellent coffees. 3990 rue St-Urbain at rue Duluth. Tel: 842-3110.

Cajun House. As you walk up the short path leading to Cajun House you can hear Billie Holliday on a discreet little speaker in the front yard singing, "All of me, why not take all of me . . ." That's exactly what you're tempted to do in the sunny interior of this establishment, with its pastel colors, jazz posters, and cheery American-style service. This is still the best place in town for the spicy and complex flavors of Louisiana, though not the cheapest. Gumbo, gator tails, and blackened fish are all featured, as are soft-shell crabs and deep-fried dill pickles. An extensive selection of California wines complements the varied menu. 1219 rue Mackay, just south of Ste-Catherine Ouest. Tel: 871-3898.

Caribec. The city's poshest West Indian restaurant offers excellent daily buffets at lunch and dinner, with rice and peas, plantain, pumpkin soups, stewed meats, *calaloo, ackee* and saltfish, and pudding all appearing regularly. Caribec's à la carte menu is fish-and-seafood heavy and predominantly Barbadian, featuring lobster, shrimp, and flying fish. The service is friendly and professional, and bread is baked on the premises. On the west side at 5942 Sherbrooke Ouest. Tel: 486-4809.

Moishe's. It's worth the usual short wait for a table at this legendary steakhouse, where at least four waiters are guaranteed to fuss mightily, plying you with water, liquor, pickles, and trimmings. The steaks are perfect and expensive, the decor plush. 3961 boulevard St-Laurent, just south of rue Duluth. Call to reserve; Tel: 845-3509.

Schwartz's Montreal Hebrew Delicatessen. The tables are narrow and shared, and the service can be brusque, but you'll soon forget all that when you taste what people from all over the world come to this boulevard St-Laurent deli for: Montréal smoked meat.

Not to be confused with pastrami, Montréal smoked meat is juicy beef cured in spices according to assorted secret recipes passed down through the family by Romanian Jews who emigrated to Montréal. No one in Montréal has a better recipe than Schwartz's. Have it hot, on rye bread, with an order of their french fries—thick, greasy, and a legend in their own right. 3895 boulevard St-Laurent, almost next door to Moishe's; no credit cards. Tel: 842-4813.

Troika. An established Russian restaurant downtown (2171 rue Crescent, just south of Sherbrooke Ouest), Troika is done up in czarist decor: lots of velvet and red plush.

There's live music here every night—some of it at your table—and expensive caviar, of course. Traditional dishes like chicken Kiev are your best bet if you're not in a decadent mood. Tel: 849-9333.

Rue Prince-Arthur

This restaurant-lined pedestrian mall is unique in Canada, especially in summer, when dozens of buskers and other street performers lend it a festive air. Many of the places are Greek, specializing in brochettes, but Vietnamese, Japanese, Indian, and Italian restaurants (bring your own bottle) are also in evidence. And while the quality of the cooking at most of these places is less than earth-shaking, the friendly ambience and affordable prices are likely to come as a pleasant surprise.

Try **Vivaldi**, which has reasonably satisfying Italian food and striking decor; **Mazurka**, a cheap and excellent Polish restaurant that was an institution long before the street acquired its present character; or **Akita**, for good sushi.

A similar gentrification is taking shape a few blocks north along **rue Duluth**. Restaurants similar to those on Prince-Arthur have sprung up, and the same rules apply. Try **Jardin de Panos**, a Greek restaurant with a charming garden and terrace, or **Tasca**, which serves superb Portuguese cuisine.

—*Ashok Chandwani*

NIGHTLIFE

There are scores of bars and cafés to choose from in Montréal, but unless you're famous or happen to know a regular, be prepared to wait in line at some of the more popular ones.

Most bars or restaurants aren't fussy about clothes, even in the posh hotels. Still, blue jeans are the most frequent cause of denied entry. Otherwise, the ambience in Montréal bars is relaxed and casual; it's easy to strike up a conversation, even make friends.

You're expected to pay for a drink at the time you receive it unless you have an honest face—or a credit card you're willing to surrender, in which case the place will run a tab for you. Almost every bar has a happy hour on weekdays. This "hour" is generally between 5:00 and 7:00 P.M., but can sometimes start as early as 4:00 P.M. and last until 9:00 P.M.

French is Montréal's principal language, but English is widely understood. Having said that, there are clear-cut Anglo and French bar areas, with a trend lately toward a cluster of cosmopolitan bars that defy labeling.

Mackay, Bishop, Crescent, and de la Montagne are four

bar-crammed downtown streets where you'll hear more English than French. The opposite is true of St-Denis and Ontario, as well as Vieux-Montréal.

Avenue du Parc and boulevard St-Laurent are late bloomers on the bar scene, with some of the trendiest locales found on one or the other, all in the cosmo class. You'll also find many low-life bars here, if you feel like slumming.

For conventional nightlife of the leg-kicking variety, your best bet is the larger hotels. Most have some sort of nightclub, with singing or dancing acts that change frequently.

There's a lively music scene outside the hotels as well: Montréal is a regular stop for many major international performers. The city also has a good selection of jazz clubs, having long been associated with that genre. Pianist Oscar Peterson is from Montréal, as is pianist Oliver Jones. In summer the city is host to one of the largest jazz festivals in the world, with more than a thousand musicians performing over a ten-day period.

The telephone area code in Montréal is 514.

In Town

Au Cépage. Favored by journalists, shipping executives, and theatergoers, this one-of-a-kind bar/bistro/restaurant in Vieux-Montréal has a super-friendly staff and a couple of cozy dining rooms. During the summer it's also a perfect spot for Sunday brunch, particularly if you're seated in the courtyard café listening to the cries of the falcons that nest high up in the buildings nearby. 212 rue Notre-Dame Ouest. Tel: 845-5436.

Biddles. Downtown at 2060 rue Aylmer, with good live jazz. You can also dine here on ribs, chicken wings, or potato skins. More fun after 11:00 P.M.

Le Bijou. An ultra-chic bar with live jazz, and a place to people-watch and be watched yourself. Lots of models and ad execs. 300 rue Lemoyne in Vieux-Montréal.

Blue Angel. Downtown at 1228 rue Drummond; old-fashioned country-music bar, Stetsons and all. Small dance floor, frayed banquettes, and waiters from the 1950s. Amateur night on Mondays is especially entertaining.

Charles Darwin. A comfortable downtown bar at 1187 rue Bishop, with a pleasant courtyard terrace in warm weather. Quiet except when an important hockey game is being televised.

Club Soda. An avenue du Parc bar-cum-concert stage in central Montréal. Check newspaper listings for upcoming events. 5240 rue du Parc.

Déjà Vu. Downtown at 1224 rue Bishop. A great place if

you like crowds and are with a group. It spreads over two-and-a-half floors and offers good live music, usually from the sixties.

Faubourg St. Denis. In the heart of the bar-and-restaurant strip at 1660 rue St-Denis. Lots of tables open to the outdoors in summer, and a cozy bar in the basement.

Le Grand Café. A large two-story jazz bar at 1720 rue St-Denis with tall glass doors open to the street in summer. Good live music.

Grumpy's. Downtown at 1242 rue Bishop. A friendly staff, and many regulars. For an older crowd; no dance floor, but people still shuffle around late at night anyway.

Lux. At 5220 boulevard St-Laurent, between Fairmount and St-Viateur. A funky Paris-style complex with bar, restaurant, grocery, and bookstore specializing in magazines from around the world. Open well past 3:00 A.M.

Moby Dick. Downtown at 1188 rue Sherbrooke Ouest; a good and busy spot for conversation. Frequented by separated or recently divorced individuals.

Thursday's. Downtown at 1449 rue Crescent. You'll find a cross-section of Montréal here, dominated by people from the advertising and fashion industries. The music is loud, and there is dancing and singles action. Thursday's is favored by the 35-plus crowd at night and by office workers of all ages between 5:00 and 7:00 P.M.

Spectrum. Downtown bar–concert hall complex that books big names on tour. Check newspaper listings for upcoming events. 318 rue Ste-Catherine Ouest.

Winnie's. Downtown at 1455 rue Crescent. A preppy Anglo crowd, with a deejay and dancing after happy hour. Lots of wood, plants, and Old English prints.

Woody's Pub. A large, generally crowded multi-bar place downtown at 1234 rue Bishop. Good English-style pub lunches. Dancing at night.

The Suburbs

If you get bored with city action, you can always head west into the suburbs to relatively new places like **Cheers** (955 rue St-Jean North, Pointe Claire), whose shopping-mall location doesn't seem to deter hundreds of upwardly mobile and mostly Anglo drinkers, or **Quai Sera** (164 rue Ste-Anne, Ste-Anne de Bellevue), a waterfront restaurant and dance bar that packs in a similar crowd—there's a small cover charge and men are required to wear a jacket. (Don't confuse the suburban Cheers with its parent bar downtown, which is popular with a 20-something crowd.)

A visit to either could be preceded by a meal at a suburban restaurant:

Le Pêché Mignon. The cuisine at this waterfront restaurant in Ste-Anne de Bellevue exhibits touches of nouvelle—a trend that isn't quite dead in Montréal. (Actually, its better elements—freshness and imagination—are likely to stick around for a while.)

In summer, ask for a table on the terrace overlooking the boardwalk. Boats chug in and out of the narrow canal here, and people promenade in the warm sunshine. Try the snails, which are served partially concealed in scooped-out brussels sprouts ringing a large plate covered with a sauce of cream, garlic, and parsley. Salmon marinated in citrus juices—in this case, grapefruit, orange, and a hint of lemon—is particularly delectable. For the main course, duck cooked two ways (thin slices of medium-rare breast and a succulent whole leg covered in a traditional rich brown sauce) is your best bet. The fish and shrimp dishes can also be recommended. 132 rue Ste-Anne, Ste-Anne de Bellevue. Tel: 457-3584.

Le Vieux-Kitzbuhel. This romantic restaurant is housed in an old mansion on Lake St. Louis in Ile-Perrot (505 boulevard Perrot). Most of the six charming dining rooms here have a view of the lake and of the garden sloping down toward it. The menu offers a fair selection of veal, pork, chicken, and fish dishes, and, of course, homemade dumplings. Perhaps the most enticing feature of the menu, however, is venison flown in from Alberta. Among the other successful dishes on the menu are a delicious Tyrolean wine soup—a heady concoction of wine, eggs, and cream with crisp croutons; venison pâté, fresh, rich and gamey; and medallions of venison, also very gamey and tender, served with a mound of red cabbage and fresh baby dumplings. Tel: 453-5521.

Highway 20 west is the way to reach these bars and restaurants. Take the Ste-Anne de Bellevue exit for Le Pêché Mignon, which is on the main drag of the little town, as well as for Quai Sera. The same highway also has an exit for boulevard St-Jean in the municipality of Pointe Claire, where you'll find Cheers. Vieux-Kitzbuhel is on an easy-to-find street in Ile-Perrot, the exit to which can also be found off Highway 20. The three exits are about a 30-minute drive west of downtown Montréal.

—*Ashok Chandwani*

SHOPS AND SHOPPING

For years Montréal ruled as the unchallenged fashion capital of Canada. Factories and sweat shops along boulevard St-

Laurent—an all-purpose thoroughfare that is, among other things, Montréal's answer to Manhattan's Seventh Avenue—produced the clothes worn by the rest of the country. The garment industry still accounts for 40 percent of the city's manufacturing jobs, but today Toronto can justifiably lay equal claim to the haute couture crown. Still, Montréal's long tradition, combined with its inhabitants' confident sense of style, has nurtured a thriving community of designers who sell their creations not only to large department stores but also from their own boutiques.

Many of the hottest design houses are clustered in Plateau Mont-Royal, an old residential and commercial district east of the mountain. **Parachute** (3526 St-Laurent, just above Sherbrooke) received wide attention a few seasons back when some of its flashy inventory appeared on the back of Don Johnson, the fashionably attired police detective on *Miami Vice*. The trendsetting store, founded by British-born designer Nicola Pelly and Harry Parnass, a former professor of urban planning from California, features rough concrete for the floor, ceiling, and walls, and looks either half-empty or elegantly uncluttered, depending on your outlook (only 30 percent of the store is given over to clothing). The expensive, heavily textured silk, cotton, and woollen garments are displayed on sloping banks of stainless steel. "Stores like these are the salons of the 20th century," says Parnass, "a place where artists, writers, filmmakers, and other creative people congregate."

Scandale (2639 St-Laurent) is the place for vintage fashions, especially rocker and biker leather-looks, as well as exquisite kimonos. Scandale also carries its own line of wonderfully imaginative women's fashions, which mix luxe fabrics, startling colors, and unusual prints in coat-of-many-color combinations, all with a somewhat retro forties look. Even the store's façade, a brightly hued wall covered with giant metal insects, is interesting.

For the last word in books, international journals, and newspapers ranging from the esoteric to the exotic, "Le Must" is **Librairie le Dernier Mot Booksellers** (3968 St-Laurent, just below Duluth). Around the corner one block west on Duluth is **Ficciones Literary Bookstore** (number 11), with Montréal's biggest selection of books by Latin American authors, as well as unusual and hard-to-find titles by North American, British, and European writers.

Upper St-Laurent
Known as Montréal's Soho area, upper St-Laurent, stretching from Rachel to Bernard, now rivals St-Denis, downtown, and

Laurier Ouest as *the* place for fashion, nightclubs, boutiques, and the rest.

Need to pen a note back home before you get started? Then drop into **Raymond des Cartes** (5171 St-Laurent), which carries beautiful and unusual postcards, notepaper, wrapping paper, posters, and all manner of artisan-crafted gift items from around the world.

The next stop for fashion-conscious shoppers should be the two-floor boutique of **Le Château** (5160 St-Laurent), whose own label leans toward knockoffs of the latest designer styles and retro fashions. Nearby **Luna** (5155 St-Laurent) sells sensuously textured, lusciously colored cotton and rayon knit jerseywear. To go with this finery, take in the **Suk-Kwan** art jewelry boutique (5141 St-Laurent) for one-of-a-kind pieces crafted by Québécois, Canadian, and international jewelry artists. From the quirky to the exotic, you'll find it here—along with Noguchi lamps, objets d'art, lingerie, millinery, and handbags.

Fashion for the home—whether avant-garde or retro—can also be found on St-Laurent. **Par le Trou de la Serrure** (number 5101) combines the practical and the unusual in beautiful door and window hardware.

Outremont

In 1976 Ariane Carle switched from designing costumes for films to creating high-fashion knitwear. Today her shop, **Les Tricots d'Ariane** (207 Laurier Ouest), stocks more than 50 styles of coordinated tops, skirts, pants, and jackets in basic colors, all in washable cotton-and-acrylic blends. Prices range from $60 to $450.

Hers is not the only "not-to-be-missed" boutique on Laurier Ouest, which long has catered to the carriage trade of Outremont—one of French Montréal's most affluent neighborhoods. From St-Laurent to côte Ste-Catherine, the eight blocks of cafés, boutiques, galleries, and restaurants lining both sides of Laurier Ouest are a shopper's paradise.

Downstairs from Tricots d'Ariane you'll find **Orchidée Sauvage**, where designer Carmen fashions leathers and knits, including outerwear, that give real meaning to the expression "wearable art."

Home furnishings abound along this stretch, from the Eurostyle lamps and lighting fixtures at **Au Courant** (number 281), to the French-Canadian pine antiques at **Boutique Confort** (number 201), to the 21st-century accessories for bath, kitchen, office, and garden at **MDI** (number 273). Leaning toward the nostalgic are **Cache-Cache**'s (number 1051) Victorian-inspired bed and table linens. Cache-Cache is also a favorite of Victorian-era fashion mavens, who each season snap up its original collection of women's and children's clothing and accessories. The unusual and the beautiful are typical of the luxe tableware, glassware, dinnerware, kitchenware, and bathwear at **Maison d'Emilie** (number 1073). For the finest French bed and bath linens try **Décor Marie-Paule** (number 1090). **Dans un Jardin** (number 1009) offers an array of personal beauty and bath products, linens, and loungewear. For men, women, and children, it all adds up to a pampered experience for the uninitiated.

For fashion, **L'Aventure pour Homme** (number 5107 du Parc) and **L'Aventure pour Femme** (number 277) are where you'll find Italian designer fashion favorites by Armani, Versace, Moschino, and others. Their **Emporio** store (number 244) carries casual wear for men, including the top-quality J. J. Farmer label—a Canadian version of the country-weekend look popularized by Ralph Lauren and Calvin Klein. **Guy Laroche** (number 1089) and **Unanyme des Georges Rech** (number 1081) carry their own lines of prêt-à-porter fashion, while **Henriette L.** (number 1031) is the place for fashions by Angelo Tarlazzi, Dorothée Bis, Emmanuelle Kahn, Lolita de Lempicka, Basile, Jin Abé, Escada, and Laurel. How to show off all this finery? Try on the precious and faux gems at the **Agatha Bijoux** (number 1054) and **Galerie Arto** (number 1083) jewelry boutiques.

Not to be missed is **Johnny, Johnny** (number 380), where would-be Madonnas and Jane's Addiction clones feel right at home. These are not fashions for the timid—see-through lace jeans and blouses, body-hugging stirrup pants, slinky cut-up-to-here-and-down-to-there lingerie, skin-tight leathers (black, naturally), and show-off accessories are the rule. The atmosphere is uptown chic and outré at the same time, with a vintage jukebox, mirrors, video screens, fluorescent-colored leather couches, and an espresso-aperitif bar on the premises. The centerpiece—one, if not two, of Gypsy Kings producer and Johnny, Johnny owner Alain Forcioli's vintage Harley Davidsons. This is fashion to the max—complete with official Harley Davidson accessories and leatherware.

St-Denis between Sherbrooke and Mont-Royal is also worth strolling. Not only will you find bistros, bookstores, and galleries cheek-by-jowl (some of Montréal's finest), you'll also find a plethora of Québécois and international fashions for the body and home. Le Château is here, as is **Revenge** (number 582), with its exclusive collection of Québécois designer clothes for women and men. For mad hatters of either sex, **Le Sieur Duluth chapeaux, bijoux et accessoires** (number 4454) is an absolute must. Most of the hats, jewelry, and accessories are designed in-house, and custom orders are accepted. Nearby **Chapofolie** (number 4129) carries an extensive range of hat styles for men, women, and children, as well as belt, glove, scarf, handbag, and hair accessories to mix and match.

One of Québec's newest designer superstars is 30-something **Marie St-Pierre**, whose fin-de-siècle-inspired fashions for men and women are available at her own atelier-boutique (number 4455) here, as well as at Holt Renfrew on Sherbrooke, Henriette L. on Laurier, and the Kyoze boutiques in Vieux-Montreal and Les Cours Mont-Royal.

Paris, Texas (number 4201B) has moved from Laurier to St-Denis, where third-generation owner/designer Robert Krief's leather fashions and casual wear continue to find favor with both sexes. In fact, Krief's colorful trendsetting jackets, trousers, skirts, and coats are regularly spotted on Montréal's fashion cognoscenti. A pair of leather pants will set you back about $350, a woman's short jacket about $570. Casual leatherware and suede unisex fashions are more affordably priced, starting at around $150 for a jeans jacket.

Avant-garde is also the byword at **Artefact** (number 4117), where the young duo of Sylvie Bergeron and Louise Girard have artfully arranged clothing collections by some of Québec's hottest young designers. Bambouche, Muse, Marco Roy, Boris Nikov, Jacques Gaspo, and Marie-Claude Rousseau are among the new wave of designers for men and women exclusive to this boutique.

For the less adventurous but equally fashion-conscious, Nafnaf, Cargo, Cache-Cache, and Kamikaze Curiosités can outfit men, women, and children from head to toe, with great footwear available from Pegabo and Sena, among other shoe boutiques on St-Denis.

The only **TinTin** boutique (number 4419) in North America is also found on St-Denis. This mecca for fans and fanatics is stuffed with a complete collection of books and paraphernalia having to do with the perennially popular Belgian cartoon character, including posters, original prints, tee-shirts, bath linens, puzzles, pins, and puppets.

For the home, the offerings of boutiques such as Zone, Après L'Eden, Bleu Nuit, Au Lit, Arthur Quentin, Crabtree & Evelyn, Aux Rêves de Morphée, Carton, Amandine, and François Decarie (all clustered on St-Denis) range in style from English manor to French château, with stops in Italy and elsewhere. These emporiums offer a fabulous choice of bed, bath, and table linens, upholstery fabrics, lace curtains by the yard, toiletries, stationery, kitchen gadgets, and tabletop and dinner ware. The only problem will be trying to fit all those "must-haves" into your suitcase.

The Underground City

Shops in the bright, airy pedestrian corridors and spacious plazas of Montreal's *ville souterraine* (underground city) offer merchandise as stylish as the city itself. Place Ville-Marie boasts some of Montréal's finest haute couture outlets. Along narrow rue Elle (a pun on *ruelle,* or alley) are 12 up-market boutiques specializing in European imports. **Lalla Fucci** sells clothes by Frank Usher of London and Parisian designer Anne-Marie Beretta. Danier Leathers and Aqua-scutum are also located in Place Ville-Marie, as is Montréal-based **Chaussures Brown**, a Canadian success story and shoe-shoppers' paradise. European labels such as Maud Frizon and Yves Saint-Laurent, as well as American names like Donna Karan and Anne Klein, share space with the company's own fashion-forward footwear, leather goods, and accessories in a range of styles. **Boutique Descamps**, just around the corner, is the only store in Montréal where you can find the entire line of bedding and accessories by the French design house Primrose Bordier. Around another corner in this elegant labyrinth of shops is **Le Body Shop**, international purveyor of environmentally friendly bath and beauty products.

At Place Bonaventure off Square Victoria, well-heeled office workers spend their lunch hours browsing in chic shops lining interior "streets" with names like Champs-Elysées and rue de Versailles. Shoe stores predominate, as a quick stroll past the shops here reveals. **Bally** has the best selection. If marriage is in the offing, drop by nearby Square Phillips, where for more than a century **Henry Birks & Sons** has catered to the tastes of Montréal's best families. Most of the jewelry is produced in limited editions; customers can also commission their own one-of-a-kind creations.

Westmount

A ride on the metro west to Atwater Station and a short stroll through a pleasant underground corridor brings the intrepid shopper to Westmount Square, which contains some of the city's finest and most expensive boutiques. **Boutique Cha-cock** features the styles of French designer Arlette Chacock, whose work seems inspired by boldly colored geometric and abstract patterns. **Lily Simon** (whose boutique is a favorite of Montréal socialites) sells more subdued styles from Sonia Rykiel and Claude Montana.

These perennial favorites go head to head with **Cacharel**, featuring that French design house's fashions for women and children; **Nelly Alexander**, which carries Nina Ricci, Pierre Balmain, and Claude Bert designs; and the Guy Laroche, Georges Rech, and Olivia Strelli boutiques (with their own labels) in the battle for fashion mavens' loyalty and purses. Henry Marks and Rodier here have the market for menswear cornered.

Not to be missed is **Galerie Opulence**'s huge showroom filled with European antiques and high-quality reproductions. Specializing in Neoclassical, Empire, and Art Deco furniture and accessories, this store has attracted a loyal following among Montrealers, Torontonians, and New Yorkers, such is its range of antiques and objets d'art. All the antique paintings, for example, are listed in the Benezit, and the selection of lamps is particularly outstanding.

Just outside Westmount Square's west entrance lies Greene Avenue—yet another mecca for shoppers seeking the refined and unusual in personal and home fashions. The street itself is a happy mix of refurbished Victorian rowhouses reborn as boutiques, food shops, pâtisseries such as **By George!** (number 1343), great bookstores, and fine restaurants. **Henrietta Antony** (4192 Ste-Catherine) and **Imperial Decorative Hardware** (number 1329) are the places for 18th- and 19th-century furniture and chandeliers, lighting fixtures, and decorative hardware. **Double Hook** (number 1235A) is Québec's only exclusively Canadian bookstore, but also be sure to check out the **Nicholas Hoare Bookstore** (number 1366) near Sherbrooke—art, travel, history, biography, and literature from around the world make this a favorite with bibliophiles.

Beaux Atours (number 1308), **Lou Goldberg** (number 1255), **Stewart Diament** (number 1355), and **Ralph Berg Jeweller** (4060 Ste-Catherine Ouest) have something to suit every taste and budget, from classy costume jewelery to custom-designed creations. **Oink, Oink** (number 1361) and the **Toy Box** (number 4160) cater to designer-label kids, while **Chaussures Tony** (number 1346), a Montréal institution, has imports from Spain, Italy, and Brazil, as well as quality Canadian and American footwear, in this year's styles but usually at lower prices than elsewhere. The **Sox Box** (number 1357), one of Montréal's most stylish hosiery boutiques, carries a variety of styles in addition to a limited selection of bathing suits, sports and exercise togs, gloves, scarves, and hair accessories. **Minks Tissus** (number 1383) specializes in beautiful and unusual imported fabrics, some of which would require a king's ransom to purchase.

Downtown

Back downtown, rue Peel is worth a visit for the boutiques in **Les Cours Mont-Royal** shopping complex, many of them as beautiful to look at as the fashions found within. Canadian superstar **Alfred Sung** has two boutiques here—a white-marbled salon featuring his day and evening wear, and his Club Monaco fashion emporium, featuring sportswear labels. There are also boutiques filled with the finery of **Ferre**, **Armani**, and **Aquascutum of London** (for the more tradition-ally inclined). **Parachute** appeals to the minimalist man or woman. Challenging Parachute's mainly monochrome theme is fellow Canadian superstar Simon Chang's **La Cricca** bou-tique for women, where color runs riot from one end of the spectrum (and showroom) to the other. **Le Château** is one of the more casual boutiques (with lower price tags for a youn-ger set of customers) that have invaded Les Cours in the last year or two. Book lovers will also want to check out **Prospero** on the main level.

At the airy, trilevel **Il n'y a que deux** boutique on rue Crescent (number 1405), the high-price fashions (especially trendy woollens) of owners Carmen Michaud and Gordon Iaconetti are displayed in a minimalist setting. But they are no longer the only ones catering to fashion trendsetters. Montréal celebrities frequent **Zoo Option** (1250 rue Cres-cent) for its Pure Sexe line as well as other over-the-edge fashions. **Grège Boutique** (2130 rue Crescent) brings the world's fashion luminaries to Montréal devotées. Grège, especially, leads the pack with clothes by Japanese superstars Yohji Yamamoto, Issey Miyake, and Rei Kawakubo, as well as those by one of the newest darlings of the international designer circuit, Italy's Romeo Gigli.

Up on Sherbrooke, carriage-trade discretion rules at **Holt Renfrew** (where a black leather Gianfranco Ferre jacket with shocking pink lining costs $4,500) in expensive designer boutiques such as Yves Saint Laurent, Gucci, Donna Karan, and Giorgio Armani. Sonia Rykiel, as well as Les Musts de Cartier, Ungaro, Clubissimo, Les Créateurs, and Polo Ralph Lauren, are all within four blocks of one another between Stanley and Bishop streets. Polo Ralph Lauren also carries the designer's Santa Fe home fashion accessories, with larger furniture items by special order.

Montréal's major department stores are located within a few blocks of each other in the heart of the central business district along rue Ste-Catherine. Although the stores carry much the same merchandise, **La Baie** (rue Ste-Catherine at Square Phillips) is the most stylish and appeals to a young clientele partial to the fashions of prominent Québec designers. It has also embraced the boutique shopping concept, with floor displays featuring merchandise by Beverley Hamburg, Yves Saint Laurent, Lancel, Mexx, Jean-Claude Poitras, Courrèges, and others. **Eaton** (677 rue Ste-Catherine Ouest) sells a wide range of fashions and has boutiques specializing in Canadian designers. When you're ready for lunch, try the ninth-floor restaurant. The food is plain cafeteria-style but the decor—35-foot marble columns, alabaster vases, Monet grills, murals, and bas-reliefs—is modeled after the Art Deco dining room of the *Ile de France,* a '30s-era luxury ocean liner.

Between Eaton and Ogilvy along Ste-Catherine are a seemingly limitless number of clothing and footwear boutiques for men and women. Notable among them are **Rodier** (number 1014); **Tristan & Iseult** and **America** (number 1107); **Jacob** (Place Montréal Trust and 1220 rue Ste-Catherine Ouest); **J. J. Farmer** (number 1187); **Bedo** (number 1253); **Stefanel** (number 1263); **Mousseline** (number 1228); and **Splash** (number 1397).

Ogilvy (1307 rue Ste-Catherine Ouest) has shed its once-conservative image, emerging as the peacock of Ste-Catherine. What began as a linen shop in 1866 has been transformed into a magnificent department store, resplendent with jewel-like boutiques on every floor. Liz Claiborne, Adrienne Vittadini, Valentino, Joan and David, La Vie en Rose, Escada, David S. Brown Antiques, Godiva Chocolates, Crabtree & Evelyn, and many more are here. In keeping with its rich heritage—the store has been a Montréal institution since it first opened—the cranberry-glass chandeliers, the sweeping staircase, and, best of all, the noon-hour ritual of a kilted bagpiper marching through the store have all been preserved.

Furs

Canada is the third-largest producer of furs in the world (after the former Soviet Union and the United States), and Montréal remains its fur capital after more than three centuries. The city's 200 fur-manufacturing firms are concentrated in a ten-block area in the center of the city, and the annual Montréal International Fur Fair is the second most important show after the fur fest in Frankfurt. The show is closed to the public, but serious buyers can visit such well-established salons as **Alexandor** (2015 de la Montagne), **Desjardins** (325 boulevard René Lévesque Est), **Grosvenor and Papillon Furs** (400 de Maisonneuve Ouest), and **Shuchat** (402 de Maisonneuve Ouest) to view Canada's forte—long-haired furs of beaver, raccoon, lynx, sable, and fox. **Holt Renfrew** (1300

Sherbrooke), established in 1837, when it was known as Henderson, Holt and Renfrew Furriers, is also among the first rank of fur salons. Its furs have been worn by four generations of British royalty. (For Queen Elizabeth II's marriage to Prince Philip in 1947, Holt's gave her a custom-designed Labrador mink coat.) Holt's also carries Denmark's exclusive and expensive line of Birger Christensen furs.

Also worth the trek is **Labelle Fourrure** (6570 rue St-Hubert). Coats, jackets, and stoles are priced from $2,000 to $50,000. Most are Canadian designs, but European houses are also represented.

Factory Outlets

In the past, a whiff of impropriety hung over shopping at factory outlets in Montréal. Manufacturers, understandably anxious about alienating retailers with discounted merchandise, opened their usually shabby premises for a couple of hours on Saturday mornings to a few select bargain hunters who knew the general manager and a password. The warehouses were run-down; elevators sometimes didn't work; changing rooms, if any, were improvised affairs. Transactions were cash only, all sales final, and don't tell your friends. This is still the case at some wholesalers, but echoing the spirit of *glasnost,* and with the institution of regular store hours, some outlets now get more traffic than stores in a suburban mall.

Most of the outlets are clustered in the Chabanel area west of boulevard St-Laurent in the north end of the city. Some are open 9:00 A.M. to 5:00 P.M. during the week, and from 8:00 A.M. to 1:00 P.M. on Saturdays; others are open only on Saturdays. Stylish leather jackets, clothes, and accessories as well as sportswear and shoes can be found in factories at the following street addresses along Chabanel: 111, 125, 225, 333, and 555.

Continental Garments (2688 St-Laurent, between Sherbrooke and avenue des Pins) is also well worth the trip. This Montréal institution carries a broad selection of women's wear, including designer labels. Suits and coats are its specialty—always the current season's styles and often the same items that you'll find in the downtown boutiques and department stores, but with lower prices and super sales.

Specialty Shopping

Like any large urban center, Montréal has its share of specialty shops. **Robert Buckland Rare Carpets** (1451 rue Sherbrooke Ouest) is the city's only gallery devoted to antique carpets and rugs. The floor coverings come from private estates all over North America, and all date from before World War I. Next door (in fact it shares the same address) is **Jardin Tissus** for antique and new kilims picked up on the owner's travels in India, Turkey, Bali, and Afghanistan. Rugs are generally priced in the $1,000–$3,000 range. The store also carries objets d'art, jewelry, and handcrafted items from these countries.

Le Cerf-Volant (30 rue St-Paul Est), in Vieux-Montréal, is Montréal's only kite store. The cheery shop is stocked with dozens of colorful kites, most designed and made on the premises. The most expensive item is the Giant Delta ($135); the most elaborate, a frail-looking Ghost Clipper Ship kite ($65), which takes more than 100 hours to build. The shop's other flying toys include boomerangs, Frisbees, and model airplanes. Hobbyists can also choose from a large selection of do-it-yourself kite kits.

As a curiosity, it's amusing to flip through the racks of outlandish outfits at **Joseph Ponton Costumes** (480 rue St-Francois-Xavier), even though most visitors probably won't return home with a kicky Julius Caesar ensemble or a Ninja Turtles outfit. Founded in 1865 by brothers Joseph and Philippe Ponton, the store is still going strong, with some 10,000 costumes in stock for theatrical productions, New Year's parties, and Halloween (pumpkin and squash getups, vampire dentures, and so on).

The **Bead Emporium** (364 avenue Victoria, just south of rue Sherbrooke in Westmount) has an astounding array of beads made of glass, ceramic, wood, metal, and even Plexiglas, along with necessities for do-it-yourself costume jewelry. The store also stocks jewelry from Africa and India.

In the Plateau Mont-Royal area, **Au Rêve de Morphée** (4123 rue St-Denis, corner of Rachel) sells lace in thousands of patterns from France, Scotland, England, and Belgium. Handcrafted jewelry, semi-precious stones, fossils, and shells are exhibited and sold at **Le Nautilus** (4840 rue St-Denis). **Lawrmet** (5666 rue Sherbrooke Ouest, in Notre-Dame-de-Grace) sells everything that has anything to do with the game of darts, including carrying cases, dartboards, and the best brand-name projectiles.

Also in the Plateau Mont-Royal area, near avenue Mont-Royal, the unusual selection of mobiles, puzzles, playing cards, and occult esoterica, as well as games of every kind, at **Valet de Coeur Jeux** (4532 rue St-Denis) makes it a browser's paradise. And with so many weird and wonderful items on hand, impulse buys are the rule rather than the exception. Chess devotees will find all the paraphernalia associated with their favorite passion—including boards, books, clocks, and computers—at the **Chess Specialists** (1356 rue Ste-Catherine Est, between rues Papineau and Amherst).

Cigar lovers can stock up at **Davidoff Tabac** (1452 rue Sherbroke Ouest), which carries a large selection of Cuban cigars in addition to pipes and tobacco from all over the world. If you can't find it at Davidoff's, you will find it at **Henri Poupart** (1331 rue Ste-Catherine Ouest). This Montréal institution, in business at the same location since 1905, features the largest selection of tobacco products and accessories in the city.

Librairie Russell Books (275 rue St-Antoine Ouest, corner of Bleury, in Vieux-Montréal) is perhaps the largest English-language bookstore in the city, with thousands of volumes—including secondhand paperbacks, out-of-print books, and antiquarian volumes—lining the shelves and another million or so in storage. Also in the Plateau Mont-Royal area, the **Bibliomania Book Shop** (4872 avenue du Parc) sells books dating back to 1660, and has a large selection of old magazines, prints, engravings, and sheet music as well. **Capitaine Québec** (5108 boulevard Decarie, corner of chemin Queen Mary) stocks eclectic collectibles, including comic books, fantasy games, obscure sci-fi books, and trading cards, while **Nebula** (1452 rue St-Mathieu, downtown) carries crime fiction, fantasy, mythology, horror, comics, and lots of other, as they say, "weird stuff" that appeals to the inquiring mind. (Nebula, which is open daily, also has a mail-order service for those who can only visit the store in spirit; time travellers welcome.)

Antiques

The section of rue Notre-Dame between rue Guy and avenue Atwater is called Attic Row because of its string of unpretentious antiques shops. **Portes & Vitraux Anciens du Grand Montréal** (1500 rue Notre-Dame) specializes in Canadian pine furniture and stained glass, while **Daniel J. Malynowsky Inc.** (1642 rue Notre-Dame) mingles Canadiana with Victorian and Chinese pieces. **Antiquitou** (2475 rue Notre-Dame) handles cash registers and old decoys. **Antiques Gisela** (1960 rue Notre-Dame) sells old toys, dolls, trains, and teddy bears. **Antiquités Landry** (1726 rue Notre-Dame) and **Antiquaires Roland Sirois, Jr.** (1970 rue Notre-Dame) deal mainly in oak and pine furniture.

To the northeast, in the Plateau Mont-Royal area, **Antiques Albert** (3762 boulevard St-Laurent) handles Victorian furniture, jewelry, and objets d'art, along with Art Nouveau and Art Deco collectibles. You'll find antique watches, clocks, and other timepieces at **La Pendulerie Antique** (5035 rue St-Denis). **Galerie Leport-Tremblay** (1802 rue Notre-Dame) specializes in jewelry, vases, furniture, and curios dating from the turn of the century to 1950. In a variation on the antiques theme, **Maison l'Ami du Collectionneur** (111 rue St-Paul Ouest), in Vieux-Montréal, sells quality reproductions of 17th- and 18th-century Québec furniture, all made by hand and without nails.

Anton Wilfer & Co. Ltd. (2002 MacKay, corner of de Maisonneuve) is the place to find antique musical instruments. Primarily handling violins, violas, basses, and classical and acoustic guitars (new, used, and old), this shop is a well-established center for the buying, selling, or repairing of instruments dating from the Renaissance period, as well as instruments used in Middle Eastern music.

Crafts

Vieux-Montréal is noted for its fine crafts stores. In bold contrast to the *quartier*'s souvenir shops, which peddle pine carvings of *habitants* and mass-produced soapstone sculpture, these respected ateliers offer limited-edition, high-quality pottery, glass, and ceramics. A few of the best include **Centre de Céramique de Bonsecours** (444 rue St-Gabriel), generally considered the best crafts gallery in the city; **Boutique L'Empreinte** (272 rue St-Paul Est), an artists' cooperative displaying a wide range of handicrafts; and **La Guilde Graphique** (9 rue St-Paul Ouest), a frame shop that offers a well-chosen selection of contemporary prints and graphics.

Also a must is the venerable **Canadian Guild of Crafts** (2025 rue Peel, in midtown), a showcase of Québécois, Canadian, and Inuit arts and crafts with a reputation for high quality and originality.

Galleries

The galleries along Sherbrooke are among Canada's most prominent. The **Galerie Walter Klinkhoff** (1200 rue Sherbrooke Ouest) is renowned for its contemporary Canadian art. **Landau Fine Art** (1456 rue Sherbrooke Ouest) is the country's toniest and most exclusive commercial art gallery, with a collection of 20th-century European and American masters rivaling those held by many public institutions. Open to the public by appointment only; Tel: (514) 849-3311.

In front of the **Galerie Dominion** (1438 rue Sherbrooke Ouest) stand Rodin's *Burghers of Calais* and Moore's *Upright Motive*. Inside, the four floors of the former graystone town house are crowded with the works of Old Masters and Canadian greats. The **Galerie Atelier Lukacs** (1529 rue Sherbrooke Ouest) has a vast selection of paintings, sculptures, and drawings, including works by Lillian Broca, Peter Aitkens, and David Silverberg.

The **Galerie Elca London** (1616 rue Sherbrooke Ouest) has a large collection of Inuit and contemporary art. Within three blocks you can find fabulous one-of-a-kind cut glass and ceramics as well as futuristic jewelry at the **Galerie Elena Lee-Verre d'Art** (1428 rue Sherbrooke Ouest); the **Galerie Jocelyne Gobeil** (2154 rue Crescent); and the **Galerie Barbara Silverberg** (2148 rue Mackay). If all this threatens to become contemporary art overkill, you can retreat into the past at **Le Petit Musée** (1494 rue Sherbrooke Ouest), where ancient *objets* and *bijoux* from Egypt, Greece, and the Far East reveal their mysteries to the curious as well as the collector.

Farther afield, **Artefact International** (102 rue Laurier Ouest) specializes in African art of the highest quality. Finally, four of Montréal's best contemporary art galleries are located at 372 rue Ste-Catherine Ouest, all on the fifth floor. They are: the **Galerie Brenda Wallace**, the **Galerie Chantal Boulanger**, the **Galerie René Blouin**, and the **Galerie Samuel Lallousz**.

—Mary Kelly

THE PROVINCE OF QUEBEC

By David E. Scott

David E. Scott was born and raised in the province of Québec, and returns there frequently. He was the travel editor of the London (Ontario) Free Press *for 15 years and since then has written* The Ontario Getaway Guidebook, A Taste of Ontario Country Inns, *and* Ontario for Free.

Canada's most culturally and historically interesting province is a vast territory comprising roughly one-sixth of the country's total area—an expanse larger than France, Spain, and West Germany combined. Included in that area is 71,000 square miles of fresh water. The northern three-quarters of the province is largely uninhabited and even unexplored, though much of it is known to contain enormous quantities of valuable minerals.

About 77 percent of Québec's population of 6.5 million is concentrated in cities, with most of that in Montréal (which has a population of more than two million) and its environs. Other urban-population pockets are found in and around the cities of Hull (next to Ottawa), Québec City, Sherbrooke, the Montréal suburbs of Laval, Longueuil, and Verdun, and the cities and towns surrounding Lac-St-Jean (St. John), source of the Saguenay River, which drains eastward into the St. Lawrence River north of Québec City.

French is the mother tongue of more than 80 percent of Quebeckers, and outside Montréal the figure rises to 93 percent. One Quebecker in four speaks English in addition to French. The visitor who is unaware of these statistics can find himself in a lather when confronted by someone who, when asked for directions, simply shrugs and walks away. Quite often the individual is walking away to fetch someone who has at least a smattering of English, but in remote areas off the established tourist tracks such individuals cannot always be found.

If you don't already know them, you should try to learn at least a dozen French words (*bonjour, s'il vous plaît, merci, où est?, combien?, comment ça va?*) before visiting the province. If you don't speak or understand French, do not assume the chap from whom you are asking directions, ordering food, or trying to buy a souvenir speaks English and is snubbing you by refusing to do so. Here's where your pleasant smile pays off. After all, his life was going along just fine until you arrived and wanted something. In return for a friendly effort, he'll probably try to find someone who can speak English and help you out.

Most Québec drivers are super macho and, unlike many of their neighbors in Ontario, know which is the passing lane of a four-lane highway. Be sure you do, too, or you may find a hood ornament stuck to the back of your car. Many local drivers will display an intense determination not to be bested in a passing match, left behind in the dash for a tiny opening in traffic, or humbled by *les spotteurs* (the Québec provincial police). Should you be challenged for that tiny hole in the traffic, give way, even if you have the right of way. Console yourself with the fact that you're not backing down but just being a gracious guest in a foreign country.

Food is taken seriously here, despite the recent proliferation of both North American and just-Québec fast-food chains. It is not unusual for the waitress at the humblest truck-stop restaurant to ask whether you want your hamburger cooked well, medium, or rare. Try to smile and laugh a lot while you're in Québec. You'll notice that's what most of the natives do. In fact, you'll encounter more joie de vivre in Québec than in any other part of North America.

MAJOR INTEREST

Eastern Townships
Fishing
Winter sports
Summer resorts

St. Lawrence South Shore
Crafts

Gaspé Peninsula
Seascapes and mountain scenery
Parc de la Gaspésie in the mountains
Parc national de Forillon on the sea
Percé village for arts and seafood

Magdalen Islands
Remoteness and tranquillity

Islands of the St. Lawrence
Old-fashioned style of living

St. Lawrence North Shore
Mountain scenery and rugged seascapes
Pointe-au-Pic summer resorts

Laurentian Mountains
Ski resorts

For touristic purposes, Québec comprises seven regions easily explored by the visitor. For internal political purposes, the province is divided into 18 touristic regions, some of which are almost inaccessible to travellers except by chartered aircraft. In this chapter the political boundaries have been ignored to simplify descriptions of the location of (and best routes through) the various geographic regions. The Magdalen Islands, included in this chapter, are somewhat difficult to reach, though the rewards for the visitor are great.

- **Eastern Townships.** A topographically varied region of rolling farmland, small volcanic mountains, lakes, rivers, and brooks extending north from the U.S. states of New York, Vermont, New Hampshire, and Maine to the south shore of the St. Lawrence opposite Montréal and Québec City.
- **St. Lawrence South Shore.** As its name suggests: Comprising the south shore of the river from Québec City and the border of the Eastern Townships northeast to the base of the Gaspé Peninsula.
- **Gaspé.** A wonderfully scenic region extending from Rivière-du-Loup on the south shore of the St. Lawrence River around the Gaspé Peninsula south to the border of northeastern New Brunswick.
- **Magdalen Islands.** A 12-island archipelago (Iles-de-la-Madeleine in French) in the Gulf of St. Lawrence approximately equidistant from southwestern Newfoundland, western Cape Breton Island, and the north coast of Prince Edward Island.

- **Islands of the St. Lawrence**. Three islands—
  Orléans, Coudres, and Grues—in the river northeast of Québec City.
- **St. Lawrence North Shore:** Also known as the
  Charlevoix area, stretching northeast along the
  river from Québec City to Tadoussac, at the mouth
  of the Saguenay River, and north from there to the
  towns and cities clustered along the shores of Lac-
  St-Jean.
- **Laurentians**. The age-old mountains north of Montréal whose family-owned inns, lodges, and resorts
  have accommodated generations of winter-sports
  enthusiasts.

Each of these regions is packed with hundreds of different
inns (*auberges*) in addition to various hotels and resorts. (See
the Accommodations Reference at the end of the chapter for
general information.) Almost all are colorful and distinctive,
and all take pride in their kitchens. Most also include dinner
and breakfast in their rates, so there is usually no need to look
further for restaurants. The French cuisine they serve is
enhanced by a "down home" Québécois flavor, and in some,
including the tiny **Auberge des Falaises** in Pointe-au-Pic, you
can sample specialties like *sauvagine,* a crossbreed of goose
and duck found only in this area.

THE EASTERN TOWNSHIPS

The Eastern Townships were so named to distinguish them
from the townships west of Montréal, which are now in
Ontario. The region is home to some 300,000 people, one-
third of whom live in the city of Sherbrooke, with the
balance scattered among the region's small towns and rural
communities. Until 1951 the area was known in French as
Les Cantons de l'Est, but it's now called l'Estrie, a marriage of
the words *est* (east) and *patrie* (homeland).

This roughly triangular area lies south of the St. Lawrence
River, and stretches from the point where Québec meets
Ontario and New York State west of Montréal to an imagi-
nary line running southeast from Québec City to the Maine
border. Comprising about 5,000 square miles of hilly country dotted with lakes and laced by rivers and streams, the
townships account for 10 percent of urbanized Québec. In
the western third of the region, north of Vermont and New

Hampshire, alluvial plains are interrupted by half a dozen volcanic peaks, the highest of which is Mont-Orford, scarcely a mountain at 2,875 feet.

The townships start less than an hour's drive east of Montréal (via Highway 10) with the flat farmland around Granby and Cowansville. Well-worn peaks of the ancient Appalachian range bearing names like Sutton, Owl's Head, Bromont, and Orford make their appearance a little farther east. At the feet of these small mountains lie pretty lakes—Brome, Massawippi, Magog, Bowker, Memphrémagog, Mégantic, Aylmer, Lyster, and St-François. The lakes haven't been polluted by heavy industry or indiscriminate dumping, and most yield an astonishing variety of game fish. Cruises are available on lakes Lyster, Mégantic, and Memphrémagog, with boats departing from the towns of Baldwin Mills, Lac-Mégantic, and Magog, respectively.

Sherbrooke is known as the Queen City of the Eastern Townships, a region whose Loyalist heritage is reflected in county names such as Wolfe, Shefford, Stanstead, and Dorchester. But while many of the towns, villages, and hamlets surrounding Sherbrooke were founded by Anglo-Saxon colonists who remained loyal to the British Crown in the wake of the American Revolution, today they're just as likely to have French prefixes or suffixes attached to their names. Since the early 19th century, French Canada's "revenge of the cradle" has resulted in a French-speaking majority in all 15 Eastern Township counties. It has been a gradual takeover, and one without the rancor that surfaced several decades ago in other parts of the province (most noticeably in the West Montréal suburbs). Today names like Ste-Catherine-de-Hatley, Ste-Hilaire-de-Dorset, and St-Jacques-de-Leeds recall the origins of the first settlers, few of whose descendants remain in this predominantly Francophone region.

Still, French and English farmers have worked this thin soil for generations, and each group has a healthy respect for the other. The movement to separate French Québec from English Canada has never been a highly emotional cause in these tranquil parts, where the Anglophone visitor will have little difficulty finding a native who speaks some English.

The western half of the region is the prettiest, reminding the visitor of England's Cotswolds, from which many of the original settlers came (though the townships are ten times the area of the Cotswolds). In the northwest, there are apple orchards and, as the land flattens to the east, fields of grain and corn.

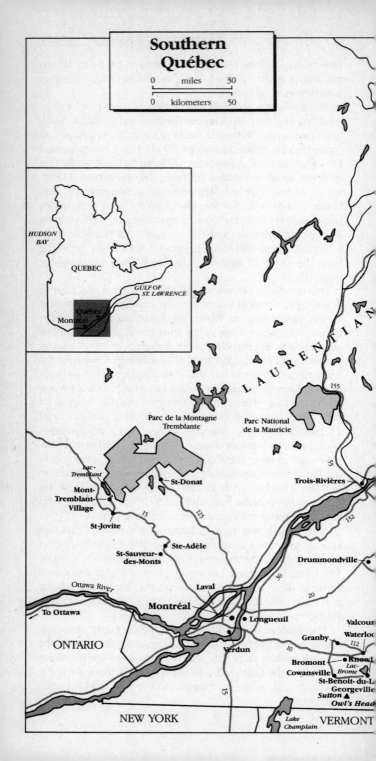

Southern Québec

0	miles	30
0	kilometers	50

HUDSON BAY

QUEBEC

GULF OF ST. LAWRENCE

Québec

Montréal

LAURENTIAN

155

55

Parc de la Montagne Tremblante

Parc National de la Mauricie

Lac-Tremblant

Mont-Tremblant-Village

St-Donat

Trois-Rivières

St-Jovite

15

125

Ste-Adèle

132

St-Sauveur-des-Monts

Drummondville

Ottawa River

Laval

To Ottawa

Montréal

30

20

ONTARIO

Longueuil

Valcour

Verdun

10

Granby

Waterloo

112

Bromont

Knowl

Cowansville

Lac-Brome

St-Benoit-du-L

Georgeville

Sutton

Owl's Head

NEW YORK

Lake Champlain

VERMONT

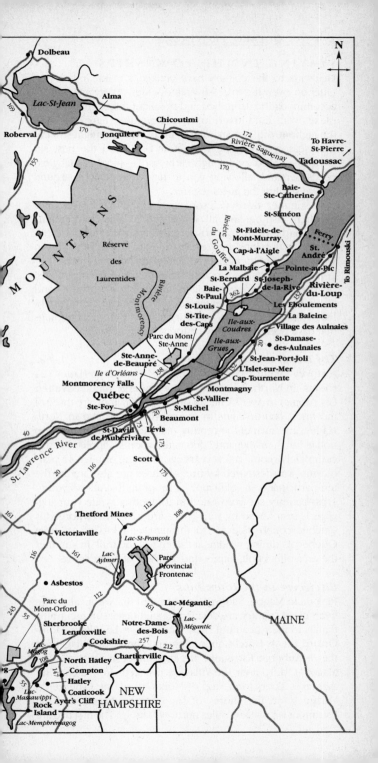

STAYING IN THE TOWNSHIPS

Getaways to the country have created a major industry in Québec over the past several decades. Every manner of accommodation, from bed-and-breakfast inns to major complexes with ultra-luxurious condominiums, have appeared throughout the province. And in all but the highest summer season—mid-June to Labour Day—and the best ski periods—February through early April—supply usually exceeds demand, allowing you to have a good look around before signing the guest register.

In summer, five-star resorts around the major lakes offer excellent fishing and all water sports. Most have tennis courts and swimming pools, and all are close to golf facilities. All major inns and resorts operate year-round, and in winter many of them cater to skiers and snowmobilers.

All the resorts we mention have their own dining rooms, of which the owners/managers are extremely proud—and justifiably so. The region teems with other fine dining establishments as well, many in Georgian and Victorian buildings that have been exquisitely restored and renovated.

The Lac-Massawippi Area

▶ Hovey Manor (35 rooms) and the ▶ Auberge Hatley (24 rooms) in North Hatley and the ▶ Auberge Ripplecove Inn (24 rooms) in Ayer's Cliff, all on Lac-Massawippi, are three of the finest country inns in the province. The two in North Hatley are turn-of-the-century mansions, and charge top dollar for their elegantly decorated rooms; Ripplecove was completely rebuilt a few years ago after the original 42-year-old inn was destroyed by fire. All three are also among the ten participants in "Skiwippi," a program that allows you to cross-country ski from one inn to another while your luggage is sent ahead by van. There are 32 miles of gorgeous Québec countryside to ski through, and lots of gourmet Québécois dining waiting at the end of the trail. In summer the area offers golf, tennis, and a variety of water sports.

Elsewhere in the Townships

Resorts in Magog, Sutton, Bromont, and Knowlton, all in the heart of ski country, are developing significant summer traffic thanks to their beautiful rural locations. ▶ Le Village Mont-Orford, the ▶ Hôtel Condominiums O'berge du Village, and the ▶ Auberge Estrimont are large modern resorts in the Magog–Orford area. (Le Village is just steps from a chair lift that takes skiers to the top of Mont-Orford, the O'berge du Village is on the shores of Lac-Memphrémagog, and the Estrimont is just a few miles north of Magog.) The first two are condominium complexes, while the Estrimont, the most deluxe of the three, offers hotel rooms in addition to condominium units, along with an indoor swimming pool, lighted tennis courts, and a fitness center.

The ► **Village Archimède de Sutton**, situated high on the slopes of Mont-Sutton overlooking the pretty village of Knowlton and Brome Lake (called Lac-Brome by the French), offers 20 modern fully-equipped wooden luxury chalets raised on stilts to capture the views. In Bromont, two of the best choices are the ► **Hôtel-Spa Le Château Bromont** and the ► **Auberge au Vieux Manoir**. The first is a modern 147-room resort with indoor and outdoor swimming pools, a physical fitness center, and rooms well above average in terms of comfort and decor. The other, one of the first deluxe accommodations in the area, is an antiques-filled hotel with 26 guest rooms and a cozy bar.

The relatively new ► **Auberge Le Malard**, a luxury complex on the northern shore of Lac-Brome, has 38 rooms and suites, all with balconies or private patios, and some with fireplaces and whirlpool baths. Other amenities here include an indoor exercise pool, a sauna, and a beach on the lake.

For a change of pace, consider the ► **Auberge Georgeville** in nearby Georgeville, a 12-room bed-and-breakfast establishment in a renovated mansion that dates to 1890.

Around the Townships

While the Eastern Townships don't have a Niagara Falls or soaring mountains, bucolic scenes frequently unfold around the next curve of a secondary highway or gravel side road. Many of Québec's remaining 150 covered wooden bridges are still in use here, and the region is dotted with elaborate Victorian mansions and wooden churches of graceful proportions.

A four-lane autoroute, Highway 10, links Montreal with Sherbrooke, 144 km (89 miles) to the east. This is the fastest route for travellers in a hurry to reach the heart of the townships and start their wanderings, but the real beauty of the townships lies north or south of this intrusion into an otherwise quiet landscape.

The town of **Granby**, about 64 km (40 miles) east of Montreal (take the autoroute to Exit 38/Highway 139), has a large zoo with 350 species of animals as well as a reptile house. At the **Lac-Boivin Nature Study Centre**, also in Granby, there are more animals as well as a variety of interesting tree and floral specimens.

For those who know and love the drowsy communities of the region, their relative obscurity is a blessing. The winding secondary roads linking towns and villages aren't crowded with tour buses and vacationers' cars, and you won't have to stand in line at the increasingly numerous restaurants fashioned from gracious old homes by entrepreneurs who can work miracles over a cooking range.

Compared with what awaits the visitor in Gaspé and along either shore of the St. Lawrence River, none of the places we discuss below (in no particular route order) is cause for a visit on its own merits. But if you have opted to savor the rural loveliness of the area and find yourself near one during your browsings, a certain town may justify a detour.

Waterloo

Waterloo, 19 km (12 miles) southeast of Granby via Highway 122, is renowned for its mushrooms, which you're likely to find in the stuffing of a duckling from nearby Lac-Brome, the duck-breeding center of Canada. Waterloo also has an unusual museum, the **Musée Québécois de la chasse**, which not only traces the history and techniques of hunting, but claims to be the only museum in North America devoted to the subject. Displays include hundreds of stuffed birds and animals, as well as a collection of antique guns. The museum, in town at 45 chemin de l'Horizon, is open daily from 10:00 A.M. to 5:00 P.M., mid-May to mid-September.

Magog

From Magog, a resort at the north end of forest-ringed Lac-Memphrémagog (which is shared by Québec and Vermont), the 55-foot *l'Aventure II* heads out on all-day buffet-lunch cruises of the lake from June through August, stopping at Newport, Vermont. A second boat makes two-hour afternoon cruises from the end of June through September 1. Both boats pass—but do not stop at—the Benedictine abbey of **St-Benoît-du-Lac**, a piece of Europe transplanted to the New World. The abbey, whose regionally famous cheese, cider, and chocolate are sold on the premises, is reached by a secondary road that runs south from Magog about 16 km (10 miles) to the hamlet of Austin. The abbey is a few kilometers south of Austin, and is signposted all the way from the autoroute.

The **Parc du Mont-Orford**, north of Magog, is the home of an important arts and cultural center where jazz and classical concerts are held during the summer season. If you're there on a clear day, take the ski lift to the top for an overview of the townships from the 2,875-foot-high summit.

North Hatley

North Hatley, at the northern end of Lac-Massawippi between Highways 108 and 147, is the prettiest of the townships' resort towns—a fact that's reflected in the locally available works by the area's many painters and artisans. Massawippi itself is only 12 miles long and a mile wide, but offers an inexhaustible supply of some 70 species of game fish. There is, in addition, an English-language summer theater at The Piggery, on Highway 108 heading east out of town.

Other Points of Interest

If Sherbrooke is the Francophone cultural center of the townships, the village of Lennoxville, only 5 km (3 miles) south, is its English counterpart. Bishops University was founded here in 1843 in buildings inspired by those at Oxford University. Just across the St. Francis River from the university complex is Bishops College School, founded in the same era for the express purpose of educating "the sons of English gentlemen."

Compton, Cookshire, Coaticook, Rock Island, Hatley, and Lac-Mégantic are other towns and villages (mostly south and east of Sherbrooke) with a slow pace and buildings that date to the early 19th century. Cookshire is particularly attractive, with its Balley and Pope houses built in 1800, an 1835 covered bridge, an 1864 Anglican church, and an 1868 post office. Rock Island has the Haskell Opera House, a scaled-down replica of the Old Boston Opera House built astride the Canada–U.S. border. From Notre-Dame-des-Bois (near Lac-Mégantic) you can drive to the 3,625-foot summit of Mont-Mégantic, where an observatory contains the most powerful telescope in eastern North America.

Just south of Chartierville, on Route 257 north of the New Hampshire border, is Québec's Magnetic Hill. Like its famous counterpart near Moncton in New Brunswick, the phenomenon is simply an optical illusion. A visit to Québec's Magnetic Hill is also a lesson in commercial promotion: While this hill is not widely known beyond the immediate vicinity, its illusion is far more dramatic than that of the New Brunswick hill.

Winter Sports

Alpine skiing is offered at eight major centers in l'Estrie. Magog's Station touristique de Mont-Orford (Tel: 819/843-

6548), with a vertical drop of 1,772 feet, has added more than $20 million worth of lift equipment and snow-making machines over the past six years.

Snowmobilers who make their way to **Valcourt**, the birthplace of Joseph-Armand Bombardier, the inventor of the snowmobile, will find a trail system measuring more than 1,250 miles. "Motoneig-Estrie" maps showing the complete system are available from any of the tourist information centers in the area.

Winter sports enthusiasts can write the Eastern Townships tourist bureau for up-to-date package and rate information. Their address and phone number are: Association Touristique de l'Estrie, 25 rue Bocage, Sherbrooke, Québec, J1L 2J4; Tel: (819) 820-2020.

ST. LAWRENCE SOUTH SHORE

The stretch of St. Lawrence River shoreline extending from Lévis northeast to Rimouski is included for the benefit of those who want to start their tour of the Gaspé Peninsula by car from the Québec City area. Information on the first half of this section—from Lévis to Rivière-du-Loup—will be of special interest for those who plan a St. Lawrence River loop: Québec City to St-Siméon on the north shore (see the St. Lawrence North Shore section below), across the river by ferry to Rivière-du-Loup, and returning to Lévis on the south shore. While the communities along this stretch offer many points of interest for the visitor, the rugged mountainous north shore route (as opposed to the flat and pastoral south shore) is by far the more scenic.

The Trans-Canada Highway (Highway 20) is the fastest south-shore route; most of the region's attractions, however, are found along Highway 132, which lies closer to the river. (The two highways run parallel to each other until just east of Rivière-du-Loup, where they merge and continue around the Gaspé Peninsula as Highway 132.) Most towns along this stretch have at least a few old buildings carefully maintained or meticulously restored. In **Lévis**, a timber export center since 1810, there are three fine Victorian mansions on rue Wolfe (numbers 2, 4, 6), as well as a magnificent view of Québec City from the **terrasse de Lévis**.

On the north side of town at Pointe Lévis you'll find **Fort No. 1**, a national historic park. The fort was built between 1865 and 1872 to defend against the possibility of an American attack on Québec City, an attack the Québécois feared would involve the railway linking the state of Maine to the city of Lévis. Fort No. 1 was one of three separate forts making up part of the fortifications of Québec City. The fort, of the Vauban type, was built behind considerable masses of earth.

BEAUMONT

The town of Beaumont, northeast of Lévis, has a beautiful 1821 mill, 20 historic homes, and a church with an interesting story. The first church on the site was built in 1694, followed in 1722 by the presbytery. In 1759 a proclamation by General James Wolfe was pinned on the door of the present church, itself built in 1733, by the general's troops. When angry villagers ripped it up, Wolfe's soldiers set fire to the church and then watched as only the door would burn.

A three-story mansard-type seigneurial mill, perched on a cliff overlooking the Maillou waterfall here, was first used as a carding mill; millstones and saws were later added so that grain and lumber could be processed. Today you can purchase muffins and bread made from flour milled on the premises.

Behind the mill a stairway leads to the remains of another mill near the river's edge, where an archaeological dig is in progress. A video explains the history of the restoration as well as the findings from the digs being carried out at both sites. The mill is open mid-June to the end of October, daily except Mondays.

ST-MICHEL TO ST-JEAN-PORT-JOLI

The church in nearby **St-Michel** dates from 1858. As you enter the village, a replica of the chapel of Lourdes will be on your left. Restoration of the 1739 presbytery near the church has erased all traces of the English bombardment intended to force the inhabitants to accept the new regime after the fall of Québec.

St-Vallier, a few miles farther north and east via Highway 132, has the **Musée des voitures à chevaux** (Horse-Drawn Carriage Museum), where 65 summer and winter carriages and assorted equestrian accessories are on display year-round.

Montmagny

Montmagny, the next community up the road, is also one of the oldest on the south shore. Thousands of snow geese stop here during their fall migration, and a snow goose festival in their honor is held during the third week in October. In town at the 18th-century Manoir Couillard-Dupuis there is an exhibit devoted to nearby **Grosse Ile**, which was used as a quarantine station for much of the 19th century. In fact, by 1910 some 50,000 European immigrants had spent time on the island. Grosse Ile's role as a bulwark against infectious diseases was superseded in the years immediately preceding and following World War II, when the Canadian and U.S. armies conducted joint experiments on the island designed to protect the North American continent from bacteriological attack. The island reverted to quasi-civilian control in 1957, and since then has been used as an animal quarantine station and international veterinary research center.

Musée maritime Bernier

About 16 km (10 miles) northeast of Montmagny is the village of **L'Islet-sur-Mer**, nicknamed the "sailors' homeland" because sailors from here have served on every ocean of the world. On July 1, 1909, one of its most courageous sons, Captain Joseph-Elzear Bernier, took possession of the Arctic islands in the name of Canada, a feat commemorated by a plaque on Melville Island in the high Arctic. The Musée maritime Bernier, located in a convent built in 1877, is the largest maritime museum in North America in terms of the size and quality of its collection. From late June through Labour Day the museum is open daily from 8:30 A.M. to 8:00 P.M.; off-season hours are Monday through Friday, 8:30 A.M. to 4:00 P.M.

St-Jean-Port-Joli

St-Jean-Port-Joli is Québec's handicraft capital. Just outside the village you'll find a cluster of wood sculptors' workshops constituting the largest assemblage of artisan-sculptors in the province. The wood-carving tradition was started here around 1936 by the Bourgault family, and since then potters and weavers in some numbers have moved to the area. Most of the shops have areas in which the sculptors work while they chat with visitors and answer questions. The caliber of work varies from studio to studio, however, and choosing a piece can be difficult; meeting and getting to know the sculptor not only makes the decision easier but also results in a work of art with a personal connection to its buyer.

The 1779 church in the village is a classified cultural property, and there's a fine mill once owned by Seigneurie de Philippe Aubert de Gaspé. There are also two interesting little museums in St-Jean-Port-Joli and a third in St-Aubert, about 13 km (8 miles) south via Route 204. The **Musée des anciens Canadiens**, in town at 322 avenue de Gaspé Ouest, has numerous wood carvings depicting the relationship of land to sea. The museum is open daily May through October. Down the street, the **Musée les retrouvailles**, 248 avenue de Gaspé Ouest, houses a collection of weaving looms, spinning wheels, dishware, agricultural and industrial machinery, and a 1953 Super-Constellation aircraft, the only one of its kind in Canada. The museum is open daily from late June through mid-September.

In St-Aubert, an 18th-century carding and flour mill filled with original machinery and the adjacent blacksmith shop are open daily year-round.

Village des Aulnaies

The Village des Aulnaies, a few miles northeast of St-Jean-Port-Joli, is the south shore's oldest seigneurial concession. Today the graceful 19th-century manor house is surrounded by wide verandahs bordered by well-kept gardens. Inside, staff in period costume recall the era. The gabled three-story communal mill of freestone has also been restored: Visitors can purchase freshly milled flour while watching the trough of incoming water power the mill. Elsewhere on the property, the miller's house has been converted into a café-terrace where refreshments are served under huge oak trees. The estate is open daily from the last week of June through Labour Day.

DINING AND STAYING IN THE AREA

There are two inns with restaurants of note in the area. In St-Jean-Port-Joli, the ▶ **Auberge du Faubourg**—which overlooks the river and is open from May through mid-October only—dishes up savory regional specialties such as lamb noisettes cooked with maple syrup and fresh mint, meat pie, and duck breast with honey and raspberry vinegar sauce. (The Auberge du Faubourg also has 90 deluxe motel units and 10 cottages.)

As you continue north and east on Highway 132 it's hard to miss the mansard-roofed ▶ **Manoir Saint-André et Chalets**, its white main building accented in turquoise trim, with red roses picked out in the window lintels of the second floor. The hotel and adjoining motel have 21 rooms, 16 with bathrooms *en suite*. But it's the hotel's seafood-dominated menu featuring locally caught sturgeon, eel, and smelt that's the real attraction.

RIVIERE-DU-LOUP TO RIMOUSKI

Rivière-du-Loup (Wolf River) was founded in 1673 on a rocky spur that juts into the St. Lawrence River. The city has a 90-foot waterfall within its limits, and is linked with St-

Siméon on the north shore by regular ferry service from March 31 through January 2 (when winter storms and drifting ice shut the service down). Two of the better accommodations in town are the 122-room ▶ **Auberge de la Pointe** and the 100-unit ▶ **Motel Lévesque**, both overlooking the river and offering nightly entertainment. The latter, at 171 rue Fraser, has 30 rooms with whirlpool baths, a heated outdoor pool, a playground for children, and a locally renowned dining room, **La Distinction**, that claims smoked salmon as its specialty. The Auberge de la Pointe, with a spa that offers Alga and Balneotherapy, is popular with dedicated health disciples. You'll find it at 10 Cartier Boulevard.

The 104-km (64-mile) stretch from here to Rimouski takes you through a procession of villages and small towns overlooking the ever-widening St. Lawrence. (At Rivière-du-Loup the river is about 12 miles wide; at Rimouski its width is 33 miles.)

Rimouski

Rimouski, midway between Québec City and Gaspé, is the last sizable city before the Gaspé loop (discussed next). The **Maison Lamontagne** here is one of the few remaining examples of half-timbered houses in Québec, and is open daily from the last week in June to the first week in September.

If you decide to spend the night before heading into the Gaspé region, you'll find a good range of affordable accommodations in town. All 165 large, elegantly appointed rooms of the ▶ **Hôtel des Gouverneurs** (155 boulevard René-Lepage Est) overlook the river, and fine French cuisine is served in the hotel's dining room. The ▶ **Centre de Congrès de Rimouski**, down the boulevard at number 225, is another five-star hotel, with 140 rooms and a swimming pool. Less grand lodgings with lovely river views can be found at the 24-unit ▶ **Motel Rimouski**, 410 boulevard St-Germain Est, and the 81-unit ▶ **Hôtel-Motel Journey's End**, 455 boulevard St-Germain Ouest.

Although you'll see signs directing you to the **Château de Rêve** along the highways, don't plan on spending the night at this turreted red-roofed castle—it's a children's amusement park with bumper cars, bumper boats, and other entertainment. The park is open from June through September.

THE GASPE PENINSULA

The Gaspé Peninsula is that part of Québec that juts into the Gulf of St. Lawrence, with the St. Lawrence River to the north and the province of New Brunswick to the south. The 150-mile-long peninsula is more or less separated from the Québec mainland by the Rivière Matapédia and Lac-Matapédia, and has 450 miles of coastline along which a narrow fringe of population is spread in tiny fishing villages. Its interior is dominated by the thickly forested Chic-Choc (pronounced sheek-shock) and Notre Dame mountain ranges, continuations of the Appalachians, which rise in places to more than 4,000 feet and provide sensational spring heli-skiing. The mountains are an obstacle to communication between the north and south coasts, and constitute a divide between the rivers flowing north into the St. Lawrence and south into the Baie des Chaleurs.

A logical starting place for a tour of the Gaspé Peninsula is Rimouski, on the south shore of the St. Lawrence River (for which see the end of the St. Lawrence South Shore section above). You can fly to Rimouski, Mont-Joli, or Matane (the last two at the base of the peninsula) from either Montréal or Québec City, and then rent a car for your tour. Or, if your time is limited, you can fly to the town of Gaspé and see the area's best sights in a single day. From Mont-Joli, 27 km (17 miles) northeast of Rimouski, you can complete the Gaspé Peninsula circle tour in two days, but forcing the pace through such spectacular scenery is ill advised. The tour merits at least twice that long, with the extra two days also giving you some insurance against bad weather. To do it in less time is to miss too many memorable little restaurants, breathtaking vistas, and friendly encounters with the region's people.

At any time of year, it's wise to make reservations in advance. Many motels are filled September to May by salespeople and government officials, and in the summer months, when those types don't travel in the region, more than a million others do. Another consideration when budgeting your time for a Gaspé tour is the weather. When an east wind blows in off the Gulf of St. Lawrence, the nasty weather can stay for days at a time. If you have some buffer time, you can use it by staying put wherever you are and catching up on your reading, or visiting nearby museums, churches, or other attractions. When the weather clears, start moving again.

Yet another thing to consider if you're bound for the Atlantic seacoast in summer is clothing. It's difficult when

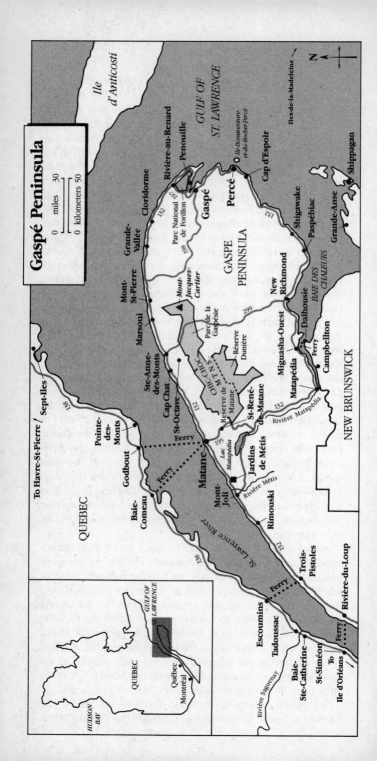

you're packing in sweltering heat even to think about warm and waterproof clothing, but you'd better have both with you on a trip around the Gaspé. The daytime highs inland can get as hot as they do anywhere else in eastern Canada, but it always cools off at night, and the average temperatures are considerably lower than they are in Montréal or Québec City.

The Gaspé: Yesterday and Today

In one version the name Gaspé derives from *gespeg,* an Indian word meaning the end of the world—a version that rings truer than the alternative. Even today it's not hard to imagine Gaspé as the end of the world . . . and besides, who ever heard of Gaspar Corte-Réal anyway?

Not only do you feel you've reached the end of the world at Gaspé, you also soon realize you truly don't want to return to the real world (unless you happen to come from a place with stunning seascapes and empty beaches, a place where social status is earned by the quality of the food you serve).

The **Micmac Indians**, known as the Indians of the Sea, have lived on the Gaspé Peninsula for more than 2,500 years. Today there are two Micmac reserves on the Baie des Chaleurs. The largest, with 1,700 residents, is at Restigouche, where a **Centre d'Interpretation de la Culture Micmac** is operated by the band. The Micmacs are known for their fine handicrafts and leather work, examples of which can be purchased at the center. Subsequent European settlers of the peninsula have included Acadians, Loyalists, Bretons, Basques, and Scots. The ethnic diversity of the Gaspé's settlers is evident in everything from its architecture to the hair and skin coloration of its inhabitants.

The Gaspé Peninsula is also one of Canada's oldest tourist regions, but one known only to wealthy and adventurous North Americans until a couple of decades ago. Visitors in those days got here by boat or by risking their lives in automobiles on the narrow, washboard roads that twisted up and down the frighteningly steep Chic-Choc mountainsides. To tour the Gaspé even in the 1950s was an adventure. You never knew when you might get stuck going up one of those incredibly steep hills and have to back all the way down again. After a couple of unsuccessful tries—each more scary than the last—you'd have to call it quits and backtrack to the nearest settlement with a hotel or boardinghouse. And there you'd stay until the road crews filled in the washouts and regraded the axle-deep washboard.

Nowadays the adventure of a Gaspé tour is confined to cuisine and scenery. The main coastal highway is well paved, and some sections are four lanes wide. Except in the most severe winter storms, people in the region's settlements set their watches by the twice-daily Voyageur bus, their chief link with the outside world.

Tourism has become an important economic fact of life in the Gaspé, with regional entrepreneurs having done their homework in preparation for the new breed of visitor. Everything is organized: Hotel and motel prices are set by the government; reservation systems are in place; menus are bilingual; and most hotel rooms have color TV.

The hospitality factor on the peninsula has never needed brushing up, having been a fact of life here since the area was settled in the late 1700s. But even though more and more visitors are crowding the highways and restaurants—to the inconvenience of the local residents—the same cheerful helpfulness is still typical of fishermen and gas jockeys, restaurant waitresses and lumberjacks.

Everything that attracted those early tourist adventurers is still here: the colorful frame houses overlooking picture-postcard inlets from their perches on steep hillsides and capes; salmon rivers, gin-clear after tumbling down gravel beds from deep in the mountains; white-capped blue Atlantic bays ringed by weatherbeaten fish shacks; sheltered coves shot through with a hundred colors of paint on lobster boats, lobster buoys, and dories.

Should you start your Gaspé tour from Québec City, take either the Trans-Canada Highway (Highway 20) or Highway 132 along the south shore of the St. Lawrence. (For information on the portion of the trip from Québec City to Rimouski, see the St. Lawrence South Shore section above.)

The Gaspé North Shore

Starting your Gaspé tour from Rimouski (discussed above), you won't have to make any decisions about highway routes. It's Highway 132 from Rimouski east to Gaspé, from there to Matapédia on the New Brunswick border, and north again from Matapédia to Mont-Joli on the St. Lawrence coast, just a few miles east of Rimouski, where you started.

Jardins de Métis

These lovely gardens about 40 km (25 miles) northeast of Rimouski should not be missed if you're fond of flowers and landscaping. The property, also known as the Villa Reford, was owned by Lord Mount Stephen, the first president of the Canadian Pacific Railroad, who enjoyed salmon fishing in the

Métis River and was part of the large English-speaking population that vacationed in family summer estates in the area.

Lord Stephen gave the estate to his niece Elsie Stephen Meighan Reford, who in turn transformed it into a magnificent British-style flower garden in the 1920s. Thanks to an exceptional microclimate and abundant resources, flowers that could be found nowhere else in northern latitudes were soon blooming here. The 37-room summer "cottage" stands in the middle of the gardens and now houses a museum, restaurant, and craft shop. The gardens are open daily from mid-June to mid-September.

MATANE TO RIVIERE-AU-RENARD

Matane, 48 km (30 miles) northeast of Métis, is the last ferry link to either Baie-Comeau or Godbout on the north shore of the St. Lawrence, which at this point is more than 64 km (40 miles) distant. The ferry runs daily throughout the year, and in summer reservations are recommended; Tel: (418) 562-2500 or (800) 463-2420 (in the 418 area code). A side trip south from Matane on Highway 195 will take you to the covered bridges of St-Jérôme-de-Matane and St-René-de-Matane.

You'll know you're in the mountains by the time you reach Cap Chat—named for its resemblance to a crouching cat—and will be for the rest of the trip to Gaspé. The highway clings to the edges of some slopes and circles the base of cliffs at sea level. The St. Lawrence is salt water here, and has been since Ile d'Orléans, about 40 miles northeast of Québec City. At times the highway may swing inland, climbing steep granite headlands before plunging down the other side to cross a stream or river flowing from deep in the mountains.

Parc de la Gaspésie

From Ste-Anne-des-Monts you can take Highway 299 south into the Parc de la Gaspésie, home to Mont-Jacques-Cartier. The park, about 56 km (35 miles) south of Highway 132, is the only place in Québec where you're likely to find moose, wood caribou, and white-tailed deer in the same general area. Accommodations are available at the 40-room ▶ **Gîte du Mont-Albert** on Highway 299. The hotel, operated by the Québec government, offers above-average comfort and very good cuisine (this is where young Montréal apprentice chefs strut their stuff), and is open from early June through mid-October.

STE-ANNE-DES-MONTS
TO GRANDE-VALLEE

In Marsoui, about 32 km (20 miles) east of Ste-Anne-des-Monts via Highway 132, there is a unique restaurant worth visiting—particularly if you have a healthy appetite for wholesome food. La Cookerie isn't listed in any gourmet restaurant guides, and it isn't advertised on highway billboards. But anybody living along this stretch of the Gaspé coast can direct you to it. (The restaurant, which is on your right as you're driving toward Gaspé, sits in a big gravel parking lot at the corner of rue Principal Ouest and the road that follows the Marsoui River inland to the mountains.) The interior decor is early practical—six long tables covered with oilcloth, each seating about a dozen, fill the room. The unadorned wooden walls are painted white and the linoleum-covered floor is spotless. Each table is crowded with four or five pies, a plate of strawberry-jam tarts, half a pound of butter on an enamel plate, and a sugar bowl. There's a menu on the wall, and a waitress will come by to tell you the special of the day. Often it's *cipaille* (pronounced sea-pie), a casserole of chicken, beef, potato, carrot, turnip, and dumpling, with a scoop of cole slaw on the side. A platter of thickly cut white bread arrives with the glass of water.

The entrée is followed by coffee and the baked goods. Customers help themselves; if you want half a pie, you eat half a pie. If you want a sliver of each to establish a favorite, that's what you're expected to do—but don't miss the sugar pie, a local specialty.

La Cookerie is a wonderful holdover from another era. It was built decades ago for the employees of the local sawmill. When the noon whistle sounded, they'd head for the restaurant, wash up in the long trough in a room outside the dining area, and tuck into the home-cooked food. The mill is closed now, but locals and knowledgeable travellers keep the place busy, and the dining room recently was made wheelchair accessible. It's open 6:00 A.M. to 8:00 P.M., seven days a week.

The hang-gliding capital of eastern Canada is a dozen miles east of Marsoui—pretty much where you'd least expect to find it. Just west of **Mont-St-Pierre** you'll come around a bend in the road and see a beautiful village site—a valley, plateau, mountain, and bay. If weather conditions are good, you'll also see a number of gaily colored hang gliders floating through the sky. Take a side trip up Mont-St-Pierre (1,376 feet) itself for great panoramic views from any of the three glider-launching pads.

There's a handsome covered bridge in **Grande-Vallée**, east of Mont-St-Pierre. A few miles farther along the road, in Cloridorme, home of a major fishing cooperative, you'll see a series of long tables, called *vigneaux,* where cod is dried in the open air. At Rivière-au-Renard, the industrial fish-processing center of the peninsula's north shore, there's no charge to watch the daily processing of cod and turbot, in season.

Parc national de Forillon

From Rivière-au-Renard you can head inland in the direction of Gaspé, about 32 km (20 miles) distant. Or you can stay on the coast and circle the Parc national de Forillon, doubling your distance to Gaspé. The park boasts one of Canada's tallest lighthouses, a 121-foot-high beauty built in 1858. (For $1 you can climb to the top.) The park also contains three plant groups left over from the ice age: flora of the Penouille dunes; flora of the briny marshes in Penouille Bay; and the arctic and alpine flora of the cliffs. From May to October whales frequently are spotted from the clifftops, and gray and common seals are usually seen disporting themselves close to shore. There's a bunker built as a lookout for German submarines during World War II to wander through as well. The lighthouse and visitor reception center are open daily, June through Labour Day; the park is open year-round.

Gaspé and Percé

The town of Gaspé overlooks an immense natural harbor into which three celebrated salmon rivers empty: the Dart-mouth, the York, and the St-Jean. The only wooden cathe-dral in North America, with a magnificent stained glass window and fresco donated by France in 1934 to com-memorate the 400th anniversary of Jacques Cartier's arrival, is another attraction. And the **Gaspé Museum** (open daily through Labour Day; Monday through Friday the rest of the year) has three rooms devoted to the history of the region.

The most spectacular sight on the Gaspé tour, however, lies 77 km (48 miles) farther south via the coast highway. You'll see **Percé Rock**, looking like an enormous ocean liner run aground with its bow facing land, long before you reach the picturesque fishing village of the same name. Waves have worn a hole through the rock near its "stern," and it's from that hole that the name Percé (meaning "pierced") is drawn. A free interpretive center in **Percé** itself will acquaint you with the heritage, history, and wildlife of the area, and naturalists are on hand to answer your questions. A number of entrepreneurs in town offer tours to and around Ile Bonaventure, where puffins, terns, and cormorants nest by the tens of thousands. Arrangements can be made for you to be left on the island and picked up later, with boats operating from the Percé beach on a regular schedule in season.

Percé is the real showplace of the Gaspé Peninsula, attracting artists, who claim the light is perfect, as well as nature lovers. In addition, the little fishing village has numerous gift shops, small museums, and art galleries.

STAYING AND DINING IN THE AREA

There is an abundance of accommodations in the Gaspé/ Percé region. Percé's ► Hôtel-Motel La Normandie, a comfortable 45-room establishment with a very good restaurant on Highway 132, commands a superb view of Percé Rock. The ► Auberge du Gargantua et Motels, also in Percé and open only during the summer season, is known for its fine food; seafood lovers should ask for the catch of the day.

If you decide to stay in the town of Gaspé, head for the 56-room ► Auberge des Commandants, 178 rue de la Reine, with a bar and dining room affording splendid views of the bay.

The Gaspé South Shore

The balance of your tour around the peninsula will be along an ever-mellowing coastline dotted with fishing villages and towns that in some stretches seem to alternate between all-French and all-English.

There's a stop worth making at Cap d'Espoir, about 22 km (14 miles) south of Percé. The Roman Catholic church here isn't the sort of building you'd expect to find in a region where the citizens traditionally have worked long and hard just to keep themselves alive. No matter. When the parish decided to build a church in 1889 they sprang for the works. The exterior is plain red brick, and there's a silvered spire and bell tower. On the outside, it isn't any different from a hundred other parish churches in rural Québec. The interior is a different story altogether.

The architecture is Roman-Corinthian; fluted white columns support the elaborately decorated arches of the 37-foot-high ceiling. The columns and ceiling are white and gold, and the gold, installed in 1912, is real. The pulpit and the doors leading to the sacristy behind the altar are priceless carved-wood artworks, and a large mural by Québec artist Charles Huot depicts the death of Saint Joseph, patron saint of the church. Though there are larger and more impressive churches in many cities of the world, the visitor is unlikely to be prepared for what he or she will find inside this one.

Cap d'Espoir, at the northeast entrance to the Baie des Chaleurs, is sometimes marked on English maps as Cape Despair. Jacques Cartier called the place Cap d'Espérance, meaning Cape Hope. In 1711 part of Admiral Sir Hovenden Walker's fleet was wrecked offshore here, resulting in the loss of all on board. The translation of Cap d'Espoir, obviously, depends on whether your background is French or English.

The land- and seascapes become ever more pastoral as you approach the New Brunswick border at the mouth of the Matapédia River. There are some fine examples of early Victorian architecture in a number of the coastal towns in this region, as well as half a dozen small museums along the way. Founded by Loyalists, New Richmond, about 150 km (93 miles) southwest of Cap d'Espoir, is remarkable for its Anglo-Saxon style of architecture. Large residences of the well-to-do are found in the center of town, while hillside farms are kept well back from the road behind a tree-lined walk, as they are in Scotland.

If the scenery and cuisine of the Gaspé Peninsula have put you behind schedule on your way to the Maritimes, you can cut roughly 100 km (62 miles) off your trip by taking the ferry from **Miguasha-Ouest** across the Baie des Chaleurs to Dalhousie in New Brunswick. Ferries run frequently in summer, and the crossing takes 15 minutes.

Travellers bound for Québec City should follow Highway 132 north up the Matapédia River valley. In just under 160 km (100 miles) you'll reach the St. Lawrence River at Mont-Joli, which itself is about 365 km (226 miles) northeast of Québec City.

THE MAGDALEN ISLANDS

The Magdalens, a 12-island archipelago situated some 135 miles southeast of Gaspé, 65 miles northeast of Prince Edward Island, and 60 miles west of Cape Breton Island, in the Gulf of St. Lawrence, are marked on most maps and in province of Québec tourism literature as the Iles-de-la-Madeleine. A population of 15,000 on the seven inhabited islands prevents them from being deserted, but you don't have to drive far to find your very own sandy beach where you can make the first set of footprints since the last storm washed the beach clean. From the air, the islands appear emerald green and ringed in white, the color of its 190 miles of beaches. In fact, if the Maggies—as they're familiarly known—were about 2,000 miles farther south and had a few resort hotels and palm trees, they would give most Caribbean islands a run for their money.

The charm of these islands lies in their remoteness from the hustle and bustle of mainland life. Because they are far from the madding crowd, the beaches aren't littered with trash and jammed with vacationers frantically trying to see and do everything during their seven- or 14-day vacation. About 20,000 visitors find their way here each summer, but the shortness of the season and the harsh weather the rest of the year have combined to discourage big investors.

That economic fact makes the Maggies the almost exclusive vacation preserve of those who know where, when, and how to make reservations for a hotel or motel room, a campsite, or one of the few chalets or houses for rent.

Shaped by Wind and Sea

The craggy coastline of the Maggies has been carved from grayish-red sandstone, gypsum, and other volcanic rock. Some of the ocher cliffs look as though a deranged giant had started his ultimate artistic masterpiece and abandoned the project partway through. Elsewhere, columns, tunnels, and caves gouged by relentless winds and waves add a touch of mystery to the scene.

Everywhere there is wind, a steady blow that averages 20 miles an hour, twice that of mainland Québec. In summer, when a hot sun bakes down on the bald hills, sand dunes, and beautiful white beaches, the breezes are welcome; in winter they tug and howl at the gaily colored square-frame houses scattered across the landscape like tantrum-tossed building blocks.

The expanses of open water around the Maggies cause the near-constant winds, but they are also responsible for moderating temperatures, which from June to September average 50° to 80° F (10° to 27° C). In winter, temperatures don't plunge nearly as much as they do on the mainland. A lot of snow falls on the islands, but accumulation isn't a problem, as most of it blows out to sea.

There are a few trees on the Magdalens, but they're short and twisted. On rounded hills, cattle graze in summer beside small fields that grudgingly surrender hay, turnips, and potatoes. Wood is so scarce that the resourceful Madelinots have developed a kind of barn found nowhere else in the world. It is called a *baraque* and consists of four stout posts supporting a four-sided roof that can be raised by ropes and pulleys as more hay is piled underneath. The roof is lowered as the hay is used up.

Although the small houses of the Magdalens may appear to be distributed with as little planning and as much color as wind-driven confetti, each faces the sea from which most families make their living. The season traditionally starts with the birth of harp and hook seal pups on the ice floes in March and April, and continues through the summer and fall with lobster, herring, cod, halibut, plaice, scallops, and mackerel. Most fishermen belong to cooperatives that sell to modern packing plants a snowball's toss from the docks, where their wives, daughters, or girlfriends have the day's catch processed and frozen or canned within minutes of its leaving the boats. After animal rights activists succeeded in banning the traditional seal pup harvest, the Madelinots turned it to their advantage. Thousands of visitors now travel to the Maggies in early spring to cuddle harp seal pups in the middle of the frozen Gulf of St. Lawrence. The new industry has proved to be an off-season bonanza for the tourism sectors of the Maggies and Charlottetown, Prince Edward Island, the most popular gateway to the islands.

Until a few decades ago, the population of the Maggies was about half French-speaking, mainly of Acadian background, and half English-speaking, mostly of Scottish descent. The population now is predominantly French-speaking, but those in tourism-related fields can and will manage some English. The few remaining English-speaking families are found on Ile d'Entrée and Grosse Ile.

AROUND THE ISLANDS

Cap-aux-Meules, a bustling town with a population approaching 2,000, is the archipelago's port of entry, main harbor, and largest commercial center. (Its name derives from *meules,* the French word for grindstone, the porous, gritty stone found throughout the archipelago.) There is, in addition, daily ferry service between Cap-aux-Meules and tiny **Ile d'Entrée**, which is home to 195 Anglophones. Although the trip takes only an hour each way, plan on setting aside a full day for exploring Ile d'Entrée; footpaths circle the island and lead to the top of Big Hill, at 557 feet the highest point in the Maggies. There's a snack bar on Ile d'Entrée, and overnight accommodations are available by advance reservation. For information, contact the Magdalen Islands Tourist Association reservations service, Tel: (418) 986-2245.

Highway 199, a paved two-lane road, links the main islands,

at times bisecting long sand spits frequented only by herons, cranes, and gulls. A dedicated sightseer could fully explore the main islands in two days, during which time he'd drive about 320 km (200 miles), visit several churches and light-houses, a windmill, a lobster- and fish-processing plant, a salt mine, and the **Museum of the Sea** in Havre-Aubert. Near the museum is a Québec government–supported handicraft center where artisans carve bowls and ashtrays from local stone, weave woollen goods, and sell paintings and photographs.

Of course, somebody racing through the islands on a schedule like that would miss their greatest attraction: the lifestyle only now being nudged aside by the 20th century; its man-made accoutrements; and the haunting beauty of those deserted dunes and beaches where the only sounds are those of wind and wave and the cries of wheeling gulls. Beautiful beaches fringe several sides of, and in some cases stretch in long spits between each of, the principal islands. Because there's always wind and no shortage of sandy spots from which to launch, the Maggies are a windsurfing para-dise. A favorite spot is **Baie de Havre aux Basques**, a com-pletely enclosed bay north of **Ile de Havre-Aubert**. Other good spots include the west-facing beaches on **Ile du Cap aux Meules** as well as the sandy isthmus linking that island to **Ile de Havre aux Maisons**.

STAYING AND DINING
ON THE MAGDALENS

Though limited, hotel and motel accommodations on the islands are relatively inexpensive. Don't expect color televi-sion in all rooms, or even your own bathroom *en suite*. Generally speaking, rooms are small, un-air-conditioned, and spotlessly clean. At several small and unpretentious restaurants you'll be able to have fresh lobster or other seafood dishes at half their usual price on the mainland.

Two of the better spots to stay are the 110-room ► **Châ-teau Madelinot** in Cap-aux-Meules, and the 28-unit ► **Motel des Iles**, on Ile du Havre aux Maisons. The latter has five units with fully equipped kitchenettes, a restaurant offering some of the archipelago's finest dining, and a lovely beach.

The finest cuisine in the Maggies is served at **La Table des Roy** (Tel: 418/986-3004) on Ile du Cap aux Meules. A choice of four dinners nightly and a warm, inviting atmosphere make this family-run restaurant a must for lovers of fine food. Closed Mondays. For that indigenous island specialty known as "pot-en-pot," a tangy mixture of fish, seafood, and potatoes baked in a flaky pie crust, try **La Saline** (Tel: 418/937-2230) in Havre-Aubert. On Ile du Havre aux Maisons, don't miss the seafood specials and mussel dishes at the aptly named **La Moulière** (Tel: 418/969-2233), in the Hotel au Vieux Couvent.

GETTING TO THE MAGGIES

Canadian Airlines International serves the Maggies with daily flights from Montréal, making connections throughout the Maritimes. Inter-Canadian Airlines has two daily flights linking the islands with other parts of Québec. Air-Madeleine offers flights to Gaspé and Mont-Joli from Montréal and Québec City.

CTMA-Voyageur, a 12-passenger freighter, makes one round trip per week from Montréal. The *Voyageur* operates from April 1 to the end of navigation, usually late autumn. The trip, which takes two days, costs roughly $400 per person, one way, or $795 round trip, and includes your cabin, all meals, and taxes. For further information, Tel: (514) 937-7656; for reservations, Tel: (418) 986-6600.

Daily ferry service to the Maggies is offered April through January from Souris, Prince Edward Island, aboard the M. V. *Lucy Maud Montgomery,* which can carry 90 cars and 400 passengers. Reservations are not accepted for the five-hour trip out of Souris, and passengers board on a first-come, first-served basis. You can, and should, reserve at least seven days in advance for the return trip. Rates for the ferry are about $50 round trip per person, and about $100 round trip for your automobile. For sailing times and additional information, Tel: (902) 687-2181 in Souris, or (418) 986-3278 in Cap-aux-Meules. (See also the Getting Around section at the end of this chapter, and the chapter on Prince Edward Island.)

THE ISLANDS OF THE ST. LAWRENCE

There are three islands in the St. Lawrence River northeast of Québec City where the 20th century has yet to make much of an impression. In fact, if you can overlook the rooftop television aerials and the automobile traffic, it isn't hard to imagine you've journeyed several centuries into the past.

The islands are Ile d'Orléans, Ile-aux-Coudres, and Ile-aux-Grues, and their residents enjoy a pace of life that's a whole lot slower than that found on the mainland. Most have time to visit and gossip and make things with their hands. Housewives buy their bread from the baker, their meat from the butcher, and their fish from the fishmonger. Vegetables and fruit come from their own gardens in season, or from jars of preserves in winter.

Ile d'Orléans

Of the three, Ile d'Orléans, about eight miles northeast of Québec City and easily accessible by car across a suspension bridge from the Montmorency area on the north shore, has yielded most to modern intrusions. Before the bridge, which opened in 1935, all traffic came by ferryboat, and that inconvenience, plus the ferry toll, hampered the development of tourism.

The island's relative isolation resulted in its inhabitants being called sorcerers, with some islanders even today proudly referring to themselves as *sorciers*. The sorcery rumor was started by French-Canadian mainlanders who were often puzzled by the strange lights they saw flickering along the shore of the island at night. At a loss to explain the lights, they began to whisper among themselves that the island was inhabited by sorcerers. English Quebeckers who saw the lights believed they were made by will-o'-the-wisps. Of course, there wasn't anything supernatural about the lights; the best explanation is that they were lanterns used by islanders to communicate with relatives or friends on the mainland.

After the bridge was built, it didn't take long for wealthy Quebeckers to decide the island's beauty made the commuting distance to downtown offices well worthwhile. In time, many built homes with sweeping views across the St. Lawrence shipping lanes to the backdrop of Québec City's Cap Diamant and the brooding Laurentian Mountains.

The island's population is now more than 6,000 and increasing, but the growth hasn't yet resulted in any shopping centers and hotels being built amid the apple orchards and strawberry fields. In part this is because the provincial government declared the island a natural and historic *arrondissement* (district) in 1970. (Whereas in a park the government owns the land, in an *arrondissement* the land remains privately owned, with the government retaining a say in what is done with it.)

Ile d'Orléans is elliptically shaped, 21 miles long, and never more than about five miles wide. The paved chemin Royal (Royal Road) skirts its shoreline and wanders through the island's six parishes. Farming is the traditional occupation, and the island's strawberries are known far and wide.

Handicrafts—among them rag-rug weaving, wood carving, spinning, knitting, and crocheting—are created in many homes.

There's a complete mix of architectural styles on the island, ranging from centuries-old stone churches and New England Victoriana to steep-roofed houses in bright colors with ski jump–shaped roofs and rows of dormer windows. (The roofs are shaped like ski jumps so that winter snow slides will not pile up against first-floor windows.) New homes are being built in the style of the *maison Canadienne* of the 1800s, many with attached two-car garages, two or three bedrooms, and most with split-fieldstone facing. The tiny generations-old roadside chapels and wayside crosses are also maintained.

STAYING AND DINING ON ILE D'ORLEANS

If you decide to spend a few days on Ile d'Orléans, especially during the colorful fall season, book early at the small—only eight guest rooms— ▶ **Auberge Le Chaumonot**. It is both quaint and quiet. For a memorable meal, ask for patio seating outside the gorgeous stone restaurant called **Le Moulin Saint-Laurent** (Tel: 418/829-3888), a renovated mill that serves the best of island seafood, wild goose, and beef dishes. A trio of troubadours strolls around the premises, entertaining diners with a combination of music and Gallic joie de vivre.

Ile-aux-Grues

This is the largest and only inhabited island of a 21-island archipelago off Montmagny, on the south shore of the St. Lawrence River about 56 km (35 miles) northeast of Lévis. The seven-mile-long island is linked by ferry, in season and depending on the tides, to Montmagny itself. Named for the cranes that use it as a stopping place on their migration south, the island was first settled by the French in 1654, then pillaged by General James Wolfe's soldiers in 1759. Prosperity gradually returned as the island found favor with those seeking peace and quiet. Today's visitors often bring their bicycles for a leisurely pedal, stopping at the cheese factory that sells its products on the premises.

There are two inns on the island, the ▶ **Auberge de l'Oie Blanche** and the ▶ **Auberge des Dunes**; both are quaint nine-room establishments with fine dining.

Ile-aux-Coudres

The pace of life on Ile-aux-Coudres is slower than on Ile d'Orléans but, thanks to its popularity with artists and vacationers, not as laid back as the very quiet Ile-aux-Grues. Located about 96 km (60 miles) northwest of Québec City and two miles from Baie-St-Paul at the mouth of the Gouffre River, the island is served by a ferry that runs every hour in daylight from St-Joseph-de-la-Rive, a north-shore village at the base of Les Eboulements, a high cape with rounded peaks.

The island was named by Jacques Cartier in 1535 for the quantities of hazelnuts he found growing here. A cross marks the location where the first Mass mentioned in Canadian history was celebrated by Cartier on September 7, 1535. The three parishes of the island each cluster around their church, and rotting *goélettes* (small wood boats) near decaying wharves tell the story of a once-flourishing coastal pulp-wood-transporting industry replaced by diesel trucks with the advent of improved and paved highways on the north shore.

Ile-aux-Coudres has its legend too. Hundreds of years ago an earthquake caused a huge chunk of Les Eboulements to fall into the deep channel between the island and the mainland, with considerable loss of life at an Indian village there. It is said that on a very still day you can see the remains of the Indian village on the bottom of the channel.

A 32-km (20-mile) road around the perimeter of the island links the parishes of La Baleine (The Whale), St-Bernard, and St-Louis. The island is almost wedge-shaped, about seven miles long, three miles wide at its west end, and tapers to a point at its northeast end. The north shore facing the mainland rises steeply from the ferry landing and continues up to a plateau running the length of the island. Fields of potatoes or wildflowers accented by fir trees slope down to the St. Lawrence; tiny chapels and wayside crosses are found along the roadsides.

The south side of the island is a pebble beach that makes for good picnicking with children—especially at low tide, when they can find all manner of sea life under the seaweed in the tidal pools.

Handicrafts flourish on Ile-aux-Coudres, as do several resort hotels, but the baker still bakes crusty loaves each morning, and social hour is at the post office each evening, when residents gather to pick up the mail brought over by boat from the north shore.

STAYING AND DINING
ON ILE-AUX-COUDRES

There are about a dozen good auberges and motels on Ile-aux-Coudres, but there is only one that is operated year-round: the 98-room ▶ **Hôtel Cap-aux-Pierres** in La Baleine, which comes highly rated and has indoor and outdoor swimming pools in addition to a good dining room (the island is only 16 km/10 miles long, so it's easy to locate). There are a number of smaller inns as well, including the 47-room ▶ **Hôtel-Motel Les Voitures d'Eau**, near the village of St-Louis; as its name implies, the hotel is situated on the coast and has wonderful views of the St. Lawrence. It is open only during the season, however.

ST. LAWRENCE NORTH SHORE

Technically, the north shore of the St. Lawrence River extends from eastern Ontario to the Labrador coast, a distance of almost 1,000 miles. The highway along the western two-thirds of that shoreline continues to inch north and east, gradually linking communities previously accessible only by ship.

For many years Highway 138 reached only as far as Sept-Isles, about 960 km (595 miles) northeast of Montréal, but in recent years it has been extended another 208 km (129 miles) to Havre-St-Pierre. Beyond this point, coastal settlements that are accessible only by air or water continue to extend their town roads, bringing closer the government and "outporter" dream of someday linking places like Blanc-Sablon— 400 km (248 miles) farther up the coast—to the rest of the mainland.

One of the most beautiful areas in this vast province of widely diversified scenery is the 225-km (140-mile) stretch between Québec City and Tadoussac. Highway 138 is now paved, the formerly hair-raising mountain traverses have been tamed, and you can make the drive today in about three hours (which includes the ten-minute ferry crossing at the mouth of the Saguenay River between Baie-Ste-Catherine and Tadoussac).

Scenery buffs would have a tough time covering the distance in two full days, while a keen sportfisherman might not get there at all, having turned inland on one of the pulp-logging roads that lace enormous Charlevoix County and then angled himself to ecstatic exhaustion in the hundreds of brooks, lakes, and rivers hereabouts, most of which abound with feisty speckled, brown, and rainbow trout.

If you have only a limited amount of time to explore this very special province, consider first visiting Québec City (described elsewhere in this guidebook), and then making a circle tour of the lower St. Lawrence. There are six "circle" tours to choose from, corresponding to the six ferry routes across the river east of Québec City. Roll your own.

In a long—and frustrating—day, you could cover the shortest loop: Québec City to St-Siméon on the north shore, across the river to Rivière-du-Loup, and back to the Québec City area along the south shore. That's a distance of about 375 km (233 miles), not counting the ferry trip. If you got an early start, you could also include Tadoussac, which would add another 64 km (40 miles) to the return trip.

Of course, the frustration would result from not being able to stop and savor the sights, not to mention the country restaurants and inns. You would also have to forgo the opportunities of meeting, if only fleetingly, some of the friendly folk along the way, many of whom have a considerable command of English owing to contact during the past century with those English-speaking North Americans who have spent summers in these parts.

All along this route you'll see roadside signs picturing a truck pointed downhill at a 45-degree angle, under which is a number and a percent sign. Some of the signs also bear the message "compression." The signs warn of an impending steep hill and the percent indicates the degree of slope. "Compression" means using a lower gear to save your brakes; you won't get a second chance on some of the 12- to 15-percent grades if your brakes burn out. Take the warning seriously.

QUEBEC CITY TO BAIE-ST-PAUL
Here's what you'd see on half the longest loop (the other half is included in the section on the St. Lawrence South Shore above):

Leave Québec City following signs for Highways 15A, 15B, 138, or Montmorency or Ste-Anne-de-Beaupré. The many stalls and shops offering handicrafts along the road east of Québec City are well worth browsing through. The dyed sheep pelts in a kaleidoscope of colors, the home-woven rag rugs, the hand-knitted woollens, and the beautifully detailed and expressive wood carvings are expensive but of good value. They're expensive because they aren't turned out by machines, instead requiring hours of patient work by skillful *habitants* whose families have handed down the tricks of the trade since they first arrived in these parts more than 300 years ago.

Montmorency Falls and Ste-Anne-de-Beaupré

This natural wonder, a thundering cascade 112 feet higher than Niagara Falls and just as spectacular, is on your left about 20 km (12 miles) east of Québec City. There's ample free parking in a lot off the highway, and from there you can walk to the base of the falls, where the spray will take the sting out of a summer sunburn. Nearby in Ste-Anne-de-Beaupré is the **shrine of Beaupré**, Canada's answer to Lourdes, where generations of believers have been cured of various afflictions. This has been a pilgrimage site since 1658, although the neo-Romanesque basilica dates only to 1923; hundreds of discarded trusses, canes, braces, and crutches testify to the miraculous cures.

From the same parking lot you can walk to the **Cyclorama of Jerusalem**, an astonishing reproduction of the Holy Land more than 44 feet high and about 350 feet long (open daily April to November). From Beaupré you can also see the graceful 5,700-foot suspension bridge to Ile d'Orléans (described in the Islands of the St. Lawrence section above).

The Laurentians

The highway climbs steeply from nearby St-Joachim onto the headland of **Cap Tourmente**. A short detour off the highway brings you to the village of St-Tite-des-Caps, named for the headlands (*caps*) that afford a panoramic vista of the St. Lawrence River. St-Tite is the gateway to the Pendragon Range of the Laurentian Mountains, which for the next 144 km (89 miles) rear their rounded granite summits to heights of 4,000 feet and more.

The headlands are separated by deep valleys carved over the centuries by rushing brooks. At the confluence of each brook or small river with the St. Lawrence you'll find a village or hamlet. Each has its wharf to which pulp logs were floated or trucked for loading onto *goélettes*. A few of these quaint and once-numerous wooden boats still carry the logs from small ports to larger ones, where they are stockpiled for loading onto lake freighters bound for paper mills on the Great Lakes.

Baie-St-Paul

Baie-St-Paul is situated about 80 km (50 miles) east of Québec City at the mouth of the Gouffre River, the latter a rushing torrent of brown water with its headwaters in the ancient forests of the Laurentian Mountains. Generations of wood-carvers have passed on their skills in this valley, and most welcome visitors to their studios knowing few can resist the local figures, faces, and scenes they have captured in wood.

The recently opened **Centre d'art de Baie-Saint-Paul**, a two-level art gallery at 4 rue Fafaro in the center of town, displays the works of local painters, sculptors, and tapestry weavers. There is no admission charge, but the number of browsers who leave without at least one purchase is small. Open daily June through September, 9:00 A.M. to 9:00 P.M., and 9:00 A.M. to 5:00 P.M. the rest of the year.

Ile-aux-Coudres, described above in the Islands of the St. Lawrence section, is off the mouth of the Gouffre River here.

TOWARD TADOUSSAC

There are two routes from Baie-St-Paul to La Malbaie. The best, but least interesting, heads inland. The most scenic is the shore road, which climbs over a cape and then winds down to St-Joseph-de-la-Rive, climbs another cape and plunges again to the village of St-Irénée, and then makes another wild climb over yet another cape before winding down into Pointe-au-Pic near La Malbaie.

An astonishing number of hostelries have developed on the stretch of north shore between Baie-St-Paul and Tadoussac, a region that, for more than a century, was a summer vacation area for wealthy Canadians and Americans. Those who didn't own their own mansions stayed at either the 380-room ► **Manoir Richelieu Hôtel** in Pointe-au-Pic, the Hôtel Tadoussac at the mouth of the Saguenay River (more on this hotel in the Tadoussac Area section below), or in pensions—the original bed-and-breakfast concept, but usually with all three meals included. Family-vacation trends have changed, as have the fortunes of some of the wealthy families who owned 30- or 40-bedroom "cottages" on the best sites along the river. As the vacation homes came onto the market, French-Canadian entrepreneurs acquired them and converted them into everything from cozy bed-and-breakfast operations to major resorts, often with additions to increase the capacity of the original historic building.

Staying and Dining in the Area

Pointe-au-Pic boasts a number of magnificent summer mansions, as well as the opulent stone fortress of the Manoir Richelieu Hôtel mentioned above and two 18-hole golf courses (open to the public) with some of the most spectacular scenery in the world. The point abuts **La Malbaie** (meaning "bad bay"), so named by Champlain because the bay is deceptively shallow and has a rank smell at low tide due to the sulfurous deposits in the estuary of the Murray River, which flows into it.

If the Manoir Richelieu is a little grand for your taste or

budget, try ▶ **L'Auberge des Falaises**, which overlooks the town and bay far below and is emblematic of Québec country-style lodging. In addition to the dozen charming little rooms in the main house, owner Denys Clouthier has built 32 modern apartment/condos nearby, most of them equipped with a whirlpool bath, fireplace, and shared balcony. The auberge is known throughout the region for its excellent kitchen, where the inventive chef creates delicacies like smoked trout and salmon in the inn's own smokehouse, vinegars from Champagne and almonds, and a surprisingly delicious onion jam. And this is one of the few spots in the world where you can taste a creation known as *sauvagine*: a fowl that is part goose and part duck. It is raised only on Ile d'Orléans, and is a treat reminiscent of chicken but with the texture of meat. Only in Québec.

In the few miles between Pointe-au-Pic and **Cap-à-l'Aigle** there are more than twenty inns, many of them ranked among Canada's finest. The cuisine at these inns is matched by only a few exceptional establishments in the rest of the province. In Pointe-au-Pic some of the best are: the ▶ **Auberge Les Trois Canards et Motels**, the ▶ **Auberge au Petit Berger**, the ▶ **Auberge Les Sources**, and the ▶ **Auberge Donohue**. Each has its own original architectural charm, and most are furnished and decorated with regional antiques, wall hangings, and paintings by local artists. Most also command wonderful views across the St. Lawrence River, and all have inviting bars and public rooms with big fireplaces. The chefs at these inns address their vocation with the dedication of rocket scientists—the competition in developing new dishes from local produce, game, and seafood is intense. The owners keep their establishments spotlessly clean and always glistening under fresh paint, so your eventual favorite may be determined by how you hit it off with your hosts and the staff.

You won't go wrong staying at any of these inns. In Cap-à-l'Aigle the 28-room ▶ **La Pinsonnière** and the 21-room ▶ **Auberge des Peupliers** offer elegantly appointed rooms, stunning views of the river and surrounding countryside, and outstanding gourmet food.

Murray River

From late June to early September you can cruise a five-mile stretch of the Murray River, which flows through a spectacularly beautiful glacier-carved canyon. The 35-km (22-mile) drive from La Malbaie to the departure point at *l'Ecluse* (the lock), at the foot of *les eaux morts* (dead waters), can take up to an hour on the rough Zec des Martres road. The operator, **Croisières Hautes Gorges de la Rivière Malbaie**, offers frequent departures in two boats, the *Maître Draveur* and *Coureurs des Bois,* with the cost per person about $20.

At St-Fidèle you face another choice of routes. The fastest turns inland, but the shore road will take you to two picture-postcard villages, each situated at the mouth of a small stream coursing between towering headlands.

River Crossings
St-Siméon is where you catch the modern ferry to Rivière-du-Loup on the south shore (frequent departures). Rates vary depending on the season, but the average one-way adult fare is $8; figure on an additional $20 for your vehicle.

Another 32 km (20 miles) downriver on the north shore is **Baie-Ste-Catherine**, where you catch the free ferry across the Saguenay River to Tadoussac. (Again, frequent departures.) At midpoint on the latter there's a splendid view up-river, with steep mountainsides plunging into the river. Those white sea creatures frisking around the ferryboat are beluga whales. They average 13 feet in length and have no dorsal fin. If you're lucky you'll also see one or more of the grampus, or killer, whales, which reach a length of 60 feet and often sound close to the ferryboats. They don't belong here, but come down from the Arctic each summer to enjoy the best of salt- and freshwater fish, both of which abound at the confluence of the two rivers.

THE TADOUSSAC AREA
The town of Tadoussac (Tad-jew-sack) gets its name from the Algonquin word for "breasts," a reference to the many rounded hills in the area. Although Tadoussac has been a vitally important Canadian seaport since the country was discovered, it has never grown larger than its present popula-tion of 1,000. Jacques Cartier was the first European to visit, in 1535, but it wasn't until 1600 that Pierre Chauvin built the first house in Canada here.

In 1615 the *recollect* (friar) Jean Dolbeau established the first mission to the Indians, which was taken over by the Jesuits in 1641. The Jesuits built a stone church in Tadoussac, which eventually was replaced by a wooden one in 1747 that is still standing. The sprawling, 140-room ▶ **Hôtel Ta-doussac**, with its trademark red roof, dominates the village above a curving sand beach. (You may recognize it as the hotel in the film version of *The Hotel New Hampshire*.) Rooms in the hotel are spotlessly clean but on the small side, and furnished functionally rather than opulently. (As is the case at Québec City's Château Frontenac, guests here are paying for the experience of staying at an internationally known address.) Yachts and pleasure craft are moored nearby at one end of the beach, and attractive native crafts are available from a cooperative artisans' outlet in front of the hotel.

In town, a variety of whale-watching outfits deliver close-up views of up to ten species of whales, including the largest creature on the planet—the 95-foot, 140-ton blue whale. One of the most popular excursions is aboard the 130-foot two-masted schooner *Marie Clarisse,* which was launched in New Brunswick in 1927. Since 1980 the refurbished schooner has been based at the Tadoussac dock, from which she departs with up to 100 passengers on Saguenay River cruises or whale-watching expeditions in the St. Lawrence. Rates are based on the length of the excursion, but usually run about $30 per person.

Beaude's Mill

Few Quebeckers are aware of it, but just a few miles east of Tadoussac is Canada's "other" desert. The Bald Head Hills near Brandon, Manitoba, are usually acknowledged as Canada's only desert, but a century ago a vast sand dune system extended from Tadoussac about ten miles east and inland. Time and man's persistence have shrunk the desert to only a few square miles. The desert doesn't have a name but is instead referred to as **Moulin Beaude** (Beaude's Mill), after a mill that operated here decades ago. In summer, artists haul their easels out this way to capture scenes more reminiscent of Egypt than Canada, while in winter the intrepid take along old skis or toboggans to court sprains and nasty burns sliding down a 200-foot-high sand dune, across a narrow beach, and into the frigid St. Lawrence River.

Lac-St-Jean and the Saguenay River

From Tadoussac, you have an assortment of choices. You can return to St-Siméon and take the ferry to Rivière-du-Loup on the south shore, from there either touring the Gaspé Peninsula or returning along the south shore to Québec City.

Or you can take Highway 172 from Tadoussac or Highway 170 from St-Siméon west to the communities of Chicoutimi, Roberval, Jonquière, and Arvida in the vicinity of Lac-St-Jean, from which the Saguenay River originates. (There are a number of outstanding trout streams in this area as well, including the Ste-Marguerite.) At least six area cruises are offered daily during the summer months. The 98-passenger M.V. *La Tournée* out of Alma (for information and reservations, Tel: 418/668-3016) is the largest cruise boat to operate on the oval lake itself, which measures some 28 miles long

and 21 miles wide, most of that characterized by an unremarkable shoreline.

The 65 miles of the cliff-lined Saguenay River, on the
other hand, have sustained tour operators since 1849. Below
Baie de Ha! Ha! the 800-foot-deep river passes a pair of
1,600-foot headlands named Éternité and Trinité. Outfitters
are also available in Lac-St-Jean ports to take fishermen out
in pursuit of ouananiche, one of the best fighting fish in the
world—and one of the trickiest to land because of its soft
jaw. (Ouananiche are Atlantic salmon that have become
landlocked.) Lac-St-Jean is the world's premier ouananiche
lake. For blueberry lovers, this is the world capital for the
fruit (*bleuet*), which surfaces in a bewildering array of regional products—including a blueberry liqueur.

Your last option is to continue north and east along the
north shore of the St. Lawrence River toward Sept-Iles (there
are actually only six islands) and Havre-St-Pierre.

TOWARD HAVRE-ST-PIERRE
The scenery along the 625 km (388 miles) of Highway 138
between Tadoussac and Havre-St-Pierre varies from rugged
seascape, to empty sand beaches, to long stretches of forest
slashed by raging rivers that thunder down from the mountains before pouring into the ever-widening St. Lawrence
River. The scattered towns and villages along the river are of
relatively recent vintage, although a lighthouse (which
houses a museum) at **Pointe-des-Monts** was built in 1830. A
restaurant now operates during the summer months in the
former keeper's house.

Between Tadoussac and Sept-Iles there are three ferry
crossings to the south shore of the St. Lawrence, so you
won't have to retrace your steps if you found the drive
boring. The crossings are: from Les Escoumins to Trois-
Pistoles; from Baie-Comeau to Matane; and from Godbout to
Matane.

The 59-room ▶ **Hôtel Le Manoir** in Baie-Comeau, about
halfway between Tadoussac and Sept-Iles, offers most of the
amenities you'd expect from a big-city hotel within its
French-colonial stone walls. A local landmark from the beginning, it was built on a site overlooking the St. Lawrence in
1937 and rebuilt in 1965 after the original structure was
destroyed by fire.

Sept-Iles
This booming little port city of 30,000 claims the second-
highest volume of shipping tonnage in Canada. It's also the
administrative and supply center for the entire north shore.

Apart from boat trips to view bird colonies on some of the offshore islands, however, it has little to offer visitors. Best accommodation bets are the two chain hotels in town—the 122-room ▶ **Hôtel des Gouverneurs** or the 71-room, three-suite ▶ **Hôtel-Motel Sept-Iles**.

SEPT-ILES TO HAVRE-ST-PIERRE

The recently opened two-lane highway from Sept-Iles to Havre-St-Pierre is well designed and presents few nasty surprises for the motorist. You can break up the trip by idling around the quiet hamlet of Magpie or strolling the beach at Rivière-au-Tonnere.

The 40-odd islands and islets of the **Réserve du parc national de l'Archipel-de-Mingan** are visible from Longue-Pointe as you approach Havre-St-Pierre. The islands are home to a wide variety of plants and bird colonies, and the limestone on some has been eroded into weird sculptures. There's a free interpretive center devoted to the park at 975 rue de l'Escale in Havre-St-Pierre (open mid-June to early September). A number of small boat operators in town offer tours of varying durations to the islands as well.

Havre-St-Pierre was founded in 1887 as a shore base by fishermen out of the Magdalen Islands, but its present raison d'être is a large deposit of ilmenite (an iron oxide with a high titanium content) discovered in the late 1940s about 25 miles north of the village.

The finest accommodation in St-Pierre—locals drop the "Havre"—is the ▶ **Hôtel-Motel du Havre**. It is also the only accommodation in town. There are 33 rooms in the main building and another 52 in converted mobile homes attached as wings. The hotel has no dining facilities, but there's a popular restaurant next door with reasonably priced though unremarkable offerings.

A bar-lounge advertised by the hotel has been closed. "People here drink in their rooms," was the explanation. There are also several *brasseries* (pubs) around St-Pierre, many of whose 3,500 residents live in mobile homes.

Ile d'Anticosti

In summer a ferry service links St-Pierre with the village of Port-Menier on Ile d'Anticosti. The island, situated some 13 miles from the north shore and 45 miles from the Gaspé coast, is 3,043 square miles in area—just 200 square miles smaller than Rhode Island and Delaware combined. As well, it is a mecca for salmon fishermen and sportsmen eager to hunt the white-tailed deer introduced to the island by the

French chocolate king Henri Menier, who made it his private domain at the end of the 19th century.

The only ship to visit Anticosti on a regular basis is a small supply freighter operated by **Relais Nordik Inc.** (Tel: 418/723-8787) out of Rimouski. Passenger space is limited, however, and the ship makes numerous stops along the north shore east of Sept-Iles and on up the Labrador coast before calling on Port-Menier. Smaller boats and private aircraft willing to make the trip may be chartered in Sept-Iles or Havre-St-Pierre; usually, these will be small operators who'll get you to Anticosti and pick you up later at a prearranged spot.

THE LAURENTIANS

"We soon found that the inhabitants were exclusively French-Canadians. In fact, we were in a foreign country, where the inhabitants uttered not one familiar sound to us." So wrote Henry David Thoreau in 1866 about the Laurentian mountain region in his classic *A Yankee in Canada*. He continued, "I got home this Thursday evening having spent just one week in Quebec and travelled 1,100 miles. The whole expense of the journey ... was $12.75."

Were Thoreau alive today, he wouldn't recognize this region north and slightly west of Montréal, and his $12.75 might buy him a good lunch—without wine.

The language has changed, too. Now it's called *hospitalité*, and it's spoken within earshot of all hotels, motels, ski lodges, and mountain ski lifts. Hospitality is a business here, and the beneficiaries pay for it. But there's a flair, or panache, and, yes, a joie de vivre that make it difficult to believe the waiters and waitresses, barmen, lift attendants, and bellboys aren't welcoming old friends to their personal playground. There are extra gestures clearly not initiated by the thought of a possible tip, and extra services that follow a routine tip when a second tip obviously won't be immediately forthcoming. There's also a lot of laughter and smiling, from those on vacation as well as those making it possible.

Wherever there is a hill near a population center in Québec, there is a ski lift and a network of cross-country ski trails. From east to west the province's major centers (with vertical drop in feet after each) are: **Le Massif**, near Baie-St-Paul east of Québec City (2,500); **Mont-Ste-Anne**, immediately east of Québec City (2,050); Orford (1,772), Owl's Head (1,770), Sutton (1,509), and Bromont (1,328) in the Eastern Townships; **Mont-Garceau** and **Mont-La Réserve** (both 1,000) north of Montréal near St-Donat; and **Mont-Ste-Marie** (1,250) north of Ottawa–Hull in the Outaouais region.

Most of these centers have been modeled after those in the Laurentians—eastern Canada's downhill skiing mecca. In fact, the region has the largest concentration of ski centers in North America, all within a 40-mile radius that starts a half hour north of Montréal and ends at Mont-Tremblant. Within this region are 26 alpine centers and 46 cross-country centers offering 1,864 miles of groomed cross-country trails.

Autoroute 15 runs north some 110 km (68 miles) from Montréal, with 19 exits serving 26 major ski areas and their accompanying lodges, inns, and motels, some of them institutions more than a century old. All but four of the ski centers can guarantee good snow conditions thanks to snowmaking equipment. Ten of the centers offer night skiing.

Vertical drops at the 26 centers range from 328 feet at Côtes in Ste-Adèle to 2,132 feet at Mont-Tremblant, a name that to many is synonymous with skiing the Laurentians.

The Mont-Tremblant Area

Tremblant, the "trembling" giant to which the Indians attributed supernatural powers, rises behind the villages of St-Jovite and Mont-Tremblant. The mountain has something for every type of skier on its 30 tree-lined runs through the forest, and from its summit at all seasons of the year visitors are treated to panoramic views of the surrounding forests, lakes, valleys, and villages.

The region itself has been a playground for more than a century: The focal point of the condominium-style ▶ **Canadian Pacific Club Tremblant**, for example, is a century-old log château overlooking Lac-Tremblant. The Club Tremblant now has 120 rooms, all with fireplaces. ▶ **Gray Rocks**, another Laurentian favorite, was developed in 1906 as a wilderness retreat. It began offering a mix of cross-country and downhill skiing in the late 1920s, with guests sliding along behind horse-drawn sleighs; a rope tow was installed in 1933. Gray Rocks now has 200 rooms, 160 with bathrooms *en suite* and 27 with wood-burning fireplaces. The resort also has an indoor swimming pool, fitness center, tennis courts, and sauna.

The Mont-Tremblant area really made it onto the international ski map in 1939 when Philadelphia millionaire Joe Ryan founded the Mont-Tremblant Lodge, now the ▶ **Mont-Tremblant Resort**. The resort fast became a favorite of American jet-setters who, because of World War II, could no longer ski Europe's Alps. Long after the war was over Americans continued to return. Today more than half the clientele of the area's lodges consists of Americans who drive past the much higher peaks of New Hampshire and Vermont on their way to Québec's Laurentians. Many of these Americans pass up the excellent ski facilities and resorts in their own country because they are drawn by the allure of Québec's *hospitalité,* which here, as elsewhere in the province, manifests itself as a fierce pride in cuisine and service as well as a natural gaiety that acts as a tonic.

While Tremblant may be the biggest and best known, the region has a number of other very popular and well-known centers, including **St-Sauveur,** with a vertical drop of 700 feet; **Mont-Blanc,** with a vertical of 1,000 feet; and **Gray Rocks,** with a vertical of 620 feet.

Even in a Québec winter at its most vicious, the four-lane autoroute north from Montréal is usually open and passable, with the first ski area only an hour away—30 minutes in good weather. Exit 60 takes you to the **valley of St-Sauveur,** where you have your choice of Mont-Avila (623 vertical feet); Mont-St-Sauveur (700 feet); Mont-Habitant (548 feet); or Mont-Christie (558 feet). Accommodations range from motels to auberges and condos, and in this one center alone there are more than 60 restaurants for après-ski fun along the main street of the village of **St-Sauveur-des-Monts.** Yes, there are discotheques too—electronic amplification has long been a fact of life in Québec.

You can still find lodging for two on the fringes of the Laurentians for under $50 a night, but at places like Gray Rocks a six-night pacakge during the ski season runs about $1,200 per person. This includes all meals—and they are superb here—lift tickets, and 22 hours of ski lessons. At ► **Le Pinoteau Village,** a well-established and popular condominium resort offering all services and modern amenities, packages range from $230 to $435, without meals, depending on the length of your stay.

The Laurentian area on both sides of Autoroute 15 is an all-season resort area, with its prime seasons autumn and winter. Though there are lakes and rivers for summer sport, they don't have the appeal of those of the more open Eastern Townships, or the rugged beauty of both shores of the St. Lawrence River and the Gaspé Peninsula.

In autumn, when the deciduous trees of the Laurentians change color, the panoramas run a close second to Ontario's Muskoka and Haliburton regions, or the forests of Vermont and New Hampshire, for spectacular beauty.

GETTING AROUND

The scenic charm and beauty of the province's countryside is best appreciated when driving your own vehicle—whether a bicycle, car, or motor home. This allows you to stop and browse in a little antiques shop or relax on the patio of the ivy-covered country auberge you just happened to spot while driving by. Although the Trans-Canada Highway (401 from Ontario) follows the north shore of the St. Lawrence, it's much more fun to explore the backcountry roads.

By Plane. Air Canada uses the Québec City airport for its connecting service (the other major domestic carrier, Canadian Airlines International, flies into Montréal), as do many of the feeder airlines that service this huge province. Quebecair, Inter-Canadian, and Air-Madeleine are among the many charter airlines that offer flights into the interior, many to remote fishing and hunting lodges.

By Bus and Train. The Bus Terminus in Québec City is the hub for bus traffic to the far reaches of the region, with connecting service offered to almost every little town and village throughout the province. The train is good for a direct transfer from Montréal to Québec City but doesn't have the "off-the-beaten-track" connections of Voyageur, the major bus company servicing the province, or the smaller Autobus Dupont.

Bus Terminus. 255 boulevard Charest Est, Québec. Tel: (418) 524-4692. *Train Information:* VIA Rail Canada, Gare du Palais, 450 rue St-Paul, Québec; Tel. (418) 692-3940.

By Boat. The most interesting mode of travel in Québec is the ferries that serve the St. Lawrence region, including the cross-river ferry between Québec City and Lévis (Tel: 418/692-0550), the island ferry to Ile-aux-Grues from Montmagny on the south shore (Tel: 418/248-3549), and the five-hour voyage to the Magdalen Islands from Prince Edward Island (which is actually closer to the Magdalens than any part of mainland Québec).

The car ferry *Lucy Maud Montgomery* leaves Souris, P.E.I., daily (except Tuesdays) from mid-June to mid-September at 2:00 P.M., and departs Cap-aux-Meules, in the Magdalens, at 8:00 A.M. (Note: On Tuesdays, the *Lucy* departs Souris at 2:00 A.M. and Cap-aux-Meules at 8:00 P.M.) *Information:* Cap-aux-Meules, Magdalens, Tel: (418) 986-3278; Souris, P.E.I., Tel: (902) 687-2181.

The passenger/cargo vessel *CTMA-Voyageur* makes a weekly trip from Montréal to the Magdalens with a maximum of 12 passengers. For information, Tel: (514) 937-7656 (in Montréal); for reservations, Tel: (418) 986-6600 (in Cap-aux-Meules).

You can also take a ferry across the mouth of the St. Lawrence at its widest point, from Matane on the Gaspé Peninsula to either Baie-Comeau or Godbout on the north shore. The daily schedule varies from June to September, so check before finalizing your travel plans. (Warning: The river here is unpredictable, so be prepared for a rough crossing, especially later in the season.) For schedules, prices, and reservations, Tel: (418) 562-2500 in Matane; Fax: (418) 562-2013.

For complete information on the ever-changing schedules, check with the province's tourism offices prior to your trip. Write: Tourisme Québec, P.O. Box 979, Montréal, Québec H3C 2W3.

ACCOMMODATIONS REFERENCE

The rates given below are projections *for peak seasons during the 1994 calendar year; at other times of the year they* may *be considerably less. Unless otherwise indicated, rates are based on double rooms, double occupancy; provincial and federal taxes are included in all rates. As rates are subject to change, always double-check before booking.*

▶ **Auberge Le Chaumonot**. 425 chemin Royal, St-François, Ile d'Orléans, Que. G0A 3S0. Tel: (418) 829-2735. $188 (includes breakfast and dinner).

▶ **Auberge des Commandants**. 178 rue de la Reine, **Gaspé**, Que. G0C 1R0. Tel: (418) 368-3355; Fax: (418) 368-1702. $78–$87.

▶ **Auberge Donohue**. P.O. Box 211, 145 rue Principal, **Pointe-au-Pic**, Que. G0T 1M0. Tel: (418) 665-4377; Fax: (418) 665-3634. $93–$161.

▶ **Auberge des Dunes**. Rue de la Basse-Ville, **Ile-aux-Grues**, Que. G0R 1P0. Tel: (418) 248-0129; Fax: (418) 248-5789. $66 (includes breakfast).

▶ **Auberge Estrimont**. 44 avenue de l'Auberge, **Magog-Orford**, Que. J1X 3W7. Tel: (819) 843-1616; Fax: (819) 843-4909; in Québec, Tel: (800) 567-7320. $110.

▶ **L'Auberge des Falaises**. 18 chemin des Falaises, **Pointe-au-Pic**, Que. G0T 1M0. Tel: (418) 665-3731; Fax: (418) 665-6194. $217–$277 (includes breakfast and dinner).

▶ **Auberge du Faubourg**. 280 rue de Gaspé Ouest, **St-Jean-Port-Joli**, Que. G0R 3G0. Tel: (418) 598-6455; Fax: (418) 598-3302; in Québec and the Maritimes, Tel: (800) 463-7045. $62–$92.

▶ **Auberge du Gargantua et Motels.** 222 route de Failles, **Percé**, Que. G0C 2L0. Tel: (418) 782-2852. $49–$94.

▶ **Auberge Georgeville.** 71 chemin Channel, **Georgeville**, Que. J0B 1T0. Tel: (819) 843-8683. $150–$160 (includes breakfast and dinner).

▶ **Auberge Hatley.** P.O. Box 330, Highway 108, **North Hatley**, Que. J0B 2C0. Tel: (819) 842-2451; Fax: (819) 842-2907. $222–$333 (includes breakfast and dinner; two-night minimum on weekends).

▶ **Auberge Le Malard.** 572 chemin Lakeside, **Lac-Brome**, Que. J0E 1R0. Tel: (514) 243-5006; Fax: (514) 243-5882. $100–$178.

▶ **Auberge de l'Oie Blanche.** Rue Principal, **Ile-aux-Grues**, Que. G0R 1P0. Tel: (418) 248-9080. $70–$74.

▶ **Auberge au Petit Berger.** 1 côte Bellevue, **Pointe-au-Pic**, Que. G0T 1M0. Tel: (418) 665-4428; Fax: (418) 665-2598. $67–$133.

▶ **Auberge des Peupliers.** 381 rue St-Raphael, **Cap-à-l'Aigle**, Que. G0T 1B0. Tel: (418) 665-4423; Fax: (418) 665-3179. $162–$210 (includes breakfast and dinner).

▶ **Auberge de la Pointe.** P.O. Box 10, autoroute 20 Jean Lesage, Sortie 507, **Rivière-du-Loup**, Que. G5R 3Y7. Tel: (418) 862-3514; Fax: (418) 862-1882; in the U.S. and Canada, Tel: (800) 463-1222. $54–$114.

▶ **Auberge Ripplecove Inn.** P.O. Box 246, 700 chemin Ripplecove, **Ayer's Cliff**, Que. J0B 1C0. Tel: (819) 838-4296; Fax: (819) 838-5541. $92 (includes breakfast and dinner; two-night minimum).

▶ **Auberge Les Sources.** 8 rue des Pins, **Pointe-au-Pic**, Que. G0T 1M0. Tel: (418) 665-6952. $135–$157 (includes breakfast and dinner).

▶ **Auberge Les Trois Canards et Motels.** 49 côte Bellevue, **Pointe-au-Pic**, Que. G0T 1M0. Tel: (418) 665-3761; Fax: (418) 665-4727. $189–$291 (includes breakfast and dinner).

▶ **Auberge au Vieux Manoir.** 871 rue Shefford, **Bromont**, Que. J0E 1L0. Tel: (514) 534-2502; Fax: (514) 534-0739. $72.

▶ **Canadian Pacific Club Tremblant.** Avenue Cuttle's, **Mont-Tremblant**, Que. J0T 1Z0. Tel: (819) 425-2731; Fax: (819) 425-9903; in the U.S., Tel: (800) 363-2413; in Québec and Ontario, Tel: (800) 567-8341. $211.

▶ **Centre de Congrès de Rimouski.** 225 boulevard René-Lepage Est, **Rimouski**, Que. G5L 1P2. Tel: (418) 725-5000; Fax: (418) 725-5725. $77.

▶ **Château Madelinot.** P.O. Box 44, Highway 199, Cap-aux-Meules, **Iles-de-la-Madeleine**, Que. G0B 1B0. Tel: (418) 986-3695; Fax: (418) 986-6437; in Québec, Tel: (800) 361-6162. $122.

► **Gîte du Mont-Albert**. Highway 299, **Parc national de la Gaspésie**, Que. G0E 2G0. Tel: (418) 763-2288 or 2289; in the eastern U.S. and eastern Canada, Tel: (800) 463-1568. $61–$67 (rooms with bathrooms *en suite*); $72 (housekeeping chalets with shared baths).

► **Gray Rocks**. P.O. Box 1000, **St-Jovite**, Que. J0T 2H0. Tel: (819) 425-2771; Fax: (819) 425-3006; in the U.S. and Canada, Tel: (800) 567-6767. $286–$315 (includes breakfast, lunch, and dinner).

► **Hôtel Cap-aux-Pierres**. 246 Highway Principal, La Baleine, **Ile-aux-Coudres**, Que. G0A 2A0. Tel: (418) 438-2711; Fax: (418) 438-2127. $208 (includes breakfast and dinner).

► **Hôtel Condominiums O'berge du Village**. 261 rue Merry Sud, **Magog**, Que. J1X 3L2. Tel: (819) 843-6566; Fax: (819) 843-2924; in the U.S. and Canada, Tel: (800) 567-6089. $100.

► **Hôtel des Gouverneurs**. 155 boulevard René-Lepage Est, **Rimouski**, Que. G5L 1P2. Tel: (418) 723-4422; Fax: (418) 724-3987; in the U.S. and Canada, Tel: (800) 463-2820. $65–$100.

► **Hôtel des Gouverneurs**. 666 boulevard Laure, **Sept-Iles**, Que. G4R 1X9. Tel: (418) 962-7071; Fax: (418) 962-8338; in the U.S. and Canada, Tel: (800) 463-2820. $65–$100.

► **Hôtel Le Manoir**. 8 rue Cabot, **Baie-Comeau**, Que. G4Z 1L8. Tel: (418) 296-3391; Fax: (418) 296-1435; in the U.S. and Canada, Tel: (800) 361-6162. $98–$109.

► **Hôtel-Motel du Havre**. 970 boulevard de l'Escale, **Havre-St-Pierre**, Que. G0G 1P0. Tel: (418) 538-2800; Fax: (418) 538-3438. $58–$119.

► **Hôtel-Motel Journey's End**. 455 boulevard St-Germain Ouest, **Rimouski**, Que. G5L 3P2. Tel: (418) 724-2500; Fax: (418) 724-6050. $65.

► **Hôtel-Motel La Normandie**. P.O. Box 129, 221 Highway 132 Ouest, **Percé**, Que. G0C 2L0. Tel: (418) 782-2112; Fax: (418) 782-2337; in Québec, Tel: (800) 463-0820. $76–$107.

► **Hôtel-Motel Sept-Iles**. 451 rue Arnaud, **Sept-Iles**, Que. G4R 3B3. Tel: (418) 962-2581; Fax: (418) 962-6918; in Québec, Tel: (800) 463-1753. $63.

► **Hôtel-Motel Les Voitures d'Eau**. 214 route Principal, **Ile-au-Coudres**, Que. G0A 1X0. Tel: (418) 438-2208. $197 (includes breakfast, lunch, and dinner).

► **Hôtel-Spa Le Château Bromont**. 90 rue Stanstead, **Bromont**, Que. J0E 1L0. Tel: (514) 534-3433; Fax: (514) 534-0514; in the U.S. and Canada, Tel: (800) 363-0363. $145.

► **Hôtel Tadoussac**. 165 rue Bord de l'Eau, **Tadoussac**, Que. G0T 2A0. Tel: (418) 235-4421; Fax: (418) 235-4607; in the U.S. and Canada, Tel: (800) 463-5250. $248 (includes breakfast and dinner).

▶ **Hovey Manor.** P.O. Box 60, 575 Hovey Road, **North Hatley,** Que. J0B 2C0. Tel: (819) 842-2421; Fax: (819) 842-2248; in the U.S. and Canada, Tel: (800) 661-2421. $250–$333 (includes breakfast and dinner; two-night minimum on weekends).

▶ **Manoir Richelieu Hôtel.** 181 avenue Richelieu, **Pointe-au-Pic,** Que. G0T 1M0. Tel: (418) 665-3703; Fax: (418) 665-3093. $255 (includes breakfast and dinner).

▶ **Manoir Saint-André et Chalets.** 196 Highway 132, **St-André,** Que. G0L 2H0. Tel: (418) 493-2082. $27–$50.

▶ **Mont-Tremblant Resort.** 3005 chemin Principal, **Mont-Tremblant,** Que. J0T 1Z0. Tel: (819) 425-8711; Fax: (819) 425-8862; in the U.S. and Canada, Tel: (800) 461-8711. $130–$315 (includes breakfast and dinner).

▶ **Motel des Iles.** P.O. Box 58, Highway 199, Havre-aux-Maisons, **Iles-de-la-Madeleine,** Que. G0B 1K0. Tel: (418) 969-2931. $54–$75.

▶ **Motel Lévesque.** 171 rue Fraser, **Rivière-du-Loup,** Que. G5R 1E2. Tel: (418) 862-6927; Fax: (418) 867-5827; elsewhere in Canada, Tel: (800) 463-1236. $89–$114.

▶ **Motel Rimouski.** 410 boulevard St-Germain Est, **Rimouski,** Que. G5l 1C7. Tel: (418) 723-9219; Fax: (418) 724-8960. $47–$65.

▶ **Le Pinoteau Village.** Lac-Tremblant, **Mont-Tremblant,** Que. J0T 1Z0. Tel: (819) 425-2795; Fax: (819) 425-9177; in the U.S. and Canada, Tel: (800) 668-7559. $230–$435.

▶ **La Pinsonnière.** 124 rue St-Raphael, **Cap-à-l'Aigle,** Que. G0T 1B0. Tel: (418) 665-4431; Fax: (418) 665-7156. $278–$388 (includes breakfast and dinner).

▶ **Village Archimède de Sutton.** P.O. Box 600, 582 rue Maple, **Sutton,** Que. J0E 2K0. Tel: (514) 538-3440; Fax: (514) 538-3540; in the U.S. and Canada, Tel: (800) 363-1226. $150–$205.

▶ **Le Village Mont-Orford.** P.O. Box 248, **Magog,** Que. J1X 3W8. Tel: (819) 847-2662; Fax: (819) 847-3635; in the U.S. and Canada, Tel: (800) 567-7315. $93–$190 (two-night minimum mid-July to mid-August.)

Guides to each region listing accommodations are available through **Tourisme Québec,** P.O. Box 979, Montréal, Québec, H3C 2W3; Tel: (514) 873-2015; in the U.S. and Canada, Tel: (800) 363-7777.

QUEBEC CITY

By Hazel Lowe

Hazel Lowe was the associate travel editor of The Gazette *and travel editor at* The Montreal Star *and* Southam News, *a Canada-wide feature service. Based in Montreal, she is now a freelance writer.*

Québec City is the beguiling Old World destination some travellers expect to find in Montréal when they visit that thoroughly modern international crossroads.

Unlike French Canada's financial hub, which recalls its colorful past in the few waterfront blocks of its historic *quartier,* the entire core of this provincial capital could pass for a postcard-pretty château town somewhere in France. At least, that's how Québec City strikes most newcomers when they first enter the gates of the only walled city north of Mexico.

Snug within its graystone ramparts above the St. Lawrence River, and still guarded by a fortified citadel, La Vieille Capitale maintains an 18th-century profile in the shadow of a multi-turreted castle most travel-poster fanciers recognize at once as the baronial **Le Château Frontenac** hotel. History buffs soon recognize other, older landmarks in a time warp of narrow streets that were planned more than 300 years ago. Lined with some of the oldest buildings in Canada, they still follow their original course through a historic district that UNESCO added to its World Heritage rolls in 1985.

These days the time-worn thoroughfares of Old Québec are convivial settings for bistros, boutiques, restaurants, and sidewalk cafés. They bustle with horse-drawn *calèche* (open carriage) traffic, sightseers, street artists, and weekday throngs of residents who refuse to abandon their small gem of a city to the tourist trade. It is their self-assured presence that dispels any notion of this city as a "living museum" kept alive only by travel literature. Québec lives because its heritage-conscious population keeps it lively. Quebeckers frankly adore their unique, French-speaking hometown, and cherish its historic role as the "Cradle of New France" founded by Samuel de Champlain in 1608.

MAJOR INTEREST

Vivid French-colonial atmosphere
Dining

The Fortifications
Citadel
National Battlefields Park

Upper Town
Place d'Armes
Rue Ste-Anne shops and cafés
Rue St-Louis restaurants
Convent of the Ursulines
Dufferin Terrace river views

Lower Town
L'Escalier Casse-Cou (Break-Neck Stairway)
Place Royale colonial townscape
Maison Chevalier museum complex
Batterie Royale
River cruises
Quartier Petit-Champlain restaurants and shops
Vieux-Port shops and restaurants

New Québec
Musée de Québec
Hôtel du Parlement

The story of Québec is a tale of two cities. The 323-acre UNESCO preserve known as Vieux-Québec (Old Québec) includes Upper Town and its fortifications, crowning a lofty promontory above Lower Town, the site of the first outpost Champlain and his doughty colonists settled between the waterfront and the sheer face of the cliff. The "new" city, beyond the 18th-century bastions, extends past elegant residential neighborhoods and industrial zones to the shopping malls of suburbia, the provincial autoroute (highway) network, and the airport at nearby Ste-Foy. Stretching out expansively from the old town's constraining walls, modern Qué-

Vieux-Québec
(Old Québec)

0   yards   275
0   meters   250

Gare du Palais

RUE ST-PAUL

Parc de l'Artillerie

BOULEVARD CHAREST EST

RUE ST-JEAN

COTE D'ABRAHAM

Porte St-Jean

RUE DAUPHINE

AVENUE DUFFERIN

Porte Kent

RUE D'AUTE

Place Québec

RUE ST-GABRIEL

COTE

BOULEVARD ST-CYRILLE EST

Hôtel du Parlement

Parc de l'Amérique-Française

RUE D'ARTIGNY

Place Georges-V

GRANDE ALLEE EST

Grand Théâtre

PLACE MONTCALM

AVENUE GEORGES-VI

To Petit Quartier

To Sillery, Airport and Ste-Foy, Laval Université

To Musée du Québec

AVENUE GEORGES-VI

AVENUE ONTARIO

AVENUE CAP-DU

National Battlefields Park

(Plains of Abraham)

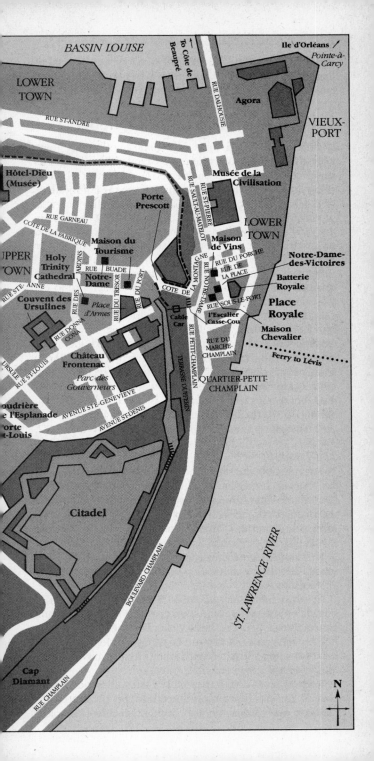

bec is the home of the provincial legislature, the provincial art museum, a civic concert hall, and an ever-growing community of high-rise hotels, office towers, and condominiums.

The Fortifications of Québec

Most travellers catch their first glimpse of Upper Town through **Porte St-Louis**, where the Grande Allée changes its name to rue St-Louis. This noble neo-Gothic entry (rebuilt in 1878) is one of the four remaining gates in the Fortifications of Québec. Now part of Canada's National Historic Parks system, the walls were raised early in the 17th century during the French-colonial regime, and later expanded and reinforced by the victorious British after France ceded her colony to England in 1763.

Sightseers hooked on military history can follow a public footpath around the wall's three-mile circumference to explore the bastions, redoubts, and cannon-guarded batteries. Guided tours depart from the **Poudrière de l'esplanade** (powder magazine), near Porte St-Louis, from May through October. Canada's parks system administers both the magazine and the military restorations at nearby **Parc de l'Artillerie**, on the wall's northwest ramparts, as reception and information centers. Artillery Park, where visitors can see a model of the city as it was in 1808, is closed during December and April. The powder magazine is open by reservation only from November through mid-May; Tel: (418) 648-7872.

The Citadel

The highlight of any wall tour is the star-shaped Citadel, on the critical southern flank of the old defense works. Crouched on the summit of Cap Diamant and commanding the river approach, the home of Canada's Royal 22nd Regiment looms over the **Parc des Champs-de-Bataille** (National Battlefields Park). The 235-acre expanse of wooded parkland is laced with scenic drives and pathways flanked by landscaped gardens, making it a popular playground for the city's residents.

But this clifftop plateau is still haunted by memories of Canada's most fateful battle. Here, on the Plains of Abraham, young British General James Wolfe won the day—and lost his own life—in 1759. Marquis Louis-Joseph Montcalm, commander of the defeated French army, was mortally wounded in the same engagement.

The Citadel is now as peaceful as the well-healed battleground and has been transformed into the city's most impressive visitor attraction. Part of the 25-building complex, which is also the official Québec residence of Canada's governor-general, is open to the public year-round (reservations required November through mid-March; Tel: 418/648-3563). A regimental museum caters to guided-tour customers, and the glamorous "Van Doos," spiffy in their ceremonial red tunics and bearskin busbies, change the guard and beat a daily retreat at 10:00 A.M. throughout the summer, weather permitting. A tattoo is also performed in July and August on Tuesdays, Thursdays, Saturdays, and Sundays at 7:00 P.M., again weather permitting.

Upper Town

PLACE D'ARMES
Côte de la Citadelle links the Citadel to rue St-Louis, the colorful Upper Town thoroughfare that follows the hillside down to Place d'Armes. Flanked by rues St-Louis, du Trésor, Ste-Anne, and du Fort, this green fountained square shaded by stands of fine old trees is still the heart of Vieux-Québec's upper level. Cheerful against the somewhat intimidating backdrop of the Château Frontenac, the little park is a favorite starting point for self-guided walking tours. Strollers can pick up complimentary brochures and maps at the Maison du Tourisme, facing the square across rue Ste-Anne, and chart their own course.

Basilique-cathédrale Notre-Dame-de-Québec
The busy pedestrian strip of **rue Ste-Anne**, lined with restaurants, stores, and café terraces, crosses rue du Trésor, a year-round rendezvous for street artists. This colorful outdoor gallery leads to rue Buade, where the Basilique-cathédrale Notre-Dame-de-Québec commands the corner of côte de la Fabrique, opposite **Place de l'Hôtel-de-Ville** (City Hall Square). Founded as a modest parish church in 1633, the richly decorated basilica today is considered the finest example of Baroque architecture in Québec, the product of more than three centuries of rebuilding and restoration. Guided tours of the crypt, where three governors of New France and all the bishops of Québec are buried, are offered daily from May 1 to November 1, 9:00 A.M. to 4:30 P.M.

The **Séminarie de Québec**, on côte de la Fabrique next to the basilica, was founded in 1663 by Monseigneur François de Montmorency-Laval, the first bishop of New France, as a training center for missionary priests; it is open to visitors daily from mid-June to the end of August. Birthplace of **Laval**

University, the first French-language Catholic university in North America, the seminary was the intellectual hub of Québec City's old Latin Quarter until 1946, when Laval moved out to its suburban campus in Ste-Foy. Summer tours of the historic seminary complex include the former refectory, kitchens, and Bishop Laval's funeral chapel.

Restaurant Row

Tracing rue du Trésor back to Place d'Armes, hungry explorers can return to **rue St-Louis** and Vieux-Québec's version of Restaurant Row. It's hard to find an unrewarding meal here, where reliable establishments such as **Le Continental** (see the Dining section below) were setting culinary standards in the 1950s. Rue St-Louis is also the home address of **Aux Anciens Canadiens** (number 34; Tel: 418/692-1627), a vintage eating house dedicated to traditional Québécois cuisine. Local and visiting devotees of *fèves au lard* (baked beans) and *tourtière* (meat pie) can enjoy these local treats in the family homestead that François Jacquet built to last forever in 1675—but only if they reserve well in advance.

Couvent des Ursulines

Around the corner on rue Donnacona, the Convent of the Ursulines was established some 30 years earlier when the indomitable Ursuline sisters moved uptown in 1642 after enduring three bone-chilling winters in primitive waterfront quarters. Part of the courtyard domain, where the good sisters presided over one of the first finishing schools for young ladies in North America, is now an endearing little museum crammed with period furniture, embroidered vestments, and memorabilia. The order still cherishes a bizarre collector's item in the skull of Montcalm, salvaged from the original shallow grave the nuns prepared for the defeated general's body the night after the battle on the Plains. If the glass-case exhibit unnerves unsuspecting visitors, they may be relieved to learn the fallen commander eventually was laid to rest in the Ursulines' chapel next door, near the tomb of the order's founder, Marie de l'Incarnation. The museum is open January 7 to November 25, daily except Mondays; the lovely little chapel, open May through October, is also closed Mondays.

Cathedral of the Holy Trinity

A few yards east of the convent complex on rue des Jardins, Holy Trinity Cathedral still serves what's left of the city's Anglican establishment. Built by royal decree in 1804 and modeled after London's St. Martin-in-the-Fields, Holy Trinity was the first Anglican cathedral built beyond the British Isles. The original pews of imported English oak are still in place, as is the Royal Pew, reserved for visiting British sovereigns and their representatives. The silver communion service was a personal gift from King George III to mark the cathedral's inauguration. Guided tours are offered daily from May through the first weekend in September, and Monday to Friday through Canadian Thanksgiving Day (October 12).

Terrasse Dufferin

City explorers can look down on the riverside community from Dufferin Terrace, a breezy boardwalk promenade that follows the wall along the clifftop from Champlain's memorial statue opposite the Château Frontenac and Place d'Armes to the foot of the Citadel. On fair-weather days (it's numbing up here in zero-degree weather), the Victorian-era terrace, with its old-fashioned lamp standards and gazebo shelters, offers memorable views of the river and the oceangoing traffic sailing past the port below. Clear days also bring lovely panoramas of the côte de Beaupré, Ile d'Orléans, and the south-shore countryside beyond Lévis.

Lower Town

A cable car at the north end of Dufferin Terrace, where Champlain's statue marks the site of 17th-century Fort St-Louis, rattles and creaks its way down to Lower Town. It's an interesting and mercifully brief ride for those who'd just as soon not follow the precipitous côte de la Montagne past Parc Montmorency and through recently rebuilt Porte Prescott, tracing a route Champlain cut into the cliffside more than three centuries ago. On the other hand, passengers who ride the glass-walled car miss the adventure of descending the notorious l'Escalier Casse-Cou (Break-Neck Stairway) into the heart of Lower Town, where rue Sous-le-Fort meets rue Petit-Champlain. Those who opt for the cable car disembark in the sturdy 17th-century house to which French explorer Louis Jolliet retired after tracing the Mississippi River to the Gulf of Mexico.

Sadly, what could be a fascinating museum piece houses a glitzy souvenir shop, an unfortunate introduction to an otherwise beautifully restored historic district. Over the past 25 years the provincial government has invested millions in a project to keep the 17th and 18th centuries alive around Place-Royale, where the first colonists staked a claim to a French empire in North America.

PLACE-ROYALE

Located a block from rue Sous-le-Fort (turn left at rue Notre-Dame), this old economic crossroads of New France is today the city's busiest tourist zone. Townspeople nonetheless live and work here in rehabilitated properties that authentically re-create a colonial townscape with their sober graystone façades and high dormered rooflines. Guided and self-conducted walking tours of Québec's birthplace generally begin at the information center on Place-Royale, the colony's first marketplace and now the showcase of the restoration.

Surrounded by the private homes, business offices, cafés, and stores of the refurbished square, the stalwart little church of **Notre-Dame-des-Victoires** has dominated the old business district since 1688. Today it's part of the stage dressing for a festival of summertime entertainment; it's also open for worship as well as sightseeing, with Mass celebrated regularly at its unusual, castle-shaped altar and a historic collection of miniature sailing vessels hanging in the nave.

Across the square, the **Maison des vins** (House of Wines) is open for 20th-century business in a building that the prosperous colonial merchant Eustache-Lambert Dumont occupied 200 years ago. Whether or not you're a connoisseur of the grape, you'll probably enjoy the Maison des vins' mini-museum of rare vintage wines and ancient cellar vaults, some of which predate the building. More than 1,000 different wines are for sale in this bountiful retail outlet—anything from an everyday table wine to a collector's item in the $700 range.

Close by, one of Place-Royale's two interpretive centers traces 400 years of history in the Fornel family's born-again town house on rue St-Pierre. A multimedia exhibit recalling the development of colonial trade and commerce is located right on Place-Royale. Both are open mid-June through September. The Place-Royale information center on rue du Marché-Finlay is the departure point for guided and audio tours of the neighborhood. It's open daily from June 7 to the end of September; off-season tours are available by reservation; Tel: (418) 643-6631.

Maison Chevalier

A stroll down rue Notre-Dame leads from Place-Royale to rue du Marché-Champlain and a trio of substantial bourgeois homesteads built for the Chevalier, Frérot, and Chenaye de la Garonne families over a span of 75 years (1675–1752). Now impeccably restored, the Maison Chevalier complex features art and theme exhibitions mounted by the **Musée de la civilisation**, a 1988 addition to Vieux-Québec's cultural scene on nearby rue Dalhousie (number 160). The brainchild of architect Moshe Safdie, who incorporated three historic buildings into his futuristic landmark in the restored port area, the museum explores all aspects of the human experience in Québec, past and present. Open daily, June 24 to September 7; closed Mondays, September 8 to June 23.

Batterie royale

Back in the Place-Royale *quartier,* the Maison Chevalier enclave was built within reassuring distance of the Royal Battery, which defended the city during Wolfe's siege of 1759. Lost for a couple of centuries under a welter of docks and warehouses, traces of the Royal Battery have been resurrected in archaeological digs at the juncture of rues Sous-le-Fort and St-Pierre. Today the restored defense site is a small park marked with interpretive signs and open free of charge daily from May through mid-October.

River Cruises

The reconstruction, complete with cannon-flanked parapets and gun ports, overlooks the Chouinard Pier cruise-boat wharf off rue Dalhousie, where the M.V. *Louis-Jolliet* embarks on three daily cruises throughout the summer. One-hour morning excursions cover the waterfront and harbor area. Ninety-minute afternoon voyages follow the St. Lawrence downstream as far as **Montmorency Falls**—one-and-a-half times the height of mighty Niagara—and around the shores of **Ile d'Orléans**, an island treasury of centuries-old farms, mills, and chapels where strawberry fields share a designated historic district with an ever-growing community of summer residents and year-round commuters.

First settled more than three centuries ago, this still-rural island wasn't linked to the mainland until 1935. Now the steel bridge off boulevard Ste-Anne, five miles east of Québec City, provides easy access for visitors to the island's inns, restaurants, handicraft outlets, and roadside markets. (For more on Ile d'Orléans, see the Québec Province chapter.)

On summer evenings the *Louis-Jolliet* makes three-hour voyages upriver to Cap Rouge (no disembarkation), where the French attempted to establish their first colony in Québec. A half-dozen cruise companies operate a variety of excursions up and down the river, embarking from the **Promenade de la Pointe-à-Carcy** wharf opposite the Musée de la civilisation, or from moorings in the **Bassin Louise**, part of the historic Old Port restoration north of Place-Royale.

Lévis

Photographers searching for the ultimate in dramatic shots of Québec's skyline can do just as well any day of the year (and less expensively) on the ferry to Lévis. Whatever the season, the commuters' special departs every hour on the half hour from its dock opposite rue Dalhousie, near rue du Marché-Champlain, between 6:00 A.M. and 7:30 P.M. Evening crossings are less frequent but even more rewarding for vista fanciers. Depending on the weather, the trip takes about 15 minutes, one way. Passengers who are not residents of the south-shore suburb rarely disembark at Lévis. However, dedicated history buffs may wish to visit the **National Historic Park** at Pointe Lévis, where British defense forces built a fort in 1865. Open May 13 to June 21, Sunday through Friday; June 22 to August 25, daily. For information on guided tours, Tel: (418) 835-5182.

QUARTIER PETIT-CHAMPLAIN

Lower Town explorers who were born to shop can retrace their steps from the wharf to Place-Royale or climb one of the stairways linking the waterfront to the various levels of Quartier Petit-Champlain, as Quebeckers call the vintage section of Lower Town west of Place-Royale. A bustling little neighborhood of specialty shops, restaurants, and snack bars, this once-slummy area between boulevard Champlain and rue Petit-Champlain recalls the 17th-century heyday of one of the oldest business districts in North America. Lined on either side with fashion boutiques, artisans' studios, and regional craft outlets, **rue Petit-Champlain** follows a picturesque course from the funicular terminal at the foot of the Break-Neck Stairway to its meeting with boulevard Champlain.

While shophounds consider Little Champlain their exclusive preserve, its best-known establishment is a nouvelle seafood restaurant founded by Serge Bruyère, one of Canada's most highly regarded chefs, who now presides over his prestigious uptown dining landmark, **A la Table de Serge Bruyère** (see Dining below). Housed unpretentiously in a centuries-old fieldstone building at the foot of the Break-Neck Stairway, **Le Marie-Clarisse** (Tel: 418/692-0857) accommodates its faithful clientele in a cozy rustic-inn setting. Customers with reservations occasionally get preferred seating—by the blazing hearth—if they arrive before the lunchtime crowd of Upper Town businesspeople and government officials, and it's just as crowded at the dinner hour.

VIEUX-PORT

Lower Town extends north beyond its residential and business community to the Old Port, where Rivière St-Charles joins the St. Lawrence. In addition to the Musée de la civilisation, the 80-acre riverfront complex includes shopping and dining facilities, a lock-serviced marina, sheltered promenades, and a huge open-air amphitheater Quebeckers refer to as the Agora. The Canadian parks department administers an interpretive center on rue St-André by the Bassin Louise marina. The **Old Port of Québec National Historic Site** here occupies four floors, and includes lifelike scenes recalling the entrepreneurial heyday of the 1800s, when Québec City was the center of Canada's lumber and shipbuilding industry and 40 percent of its population was English. Hours vary with the season; for information, Tel: (418) 648-3300.

Vieux-Port really is a misnomer for the business, residential, recreation, and entertainment zone that the federal, provincial, and municipal governments are developing, at a cost of $100 million, around Promenade de la Pointe-à-Carcy. Although the complex is steeped in maritime history, this oldest part of the city's waterfront district has a brand-new look. Its aerial walkways are futuristically designed and the Port of Québec interpretive center, housed in a former cement plant, has been refurbished in a cool, contemporary style, with glass-wall views of Lower Town and the marina.

New Québec

The 19th century ushered in a fortune-founding era during which Québec's Anglo-Scottish lumber barons and wealthy shipbuilders pushed the city limits beyond the western walls toward the landed-gentry realms of **Sillery**, sitting pretty above the St. Lawrence between Parc du Bois de Boulogne and Ste-Foy. No longer an Anglo stronghold in a metropolitan region where 96 percent of the population claims French as its mother tongue, the old country-estate district is still an attractive residential suburb, and is linked to the town-within-the-walls by chemin St-Louis, the western extension of the Grande Allée.

Musée du Québec

From Porte St-Louis, the Grande Allée sweeps grandly past avenue Dufferin, Parliament Hill, and the Hôtel du Parlement (Parliament Building), seat of Québec's National Assembly, toward National Battlefields Park and the Musée du Québec. Closed on an off-and-on basis since 1989 for a lengthy expansion and development project, the museum officially reopened in 1991, having doubled its display and administrative space. A new atrium entrance off the park links the original Neoclassical building to the old jail, which has been restored to accommodate offices, exhibition rooms, a library, and an interpretive center. The so-called "Prison on the Plains" now opens onto the Grand Hall, a work of art in itself with its glass walls and soaring cruciform skylight. The dramatic new entrance hall houses the museum's public facilities, including a 180-seat auditorium, a gift shop, and a restaurant opening on sweeping café-terrace views of the park and riverfront skyline. Nearby, a sculpture garden blossoms in an inner courtyard between the Grand Hall and the original **Gérard Morisset Pavilion**, where six galleries are devoted to a permanent collection comprising more than 18,000 works dating from the 18th century to the 1990s. The museum is located at the western end of the park at 1 avenue Wolfe-Montcalm, just a short stroll from the **Wolfe Monument** (marking the spot where the British general died on September 13, 1759), and is open daily, May 17 to Labour Day; closed Mondays the rest of the year.

Grande Allée

This handsome boulevard begins (or ends) opposite the Wolfe Monument. Flanked by tall shade trees, sidewalk cafés, and the fashionable restaurants that have taken over blocks of dignified Victorian and Edwardian homes, the Allée is Québec's answer to the Champs-Elysées. Still residential in its western reaches, it channels Highway 175 traffic in and out of the walled town through the oldest part of the new city. Indian braves followed what was then just a trail to the trading posts of "Kebec" centuries before the **Hôtel du Parlement** cast its graceful Second Empire shadow over Parliament Hill. The Louvre-inspired quadrilateral building has been a New Town presence at the corner of avenue Dufferin and the Grand Allée since the 1880s, and is open to the public most days of the year. For information on free guided tours, Tel: (418) 643-7239.

For people watchers with an eye for political power lunches, **Le Parlementaire** restaurant in the Hôtel du Parlement is open to the general public for lunch and until 9:00 P.M. when the national assembly is in session. Outsiders can't make reservations at this palatial official dining room, and they often have a long wait before finding a table. Still, the price is right, the menu is traditionally French, and many visitors find it interesting to dine in the precincts of power.

The home of Canada's oldest symphony orchestra, the

Orchestre Symphonique de Québec, is a close neighbor of the Parliament Building. Concert and theater lovers who can't make a performance at the **Grand Théâtre de Québec** (theatrical productions are presented in French) can always drop by to admire Jordi Bonet's massive cement mural and inspect the two auditoriums. Daily guided tours for groups are conducted through this performing-arts center at 269 boulevard St-Cyrille, two blocks north of the Grande Allée. Reservations required; Tel: (418) 643-8131.

GETTING AROUND

By Air. Although Québec City is linked to the United States and the rest of Canada by major highways, there is no scheduled international air service to the provincial capital. Air Canada/Air Alliance, Canadian Airlines International, and Intair offer frequent daily flights (35 minutes) to Québec Airport in Ste-Foy through Montréal's Dorval gateway.

Passengers can pick up rented cars at the Ste-Foy terminal, a 20-minute drive from the city center. Taxi queues form just outside the terminal building, where the Maple Leaf Tours shuttle bus serving the city's larger hotels meets incoming flights. The taxi ride to town costs about $20, the shuttle bus $8.50.

By Train and Bus. VIA Rail operates at least two daily round-trip trains (three and a half hours, with additional service on weekends) between Montréal's Central Station and Québec's Gare du Palais railway terminus on rue St-Paul, just beyond the walls. Voyageur Bus provides express service on the hour between Montréal (505 boulevard de Maisonneuve Est) and the main Québec City depot on boulevard Charest northwest of Upper Town. The 270-km (167-mile) trip takes three hours.

Travellers with a car should leave it in the hotel garage and explore this most walkable of capital cities on foot. City-operated and private parking lots are jammed throughout the tourist season, especially on weekends, and the local gendarmerie takes a dim view of violators in no-parking zones. The number 11 city bus follows a direct route down the Grande Allée from the Ste-Foy motel strip to the center of Upper Town.

The Gray Line and seven other companies operate year-round coach tours of the city. Spring through late fall, half- and full-day excursions are available to the shrine at Ste-Anne-de-Beaupré, Montmorency Falls, and the venerable farm villages of Ile d'Orléans. Mont-Ste-Anne, 38 km (24 miles) to the east, is one of four ski areas located within a 30-minute drive of the city.

Tourist Information. The Québec City Region Tourism and Convention Bureau's information center on rue d'Auteuil, just east of Porte St-Louis, offers an invaluable guidebook to the city and surrounding region. Information officers are also on hand with all the answers about *calèche,* bus, and taxi tours; professionally guided walks; accommodations and restaurants; and entertainment and shopping options. The staff is bilingual, as is almost everyone else involved in city tourism, and English-speaking visitors rarely encounter a language barrier in the heart of the tourist zone. If you do happen to lose your way or encounter a problem, motorized guides assigned to assist strangers in need patrol the historic district daily from mid-June through Labour Day. Just look for the green mopeds flying question-mark pennants.

Québec's best-publicized festival is its pre-Lent Mardi Gras, the **Carnaval de Québec,** a wintry ten-day revel during which even the most sophisticated Quebeckers lose their inhibitions in a whirl of sports events, parades, parties, and hoopla. However, visitors to the February festivities really shouldn't expect to see the gracious old city at its best then, as it's usually overcrowded and overstimulated. Fun seekers who hope to meet Bonhomme Carnaval, the February festival's mascot snowman, should reserve accommodations well before Christmas.

Quebec winters are bone-chilling: Plan on bundling up from November through the end of March. May to mid-October is the peak tourist period, with average temperatures hovering between 60° and 70° F (15° to 21° C). Midsummer "heat waves" in the low 80s° F (26° C) rarely break any records. Overall, temperatures here are always a few degrees cooler than in Montréal.

ACCOMMODATIONS

The city's big new hotels are all located beyond the walls and in the motel community of Ste-Foy—close to the airport, the Laval University campus, and the metropolitan area's two largest shopping malls. Accommodations *within* the fortifications are limited to small, old-fashioned hostelries and private guest houses—with one outstanding exception.

The rates given below are *projections* for peak seasons during the 1994 calendar year. Unless otherwise indicated, rates are based on double rooms, double occupancy; provincial and federal taxes are included in all rates. As rates are subject to change, always double-check before booking.

The telephone area code for Québec City is 418.

Within the Walls

▶ **Le Château Frontenac.** Once they've laid eyes on it, few first-time visitors can resist the neo-Renaissance appeal of this magnificent old Canadian-Pacific structure. Certainly it's hard to ignore, looming as it does over Vieux-Québec like a ducal palace, its soaring towers, turrets, and spires dominating the skyline in all directions. It's hard, in fact, to compose a photograph of the historic *quartier* and its outskirts without including the hotel's famous verdigris rooftops.

The Canadian-Pacific Railway raised the first wings of its stately home for discriminating travellers in 1893, adding the finishing flourish of a 17-story tower 30 years later, when guests still were more concerned with "*le bon ton*" than executive floors and gold keys. Today there's no lack of executive suites in this grande dame of Québec City hostelries, all of which—including an opulent royal apartment—have been recently renovated in the spirit of the posh old days. The five-year, multimillion-dollar renovation and expansion project has brought the guest unit total to 620, including 20 suites. Rooms are now decorated in French-provincial style, while the suites, all of which open on river views, are either ultra-traditional, with the expected baronial trappings, or ultra-contemporary. Many of the standard rooms are tucked into towers, or else are split-level aeries under the roof of the central block. Recently added facilities elsewhere in the hotel include an additional wing with terrace, a fitness center, an indoor swimming pool, and expanded parking.

Management did not forget the hotel's handsome public rooms, which now live up to the standards set by the impressive oak-paneled lobby. For the romantically inclined, the grand ballroom has likewise been restored to its original splendor, while the piano bar and Bar St-Laurent lounge overlooking Dufferin Terrace are popular rendezvous spots. And for those who believe a hotel is only as good as its dining room, **Le Champlain**, the main dining room in the Frontenac, is without doubt the most elegant restaurant in town (see Dining below).

1 rue des Carrières, G1R 4P5. Tel: 692-3861; Fax: 692-1751; in the U.S., Tel: (800) 828-7447; within the province, (800) 268-9420; elsewhere in Canada, (800) 441-1414. $200–$255; $400–$650 (suites).

The ▶ **Hôtel Clarendon** was Québec's first "high-rise" hotel. Older even than its world-famous neighbor, the Frontenac, this 93-room landmark assumed a bold new Art Deco personality in the 1930s and has clung to a good thing ever since. Not surprisingly, given the fact it has been more than 50 years since its last face-lift, the Clarendon's guest rooms

retain the slightly worn but nevertheless clean and comfortable atmosphere of an old-fashioned residential club, with
narrow corridors and decor leaning heavily toward dark-
colored plush. Management isn't planning to modernize
again after a mere half century, but the price is right and the
hotel still has a loyal clientele.

Local diners swear by the hotel's **Charles Baillairgé** room
and the innovative dinnertime offerings from the kitchen of
chef Christian L'Estriez. Unfortunately, lunch in the same
paneled and mirrored dining room is a disappointment.
Still, it's an experience to visit Canada's oldest continuously
operating restaurant, which dates back to 1866, the year the
hotel was built.

57 rue Ste-Anne, G1R 3X4. Tel: 692-2480; Fax: 692-4652; in
Canada and the eastern U.S., Tel: (800) 361-6162. $138.

The ▶ **Hôtel Manoir Ste-Geneviève** boasts an even longer
history than either of the above-mentioned hotels. Born at the
height of the Victorian era, when British regiments still garri-
soned the Citadel, it was one of a row of town houses
occupied by senior officers and their families.

Today this well-preserved relic of the city's imperial past
represents the best of a unique Québécois tourist tradition.
Old World, *pension*–style guesthouses really don't exist in
the rest of Canada, but they flourish around the Parc des
Gouverneurs, where Mme. Marguerite Corriveau's impeccable little establishment looks across the green to Le Château
Frontenac. The Manoir attracts guests who prefer peaceful,
homey surroundings to crowded hotel lobbies, and quiet
comfort does indeed prevail here. Each of its nine spacious,
high-ceilinged rooms is furnished and decorated individually (compulsive housekeeper Corriveau has a passion for
fresh paint, new wallpaper, and new draperies), and all have
bathrooms *en suite* and color TV. Prices are expensive
enough, considering that none of the rooms has a phone
and no meals are served. Even so, genial hostess Corriveau
turns customers away from her fully booked house at the
height of the season.

13 avenue Ste-Geneviève, G1R 4A7. Tel: 694-1666; Fax:
694-1666. $96–$133.

The ▶ **Hôtel au Château Fleur de Lys** and ▶ **Le Château
de Pierre** are two other avenue Ste-Geneviève properties
worth considering if Mme. Corriveau can't accommodate.
Both are in the same price range, and the Fleur de Lys,
which has facilities for the handicapped, has won a Four
Fleur de Lys rating from Québec Tourism for "very good
comfort."

Hôtel au Château Fleur de Lys. 15 avenue Ste-Geneviève, G1R 4A8. Tel: 694-1884. $83–$122.

Le Château de Pierre. 17 avenue Ste-Geneviève, G1R 4A8. Tel: 694-0429. $95–$122.

Around the corner on Place Terrasse Dufferin, next door to the United States consulate, the four-story ▶ **Hôtel Château de la Terrasse** has been welcoming overnight guests for the past quarter century. Overlooking the Dufferin Terrace boardwalk and the St. Lawrence, this small, well-maintained 19th-century neighbor of the stately Château Frontenac has been divided into 18 rooms, each with private bath, color TV, and telephone, but no air conditioning. Guests pay a premium for river-view rooms at the front as well as for the suite with kitchenette, but the overall tariff is modest.

6 Place Terrasse Dufferin, G1R 4N5. Tel: 694-9472; Fax: 694-0055. $75–$98.

The 17-room ▶ **Manoir d'Auteuil**, across rue d'Auteuil from the tourism and information center, is another popular small hotel, with private baths, color TV, and telephones *en suite*. Air conditioning isn't considered a necessary amenity in this moderately priced guest house and, like the other small properties mentioned above, the Manoir provides parking facilities for an additional fee.

49 rue d'Auteuil, G1R 4C2. Tel: 694-1173. $89–$145.

Outside the Walls

Frequent business travellers who rely on guaranteed corporate comfort to make their day insist that the ▶ **Québec Hilton**, a member of the Canadian Hilton group, is the best hotel in town.

Conveniently situated near the Hôtel du Parlement, just west of the walls and only a five-minute walk from the city gates, this 565-room high-rise hotel is linked to the convention center and opens into Place Québec's underground shopping world of 75 stores and various services. The 17th and 18th floors are reserved for guests who pay executive-floor prices for extra pampering, and the service throughout is cheerful and efficient. The Hilton also has a pool and health club, as well as an attractively appointed restaurant, **Le Caucus**.

3 Place Québec, G1R 4X3. Tel: 647-2411; Fax: 647-6488; in the U.S. and Canada, Tel: (800) HILTONS. $155–$245.

The ▶ **Radisson Gouverneurs Québec** (not to be confused with the Hôtel des Gouverneurs on boulevard Laurier) specializes in reasonably priced hospitality. That said, the per diem at the Radisson is nearly as high as the nearby

Hilton's, and visitors who expect better things of a city-center hotel probably will feel they're paying plenty for their comfortable—but otherwise charmless—guest rooms. (The rooms on the executive floors are the exception.)

Still, Radisson chain members don't make any claim to Grand Hotel status. Instead, the 377-room high rise is favored by both business and leisure travellers because of its convenient location. Among the added bonuses are the recently renovated public areas and a range of amenities that includes a health club, indoor parking, and an outdoor pool.

690 boulevard René-Lévesque Est, G1R 5A8. Tel: 647-1717; Fax: 647-2146; in the U.S. and Canada, Tel: (800) 333-3333. $137–$200.

The ▶ Hôtel Loews Le Concorde made the Grande Allée scene some 15 years ago, an unlikely space-age addition to a neighborhood steeped in 19th-century traditions. By now, however, the geometric wedge of glass and concrete (topped by a restaurant that looks like an airport control tower) is well grounded on Place Montcalm. Inside, management has completed a floor-by-floor renovation, with rooms and suites having been elegantly refurbished and the public areas on the lobby floor looking brand-new.

Guests award Le Concorde high marks for the generous size of its 400-plus rooms (all with river views), as well as for the honorary club membership they receive when they check in during the winter months. Facilities at the nearby Club des Employés Civils are open to guests of the hotel, and include a health club, swimming pool, badminton and squash courts, and a curling rink. While membership privileges are not extended during the summer months, guests can cool off in Le Concorde's heated outdoor pool after a workout and sauna in the hotel's very own fourth-floor health club.

Overlooking National Battlefields Park, Le Concorde also boasts the city's only revolving rooftop restaurant. Long gone, however, are the days when the view from L'Astral generated nearly as much enthusiasm as its buffet and à la carte offerings. Although the chef's toque has passed from Nanak Chand Vig to Jean-Pierre Sauval, the seasonal food festivals and Sunday brunch buffet make this one of the most popular rendezvous spots in town.

1225 Place Montcalm, G1R 4W6. Tel: 647-2222; Fax: 647-4710; in the U.S. and Canada, Tel: (800) 23-LOEWS. $150–$216.

The 127-room ▶ Hôtel Germain-des-Prés, one of the niftier new properties in the city, adds a touch of European-style class to the crowded old motel strip in suburban Ste-Foy.

Popular with business travellers who do business in this suburb's ever-expanding industrial zone, the Germain-des-Prés offers cool, uncluttered public areas as well as a number of executive-class perks as part of its standard tariff. A secretarial pool, photo copier and fax machines, and meeting rooms that can accommodate up to 200 people contribute to its appeal, as does the free shuttle service to and from the airport, some 10 minutes away. An added bonus is **Le Bistango**, its pleasantly laid-back restaurant, which makes for a welcome bistro alternative to the downtown restaurant scene, the latter a quarter hour away by cab.

1200 avenue Germain-des-Prés, Ste-Foy G1V 3M7. Tel: 658-1224; Fax: 658-8846; within the province and eastern Canada, Tel: (800) 463-5253. $99–$167.

The ▶ **Château Bonne Entente** started out as an eight-bedroom inn back in the 1950s after country squire Mowbray Le Pailleur Jones decided to open the family seat and 120 acres that went with it to the tourist trade. While the property—complete with trout pond, tennis courts, outdoor pool, jogging trails, and children's playground—has since shrunk to 11 landscaped acres, the original building has expanded to include 170 rooms and suites. Located just off traffic-congested chemin Ste-Foy, this mini-resort is a boon for business travellers and convention-goers who have brought the family along on a working vacation. "L'Autre Château," as the new owners call their recently renovated version of a rambling New England–style resort hotel, combines business center and conference amenities with free baby-sitting and family-style dining in one of two main restaurants. Senior citizens qualify for a 10-percent discount.

3400 chemin Ste-Foy, G1X 1S6. Tel: 653-5221; Fax: 653-3098; in the U.S. and Canada, Tel: (800) 463-4390. $115–$215.

DINING

Secretly convinced they know more about good food and drink than their compatriots, Quebeckers will grudgingly admit that the rest of the country is catching up to standards they set more than a century ago. Meanwhile, they shrug off Toronto's self-conscious gourmandism and the number and variety of Montréal's fine restaurants. Civic boosters, to whom the art of dining is practically a religion, still claim Québec City can count more haute-cuisine establishments per capita than any large population center in Canada and, perhaps, the United States.

Excellence isn't necessarily expensive in a town where even a modest meal is an occasion. Québec has its share of fast-food emporiums and snack parlors, and of course it's possible to order a disappointing dinner here. Still, the capital stakes its international reputation on the uniformly high quality of its restaurants, large and small. Many of the establishments with the priciest reputations offer a reasonable *table d'hôte* menu, especially at lunchtime. If you choose from the prix-fixe selections you can avoid running up a budget-breaking tab. It's getting into the grape and the à la carte specialities that run up *l'addition*.

Québec chefs and most Quebeckers subscribe to the principles of classic French cuisine, which is one reason diners won't find many first-rate ethnic restaurants here, although more appear within and without the walls every year. Innovators commanding the better kitchens have all embraced the philosophy of nouvelle cuisine, but most have taken a distinctive Québécois approach to the new school, especially in regard to regional produce.

A word to the hungry: No right-minded citizen hurries through lunch, which is a large, long meal in Québec, and almost as important as dinner itself. Early reservations for both meals are a must in the most popular restaurants (including all those listed below), the majority of which stay open seven days a week during peak tourist periods. During off-season periods (November, January, March, and April), many close for lunch on Mondays and Saturdays.

The telephone area code in Québec City is 418.

Within the Walls

When resident bons vivants want to celebrate a special occasion, and hang the expense, they call 692-3861 and book a table at **Le Champlain**. Le Château Frontenac's main dining room has to be the most elegant restaurant in Québec, and certainly is one of the most handsome in Canada. A kind of seigneurial serenity envelops this graceful, richly paneled room, with its majestic oak pillars and stenciled ceiling. Soothed by a harpist's serenade, diners relax in high-backed tapestry armchairs while they review chef Jean Soulard's extensive menu. House specialties, which tend toward a conservative interpretation of traditional haute cookery, include such gamey delights as pheasant consommé, buffalo filets, and quail in a delicate port wine and grape sauce. A seven-course fixed-price ($48) menu dégustation features honey-buttered scallops and coral perfumed with fresh ginger, sorrel-spiced filets of Gaspé salmon, and heart of beef tenderloin enriched with truffles and a Madeira sauce. The hotel also maintains a reliable cellar; the service is calm and caring; and the general ambience is exactly what knowledgeable diners expect of a dignified, Old World–style dining room.

Specializing in nouvelle-style seafood dishes, **Gambrinus** (Tel: 692-5144), a clubby hideaway under the Musée du Fort on the corner of rue du Fort, is one of the more appealing restaurants in Upper Town, and offers bright young men and women about town an upscale luncheon spot at prices they can handle. (The restaurant has no connection with the commercially operated sound-and-light museum upstairs.) In the evening, when prices are higher, a mixed group of discriminating diners takes over.

When it made its debut eight years ago, Gambrinus opted for contemporary decor as a change of pace from the rough stone walls, exposed brick, and crackling hearths most of its older neighbors favor. Bright floral tapestry, crisp café curtains, and green plants brighten a mellow background of mahogany paneling and polished brass. Although the split-level dining room is always full, it never seems crowded. In addition to his innovative ways with seafood, young chef Marc Belanger turns out a variety of excellent veal dishes, not to mention his wicked chocolate-mousse *gâteau*.

The **Café de la Paix** (Tel: 692-1430), two blocks to the west along rue Ste-Anne, has been carrying on at the same old stand at 44 rue Desjardins for more than three decades now. Although it first made a name for itself as a noonday refuge for members of the legal profession, it wasn't long before it came to the attention of travel writers and visiting celebrities, most of whom, like its regular patrons, were charmed by the clutter of wine racks and antique hutches, lamp-lit tables and Desrosier landscapes.

These days the place is a regular stop on most tourist itineraries. Still, it manages to remain amiable and unpretentious (owner Benito Terzini often regales his clientele with impromptu bursts of song), even though it has expanded to include a large pastel-tinted second-floor room that lacks the country-auberge intimacy of the original ground-floor café. Dinner prices on the upper level have soared as well. Beef Bourguignon, rack of lamb, quail in cherry sauce, seasonal game, and seafood are some of the house specialties.

Over on the rue St-Louis Restaurant Row, **La Caravelle** (Tel: 694-9022) clings to its 18th-century decor of graystone walls and rustic furniture. A *chansonnier* performs through the dinner hour, as local customers mingle with visitors while enjoying traditional French cuisine and an interesting selection of Spanish dishes.

Up the street, the **Restaurant au Parmesan** (Tel: 692-0341) chooses to ignore the French, concentrating instead on robust Italian fare. Owner Luigi Leoni plays host nightly in a friendly, firelit room he's decorated with an eclectic collection of wine bottles. An in-house troubadour keeps the dinner hour lively.

As the grande dame of the rue St-Louis Restaurant Row, **Le Continental** (Tel: 694-9995) has been perfecting its variations on the haute-cuisine theme for more than 30 years. Two generations of the Sgobba family now reign over the kitchen and a quiet, formal dining room patronized by longtime customers from government circles, as well as journalists, visiting dignitaries, and down-to-earth gourmets who like to eat well at reasonable prices.

Le Saint Amour (Tel: 694-0667), a pretty hideaway around the corner on rue Ste-Ursule, is light-years removed from the bonhomie of Restaurant Row. Romantic as a hearts-and-flowers valentine, the modish little salon that partners Jacques Fortier and chef Jean-Luc Boulay tucked into a restored Victorian town house more than a dozen years ago lives up to its loverly name in every seductive detail. The main dining room fairly blushes with tenderness—pink tablecloths, napkins, and walls; rosy candle glow—and Renoir reproductions set the tone. A glass-enclosed dining terrace opens off the main room, adding a touch of hot-house green to the roseate *mise-en-scène*.

For all its sentimental decor, Le Saint Amour couldn't be more contemporary, and attracts a following of mostly young, worldly-wise patrons, the majority of them local devotees of Jean-Luc—with good reason. The master chef from Normandy adds other dimensions to the new school with his original, sometimes unorthodox presentation of classic French dishes. His combination of rare beef fillet with a white sauce of Roquefort cheese, almonds, and hazelnuts has become legend.

When expense-account hosts want to impress their clients, they introduce them to the joys of Serge Bruyère's table on rue St-Jean. The upper floors of the Livernois family's 1855 home, where Canada's first professional photographer practiced his art, now houses the best restaurant in Québec City. All things considered, **A la Table de Serge Bruyère** (Tel: 694-0618) isn't expensive when compared with similar places in Montréal, but this isn't the spot for a folksy night out with the children.

Bruyère, a Lyon-born disciple of Paul Bocuse, opened la Table 12 years ago after buying the old building and dividing it into three levels. The ground-floor café, **A la Petite Table**, serves inexpensive lunches and afternoon tea. So does **La**

Serre, a little glass-walled *salon du thé* and snackery that shares the ground floor complex with **Le Petit Caveau** wine bar; Roger Geslin's confectionery corner of pastries and hand-dipped chocolates; and Bruyère's own gourmet shop of take-out delights. The upstairs floor is divided into two small dining parlors and a piano bar, the third floor into two private salons. In all, Chef Bruyère can serve no more than 50 customers at a time on the upper floors, so reservations are a must.

Bruyère sets his tables with peach-tinted linen, fresh flowers, and fine china and crystal against a contrasting background of exposed brick and stone. Prints and paintings soften the raw walls, and log fires burn in the hearths of both rooms, burnishing the chef's collection of copperware and adding wintertime warmth to the subdued lighting.

Winter or summer, Bruyère cossets his patrons with dishes like tender young Québec lamb "with just a perfume of sweet garlic," a wreath of tiny pheasant slices in blueberry sauce, poached salmon in a delicate sabayon with black pepper, fresh scallops from the Iles-de-la-Madeleine, and a "sausage" of salmon sauced with leek-flavored cream and white wine. An eight-course *table d'hôte* "Discovery" menu is a good value (under $60), and Bruyère stocks one of the best wine cellars in Québec City (which is where the tab adds up).

Still clinging stubbornly to the slope of côte de la Montagne where the road tumbles through Prescott Gate on its way to Lower Town, **Le Vendôme** (Tel: 692-0557) has been open for business under the sign of the horsedrawn carriage for 40 years now. No surprise then that it's familiar territory to legions of globe-trotters who've happened upon its close cousins in the back streets of Parisian *arrondissements* or the market squares of sleepy provincial towns, their prim lace curtains masking storefront windows and the cluster of white-clothed tables around a one-man bar. Le Vendôme cherishes other mementoes of its 1950s heyday as well: murals of the Eiffel Tower and the Seine, a wainscoting of maroon tile, a hanging garden of ferns. Though it's often overlooked by travel snobs because it caters to large tour groups, trendy it is not, and no one here is concerned with nouvelle cuisine. The kitchen *is* concerned with such hearty, calorie-rich standbys as crusty onion soup gratinée, savory ragoûts, casseroles of chicken Bourguignon, succulent steaks, and Dover sole served with a simple lemon garnish and boned with surgical expertise. Nor will there be any unpleasant surprises when the bill is presented. The restaurant was much cozier before the new management extended a small café into a two-level dining hall, but lunch in the old front section—with a glimpse of river through the curtains—is still a nostalgic delight.

Outside the Walls

The **Auberge Louis Hébert** (Tel: 525-7812) has been a distinguished presence on the Grande Allée for years. As advertised, it really is a small, European-style hotel of 10 rooms housed in one of the avenue's gracious old dwellings. However, it is better known for its café terrace and restaurant than for its three floors of *pension* accommodations. Senior civil servants and power brokers from Parliament Hill tend to take over the dining room at lunchtime, but a mixed crowd of gastronomes reserves for dinner. Chef Hervé Tousin brings a nouvelle approach to a traditional French kitchen, locally renowned for seafood and gamey treats such as wild boar, venison, and moose. Prices here vary considerably according to the choice of specialties and wines, but the *table d'hôte* menu is always manageable.

Just off the always busy Grande Allée, avenue Cartier turns north into the **Petit Quartier**, a lively neighborhood of cafés, boutiques, and small-business firms where adventurous chef Robert Saunier is exploring new avenues of *cuisine légère*. Presiding over voguish **Le Graffiti** (Tel: 529-4949) in the heart of the *quartier*, Saunier "designs" meals that look as delectable as they taste. His house specialties in particular are delicious, light, imaginative, and artistically presented. Best of all, it's easy to hold the dinner tab here to a reasonable level.

Down in the Vieux-Port district on rue Dalhousie, **Le Café du Monde** (Tel: 692-4455) upholds the traditions of a sophisticated Parisian bistro in a restored waterfront building overlooking the St. Lawrence River's seagoing traffic. Chef Robert Prigent adds distinctive zest to classic French cuisine with specialties from his native Brittany. Other members of the staff double as *chansonniers* during the dinner hours.

A new cluster of charming neighborhood restaurants in the garden community of Sillery, a 10-minute cab ride from the walled city, is luring adventurous table-hoppers away from the traditional gourmet haunts of Upper and Lower Town. **Le Melrose** (Tel: 681-7752), the cornerstone of a chic little shopping complex on chemin St-Louis, is the domain of award-winning chef Mario Martel and his partners, who entertain a maximum 60 customers per sitting in the candlelight intimacy of their lace-curtained, flower-banked cottage. In addition to à la carte delectables au Martel (caribou filets in a peach-ginger sauce, fresh salmon delicately braised in dill butter and olive oil, a foie gras of duckling in chestnut cream for starters), there's a six-course menu découverte for $41 (wine not included).

NIGHTLIFE

Québec City doesn't indulge in the kind of after-dark activities that travellers might expect of a popular tourist center. Conscious of its status as the seat of provincial government, it is a conservative town given to sedate pleasures, and never feels the need to compete with freewheeling Montréal.

Capital dwellers who aren't part of the government social circle consider an evening well spent at the Grand Théâtre. Once the season opens, sports-minded Quebeckers converge on the Coliseum in suburban Exhibition Park to cheer the Nordiques on to higher National Hockey League heights. In summer the sidewalk cafés lining the Grande Allée are the city's most popular rendezvous. The high-spirited enclave between Place Montcalm and Place Georges-V is transformed into one long block party by late afternoon, when the terraces fronting the Auberge Louis Hébert and Brandy start welcoming the pre-dinner crowd, and the action usually continues into the wee hours. Lingering over a long candlelit dinner and humming along with the *chansonnier* is a year-round diversion. Late-night revelers top off the evening at Le Château Frontenac's piano bar (always sprightly) or watch the city lights from the revolving restaurant-bar atop the Hôtel Loews Le Concorde.

Discotheques and Singles Bars

Discotheques are mainly for the young, although **Chez Raspoutine**, a Ste-Foy disco bar at 2960 boulevard Laurier (Tel: 659-4318), caters to the 30-to-45-year-old crowd. The house disco at **Loews Le Concorde** spans the generation gap as well. Newly renovated **Chez Dagobert** (Tel: 522-0393), the bright star of the Grande Allée constellation, is where *les gens huppés* congregate to see and be seen. Its second floor disco is popular with the 20-something crowd. Party people of all ages dance to live music downstairs. **Vogue** (Tel: 647-2100), on the corner of d'Artigny and the Grande Allée, is another split-level emporium, with a café bar on the ground floor and a disco *en haut*.

Back in the walled city, **rue St-Jean**, the main drag of the historic Latin Quarter made famous by students from Laval University before it moved to its suburban campus in Ste-Foy, still attracts the young and the restless to its somewhat raunchy community of pubs, discos, and singles bars. Strangers in the night can find plenty of action here in establishments like **Bistro Plus** (Tel: 694-9252), a friendly singles hangout, or **L'A Propos** (Tel: 529-1242), which adds *"spectacles"* and music to its all-night bar service. So does **Les Yeux Bleus** (Tel: 694-9118), along with the added attraction of a *chansonnier*. Other crowded rue St-Jean watering holes include **Bar Ballon Rouge** (Tel: 647-9227), **L'Improviste** (Tel: 529-7868), **Fausse Alarme** (Tel: 529-0277), and **L'Etrange** (Tel: 522-6504).

To accommodate the collegians of the nineties and their camp followers, **Le Palladium** (Tel: 682-8783), 2327 boulevard Versant Nord, near Laval's Ste-Foy campus, has room for 2,000 patrons, and is one of the "in" places for disco devotees. **Beaugarte** (Tel: 659-2442), Ste-Foy's upscale singles bar, is a pricey disco destination for slightly older table-hoppers who don't mind the trip out to boulevard Laurier.

Jazz

Although the city's last serious jazz club folded more than five years ago, groovers still gather at the Clarendon Hotel's art nouveau **Bar l'Emprise** (Tel: 692-2480), 57 rue Ste-Anne, where the beat goes on from 11:00 P.M. to 1:00 A.M. seven nights a week. During Québec City's annual summer jazz festival (usually June 23 to July 2), the faithful gather at almost every bar, restaurant, and available hall in town.

Pubs

Pub life is something new and different in Vieux-Québec. Local snuggeries modeled after British originals are springing up all over town, purveying imported ales and Ye Olde England conviviality in the heart of Canada's French-speaking province. **Aviatic** (Tel: 522-3555), a clubby pub-restaurant in the Gare du Palais railway station, specializes in imported beers. **Thomas Dunn** (Tel: 692-4693), a rue St-Paul pub across the street, also stocks imported ales. **Sherlock Holmes** (Tel: 529-9973), tucked away under the Vogue disco on the corner of d'Artigny, is a recent addition to the Grande Allée bar scene. A clone of London's own late-lamented locale of the same name, the veddy British Holmes is cozily at ease in its French milieu.

Back within the walls, the owners of **D'Orsay** (Tel: 694-1582), opposite City Hall, maintain a restaurant above their sophisticated version of a clubby British pub, with mellow paneling and polished brass fixtures adding to the authentic atmosphere. **Le Pub St-Alexandre** (Tel: 694-0015), on rue St-Jean, depends less on imported atmosphere than imported suds (it stocks 175 varieties of beer and ale, imported and domestic) to attract a young, Latin Quarter clientele. **L'Inox**

(Tel: 692-2877), on the Vieux-Port's rue St-André, operates the only authentic brewery in Québec City. Patrons can watch as three original brands are brewed before their eyes, then choose one to wash down the giant hot dogs the pub features as a house specialty.

SHOPS AND SHOPPING

Québec doesn't pretend to be a shopper's paradise. Its six major shopping malls support close to 1,000 stores of all kinds, but a mall is a mall by any name, and visitors aren't likely to discover much in Place Québec's underground mart, Place Fleur de Lys, or Place Laurier that they can't find at home.

The newest addition to the suburban shopping scene in Ste-Foy is an exception. With more than 230 boutiques, seven department stores, movie theaters, a recreation complex for all seasons, and a variety of restaurants spread out over a sprawling, three-level building, **Les Galeries de la Capitale**, 5401 boulevard des Galeries, has something for everyone. While compulsive bargain-hunters prowl the retail corridors, fun-seekers can ride a roller coaster, carousel, or ferris wheel, try their hand at an 18-hole miniature golf course, or cut a few figure eights on a regulation-size skating rink. Baby-sitting is available at the children's play area, and there's ample parking space.

Within the walls, côte de la Fabrique and rues Buade, Ste-Anne, and St-Jean are the main shopping avenues of the old commercial center around City Hall. Visitors on the prowl for a souvenir can buy art hot off the easel along the minibohemia of rue du Trésor, where Québec's indefatigable street artists display their canvases. Serious collectors will discover happier hunting grounds along rue St-Paul below the walls in Lower Town, where a growing community of galleries is devoted to the exhibition and sale of works by established and up-and-coming Québec artists. Works by such well-known Canadian painters as Jean-Paul Lemieux, Marc-Aurèle Fortin, Jean-Paul Riopelle, and F. S. Coburn are showcased at the **Galerie Eliette Dufour**, 169 rue St-Paul, one of the street's larger galleries. Open seven days a week, the Dufour salon exhibits works by more than 30 Canadian-based artists, including sculptors Jordi Bonet, Donald Liardi, and Claude Dufour.

Rue Buade

Rue Buade, at the bottom of rue du Trésor, is the business address of a fairly new enterprise in the old commercial core. **Promenade du Vieux Québec**, 43 rue Buade, houses four floors of chic boutiques for men and women, as well as an art gallery. Just up the street, **Frederik et Cie**, 49 rue Buade, specializes in imported toiletries, British woollens, and sports attire from Austria. **La Maison Darlington**, on the corner of rue du Fort at 7 rue Buade, expanded its long-established operation not too long ago, the better to display its collection of imported woollens, tweeds, fine cashmeres, and Canada's widest selection of hand-smocked dresses for little girls.

Rue St-Louis

Les Trois Colombes, 46 rue St-Louis, looks like a tourist trap from the outside, but once over the threshold you'll discover a three-story treasure chest of handcrafted collectibles from artisans' studios in Québec, Newfoundland, New Brunswick, Nova Scotia, Ontario, and the Canadian North. Pottery, paintings, Inuit art, and sculpture share space here with designer household accessories and fashion. The sweaters by Marilise/Couture are one-of-a-kind confections of handwoven mohair handsomely combined with leather, silk, lace, or fringe. But the big fashion item here is the selection of reversible coats, each an original, designed and woven in mohair and wool by Lise Dupuis and her daughter. Available in a rainbow of color combinations, each is hand-decorated with embroidery or appliqué work, guaranteeing that customers will never meet their double in a Dupuis creation.

Across the street at 49 rue St-Louis another treasure trove of French Canadiana tempts window-shoppers and collectors into stepping inside **La Corriveau**, an arts-and-crafts gift shop specializing in everything Québécois, from hand-carved waterfowl decoys to homemade preserves. Like its partner of the same name on rue Garneau, La Corriveau's shelves overflow with the works of Québec artisans and Inuit carvers.

On the threshold of the Vieux-Port, rue St-Paul is lined with antiques stores. Hopeful amateur collectors should remember, however, that heirlooms from the seigneurial era—hand-carved armoires and four-posters, regional cottage furniture, and naïve religious statues—were snapped up by the professionals a generation ago. Genuine antiques are hard to find if you're a casual shopper. Still, rue St-Paul is fascinating browsing territory for those who don't take their collecting too seriously. Knowledgeable shoppers often strike excellent bargains at **Antiquités Zaor**, 112 rue St-Paul, a collectors' crossroads for more than 30 years that specializes in *objets d'art*, fine porcelain, silver, and bronze. **Gérard Bourguet Antiquaire**, 97 rue St-Paul, is the place for 18th-century Québec furniture and antique ceramics, while **Antiquités aux**

Quatre Epaules at number 133 buys and sells 19th-century pine pieces and wooden toys. Louis Bolduc's **Aux Memoires Boutique**, 105 Antique Row, is another reputable source of Victorian-era collectibles.

Rue Ste-Anne

Up on rue Ste-Anne, the Brousseau family's **Aux Multiples** specializes in authentic (guaranteed) Inuit sculptures, Qué-bécois furniture, quilts, hooked rugs, woodwork, and other artifacts from a not-too-distant past. The Brousseau family operates two branch galleries, a recently opened **Aux Multiples** at 43 rue Buade and the **Galerie Brousseau et Brousseau** on the terrace-level boutique row in Le Château Frontenac. More than 500 signed works by Inuit artists are on display at the latter, from small keepsake figures to museum-quality (and priced) collector's items. The gallery will pack and ship your purchase to just about any point on the planet.

QUARTIER PETIT-CHAMPLAIN

Of all the city's shopping areas, the Quartier Petit-Champlain in Lower Town is the most rewarding for out-of-towners. The *quartier*'s retail community is a cooperative association of owner-artisans who either create the merchandise in their own ateliers or import collectibles from the studios of regional weavers, ceramists, and carvers. The following is a listing of some of the more interesting shops and boutiques organized by category.

Collectible Dolls

Michèle Prasil doesn't cater to the nursery set. Her dolls are works of art, each an original and designed for serious collectors who can afford to indulge their fancies. Prasil dolls are carried by **La Galerie Le Fil du Temps**, 88 rue Petit-Champlain, where the artist has created a fantasy world of *poupées*—baby dolls, grandma dolls, Victorian belles, and disco swingers—dressed to the nines in hand-sewn garments. Clients can also order replicas of their favorite person if nothing in the gallery collection suits them. Working from photographs, Michèle will create a reasonable facsimile of the real thing and dress it to order.

Fashion

Atelier La Pomme, 47 rue Sous-le-Fort, is the place for couture leather. Customers can choose from a high-fashion *prêt-à-porter* collection or order custom-designed jackets, skirts, dresses, pants, and accessories in the finest Argentine leathers. Practically everything is produced in the house studio, where La Pomme designers work with lusciously colored suede, pigskin, and silk-smooth leather. **Atelier Ibiza**, 47 rue Petit-Champlain, also specializes in fine leather, while **Peau sur Peau**, with stores at 85 rue Petit-Champlain and 70 boulevard Champlain, offers "leather from head to foot" in high-style fashions for both men and women.

Next door to La Pomme, **Les Vêteries-Blanc Mouton**, 31½ rue Petit-Champlain, creates fashions in wool, silk, mohair, and cotton. Among the big sellers here are the comfortable, packable suits and dresses in handwoven cotton (available in delicate pastels for summer and as resort wear, as well as citified color combinations in warm winter shades). Couture sweaters, beaded and embroidered for cocktail or *après-ski* occasions, can be created to order if nothing in the ready-made line appeals to you. The same is true for the heavier sports pull-ons that come with matching scarves and little caps. They carry a good selection of sweaters for men too. Some of the combinations of color and material the shop's suppliers achieve are as unusual—and irresistible—as anything of the kind in the province.

Crafts

Stocked with tasteful mementoes of a Lower Town excursion, all in a reasonable price range, **Le Jardin de l'Argile**, 51 rue Petit-Champlain, is a souvenir shop with a difference. Owners Thérèse and Jacques Tessier have developed something of a following for their "Lorteau" figurines, schmaltzy-sweet but endearing little ceramic people captured in loving twosomes or dreamy solitude. The store also carries regional pottery, carvings, wooden toys, and inexpensive take-home items such as bottle corks with carved wooden faces and traditional *gigueurs*, loose-jointed wooden puppets that clog-dance on a string.

Down the street at 27 rue Petit-Champlain, **Pot-en-Ciel** takes Québec crafts more seriously. This gallery shop displays and sells the works of more than a dozen artisans specializing in pottery, ceramics, sculpture, and carvings. **Studio Georgette Pihay**, 53 rue Petit-Champlain, is the atelier of an award-winning Belgian sculptor whose works in bronze are popular with an international clientele. Neighboring artist Pauline Pelletier is one of the region's most innovative ceramists. Pelletier shares her **Petit Galerie** boutique at 30 rue Petit-Champlain with fellow artists and artisans from around the world. The result, Lower Town's most fascinating crafts collection, includes exotic imports from India, China, Thailand, and Bali, as well as unusual works from studios in Québec City and Montréal. Réjean Burns creates stained glass ornamentation at nearby **Verrerie d'Art**, 88 rue Petit-Champlain.

Collectors of native crafts can find authentic Inuit carvings (each piece guaranteed genuine and signed by the artist) at **L'Iroquois**, 39 and 41 rue Sous-le-Fort, as well as unusual Indian handicrafts and signed prints by a variety of Arctic-zone artists. Inexpensive but attractive souvenir items are also for sale here.

Visitors who admire the traditional lace curtains framing the windows of farmhouses, country cottages, and pictur-esque cafés throughout Québec can buy the same patterns by the yard at **Boutique la Dentellière**, 54 boulevard Champlain. This frothy little outlet for domestic and imported wares also sells ready-made curtains, tablecloths, boudoir frivolities, bathroom accessories, clothing, and a variety of lacy trimmings for all occasions.

Jewelry

Les Bijoux Décade, 48 rue Petit-Champlain, is one of the gems of Petit-Champlain's main shopping street. The small, unassuming shop is the retail outlet for a number of young Québec designers whose work features unusual settings in silver, gold, wood, leather, and ceramics. One-of-a-kind wrist-watches framed in enamel and copper are showcase items unique to the store, as are the costume-jewelry collections of Montréal-based Israeli artist Jacob Neeman, who creates contemporary adornment in a traditional Middle Eastern style.

OTTAWA

By Maura Giuliani

Maura Giuliani, a freelance writer and editor for various publications and the federal government, has lived in the Ottawa area for the last decade.

Yes, it *is* the coldest national capital in the Western hemisphere (the worldwide title goes to Ulan Bator, Mongolia), but it is also possibly the most attractive. A relatively tiny city perched on the edge of the Ottawa River, Canada's capital is the perfect stopping point between Montreal and Toronto.

Its appeal lies in charms quite different from those of most urban centers. Ottawa is very much a "company town." Signs of federal occupancy are everywhere: in its neo-Gothic buildings, landscaped riverbanks, and fine museums. It is a place to put on walking shoes for perhaps two days and enjoy the benefits of federal government investment.

One of the nicest times to visit is mid-May, when the Festival of Spring celebrates the blooming of millions of tulips (a gift from Queen Juliana of the Netherlands—the queen and her family found refuge in Ottawa during World War II) massed in beds throughout the city. The flowering tulips are a hallmark of winter's end here. The festival has grown over the years, and now includes fireworks, a flotilla on the canal, a marathon, and an ever-changing assortment of activities.

MAJOR INTEREST

Parliament Hill
Rideau Canal
Winterlude Festival
Byward Market and Lower Town street life
National Gallery of Canada and other national
   museums

Nightlife and dining in Hull, Quebec
Gatineau Park

A Strategic Location

Ottawa is dominated by waterways that divide and define the city. The Ottawa and Rideau rivers, as well as the Rideau Canal, are constant points of reference for inhabitants. The Ottawa River is the big one—a major water route that offered early explorers access to the center of a new continent. In Quebec the river is known as the Outaouais, the name of a large tribe of Algonquin Indians whose hunting area once spanned the stretch from the Ottawa River to Lake Superior. English settlers later changed the pronunciation to Ottawa, but both names are still in use by English and French Canadians.

Along this river and under the limestone cliffs on which Canada's parliamentary buildings now stand passed missionaries and adventurers bound for the western wilderness. English and French explorers, Jesuits, and fur traders used the river from the early 1600s on. Still, the United States was already an independent nation before the site on the Ottawa River became anything more than a temporary camping spot.

It was 1800, in fact, when an American from Massachusetts, Philemon Wright, trudged up the frozen river with five other families to establish a homestead on its north bank. Wright had been on the river the year before and recognized in the combination of dense forest and ample water power the elements of a profitable lumber trade. First called Wrightsville, then Hull, the settlement rapidly became a center for assembling rafts of white pine logs, which were sailed downstream to Montreal, then shipped to England.

Even in those days, before Canada had become a nation, its relationship with the United States was a constant political concern. After the War of 1812 the British were decidedly nervous about the St. Lawrence River being the only military supply route between Montreal and the province's strategic naval dockyards at Kingston, on Lake Ontario. U.S. forts along the St. Lawrence east of the lake defended that border all too well, offering a constant threat to British gunboats and supply ships.

Westminster saw the Rideau River as a viable alternative to the St. Lawrence. Linked through a chain of lakes to Lake Ontario, it promised safe passage from the east to Kingston. Eventually, the British government committed itself to opening the 125-mile route with a series of locks and an entrance canal leading from the Ottawa River to the Rideau (thereby circumventing the falls at the mouth of the latter). Colonel

John By of the Royal Engineers was dispatched to Canada in the spring of 1826 to oversee construction of the project.

Of course it was the best thing that could have happened to the tiny settlement on the Ottawa River. Many of the military and civil personnel dispatched from England to build the canal were persuaded by land grants to stay in what was soon known as Bytown, and the area grew rapidly. By the mid-1830s, Wrightsville and Bytown were the center of the Ottawa River valley's squared-timber trade. Raftsmen found rowdy relaxation in Bytown on their way to Quebec, fostering the town's turbulent reputation—a reputation the settlement tried to shed in 1855 by changing its name from Bytown to Ottawa when it applied for consideration as the new capital of Upper and Lower Canada (upper meaning upriver, lower meaning nearer the mouth of the St. Lawrence).

There were cogent arguments in favor of Ottawa as the provincial capital: Its distance from borders made it safe from hostile attack; communications with Montreal and Kingston were well developed by water; it was almost equidistant from Quebec and Toronto, as well as being situated on the border of the two provinces; and—no mean point—its location was one of undeniable beauty. And so in 1858, Queen Victoria named Ottawa permanent capital of the Province of Canada—causing an American newspaper to acknowledge the wisdom of the choice by noting that "invaders would inevitably be lost in the woods trying to find it."

Lost in the woods or not, Ottawa's character was established by Her Majesty's decision. With the opening of the Parliament Buildings in 1866, the "civil" side of life in the new capital gained ground.

EXPLORING OTTAWA

Ottawa is a small town that breaks easily into three basic chunks: Upper Town, Lower Town, and Sussex Drive. Traditionally the Rideau Canal has divided Ottawa into Upper Town and Lower Town. Upper Town, above the limestone cliffs overlooking the Ottawa River west of the canal, is dominated by the federal government and originally was the site of British military barracks and, later, of Canada's Parliament Buildings. Lower Town, below the cliffs east of the canal, was home to the enlisted men and canal laborers, as well as Byward Market and a great many taverns. Sussex Drive, running from Wellington Street along the Ottawa River to Rideau Falls and beyond, connected the two areas and provided a conduit for incoming and outgoing shipments on the river. Today everything merges near Confederation Square.

Upper Town

Confederation Square, more triangular than quadrilateral and dominated by the National War Memorial to Canada's armed forces, is the heart of the city. From this junction of Ottawa's oldest streets—Wellington, Sparks, and Elgin—most points of interest are within easy walking distance. The urban area of Ottawa is compact, and driving and parking downtown offer more frustration than convenience. Taxis are easy to come by and, because of the short distances involved in the downtown core, are as practical as city buses.

The **Ottawa Tourism and Convention Authority** (Tel: 613/237-5158) is located at 65 Elgin Street in the National Arts Centre facing the square. Tour buses of the city also run regularly from Confederation Square, but you can start on your own with Ottawa's raison d'être: the Parliament Buildings.

PARLIAMENT HILL

In front of Parliament's Centre Block, the **changing of the guard** ceremony, an irresistible tourist attraction, takes place on the lawn every morning at 10:00 A.M. (from the last Sunday in June to Labour Day weekend). The scarlet coats and bearskins of the Governor General's Foot Guards set the tone for what follows.

Before going inside, take a half hour to explore the grounds. A path behind "the hill" offers a spectacular view of the river (not to mention an assortment of statues). Guided tours of the various buildings are offered daily, although the best time to visit is when Parliament is in session. (Parliament usually recesses for the summer months, Easter, and Christmas.) At two o'clock most afternoons you can watch the prime minister and his cabinet field questions from the "loyal opposition." A no-holds-barred confrontation, it's probably the best entertainment in town and worth the time spent standing in line to get into the public gallery. If Parliament is in recess, console yourself with a tour of the restored 19th-century offices in the East Block. The rooms, open to the public only when Parliament is not in session, date back to 1872. A logical follow-up to your Parliamentary meanderings is formal tea at the Château Laurier, a short walk east on Wellington Street.

A neo-Gothic delight topped by a variety of spires and

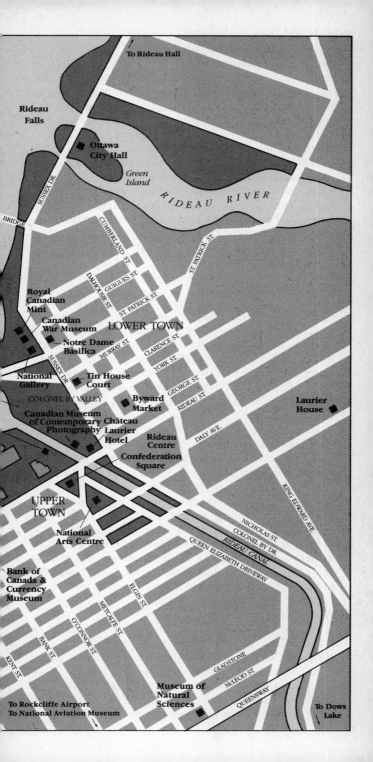

To Rideau Hall

Rideau
Falls

Ottawa
City Hall

*Green
Island*

RIDEAU RIVER

BRIDGE

SUSSEX DR.

CUMBERLAND ST.

DALHOUSIE ST.

GUIGUES ST.

ST PATRICK ST.

ST. PATRICK ST.

Royal
Canadian
Mint

Canadian
War Museum

LOWER TOWN

Notre Dame
Basilica

MURRAY ST.

CLARENCE ST.

YORK ST.

National
Gallery

SUSSEX DR.

Tin House
Court

GEORGE ST.

Laurier
House

COLONEL BY VALLEY

Byward
Market

RIDEAU ST.

Canadian Museum
of Contemporary
Photography

Château
Laurier
Hotel

DALY AVE.

Rideau
Centre

KING EDWARD AVE.

Confederation
Square

UPPER
TOWN

National
Arts Centre

NICHOLAS ST.

COLONEL BY DR.

RIDEAU CANAL

QUEEN ELIZABETH DRIVEWAY

Bank of
Canada &
Currency
Museum

ELGIN ST.

METCALFE ST.

O'CONNOR ST.

BANK ST.

KENT ST.

GLADSTONE

McLEOD ST.

Museum of
Natural
Sciences

QUEENSWAY

To Rockcliffe Airport
To National Aviation Museum

To Dows
Lake

towers, the ▶ **Château Laurier** was built about the same time
as the Parliament Buildings (1916) and is typical of hotels
constructed by the national railroads in their heyday—a great
place to stay for comfort, location, and a sense of history. If
you like odd spaces, ask for a turret room; otherwise, specify a
room overlooking the river. One of the city's best handicraft
shops, **Signatures**, is located on the first floor of the hotel,
with top-flight work by several local artisans in leather, glass,
gold, and silk. Traditional British tea—finger sandwiches,
cakes, and clotted cream included—is served between 3:00
and 5:00 P.M. every day in **Zoë's**, a pretty palm-strewn dining
area just off the main lobby. Make a note, though, to return to
Parliament Hill in the evening (summer months) for a well-
designed sound-and-light presentation on the lawn directly in
front of Centre Block.

West of Parliament Hill

From the Château Laurier, head west on Wellington Street
past the parliamentary buildings themselves to the **Supreme
Court of Canada**, the lobby and courtroom of which are
open to the public on weekdays. The **Bank of Canada**,
nearby on the south side of Wellington, is an architecturally
interesting meld of two worlds: Modern glass towers flank
the original bank building, in which an attractive **Currency
Museum** now resides. The **National Library and Public Archives** are housed in the last building before Portage Bridge;
there are often exhibits on the first floor, which is open
daily, but the library itself is strictly a reference facility.

At this point you are close to two reliable hotels: the
▶ **Delta Ottawa** at 361 Queen Street, and the ▶ **Radisson
Hotel Ottawa Centre** at 100 Kent Street. Both offer comfortable, if predictable, accommodations at Ottawa's usual high
prices. For something a little less typical, try the tiny
▶ **Doral Inn Hotel** on Albert Street. This restored 1879
hostelry combines a welcoming Old World ambience with
modern amenities such as air conditioning at very reasonable rates. A good Spanish restaurant, the **Costa Brava** (Tel:
613/563-8255), is also located in the inn.

Sparks Street

It isn't far back to Confederation Square, but instead of
walking along Wellington take Sparks Street, which runs
parallel to Wellington. The first pedestrian mall in Canada,
Sparks Street is still an important shopping district. Check
out **Canada's Four Corners** (at Sparks and Metcalfe) for
traditional Canadian crafts. Another excellent spot is **The
Snow Goose**, 83 Sparks Street, which offers a variety of

native Canadian art and is a good source of Inuit graphics. The **Plaza Café**, 101 Sparks Street, offers good food, an excellent view of Parliament Hill, and a patio that's a perfect perch for people-watching. Tel: (613) 563-0636.

Colonel By's Canal

It's impossible to ignore the **Rideau Canal** in Ottawa. From its start at the Ottawa River, the canal runs roughly south, bisecting the core of the city. Bicycle paths and parklands, of which Ottawans make constant use, line both sides of the canal from **Entrance Bay** (now called Colonel By Valley) to the point where it joins the Rideau River. But start at the beginning: From Confederation Square, cross Wellington Street to the north side and the gully tucked in between Parliament Hill and the Château Laurier.

Mere feet from the centers of government and commerce, the Rideau Canal begins in this gully. Here the Ottawa River, its limestone cliffs, and the first few Rideau locks seem isolated from the rest of the city. There is delight in just watching small boats being lifted in the locks, in seeing the old road that runs along the cliff wall, or in exploring the Commissariat.

Canadian Museum of Contemporary Photography

The oldest surviving stone building in Ottawa, the Commissariat was built in 1827 as a military supply depot. Now the **Bytown Museum**, it houses a collection of artifacts from the city's earliest days. Directly opposite at 1 Rideau Canal, a new museum has been wedged between the east bank of the canal and the Château Laurier. Built into what was once a railway tunnel, the Canadian Museum of Contemporary Photography makes very effective use of an unlikely space, with frequently changing exhibits highlighting Canadian photography from the museum's extensive collection. While federal museums in Ottawa generally are open daily from 9:00 A.M. to 5:00 P.M. (and until 8:00 P.M. on Thursdays) during the summer, these two keep slightly different hours. For their exact hours, check with the Tourism and Convention Authority in the National Arts Centre (see above).

Canal Excursions

On Wellington Street itself it's hard to avoid hawkers for canal tours. And why should you? The sightseeing boats ply the canal all day, so choose a time when you're ready to relax and use an hour to see Ottawa from a watery vantage point. Or tour the same areas the way the locals do, by bicycle. Bikes can be rented at the Château Laurier (by the hour or by the day). Although escorted tours are available, it's easy enough to follow the bicycle paths heading south beside the canal to **Dows Lake** (about a six-mile round trip). A marina at the lake offers the choice of several restaurants—or you can save yourself for the **Canal Ritz** (Tel: 613/238-8998), located about halfway to Dows Lake on the west bank of the canal. The latter's setting is almost as good as the tiny specialty pizzas it serves.

Cycling along the canal in good weather you'll encounter Ottawans of all ages bicycling, walking, or just sunning themselves on the grass. In fact, the city seems to live beside the canal during the summer months. Come winter and the waterway takes on another life. The grass and bicycle paths are defeated by snow, but the canal itself is cleared to form the longest skating rink in the world. Ottawans love it! They skate to work during the week and skate with their families on weekends. And for ten days every February the canal becomes the main venue for **Winterlude**, a festival of snow sculptures, harness racing, dog sledding, and general foolishness on ice. At night, lights line the canal and music plays for the thousands of skaters who turn up. Visitors have no excuse: Skates can be rented from kiosks at several points right on the ice.

NATIONAL ARTS CENTRE AREA

Just south of Confederation Square stands the massive **National Arts Centre** (Tel: 613/996-5051, ext. 280), housing three performance halls in which concerts, theater, and ballet are staged year-round. A pleasant restaurant, **Le Café** (Tel: 613/594-5127), is part of the complex, and offers good food before or after a performance. During summer months the tables spill out onto a canalside terrace, making it a comfortable place to stop for a spritzer or cup of tea.

Just around the corner on Albert Street near Elgin is the ▶ **Ottawa Hilton**—very much an "establishment" oasis, with a reputation for good service. Cabinet ministers and senior bureaucrats are often seen here at breakfast and luncheon meetings.

Things change when you cross the canal—including, quite often, the names of Ottawa's streets. Wellington, for example, becomes Rideau Street east of the bridge facing Confederation Square. Easily seen from the bridge is the **Rideau Centre**, Ottawa's latest shopping complex, which in true suburban fashion gathers together some 200-odd establishments—from boutiques to department stores to fast-food outlets—under one roof (good for a rainy or freezing day).

There are, of course, alternatives to eating in a shopping center. Those who manage to track down the second-floor walk-up location of **Santé**, 45 Rideau Street, near Sussex Drive, will find a menu with Thai overtones served in comfortable surroundings. Denizens of the nearby parliamentary world know Santé; you'll need reservations (Tel: 613/232-7113).

Adjacent to the Rideau Centre at 11 Colonel By Drive is the ▶ **Westin Hotel Ottawa**. Well located and equipped with all the modern amenities (including squash courts), it's another convenient place to stay, and within easy reach of everything.

On the north side of Rideau Street, just behind the shopping behemoth, is the oldest—and liveliest—part of Ottawa.

Lower Town

Traditionally known as Lower Town or the **Byward Market** area, this is where the city's first houses—and taverns— were built 150 years ago for the men who worked on the Rideau Canal. Bounded by Sussex Drive, Rideau, Cumberland, and St. Patrick streets, it's a compact area that has never lost its central role in Ottawa's commercial life, although it has moved up and down the social ladder over the years.

If Quebec lumbermen favored the area's bars in the mid-1800s, so do Ottawa's young professionals in the 1990s. Lower Town is busy during the day, and just as busy at night. Much of the city's nightlife (the rest of it can be found on Elgin Street, which runs south from Wellington Street) happens in wine bars, pubs, and clubs like the **Rainbow Bistro** at 76 Murray Street. At many of these places the sounds of rhythm-and-blues bands obscure conversation inside, and unless you get in early the most you can hope for on a Saturday night is a bit of bar to lean against. The clubs all close at 1:00 A.M., but no need to despair: The bar crowd just moves over to Hull (more on Hull later).

The actual market still thrives, with many Ottawans, particularly on weekends, flocking to stores that specialize in cheeses, meats, fish, or fruits. During the summer months local farmers set up stalls in the streets between the principal market buildings and sell fresh fruits, vegetables, and flowers.

Although the basic market function of the Byward area endures, it has been embroidered in recent years. Many of the older buildings now harbor chic boutiques and restaurants, making it a favorite haunt for locals on Sundays. In fact, a stranger to the city might well presume that no one in Ottawa eats breakfast at home on weekends, the brunch habit is so prevalent here. After brunch the logical thing to do is browse. Possibilities range from secondhand bookstores to designer clothing shops. One distinctively Canadian shop is **Suttles and Seawinds** (535 Sussex Drive), which sells handcrafted clothes and quilts from Nova Scotia.

Back lanes and small courtyards contribute to the market area's ambience. **Tin House Court**, a particularly charming cobblestoned spot between Clarence and Murray streets, includes the façade of an old front wall affixed to the side of another stone building. The house from which the façade came was owned in the early 1900s by a city tinsmith named Foisy, and his skill at his trade is evident here. The **Courtyard Restaurant**, 21 George Street, is a good Sunday brunch bet, with live classical music an added bonus. Tel: (613) 238-4623.

If you find yourself in Tin House Court, you won't be far from **Memories**, 7 Clarence Street, a café famous for desserts too good to pass up. Of course, the market area abounds in restaurants of every persuasion. From Tex-Mex to nouvelle cuisine, you'll find a quick or leisurely meal easy to locate. One that might—but shouldn't—escape your attention is the tiny café that is part of **Domus**, a kitchen-supply shop at 269 Dalhousie Street. (The café is open only for lunch.) For a special dinner or lunch, **Le Jardin**, 127 York Street, serves classic French cuisine in an old, beautifully renovated house. Tel: (613) 238-1828. Or just wander until something strikes your fancy.

Any exploration of this part of the city would be incomplete without a walk down **St. Patrick Street**, where two of the first houses to be built in Ottawa still stand. Typical of the small wood-frame homes once common in Lower Town, number 138 dates back to 1850 and was the home for many years of Flavan Rochon, a wood-carver whose skills embellished the Library of Parliament. By the time of Confederation (1867) the more usual style of house was the one standing at 142 St. Patrick—three stories in stone, with a second-floor verandah.

Sussex Drive

Sussex Drive has been an impressive boulevard since Ottawa's pioneering days. During the city's first century it was a commercial center, lined with hardware and grocery stores, hotels and haberdashers. Running parallel to the Ottawa River, the street carried traffic to Queen's Wharf (long gone) and the sawmills (equally extinct) at Rideau Falls, where the Rideau River empties into the Ottawa. As river traffic gave way to road and rail, however, the street lost its status as a business thoroughfare.

In the early 1960s the federal government decided to preserve the old commercial structures on the east side of Sussex between George and St. Patrick streets with the idea of creating a Confederation-period streetscape. Original façades were refurbished while interiors were gutted and rebuilt. Today these old buildings are occupied by toney shops that line part of the well-used ceremonial route leading to Rideau Hall (see below).

A walk along Sussex has the potential to be time-consuming—not because of its length (from Confederation Square to Ottawa City Hall is just over a mile) but because there is so much worth seeing. The restored buildings between George and St. Patrick streets are on your right as you stroll down Sussex, but the skyline is dominated by the spires of **Notre Dame Basilica** (at St. Patrick Street) and the glass domes of the National Gallery. Consecrated in 1846 (making it the oldest church in the capital), Notre Dame is the spiritual heart of Lower Town's Irish Catholic population.

National Gallery of Canada

Across the street, overlooking Nepean Point and the river, is the National Gallery of Canada. Designed by Moshe Safdie, it echoes in granite and glass the lines of the parliamentary library visible in the background. A stunning building, the National Gallery offers first-rate exhibit spaces, good restaurants, and a number of quiet courtyards. Predictably, its collection of Canadian art is its strength, and while it offers a historical perspective, the gallery's best-known holdings are early-20th-century works by the **Group of Seven**. (See the Northern Ontario section in the Ontario Province chapter below.) Be sure also to see the reconstructed chapel from the Rideau Street Convent—an outstanding example of 19th-century French-Canadian architecture—and try to save a half hour for the museum's bookstore. The National Gallery is closed Mondays from Labour Day to April 30.

Canadian Museum of Civilization

From the National Gallery site, you cannot miss the curved profile of the Canadian Museum of Civilization on the opposite bank of the Ottawa River in Hull. (It's an easy walk across the Interprovincial Bridge, also called the Alexandra Bridge.)

This relatively new museum is the work of Canadian

architect Douglas Cardinal, who describes its curving walls and domed roofs as evocative of a Canadian landscape sculpted by the natural forces of glaciers, wind, and water. State-of-the-art exhibits detailing the history and prehistory of humans in Canada abound, and the museum's world-famous collection of totem poles is reason enough for a visit. Like the National Gallery, the Museum of Civilization is closed Mondays from Labour Day to the end of April. There are a café and restaurant on the premises.

Canadian War Museum and Royal Canadian Mint

When you're finished at the Canadian Museum of Civilization, return via the bridge to Sussex Drive, where there is more territory to explore. Just north of the National Gallery is the Canadian War Museum, whose collection includes not only the expected paraphernalia of conflict—torpedoes, tanks, cannons, and the like—but more than 7,000 artworks that reveal war in all its guises through the eyes of artists from several countries.

Just beyond the War Museum is the turreted Royal Canadian Mint, behind whose neo-Gothic walls commemorative coins and medals, as well as the gold maple-leaf coins, are manufactured. Tours (by appointment; call 613/993-8990) are available May through August.

North on Sussex Drive

Continuing north on Sussex, in ten minutes you'll reach Green Island and Ottawa's City Hall, where works by local artists are frequently exhibited in the first-floor lobby. Across the street and flanked by a pleasant park, Rideau Falls mark the spot where the Rideau River empties into the larger Ottawa River. If you turn around and head south on Sussex, you'll be facing a pleasant 20-minute walk back to Confederation Square.

If you decide to explore Sussex Drive farther to the east (where the diplomatic community has set up shop), a car or bicycle will come in handy. The Department of External Affairs (tours available on weekdays) is housed in a multi-tiered structure at 125 Sussex; the French embassy and the prime minister's residence (24 Sussex) both command attention, although neither is open to the public. At the end of Sussex (number 1), about three miles from Confederation Square, is Rideau Hall, residence of the governor general since 1865. Superbly situated on 80-odd acres, the house and grounds are open to the public (hourly tours available in summer; Tel: 613/998-7113 for reservations).

Elsewhere in Ottawa

While the city is small and does break into three basic units, there are a few things worth seeing that don't quite fit into this scheme. Because Ottawa is a national capital it enjoys a higher concentration of museums than most cities. Many museums are closed on Mondays (check at the tourism-information kiosk in the National Arts Centre—some museums make exceptions during the summer months), and most offer free admission one day a week.

The **Canadian Museum of Nature** is located on the edge of the downtown core in the Victoria Memorial Building, a 20-minute walk south of Confederation Square at the corner of Metcalfe and McLeod streets. The building itself (which was used to house Parliament when the Centre Block was destroyed by fire in 1916) is beautiful, and the plant gallery on the fourth floor is a special treat.

Laurier House, 335 Laurier East (the canal divides Laurier Street into east and west), is not a museum per se but rather an interesting Victorian-era house open to the public. Formerly the residence of two Canadian prime ministers, Wilfrid Laurier and William Lyon Mackenzie King (Laurier's successor as leader of the Liberal Party), it has several rooms furnished with period pieces.

The **National Aviation Museum** at Rockcliffe Airport has more than a hundred aircraft on display; the collection traces the progress of aircraft development from early bamboo-and-balloon-cloth structures to the present.

HULL

Ottawa is located in the National Capital Region, an area that includes both Ottawa itself and, across the Ottawa River in Quebec, Hull. Many Canadians would like to see the capital region become a distinct political unit (in a manner similar to the District of Columbia in the United States or the Australian Capital Territory in Australia), but Quebec has been reluctant to yield sovereignty over any of its territory.

Although linked by several bridges, the two cities are far from being integrated. Hull remains a French-speaking city and has retained its small-town working-class character. Inhabitants of the two towns interact in a couple of arenas: as employees of federal government departments, some of which have been moved to Hull in recent years, and in Hull's late-night bars.

The Strip

When Ottawa's bars close at 1:00 A.M., serious revelers head across the bridges to Hull's **Promenade du Portage**, a broad thoroughfare sporting a collection of bars and discos that stay open every night until 3:00 A.M. (and hardly warm up before 11:00 P.M.). The names along the Strip change frequently, but the general character of the area remains the same: The crowd is young, the music is loud, and the bouncers have no necks. The current favorite here is the **Citi Club** (179 promenade du Portage), replete with laser lights and smoke machines. The "older" crowd (read over 22) drifts toward **Le Bistro**, just around the corner at 3 Kent Street.

Food can also be found along the Strip. One tiny, inexpensive restaurant worth stopping at is **La Grenouille** (80 promenade du Portage; Tel: 819/776-4515). The *table d'hôte* menu is limited, but the food is imaginatively and carefully prepared.

In fact, Hull has a number of good French restaurants. Among the best is the casual **Le Pied de Cochon** (248 Montcalm; Tel: 819/777-5808), located in the heart of a commercial area and well worth a detour. For a more formal atmosphere, the number-one spot in Hull is the **Café Henry Burger** (69 rue Laurier; Tel: 819/777-5646). Go for the evening or schedule a long lunch—it will be both expensive and memorable.

GATINEAU PARK

If you have a car, a 20-minute drive from Parliament Hill will take you to the well-cared-for wilderness of **Gatineau Park**. From Confederation Square, take Wellington Street west to the Portage Bridge and turn left at the first intersection in Hull (Taché Boulevard). Follow Taché west for about a mile to the **Gatineau Parkway**, which is a righthand turn off Taché. Points of interest are marked by signs along the route. Totaling some 88,000 acres belonging to the federal government, the park offers hiking trails, bikeways, and swimming in freshwater lakes. In the winter, superbly maintained cross-country ski trails crisscross the park, with cabins where skiers may stop to warm up or cook their lunch on wood stoves dotting the landscape.

While you're in the park, stop at **Kingsmere**, the country estate of former Canadian prime minister William Mackenzie King. An eccentric man, King was given to trafficking with spiritual mediums and collecting "ruins," with which he festooned his estate. Among numerous bits and pieces gracefully scattered throughout the gardens are parts of the old Parliament Buildings that burned in 1916 and some Corinthian columns from a 19th-century bank building. A pleasant tearoom operates here during the summer months.

GETTING AROUND

By Air. Ottawa International Airport is a 20-minute drive from Parliament Hill. City buses run every half hour between the terminal and downtown. Taxi fare to a downtown hotel from the airport costs about $15. An airport shuttle bus to several major hotels runs at half-hour intervals for about $9.00 per person. Ottawa is served by commuter airlines from most major Canadian cities.

By Rail and Bus. Despite the city's location in the "central corridor" of Canadian passenger rail service, most Ottawans have a jaundiced view of train service. While several trains run daily between Ottawa and either Montreal or Toronto, they are frequently late—especially during the winter. The station is not downtown (it's located a couple of miles southwest of Parliament Hill), but it is linked to the city center by regular city bus service. Taxis are always available, with the fare from downtown about $7.

By Car or Bus. From Montreal, the stretch of Highway 417 heading west to Ottawa may be the most boring road on the North American continent. The 192-km (119-mile) drive is far more pleasant if you take Highway 17, which follows the course of the Ottawa River. Highway 401 links Montreal to Toronto. Ottawans driving the five hours to Toronto will usually use Highways 16 or 31 south to 401.

The intercity bus terminal is located on Catherine Street, with city bus stops close by. If luggage isn't a problem, it's a 15-minute walk to the downtown core.

Because so many of its attractions are clustered in the downtown core, walking is the most practical way to see the city. A lack of adequate space has made parking a car in Ottawa both difficult and expensive. City bus service is extensive and reliable but operates on a strange two-tier fare structure. During morning and evening rush hours (6:00 to 8:30 A.M. and 3:00 to 5:30 P.M.) it costs $2.75 to get on an Ottawa bus—the highest bus fare in Canada. At less busy times the fare is $2.00. Unless you are going a considerable distance, a taxi is far more convenient.

ACCOMMODATIONS REFERENCE

Hotels in Ottawa can be expensive, although most offer substantial reductions on weekends. The rates given below are projections *for peak seasons during the 1994 calendar year. Unless otherwise indicated, rates are based on double rooms, double occupancy; sales and federal taxes are included in all rates. As rates are subject to change, always double-check before booking.*

The telephone area code in Ottawa is 613.

► **Château Laurier.** 1 Rideau Street, **Ottawa**, Ont. K1N 8S7. Tel: 232-6411; Fax: 232-3492; in the U.S., Tel: (800) 828-7447; in Canada, (800) 268-9411. $156–$178.

► **Delta Ottawa.** 361 Queen Street, **Ottawa**, Ont. K1R 7S9. Tel: 238-6000; Fax: 238-2290; in U.S., Tel: (800) 877-1133; in Canada, (800) 268-1133. $110–$160.

► **Doral Inn Hotel.** 486 Albert Street, **Ottawa**, Ont. K1R 5B5. Tel: 230-8055; Fax: 237-9660; in the U.S. and Canada, Tel: (800) 263-6725. $77–$88 (suite with kitchenette).

► **Ottawa Hilton.** 150 Albert Street, **Ottawa**, Ont. K1P 5G2. Tel: 238-1500; Fax: 235-2723; in the U.S. and Canada, Tel: (800) HILTONS. $178–$234.

► **Radisson Hotel Ottawa Centre.** 100 Kent Street, **Ottawa**, Ont. K1P 5R7. Tel: 238-1122; Fax: 783-4229; in the U.S. and Canada, Tel: (800) 333-3333. $95–$162.

► **Westin Hotel Ottawa.** 11 Colonel By Drive, **Ottawa**, Ont. K1N 9H4. Tel: 560-7000; Fax: 234-5396; in the U.S. and Canada, Tel: (800) 228-3000. $196–$207.

If bed and breakfast is a more appealing arrangement you might choose to stay in one of Ottawa's dozen or so guest houses. A listing is available from **Ottawa Bed and Breakfast Association**, 488 Cooper Street, Ottawa, Ontario, K1R 5H9. Tel: (613) 563-0161.

TORONTO

By Steve Veale

Steve Veale is a freelance travel writer living in Toronto. He contributes to various newspapers and magazines in both Canada and the United States, including the Toronto Star, *the* Buffalo News, *the* Detroit Free Press, Michigan Living, *and* Yankee Magazine. *For almost a decade he was the promotion officer in the travel media department of the Ontario government's Ministry of Tourism, and since 1982 has been a member of the Society of American Travel Writers.*

Toronto is a city that has finally shed its dull-duckling image and turned into a rather glorious swan; gone are the gawky days as a rather provincial British colonial outpost where gray flannel was the only fashion and roast beef the only cuisine. Toronto, in fact, has become so chic and trendy that a tourist who last visited in the early 1960s would fail to recognize the place, both in style and spirit. The changes have taken place with a vengeance, as if Toronto were trying to make up for years lost while chained in bondage to someone else's traditions.

And yet these changes, although they appeared to take place overnight, have been the result of careful urban planning. Toronto watched the blight that descended on other North American cities in the 1950s and 1960s, when their core areas slumped as people escaped to the suburbs, and took the opposite tack; it revitalized and rejuvenated its downtown (led by the huge Eaton Centre shopping complex), which in turn led to an explosion of restaurants, nightclubs, bars, theaters, and venues for concerts and other performing arts—all of which recaptured downtown dwellers in record numbers.

Today Toronto is a thriving city of business, from stock and bond trading, to legal and government work, to film and

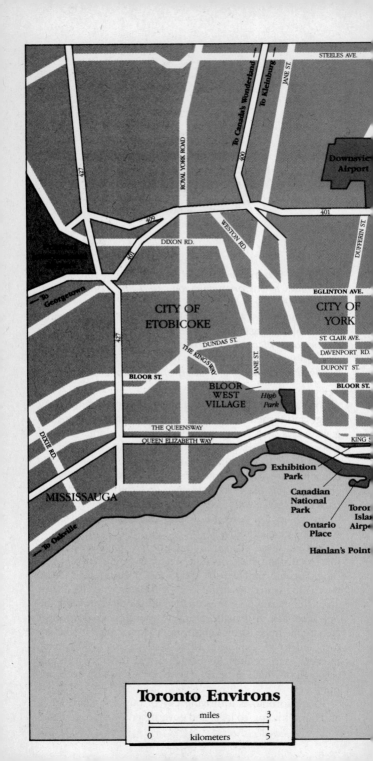

Toronto Environs

| 0 | miles | 3 |
| 0 | kilometers | 5 |

theater activity. It is also the safest and cleanest city of its size in North America.

As well, it is a city under constant construction, with the downtown landscape changing daily at the whim of major developers. Architectural landmarks are seemingly demolished overnight while others, phoenix-like, rise the following day to take their place. The city has been in a constant state of flux and change for more than a decade now, which means if you haven't been to Toronto for several years, much of what was familiar to you may have disappeared or been transformed into something else.

However, fair warning: Toronto has paid for its popularity with a steady rise in prices. It seems everyone wants to be here, whether to live or visit, and the soaring prices reflect what the market will bear—which seems to be quite a lot these days.

MAJOR INTEREST

CN Tower
Harbourfront and the Toronto Islands
Ontario Place
Eaton Centre and the Underground City
The Beach (shopping, cafés)
Yorkville shops, cafés, bars, nightclubs
Casa Loma
Ontario Science Centre
Performing arts: theater, concerts, opera, symphony, dance, cabaret
Festivals (Caravan, Caribana, Film Festival of Festivals)
Canada's Wonderland theme park
Dining and nightlife
Shopping

Mudhole to Metropolis

Although Toronto has been hailed in recent years as "the North American city that works," initial descriptions of the settlement on Lake Ontario's shores were anything but favorable. "The city's site was better calculated for a frog pond or a beaver meadow than for the residence of human beings," wrote John Graves Simcoe, the first lieutenant governor of Upper Canada, who discarded the original Turontu in favor of York, after the duke of York, second son of the reigning monarch, George III. (It is not known whether this ingratiating name change aided Simcoe's career.)

The site soon became known as Muddy York by those

who had to walk its streets. For a while the name Hogtown, proposed because of the increase in farmers' markets and livestock trading (as at today's St. Lawrence Market), seemed a viable alternative, but fortunately cooler heads prevailed, and in 1834 the official, final name for the growing community became Toronto.

The name itself stems from the similar sounding Huron word meaning "meeting or gathering place," thus making Toronto the world's first convention center. (Today's inhabitants pronounce their city's name "Trawna," completely ignoring all the *o*s and the final *t*; this is closer, perhaps, to the original Huron dialect, but it's a far cry from phonetic English.) The French voyageurs were the first to meet with the native Indians, and traded beads for furs at Fort Rouille, on the site of what today is Exhibition Park, still the venue for annual fairs and sporting events. When the British assumed control of the area in 1788, the land was purchased from the Mississauga Indians for more beads, cloth, and blankets totaling about $1,700.

Contrary to Simcoe's pessimistic predictions, Toronto continued to grow and expand; at last count the metropolitan area claimed well over three million inhabitants (the city of Toronto proper has about 700,000). It remains the province's capital city, the financial center of the country, and in the late 1970s surpassed Montreal as the largest city in Canada.

For many years the city was definitely Toronto the Good, a euphemistic add-on that translated as boring, dull, and staid; or, as W. C. Fields once drawled, "I went to Toronto last Sunday; it was closed."

Things started to change following World War II as waves of immigrants flooded the New World: Italians, Chinese, Greeks, Japanese, Hungarians, Portuguese, Poles, and others combined to change the shape and ethnic composition of the burgeoning community. In recent years immigrants from the West Indies, East Indies, Pakistan, Vietnam, and elsewhere have joined them, swelling the metro area's population from the 1958 figure of 750,000 to today's total. Nowhere is the resulting transformation more evident than in the old-line Jewish garment district of Spadina, where bagels and knishes have given way to egg rolls and noodles, Shopsy's deli to Peking Court.

Along the way, Toronto became not so much a melting pot as a mulligan stew, with a blend of ingredients—a touch of this culture, a pinch of that—that has created a spectacular mixture of sight and sound, color and style. And new arrivals daily add to the flavor of this polyglot world capital.

Exploring Toronto

TORONTO'S NEIGHBORHOODS

True to the cliché, Toronto really is a city of neighborhoods, although as often as not they have outgrown their old boundaries and blended with other distinct neighborhoods. For example, the Fashion District along Spadina (Spa-DINE-ah) sells clothes and accessories. It runs into the Chinatown of Dundas Street West, which looks like a typically crowded street in Hong Kong. Yet for a few blocks you will be bewildered by the cultural mixture. A third-generation Russian/Polish/Armenian designs coats in one store while a recently arrived Chinese/Thai/Filipino teenager creates some terrific wok concoction in the restaurant next door.

Though the nationalities do mix, certain neighborhoods are recognized for a particular cuisine or style: the *schmatta* district of Spadina; the bright lights of Chinatown on Dundas West; the Portuguese market of Kensington; the Greek souvlaki along the Danforth; the Italian spumoni shops lining College Street; the monied mansions of conservative Rosedale and Forest Hill; the thousands of students in the Annex; the young professionals of Cabbagetown. The city often seems like a patchwork quilt of small neighborhoods threaded together by its diverse mix of people.

The laid-back yachting life of the harborfront segues into the concrete and steel of the city's Bay Street stock-market area to the north; the boardwalk and racetrack of the Beach meld with the gritty industrial area of Queen Street; the Little Italy of College Street West soon runs into the gentrified shopping section of Bloor West Village; the stately, century-old homes of the Annex give way to the chic condos of Yorkville; and the million-dollar mansions of Rosedale meet the Greek tavernas of Bloor Street when the latter becomes the Danforth.

For many Torontonians, the intersection of **Yonge** and **Bloor** streets is the center of their universe; this is where the commerce of north–south Yonge (pronounced "young") meets the high prices and fashion of east–west Bloor. Yonge is, in fact, the longest street in Canada, actually ending far to the north at James Bay, with every little town along the way able to boast its own "Yonge Street." **King Street**, downtown, is the financial core of the city, while **Queen Street**, a few blocks north of and running parallel to King, is the avenue for funky fashions and music. **Yorkville**, just north of Bloor Street, is for the chic and trendy, as well as for those who have made a weekday art out of lingering over lunch. And the **Harbourfront** area is a strange mixture of yachts and parkland, sidewalk vendors and pricey lakeside restaurants, with a dash of out-of-control condominium development.

The Annex, in the middle of the city; **Forest Hill** to the north; and **Rosedale** to the east are all residential areas, with the latter claiming most of the city's mansions. **Queen's Quay** is home to the arts and crafts of Harbourfront as well as the three island yacht clubs; **The Beach**, at the eastern end of Queen Street, is lined with trendy shops; and **the Danforth**, a continuation of Bloor Street east of the Bloor viaduct, is crowded with Mediterranean restaurants.

Chinatown on Dundas West provides all the flair and food of the Far East, while **Spadina** mixes discount fashion with bagels and lox. **Kensington Market**, filled with kiosks and stalls where you can shop on Saturday mornings for the freshest produce, could be a street bazaar in Portugal, whereas only the trendy and gold-card rich casually shop the designer boutiques in chic midtown Yorkville.

The formerly downtrodden **Cabbagetown** at the north end of Parliament Street (so named because poor Irish immigrants grew cabbage to eat instead of grass on their front lawns) is now all sandblasted brick and cozy cafés, though it runs south into **Regent Park**, a poorer inner-city area of housing developments and street derelicts (not all of Toronto has been renovated).

Each area is proud of its unique character; in fact most areas are well marked with street signs that include their unofficial designations; College Street signs say "Little Italy"; Dundas Street signs bear Chinese characters; Cumberland Street is in the upscale Yorkville–Bloor shopping district; Queen's Quay West is Harbourfront; Greek letters underscore the Danforth signs; Spadina is brightly marked with a red "Fashion District" insignia; and so on. You'll know immediately which area of the city you're in.

In short, Toronto is a vital, continually growing city where the sights and sounds of a neighborhood can change merely by turning a street corner. If it all sounds a bit overwhelming to the prospective first-time visitor, don't despair. All you need is a little perspective.

CN TOWER

Most people visit Toronto for its permanent attractions, and there is none more noticeable than the CN (Canadian National) Tower, at 1,815 feet the world's tallest free-standing structure (New York's Empire State Building is 1,250 feet and Paris's Eiffel Tower a mere 984 feet). The tower, at 301 Front Street, should be one of your first stops in Toronto, if only because the view from the observation deck or the **Top of**

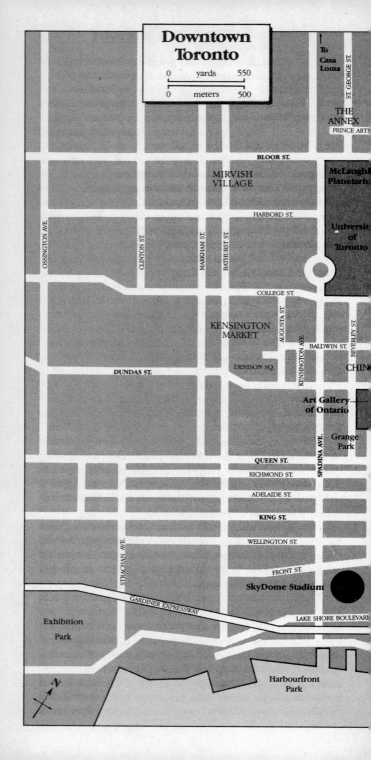

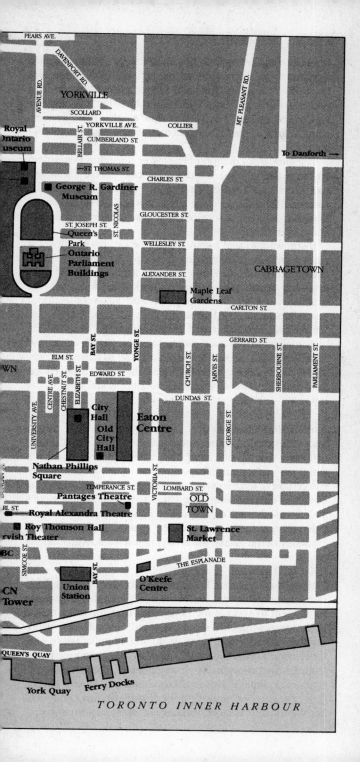

Toronto revolving restaurant will give you a wonderful orientation to the layout of the city far below. On a clear day you'll even be able to see past the hundreds of sailboats and yachts in the Toronto harbor to the mist rising from Niagara Falls, some 100 km (62 miles) to the south. The night view from **Sparkles**, the world's highest nightclub, is similarly impressive.

The view from the top of the tower illustrates better than anything the gridlike layout of the city: Everything below seems to be square, perpendicular, or parallel. You'll also be surprised at how green the city is; not just the parkland but even the downtown core has trees planted along its streets and boulevards.

If you want to take a spin around the city, book a table for sunset cocktails (a complete revolution takes about an hour and 12 minutes); Tel: (416) 362-5411 for reservations. For a revolving dinner, it's better to check out the **Lighthouse Restaurant** (Tel: 416/869-1600) in the lakefront Harbour Castle Westin at One Harbour Square; the view, while not as lofty, is still spectacular, and the food is better.

A final word of advice: Get to the tower early. On a clear summer day it can take more than an hour to make your way through the line at the elevators. The Metro Convention Centre is the chrome-and-glass building at the base of the tower.

Tour of the Universe

Another attraction at the base of the tower is the Tour of the Universe, a blast into outer space, compliments of a flight simulator and visual effects that will have you firmly convinced you've left the planet. An elevator transports you to the bowels of the CN Tower, where you are led, by human guides and robots, through computerized passport controls and past video screens into a 40-passenger "spaceship" that takes you on a tour of the galaxy while staying safely underground.

SKYDOME

Right next door to the CN Tower is the world's first retractable domed stadium, better known as SkyDome. This 56,000-seat monument to sport is the home of two of Toronto's major-league teams: baseball's Blue Jays and football's Argonauts. (Hockey's Maple Leafs remain in the historic Maple Leaf Gardens at Carlton and Yonge streets, preferring ice to Astroturf.) SkyDome, truly an engineering marvel, officially opened on June 3, 1989, with the first ballgame played two days later (historic note: the home team lost). SkyDome could accommodate a 31-story building if it were set down in center field, and the dome itself can rotate 180 degrees. A 450-room hotel (see the Accommodations section below) is attached to the stadium, with 70 rooms overlooking the field, an entertainment complex, and various restaurant and bar areas. The major problem is traffic congestion. Take public transport, or, better still, walk to the game on one of Toronto's glorious summer days.

HARBOURFRONT
AND THE TORONTO ISLANDS

For more than a decade now Toronto has been transforming its once dingy harbor area into a district that features arts and crafts; children's activities; theater, dance, and film; marinas; waterfront cafés and restaurants; and a lush two-mile waterfront promenade. The area quickly became popular for summer strolling, although in the past couple of years the burgeoning condos have greatly increased pedestrian traffic and density. York Quay (pronounced "key") Centre remains true to its roots, however, with artists creating kiln-fired pottery and the like. The original "people place" is bordered on the east by the expensive shops of the **Queen's Quay Terminal Building**, actually a spectacular renovation of an old, unused grain terminal, and, to the west, the Radisson Plaza Hotel Admiral (this is one area where the council failed to stop developers).

Chips wagons selling fat french fries and hot dogs line the roadside (watch for the police citing them for illegal vending). If you want something more substantial, scenic, or alcoholic, try the lakefront **Spinnakers** café (Tel: 416/203-0559) in the Terminal Building or the restaurants at Pier Four beside the Hotel Admiral.

For a day of picnicking, sunbathing, and swimming on the **Toronto Islands** (Ward's, Centre, Olympic, and Hanlon's Point), take the ferry from behind the Westin Harbour Castle ($5 per person). Once on the islands (which are separated by narrow channels), you can rent bicycles, canoes, or rowboats, or simply stroll among their manicured acres. (There are also three private yacht clubs here.)

If you don't wish to spend the entire day on the islands, you can take a harbor tour through the islands' interconnected lagoon system with either **Gray Line Boat Tours**, 5 Queen's Quay West (Tel: 416/364-2412), or **Toronto Tours Ltd.**, 145 Queen's Quay West (Tel: 416/869-1372). Gray Line tours depart hourly during the summer months from the foot of Yonge Street, Toronto Tours from the foot of York Street.

ONTARIO PLACE

A 96-acre amusement park built on three man-made islands created, owned, and operated by the Ontario government, Ontario Place is the most popular spot on the waterfront by virtue of its six-story **Cinesphere**, outdoor Forum concert stage, separate children's island with water slide and huge wading pool, cafés, pubs, and venues for starlight dancing.

The park is open from the third weekend in May to Labour Day; admission was made free in 1991, while varying fees are still charged for the Cinesphere and concerts at the Forum, where the entertainment ranges from the Neville Brothers to the National Ballet. Ontario's provincial government was the developer of the IMAX film system, and there are continuous showings of several different features in the 800-seat Cinesphere, a geodesic dome that seems to float on the waters of the lake. Running about 40 minutes each, these films have been specially produced to demonstrate the dizzying visual effects of IMAX—effects that include silently soaring in a glider, zooming down a wooded ski slope, or feeling the heat from within a northern Ontario forest fire. During the winter, Ontario Place presents its 70-mm film festival, with such visually striking films as (in previous years) *Apocalypse Now* and *Die Hard.*

Ontario Place is also the locale of **Trillium** (Tel: 416/314-9831), an upscale restaurant on the water that caters to local businessmen looking to beat the city's summer heat. In fact, on sunny afternoons you will often see them playing hooky, shoeless in their three-piece suits as they navigate little paddleboats through the park's many canals.

The Trillium menu ranges from noontime hamburgers to dinner surf and turf; parents with kids in tow might want to opt for one of the park's many fast-food stands instead.

CITY HALL AND
NATHAN PHILLIPS SQUARE

City Hall, one of Toronto's major architectural landmarks, stands in striking contrast to the stately old municipal headquarters across the street on Nathan Phillips Square. The huge arched towers designed by Finnish architect Viljo Revell were completed in 1965 amid great controversy. Toronto the Good was shocked that the new structure didn't look like an official building should; it should look like, well, the old City Hall.

However, after it opened and the city wasn't destroyed in a flash of thunder and lightning, people started to realize that perhaps there was more to life than the staid and stodgy. Buildings could be modern and inventive and still function properly. Since then, the look of Toronto has never been the same, as older structures have been harmoniously integrated with the latest in architectural design.

EATON CENTRE AND
THE UNDERGROUND CITY

If City Hall is Toronto's political mecca, then the Eaton Centre is absolute nirvana for its shoppers. You enter this shrine to consumerism, which has become a major visitor attraction as well, just a few steps east of Old City Hall at the corner of Yonge and Queen streets. Inside, hundreds of shops, restaurants, and pubs fill three floors all the way up to Dundas Street—a four-city-block area where, as at Alice's Restaurant, "you can get anything you want," from fur coats to grocery greens, souvenir sweatshirts to deli delights, all in a vast complex modeled after the famed Galleria in Milan.

As you head south from the Dundas Street subway stop this portion of the complex is actually **Eaton's** department store—six levels running the full consumer gamut from specialty foods, to casual and formal clothing, to electronics, hardware and kitchen appliances. And where Eaton's ends, the individual shops of the Centre begin. This second section has only three levels, with the general rule of thumb being that the less expensive items (i.e., records, books, fast-food alley) are located on the lower level while the quality and prices (i.e., jewelry stores, exclusive clothing shops, full-course dining) climb as you ascend the escalators. Coffee is in the basement, cappuccino on the third-level deck.

When you run out of Eaton Centre at the Queen Street subway station, you segue into another vast consumer cornucopia, **The Bay** department store. The former Simpson's—which underwent a name change when Canada's first department store, an offshoot of the original Hudson's Bay fur trading company, acquired the chain—wisely decided not to compete with the ultramodern Centre but instead set about preserving the beauties of the past by spending millions cleaning and renovating its old downtown department store. Whether you wish to shop in space-age splendor or among the polished gargoyles of the past, you'll find whatever you need between these two mega-stores.

Bounded by Dundas Street to the north and Front Street's **Union Station** to the south, Toronto's **Underground City** offers miles of clean, brightly lit shopping; in fact, this is the world's largest subterranean complex, complete with green trees and waterfalls as well as restaurants, bars, banks, medical and dental offices, and more than 1,000 stores. It's also a commuter's wintertime dream: You can drive to the GO

suburban train, arrive at Union Station, walk underground to
one of the connecting office complexes, lunch, shop, entertain, and return home without ever having to don an overcoat.

SPADINA, CHINATOWN, AND KENSINGTON MARKET

For a complete change of pace, head west toward the streets
and stalls of three of the city's best-known ethnic areas.

Spadina Avenue used to be the Jewish garment and food
district. As members of the younger generation moved north
into more affluent neighborhoods, however, the vacant storefronts they left behind gradually filled with Chinese-owned
noodle houses, vegetable stands, herbal medicine stores,
and silk outlets. As a result, today the cross streets around
the intersection of Dundas and Spadina are a harmonious
blend of cultural and consumer delights. And though the
debate still rages as to where to go for a decent bagel
(Montreal seems to have the edge on Toronto), there is no
debate about Asian cuisine; culinary experts have pro-
claimed Toronto one of the Chinese food capitals of North
America. Try the second-story **Sai Woo** (no decor but wonderful food; Tel: 416/977-4988) at 130 Dundas Street West, or
the acclaimed **Hunan Palace** (Tel: 416/593-9831), around the
corner at 412 Spadina Avenue. Or visit one of the many
nondescript, dingy-looking noodle houses; usually, the shab-
bier the decor, the better the food.

If you head west on Dundas and turn right on Augusta
Street, you'll soon find yourself on what feel like the back
streets of Lisbon. The Portuguese marketplace here is the real
thing: an Old World bazaar selling live chickens and fresh fish,
fruits and vegetables, seeds and beans, delicious pastries and
homemade sandwiches. **Kensington Market** lies west of
Spadina between Dundas and College streets, where it over-
laps with the student neighborhood around George Brown
Community College. The market, especially on Saturday
mornings (it's deserted on Sundays), is a shopper's and
browser's delight, a crowded cacophony of haggling in Portuguese and English. This is a definite walking tour; besides, the
market is too crowded to drive through. When you're ready to
take a break, try the outdoor patio of the **Casa Abril em
Portugal** restaurant at 159 Augusta for a tangy Portuguese-
style coffee, an afternoon *cerveja*, or a platter of calamari. Tel:
(416) 593-0440.

QUEEN STREET WEST

Wander south on Spadina a few blocks to Queen Street and
the scene changes again; this is a more vibrant, youth-

oriented area that has become synonymous with the latest in music, style, and fashion. Queen Street between Bathurst to the west and University Avenue to the east is lined with tiny restaurants (Peter Pan, Queen Mother Café), sidewalk cafés and bookstores (lounging around Edward's Bookstore on Sundays is a favorite pastime for many), art galleries, second-hand clothing stores, overpriced designer boutiques, and, for some reason, dozens of electronics stores and low-priced furniture outlets.

But the soul of Queen Street West is music—whether the eclectic variety (from reggae to jazz) of the vanguard **Bam-Boo Club** (number 312), the country-and-western twang of the **Horseshoe Tavern** (number 370), or the driving hard-rock sounds of the **Cameron House** (number 408). The dance-palace/disco scene is ably represented by the **Big Bop**, at the corner of Queen and Bathurst—two floors of earth-shaking music that attract long lines every weekend.

This is Toronto's very own "bohemian" area, filled with musicians, artists, and writers who help stoke the city's creative fires. And like bohemian scenes anywhere, the prevailing attitude is one of live-and-let-live: You'll feel just as "at home" in a tweed jacket as you will in a spiked hairdo.

For yet another contrast, take a drive or stroll through conservative **Rosedale** (take Sherbourne Street north of Bloor Street East) or **Forest Hill** (north of St. Clair Avenue, west of Yonge Street) to get a taste of how Toronto's old money lives. Thinking of buying? Better have a million or so to start. If you decide to explore the area, don't dawdle in front of the mansions; the landed gentry don't take kindly to people lurking on their sidewalks.

THE BEACH

Controversy long raged over whether the small, thriving village at the easternmost end of Queen Street (past Wood-bine Avenue) should be known as "The Beach" or "The Beaches." Eventually, the city council legislated in favor of the singular form, and longtime residents were able to rest easy. "Once a beacher, always a beacher" is the rallying cry for all those who live between Woodbine and the end of Queen at the trolley turnaround—older, longtime residents, up-and-coming young professionals, and some long-haired remnants of the 1960s. Some people literally never leave the confines of the Beach.

Located only a 20-minute Queen Street trolley ride from the center of town, the Beach offers several miles of sand fronting the cold waters of Lake Ontario and a lovely board-walk area crowded with strollers, joggers, and beautiful bodies during the summer. (There are also tennis courts and green parks en route.)

The area, which, before the city swallowed it up, was a "resort" for harried urban dwellers, is dotted with gorgeous old homes on either side of Queen Street, although rents soar on the south (water) side. Queen Street itself looks like a summer tourist town, complete with functional grocery stores for the locals and trendy gift and clothing stores for the tourists. In summer, bathing suits seem to be de rigueur.

For burgers and standard bar fare, try **Licks** (1960 Queen Street East; Tel: 416/362-5425), consistently rated among the best burger joints in the city, or, in the renovated old bank building across the street, the **Lion on the Beach** (1958 Queen Street East; Tel: 416/690-1984), an upscale English pub where a meal will put a dent in your wallet but at least provide the interest of an inventive menu.

The classic diner here, however, is the **Garden Gate** (2379 Queen Street East; Tel: 416/694-3605), known to all as the "Goof." This is the definitive small-town Chinese restaurant: wonderful food, huge portions, low prices. It is also across the street from a grungy old repertory movie house called the Fox, which itself is right beside a laundromat. A "beacher" can put the wash in, have dinner at the Goof, switch to the dryer, watch a film for $2, pick up the laundry, and walk home, stopping for an ice-cream cone on the way. A typical night in the Beach.

Other Beach highlights are provided by the **Sunset Grill** (2006 Queen Street East; Tel: 416/690-9985), one of the best-ever upscale greasy spoons, with long weekend lines for their huge breakfasts (served all day), and the tiny, informal **Spiaggia Trattoria** (2318 Queen Street East; Tel: 416/699-4656), which serves excellent Italian cuisine at the east end of Queen Street.

YORKVILLE

The major downtown area, at least for nightlife, bars and restaurants (Bellair, Bemelman's, Remy's), exclusive shopping (Holt Renfrew, Bretton's, David's), and hotels (the Intercontinental, Four Seasons, Park Plaza) is the Yorkville–Bloor area, in the center of the city just west of Yonge Street. This is chic and trendy at its finest, an area where you wear $200 jeans advertising someone else's name, and BMWs, Corvettes, and Cadillacs all jockey for the same illegal parking spots. (The police who have to work the weekend shift take great glee in towing cars off the streets every Friday and Saturday night, the theory being that anyone driving that type of car should be able to pay for it.)

Yorkville blooms with outdoor cafés and rooftop bars during the spring and summer, when Toronto emerges from its winter hibernation; quite often lunch becomes dinner and rolls on into the night. The wining and dining establishments are filled with the rich and those hoping to be.

On warm summer weekend nights, both Yorkville and Cumberland take on the atmosphere of a midway, with clowns, acrobats, street jugglers, and fortune tellers mixing with the bar-and-disco crowd.

Twenty-some years ago the area was a slum, a hangout for the hippie generation, headquarters for the city's burgeoning folk-club and coffeehouse scene, and rife with marijuana. It was also filled every weekend night, mainly with parents looking for their runaway children. In one of life's ironic twists, those same "lost" children are now buying expense-account lunches and designer leather jackets here with their American Express gold cards.

Yorkville also plays host to the **Festival of Festivals**, the world's largest film festival. Every September, movie fans and celebrities spend ten days packing theaters in the Yorkville–Bloor neighborhood to see more than 250 movies from around the world, including "gala" premieres from Hollywood, retrospectives, long-lost cinematic treasures, and the best of world cinema. Prices range from $275 for a gala pass (all films and parties) to a $125 daytime pass, good until 6:00 P.M.; for information, Tel: (416) 967-7371.

CASA LOMA

If you want to see a bit of old Toronto, there is no better spot than the city's famous 98-room castle, located at 1 Austin Terrace, northwest of Yorkville. Erected in 1914 at a cost of more than three million dollars by Sir Henry Pellatt, Casa Loma would be all but impossible to build today.

Sir Henry actually had the castle shipped over from Scotland, brick by brick, and then had it rebuilt, complete with secret passageways and hidden staircases. He even had carpeting put in the stables for his horses, which doubtless caused the cleaning staff no end of difficulties. All that effort and expense was not without its point, however. With its suits of armor, magnificent old pipe organ (conjuring up images of *The Phantom of the Opera*), turrets, and gargoyles, Casa Loma truly is a marvel—albeit one out of place and time, a tribute to one man's obsession. Today the huge edifice is operated by the Kinsmen Club and is open daily for tours; it also seems to be a popular spot for Saturday-night ballroom dancing and wedding receptions.

Museums and Galleries

Royal Ontario Museum

Toronto has a goodly number of museums, from the majestic Royal Ontario Museum (the ROM), at the corner of Bloor and University, to the tiny **Museum of the History of Medicine**, just around the corner on Bloor Street West. The ROM is by far the largest and most impressive. Renowned for its collection of Chinese antiquities, the ROM is also connected to the adjoining McLaughlin Planetarium, with its spectacular light show set to rock music, and has recently joined forces with the **George R. Gardiner Museum** across the street (open daily except Mondays), known for its delicate and colorful collections of ceramic art.

Ontario Science Centre

Located just northeast of the downtown core on Don Mills Road (call the Centre for bus information—Tel: 416/429-4100—or take a taxi, which will cost you about $10), this is one of the most fascinating museums in the country. Forget your eighth-grade science class; this is an all-day hands-on excursion that demonstrates the wonders of modern technology. As well, there are constantly changing displays throughout the pavilion, whose various escalator-linked levels cling to the side of the Don Valley ravine.

Art Gallery of Ontario

The AGO boasts the world's largest collection of Henry Moore pieces (look also for Moore's *The Archer* outside City Hall) as well as constantly changing touring exhibits. The museum sits on the corner of Dundas Street West and Beverley, four blocks west of the Eaton Centre, and also serves as an unofficial landmark marking this stretch of the city's Chinatown.

McMichael Gallery Canadian Collection

To see Canadian art at its best, be sure to visit this world-renowned gallery in Kleinburg (about 30 km/19 miles north of Toronto; take Highway 400, then head west on Major Mackenzie Drive). The gallery's collection of works by the so-called Group of Seven, those famous early-20th-century painters of the Canadian North, is second to none.

Libby's of Toronto

In Toronto itself, there are two major areas for art galleries: One is Yorkville, the second is on Queen Street West.

Serious collectors would be well advised to contact

Libby's of Toronto (Tel: 416/364-3730) for a gallery perusal or invitation to one of its soirées. Libby's represents some of the best up-and-coming Canadian artists in addition to its stable of well-established painters; representatives are available by appointment at their King Street East (number 463) gallery.

Performing Arts

Whether it's the performing, visual, or film arts, Toronto has joined the big leagues seemingly overnight. With the exception of New York City, there are more theaters here—ranging from the grandeur of the Royal Alex to the wooden benches at the Tarragon—than in any city in North America. Toronto is also the home of the **National Ballet Company**, headed by Reid Anderson; the **Canadian Opera Company** (COC), in search of a new director as this book went to press; and the renowned **Toronto Symphony**, conducted by Gunther Herbig.

Both the COC and the ballet use the 3,200-seat **O'Keefe Centre** (Yonge and Front streets) for their performances, as do most touring Broadway shows that come through town. Many English-theater imports play at the **Royal Alexandra** (perhaps because owner Ed Mirvish also owns the Old Vic in London), on King Street West across from the visually striking and acoustically perfect **Roy Thomson Hall** (home of the symphony). In May 1993 Mirvish opened his new 2,000-seat **Princess of Wales Theatre**, the first free-standing theater built in North America in 30 years, on the corner of King and John streets, where it will host an extended run of *Miss Saigon*.

The nearby **Pantages Theatre**, on Yonge Street, underwent a multimillion dollar renovation a few years ago, and is currently home to *The Phantom of the Opera*. The restoration was the brainchild of Toronto movie-mogul Garth Dabrinsky, father of the multiscreen cineplex theater. Dabrinsky recently announced his intention to leave the movie business in order to concentrate his energies on the municipally owned **Performing Arts Centre**, which opened in 1993 in the borough of North York. Designed by architect Eberhard Zeidler, the complex includes an 1,800-seat theater, a 1,000-seat recital hall, a smaller experimental theater, and a two-story art gallery.

On any given night there are dozens (hundreds, counting smaller cabaret and musical venues) of stage performances and musical concerts to choose from; check the three local papers (for entertainment, the *Toronto Star* is the best, followed by the *Toronto Sun* and the *Globe & Mail*) or the free *NOW* magazine, a weekly entertainment guide found on newsstands and in restaurants everywhere. The monthly *Toronto Life* and *TO* magazines are also available at newsstands.

For half-price tickets on the day of the show, visit the Five Star ticket booth on Yonge Street outside the Eaton Centre, just south of Dundas Street. The booth also provides a free magazine listing theater locations.

Festivals

There are more Italians living in Toronto than in Milan; Toronto also has the second-largest Chinese population on the continent and more West Indians than anywhere else outside those sunny islands. The city recognizes these elements and celebrates them annually with various ethnic festivals, ranging from the colorful crowds of Caribana and the mini–United Nations known as Caravan to the weekend Italian picnic on the Toronto Islands.

Caravan

For the two-week festival in June known as Caravan, the more than 70 ethnic groups that call Toronto home set up pavilions throughout the city in order to introduce metropolitan residents to the finest from their native countries. Demonstrations include Ukrainian dancers, an Oriental tea ceremony, and Jamaican reggae. For a mere $14 you can buy a Caravan passport, which is stamped as you enter the domain of each new country and entitles you to unlimited entry to dozens of buildings and tents during the festival. (You can also purchase individual tickets, but after three different pavilions you'll find you should have bought the passport.) The "location" of each country is listed on maps at the Caravan office (263 Adelaide Street West; Tel: 416/977-0466) as well as in the daily newspapers. There can be long lines at the most popular pavilions, which change annually: Check the papers and listen to local gossip for the best ones.

Caribana

Though a relative newcomer, the first-weekend-in-August celebration known as Caribana already attracts more than half a million people annually. (Heritage Day, the first Monday in August, creates a long weekend for Canadians; all banks and government offices and many stores close.) Caribana starts off with a parade along the lakeshore drive (see local newspapers for parade times and routes) and usually ends near the Harbourfront area, where the party continues all weekend. Food wagons en route dispense roti and rice, and the police often turn a judicious eye should they spy an occasional bottle of a substance meant to be consumed only on licensed premises. Caribana is not just for the West Indian population; it appeals to all who enjoy the reggae beat of the islands. The highlight of the festival comes on its final Saturday night with the Miss Caribana Ball on the Toronto Islands.

Other Festivals

The "Miss Bikini of the Year" contest is the highlight of the annual Italian-language **CHIN Radio Station Picnic** at the Exhibition Grounds (west of downtown, at the southern end of Bathurst Street) the first weekend in July. Advance photos of the contestants in local newspapers guarantee a good turnout of non-Italians, and of course the local Italian community comes out in full force for the four-day celebration of their heritage, complete with pasta, bocce balls, and (unofficial) homemade vino competitions.

Numerous other ethnic celebrations are held throughout the year, from a Portuguese music festival in a Dundas Street park to a Greek Orthodox street parade along the Danforth. Toronto is proud of the many "new Canadians" who have chosen to live here yet take pride in remembering their native heritage, in the process adding much to the cultural life of the city.

Street Scenes at Night

There are thousands of restaurants, bars, and cafés scattered throughout the city, but only certain areas are automatically recognized by locals as places where they can barhop. The most notorious scene is the **Eglinton Avenue** "strip" between the Berlin nightclub on Yonge Street east to Mount Pleasant. The bars and clubs in this area have all sprouted in the last decade or so to accommodate the singles who live in the houses and apartment buildings along the quiet streets surrounding the bustling Eglinton–Yonge intersection.

The **Esplanade** area, bounded by Yonge Street and the O'Keefe Centre to the west, Jarvis Street to the east, and Wellington Street to the north, is also rife with bars that have taken up residence in the old, now renovated, warehouses facing Front Street.

King Street West features the Roy Thomson concert hall, home of the Toronto Symphony, just across the street from a restored Victorian theater, the Royal Alexandra (or "Alex"), a

2,400-seat venue for the likes of Broadway road shows and the Royal Shakespeare Company. Owner Ed Mirvish, who also runs the quaint complex known as Mirvish Village behind his huge, garish Honest Ed's Discount Store on Bloor Street (see the Shopping section below), manages a number of restaurants in the area known for their size, reasonable prices, and acres of kitschy decor.

The newest hot spot, however, is the **SkyDome** area, thanks in part to the nightly crowds of 60,000 or so who flock to the Dome for sports events and concerts. Dozens of bars, restaurants, and cafés have opened in the area in the past several years, and the scene recently got even more feverish as about 6,000 CBC employees previously scattered around the city were relocated here.

(See the Bars and Nightlife section below for more on Toronto's after-dark scene.)

Paramount Canada's Wonderland

Located 30 km (19 miles) north of the city off Highway 400 in Maple, this theme park featuring three dozen rides is Toronto's five-month (May through September and weekends in October) version of Disneyland. For those more comfortable with their feet firmly planted on terra firma, there's plenty of entertainment to be had in the 370-acre park, including a Broadway-style musical theater, an aquarium show, a variety of performance venues, and plenty of restaurants. For ticket and pass information, Tel: (905) 832-7000. Connected with the park is the **Kingswood Music Theater**, a canopied concert stage that features musical acts; check the local papers for daily performances and prices.

GETTING AROUND

Toronto's **Pearson International Airport** (named for former Prime Minister Lester B. Pearson, but usually called simply Toronto International) has three terminals: Terminal One is the original airport; Terminal Two is the home of Air Canada, the national carrier, although a number of other airlines also use it; and Terminal Three, also known as the Trillium Terminal (the trillium is the official flower of Ontario), is the home of Canadian Airlines International, Canada's number-two carrier, as well as a number of other major carriers, including American Airlines, British Airways, Air France, KLM, and Lufthansa. Terminal Three is a state-of-the-art "people-friendly" terminal filled with ritzy stores for those who have some time to kill before takeoff.

The small **Toronto Island Airport** (at the base of Bathurst

Street) is mainly used for business commuter flights (for example, to Ottawa and Montreal) and STOL (short takeoff and landing) aircraft.

During peak times there is always a dearth of taxicabs at Toronto International; avoid arriving on a Sunday night if possible. The average fare downtown, approximately 30 km (19 miles) to the south and east, is about $40, including tip. For the same price you can take a limousine. Stands are found outside each terminal building. The best public transit deal in town, however, is the Airport Bus, which runs direct to the Royal York Hotel, at the corner of Front and University streets, across from Union Station, for a mere $10.

Toronto Transit Commission

The TTC is one of the fastest, cleanest, safest, and—most important—easiest-to-use transit systems in the world. Quite a claim, but true. Every year the subway/bus/trolley system wins awards for these distinctions. (In fact, the transit system mirrors the city, causing no less a personage than globe-trotting Renaissance man Peter Ustinov to remark that "Toronto is New York run by the Swiss.")

There are two main subway routes, the north–south Yonge Street line and the east–west Bloor line; the two meet at the corner of Yonge and Bloor, the commercial crossroads of downtown Toronto. The regular price of a ticket is $2.00; a package of five tokens can be purchased for $6.50, and a monthly "metro pass" goes for $64. Buses and trolley cars connect with each subway stop, which means you can get virtually anywhere in the city from anywhere else with the help of free transfers (there are machines placed thoughout the subway system, or ask the driver as you board a bus or trolley). You can also pick up free TTC Ride Guides at any subway entrance, as well as enlarged maps of the entire system. Subway entrances are readily identifiable by the TTC logo.

For many years the old streetcars, with their tracks imbedded in the concrete and power wires overhead, formed the spine of the TTC; when it was suggested they be replaced with buses, there was a great hue and cry from the public. So the TTC decided to order modern trolley cars instead, making Toronto one of the few North American cities still operating a viable, pollution-free trolley system. Watch for the relatively new articulated (or "accordion") trolleys and buses—double cars with flexible centers to accommodate their increased length.

A new light-rail transit line from Union Station services the growing Harbourfront area.

The TTC "GO" trains, the green and white double-decker trains that bring daily commuters into the downtown core, extend from Oakville in the west to Pickering in the east, a distance of some 68 km (42 miles). GO trains and buses also service 140 km (87 miles) of northern routes, from Richmond Hill to Georgetown. All GO trains, subways, and rail lines use Front Street's Union Station as their home base.

Taxis and Cars

Taxis are plentiful and readily available night or day. The rate set by the licensing commission is a flat $2.40 for the first 350 meters (approximately ¼ mile) and 25¢ for each succeeding 350 meters, up to four people. Standing adds another 25¢ every 65 seconds.

You should have no problem hailing a cab, especially in the downtown core, but if you need to call one, just check the Yellow Pages under "Taxicabs."

Drivers will find Toronto's gridlike layout easy to navigate. Street maps are available at any tourist information booth or corner newsstand (*The Perly's Guide* is the most comprehensive). Some streets may occasionally fool you; for instance, University Avenue changes its name to Avenue Road north of Bloor Street; Bloor Street East becomes the Danforth once it crosses the viaduct; College is Carlton east of Yonge. There are some one-way streets downtown off Yonge, and for a couple of blocks south of Dundas (Eaton Centre) you cannot make any turns off Yonge. But except for a few minor difficulties, Toronto is a very easy city to drive.

Avoid Yonge Street south of Bloor in the summer months. This is a "cruising" strip (misnamed—there is so much traffic you can hardly move), and one of the areas where Toronto shows a bit of its true face to the world—a visage that mirrors nothing more than small-town Canada on a Saturday night.

ACCOMMODATIONS

In Toronto, as in any major city with more than three million people, you get what you pay for in a hotel. Quite often, it seems, you pay for much more than you actually get, but that's the price of visiting an attractive city filled with tourists, conventioneers, travelling government officials, and business executives.

The rates given below are *projections* for peak seasons during the 1994 calendar year. Unless otherwise indicated, rates are based on double rooms, double occupancy; provincial and federal taxes are included in all rates. Few visitors ever pay these prices, however. Every Toronto hotel offers special summer rates, either for an extended stay or a weekend getaway; indeed, some of these savings are exceptional. Before booking a room, always double-check for special rates and packages.

When booking a room, have your credit card number at hand. The vast majority of Toronto hotels will refuse to hold a room for you without this magic little number. Cash will be accepted when it comes time to square the bill, of course, but the simple act of booking a room requires a major credit card.

The telephone area code for Toronto is 416.

Bloor Street/Midtown Chic

The ► **Four Seasons**, a glitzy gold-and-chrome palace, claims a landmark location at the beginning of the strip known as Yorkville, a stylish, expensive, and trendy enclave of restaurants and boutiques. Bring money, for both the neighborhood and hotel embody the glamour and affluence of a certain kind of lifestyle. Of course, the luxuriousness of the rooms and the quality of the service should soften the inevitable blow of the bill, while **Truffles** and the **Studio Café** both rate among the city's best dining rooms. Likewise, the hotel's street-level bars make for excellent, if pricey, people-watching spots. Voted one of the Leading Hotels of the World.

21 Avenue Road, M5R 2G1. Tel: 964-0411; Fax: 964-2301; in the U.S., Tel: (800) 332-3442; in Canada, (800) 268-6282. $308; $380 (deluxe suite).

The Four Seasons also operates the ► **Inn on the Park**, a total luxury complex with everything from barbershops to bars just 15 minutes north of the downtown core. Because it borders greenbelt parkland, guests can enjoy the added convenience of jogging trails or cross-country skiing right outside the hotel's back door.

1100 Eglinton Avenue East, M3C 1H8. Tel: 444-2561; Fax: 446-3308; in the U.S.; Tel: (800) 332-3442; in Canada, (800) 268-6282. $150–$218.

As one might expect of a hotel with a downtown location bordering Bloor Street and trendy Yorkville, the 213-room ► **Hotel Inter-Continental** has rates that start at $155 for a small double and go as high as $2,000 for a deluxe suite. That kind of money brings with it a wealth of stylish facilities and amenities, including well-appointed rooms, elegant public areas, 24-hour room service, a rooftop lap pool and tanning deck, a fully equipped gym, and a complete business center. Tired after a day spent touring the city? The hotel's wood-paneled **Harmony Lounge** is a soothingly refined retreat, as is the split-level **Signatures** restaurant, which offers its own inventive "moderne cuisine," featuring whatever is fresh at market that day.

220 Bloor Street West, M5S 1T8. Tel: 960-5200; Fax: 960-8269; worldwide, Tel: (800) 327-0200. $155–$275; $2,000 (deluxe suite).

Although located right across the street from the Four Seasons, the ▶ **Park Plaza** is a world away in style. More familiar than formal (although it did enjoy a multimillion-dollar refurbishing a few years ago), it has long been known as one of the city's grand hotels and for years played host to an old-line clientele that dined every Sunday evening in its stately **Prince Arthur Room**. Regulars are partial to its large, distinctly untrendy rooms, while locals frequent the hotel's rooftop bar for the splendid views of the city it offers. In recent years the Park Plaza has also become the unofficial September home of the city's ten-day film festival, listing everyone from Warren Beatty to Bette Midler among its guests.

4 Avenue Road, M5R 2E8. Tel: 924-5471; Fax: 924-4933; in the U.S. and Canada, Tel: (800) 268-4927. $133–$275.

The ▶ **Hotel Plaza II** is situated in the heart of the downtown area, with the stores and restaurants of Bloor Street and Yorkville within easy strolling distance. The 256-room hotel offers completely remodeled guest rooms and standard big-city-hotel amenities, including a health club, room service, and a brand new restaurant called **Matisse**.

90 Bloor Street East, M4W 1A7. Tel: 961-8000; Fax: 961-4635; in the U.S. and Canada, (800) 267-6116. $157.

Formerly a meeting place for Tory politicians, lawyers, and lobbyists because of its proximity to Ontario's Parliament Buildings, the ▶ **Sutton Place Grand Le Meridien** is today just as likely to attract visiting movie stars and pop-music celebrities. The millions of dollars that have been spent on renovations are evident in the hotel's gilded lobby, its dining and bar areas, as well as the rooms themselves. Several recent changes in ownership have not done much to alter the hotel's rather formal atmosphere, and lawyers and lobbyists in discreet conversation are still a staple of the scene here.

955 Bay Street, M5S 2A2. Tel: 924-9221; Fax: 924-1778; in the U.S. and Canada, Tel: (800) 268-3790. $150–$285.

On the Waterfront

The 980-room ▶ **Westin Harbour Castle** commands a magnificent view of the harborfront area—a good thing, too, because the hotel is rather inconveniently situated to the downtown core. Still, it does offer a complete range of amenities and facilities, including the **Regatta and Terrace** and **Grant Yacht** dining rooms, as well as the 35th-story **Lighthouse Restaurant**, which makes a complete 360-degree revolution every hour or so. And for a quick escape from everyday urban headaches, the Westin can't be beat: Ferries to the Toronto Islands leave from its back door every half hour throughout the summer months.

One Harbour Square, M5J 1A6. Tel: 869-1600; Fax: 869-0573; in the U.S. and Canada, Tel: (800) 228-3000. $200–$280.

While the 157-room ▶ **Radisson Plaza Hotel Admiral** is also incoveniently located to the downtown core, it is within strolling distance of SkyDome and well situated for a refreshing walk along the clean, green waterfront area to the arts, crafts, and entertainment offered in the Harbourfront complex. In addition to its superb kitchen and well-appointed rooms, it has a lovely fourth-floor outdoor pool area and glassed-in whirlpool with great views of the harbor.

249 Queen's Quay West, M5J 2N5. Tel: 203-3333; Fax: 203-3100; in the U.S. and Canada, Tel: (800) 333-3333. $82–$190.

Front Street to Midtown

Located directly across the street from Union Station, the ▶ **Canadian Pacific Royal York**, the 1,400-room grande dame of Toronto hotels, underwent a $95-million renovation a few years back. Still known as the largest hotel in the British Commonwealth, this CP Railway hotel epitomizes the term "faded elegance": The rooms have been redone, the service is good, there's an indoor pool, and the public areas are comfortable. Filled with restaurants and bars, it is also the home of the famed **Imperial Room**, the oldest continuously operating nightclub in North America, now used only for special functions.

100 Front Street West, M5J 1E3. Tel: 368-2511; Fax: 368-2884; in the U.S., Tel: (800) 828-7447; in Canada, (800) 268-9411. $180–$191.

Billed as the world's first hotel–cum–sports-and-entertainment complex, the ▶ **SkyDome Hotel** opened in time for the Blue Jays' 1990 season and has been turning heads ever since. Indeed, 70 of its 346 guest rooms offer magnificent panoramic views of SkyDome's playing field, with the tariff per night from $255 to $335 (and suites going as high as $1,430—it helps if you like baseball). Standard rooms with views of the city, on the other hand, start at about $150. In addition to all the usual business amenities and health-club facilities, the hotel has a good restaurant overlooking the playing field, and guests have the privilege (for an added fee) of reserving any of the four SkyDome boxes belonging to the hotel.

45 Peter Street South, M5V 3B4. Tel: 360-7100; Fax: 341-5090; in the U.S., Tel: (800) 828-7447; in Canada, (800) 268-9411. $130–$220.

Located behind the O'Keefe Centre at the corner of Yonge and the Esplanade, one block south of Front Street, the rather austere exterior of the ▶ **Novotel Toronto Centre** hides a most pleasant interior. The 266 rooms here are basic but well appointed, and the rates are reasonable, especially given the hotel's many first-rate amenities—from a health spa to fine dining in the **Café Nicole**. Its location near the bars of the Esplanade and the restaurants and nightlife along Front Street is another plus. And for those looking to make a quick getaway, it offers easy access to the Gardiner Expressway.

45 Esplanade, M5E 1W2. Tel. 367-8900; Fax: 360-8285; worldwide, Tel: (800) 221-4542. $125–$185.

The first eight stories of the 17-story tower housing the ▶ **Holiday Inn on King** are occupied by offices and parking lots; the hotel itself actually starts on the ninth floor. Rates for the 425 rooms here start at $150 and go as high as $215 a night for the deluxe suites, all of which have a Jacuzzi and wet bar. The hotel's two restaurants, the famous **Matsuri** and **Judy of Toronto** (with a menu ranging from lighter fare to more traditional cuisine), are both good, and its location just blocks from SkyDome in the middle of the fashion district— the name Judy refers to the annual fashion awards statuette—makes it popular with out-of-town sports fans as well as up-and-coming designers.

370 King Street West, M5V 1J9. Tel: 599-4000; Fax: 599-7394; worldwide, Tel: (800) 465-4329. $150; $215 (deluxe suite).

▶ **Crowne Plaza Toronto Centre**, the glass-and-steel structure just west of the Royal York, is connected to the huge Metro Convention Centre, which makes it a convenient convention property. The hotel's 555 rooms and 32 suites are tastefully decorated and come with all the standard CP amenities. Guests can treat themselves to four-star dining at **Chanterelles** (reserve; Tel: 597-8142), and there's all-day service under the soaring glass atrium of the hotel's **Orchard Café**. Such amenities notwithstanding, be prepared for slow service during peak hours.

225 Front Street West, M5V 2X3. Tel: 597-1400; Fax: 597-

8128; in the U.S. and Canada, Tel: (800) 465-4329. $155–$190.

Recently resurrected from its rather seedy state, the little 48-room ► **Hotel Victoria** has been given new life with an improved decor and comfortable lounge area. The rooms are small but cozy, and the rates reasonable. Its proximity to the Front Street theaters (the O'Keefe and St. Lawrence centers), the upscale bars of the Esplanade, and the St. Lawrence Market is an added bonus, especially as the hotel's restaurant serves only breakfast and lunch.

56 Yonge Street, M5E 1G5. Tel: 363-1666; Fax: 363-7327. $84–$105.

Despite its Old World grandeur and style, with porters offering white-glove service and desk clerks resplendent in morning suits, the old ► **King Edward Hotel** (or King Eddy, as it's affectionately known) had fallen on hard times when England's Trusthouse Forte restored it to its former glory in 1979. (As you enter the luxurious lobby, try to determine which are the new pillars and which the restored 90-year-old originals.) As for price, well, as the man said, if you have to ask. . . .

The various bars, especially the **Consort Bar** with its leather wingback chairs, are usually busy, and the excellent **Chiaro's** (pronounced with a *K*) and **Café Victoria** fill with old-establishment types and business executives during the lunch hour.

37 King Street East, M5C 1E9. Tel: 863-9700; Fax: 367-5515; in the U.S. and Canada, Tel: (800) 225-5843. $157–$263; the Royal Suite, with five bedrooms, boardroom, and sunken living room, is yours for $2,000 a night.

For a room with a view, cross Yonge Street to the west side of King, where the 53-suite ► **Camberley Club Hotel** occupies the 28th and 29th floors of the Scotia Plaza. Linked directly to Toronto's Underground City, this recent addition to the hotel scene has fast become a favorite with visiting bankers, lawyers, and brokers. Equipped with whirl-pool baths, color TVs, and VCRs, the Camberley's suites are tastefully decorated and large enough to serve as mini-boardrooms or private dining rooms. And because it's in the middle of Toronto's financial district, the hotel reduces its rates by 50 percent on weekends.

Scotia Plaza, 40 King Street West, M5H 3Y2. Tel: 947-9025; Fax: 947-0622. $246–$336.

Located across from City Hall on Queen Street West, the ► **Sheraton Centre Hotel and Towers** is known for its meeting rooms and exhibition halls galore, classy shops and cinemas (another link in the Underground City), and the elegant **Russian Winter Palace** dining room on the 42nd floor (temporarily closed at press time). Amid all this are scads of clean, functional rooms (1,399 of them), and bars and restaurants that won't break a vacation budget. Due to its location and size, the Sheraton is hard to miss, but to assist the visitor the hotel is now outlined at night with a one-mile string of lights.

123 Queen Street West, M5H 2M9. Tel: 361-1000; Fax: 947-4854, ext. 4689; in the U.S. and Canada, Tel: (800) 325-3535. $115–$230.

Ensconced in the heart of the city's legal/financial district, the 601-room ▶ **Toronto Hilton** (formerly the Toronto Westin) is a comfortable hotel designed for the expense-account traveller. The hotel has undergone some renovations since being taken over by the Hilton chain, and now features spacious and well-appointed rooms and suites along with a pool and gymnasium to help type-A personalities unwind after a busy day navigating the shoals of international finance. The **Garden Court** lobby restaurant is a popular spot at lunchtime and after five, as are **Trader Vic's** downstairs and the aptly named **Barristers Lounge**.

145 Richmond Street West, M5H 2L2. Tel: 869-3456; Fax: 869-3187; in the U.S. and Canada, Tel: (800) HILTONS. $118–$302.

Once known as an inexpensive downtown hotel, the ▶ **Delta Chelsea Inn** has raised its rates as its popularity has grown, and recent renovations have increased the number of rooms here to 1,600 (some with kitchenettes). The pool and sauna area seems to be especially popular with vacationing families. Elsewhere on the premises, the **Chelsea Bun** lounge, with some of the best Saturday afternoon jazz sessions in town, also has a local following as an after-five watering hole.

33 Gerrard Street West, M5G 1Z4. Tel: 595-1975; Fax: 585-4362; in the U.S. and Canada, Tel: (800) 268-1133. $125–$135.

With its entrance off Bay Street south of Dundas, just a short distance from historic Trinity Church and the city's largest shopping center, the newest addition to the Toronto hotel scene is the 18-story ▶ **Toronto Marriott Eaton Centre**. In addition to 459 spacious and brightly decorated rooms, the Marriott has a rooftop pool with panoramic views of the city, a fully equipped fitness center, a sunny atrium-style restaurant, dancing in its **Characters Bar**, and 24-hour room service for guests who don't feel like leaving their rooms in search of the all-night action along nearby Yonge Street.

525 Bay Street, M5G 2L2. Tel: 597-9200; Fax: 597-9211; in the U.S. and Canada, Tel: (800) 228-9290. $122–$162.

The ▶ **Ramada Downtown**, located behind City Hall, offers well-appointed rooms, a friendly bar (Dewey, Secombe, and Howe—which sounds more like an old-line law firm), a pleasant dining room, and an indoor and outdoor pool. And if you love Chinese food, you're in luck: The hotel is only steps from the culinary delights and Asian sights of the city's Chinatown on Dundas Street.

89 Chestnut Street, M5G 1R1. Tel: 977-0707; Fax: 585-3157; in the U.S. and Canada, Tel: (800) 2-RAMADA. $122–$162.

Recently acquired by the Best Western group, the almost-new ▶ **Best Western Chestnut Park** packs 522 rooms, a complete gym and health club, a large ballroom, several restaurants, and 20 meeting rooms into its 26 stories. It's also got a great central location, with the lights of Chinatown visible through your window.

108 Chestnut Street, M5G 1R3. Tel: 977-5000; Fax: 977-9513; in the U.S. and Canada, Tel: (800) 528-1234. $95–$215.

For out-of-town hockey fans and concert-goers, the moderately priced ▶ **Days Inn Toronto Downtown** is conveniently located just east of Yonge Street next to Maple Leaf Gardens. Management spent $4 million renovating its 536 rooms—as well as the lobby areas—a few years ago, and though the rooms may be on the small side, they are equipped with all the usual amenities. The hotel also has a sixth-floor pool and sauna, with adjoining summer sundeck, along with several bars and restaurants.

30 Carlton Street, M5B 2E9. Tel: 977-6655; Fax: 977-0502; in the U.S. and Canada, Tel: (800) DAYSINN. $77–$145.

The ▶ **Best Western Primrose Hotel**, a little farther east at the corner of Carlton and Jarvis, is another good moderately priced accommodation downtown. The glitzy lobby comes as a pleasant surprise after navigating the slightly seedy yet vibrant street scene outside, and the rooms are comfortable if a bit on the small side. The Primrose also has a great piano bar called the One Eleven Lounge, a café with an extensive menu, and an outdoor pool.

111 Carlton Street, M5B 2G3. Tel: 977-8000; Fax: 977-6323; in the U.S. and Canada, (800) 268-8082 or (800) 528-1234. $73–$167.

The ▶ **Quality Hotel by Journey's End** chain has been making major inroads into the Toronto market by providing affordable, no-frills accommodations in the heart of the city. Their 195-room downtown property on Lombard Street is across from the famous Second City/Firehall Theatre and just

east of bustling Yonge Street, while their newest venture is
located on Bloor Street West across from the Royal Ontario
Museum and close to the upscale shopping neighborhoods
of midtown. Neither is the Ritz, but they do offer good,
dependable lodging with all the standard amenities.

111 Lombard Street, M5C 2T9. Tel: 367-5555; Fax: 367-
3470; in the U.S. and Canada, Tel: (800) 668-4200. $95.

280 Bloor Street West, M5S 1V8. Tel: 968-0010; Fax: 968-
7765; in the U.S. and Canada, Tel: (800) 668-4200. $115.

Located one block east of the Eaton Centre, the very
affordable ▶ **Bond Place** is an ideal accommodation for the
out-of-town shopper who'd rather spend his or her time and
money searching out bargains in Toronto's myriad stores
and boutiques. Rooms here are small but comfortable, and
the public areas more than adequate. The immediate neighborhood is somewhat seedy but still scenic in a big-city way,
with a changing cast of colorfully dressed women strolling
the streets at all hours.

65 Dundas Street East, M5B 2G8. Tel: 362-6061; Fax: 360-
6406; in the U.S., Ontario, Quebec, and the Maritimes, Tel:
(800) 268-9390; elsewhere in Canada, (800) 387-1557. $77–
$88.

Want to sleep in the room Hemingway occupied as a cub
reporter for *The Toronto Star* during the 1920s? You can at
the ▶ **Hotel Selby**, a former Rosedale mansion built for the
Gooderham family. After falling on hard times, the Selby was
recently restored to its former glory while keeping its bargain rates. Many of the 67 rooms here boast their original
stained glass and 15-foot ceilings, and the chandelier in the
lobby was acquired from the Chrysler mansion in Michigan.
Other welcome changes at the so-called "Rosedale Valley
Inn" (just south of Bloor) include a refurbished outdoor
patio and a new menu. You may also notice that the hotel's
basement bar, **Boots and Buds**, caters to a largely male
clientele in the evenings. (For the record, the *Star* fired
Hemingway for failing to file his copy on time.) The Hotel
Selby now also offers health club privileges at the Bloor
Valley Health Club across the street as well as shared kitchen
facilities and a coin-operated laundry.

592 Sherbourne Street, M4X 1L4. Tel: 921-3142; Fax: 923-
3177; in the U.S. and Canada, Tel: (800) 387-4788. $69–$117.

Something Different

Situated slightly off the beaten track at Avenue Road and St.
Clair Avenue, the ▶ **Bradgate Arms** was created several
years ago when two adjoining apartment buildings were
enclosed under a glass dome. After extensive renovations,

the six-story lobby now has an airy look and feel to it, and the former apartments have been converted into small suites complete with kitchen facilities. The hotel is bright, clean, and surprisingly inexpensive.

54 Foxbar Road, M4V 2G6. Tel: 968-1331; Fax: 968-3743; in the U.S. and Canada, Tel: (800) 268-7171. $118–$129.

Airport Hotels

Toronto's airport strip has an array of good hotels that are mainly used by airport personnel, late-arriving or early-departing travellers, businesspeople, salesmen, and tourists who arrive in high season without advance bookings for a downtown hotel. Some offer a full range of amenities, from nightclubs to swimming pools, while others offer only the basics. The largest of the lot (with the most facilities) are:

▶ **Bristol Place**. 950 Dixon Road, M9W 5N4. Tel: 675-9444; Fax: 675-4421; in the U.S. and Canada, Tel: (800) 268-4927. $100–$190.

▶ **Regal Constellation**. 900 Dixon Road, M9W 1J7. Tel: 675-1500; Fax: 675-1737; in the U.S. and Canada, Tel: (800) 268-4838. $78–$100.

Others (all within sight of the airport) include the ▶ **Airport Hilton**, 5875 Airport Road, L4V 1N1; Tel: 677-9900; Fax: 677-7782; in the U.S. and Canada, Tel: (800) HILTONS; $145–$185. The ▶ **Best Western Carlton Place**, 33 Carlson Court, M9W 6H5; Tel: 675-1234; Fax: 675-3436; in the U.S. and Canada, Tel: (800) 528-1234; $113–$128. ▶ **Howard Johnson's**, 600 Dixon Road, M9W 1J1; Tel: 249-7671; Fax: 249-3561; in the U.S. and Canada, Tel: (800) 654-2000; $83–$168. And the ▶ **Holiday Inn Crowne Plaza**, 970 Dixon Road, M9W 1J9; Tel: 675-7611; Fax: 674-4364; in the U.S. and Canada, Tel: (800) 465-4329; $151.

Executive Travel Apartments/Suites

Apartments for couples, with or without children, and no limit (within reason) to the number of overnight guests, have also become popular with visitors. Executive Travel has various locations throughout the city; for example, their Bay Bloor Suites, right downtown, are fully equipped studios and one- and two-bedroom suites with complete kitchen, maid service, exercise facilities, pool and sauna, and 24-hour security. All accommodations are clean and well maintained. At about $100 per night, a bargain, especially for families or groups intending to linger for the better part of a week.

40 St. Mary Street, M4Y 2S8; Tel: 923-3000; Fax: 924-2446.

Bed and Breakfast

For those who prefer a homier atmosphere, **Metropolitan B & B Registry of Toronto** will send you a booklet containing their complete listings. To order, write or contact them at Suite 269, 615 Mount Pleasant Road, Toronto, M4S 3C5; Tel: 964-2566; Fax: 537-0233. Another source of information is **Toronto Bed and Breakfast**, P.O. Box 269, 253 College Street, Toronto, M5T 1R5; Tel: 588-8800 or 961-3676; Fax: 964-1756. Rates usually run about $50 to $60 for a double room, including breakfast, in a private home.

The quality, of course, may vary. To be on the safe side, contact the very friendly Linda Lippa at the **Downtown Toronto Association of Bed & Breakfast Guest Houses** (P.O. Box 190, Station B, Toronto, M5T 2W1, Tel: 690-1724; Fax: 690-5730). Her organization reserves large rooms in 30 refurbished Victorian homes throughout the city. Doubles start at $60 to $75, including breakfast. If you need recommendations on restaurants or theater, just ask Linda.

For a Complete Listing

Complete listings of Toronto accommodations for every style and pocketbook, from deluxe suites to little self-contained units, are available through the **Metro Toronto Convention and Visitors Association**, located at the Queen's Quay Terminal, 207 Queen's Quay West, P.O. Box 126, Toronto, M5J 1A7; Tel: 203-2600 or (800) 363-1990; Fax: 867-3995.

—Steve Veale

DINING

If we're talking about serious eating out, understand that Toronto dining shares in the general evolution of many—if not most—noncoastal North American cities. Pesto, garlic, mussels, calamari, satay, duck breast, goat's cheese, and the like have been well integrated into local menus; no longer do restaurants depend primarily on the stockyard. There's been an especially large increase in the popularity of fish, and even diner food tends to be leaner.

Grilling is probably the favorite method of cooking, with Franco/Italocized California the ideal, followed by a certain ethnic mania largely directed toward Southeast Asian cuisine in general and Thai food in particular (China and Japan prepared local palates ages ago). Ethiopian and Mauritian creole also find a place. But there is surprisingly little *real* Mexican or satisfactory Caribbean food to be had in Toronto, while Indian food is mostly Punjabi. Organic is the latest moniker to appear on local menus, which indicates at least an attempt to be sincere.

Many Torontonians eat out as a matter of course—before the theater, to entertain, just for a change—dress as they happen to be, and are usually just as particular as anyone else about value for money. Dining hours are fairly conventional, with most kitchens closing or closed by 10:00 P.M.; after that it's just snacks, though a few places serve meals up to about midnight. Most are completely dark on Sundays, though this is changing as pressure (mainly from business) increases to treat the day less sacrosanctly. The number of licensed dining establishments in the region, including pizza parlors and neighborhood eateries, is 3,400 or so. Which ones, then, really matter?

The dining-out trend has shifted from hotels (though some of their rooms do hold up well) and elaborate steak/lobster baronies to small 40- to 50-seat restaurants. It's mainly in places such as these that Toronto chefs are trying to make a name for themselves by bringing a signature touch to the anonymity of international cooking.

Another remarkable change is in the attitude toward the vocation of chef. It's no longer unusual for exceptionally bright physicists to abandon promising careers and apprentice in a kitchen—and this applies equally to both sexes. For those who eat out, this is a fortunate development, not to mention one that has resulted in a very welcome rise in the number of first-rate chef-owned restaurants—the pattern in France and Italy.

In general, Toronto's restaurants are much like its transportation system: dependable enough in attending to the basic requirements, often surprising in the method of delivery. Bad meals (or, at any rate, disgusting ones) are rare. The real problem now is survival, as a palpable fear has arisen among restaurateurs that the public just won't spend the way it used to on caviar and Bollinger. What to do: lower prices, lower standards, lower the blinds? Any restaurant that's undercapitalized, mismanaged, unwarrantably expensive, or operated by the fainthearted is unlikely to last in the 1990s.

Service in Toronto restaurants is usually good—up to a point. It's not unusual, even in the most expensive places, to find the salt cellar and pepper shaker on the table when dessert is being served, or to have plonk served like expensive bubbly (or vice versa).

As for wines, local restaurant lists all too often rely on basic blends, but there are an increasing number that are breaking out of these unimaginative confines, almost always where the cooking is trying to do the same. Markups tend to represent greed; there's really no reason to charge more than 100 percent above cost, especially for low-end, high-volume products in low-end, high-volume restaurants.

Summer is a beloved time of the year in Toronto, and many restaurants here make it a point to have a suitable open-air area for consuming edibles and potables. Obviously, the most comfortable are away from noxious street fumes, preferably in a back enclosure shaded by trees.

All the major hotels have dining rooms; if we mention particular ones, it's because they are worthwhile for nonresidents to consider. Barring closure or a complete change in ownership, the following restaurants, their order alphabetical, deserve the most serious attention: Barolo, Centro, Ia Fenice, Le Bistingo, Lotus, N44°, Notorious, Orso, Palmerston, Seasons, and Truffles. Among the leading dispensers of non-Western cuisines, pay special attention to Lee Garden and Roppongi for Chinese; Babur and the Moghul for Indian; Ematei, Nami, and Yamase for Japanese; and Bangkok Garden, the Original Vietnam, Thai Magic, and Vanipha for Southeast Asian.

Those restaurants discussed below without an indication of price, subtle or otherwise, fall into the moderate category, which would mean $70 to $90 (Canadian) for two, including wine, gratuity, and tax. The last will add an average of 15 percent to the basic tab.

The telephone area code for Toronto is 416.

Downtown/Harbourfront to Dundas Street

The King Edward Hotel on King Street East has within its bosom the **Café Victoria** (Tel: 863-9700), whose large windows offer street views; best for Sunday brunch, weekday lunch, or a novel pre-theater prix fixe that allows you to return for dessert after the performance. Afternoon tea is served in the lounge.

Located behind it are **Tom Jones** (Tel: 366-6583), a steakhouse with all the trimmings, from shrimp cocktail and Black Forest cake to fawning service and ranked French growths; and **Maccheroni** (Tel: 515-7560), for cheapo bruschetta, pastas, and salads. The latter's forecourt provides alfresco environs, particularly pleasant come late afternoon, and there's a midtown branch at 83 Bloor Street East. **Vines** (Tel: 869-0744), east of Maccheroni along Wellington Street, is a cellar seriously devoted to the grape (a good selection, and oftentimes a regional promotion); food is not so gravely considered here, but cold trout and cheese plates shouldn't disappoint.

Though quite different in style, **Shopsy's** (Tel: 365-3333) and **Penelope** (Tel: 947-1159), which occupy the same office building opposite the O'Keefe and St. Lawrence performing arts centers (Yonge and Front streets), share a street-side outdoor area: The first is a deli, with roots in what was once the Jewish quarter along Spadina, and with aspirations (sometimes salty) to New Yorkese; the second touts Greek cuisine in a modern way.

For Italian in the high-butterfat manner, there's **Amalfi** (227 Church Street; Tel: 861-0643), which is also much favored by partying groups. **Florentine Court** (97 Church Street; Tel: 364-3687) follows suit in more gilded environs. Nearby **Golden Thai** (105 Church Street; Tel: 868-6668) appeals to penny-pinchers bent on satay and such for lunch, and in the right light is not completely unsmart. Aficionados of Japanese cuisine will probably enjoy **Nami** (55 Adelaide Street East; Tel: 362-7373), with its excellent *robata* counter and a most attractive midnight-blue setting, as well as the plainer-looking **Takesushi** (22 Front Street West; Tel: 862-1891), particularly if making it to the theater on time is important. When children are part of the group, the all-beef burgers at **Hughie's** (22 Front Street West; Tel: 364-2242) should keep everyone happy.

La Maquette (111 King Street East; Tel: 366-8191), in a historic 19th-century property, adjoins the Sculpture Garden and offers views of St. James Cathedral across King Street at Church—most advantageously appreciated over a French-ified lunch from a second-floor conservatory abutment (or in summer on the patio underneath it). Summer, too, finds a fountain-centered back terrace at **Biagio** (157 King Street East; Tel: 366-4040), with the restaurant proper on the ground floor of Toronto's first public meeting place, St. Lawrence Hall, built in the 1850s. Intelligent cooking (risottos, much seafood) in the best Italian tradition; ditto service.

Although a branch of an international chain, **Bombay Palace** (71 Jarvis Street; Tel: 368-8048) exhibits enough individuality, particularly at its buffet lunch. Around the corner, **Rodney's Oyster House** (209 Adelaide Street East; Tel: 363-8105) purveys the named bivalve and other crustaceous sea creatures (kept fresh in back-room holding tanks after their journey from the Maritimes) at a bar with a few tables in the plainest of basement areas; crowded at lunch, a bit less so at night. Note: Its anonymous street frontage makes it hard to locate.

The venerable **St. Lawrence Market South**, at Front and Jarvis streets, certainly merits a tour (closed Sundays and Mondays), and also offers all the makings of an unforgettable picnic lunch, from peameal bacon on a kaiser roll to barbecued chicken Portuguese-style to unusual soups, cashew baklava, and various cheeses. Come Saturdays, the north building is transformed into an exhibit hall and market for the products and crafts of local farmers and food entrepreneurs, with everything from maple syrup to quail's eggs for sale.

The dining room in the Hotel Victoria (dubbed **56 Yonge** after the street number; Tel: 363-1666) offers a comfortable environment for a decent lunch, as does **Orestion** (20 Adelaide Street East; Tel: 368-7571), which welcomes with Greek food (mainly) in large portions (always). Weekday afternoons from 2:30 to 5:30 the dowager Royal York Hotel (100 Front Street West, Tel: 368-2511) serves a formal tea (three-tiered plates and all) in its **Acadian Room**. **Chanterelles** (225 Front Street West; Tel: 597-1400) is the Crowne Plaza Toronto Centre's successful effort to provide cosmopolitan luxe amid impressionistic oils, with seafood and white meats its best main dishes. One block to the north, at the corner of Emily and Wellington, glass-fronted **Chez Max** (Tel: 599-9633) practices solid bourgeois cooking, freely mixing the regional cuisines of France.

Down by the harbor, **Commodore's** (Tel: 203-3333) in the Radisson Plaza Hotel Admiral offers lovely views over the water to Hanlan's Point and the Island airport (where smaller aircraft take off and land), as well as a pricey international menu. You'll find the **Pink Pearl Harbourfront** (Tel: 203-1233) for decent dim sum, and **Spinnakers** (Tel: 203-0559) for afternoon tea or a drink at sundown, in Queen's Quay Terminal. If you do take the ferry over to Centre Island, a nice place for an ice-cold beer and a hamburger is **Island Paradise** (to the right of the docks); from here you can see the city's skyline, as well as the comings and goings of amateur rowers and sailors, in temperatures at least ten degrees cooler than on the mainland. Open mid-April to mid-October.

The very up-priced Art Nouveau-ish **Winston's** (Tel: 363-1627), at 104 Adelaide Street West, has long been a hangout for corporate types, with beef and Dover sole served in ritzy surroundings, and a wine list to match. The restaurant was given a facelift recently, and is now a somewhat friendlier, more informal place, thanks to the management style of Joe Allen's John Maxwell.

Around the corner on York, **Mövenpick on York Street** (Tel: 366-5234) surprises right away by contradicting the rule that dining spots found near hotels are, by definition, ho-hum. This one offers alfresco dining (both facing the street and in an inner court), breads and cakes baked on the premises, full breakfasts and extensive buffets, and a solid wine list. Its Belle Terrasse is informal but not inexpensive, while its Rössli dining room is the place for more refined and expensive Swiss/Continental dishes. Open daily year-round, including Christmas.

Marché (Tel: 366-8986), Mövenpick's other downtown eatery, is located in BCE Place, an attractive galleria-style complex occupying most of the Bay–Wellington–Yonge block. Wine, beer, and food are dispensed from staff-worked stations (pasta booth, salad bar, bakery, meat grill, etc.) in this food emporium, with patrons toting trays from one to the other, then choosing a seat in one of the many themed areas. Open from 7:30 A.M. till 2:00 A.M., it's a very busy place, with off-peak hours the most comfortable; a fascinating experience for children as well.

The Bay, a grand—meaning proper—department store opposite Old City Hall, has on its eighth floor the elegant **Arcadian Court**, where a pianist plays melodies beneath crystal chandeliers. Go for lunch and the buffet on Thursday evenings. **Senator** (Tel: 364-7517), opposite the Pantages Theatre's Victoria Street entrance, has turned itself into a retro theme park, with diner fare in a like setting, huge steaks served in a room of curtained booths (complete with little bells to summon staff), and a jazz emporium upstairs. Much beloved by visitors from outside North America, it also has an extensive list of California wines. **Denison's Brewing Company and Restaurants** (Tel: 360-5877), located two blocks south of St. Michael's Hospital on the same street, is bifurcated by gleaming kettles in which its own commendable potables are brewed. Its pastas and grills will also interest diners. Across the way, **Portico Bar and Restaurant** (Tel: 601-3774), at the corner of Richmond and Victoria in the Cambridge Suites Hotel, specializes in a sort of California-style cookery, deftly handled and with a hint of the Orient. The **Silver Rail** (225 Yonge Street; Tel: 368-8697) was born a steakhouse in 1947, and so it remains. Popular with legal types at lunch, and with Pantages Theatre–goers before the curtain goes up.

King Street West/Theater and Concert Dining

It's westward-ho to an area bounded by the Royal Alexandra Theatre to the north and SkyDome to the south for the next concentration of dining establishments. Where there are circuses there must be bread, so naturally, the northern side of the huge stadium offers **Windows on SkyDome** (Tel: 341-2424), serving (buffet-style) real (as opposed to fast) food on marbled tables along with views of the outfield. **Barootes** (Tel:

979-7717), on King Street near the Royal Alex, serves a varied menu, from noodles to poached salmon, in confines vaulted like a wine cellar. Neighboring Il Fornello, part of a mini-chain, is a local pioneer of the oven-baked pizza, and offers enough variety in its toppings to please fussy aficionados, especially children.

Orso (106 John Street; Tel: 596-1989) and La Fenice (319 King Street West; Tel: 585-2377) do Italy proud: Orso, in an ex-Victorian farrier's, has a delightful second-floor patio, lots of folkloric pottery, and trout and rapini doing their share to keep one and all happy, some nights unto the stroke of twelve; La Fenice, in a designer's echo chamber, is the home of breathtaking risottos, an hors d'oeuvre trolley of flavorful simplicity, and olive oil–anointed grills of the freshest fish. In Milan-smart basement quarters downstairs, La Fenice becomes a pasta and wine bar, with the sophisticated menu choices undiminished and the final tab most definitely so.

Located between John and Spadina on King Street West, Marcel's and Guadeloupe do France—and the French West Indies—proud, not to mention comfortably. At high-ceilinged Marcel's Bistro (Tel: 591-8600), upstairs at number 315, regional cooking is often showcased, and the restaurant's hours are wonderfully civilized (lunch is served until 4:00 P.M., as are desserts and attendant beverages after the theater). As of June 1993, the space downstairs from Marcel's has been taken over by Guadeloupe (Tel: 591-3600), which serves, as its name suggests, French island cuisine.

The chops at Lazoff's Meteor Chophouse (41 Peter Street; Tel: 979-7825) are veal, of course, the favored accent lemongrass. Prices at this largish, snazzy 1940s-style room are reasonable, as they are at Alice Fazooli's (294 Adelaide Street West; Tel: 979-1910), a favorite of boisterous sports-loving crowds. The extensive menu features things like Southern-style seafood (alligator bisque), American-style Italian dishes (cannelloni with scallops, shrimp, and crab stuffing, ricotta cheese, and spinach), wines (100 or so) by the glass, and umpteen beers on tap—making it especially suitable for younger diners who like to mix and match appetizers. Crowded but manageable most nights—unless, of course, the Blue Jays are in town.

Attentive service, private dining rooms, and elegantly restrained decor are part of the experience at Roppongi (230 Richmond Street West; Tel: 977-6622). Named after a fashionable district of Tokyo, Roppongi aims for sophistication throughout. It begins in the kitchen, which produces marvelous renditions of Szechuan, Cantonese, and Chiu-Chow dishes with little oil, no MSG, and no discordant ingredients. The menu is interesting and extensive (but not daunting), and ranges from sea slug in mayonnaise to shark's fin soup and Peking duck. One of the best Chinese restaurants in the city, Roppongi is a favorite of Japanese business travellers.

With its slitted window of plastic food replicas, **Yamase** (317 King Street West; Tel: 598-1562) could be mistakenly judged set-menu Japanese; the approach here, however, is to serve a range of appetizers and lesser-known dishes, including lots of salt-cooked food. Grazers head for **Fred's Not Here** (Tel: 971-9155), Yamase's near neighbor, for cheddar-duck enchiladas, grilled rabbit, and a much-admired wine list; it's all quite jolly.

Filet of Sole (Tel: 598-3256), at 11 Duncan Street (one of the boundaries of the Royal Alex's block), is a busy concourse at lunch and between 6:00 P.M. and curtain time. You may have to speak more forcefully than usual—the sound bounces around quite a bit in this big-windowed former warehouse—when ordering something from its extensive menu of sea creatures (fried, steamed, broiled, or barbecued) or its wine list, whose prices show a praiseworthy restraint in markup. Across the way at number 20, the **Duncan Street Grill** (Tel: 977-8997) improbably—but successfully—combines eclecticism (deep-fried this, Thai-healthy that, sugary finishes) with a singles bar and children's menu.

Amsterdam (133 John Street; Tel: 595-8201) is full of metropolitan razzmatazz, as befits a brew-pub of this size. The same can be said of **Rotterdam** (600 King Street West; Tel: 868-6882), a kindred enterprise. The food at both tends to strong flavors (it's better at Amsterdam), and each has seating on the boulevard for the enjoyment of good weather.

Queen Street West

There are some serious gastronomic islets in this laid-back sea of spiked hair and uninhibited opinions, generally between John and Spadina. Most expensive as well as most accomplished is **Le Bistingo** (number 349; Tel: 598-3490), where freshness and verve à la Française can astound, and the regular clientele, attended by a staff possessed of an accomplished restaurant pedigree, brings plenty of glamour to the scene. With a menu that includes some bistroisms (toulouse sausage), some trendiness (five-spice chicken with Chinese noodles), a few classics (hot apple tart with Calvados ice cream), and some crackerjack wines, it's unlikely that Le Bistingo will disappoint.

Beautiful scenery and attractive food arrangements are

integral to the pleasure of eating at **Ema-tei** (30 St. Patrick Street; Tel: 340-0472). Absolute freshness, however, is the prime reason its Japanese repertoire is reckoned to be outstanding, with seafood the key indicator in this regard. The tradition of pure tastes is confidently upheld here, as are those of having discreetly sectioned rooms and unhurried service.

The crowd at **Le Sélect** (328 Queen Street West; Tel: 596-6405 or 6406) spills onto Queen Street when the weather warrants, and there's added merriment come Beaujolais nouveau time, when it's a sea of blue suits and striped ties. The menu, which carries traces of many foreign accents, is anything but predictable, on the other hand. Across the street at **Raclette** (number 361; Tel: 593-0934) wine is serious business. The usual cheese/fondue dishes as well as chicken and fish in the contemporary mode dominate its modest menu.

Queen Street West is an area worth strolling, especially if a diversity of human interests or secondhand books and odd little edibles makes your day. A study in sea-green tranquillity, **Sushi Bistro** (number 204; Tel: 971-5315) caters to the vogue for small bites in the Japanese manner, while the **Queen Mother Café** (number 208; Tel: 598-4719) attracts a casual crowd with its chicken and shrimp with Laotian-Thai spicing. Its relative, the **Rivoli** (number 334; Tel: 596-1908), uses the same Southeast Asian accents in a more sophisticated way (it also has more ponytails per square inch), and its front terrace is *the* place to view the passing parade. **Zaidy's** (number 225; Tel: 977-7222) offers a taste of New Orleans and Cajun country, those accents always on fish and sometimes, surprisingly, on osso buco. The crowd at **Express** (number 254; Tel: 596-0205) stays ahead of the curve with Mediterranean-cum-California pizzas and pastas, in basic surroundings. The **Epicure Café** (number 512; Tel: 363-8942) pulses with the concentrated din and aromas of a left-bank *boîte;* portions are filling, the wines youthfully vigorous. If it's tripe soup and other Czech favorites you crave, nearby **Pepo's** (number 676; Tel: 860-0514) will humbly provide same, while **Cities** (number 859; Tel: 594-3762) is every foodie's neighborhood dream—inventive (try the filo stuffed with goat cheese in a cashew sauce), urbane (coral-colored walls and an Elvis bust in the bar), and reasonably priced.

Queen's parallel thoroughfare, Richmond West, becomes particularly dreary in this neighborhood, although there is a restaurant that might interest: **Masa** (number 205; Tel: 977-9519) is reliable for things like tempura soba and seafood yosenabe. Tucked in an aged off-Queen warehouse district, **Mildred Pierce** (99 Sudbury Street; Tel: 588-5695) affects the campiness of a mock film set; the cooking, however, is most assured—duck confit with peach coulis, chickpea-battered eggplant with mayo—the dishes typical of a sort of well-considered unorthodoxy that passes for bistro moderne.

Chinatown/West of Yonge

First- and second-generation Chinese no longer restrict themselves to the Spadina/Dundas axis, and their restaurants are scattered throughout the metropolitan area as a result. These days the Vietnamese (mainly ethnic Chinese) have moved in to take their place. Still, enough Chinese establishments remain to give assurance that the district has not been misnamed. (For the best Shanghai cooking, though, you'll have to trek to **Fon Son**, 356 Eglinton Avenue West, Tel: 489-7766, a 20-minute cab ride north of Chinatown.)

As drab and harshly lit as any restaurant in Chinatown, **Lee Garden** (358 Spadina Avenue; Tel: 593-9524) remains the benchmark of Cantonese cooking in the city. The selection of ingredients at its disposal is vast, with the offerings running the gamut from exotica (pig entrails) to seafood to sticky-sweet ribs, lily bulbs, and always fresh pineapple. Lines are the rule—even with a reservation you might have to wait—but once ordered, your meal comes quickly. There's no charm here whatsoever, but neither is there any rudeness or crudeness. **Chinatown International** (421 Dundas Street West; Tel: 593-0291), more expensive, is best appreciated for its trolley-served dim sum. Behind a window filled with lacquered birds, **Kom Jug Yuen** (371 Spadina; Tel: 977-4079) buzzes with customers partaking of their very affordable northern-style items. **Champion House** (480 Dundas Street West; Tel: 977-8282) and **Lucky Yu** (536 Dundas Street West; Tel: 598-7823) also offer northern-style cooking; the former is more comfortable and is renowned for Peking duck and a vegetarian-only menu on Mondays. **Yueh Tung** (Tel: 977-0933), which has a particularly fetching way with oysters in black bean sauce, occupies a barn of a room dominated by a huge television set at 111 Elizabeth Street, near City Hall. The red, yellow, and green curries of Thai cookery liven up the menu at tiny **Chieng Mai** (112 Dundas Street West; Tel: 599-8308), which also does wonderful things with chicken wings (they're boned and stuffed with pork and mushrooms).

Wah Sing (Tel: 596-1628), one of several diverse restaurants along a short tree-shaded stretch of Baldwin Street (which runs parallel to Dundas Street), is a real seafood treasure (at number 41–43). You'll find a varied French-style menu at antiques-filled **La Bodega** (number 30; Tel: 977-1287), more forthright French food at **Gaston's** (its onion soup is a local legend; number 35; Tel: 596-0278), the curries and chilies of the Malaysian-Singaporean tradition at **Ole Malacca** (number 49; Tel: 340-1208), and excellent little heart pleasers at **Kowloon Dim Sum** (number 5; Tel: 977-3773), which also has a regular, mainly Cantonese, menu.

Lots of white plastic brightens **Sri Malaysia** (number 1; Tel: 585-9052); more to the point, so does its Chinese-Malay cooking. **La Soirée** (number 17; Tel: 581-1676), where salmon might be merrily partnered to strawberries on a given evening, offers an economical prix fixe, while **Café La Gaffe**'s (number 24; Tel: 596-2397) eminently digestible bistroisms run to steamed mussels and dijon chicken. In addition to its other Cantonese items not usually encountered, **Sam Yuet**'s (number 45; Tel: 351-0398) specialty is sautéed scallops garnished with deep-fried milk orbs. For the late-night boho, **John's Italian Café** (number 27; Tel: 596-8848) serves up lots of pizza and grappa, along with a bizarre, if amiable, crowd that fills the tables around the jukebox or on its Baldwin Street patio.

Gentle little **Babur** (279 Dundas Street West; Tel: 599-7720) impresses with the range of its culinary ambitions. The tandoor-based cooking is often brilliant, with the clay oven giving a wood-smoke edge to breads and meats alike. Curries are also well represented on the menu, and even the mango chutney is more interesting than the norm. Just around the corner at 122 St. Patrick Street, **Young Lok Garden** (Tel: 593-9819) caters to Western tastes with all-day, open-kitchen dim sum and dishes inspired by many regions.

Slightly north of Dundas Street, at 18 Elm Street, is the Thai-oriented and glamorous **Bangkok Garden** (Tel: 977-6748). No expense was spared in converting the Victorian-era premises into stage-set tropicana. Spirit house, masses of teak, even a babbling brook—it's all here, and without any of it seeming spurious. The menu encompasses all the cooking techniques of Thailand, making it very easy for patrons to order a balanced meal, and the always fresh ingredients are blended with skill and inventiveness. The **Moghul** (Tel: 597-0522), across the street at number 33, specializes in the cuisine of northern India. The breads here are particularly fine, and the desserts are second to none.

On the same short stretch of Elm, at number 7, high-quality grilled meats and a late-night menu star at **Barberian's** (Tel: 597-0225); a hybrid—and pleasingly executed—menu of filet mignon, satay, and southern Italianisms suit smartly tiled

Teula (number 35; Tel: 597-0020); cold cherry soup and similar Hungarian fare are featured at **Csarda** (number 43; Tel: 971-8843), where a wandering violinist adds color; and modern Italian *cucina* is the order of the day, as it has been for 60-odd years, at dependable **Old Angelo's** (number 45; Tel: 597-0155).

Maple Leaf Gardens/East of Yonge

Maple Leaf Gardens is the venue for thousands of events, including hockey games, track meets, Pavarotti recitals, rock concerts, and the like, and so has occasioned the establishment of eateries throughout the Yonge/Carlton/Church area. Most of them are ordinary (to be charitable) and a few—the expensive ones—worthy.

   Carman's Club (26 Alexander Street; Tel: 924-8697) is a club in name only, for all are welcome to partake of its steaks and some nice Greek-style go-withs. **George Bigliardi's** (463 Church Street; Tel: 922-9594) is another grand emporium for lobster or a favored cut of beef, this time Italian-accented. Across the way at number 504, **Gatsby's** (Tel: 925-4545) highlights the century's earlier days, with Tiffany lamps and substantial portions two of the best things about it.

Midtown Chic

There is a clutch of major hotels in the vicinity of Bloor and Avenue Road, many with fine dining rooms. For example, the Inter-Continental's **Signatures** (220 Bloor Street West; Tel: 324-5885) is well liked for its cosmopolitan touches and rather formal offerings. As an added bonus, afternoon tea in the hotel's **Harmony Lounge** (Tel: 960-5200) has all the desired components (including a crackling fire). The Park Plaza (4 Avenue Road) successfully essays both familiar and current styles in its magical glassed-in room on the 18th floor, now christened **The Roof** (Tel: 924-5471); there are also a few tables outside on the terrace for drinks and views of capital interest (over the Ontario Parliament Buildings, for instance). **Prego** (Tel: 920-9900), opposite the Park Plaza on Renaissance Plaza, strives for modernity the California way, using mock Chagallery to catch the eye. **Enoteca**, with which it shares an entry (and a telephone number), offers white walls and the warmth of wood, quality wines, and comparatively inexpensive nosh, the inspiration being Tuscany.

   Bemelmans (Tel: 960-0306) and the **Bellair Café** (Tel: 964-2222), both off nearby Bellair Street on Bloor and Cumberland respectively, flirt with the ingredients of sunnier climes. Both are also noisy, but then the bar is their primary money-maker. Which may very well be the case at **Acrobat** (1221 Bay Street; Tel: 920-2323), where weekend waiting lines can get downright discouraging (the-young-and-the-hip take over by 9:00 P.M.). The decorative flourishes on a basic theme of warm woods and brushed stainless steel are extraordinary, and include fish tanks shaped like Champagne flutes, a wavy installation of grappa bottles, and a ceiling cluster of cherubs and vine leaves. The menu is varied and extensive (tempura, pizza, fish, grills, etc.)—providing you can afford it.

The Four Seasons Hotel, at Avenue Road and Yorkville, has the very expensive **Truffles** (Tel: 928-7331), from whose banquettes can be seen a passing parade of Eurodignitaries, usually dressed to the nines. Food and wine of a very high standard are the norm here. Twinned with it is the hotel's **Studio Café**, where the Japanese breakfast, halibut burgers, and buttermilk-mashed potatoes reign supreme in a pearly-white art gallery setting. A blue-checkered respite from such splendor can be found on the other side of Avenue Road at **Fieramosca** (number 52; Tel: 323-0636), where sausages and cream come together with pasta, and the squid is decidedly fried.

Yorkville Avenue and vicinity, east of Avenue Road, harbor a diversity of establishments. **Il Posto** (148 Yorkville; Tel: 968-0469) cocoons those dining outside in the confines of shop-enclosed York Square; inside, it handles northern Italian cuisine well enough in what feels like a swank club for residents of the ritzy condos nearby. Mövenpick's two uptown restaurants, **La Pêcherie** (Tel: 926-9545) and the more moderately priced **Bistretto** (downstairs from La Pêcherie; same phone), offer, respectively, seafood (mainly) ordered off a chalkboard and done every which way, and the informality of mussels, *frites,* and the like—until 1:00 A.M. at both places most nights. **Zero** (as in aircraft, not valuation; 69 Yorkville; Tel: 961-8349) surprises with budget Japanese cuisine served in stark surroundings.

Only a few steps away on the west side of Bay Street at number 1280, the **Sultan's Tent** (Tel: 961-0601), with a tidy prix fixe, is the place for indulging in Moroccan fare—and viewing belly dancers—while lolling on comfortable cushions. On Bay Street's east side, modest **Gilles' Bistro** (number 1315; Tel: 923-1005) is cannily run by alumni from Mövenpick's Yorkville operation.

Behind the Park Plaza on Prince Arthur Avenue, **Yves Bistro** (Tel: 972-1010) is all about modernized French fare (say, creole-inspired marmite), debonair service (enough so to warrant wearing a tie, although it's not required), and prix-fixe value for your money. **Le Rendez-Vous** (14 Prince Arthur Avenue; Tel: 961-6111) inclines to Provence—and expertly so—as well as to calorie-rich opulence; it also has an impressive wine cellar, and is suitable for Sunday brunch.

Cumberland Street has its share of hooks for hungry passersby. Spacious and amiable **Shogun** (number 154; Tel: 964-8665) has sushi-based set dinners, beauteous fruit plates, and gaudy cocktails. Its neighbor, **Jacques' Bistro du Parc** (number 126A; Tel: 961-1893), specializes in omelettes, though there's much else to choose from on the menu. There is also a view of the street from its second-floor windows, as well as of the new park opposite.

The **Pink Pearl** (120 Avenue Road; Tel: 966-3631) has all the smart accoutrements of a big-city restaurant, with chopsticks on the table the only indication that Cantonese and other regional dishes are the fare. On the same block is **Arlequin** (Tel: 928-9521), which boldly rummages through the Mediterranean, particularly Provence, with panache in a pretty little pink room at 134 Avenue Road.

Though the surrounding clamor is pure Anglo, **Le Paradis** (166 Bedford Road; Tel: 921-0995) does a very good imitation of a popular Paris bistro, with solid wines, well-crafted and robust food, and fair prices. The titillating artwork at **Joso's** (202 Davenport Road; Tel: 925-1903), around the corner, does not upstage the fresh seafood on the menu, though the mega-garlicky black Sicilian spaghetti almost does. A short cab ride west takes you to the **Indian Rice Factory** (414 Dupont Street; Tel: 961-3472), whose California-café exterior belies the authenticity of its subcontinental specialties.

Metropolis (838 Yonge Street; Tel: 924-4100) uses local produce and products, on the whole effectively. The main room, bright with sunny colors, leads to a back patio, and the wine list—much of it offered by the glass, and much of it Canadian—is interesting. For those who find excessive chile heat tiresome, if not intolerable, **Thai Orchid** (813 Yonge Street; Tel; 925-2599) is most understanding in this respect, with no apparent lack of authenticity in its cooking.

On Bay Street, the Sutton Place Hotel is very smart, and **Sanssouci** (Tel: 324-5633), its summery main dining room, follows suit by offering inventive, intricate cooking. It's also a good option for afternoon tea. **Bistro 990** (Tel: 921-9990), across from the hotel, opens its French doors out onto Bay, inviting passersby in for such seasonally adjusted specialties as sweetbreads, lamb, fish, and venison. It looks a bit like a cave (ocher vaulted ceiling, lots of wood trim), and, in fact, does have a good wine list. **Mammina's** (6 Wellesley Street

West; Tel: 967-7199) is diminutive in size and menu, but capable of offering freshness in the great Italian mode of simple, down-to-earth cookery. Tiny **Segovia** (582 Yonge Street; Tel: 960-1010) is its equal, the inspiration in this instance being Spain.

A manageable number of blocks north of Bloor, Yonge Street forms the western boundary of Rosedale, Toronto's original chic neighborhood, and so has become the principal dining venue for the inhabitants of this rarefied realm. The options begin at slim-dimensioned **Lakes Bar and Grill** (number 1112; Tel: 966-0185), which serves nouvelle grills and sautés. Tons of color and loads of fire—just what this area needs—are the specialties of **Thai Magic** (number 1118; Tel: 968-7366); that the local hoi polloi agree is evident from the nightly crowds that gather outside, so plan accordingly. The nose is the first thing to discover the superior quality of the breads, cheeses, and takeout at **All the Best Fine Foods** (numbers 1097A–1101; Tel: 928-3330); in fact, if it has to do with edibles, you'll find it fastidiously chosen and presented here. For the thrifty, the **Rosedale Diner** (number 1164; Tel: 923-3122), in cramped but campy quarters, offers Tonawanda wings (Tonawanda is a rough suburb of Buffalo), smoked scallops, and other savory American classics.

Brownes Bistro, on a nearby cross street (4 Woodlawn Avenue East; Tel: 924-8132), is where folks who don't feel like cooking eat glamorized sausage (lamb) with mashed spuds and pizza bread at closely spaced tables. There is much else to admire here—the freshness of the ingredients, the sauces, the wine list, and the well-behaved crowd.

Eclectic and Ethnic

Lotus (Tel: 368-7620) carries the fresh-from-the-market concept to the extreme, its chef shopping maybe twice a day; the result is Amero-Eurasian combinations that intrigue at the least and often hit the mark. The restaurant, at 96 Tecumseh Street, west of the downtown area, occupies an excessively plain storefront—a fact that's not reflected in its prices, however.

In the same general neighborhood, one in which immigrants from all over the globe have settled, **Palmerston** (488 College Street; Tel: 922-9277) stands as a temple (albeit a modestly furnished one) to forthright urban cookery for forthright urbanites who like everything at table—as in life—to be meaningfully correct. Thus, you get rich brown flavors, sourdough, frites with mayo, the bite of arugula, and strawberry shortcake, among other treats. There's also a pleasant back terrace to idle on when the temperature is right. **Chiado** (864

College Street; Tel: 538-1910) is a sophisticated purveyor of Portugal's wine and food, and enjoyably so.

Situated in modest below-stairs quarters, the family-run **Vanipha Fine Cuisine** (193 Augusta Avenue; Tel: 340-0491) caters to the current fancy for Southeast Asian cuisine; it's within the boundaries of Kensington Market, which stretches up and down several streets like an Oriental bazaar. The market's diversity is partly reflected in the menu at **Kensington Kitchen** (214 Harbord Street; Tel: 961-3404), which favors Mediterranean and Middle Eastern cuisine and has much to interest the vegetarian in addition to a relaxing rooftop patio. Though still primarily residential, Harbord boasts a number of other eating places. The **Boulevard Café** (number 161; Tel: 961-7676) will delight the seeker of strong flavors, now and then Peruvian, and offers the added bonus of outside seating in leafy environs when the weather allows. **Porretta's** (number 97; Tel: 920-2186) has long provided the student body at the University of Toronto with pizza, but also does other praiseworthy dishes, mostly in the Italian tradition, and has a good wine list.

Opposite, **Splendido** (number 88; Tel: 929-7788) has no neighborhood rival—as witnessed by the hordes of fashionably dressed patrons who fill it night after night. The menu leans toward California-style Italian cooking, with some rustic European dishes. A superior wine list (many by the glass), swift service, and a warehouse space warmed by paintings of huge flowers seem to guarantee its continued popularity for the foreseeable future. Informal like cashmere, and about as costly.

From here it's on up to Bloor Street West for another string of interesting places. The **Renaissance Café** (number 509; Tel: 968-6639) is for unsolemn vegetarians who like to sup on multinational dishes at a sidewalk terrace; inexpensive. Gentle to the purse, too, is the **Original Vietnam** (number 842; Tel: 531-8763), the cheery home of quail in a sweet crunch of honey and chicken packaged in a half-pineapple. And home is right, for the restaurant is family-run, with toddlers very much a part of the to-ing and fro-ing. The food is a Chinese-Vietnamese hybrid, not particularly subtle, perhaps, but fresh, rich, and delicately textured. The entranceway kitchen also provides entertainment to those waiting on line. **Southern Accent** (595 Markham Street; Tel: 536-3211) approximates the coastal style of Louisiana in a storybook house with a sidewalk patio, and is great fun most nights.

Perched on the brow of a hill at 1 Benvenuto Place, just off Avenue Road, **Scaramouche** (Tel: 961-8011) has a diamanté view of downtown, impressively solid though expensive fare,

a lounge for pasta and simple grills, and capital desserts.
Centro (2472 Yonge Street; Tel: 483-2211) looks like a fancy
jeweler's from the outside—which, given the fact its Italo-
California menu attracts much interest from the BMW/Jaguar
set, is entirely appropriate. Inside it has, among other things, a
wine "library" wherein bottles replace books. (You can imagine how extensive—and expensive—the offerings.)

Named after Toronto's hemispheric latitude, with the compass metaphor very much in evidence in its startling design,
North 44° (2537 Yonge Street; Tel: 487-4897) masterfully
charts the modern North American course, the cooking a
revelation about its many components, from tuna carpaccio
and roasted sweetbreads to desserts for chocolate devotees.
There's depth in the wine list, too, and intelligent service
ensures that all this is not in vain. Expensive, but not so
much that it hurts.

A basement bakery provides **Grano** (2035 Yonge Street;
Tel: 440-1986) with wonderful breads to go with its lusty
antipasti and fragrant grills. Snowshoes on the cool beige
walls at **Trapper's** (3479 Yonge Street; Tel: 482-6211) underscore its ongoing search for a Canadian cooking style (say,
maple syrup as a soup flavoring). The restaurant achieves
what it sets out to do, and that means attention is paid to
wines, too.

Philoxenia (519 Danforth Avenue; Tel: 461-1997) is an
excellent introduction to the Greek food that is so character-
istic of the Danforth, except that here it is light and digestible. Neighboring **Ouzeri** (number 500A; Tel: 778-0500) is
the pot at the end of the rainbow for many patient diners,
who stand in line for its generous portions and more than 50
wines by the glass. Another gently priced Danforth favorite is
Waves (number 347; Tel: 466-4644), where olive oil is the
common denominator among a variety of Mediterranean
styles and the operation itself is refreshingly unjaded.

Among the Cabbagetown restaurants that warrant consideration, **Barolo** (193 Carlton Street; Tel: 961-4747) is a standout
for its Italian food, with a menu that's trendy (balsamic vinegar, roasted garlic, fresh mango), unusual (especially the
pasta combinations), and expertly done. The room has some
nooks, and many levels, which by candlelight just add to the
intimate atmosphere. **Tapas** (226 Carlton Street; Tel: 323-
9651) offers *tapas* by the legion in noisy surroundings.

Drawn by its inexpensive shrimp and lobster dishes as well
as little canapes, appropriately spiced, the multitudes line up
patiently outside the doors of **Young Thailand** (111 Gerrard
Street East; Tel: 599-9099), all the while shuffling past exoti-
cally dressed women who appear to be waiting for buses that

never come. Intrepid seekers of Caribbean spicing will find it at the **Real Jerk** (709 Queen Street East; Tel: 463-6906), amid palm trees decorated with flashing Christmas lights, and at **Mobay** (200 Carlton Street; Tel: 925-7950), where mutton soup and black fruitcake do star turns.

At Eglinton Avenue East and Leslie Street (15 minutes from downtown), the Inn on the Park's principal room, **Seasons** (Tel: 444-2561), is convenient to the bedroom communities of the eastern suburbs and offers a wide-ranging menu of mods and trads in a classy setting. Expensive, but worth it.

On Queen Street East you can choose between the storefront informality of Italian **Spiaggia Trattoria** (number 2318; Tel: 699-4656) or the down-home Southwestern cooking of **Tejas** (number 2485; Tel: 694-2643), followed by a stroll along the boardwalk paralleling the Lake Ontario shoreline.

Near Enough to the Airport

Lake Ontario forms the southern boundary of the municipality of Mississauga, which encompasses a huge chunk of territory west of the city, including Pearson International Airport. **Babsi's** (1731 Lake Shore Road West; Tel: 823-3794) provisions quality ingredients, usually with flair and almost always at prices a little higher than average. Uncowed by its dreary neighborhood, **Sammy's** (3409 Lake Shore Boulevard West; Tel: 251-2036) bifurcates its menu into familiar grillwork and deft Louisiana cooking; a tropical theme is favored, even unto the drinks. **Rogues** is located in a shopping mall called Sherwood Forest Village (1900 Dundas Street West; Tel: 822-2670)—hence the restaurant's name—but serves first-rate Italian food from an open kitchen.

Last but not least, Brampton provides an elegant duo to choose from, although both require a detour on your way to or from the airport: **Antonelli's** (200 County Court Boulevard; Tel: 450-5322) serves up vivid Italian cuisine, while the **Bassano Café** (485 Main Street North; Tel: 451-2600) stakes its reputation on the lightness of its frittatas and the richness of its Crespelle Fiorentina stuffed with ricotta cheese and spinach in a light cream and tomato sauce.

—Joseph Hoare

BARS AND NIGHTLIFE

Like any city of more than three million people, Toronto has a vast and varied social life that supports thousands of meeting and greeting spots, from the "friendly neighborhood" to the ritzy on-the-town nightclub, the cut-off-jeans crowd of the Balmy Arms to the tuxedoed swells of the

Imperial Room. In Toronto you'll find the world's highest dance floor; a bar where the Rolling Stones drop in to play; real English pubs with imported beer and barstools; uptown nightclubs, downtown bars, and rowdy student pubs.

There are, as well, comedy pubs, dinner theaters, jazz clubs galore (Toronto is known for its jazz spots), "down-home" Maritimer boot-stomping fiddle-music venues, new-wave nightclubs, chic and trendy hot spots, dance palaces filled with thousands of young people, bars for singles, sedate lounges, and clubs for those of alternative sexual lifestyles.

Although most hotels have their own lounges, some a cut above the average (for example, the Chelsea Bun in the Delta Chelsea Inn, frequented by locals for good jazz), we concentrate mainly on the independent spots, both new and established, that seem likely to survive.

Yorkville/Bloor

Home of the chic and trendy, and those wishing to be, this area on the northern fringes of midtown (bordered by Bloor, Yonge, Avenue Road, and the Davenport) contains some of Toronto's hottest partying grounds, with prices to match. With its constantly crowded bar, and drinking, dining, and dancing on two levels, the epicenter of the scene is the **Bellair Café**, on the corner of Cumberland and Bellair. The food is surprisingly good and always inventive; the glass panes are removed in summer; and, when the weather allows, the café tables lining the sidewalk are filled from lunch on.

Farther down the street is the casual yet equally crowded pub atmosphere of **Hemingway's**, an upscale burgers-and-beer bar with two levels of rooftop dining and a steady stream of regulars.

Around the corner on Yorkville proper (an expensive view can be had from the opulent ground-floor lounge of the Four Seasons Hotel) you'll find such diverse spots as **Remy's** (check out their second-floor roof deck) and the back garden of **South Side Charlie's**, off Old York Lane, a walk-through connecting Cumberland and Yorkville. A block farther east, amid all the sidewalk cafés, look for the **PWD** sign (88 Yorkville Avenue) and the cozy cellar nightclub of the same name. Actually, you'll be able to hear it from the street: When they're not hanging around the bar, the 30-something crowd here hits the dance floor to the eclectic sounds of reggae, salsa, and r&b.

Across the street is **Meyer's**, a deli by day, jazz club by night. Many people make this their last stop of the evening, wandering in for great after-hours jazz or blues by adver-tised headliners and an ever-changing cast of musicians who drop in after their own gigs are over for the evening.

You'll find the **Barracuda**, a former warehouse that can hold about 2,000 dancers and drinkers on its two levels, at the intersection of Yorkville and Yonge. The Barracuda (for-merly the Copa) is a barn of a place, with a flashing light show and multiscreen videos, and its patrons range from those who have just recently begun to drink legally (19) to three-piece-suit types. A deejay spins the music, though often a live band takes over; the cover charge varies.

For something a little quieter, walk down Yonge to **The Pilot** (22 Cumberland Street), a well-established bar with its own well-established clientele. On sunny days the sidewalk café in front pulses to a bluesy beat, while the main room inside continues to be known for its relaxed atmosphere, excellent bartending, and good bar fare.

There is no cover around the corner at **Balmuto's** (17 Balmuto Street), where you can enjoy a jazz brunch, dance to a deejay on Friday nights, or belt out your favorites at weekday karaoke contests.

With its chrome-and-brass decor, **Bemelmans**, just around the corner on Bloor, is a completely different scene. The bar area is filled from noon on, as are most of the restaurant tables (ask for the outdoor patio), and the place remains open until after 3:00 A.M. (though you can't order alcohol after that hour, you can get a great eggs Benedict and cappuccino). The crowd is very much a mixed bag, from punkers to businesspeople, although you may notice a pre-ponderance of good-looking males at the bar.

Queen Street West

From glitz to funk, Queen Street West (University to Bath-urst, and slowly spreading) is an eclectic blend of artists, literati, and progressive music clubs. From the new-wave explosion of the **Rivoli** to the three-tiered dancing at the multicolored **Big Bop** (with nightly lines), the keynote here is casual. The heart and soul of Queen Street West belongs to **BamBoo** (number 312). So named for the former "Wicker World" basket shop it once was, BamBoo defies categoriza-tion; nightly music acts range from rock to reggae, fusion jazz to country blues, and the excellent menu features a unique combination of Caribbean and Indonesian food. The cover charge varies with each act, but the full houses under-line the fact that owners Patti Habib and Richard O'Brien always hit the right note.

Several new dance clubs, complete with bars and lounge

areas, have made their debuts along the strip, among them the **Boom Boom Room** (number 650½) and the **Bovine Sex Club**—near the always popular Big Bop at the corner of Bathurst. Both clubs appeal to a younger set that tends to favor Queen Street West "alternative fashions" in clothing and musical taste. The latter is open nightly from 9:00 P.M. "until the cows come home."

Farther east is the **Horseshoe Tavern**, a 44-year-old Toronto rock mecca featuring mainstream local groups and legendary r&b masters. There's usually a cover (which obviously doesn't go toward improving the slightly seedy decor), and the crowd includes everyone from kids in faded blue jeans to tuxedo-clad refugees from stuffy parties.

To find truly seedy, you have to visit the **Cameron Public House** (408 Queen Street West), which has all the charm of a broken-down northern fishing lodge—until you order your first draft. The Cameron is like a crowded house party, with its front room the place where people always seem to congregate. The back room holds a tiny stage and a crush of people listening to good-time rock. The Cameron has its regulars, but if there's room they'll gladly accept a guest.

Chicago's Diner (335 Queen Street West), which always served a good solid lunch in its dark-wood bar, has added intimate evenings of jazz and blues to its offerings, perhaps in tribute to its Windy City pedigree. A good Queen Street establishment that avoids the normal bar clichés.

Two more Queen Street West offerings are **X-Rays** (number 271), a rather stark-looking space (comedian Dan Ackroyd is a silent partner) that caters to the street's new-wave contingent, and **Stilife**, just south of Queen at the corner of Richmond and Duncan. It's easy to miss Stilife because its exterior says "warehouse"; inside, however, the decor screams ultra-chic. That also describes the clientele, who line up every Friday and Saturday night to pay the $10 cover and dance until 3:00 A.M. to tunes spun by a deejay. Just seeing this club is an experience, but you'll need to arrive early; entry is limited to 300 revelers. Stilife also offers a bar menu seven nights a week; if you get here before 9:00 P.M., you can order a fairly tasty dinner *and* avoid the cover.

King Street West

Located only two short blocks south of the funky Queen Street strip, "uptown" King Street West might as well be a world away.

The former star of the King Street neighborhood, Joe Allen, has closed its doors, although it is relocating, perhaps farther west on King. Manager John Maxwell hasn't announced the new location as of this writing, but loyal fans are lying in wait for its rebirth. The Joe Allen group still runs **Orso**, however, its Italian dining cousin with a far-flung beer list, on the corner of John and Richmond streets.

The local pub with the most action nowadays is the **Loose Moose** on Adelaide Street; in fact, on a traditionally slow Tuesday night elsewhere in the city you may have to wait outside for a table at this two-story establishment. The finger food ranges from pizza to wings, and the crowds are young, trendy, and raucous, with plenty of young stockbrokers and scores of secretaries on the prowl.

At the "brew pub" **Amsterdam**, across the street, you can watch the staff create the establishment's beer and ale in the basement, then sample the wares upstairs in its four-story, cathedral-ceilinged bar. Although the menu and food are good here, most people come for the crowded bar scene, with the outdoor seating jam-packed in summer. It's fun for a while, but the din created by the terminally trendy may eventually force you to seek quieter drinking pastures. The same holds true for the Amsterdam's brew-pub cousin, the **Rotterdam**, just around the corner on King Street. And though it's not any quieter, you can still have fun while being a whole lot less pretentious at **Studebaker's**, a 1950s-style rock 'n' roll platter place around the corner on Pearl Street. Yes, they do have a real Studebaker on display.

Though located next door to each other, the Go Go and the Jerk Pit are worlds apart in spirit. The five-story **Go Go** at 250 Richmond Street West is a vast club featuring different musical eras on its various floors, some dancing, some lounging and listening, all topped off by a lovely rooftop bar. A cover charge usually applies on weekends unless you bring along their ad from either *NOW* or *EYE* magazine. The **Jerk Pit**, 240 Richmond Street West, serves up generous helpings of spicy ("jerked") Caribbean-style pork and chicken to go along with its selection of beers from the islands. If you're not careful, its calypso and reggae dance parties will soon have you longing for a sunny Jamaican retreat.

Ever since ground was broken for the SkyDome, new bars and restaurants have moved into the area and tried to establish loyal followings. These range from **Filet of Sole** and the **Duncan Street Grill** on—you guessed it—Duncan Street, to the exquisite **Tidal Wave** on Simcoe Street, **Fred's Not Here** on King Street, and **Don Cherry's Grapevine** (diehard sports fans only) farther along King Street. The cost of parking in this neighborhood is appalling, however; walking, taking a cab, or catching the trolley are the better options for all but those with the deepest pockets.

The theater and music crowds frequenting the Royal Alex or Roy Thomson Hall on King (and Simcoe) Street will often stop at one of Ed Mirvish's restaurants (which include **Ed's Warehouse**, **Ed's Seafood**, and **Ed's Chinese**—total seating of 3,000) or **Peter's Backyard**; for a relaxed brandy, stop at the lounge of **Telfer's**, on the corner, or stay longer for an excellent *après*-theater dinner.

Overlooking all this—this being the entire city—is **Sparkles**, the world's highest nightclub and bar, in the CN Tower, where you can drink and dance 1,136 feet above the city's carpet of lights. The $12 cover charge includes the elevator ride and club's light show, although the nighttime view of the Toronto Islands alone is worth the cover.

Esplanade and Front Street

The spiffed-up warehouse district just east of Yonge Street now boasts several major theaters (the O'Keefe, St. Lawrence Centre, Young People's Theatre), the huge St. Lawrence Market, and many new office buildings—and, therefore, many new bars and restaurants. **Brandy's**, at 58 Esplanade, was the first in the area and remains the most popular; businesspeople come for lunch and after work, before the evening dance crowd lines up. It's a comfortable bar during the day, with large wingback chairs, brass, and ferns; at night the stylish patrons provide their own decor. The adjacent **Scotland Yard** is another popular spot, with plenty of cranked-up music and a well-heeled crowd. **Muddy York**, just across the street, gets crowded only when there's an overflow. Too bad, because it's a friendly bar with dancing, and you can actually converse over the music.

The appropriately named **Underground**, around the corner where Front and Wellington split at the historic Flatiron (or Gooderham) Building, serves great finger food and generous libations in its basement bar as well as on its streetside patio (weather permitting). For something a little different, wander across Front Street and into the depths (another basement bar) of the electically eccentric **C'est What?**, where a very late-night crowd can usually be found sitting on comfortable old sofas playing an assortment of board games.

For a quiet nightcap, try the "old club" atmosphere of the very upscale **Consort Bar** in the King Edward Hotel, with its wingback leather chairs and white-glove service. Not to everyone's taste, certainly—and gentlemen will feel more comfortable in a jacket and tie—but it can be a welcome change from a crowded, noisy bar scene.

This area is also home to the former Gimlet's (of

Flashdance fame), which has been magically transformed (with massive renovations) into the upscale **Denison's**, at the corner of Lombard and Victoria streets, with fine dining upstairs and a convivial brew-pub atmosphere downstairs. The brew, by the way, is from an old family recipe belonging to Prince Leitpold of Germany (a partner in the venture), whose family started the Oktoberfest tradition.

Pat & Mario's, just steps east at Wellington and Church streets, is the premier singles bar in the area, with youngish weekend crowds lining up to hit the fast-paced dance floor. A slightly older crowd jams into **RPM**, a cavernous bilevel hall at the bottom of Yonge Street (just east of the Toronto Star building on Queen's Quay).

The Beach

A ten-minute cab ride to the east puts you in the middle of the two-mile strip of Queen Street East that, with its gracious old houses, lakeshore boardwalk, and, of course, beach, seems like a little summer resort unto itself. Several blocks east of Woodbine (the official start of the Beach) you'll find the **Lido**, usually filled with a local crowd, but one geared to top-40 music and video screens. (There's no cover charge for the nightly deejay, nor for the live jazz groups on Sunday and Monday evenings.) This is a 25-to-35-year-old crowd that likes to party. And eat: The menu is a substantial one, with great combo baskets of shrimp and chicken.

A stroll east on Queen Street will take you past various bars and informal dining spots, including the former bank that in its new guise as the publike **Lion on the Beach** makes customers happier than the building's original occupant ever did; the **Beach Bar**, with its side-street outdoor patio; the ever-popular **Scratch Daniels**, filled with a slightly younger, rowdier crowd ordering pitchers of draft beer; the **Balmy Arms**, the quintessential "local" pub serving draft and darts; and the raucous **Quigley's**, **Babbage's**, or **Fitzgerald's**, all three oriented to local Beach residents, a diverse group that includes everyone from upscale professionals to windsurfing jocks to long-haired sixties leftovers. Fitzgerald's, the last pub on the trolley line (one more street and you hit Scarborough), may have the best—and cheapest—chicken wings in town, as well as a cozy corner fireplace.

Yonge–Eglinton

North of Bloor, Eglinton Avenue east of Yonge to Mount Pleasant has, for the past decade, been the epicenter of Toronto's singles scene.

To explore the area yourself, take the subway to the

Yonge–Eglinton station. Starting at the corner of Yonge Street, check out **Berlin**, where the music, supplied by BOB (Berlin's Own Band), usually attracts an early crowd, with anxious lines outside waiting to get in. Best to make dinner reservations to ensure a seat and avoid the $10 weekend cover charge; Tel: (416) 489-7777.

For a different, though no less raucous, evening, the adjacent **Duke of Kent** provides a typical English pub atmosphere, complete with imported beer, Cornish pasties, and a blend of United Kingdom accents.

Many of the trendy pick-up bars that sprang up in the seventies and eighties have closed or evolved as the young-singles crowd they used to attract turned into middle-aged marrieds. As befits the times, the establishments that remain tend to be more traditional bar settings, with a little nostalgia thrown in for good measure. Places like **Original Hector's** (49 Eglinton East) are usually crowded with more suits than blue jeans, while the "malt shoppe" design of **Pete and Marty's Uptown** (160 Eglinton) attracts the baby-boomer crowd as well as younger folks who just want a malted. For something a little different, the **Spruce Goose Brew Pub** at 130 Eglinton West guarantees its evening patrons some of the best brewed-on-the-premises suds in Toronto—the perfect complement to its fiery Texas-style chili.

The cheery, unpretentious **Chick n' Deli**, around the corner at 744 Mount Pleasant (just south of Eglinton), is a minor city legend where aficionados can be assured of hearing some of the best jazz in North America. It's especially pleasant on rainy Sunday afternoons, and also serves some dynamite chicken wings. Very popular.

The Danforth

An old, established area, the Danforth (this is actually Bloor Street East; the name changes when you cross the Bloor viaduct at Broadview) has long been known as Toronto's Greek ghetto, and is famous for some of the best Aegean food in North America. And although the puritanical provincial government has prohibited the serving of alcohol past 1:00 A.M., the Greek restaurants here dish up succulent souvlaki and crispy calamari until 3:00 or 4:00 A.M., which keeps the street bright and lively all night long. In fact, lately a younger group of urban professionals has been frequenting the area, paving the way for ever-trendier bars.

Located next to the Music Hall Theatre at 143 Danforth is **Allen's**, an offshoot of the popular Joe Allen chain (New York, Los Angeles, London, Paris), a casually classy spot with dark wood paneling and a deep blue interior. Allen's has a burger bar opposite the regular bar as you enter, an extensive imported-beer list, and a full kitchen to take care of its regular menu. And out back there's a wonderful garden under weeping willows with seating for 100.

Across the street at **Panama Joe's** (affectionately known as PJ's), the scene is slightly more rowdy and a little louder. The building used to be an old movie theater, which has allowed the designer to be especially inventive, from the balconies to the Art Deco cornices. Lines form on the weekends, so you'll want to get here early in order to get a table on the rooftop patio. And whatever your choice of libation, be sure to try the charcoal-cooked chicken satay or one of the stir-fried delicacies.

The most recent addition to the Danforth lineup (number 500A) is **Ouzeri**, the brainchild of Greek restaurateur Aristedes, who half a dozen years ago opened this spot to instant and immense popularity. Ouzeri is a windowpane-less, doorless (summer only) restaurant/bar where the crowd spills onto the sidewalk on warm summer nights. The food is excellent, although it's likely to set you back double what most of the other Greek restaurants in the neighborhood charge for the same thing.

The **Hargrave Exchange**, slightly to the east, is a nearly perfect neighborhood local. The friendly staff seems to be on a first-name basis with most of the customers, and newcomers quickly will be made to feel at home by the casual, easygoing crowd. Feel free to dawdle in the booths or join the ongoing dart tournament. And try their famous chicken wings (although only the brave order the "suicide" strength).

With its sidewalk tables and tiny backyard patio surrounded by high barn-board walls, **Maverick's Urban Saloon** is the epitome of a neighborhood restaurant/bar. The atmosphere here ranges from quiet weekend brunch spot to friendly house party whenever owner Peter Tsiaras invites a few of his musician friends to drop in for an impromptu gig. At all times, however, the draft beer flows freely (ask for Duffy's, a Canadian beer dark in color and rich in flavor) and the prices on the menu are among the most reasonable in town. In fact, Tsiaras's Greek ancestors would surely approve of his being able to serve a delicious daily special— from a three-egg omelet to chicken and ribs—for an unheard-of $5 a plate.

Spectrum (2714 Danforth), the largest club in the neighborhood, also has the best light show in town. There's live entertainment on Thursdays, and weekend dancing on the huge dance floor goes on until 4:00 A.M. The second-floor dining room alone holds 200, and the over-25 crowd willingly lines up each weekend for dinner and a long evening of dancing. As a change of pace, Spectrum features ballroom dancing on Tuesdays.

Other Entertainment

The above are just some of the bars, pubs, and night spots clustered in several popular—and populated—neighborhoods; countless others are scattered throughout the city. Other recommended clubs include **Albert's Hall** in Ye Olde Brunswick House, 481 Bloor Street West, for r&b; Yonge Street's **Café New Orleans** (618 Yonge, just north of Wellesley), with its outdoor patio; the **Clinton Tavern** at 693 Bloor Street West; the hot jazz and overstuffed sofas at the **Montreal Bistro**, 65 Sherbourne Street; the rock 'n' roll at the **Hard Rock Café**, 283 Yonge and Dundas, across from the Eaton Centre; the **Bohemian Embassy Coffee Club** at 318 Queen Street West for midnight jazz and Poetry Tuesday; and the eclectic musical offerings from the tried-and-true **Club Blue Note**, 138 Pears Avenue.

Major dance clubs featuring deejays and current videos include **Krush**, on Kingston Road (north Beach area), and **Lee's Palace**, on Bloor Street West in the Annex area. After-hours (no alcohol after 1:00 A.M.) spots include the **Twilight Zone**, on Richmond Street West, and St. Joseph Street's **Club Z**, near the busy corner of Yonge and Wellesley.

Dining entertainment abounds in Toronto, from the first-class elegance of the Royal York's **Imperial Room** (Tony Bennett to Tina Turner) to dinner theater at **Garbo's** on Queen Street West, **His Majesty's Feast** down on Lakeshore Boulevard West, the **Limelight** on Yonge (just south of Davisville), and **Stagewest**, in the northern reaches of the city just south of Highway 401.

Comedy clubs include the world-famous Second City troupes at the **Old Firehall**, and **Harper's Night Magic**, both downtown on Lombard Street, as well as the still-popular and ever-expanding **Yuk Yuk's**, now with four locations around metro Toronto.

Toronto has other nocturnal pastimes, of course (it is not "Toronto the Good" all the time), and these might include visits to the **Brass Rail**, on Yonge just south of Bloor; **Cheaters**, at Yonge north of Davisville; or the **Filmore**, along Dundas East, for some research into the city's ecdysiasts, more commonly known as strippers.

As previously mentioned, check the local newspapers for the nightly entertainment scene. The most complete listing, however, can be found in the weekly tabloid *NOW*, available free of charge at most restaurants and bars throughout the city.

Micro Breweries

A recent trend across Canada, from Vancouver to Nova Scotia, is the growth of breweries that produce a very limited quantity of high-quality beer, ale, and lager. These so-called micro breweries constitute a cottage industry that now spans the country (although each brewery is individually owned); in fact, some seem to have sprung up as the result of a neighbor's basement homebrew that became so popular they built a little shop around it. Canadians have always had "the Big Three"—Molson's, Labatt's, and Carling-O'Keefe—as well as the odd popular export such as New Brunswick's Moosehead brand—but today other names such as Castle Brewing, Sleeman's, Les Brassauers du Nord, Okanagan Springs, and Ottawa Valley are finding regional acceptance across the country.

With an alcohol content around 5.5 percent, regular Canadian beer is stronger than American beer, yet weaker than many English brews. The typical microbeer (if such a thing exists) boasts a more distinctive, European flavor. One reason for this is that a batch of regular beer is brewed for three to five days, whereas microbeers are brewed for a minimum of five *weeks* (usually seven before they are bottled). The micros use pure spring water as well, which helps ensure a distinctive taste. For further information on the micro brewery phenomenon in Canada consult expert Jake McKay, who produces the *Northern Brewer* magazine dealing with all facets of the industry. The magazine is free and available at most pubs in the city.

Toronto is blessed (for beer drinkers, that is) with four of these micro breweries: Upper Canada (the largest "micro" in the country), Conners, Northern Algonquin, and Great Lakes. All offer free public tours and tastings; if you're looking for something different to do on a rainy day (or a hot, sunny one for that matter) just give them a call.

Conners Brewery, 544 Eglinton Avenue East; Tel: 488-1406.

Great Lakes Brewing Company, 30 Queen Elizabeth Boulevard, Etobicoke; Tel: 255-4510.

Northern Algonquin Brewing Company, 1270 Central Parkway West, Cooksville; Tel: 949-0790.

Upper Canada Brewing Company, 2 Atlantic Avenue; Tel: 534-9281.

—*Steve Veale*

SHOPS AND SHOPPING

The best buys in Toronto are those with a distinctly Canadian flavor: duck decoys by Canadian woodcarvers, Inuit carvings, an Ojibway quill basket, Mennonite and Amish quilts, early Canadian country-style pine furniture, Quebec folk art, a delicate handblown glass vase, a trendy outfit from one of Queen Street West's avant-garde designers.

By far the most interesting places to shop are the neighborhoods that fan out from the city center: Bloor/Yorkville, Mirvish Village, the Kingsway, Bloor West Village, St. Clair Avenue West, the Danforth, the Beach, Queen Street West, Village by the Grange, Chinatown, Kensington Market, Harbourfront, Yonge Street, Mount Pleasant, and Bayview from Davisville as far north as the city limits.

Bloor/Yorkville

Bloor/Yorkville, where Toronto's first coffeehouses and clubs (host to the likes of Gordon Lightfoot, Neil Young, and Joni Mitchell) have given way to extravagant renovations and elegant shops, is where you'll find Armani, Gucci, Valentino, and Saint Laurent, along with a few others you may not have heard of. A recent entry in the opulence stakes is **Fetoun**, 55 Avenue Road in Hazelton Lanes, a lavish boutique all a-shimmer and a-glitter with hand-embroidered gowns by the Saudi-born owner, who also breeds racehorses. Her pampered clients enjoy smoked salmon, caviar, and white and red wine as they shop. Even if you don't feel up to buying anything, it's worth a visit just to see the pale pink, black, and gold-leaf decor.

Hazelton Lanes is Toronto's version of Rodeo Drive, a series of lanes winding in a figure eight around a skating rink in winter, a garden restaurant in summer. **Valencienne**, 25 Bloor Street West (upstairs), is a tiny hidden-away boutique that sells pure silk heirloom wedding dresses to princesses and movie stars. Prices range from $1,200 to $30,000.

Bloor West Village

Bloor West Village, one of the pleasanter places to shop in the city, was created by local ingenuity—it's a friendly, tree-lined part of Bloor Street, running from Jane to Runnymede, known for its meat markets, delis, pastry shops, flower stalls, and fashionable boutiques, all just steps from High Park and easily accessible by subway.

The Kingsway

The upscale Kingsway area, farther west along Bloor Street extending from Prince Edward Drive to Montgomery Road, is definitely worth a visit. Check out the **Lambton Mills Country Store** at 2940 Bloor Street West for unusual hand-made dolls and keepsake boxes, and **Keltic Touch** and the **Pant Bin**, at numbers 2998 and 3078 on the same street, for well-made clothing. **Side Step**, number 2988, is the place for low-priced linen clothes and handcrafted leather belts. **The Bookmark**, an excellent bookstore at 2 Jackson Avenue, is just around the corner.

St. Clair Avenue West

St. Clair Avenue West, or Westclair, is Toronto's Little Italy. Italian designer clothes, linen and laces, leather and linguini, Pavarotti and Fellini—all can be found here. Within seven blocks, from Westmount Avenue to Lansdowne Avenue, you'll find more than 40 shoe stores. The best buys are at **Venetian Shoes**, 1262 St. Clair Avenue West. You'll see a lot of the neighborhood if you travel through on a St. Clair Avenue West streetcar; just be sure to get off to visit **Genesis** and **La Scala** (numbers 1188 and 1190) for elegant Italian menswear, and **Richards Babies Place Limited** (number 1242), the best place in town for designer children's wear. Cappuccino and espresso are always on the house in this neighborhood.

The Danforth

The Danforth, bounded by the Don Valley and Woodbine area to the east, might just for a minute remind you of Athens, what with the smell of lamb roasting on a spit, the sound of bouzouki music, and the sight of all-night fruit stands. The oldest shop here is **Thuna Herbalist**—established in 1900 and still going strong. **Artesano**, 176A Hampton at the Chester subway station, just south of Danforth Avenue, specializes in Central American folk art and jewelry.

Gifts from the Earth, 320 Danforth Avenue in Carrot Common, stocks an assortment of crystals, pyramids, dream catchers, fossils, tranquillity tapes, and books on self-healing.

Chinatown and Kensington Market

Chinatown, bounded by Bay Street to the east, Spadina Avenue to the west, and College Street south to Dundas, is divided into old and new, a neighborhood of fish and meat stores, bakeries, herbalists, bookstores, discount clothing, crafts, and discount art-supply stores like **Picasso's** and **Gwartzman's**, not to mention more than 100 restaurants.

Kensington Market, bounded by Bathurst and Spadina, Dundas and College, with the main market streets being Augusta, Baldwin, and Kensington Avenue, is a jumble of noise, movement, and extraordinary smells. Everything is compact here, from the gaudy Portuguese hardware stores on Denison Square to the endless stalls of fruit, vegetables, dried beans, fish, and cheese.

Mirvish Village

Mirvish Village, on Markham Street in midtown near the intersection of Bloor and Bathurst streets, is a block of renovated Victorian houses inhabited by artists, antiques dealers, and booksellers. The "village" was the brainchild of Toronto's most famous entrepreneur, Ed Mirvish, who owns **Honest Ed's** (a bargain-basement store at the corner of Markham and Bloor with the world's biggest electric sign) and, downtown, the Royal Alexandra Theatre and a number of nearby restaurants.

The Beach

The Beach area was the city's first summer retreat; Queen Street East is just a few blocks from the lake, and home to some of the city's most interesting shops. It runs east from Woodbine as far as Victoria Park, and has everything from antiques and junk stores to health and beauty emporiums and good secondhand bookstores. From east to west, some of the more interesting are: the **Animation Gallery**, 1977 Queen Street East (second floor), which sells original hand-painted animation art, one of the fastest-appreciating art forms on the market. **Tambuli**, 1915 Queen Street East, sells church art, African masks, and Oriental rugs. The **Old Lamp Shop**, 1582 Queen Street East, is owned by antiques dealer Dominique Douillet, who restores and sells the elegant solid brass fixtures that graced the homes, businesses, and churches of turn-of-the-century Toronto. To add the right finishing touches to his lamps, he also has the largest selection of art-glass shades in Canada, many of them bearing the name of the famous Steuben glassworks, as well as a 1910 Art Nouveau lamp with stained glass shade. Farther west is **Antiques in Time**, 211 Queen Street East, which specializes in old clocks.

The Harbourfront

The Harbourfront, which stretches along the lakefront south of Queen's Quay, is a miracle of retrieved park space and warehouses that have been converted into galleries, shops, theaters, and living spaces. This is where you'll find **Harbourfront Antique Market**, a great place to browse for bargains on Sundays.

Queen Street West

Queen Street West, starting at McCaul Street and running west of Bathurst, may at first inspection seem intimidating, what with all the punk haircuts and new-wave youths, but it's also full of surprises and intriguing shops. Once it was the exclusive home of discount stores and jobbers; they now exist side by side with the boutiques, galleries, and bookstores that have become the hallmark of the street. In rooms and apartments over the stores, a good mix of students from the nearby Ontario College of Art, musicians, photographers, and young people are busy trying to find themselves. All the trendy young avant-garde Canadian designers are here as well, including **Ms. Emma** (number 275); **Marilyn Brooks** (number 391); **Alfred Sung** at Club Monaco (number 403); Pam Chorley at **Fashion Crimes** (number 395); Big Fish, Comrags, Zapata, and Lucas at **Parade** (number 557); **Hoax** (number 456); and **Price Roman** (number 267). The area is also a gold mine for vintage clothes, with **Black Market** (number 323A) specializing in men's tuxedos from the 1940s and 1950s (popular with Toronto rock bands), **English Eccentrics** (number 477) filled with Victorian clothes, and **Libido Lil** (number 753) the place to go for retro fashions from the sixties and seventies. Farther west on the same street is **Romni Wools Ltd.** (number 658) for the best selection of yarns in town; the **Algonquins Sweet Grass Gallery** (number 670) for Native American artwork; the **Atelier Ceramique** (number 709) for raku pottery, handblown glass, bronze sculptures, papier-mâché figures, silk paintings, and jewelry; **Ragnarokr** (number 758) for handmade leather goods; and the **Japanese Paper Place** (number 966) for exquisite handmade Japanese paper and origami.

These are the neighborhoods where you'll find most of the interesting shopping. Now we'll zero in on the rest of the best by specialty.

Antiques

Crème de la Crème Vintage Plumbing Inc., 332 Geary Street near Dufferin and Davenport Avenue, sells antique plumbing fixtures. **Doc John's Antique Doll Clinic**, 194 Carlton Street East, is owned by John Hawkslaw, a pattern-maker who loves collecting old dolls; his oldest dates from 1830. **Garden of Eden Antiques**, 2644 Danforth Avenue, is a bargain hunter's paradise crammed with beautiful merchandise, including an unfinished pine occasional table for less than $100 and a stately 1930s sideboard for only $365. **Harbourfront Antique Market**, 390 Queen's Quay West, is billed as Canada's largest quality antiques market. It has 70 permanent dealers, with another 200 dealers converging on it from all over the province, and is open on Sundays. **Linda Howard Antiques**, 581 Mount Pleasant, has a great supply of antique Mennonite and Amish quilts, early and contemporary Quebec folk art, decoys, wall hangings, hooked rugs, and early-Canadian pine furniture. **Sandy's Antiques**, 3130 Bathurst Street, is tucked away at the north end of Lawrence Plaza up some nondescript stairs. Once you've arrived, however, there's no mistaking the quality of the merchandise and the good prices. The bargain here is the 50 to 60 percent discount on Birks estate sterling-silver flatware patterns as well as that on Wallace, International, Northumbria, and Jensen. The Royal Crown Derby china, crystal, cloisonné vases, tea sets, and trays make Sandy's a browser's paradise. **Somerville Antiques**, 390 Queen's Quay, is filled with unusual items, including a Victorian croquet set, antique buttons, and ladies' fans.

Arts and Crafts

Indian Art. The Ojibway-owned **Algonquins Sweet Grass Gallery**, 670 Queen Street West, is an authentic arts-and-crafts store (a rare find these days) featuring items selected with excellent taste: carvings and prints, hand-sewn moccasins, beading, baskets made from porcupine quills, tamarack birds, birchbark bitings, duck decoys, and Cowichan sweaters from the West Coast.

Inuit Art. The **Guild Shop**, 140 Cumberland in the Bloor/Yorkville district, has the best selection and prices for Inuit art. Owned and operated by the Ontario Craft Council, it is nonprofit, hence no hefty markup. A delightful little polar bear tapestry on a teal blue background by Veronica Manilak of Rankin Inlet is only $150, but you can go as high as $6,000 for a mother-and-child soapstone carving by Tutya Ikkidluts of Cape Dorset. **Fehely Fine Arts**, 45 Avenue Road, and the **Inuit Gallery of Eskimo Art**, 9 Prince Arthur in the same neighborhood, are commercial galleries with good selections. Older pieces from the 1950s and 1960s are sometimes available at **Waddington McLean** auctions, 189 Queen Street East, held Wednesdays and Saturdays.

Crafts. The **Guild Shop** (see above) has top-quality Canadian crafts: leather, textile, glass, woodcarving, jewelry, pottery. The **Gardiner Museum Shop**, 111 Queen's Park (opposite the Royal Ontario Museum), offers one-of-a-kind Canadian pottery pieces that complement the museum's outstanding collection of ceramic art. **A Show of Hands**, 1947 Avenue Road (entrance on Felbrigg Road), has an eclectic collection of Canadian crafts—ceramics, glass, leather, wood, papier-mâché, and fibers—as well as the best assortment of folk art in the city. A one-of-a-kind craft can be bought for as little as $50. **Early Canadian Furniture**, 8 Cumberland Street, has handcrafted pine and oak reproductions; requests for custom work are welcome.

Birds

The **Canadian Wild Bird Company**, 317 Millwood Road, just off Mount Pleasant, is bird heaven, with an astonishing selection of feeders—some hand-carved—and birdseed. Owners Paige and Julia Cowan, who always have time to talk about birds, strongly believe bird-watching is a favorite Canadian pastime and that Toronto is one of the nation's "birdiest" cities due to its miles of wooded ravines along the Don River.

Books

Toronto has a mind-boggling array of bookstores, reflecting a certain eclecticism among its citizenry. The almost 100-year-old **Albert Britnell Book Shop**, 765 Yonge Street, is the oldest in the city, and still family owned and operated; they say they can find any book in or out of print. **Ballenford Architectural Books**, 98 Scollard (in the Bloor/Yorkville district), has collector's items as well as contemporary books and exhibits of architectural drawings and models. **Can-Do Bookstore**, 311 Queen Street West, is do-it-yourself heaven. Owner Stan Adelman, a Mr. Fix-It himself, claims to have more than 400 books on woodcarving alone.

David Mirvish Books on Art, 596 Markham Street, in the heart of Mirvish Village, stocks more than 40,000 titles (in and out of print), all valuable. **Longhouse Book Shop Limited**, 497 Bloor Street West, carries only Canadian books, some 20,000 titles in stock, including an excellent children's section, a Toronto section, history, political science, and sociology. **Sleuth of Baker Street**, 1595 Bayview Avenue (in the Bloor/Yorkville district), offers detective and spy thrillers as well as collectors' editions and a good selection of Sherlockiana. **That Other Bookstore**, 745 Queen Street West, is also a café. Owned by a former heroin addict turned drama therapist, the store's specialty is recovery and self-help books on every addiction, obsession, and unhealthy relationship known to man. **Theatrebooks**, 25 Bloor Street West (entrance on Balmuto Street, upstairs), specializes in theater, film, photography, and dance. The **Garden Bookstore**, 5 Yorkville Avenue, is Toronto's only bookstore devoted exclusively to gardening. As its name suggests, the place to go for healthy reading is **Toronto's Most Comprehensive Health Book Store**, on the lower level at 110 Cumberland Street.

If you like quantity, **Coles the World's Biggest Book Store**, at 20 Edward Street, one block north of the Eaton Centre, has 17 miles of bookshelves and more than one million books in stock. Its 55 specialty departments cover everything from accounting to zoology.

Antiquarian dealers of note include: the **Village Book Store**, 239 Queen Street West; **About Books**, 83 Harbord Street; **David Mason Books**, 342 Queen Street West (second floor); the **Abelard Book Shop**, 519 Queen Street West; **McBurnie & Cutler**, which specializes in Canadiana and books about music, 698 Queen Street West; **Hugh Anson-Cartwright Books**, 229 College Street, with a good selection of fine leather bindings; the **Old Favorites Book Shop Ltd.**, 250 Adelaide Street West; and **Ten Editions Books**, 698 Spadina Avenue, which sells vintage sheet music as well as old books.

Chess Sets
The **ROM** (Royal Ontario Museum) **Shop**, 100 Queen's Park, has the best and most interesting selection in town; sets represent different cultures and historical periods, and are reasonably priced. Among the rarities here is an Etruscan reproduction set from Italy in bronze for $1,975. The big sellers are handpainted stone resin sets from England— everything from *Alice in Wonderland* characters to Camelot to Egyptian, Chinese, Elizabethan, and Victorian costume sets, ranging from $100 to $700.

Children
Absolutely Diapers, 940 Queen Street West, has opened just in time to help the environmental crisis. This is Toronto's first and only source for all-cotton diapers. Worth checking out for its wide assortment of designs, including an expandable diaper good for the newborn baby right up to two years old. The **Museum Children's Shop** (in the Royal Ontario Museum), 100 Queen's Park, is a gold mine of gift ideas for children. The biggest sellers are the plastic dinosaurs, accurately modeled on the museum's own collection; the shop also carries dinosaur kits and wooden skeletal dinosaurs. **Science City Inc.** (Holt Renfrew Centre, lower level, 50 Bloor Street West) is the place for children with a scientific bent. You'll find everything scientific and educational for all ages here, from telescopes to chemistry sets. Science City has two more shops nearby for adults. The **Children's Book Store**, 604 Markham Street (in Mirvish Village), boasts the world's largest selection of quality books, records, and tapes for children up to age 14, as well as a staff of helpful librarians and teachers. **Mabel's Fables**, 662

Mount Pleasant, is a tiny, perfect place for young readers, with resident cat Mabel presiding. The **Last Wound Up**, 91 Cumberland Street, Bloor/Yorkville, is strictly windup toys and music boxes for children and adults who never grew up. The **Toy Shop**, 62 Cumberland Street, offers two floors chock full of toys, books, and games from around the world. **Touch the Sky, Inc.**, 207 Queen's Quay West, is Canada's largest seller of kites, wind socks, wood chimes, mobiles, Frisbees, and hotair balloons.

Clocks

Abernethy & Son, 3235 Yonge Street, is a father-and-son operation that grandfather started in Manchester, England. Each old clock is clearly dated, priced, and guaranteed for a year. The store has an extensive selection that includes clocks from England and Scotland, Long Case clocks, mantel clocks, a few early American clocks, and a sterling silver pocket watch from the mid-18th century that's priced at $1,250. Other prices range from $100 for an antique Victorian mantel clock to a William Cattell–built Marquetry Long Case clock circa 1664 for $30,000. Reproductions are also sold.

Collectors

Toronto caters to collectors with stores like **Autophile Car Books**, 1685 Bayview Avenue, with its stock of miniature cars and motoring books, and **Doc John's Antique Doll Clinic**, 194 Carlton Street East (both in north Toronto). **The Dolly Madison Co.**, 170 West Beaver Creek, Thornhill, has a porcelain doll-making studio complete with finished dolls, kits, accessories, and collectible teddy bears. **Geomania**, at the Holt Renfrew Centre on the lower level, is a fascinating store filled with high-quality rocks, Mexican desert roses, and rare butterflies. **George's Trains**, 510 Mount Pleasant in north Toronto, is Canada's biggest model train store, with readymade trains in all sizes as well as kits, collectible brass locomotives, and antiques. Owner Robert Jerred of **Tall Ships** has a Royal Marine background and a fascination for all things nautical. You'll find handcrafted scale-model ships, kits, nautical antiques, ships in a bottle, and nautical books in his store at 1545 Bayview Avenue.

Duck Decoys

Atelier Fine Arts, Inc., 588 Markham Street, has Toronto's biggest selection of decoys by first-class carvers such as Phineas Charles Reeves. Owner Fred Tymoshento is considered the godfather of Canadian decoys and has a soft spot for folksy Nova Scotia lures. Best of all, the prices here and at the three stores mentioned below are quite affordable in relation to prices in the United States.

Avendale Antiques, 1626 Bayview Avenue, specializes in appealing, well-made decoys that aren't necessarily the work of well-known carvers. Prices range from $62 up to $498. **Perkins Antiques,** 1198 Yonge Street, favors the trim birds designed for the placid waters of eastern Ontario, which Perkins believes are the finest decoys in North America. The **Port Dalhousie Trading Company,** 104 Avenue Road, carries up to 20 birds at a time, ranging in price from $54 to several thousand dollars.

Furs

Apart from pricey fur salons such as Holt Renfrew and Creeds, there are plenty of bargains to be had on Spadina Avenue between King and Front streets in stores like **Cosmopolitan Fur Co. Ltd.,** 204 Spadina Avenue; **House of Appel Fur Company,** 119 Spadina Avenue; **Leader Furs,** 686 Bathurst Street; **Norman Rogul Furs,** 480 Adelaide Street West; and **Paul Magder Furs,** 202 Spadina Avenue (with more than 3,000 furs to choose from). The very best deals are found at **Formerly Yours,** a consignment shop at 1907 Avenue Road. Owner Nancy Gillick's in-laws are Montreal furriers who supply her with low-priced samples. She's even been known to provide limousine service for out-of-town clients, who sometimes buy two or three coats at a time.

Jewelry

Emotional Outlet, 2487½ Yonge Street, sells jewelry by Canadian designers on consignment and at good prices. **Fortune's Fine Jewellery,** 1901 Avenue Road, owned by designer Michael S. de Costa, handles everything from start to finish on the premises. The **Jewellery Shop,** in the Art Gallery of Ontario, 317 Dundas Street West, has a reputation for carrying the best handcrafted sterling-silver jewelry by contemporary Canadian artists. Last but not least, the **Lapis Touch,** 80 Front Street East, is known for unusual gold and silver jewelry designed with lapis lazuli from Afghanistan.

Lace

Filigree Linens and Lace, 1210 Yonge Street, sells heirloom lace made up in sheets, pillowcases, curtains, bedspreads, and dress collars. The **Irish Shop,** 110 Bloor Street West, also has old lace collars, accessories, and blouses.

Military Insignia and Miniatures

Toys for Big Boys, at the Harbourfront Antique Market, has a wide range of militaria, including antique guns. **Labell's Toy Soldiers**, 100 Front Street West (Royal York Hotel, arcade level), sells a bewildering array of military miniatures perfect in every detail. You name it, Labell makes it: French cavalry figures, British soldiers from the Napoleonic Wars, Canadian regulars from the War of 1812 to World War II, and Prussian hussars circa 1907. What better souvenir of Canada than a miniature Mountie, on horseback or standing with a lance? The range is enormous, and includes figures marching, running, firing, kneeling, even dying.

Museum Shops

The **ROM** (Royal Ontario Museum), 100 Queen's Park, has three shops replete with treasures and bargains. Best buys are the Thai tapestries, handcarved chess sets, reproduction jewelry treasures, handblown glass, Chilean folk-art miniatures, and Balinese masks and flying figures. The tiny **Reproduction Shop** at the entrance has a cast of a dinosaur's foot (perfect for the garden) for $65 and an ichthyosaurus wall hanging for $225, not to mention jewelry, scarves, calendars, needlepoint kits, and sculptures—all reproduced from the museum's collection.

Old Maps and Engravings

Beach Antique Maps and Prints, 390 Queen's Quay West, specializes in North American maps from the 18th and 19th centuries—at bargain prices. They also have a complete collection of Canadian and American landscapes for as little as $50 all the way up to $1,000. The **Map Room** at Exploration House, 18 Birch Avenue, also has a good selection, but at much higher prices.

Rare Musical Instruments

Remenyi House of Music, 210 Bloor Street West: Michael Remenyi represents the third generation of Remenyis to stand behind the counter at this family-owned business, which started in Budapest in 1890 and moved to Toronto in 1959. The Remenyis specialize in antique instruments—stringed instruments, plucked instruments, brass, and woodwinds. (It's also the only music store in Canada with a harp salon.) The oldest instrument here is an early 17th-century violin; there's also an artists' room in the basement where concert musicians come to practice when they're performing in town.

Southpaws

The **Sinister Shoppe** (by appointment and mail order only; Tel: 416/366-1790) has everything for left-handed people, including all kinds of kitchen supplies and instruction books on a wide range of subjects, from needlepoint to woodcarving.

Vintage Clothing

These are a few of the best places to find what your grandmother wore: **Black Market**, 323A Queen Street West; **Courage My Love**, 14 Kensington Street; **Divine Decadence Originals**, 7 Charles Street West; and **Flying Down to Rio**, 614 Yonge Street.

—*Sherry Boeckh*

ONTARIO PROVINCE

*By David E. Scott, Jean Danard,
and Steve Veale*

*David E. Scott, the author of the Southwestern Ontario
section, also wrote the section on the French islands of St.
Pierre and Miquelon as well as the chapter on Quebec
Province. Jean Danard, who contributed the section on
Muskoka and Ontario's Cottage Country, has lived in many
parts of Ontario and is now based in Toronto. She was travel
and tourism editor of Canada's* Financial Post *before becoming a freelance writer. Steve Veale, the author of the Northern
Ontario and Eastern Ontario sections, also contributed several sections on Toronto.*

Ontario is a vast province—not only south to north, up to
Hudson Bay, but east to west, stretching from near Montreal
in the east to close to Winnipeg, Manitoba, in the west. In the
United States, this would be the equivalent of a single state
with New York City on its eastern border and Minneapolis,
Minnesota, on its western border.

An area this large—and diverse—will of course have
various regions, each offering a different experience to
visitors. For Ontario, there is first of all semi-urban *Southwestern Ontario,* a peninsula-like piece of land southwest of
Toronto that is surrounded by the Great Lakes.

Then there's *Muskoka and Ontario's Cottage Country* to
the north of Toronto and Lake Ontario. Next is *Eastern
Ontario,* the water-oriented region stretching along the St.
Lawrence River northeast of Toronto and north to Ottawa.
Finally, all the rest: *Northern Ontario* (which some call
Western Ontario), the distinctly non-urban area north of
Lakes Huron and Superior.

SOUTHWESTERN ONTARIO

Southwestern Ontario is the commercial center of Canada, and the part of the country where business-oriented people will feel most at home. Nowhere is this more manifest than in the "golden horseshoe," the nickname for the arc of land at the western end of Lake Ontario that runs from Oshawa in the east through Toronto to Hamilton in the west. "Golden" is not a reference to summer sunsets or autumn leaves in this, the region where most of Canada's big business deals are struck. Golden refers instead to the costly mineral mined several hundred miles north of the area, its buying power converted into tons of paper share certificates in the south, where money talks louder than in any other part of the Dominion.

It is not until you get about 80 km (50 miles) north of the Macdonald-Cartier Expressway (Highway 401)—the umbilical cord of southern Ontario's economy—that people generally embrace a less acquisitive lifestyle. Though some may resent to a degree the intrusion of strangers in their quiet communities, most will nonetheless pause to exchange greetings and comment on the weather.

The weather in Southwestern Ontario is, in fact, the despair of its forecasters. The region is virtually an island, and winds sweeping toward it over large bodies of water pick up unpredictable amounts of precipitation. The region's southern boundary is Lake Erie; on the west it is separated from the state of Michigan by the Detroit River, 460-square-mile Lake St. Clair, the St. Clair River, and Lake Huron, which wraps around the northern limit of Southwestern Ontario in the form of Georgian Bay. Easterly winds blowing into the region pass over Lake Ontario; those from the northeast cross Lake Simcoe, and east of that is an area riddled with lakes and waterways.

MAJOR INTEREST

Niagara Falls
Niagara-on-the-Lake's George Bernard Shaw
    Festival
Kitchener–Waterloo Oktoberfest
Mennonite country
Shakespearean Festival at Stratford

Point Pelee National Park
Pelee Island resort area
Lake Huron coastline resort towns and
  deepwater fishing
South Georgian Bay resort towns for
  hunting and fishing

Southwestern Ontario is a difficult region to describe in any logical sequence. The places of most legitimate touristic interest are either close to its entry points from New York State and Michigan, or along its perimeters—the lakeshores of Erie, Huron, and Georgian Bay. In the central part of this region, which is roughly the size of the state of Vermont, there are some scattered points of interest for the discerning traveller. There are also some real gems in terms of country inns for lodging or dining, but little else.

Nor will Ontario's excellent (and free) road map help the first-time visitor plan a worthwhile sightseeing itinerary. The map draws your eye to the sizable cities of Woodstock, Chatham, St. Thomas, Windsor, St. Catharines, Welland, and Sarnia. But despite the protestations of the well-funded tourist promotion boards in those cities, no two of them share what awaits the visitor in many of the small towns and villages scattered like pearls across the region.

With only two or three days available to sample Southwestern Ontario, you would be smart to pick one corner with worthwhile attractions and get to know it well. To try to explore the entire area, even within a week, is to spend most of that week on heavily trafficked Highway 401, the region's principal east–west link, and on the vehicle-cluttered north–south secondary highways, all of which are two-lane and often shared by farm machinery in summer and fall.

THE NIAGARA FALLS AREA

The greatest concentration of attractions is found in the extreme southeastern corner of the region, on either side of Niagara Falls. Since 1885 the 35-mile length of Ontario's border with New York State has been showcased by the Niagara Parks Commission, an organization that operates on its own revenues and is not beholden to any political body for funds or direction.

The NPC has, over the years, acquired most of the riverfront property along the Niagara River and turned it into a long, narrow parkland where picnickers, cross-

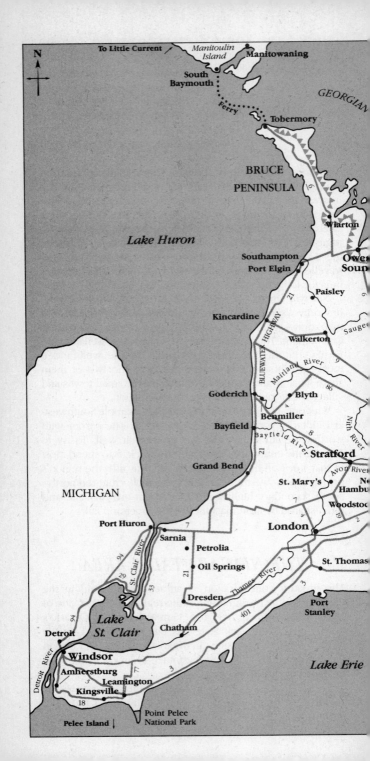

Southwestern Ontario

| 0 | miles | 24 |
| 0 | kilometers | 40 |

MUSKOKA LAKES

BAY

PENETANG PENINSULA

NOTTAWASAGA BAY

NIAGARA ESCARPMENT

Collingwood

Wasaga Beach

Nottawasaga River

26

River

Lake Simcoe

11

Oshawa

To Montréal

2

401

QUEEN ELIZABETH WAY 2

Toronto

Lake Ontario

mira

Elora
West Montrose
St. Jacobs
Heidelberg
Waterloo
Kitchener

Hamilton

8

404

Niagara-on-the Lake

St. Catharines

Ft. George
Virgil
Queenston

2

Jordan Station

Thorold

Paris

Brantford

Grand River

33

Port Dover

3

59

24

Long Point

t wan

Turkey Point

Niagara Falls

Welland

Niagara River

NEW YORK

Fort Erie

• **Buffalo**

NEW YORK

ONTARIO

Toronto Ottawa

country skiers, bird-watchers, and sunbathers are welcome at no charge. What used to be a six-month-long traffic snarl in the immediate area of the falls has been remedied; now visitors park in spacious lots and are taken to the falls by rubber-tired people movers.

Niagara Falls

The city of Niagara Falls has spent a lot of money cleaning up its core area, which used to be a glare of neon signs and shabby billboards directing the unwary to a variety of sleazy operations where they'd be fleeced for tacky kitsch and served the kind of food that incites prison riots. There still exist a number of questionable attractions for which admissions are charged, but most visitors with intelligence can easily determine what's worth shelling out a fistful of dollars to see.

THE FALLS
The city's premier attraction is free. Each night throughout the year the three famous falls of Niagara are floodlit with moving colored lights, courtesy of the NPC. One of the best observation points for night viewing is the dining room of the 50-story **Skylon Tower**, which also offers some of the best dining in the area; as you linger over a reasonably priced bottle of wine whose grapes were grown just down the road, the dining room will slowly revolve 360 degrees. For reservations, Tel: (905) 356-2651.

That experience is doubly enjoyable from mid-November to mid-February, when the owners of various businesses, hotels, private residences, and other towers vie to outdo each other with variations on the Christmas-season lighting spectacle.

During cold winters spray from the 162-foot-high Horse-shoe Falls freezes on everything nearby, creating grotesquely attractive ice formations on trees, buildings, railings, lamp-posts—and your car, if you've parked too close. Most years, ice floes carried down the Niagara River from Lake Erie form a bridge across the river below the falls. Walking across the ice bridge was one of Niagara's winter tourist musts until one such bridge collapsed unexpectedly in 1912, sweeping three visitors to their deaths.

Since the first European, Jesuit missionary Louis Hennepin, saw Niagara Falls in 1678, the spectacle has drawn millions of tourists—and a considerable number of daredevils and suicides. Museums around the city chronicle the adventures of the 13 daredevils who have survived the plunge, those who have walked tightropes across the falls' face, and those who paid the ultimate price for their escapades. No matter how carefully the various police forces patrol the area, however, an average of six bodies turn up each year in the giant whirlpool several miles below the falls.

(A word of warning for those viewing the Horseshoe Falls from their closest edge on the Canadian side. Staring for any length of time at the smooth curve of water as it rushes over the lip of the falls can exert a magnetism—a fatal magnetism believed to have lured a number of people to their deaths. This observation point recently was moved back a distance from the edge, and a higher fence erected between it and the falls.)

Area Attractions

If you're going to visit only one museum in the area, make it the **Niagara Falls Museum**, 5651 River Road, next to the Rainbow Bridge. It's North America's oldest and has a bit of everything—including seven authentic Egyptian mummies as well as the Daredevil Hall of Fame. The museum is open daily, April to October, and weekends November through May; Tel: (905) 356-2151.

The visitor to Niagara Falls shortchanges himself if he doesn't take in the view from below the falls. A trip under the falls (**Table Rock Scenic Tunnels**) starts beneath Table Rock House, a limestone building near the lip of the Horseshoe Falls. Participants are outfitted with rubber boots, slickers, and hats, and then led down a tunnel blasted through the rock behind the falls. Openings in the tunnel allow you to experience up-close the volume and violence of the roaring wall of water. A second viewing station halfway down the cliff is usually battered by heavy spray—a refreshing way to cool off on a hot summer day.

A short distance below the falls is a small pier from which sightseeing boats take visitors up the Niagara Gorge to the foot of the falls. The **Maid of the Mist** boats get as close as they can—what appears as water directly in front of the wall of falling water is mostly air. Again, sightseers are dressed in rain gear against the capricious sheets of spray. For information, Tel: (905) 358-0311.

Yet another way to view the falls is by helicopter. **Niagara Helicopters**, on the river at the end of Victoria Avenue, offers frequent flights across the giant whirlpool several miles downstream from the falls and then up the gorge of sheer rock cliffs to the falls themselves. The ultimate test of your heart occurs when the pilot banks the chopper around the lip of the Horseshoe Falls. The cost per person is $65; couples can fly as a team for $120, and children under 12 are welcomed aboard for $25, or $45 for two. Tel: (905) 357-5672.

Another Niagara thrill is the trip across the Giant Whirlpool in the **Spanish Aero Car**. Located several miles below the falls, the whirlpool is traversed by a large, open cable car that tends to swing and sway as it carries passengers across the river at a dizzying height above the foam-flecked maelstrom below.

STAYING NEAR THE FALLS

Though it may not be the "honeymoon capital" of the world anymore, Niagara Falls still has hundreds of hotels, motels, cottages, and guest houses for honeymooners or anyone else. These range from the ▶ **Skyline Brock Hotel**, ▶ **Skyline Foxhead Hotel**, and ▶ **Skyline Village Inn**, with 250, 400, and 200 rooms, respectively, to the homier ▶ **Holiday Inn by the Falls** and the ▶ **Old Stone Inn**, both near the Skylon Tower. Lovers of kitsch might want to try the ▶ **Honeymoon City Motel**, next to the House of Frankenstein among the garish neon of Clifton Hill. Or for a very special night consider ▶ **Michael's Inn**. More than 20 of the motel's 130 rooms, which overlook the American Falls and the sheer rock face of the Niagara Gorge, are elaborately themed; you can imagine you're in deepest Africa, the Far East, or the Old South.

As a general rule, the closer a hotel is to the falls, and thus the better the view, the more expensive it will be. Budget motels with fine views do exist but rarely have vacancies. Still, for all the accommodations in the immediate area, perhaps the most desirable option is to head "down" to one of the lovely inns in Niagara-on-the-Lake. Here, too, you'll want to book well in advance; the great majority of these places are often filled with Shaw Festival theatergoers during the summer months.

Fort Erie and Fort George

From Niagara Falls you can drive south to Fort Erie, facing Buffalo across the Niagara River, or north to Niagara-on-the-Lake. If time is short, skip the Fort Erie section, the highlight of which in summer is the restored fort (originally built in 1764) with a military museum staffed by students dressed in period costume. In the opposite direction, just outside Niagara-on-the-Lake, is Fort George (1796), also facing New York State across the mouth of the Niagara River, and also staffed by students in period costume.

Niagara-on-the-Lake

Originally the site of an Onghiara Indian village, Niagara-on-the-Lake was settled by Loyalists from upstate New York, Connecticut, and Pennsylvania—many of whom had been members of British Col. John Butler's much-feared Rangers—at the close of the American Revolution. In 1792, newly appointed lieutenant-governor John Graves Simcoe declared the village the capital of Upper Canada and ordered its name changed to Newark. The first legislature met that September in Freemasons' Hall, and continued to meet there for four more sessions before Simcoe ordered the capital moved to York, now Toronto, because the latter was farther from the American border. The town he left behind was renamed Niagara by an act of Parliament a few years later.

The thriving little community suffered heavily during the War of 1812, its buildings razed by American troops in the second year of the conflict. (As a result, none of its extant buildings predate 1813, even though the town itself is more than 200 years old.) It was renamed again in 1906, this time Niagara-on-the-Lake, to avoid confusion with nearby Niagara Falls.

Today Niagara-on-the-Lake is a delight, although the reluctance of some of its influential residents (outside the retail sector) to share their lovely and historic town with the rest of the world makes for traffic snarls at the height of the summer-long tourist season, particularly on weekends. There isn't enough room for the invasion of buses, motor homes, cars, and campers to park along the streets of this community of 12,000 people, and the town fathers have not seen fit to establish a parking lot outside town—that would only encourage more visitors to flock to the already crowded sidewalks, shops, restaurants, and pubs.

Theatergoers know the village for the **George Bernard Shaw Festival**, the only professional theater company in the world devoted to the works of Shaw and his contemporaries. This cultural magnet had its humble origins in 1962, with underpaid thespians strutting the boards of an improvised stage in the old Victorian-era town hall. The patrons were loyal, and the productions attracted increasingly impressive casts—Jessica Tandy, Paxton Whitehead, and Kate Reid, among others. These days the festival draws almost 300,000 people a year to a theater built on the southern edge of town in 1973. The brown-brick building is mercifully shielded by landscaping and mature trees from the scenic Niagara Parkway drive, as its modern architectural style suits the town as gracefully as do the Golden Arches at the north end of Picton Street, the town's main street. For box-office information, Tel: (905) 468-2172.

STAYING AND DINING IN NIAGARA-ON-THE-LAKE

The relaxed Old English atmosphere of the ▶ Oban Inn, 160 Front Street, has been preserved despite the addition of modern conveniences. But book early; the inn only has 23 rooms—all different in terms of size and layout, and all furnished with antiques and decorated with arrangements of fresh cut flowers—to accommodate its permanent waiting list. It's also just steps from the local golf course. (Lunch in the inn's dining room, which caters to crowded bus tours, can be skipped at no great loss.)

The ▶ Prince of Wales, in the center of town, is a large luxury hotel whose 105 rooms usually are filled with theatergoers. Guest rooms are furnished in reproduction French provincial or traditional English country furniture, and range in size from a smallish standard room with two queen-size beds to a one-bedroom tower suite with fireplace, living room, and kitchen area. This is also the place to book a five-star dinner, to stop in for a light piano-bar buffet après-theater, or to get cozy in front of a crackling fire.

For more casual dining, cross the street to the front porch of **The Buttery** (Tel: (905/468-2564), a deservedly popular place for dining and people-watching. The Buttery serves lunch, afternoon tea, dinner, and an après-theater menu daily, but is perhaps best known for its Henry VIII feast, a four-course medieval-style banquet with music and much roistering held every Friday and Saturday night year-round.

Another establishment in the same price range is the ▶ Pillar & Post Inn, located just a few blocks from the town square at King and John streets. All 91 rooms here are decorated with handmade pine furniture and patchwork quilts, and about half of them have wood-burning fireplaces. Not all the fireplace rooms have queen-size beds, however; you'll want to reserve well in advance to guarantee a room with both.

Those seeking something cozier in the $85-to-$120 range should check out the 22-room ▶ Moffat Inn, 60 Picton Street, which was built as a hotel in 1835 and fully renovated in 1983. Some of the rooms have brass beds and fireplaces, and downstairs there's a tearoom and a friendly bar. The 10-room ▶ Gate House Hotel, 142 Queen Street, has retained most of its original appearance—on the outside. Inside, the design and decor (in a departure from the norm in this Victorian-flavored village) is contemporary Italian. The pasta is made fresh daily for the **Ristorante Giardino** (Tel: 905/468-3263) here, which offers a menu and atmosphere as European as its name.

You'll find the ▶ **South Landing Inn** a few miles upriver, in the quiet, historic village of Queenston. In the mid-1800s, when Queenston was a busy trans-shipment point on the Great Lakes, there were 13 inns here; today the South Landing is the only one still in operation. There are five rooms in the original inn, all furnished in traditional Canadian-style pine but with modern bathrooms *en suite* and air-conditioning. The 18 rooms in the two-story annex are similarly furnished, and open onto a wide verandah overlooking the original inn and the Niagara River.

THE NIAGARA PENINSULA

From late summer to the first frost, the Niagara Peninsula is a cornucopia of fresh fruits and vegetables, with stands along the major highways selling everything from fresh apple cider and grape juice to pumpkins and potatoes. The most comprehensive display is found on Lincoln County Road 55, the route you'd take from Niagara-on-the-Lake to Thorold, the next major tourist attraction heading west. Just past the hamlet of Virgil, on the right and behind well-tended flowerbeds, the **Harvest Barn Country Market** stocks everything grown locally as well as fruits and vegetables from around the world. There's a small bakery on the premises, and tables are provided so you can tuck right into the fresh produce, baked goods, and salads.

Welland Canal

The town of **Thorold**, about 24 km (15 miles) southwest of Niagara-on-the-Lake, and a bit west of Niagara Falls, has only one feature to recommend it to visitors. The paper-mill town of 16,000 is on the Welland Canal, a 26-mile-long system of locks that raise ships 326.5 feet from Lake Ontario to Lake Erie. The 24-unit ▶ **Lock 7 Motel** here was built to overlook the final lock in the system. The motel is popular with ship watchers from April to the end of December, during which time approximately 4,000 ships—some up to 730 feet in length—transit the lock right in front of the motel's picture windows. Breakfast only is served in the motel's modest dining room, and during the shipping season room reservations are essential.

The four-lane Queen Elizabeth Way (QEW) links the Niagara Peninsula with Toronto, where you can catch Highway

401 heading east along the north shore of Lake Ontario and the St. Lawrence River to the Quebec border. To head west from the peninsula, leave the QEW for Highway 403 just west of Hamilton. Highway 403 bypasses Brantford and joins Highway 401 just east of Woodstock.

Hamilton

This city of 300,000 is built under and upon an outcrop of the **Niagara Escarpment** west of Niagara Falls. It is the steel capital of Canada but, somewhat paradoxically, also home to a 2,500-acre **botanical garden** and the third-largest art gallery in Ontario. Hamilton has two noteworthy museums as well: the **Canadian Football Hall of Fame and Museum**, which traces the history of the game since it was first played in Canada in 1870, and the **Canadian Warplane Heritage Museum**, whose 35 aircraft are all capable of flying.

The city's foremost attraction is **Dundurn Castle**, the 35-room 19th-century mansion built by Sir Allan Napier McNab, prime minister of the United Provinces of Canada from 1854 to 1856. The castle is open daily, 11:00 A.M. to 4:00 P.M., June through Labour Day, and 1:00 to 4:00 P.M. the rest of the year.

African Lion Safari, a drive-through wildlife park with rail and cruise-boat excursions, petting zoo, and daily animal and bird shows, is located 19 km (12 miles) northwest of the city off Highway 8 near Rockton. Open daily mid-April to late October. Excellent, reasonably priced lunches and dinners are available in the **Ancaster Old Mill** (Tel: 905/648-1827), a restored grist mill in nearby Ancaster; try to get a seat overlooking the dam and millrace.

Visitors who decide to stay overnight in Hamilton will find a range of accommodations in the downtown area, from the sparkling 300-room ▶ **Sheraton Hamilton**, 116 King Street West, to the refurbished old-style luxury of the ▶ **Royal Connaught Hotel**, 112 King Street East. The food at **The Grill** in the Connaught gives it the edge.

Brantford

Alexander Graham Bell Homestead

The man whose genius resulted in Brantford (southwest of Hamilton via Highway 403/Route 2) being called the Telephone City lived here with his family between 1870 and 1881, during which time he made the world's first long-distance telephone call to Paris, eight miles to the northwest.

The Bell Homestead, on the outskirts of town at 94 Tutela Heights Road, on the banks of the Grand River, is a national historic site. About 90 percent of the period furnishings are authentic, although the instrument with which Bell made history is a replica; the original is in the United States. Next door is the house of the Rev. Thomas Henderson, the first telephone business office in Canada. It was moved to the museum site from downtown Brantford, and now houses a number of displays tracing the evolution of the telephone from 1876 to the present. The Bell Homestead is open daily except Mondays, year-round.

Paris

For technology buffs, the trek to Paris is likely to be disappointing; the momentous event is noted only by an unobtrusive storefront plaque. Along the way, however, you'll pass the turn-of-the-century structure that houses the **Olde School House Restaurant** (Tel: 519/753-3131), one of Ontario's finest. Steaks, salads, fish, and chops dominate the menu, and the chocolate mouse—that's right, mouse—is as good as it gets. Paris itself, population 7,500, is situated at the confluence of the Nith and Grand rivers, which together have carved a steep-sided valley through the Niagara Escarpment. It is one of a number of communities calling itself "the prettiest town in Ontario," and certainly qualifies as one of the scenic highlights of Southwestern Ontario, a region that is alternately densely populated or rolling farm country. The town has a dozen houses, two churches, and several walls typifying cobblestone architecture—a rare building style utilizing small water-worn stones laid in horizontal rows. You'll find **John M. Hall's Linen Store**, a living museum of the retail dry-goods business with an unsurpassed stock of quality linen and textile goods just up the street from the plaque commemorating Bell's feat.

THE KITCHENER–WATERLOO AREA
Kitchener–Waterloo

Located about 48 km (30 miles) northwest of Hamilton, the twin cities of Kitchener and Waterloo are the gateway to Mennonite country. For ten days in early to mid-October the cities, whose combined population is about 200,000, draw up to 600,000 people to **Oktoberfest**, a harvest blast floated on beer and held in 30 festival halls and tents, with related sporting events and a three-mile-long parade.

The Farmers' Market

Of all the many farmers' markets in the province, Kitchener's is easily the most impressive. These days it is incorporated into the vibrant new **Market Square**, a glass-enclosed complex with its own clock tower and about 70 shops and boutiques. The market's 100 vendors offer the usual meats, fish, and vegetables, as well as plants and a wide range of handicrafts. Hours are every Saturday from 5:00 A.M. to 2:00 P.M., with a second day, Thursdays from 7:00 A.M. to 2:00 P.M., added from May to December.

The square is connected by a glass-wrapped second-floor walkway to the 203-room ▶ **Valhalla Inn**, one of two lodgings in downtown Kitchener recommended as a base from which to explore this historic area. Facilities and amenities here include two five-pin bowling alleys, three squash courts, a nine-hole miniature golf course, a sauna, a swimming pool, and three dining areas.

The glockenspiel directly across the street from the Valhalla Inn sounds sporadically throughout the day. Immediately adjacent is the **Kitchener Chamber of Commerce** office, well-stocked with detailed information about area attractions.

The ▶ **Walper Terrace Hotel**, 1 King Street West, is one block north. After standing empty for several years, the 83-room hotel has been completely restored to its former elegance. Original features—from wooden trim moldings and carved marble pillars to the ornate brass banister of the main staircase—have been faithfully refinished, and every room has at least one piece of period cherrywood furniture. A restaurant and a pub, a lounge, and a mini-mall on the hotel's lower level ensure that guests never have to stray far to keep themselves well fed and amused.

Woodside National Historic Park
and the Seagram Museum

Kitchener's Woodside National Historic Park (open daily year-round) surrounds the boyhood home of William Lyon Mackenzie King, the tenth prime minister of Canada. The home is situated in a pleasant park setting and has been faithfully restored in 1890s-period style.

In **Waterloo**, which is really the northern extension of the city of Kitchener, you'll find the Seagram Museum at 57 Erb Street West. The museum promotes the Seagram company product—alcoholic beverages—but also does a nice job explaining the wine-and-spirits industry with artifacts from around the world, and has an excellent restaurant. Open daily May through October; closed Mondays the rest of the year.

St. Jacobs

St. Jacobs, several miles north of Waterloo and immediately west of Highway 86 on County Road 17, is located in the heart of Ontario's Mennonite country. You'll first notice the extra-wide graveled shoulders of the secondary highways in the region, and before long you're bound to spot one of the black horse-drawn buggies. After an hour or two you'll find that you're not driving as fast as usual and that you've decided there's time for that second cup of coffee after lunch or dinner.

To watch the Mennonites go about their daily business is to watch a way of life from another era, the way of life of our forefathers, which might have involved harder and more sustained physical labor but was not as complicated, fast-paced, and downright hectic as life seems to be nowadays.

STAYING AND DINING IN THE AREA

▶ Benjamin's Restaurant & Inn (Tel: 519/664-3731), a beautifully renovated 1850s-vintage inn with nine guest rooms on King Street, is a great place for lunch or dinner, or to stay overnight. Rooms are furnished with local antiques, and each bed is covered with a handmade Mennonite quilt. In the morning, a Continental breakfast is served on a closed verandah. The turn-of-the-century red-brick ▶ Jakobstettel Guest House, on Isabella Street, has 12 rooms on five landscaped acres, along with a swimming pool and a clay tennis court. Handicraft aficionados will want to check out Village Silos, across the street from Benjamin's, where former grain storage silos have been converted into boutiques for local artists and artisans.

In any direction from St. Jacobs you'll stumble upon small villages, many with country inns where you can enjoy Mennonite cooking. The hitching rails in front of the stores in this area are not for effect; you'll see horses attached to black carriages tethered to them with some frequency.

One of the best dining rooms in the area belongs to the 1838-vintage ▶ Heidelberg Brewery and Restaurant Motel (Tel: 519/699-4413), located a few miles south of St. Jacobs and about 5 km (3 miles) west of Highway 86 on County Road 15 in the hamlet of Heidelberg. Meals are served on 9-by-13-inch platters, with hardly any room left over for the side dishes. The Bavarian lager beer brewed and served here has a loyal local following as well. The adjoining 16-unit motel has rooms in the $45-a-night range; the far-more-than-you-can-or-should-eat dinner platters average about $12.

If you bought goodies at the Kitchener or Waterloo farmers' markets and are ready for a picnic, consider one of the region's very special places: Take Highway 86 north from Kitchener–Waterloo and turn off onto County Road 21, following signs for Elmira. In Elmira, turn right on Waterloo County Road 86 to **West Montrose**, just a speck on the map a few miles east of Elmira. Ontario's only covered bridge spans the Grand River here, and the setting is bucolic. The lawns surrounding the approaches to the bridge are privately owned, but picnickers who respect the environment are welcome.

Elora

The picture-postcard village of Elora, where pre-Confederation limestone buildings cluster around the banks of the Grand River as it froths through the jagged Elora Gorge, is about 16 km (10 miles) north of West Montrose. The village is anchored by an old grist mill turned swank hostelry now called the ▶ **Elora Mill Inn** (Tel: 519/846-5356). The inn has a well-deserved reputation for serving excellent Canadian and international cuisine, and also has 35 guest rooms in four stone buildings. Each of the rooms is different in its floor plan and decor, but all have period pine furniture and quilts handmade by area Mennonites. No room or hallway is without some section of original stonework or hand-hewn wooden beams.

Within the immediate vicinity of the inn there's a profusion of boutiques, pottery and antiques stores, and half a dozen European-style restaurants in original stone or frame buildings, most dating from the 1850s. The quiet, tree-lined streets invite strolling, and the boutiques welcome browsing.

If the weather is good, consider hiking the **Elora Gorge**, a pretty stretch of the Grand River flanked by sheer limestone walls trimmed with leafy cedar trees. Narrow trails with sturdy guardrails follow the gorge, although the ground is often wet and littered with sharp stones and loose gravel. Best to leave your leather-soled shoes behind if you decide to tackle it.

New Hamburg

New Hamburg, which many travellers make the mistake of bypassing, is about 24 km (15 miles) west of Kitchener, just off Highway 7. The ▶ **Waterlot Inn** (Tel: 519/662-2020) here, in a building erected by the local mill owner around 1846, overlooks a millpond off the Nith River. Most of the brick building is Victorian in style, but a nonfunctional cupola adds an Italian flavor. The inn's restaurant, with four dining rooms and a café-style patio-lounge, enjoys a wide reputation for excellent French cuisine and has earned numerous culinary awards. Ask for a table overlooking the millpond and the beautiful lawns shaded by huge willows. Three reasonably priced guest rooms are also available, one of which is a large suite that's ideal for two couples. The other two rooms share a large bathroom and a sitting area lighted by the cupola.

The **Selfhelp Crafts Canada** outlet, a Mennonite project designed to help Third World countries by selling goods produced in 20 such countries, is located three blocks north of the center of town. Selfhelp is a nonprofit program: The individual wood-carver, metal-worker, weaver, embroiderer, or jeweler sets the price of the article he or she has created, with any markup applied solely to the added cost of transportation, customs, warehousing, and administration. There are more than 100 Selfhelp outlets across Canada and the United States. The New Hamburg store, at 175 Waterloo Street, carries brassware, hand-carved wooden articles, batik items, jute mats, tooled leather, embroidered and hand-woven linens, handcrafted greeting cards, baskets, wicker-work, jewelry, dolls, and toys. Next door the Mennonites operate a used-clothing store, and on the other side is **Riverside Brass**, which advertises its four rooms full of Canadian-made and imported brass items as the largest selection of brassware in Canada.

STRATFORD

From a modest but ambitious start in 1953, the **Stratford Shakespearean Festival** has become a major world theatrical event, attracting more than 400,000 people annually to this city of 26,000 on the Avon River. Any physical resemblance to Stratford-upon-Avon in England is deliberate . . . and there are many.

The city now has three theaters. Festival Theatre, with its Shakespearean productions, is the major operation, but the Avon Theatre and Third Stage, which offer music, opera, and contemporary drama, also draw their share of visitors. Tickets to Festival Theatre productions can be ordered through the box office; Tel: (519) 273-1600.

The city has more than 500 hotel and motel rooms to accommodate theatergoers during the season (May 1 to mid-October). One gem is the 30-room ▶ **Queen's Inn at Stratford**, 161 Ontario Street, a local landmark dating to the mid-19th century that was completely renovated a few years ago.

One of Stratford's most interesting bed-and-breakfast operations is ▶ **Woods Villa**, 62 John Street North, an 1870 mansion in whose public rooms owner Ken Vinen displays his colleetion of more than 20 working player pianos, vintage jukeboxes, and music boxes. Vinen has lovingly restored both the instruments and the mansion (which has an enormous ceramic-tiled swimming pool), and has the piano rolls or original recordings of any old favorite you care to request. If he hasn't got it, he'll play it for you as he played it with the greats during his show-business days. Rooms go for about $75 a night; no children or pets, and no smoking.

Stratford has far more pubs and top-notch dining establishments than most cities its size. Many stay open year-round. At **Jay's** (Tel: 519/271-1023), next to the Albert Place Hotel at 23 Albert Street, you can have your drinks on sofas set around a blazing fire. Stratford's **Olde English Parlour** (Tel: 519/271-2772), 101 Wellington Street at St. Patrick, offers family dining, after-theater fare, and a full menu on an outdoor patio. The younger set congregates at **Classics** and **Rumors**, both at City Hall, 27 Market Place.

About ten miles southwest of Stratford, in the prosperous 19th-century town of **St. Mary's** (follow Highways 7 and 19 to County Road 28), you'll find a well-preserved Victorian-era business district as well as another fine country inn. The ▶ **Westover Inn** opened in 1987 and has 22 bedrooms in three buildings—one used to be a dormitory when the estate was a Roman Catholic seminary—as well as a chef who is gaining a dedicated following for his nouvelle-style creations.

LONDON

This city of 300,000 people is situated almost exactly midway between Toronto and Windsor on the banks of—you guessed it—the Thames River. Colonel John Graves Simcoe chose the site in 1792 for the future capital of Upper Canada, but was subsequently overruled by a superior who opted instead for Newark, now Niagara-on-the-Lake. (The legislature met for four sessions in Newark before moving to York, now Toronto, a site considered safer because it was farther from the U.S. border.) London is nicknamed the Forest City because of the many old trees that shade its lovely residential streets.

Old money is alive and well here, and it shows. As the chief metropolis of Southwestern Ontario, London is a manufacturing, distribution, and financial center of considerable importance. The city boasts more than 300 major industries, the headquarters of two major life insurance companies and two trust companies, and the main campus of the **University of Western Ontario**. At the same time, you won't find any famous tourist attractions here, except perhaps for the architecturally striking **London Regional Art and Historical Museum**, 421 Ridout Street, which offers a series of changing exhibitions. (Open year-round, daily except Mondays, noon to 5:00 P.M.) Instead, visitors delight in exploring London because it is clean, well maintained, and riddled with lovely parks.

STAYING AND DINING IN LONDON

The city core is presently undergoing a construction boom that will add several new hotels and a convention center. The newest showpiece downtown is the ▶ **Sheraton Armouries**, a glass tower rising from the former armories building on Dundas Street. For five-star comfort at a slower pace consider the ▶ **Idlewyld Inn**, on Grand Avenue, an 1878 mansion converted into a 27-room hotel with all the comforts of home.

The **Marienbad Restaurant** (Tel: 519/679-9940) and **Chaucer's Pub**, both at 122 Carling Street, serve up Czechoslovakian specialties in a central courtyard area (weather permitting). For especially good food with a view and service to match—tableside cooking, flaming desserts, and the like—try **Michael's on the Thames**, overlooking the river at 1 York Street; Tel: (519) 672-0111.

Just east of the city there's a pioneer village on the shores of **Lake Fanshawe**, a man-made lake suitable for sailing, fishing, and swimming. The London International Air Show, held in early June for two days, has become one of the biggest air shows in North America, drawing the air forces of many countries and more than 50,000 spectators.

THE LAKE ERIE SHORE

Port Stanley

Port Stanley, on Lake Erie about 32 km (20 miles) south of London via Highway 4, is one of the region's warm-weather playgrounds. A village of just under 2,000, it jumps in the summer and snoozes through the winter. On weekends year-round or daily July through October, visitors can make the 50-minute round trip to the hamlet of Union or the longer trip to the city of St. Thomas on the antique railcars of the **Port Stanley Terminal Rail Inc.**

Back in Port Stanley, the elegant ▶ **Kettle Creek Inn** just off Main Street has ten rooms, five suites, a hospitable bar-lounge, and superb cuisine served year-round. (In fine weather you can dine on an outdoor patio.) All rooms have bathrooms *en suite,* and the luxury suites also have two-person whirlpool tubs and gas fireplaces in the sitting rooms.

Port Stanley is fairly typical of the tiny ports and towns that dot the northern shore of Lake Erie. In fact, if you leave Highway 401 and dawdle along the lakeshore of Southwest Ontario, you'll find some great little fishing villages, sand beaches, and summer festivals. These include the resort beaches of **Long Point**, a sandy peninsula jutting some 40 miles into Lake Erie, and the cottages and marinas of **Port Rowan** and **Turkey Point**, the latter about 65 km (40 miles) east of Port Stanley via County Roads 42 and 24.

Port Dover

Located 46 km (29 miles) east of Long Point via Highways 24 and 59, Port Dover is the quintessential Lake Erie beach town. As such, it comes alive in summer, when tourists and cottagers parade up and down the boardwalk, line up to munch foot-long hot dogs and steamy french fries at the **Arbor** (a local institution for more than 60 years), sprawl on the beach, or sip a libation on the deck at **Callahan's** lakefront restaurant.

With a major fishing fleet calling Port Dover home, there's never a shortage of fresh fish. You can sample it at **Knechtel's** (Tel: 519/782-3315) on the beach at 291 Colbourne Street, or head over to the ▶ **Erie Beach Hotel** (Tel: 519/583-1391), on Walker Street, where those in the know fill up on platters of perch, shrimp, scallops, the hotel's special celery bread, and pitchers of various liquids. The place is always crowded and the lines are long, but no one seems to mind.

Port Dover is about more than food and fish, however. One of the most popular tourist stops is **The Sandalmaker**, where Johnny Miller has been handcrafting made-to-measure leather sandals in a renovated fisherman's hut beside the pier for more than two decades. His talented staff also creates leather belts, briefcases, jackets, vests, and almost anything you care to design yourself.

Scuba divers will want to drop by the **Outer Reef Dive Shop**, a little shop at the foot of Main Street that never fails to surprise with its wide-ranging selection of diving gear (rentals as well as new), bathing suits, and beachwear. Outer Reef also offers excursions to some of the old shipwrecks in Lake

Erie, as well as an intensive weekend PADI certification course.

Finally, no visit to Port Dover would be complete without a shopping spree at the **Surf Shop**, on the boardwalk adjacent to Knechtel's. This summertime hangout is packed with the latest in swimsuits and beach gear, sunglasses and suntan lotions, beach towels and summer dresses.

There are plenty of rental cottages in the area, but if you stay at the Erie Beach, with its 18 motel-style rooms, you won't have far to walk after dinner.

THE WINDSOR AREA

Point Pelee National Park
Essex County, at the extreme western end of Southwestern Ontario, has a number of worthwhile attractions. (From London, take Highway 401—or Highway 4 to Highway 3—to Leamington and Highway 77.) Extending like a stout icicle into the waters of Lake Erie, Point Pelee National Park (pronounced "pee-lee") comprises 4,000 acres of sand, marsh, trees, and grass, as well as the southernmost point on the Canadian mainland. The point is also on the flyway for many species of birds, notably Canada geese, as well as the monarch butterfly. You'll find an interpretive center, transit trains, nature trails, picnic grounds, and a mile of boardwalk running through the marsh here, with observation towers for bird-watchers. Bicycle and canoe rentals are also available, and are good ways to explore the park's 14 miles of sandy beach; because of the delicate ecology of the point, bans on camping and leaving the boardwalk are strictly enforced. Efforts are also being made to encourage birders and others to visit equally productive conservation areas in the region.

Motel accommodations are available in Leamington, 10 km (6 miles) to the north, but are usually fully booked well in advance of the butterfly and bird migrations. If you're feeling lucky, try either the ▶ **Journey's End Leamington**, 279 Erie Street South, or the ▶ **Days Inn**, about a mile southeast of town on Highway 77.

The **Jack Miner Migratory Bird Foundation**, open to the public Monday through Saturday from October 1 to April 10 (closed Christmas Day, Boxing Day, and New Year's Day), is a few miles west and north of Leamington, and well signposted. Miner was a pioneer conservationist active in a variety of causes from 1910 to 1940, and his home here has been turned into a museum filled with Miner memorabilia.

The sanctuary, popularly known as "Jack Miner's," is a resting area and feeding ground for large flocks of geese and other waterfowl.

Pelee Island

Located southwest of Point Pelee, halfway between Ontario and the U.S. state of Ohio, Pelee Island is the largest island in Lake Erie and, with the exception of Middle Island (which is negligible in size), Canada's southernmost possession. It's also a charming escape from either mainland (reached by ferry from either Leamington, Kingsville, or Sandusky in Ohio).

Unpaved roads circle and cross the island, which is about eight miles long and four miles wide. On the entire island there is only one stop sign and one speed-limit sign: Pelee is a laid-back sort of place where nobody ever seems to hurry. Although there are a number of small, comfortable motels here (try the ► **Westview Motel**, open May to November), it really is cottage country for families from both mainlands. The 14-room ► **Pelee Island Hotel**, owned and managed by Darith and Bruce Smith, has become the island's social center. Rooms are small and basic, and priced accordingly. (You won't be spending much time in your room anyway.)

Because the municipality raises pheasants and charges wealthy hunters a stiff fee for the right to shoot them in the fall, taxes are low. The interior of the island is given over to the production of grapes for a local winery. You can tour Pelee by car or bicycle (the island is flat and rentals are available), but whether walking or bicycling, be prepared to receive—and return—friendly waves from the driver of almost every passing vehicle. Information on ferry sailings, fares, and reservations (which are strongly recommended for vehicles in summer) is available by calling Pelee Island Transportation Services, Tel: (800) 661-2220 or (519) 724-2115; they're also your best bet for booking air transportation to the island. In winter the only way to reach the island is by air: from Windsor, contact **Southwest Air** (Tel: 519/966-5727); **Simo Air** (Tel: 519/969-0007), which provides charter service; or **Griffin Flying Service** (in Sandusky, Ohio; Tel: 419/626-5161).

Amherstburg

This town of 8,500 residents at the mouth of the Detroit River, about 24 km (15 miles) south of Windsor and 38 km (24 miles) west of Kingsville via Highway 18, has several points of historical interest as well as a pleasant riverside motel with excellent dining facilities— ▶ **Duffy's Motor Inn**, 306 Dalhousie Street, where almost every room has a river view. **Fort Malden National Historic Park**, first known as Fort Amherstburg, played important roles in the War of 1812 and the Rebellion of 1837–1838. The 11-acre park includes remains of the original earthworks, a restored barracks, a military pensioner's cottage, two exhibit buildings, and picnic facilities; open daily year-round.

Two Museums of 19th-Century Life

The **North American Black Historical Museum**, 277 King Street, tells of daring escapes from the U.S. by black slaves and of the underground railway system that brought many such slaves to freedom in Canada. An 1848-vintage church and log cabin contain artifacts from the era, with photographs, crafts, and art displays tracing the history of black people in the Western Hemisphere from slavery to freedom; the museum is open Wednesday through Sunday year-round.

Also of interest in Amherstburg is the **Park House Museum**, originally built in 1796 on the U.S. side of the Detroit River. The owner, a Loyalist who objected to the terms of the Jay Treaty of 1798, preferred not to leave his new home on the American side of the river, and so dismantled it, floated the materials downriver, and then reassembled them in Amherstburg. The solid log home with clapboard siding and cedar-shake roof has been restored to depict the lifestyle of the Park family, who occupied it for years. An exhibit area contains pioneer artifacts, and there are on-premises demonstrations of tinsmithing and a hand-operated printing press—the same press that turned out the first copies of the *Amherstburg Echo* weekly in 1874. From June 1 through August 31 the house is open daily; check the posted schedule for off-season hours.

Windsor

Although the Automotive City, as Windsor is nicknamed, has done a wonderful job cleaning up its formerly tatty, junk-littered waterfront, major tourist attractions here are still few and far between. (The big draws are found in and around Detroit, on the opposite bank of the Detroit River.) Windsor is the only convenient option hereabouts for deluxe lodgings, however, not to mention a wide range of services. For four-star, if somewhat impersonal, accommodations, the 22-story ▶ **Hilton International Windsor**, 277 Riverside Drive

West, a couple of blocks from the heart of downtown, has 303 rooms and suites overlooking the Detroit River (touted as the world's busiest inland waterway), and is the best hotel the area has to offer.

At the other end of the lodging spectrum, the ▶ **Ivy Rose Motor Inn**, 2885 Howard Avenue, is one of the most unusual in the province. Owner Walter Skally runs the place as though his guests were friends of the family—and many of them are. Skally doesn't care much for mass-produced furniture and doesn't see why his guests have to put up with it. As a result, each of the 91 personalized motel-style units is furnished like a bed–sitting-room in someone's home. The Ivy Rose also has an outdoor swimming pool, picnic areas, and a barbecue patio where guests can cook their own meals, as well as a restaurant that attracts a steady stream of locals and out-of-towners with its home-style cooking.

Sarnia and Vicinity

This city of 50,000 faces Port Huron, Michigan, across the St. Clair River, which flows south into Lake St. Clair and then becomes the Detroit River on its way to Lake Erie. There are three points of interest near Sarnia: The first, on Highway 21, is **Oil Springs**, a hamlet of 630 people once known as the oil capital of Canada. The Oil Museum of Canada here has working models of, and actual drill rigs from, North America's first commercial oil fields. The museum is open daily May through October, and Monday through Friday the rest of the year.

Petrolia

When 19th-century drillers hit oil at Oil Springs, Petrolia, now a pretty town of 4,500 people about 8 km (5 miles) to the north, became the world's first oil boomtown. In fact, by 1890 it was the hub of an intercontinental refining empire, with the world's first oil exchange housed in a building that still stands. **Petrolia Discovery**, a 60-acre, fully operational oil field, looks and operates much as it did in the second half of the 19th century. Interpretive exhibits and a film describe the discovery and development of the area's petroleum reserves. The display area is open daily from early May to late October.

Uncle Tom's Cabin National Historic Site

Dresden, about 35 km (22 miles) south of Petrolia, is the site of Uncle Tom's Cabin, a magnet for thousands of visitors annually. In real life, "Uncle Tom" was the Rev. Josiah

Henson, himself an ex-slave who, with the help of abolition-ists in the States, purchased 200 acres here and founded a vocational school for runaway slaves in 1841. His cabin and five other buildings are open daily from May to the end of October. In addition to the main cabin, visitors can see a church dating to the 1850s, an agricultural building contain-ing early farming and logging equipment, a smokehouse carved from a six-foot-thick sycamore tree, and a museum containing rare books and documents on the abolitionist era. Scattered throughout the museum are balls-and-chains, head irons, slave whips, handcuffs, and clubs—graphic re-minders of man's inhumanity to man slightly more than a century ago.

THE LAKE HURON COASTLINE

Ontario's lower Lake Huron coastline stretches 350 km (217 miles), from Sarnia north to the tip of the Bruce Peninsula, the latter forming the western shoreline of Georgian Bay. Much of this coastline consists of fine sandy beaches and small summer resorts that draw vacationers from neighbor-ing Michigan and inland Ontario.

From south to north, the main resorts are strung along Highway 21, also known as the **Bluewater Highway**, which runs from Ipperwash Beach, about 60 km (37 miles) north-east of Sarnia, north to Southampton, where it turns east and crosses the base of the Bruce Peninsula to the town of Owen Sound. Highway 6 runs north from a point halfway between Southampton and Owen Sound to Tobermory, at the tip of the peninsula. Tobermory itself is linked by two large mod-ern ferries to South Baymouth on **Manitoulin Island**, a shortcut to Northern Ontario from Southwestern Ontario. (See the Northern Ontario section for details on the ferries and the island.)

Grand Bend

Grand Bend, about 80 km (50 miles) northeast of Sarnia, is one of the area's more popular resorts. In winter it has a population of 800; on summer weekends the beach and streets are choked with tens of thousands of people lured by the sand, the marinas, the hot-dog stands, and all the other people. Grand Bend also supports two straw-hat summer theaters, the Huron Country Playhouse and Playhouse II, which offer cabaret theater from late June to early September.

Grand Bend got a "new" resort in 1988 when the
► **Oakwood Inn Resort** was completely renovated. There are

now 89 rooms, suites, and cabins available here, some in a new lodge, others in motel-like units. The resort's showpiece is an indoor swimming pool surrounded by spacious aprons, brightened by skylights, and decorated with black-and-white blowups of turn-of-the-century Grand Bend scenes. In summer golfers from Michigan and southern Ontario lose balls in a creek that seems to cross every fairway, while in winter sports enthusiasts swap stories around a big fireplace in the always-popular bar, enjoy excellent meals in the Oak Room dining room, and retire to their cabin for romantic evenings in front of gas-lit fireplaces. Daily rates start at under $100, depending on the type of room.

Bayfield

Bayfield, a pretty village of old-money summer cottages some 29 km (18 miles) north of Grand Bend, has a main street lined with trendy boutiques and Victorian-era frame buildings. The historic ▶ Little Inn of Bayfield is an outstanding country inn popular with the yachting set that flocks to a modern marina at the mouth of the Bayfield River. Elsewhere on Main Street, the Admiral Bayfield, a walk-up window beside the ▶ Albion Hotel, serves some of the best french-fried potatoes in the world. For something a little more substantial, the dining room in the Albion is a great place for lunch, with a laid-back pub ambience guaranteed to charm. The 135-year-old inn also has seven modest rooms upstairs. You'll have to book in advance, however: In a quaint village of "in" spots, this is *the* in spot.

For a truly memorable dining experience, plan to have dinner at ▶ La Brassine (Tel: 519/524-6300), a self-styled bed and breakfast with an outstanding dining room. To find it, take Highway 21 north to Kitchigami Camp Road, a few miles south of Goderich, and turn left (west) in the direction of Lake Huron. The first right off this road leads to the inn. Dinner reservations (Wednesday through Sunday only) must be booked 24 hours in advance, although if you reserve far enough ahead owners Tom and Nicky Blanchard-Hublet will send you a four-page menu listing the gastronomic delights they offer. The five-course meal is served on fine china in a dining room that's a treasure trove of antiques and curios collected by Tom and Nicky. La Brassine also has five reasonably priced rooms (breakfast included) overlooking farm fields and a fish pond or Lake Huron itself.

Goderich

With an uncharacteristic lack of diplomacy, Queen Elizabeth II once called Goderich, located some 21 km (13 miles) north of Bayfield, "the prettiest town in Canada"—a claim that can be legitimately disputed by several dozen chambers of commerce. Notwithstanding, Goderich is certainly pretty, and its octagonal town green gives it a one-of-a-kind center, with a handsome stone courthouse in the middle. The town sits atop a bluff overlooking the Maitland River and Goderich Harbour, the largest harbor on the Canadian side of Lake Huron. Visiting freighters load grain and salt, which is mined from deposits beneath the lake bed. Artifacts from Ontario pioneer life are assembled in the 20,000-piece **Huron County Pioneer Museum** collection at 110 North Street. The museum's exhibit space has tripled in recent years, so allow at least two hours for an overview of the collection, which includes a restored log cabin. (Open daily in summer; closed Saturdays Labour Day through April.) Admission to the museum also gets you into the **Huron County Marine Museum**, a collection of shipping artifacts and photographs housed in the former forward cabin of an old lake freighter down by the harbor.

The old Goderich jail, 181 Victoria Street, dates to 1841 and is also octagonal. Officially known as the **Huron Historic Gaol**, the jail commands the finest site in town, overlooking both the harbor and the mouth of the Maitland River. A stroll through this well-preserved facility might very well cause the visitor to reflect that crime wouldn't have reached today's epidemic proportions had not so many improvements been made to North American jails over the years.

The ▶ **Hotel Bedford**, anchoring one corner of the town's square, has recently been refurbished. While the pine wainscoting, pine-frame beds, and air-conditioning are recent additions, each room also contains at least two original pieces. The hotel, built in 1896, combines the local watering hole, the **Duke of Bedford Cocktail Lounge**, with the upscale **Bruno's** (Tel: 519/524-7337), across the lobby. Bruno's is a *ristorante* with Italian cuisine by day and a New York–style nightclub by night. The hotel also has a traditional dining room that offers a reasonably priced menu heavy on fresh lake fish and seafood.

Kincardine and Port Elgin

Kincardine, a town of 6,000 some 52 km (32 miles) farther north, has its own fine beach on Lake Huron, to which thousands of summertime visitors flock. But because it also has a relatively large year-round population, it tends to be quieter than Grand Bend during the warm-weather months.

Deepwater-fishing charters in boats with all the latest scientific gadgets (for taking the guesswork—and sport—

out of salmon fishing) are available the length of the Lake Huron shoreline, with the largest concentration of outfitters in Port Elgin, a small town 37 km (23 miles) north of Kincardine. The electronics available to outwit fish are so baboon-proof that some outfitters even advertise partial money-back guarantees if they're unable to get your hook into the mouth of one.

Southhampton

The Saugeen River flows into Lake Huron at Southampton, another small town on yet another fine sandy beach just 9 km (5½ miles) north of Port Elgin. Southampton is a re-served resort town where old-money types maintain all-season "cottages" and the tennis club has one of the largest membership rolls in Canada. The 1850s ▶ Chantry House Inn at 118 High Street, Southampton's main street, is a small country inn with three suites and seven bedrooms; all rooms are decorated with family heirlooms and antiques, and have coffee makers, mini-refrigerators, and microwave ovens. The afghans are made by the innkeeper, and the lunch and dinner menus feature Mennonite recipes handed down through the generations. In season vegetables are harvested from the inn's garden, and all dishes, including the jams, jellies, and preserves, are prepared from scratch.

The Bruce Peninsula

The remote town of **Tobermory**, at the tip of the Bruce Peninsula some 120 km (74 miles) north of Southampton, is developing a substantial reputation as a winter-vacation desti-nation. (Wiarton, at the base of the peninsula facing Geor-gian Bay, recently set Ontario's record for annual snowfall— more than 20 feet.) The almost guaranteed annual snowfall in this neck of the woods allows the Bruce Peninsula Snow-mobile Trail Association to maintain some 1,000 miles of groomed snowmobile trails, and cross-country ski packages to the area are gaining in popularity. Tobermory is also the terminal for the *Chi-Cheemaun* and *Nindawayma* car ferries to South Baymouth on **Manitoulin Island**, off the north shore of Lake Huron (see the Northern Ontario section below).

During its short summer season, hearty scuba divers take advantage of Tobermory's unmatched access to the crystal-clear waters of Lake Huron and Georgian Bay to explore the many shipwrecks in the area. A bird's-eye view of some of the same wrecks can be had by taking one of the glass-bottom boat trips offered in town. Other visitors head out to the "flowerpots"—stone monoliths carved by the wind and waves.

INLAND FROM LAKE HURON

Inland from the Bluewater Highway you'll find rolling farm country dotted by quiet, long-settled hamlets and villages. The region is laced by small rivers, many ideal for canoeing, and all excellent for bass, trout, and salmon fishing. Most towns still have their downtown hotel, many of them 150-year-old buildings of quarried stone where farmers and townsfolk socialize in Canada's answer to the rural British pub. Most of these hotels also rent rooms in the $45-to-$60-per-night range. You'll get what you pay for at those prices, but it's still possible to find a clean, no-frills room—usually with a bathroom down the hall—for $45 a night. Several towns in the region rate a brief mention.

An old stone mill on the Maitland River at Benmiller, a few miles south and east of Goderich, has been developed into a showcase rural retreat for the well-to-do. The ▶ Benmiller Inn offers modern, fully equipped rooms and suites overlooking either the river or the lovingly restored mill buildings. Wood-burning fireplaces, Jacuzzis, saunas, walking trails, an indoor pool, and an extensive international menu in the beautifully decorated dining room of the main building all contribute to the inn's excellent reputation.

The village of **Blyth**, about 16 km (10 miles) east of Benmiller via Highways 8 and 4, has two major leather-goods outlets that draw customers from a wide radius. In addition, from mid-June to mid-September the Blyth Festival Theatre specializes in contemporary Canadian drama. Lack of any kind of hotel or motel accommodations in the immediate area has inspired at least 30 country bed-and-breakfast operations. For information call Ontario Travel; Tel: (800) 668-2746 or (416) 314-0944.

Paisley, located 40 km (25 miles) northeast of Kincardine, is nicknamed the Village of Bridges after the six inside the village limits that cross the four rivers converging here. Outfitter Ted Cowan, who makes his own canoes and a unique bent-shaft wooden paddle, will rent canoes for use on the **Saugeen River**, the best canoeing river in Southwestern Ontario.

OWEN SOUND – NOTTAWASAGA BAY

The town of **Owen Sound** looks as if it was built in a huge bowl with a piece missing. The missing piece is Owen Sound itself, a deep inlet off the southern end of Georgian

Bay. The community climbs the slopes surrounding the inlet on three sides. Geography makes it a compact site; its distance from any major city makes it a tightly knit community. This is fishing country year-round, hunting country in season, and, when the ice is gone, a watery playground for canoeists, kayakers, sailors, and motorboaters. The ▶ **Inn on the Bay** here has 56 rooms and four suites, all overlooking the sound. For dining at its finest try **Louis' Steak and Seafood House** (Tel: 519/376-4430), just east of the town center on Highway 26.

Collingwood, which sits below the highest section of the Niagara Escarpment, is the downhill ski center of Southwestern Ontario. In recent years a number of summer attractions have been developed in an attempt to defray the overhead on the substantial number of rooms built for skiers. These include a 3,000-foot alpine slide, a water slide, and a tube ride, all located 13 km (8 miles) west of town.

East of Collingwood, **Wasaga Beach**, a small resort town of 4,600 built on a sandspit between Georgian Bay and the Nottawasaga River, draws cottagers and vacationers alike with its nine-mile sweep of sandy beach. In summer, kids and teenagers flock to the two water theme parks here, while some of the most comfortable lodgings in Southwestern Ontario are found at the ▶ **Dyconia Resort Hotel** on Mosley Street, which has 32 rooms in a variety of shapes and sizes, all with wood-burning fireplaces and many with oversize Jacuzzis.

MUSKOKA AND ONTARIO'S COTTAGE COUNTRY

Southern Ontario may be the industrial heartland of Canada, but in its hinterland most people seem to be in the business of having a good time. The part of the Laurentian Shield between Georgian Bay and the Ottawa River is the playground of the province. Many Americans and a few British discovered the holiday pleasures of the area more than a century ago, and in recent years increasing numbers of Europeans have also been coming on the scene.

Starting about 100 km (62 miles) north of Toronto (and half that distance again from Hamilton), a spectacular lakeland spreads out, one that gets more wooded and less populated the farther north you go. The foliage and evergreen trees screen a vast array of inns, cottages, marinas, and all those facilities that—regardless of the time of year—make outdoor life so irresistible. As a result, on weekends, particularly in summer, thousands of city people flee the urban jungle, and main highways that lead north are heavy with traffic as early as noon on Fridays.

MAJOR INTEREST

Lake resorts
Lake cruises and houseboat touring
Trent–Severn Waterway
Fishing, even in winter
Arts-and-crafts shows
Significant historical restorations
Fairs during fall foliage season
Canoeing and camping in Algonquin Park

A Brief History of the Region

Quiet retreats by lakes or streams are relatively easy to find today, but think what this land must have been like in 1610, when the Huron Indians brought Etienne Brûlé, then a lad of 16, from Quebec to their village on Georgian Bay to take the place of a young Indian sent to France by Samuel de Champlain.

The vacation pleasures of the lakes at the center of the region—Rosseau, Joseph, and Muskoka—were discovered in 1860, when two young men came from Toronto, hiking much of the way. They subsequently brought friends, and eventually many of them bought property on the islands in the lakes. Much of the land bought then—even into the 1890s—has now been passed on to the third and fourth generations.

By the 1880s the area had become a summer magnet for affluent families from the United States and England as well as southern Ontario. At first they came only to fish or to escape hay fever, but that changed quickly, and soon many came for two months, often with guests, taking the Muskoka Express from Toronto to Gravenhurst, a three- to five-hour trip, before boarding a lake steamer to their cottages. Boating then took up much of their time.

In 1894 Toronto, with a population of 200,000, celebrated its 60th birthday. One February night that winter, 19 Muskoka property owners gathered downtown to form the Muskoka Lakes Association. Today it has about 3,000 mem-

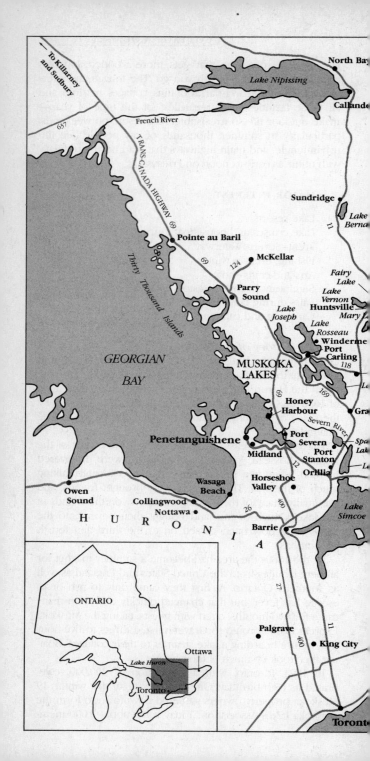

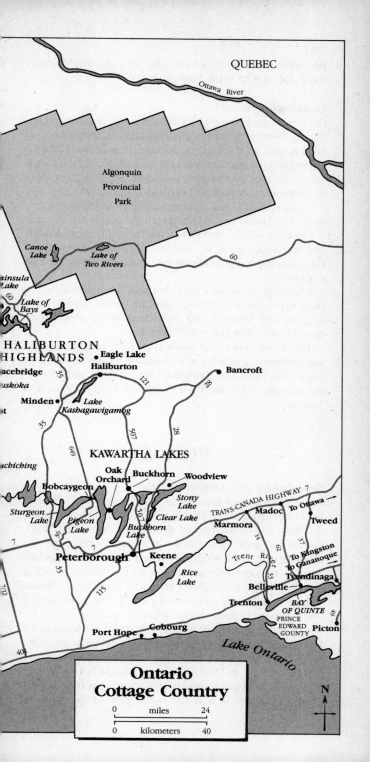

Ontario
Cottage Country

```
0        miles        24
0        kilometers        40
```

N

QUEBEC

Ottawa River

Algonquin

Provincial

Park

Canoe
Lake

Lake of
Two Rivers

60

ninsula
Lake

Lake of
Bays

HALIBURTON
HIGHLANDS

Eagle Lake
Haliburton

acebridge

Bancroft

35

121

28

uskoka

Minden

Lake
Kashagawigamog

st

35

507

28

649

KAWARTHA LAKES

chiching

Oak
Orchard

Buckhorn
Woodview

Bobcaygeon

Stony
Lake

TRANS-CANADA HIGHWAY 7

Madoc

To Ottawa

Sturgeon
Lake

Pigeon
Lake

Clear Lake

507

Marmora

Tweed

Buckhorn
Lake

14

62

37

7

9c

7

Trent River

To Kingston

Peterborough

Keene

To Gananoque

33

35

Rice
Lake

Tyendinaga

115

Belleville

7/12

Trenton

BAY
OF QUINTE

40

Port Hope

Cobourg

PRINCE
EDWARD
COUNTY

49

Picton

Lake Ontario

ber families and a vigilant executive to make sure development does not spoil the Muskoka way of life.

Orientation

Only two other areas in Ontario were popular as resorts before 1900: to the west, Georgian Bay's Thirty Thousand Islands and, to the east, Stony Lake, one of the Kawartha Lakes used by the Indians as a natural "hospital." In the 1890s Toronto newspapers would be filled with news of summer activities at these fashionable spots.

Today central Ontario has several large and distinct resort areas. The largest and most popular—as well as the oldest—is **Muskoka**, which, centered on the lakes of Rosseau, Joseph, and Muskoka, runs from Gravenhurst and the lower end of Georgian Bay to Huntsville in the north and **Algonquin Park** to the east.

Adjoining Muskoka's southern end is **Huronia**, which takes in the lower end of Georgian Bay west to Collingwood and, around Midland and Penetanguishene, contains the most historic sites in the province.

The lesser-developed **Haliburton** area, east of Muskoka and northeast of Lake Simcoe, abuts the southwest corner of Algonquin Park. The **Kawartha Lakes** are just north of Peterborough, which itself is 135 km (84 miles) northeast of Toronto.

MUSKOKA

Bracebridge and Gravenhurst

The small towns of Bracebridge and Gravenhurst, about 19 km (12 miles) apart off Highway 11, are the main hubs at the southern end of the region. **Bracebridge**, now with 12,000 people and growing fast, is the more aggressive of the two, courting industry as well as tourists. It is also the municipal, judicial, and health services center for the district, as well as home of the South Muskoka Memorial Hospital and **Santa's Village**, a children's amusement park. Cottagers on several lakes do most of their shopping here as well.

Gravenhurst, slightly smaller, revels in its location on lakes Muskoka and Gull, as well as in its status as an artists' colony and cultural community. Many artists do live here (and elsewhere in Muskoka), and its opera house, built in 1901 with hammered-wood beams, attracts international artists. Gravenhurst is also the home base of the **Muskoka**

Festival, which stages Canadian plays, musicals, some children's theater, and a winter series. (In summer, its productions travel to Port Carling and occasionally to Huntsville.) The festival is a training ground for young theater professionals and its Young Company performs at resorts, parks, and museums. Gravenhurst also has **Music on the Barge**, free weekly concerts by the side of Gull Lake, and both communities offer a wealth of antiques and craft shows throughout the summer. And of course here, as in all parts of this vacationland, the fall foliage is spectacular.

Huntsville

Muskoka's largest town, Huntsville, lies 50 km (31 miles) north of Bracebridge near the region's northern boundary. Because the Muskoka Road, the area's principal link to Toronto in the second half of the 19th century, wasn't pushed this far north until 1871, Huntsville became a popular summertime destination somewhat later. Today it's a vibrant town of 15,000 (and three times that number in summer), with all the services and facilities necessary for the good life. The last five or six years, in particular, have brought a burst of growth, with retirees as well as young urban refugees moving into town in record numbers. This growth has resulted in the opening of several new restaurants and boutiques, a huge shopping mall at the north end of town, and a community recreation center. Yet another reason people visit Huntsville is its accessibility to Algonquin Park, Ontario's oldest (dating to 1893), and a pristine wilderness area cherished by outdoors enthusiasts. The park's western entrance lies 49 km (30 miles) east of town via Highway 60.

The attractions that make Muskoka so popular are easily found. A number of tourism associations publish events booklets four times a year; you can find them in most stores, marinas, and restaurants. Local papers and leaflets also list theater, arts-and-crafts shows, tours of artists' studios, and the like. From late January to early March, half a dozen winter carnivals capture the fun of the season, with ski and motorcycle races, hay rides, cookouts, hot-air balloons rides, and the like.

On the Water

Wherever there's a body of water, you're bound to find a cruise; information usually can be found at dockside or in the nearest lakeside town. Some operate from late June to Labour Day only, while others run until mid-October.

The area favorite is the 99-passenger RMS *Segwun,* which is based in Gravenhurst and turned 100 years old in 1987. Sunset dinner cruises may sell out early. On Georgian Bay, where the **Thirty Thousand Islands** and rocky cliffs make the scenery even more spectacular, cruises leave from Penetanguishene, Midland, and Parry Sound. The latter is home port for the 550-passenger *Island Queen,* the largest cruise boat in cottage country, and a popular option with foreign visitors. A new model, with more comforts and a sound system to carry music as well as voice, took to the water in 1990.

The biggest event in Muskoka is the **Antique Boat Show,** held in Port Carling on a July weekend. In recent years as many as 150 boats, some from as far away as Florida, have been displayed. For three weeks starting in mid-July, music lovers head for Parry Sound (at the midpoint of Georgian Bay) and the **Festival of the Sound,** during which visitors can enjoy chamber music interspersed with lighter musical fare, in addition to cruises on the bay (reserve well ahead) and nature walks.

Muskoka Resorts

The ▶ **Deerhurst Resort,** built in the last years of the 19th century and today Ontario's largest resort, is located on Peninsula Lake near Huntsville. A member of the Canadian Pacific Hotel and Resorts chain, Deerhurst accommodates 900 people luxuriously in its main lodge, condominiums, and time-sharing units. The newest addition to its lineup of facilities (which includes five pools, a stable, a sandy beach, and a water-sports center) is the Pavilion, a giant indoor recreational complex that offers tennis, squash, and racquetball courts, a health and beauty spa, and a theater-banquet room capable of seating 400. Nearby are the so-called Sports Villas, bright, comfortable, and well equipped. Variety in lodgings is the keynote elsewhere on this 1,000-acre property, with the decor in some rooms knotty pine, in others oak with floral-printed duvet covers. In addition, all suites are equipped with kitchens and fireplaces, and some have Jacuzzis.

Since everything in the way of recreation and entertainment (including a lavish Broadway-style show) is available on or near the premises, Deerhurst's guests simply design their own vacations. Golfers, for example, have a choice of two layouts: the par-72 Deerhurst Highlands course, which opened in 1990 and incorporates Muskoka's rugged terrain and craggy rock outcroppings to beautiful effect, or the older Lakeside course. Greens fees at the Highlands course run about $65 (including cart); they're about $25 at the Lakeside layout.

The surrounding area has a dozen or more less elaborate resorts. These include everything from housekeeping cottages (Blue Water Acres), to a luxury lodge (Pow-Wow Point), to a smaller version of Deerhurst. The latter is the 160-room ► **Grandview Inn**, located less than a mile from Deerhurst on Fairy Lake. (Do not confuse it with the Grandview Lodge, a moderately priced family resort south of Gravenhurst on Sparrow Lake.) The Grandview Inn has grown considerably in the last several years, most recently adding an indoor pool and sports center. The $17 Sunday brunch is popular with guests and nonguests alike, and during the winter, when some 2,000 lights illuminate its nine-hole golf course and tennis courts, it's extremely picturesque.

The 93-unit ► **Best Western Hidden Valley Resort Hotel**, bought and refurbished in early 1992 by the Best Western chain, is situated on the other side of Deerhurst's Lakeside golf course. In fact, when there's snow on the ground, guests at the bigger resort use Hidden Valley's eight downhill ski runs (with a modest vertical drop of 300 feet). The staff here is young, as are the guests, most of whom have children in tow. (A new program for youngsters, ages 2 to 15, was introduced in 1991.)

Visitors searching for a smaller place with a spectacular lake view and excellent meals should look into the ► **Gryffin Lodge** on Mary Lake, about 5 km (3 miles) south of Huntsville and another 5 km (3 miles) east of Highway 11 (the turnoff is marked by a sign). The rooms at this stone lodge are homey, and its small book-lined library is a great place to relax. Guests have a variety of activities to choose from, including swimming, canoeing, windsurfing, fishing, hiking, tennis, and billiards.

Visitors to the Bracebridge–Gravenhurst area often prefer to stay in cottages that each year become more like second homes. But there is a top-notch inn on each of the three lakes here.

On Lake Rosseau you'll find ► **Windermere House**, a stately white structure with a long second-story verandah overlooking a sloping lawn and marina. Windermere House started as a simple fishing lodge in 1864 but eventually developed into a haven for the gentry. Today it has a wider, and younger, appeal, although it's still an elegant establishment with impeccable service. Rooms, which look appealingly fresh, feature white iron bedsteads and flowered bedspreads; doors are painted a teal green. Lunch may be eaten on the verandah overlooking the lawns, and luscious cakes and desserts are served in the living room from 11:00 A.M. to 4:00 P.M. daily. Reservations are required for dinner, where a modified dress code rules out jeans or shorts. On Mondays in July and August, the RMS *Segwun* docks here at noon and, while its passengers eat lunch at the hotel, takes guests of the hotel on a two-hour cruise of the lake. Open from May to October only.

The ► **Muskoka Sands Resort**, at the southern tip of Lake Muskoka, also had a recent multimillion-dollar makeover: The inn was gutted in 1987 and transformed into a resort property with 48 units (62 bedrooms). One wing has golden pine furnishings with either jewel-toned or country-style decor; the other is done in soft, warm tones, and features deluxe one- and two-bedroom suites with fireplaces and refrigerators. All have balconies. The resort also has two- and three-bedroom cottage condominiums, five swimming pools, two squash and five tennis courts, and facilities for golf and horseback riding nearby. Other activity centers on the dockside **Boathouse** and its whirlpool bar. And on summer weekend nights **Steamer Jakes**, the downstairs lounge built around a huge chunk of Muskoka granite, is usually crowded.

If you want a quiet, restful time in Muskoka at a place where privacy is paramount and the food and wine exceptional, reserve a room (two have whirlpool baths) at the ► **Sherwood Inn** on Lake Joseph. The inn is fabulously situated on a pine-shaded rise overlooking the lake. The first choice of many guests is one of the nine winterized cottages with fireplaces nestled under the property's pines. .

Most tennis buffs have heard of Muskoka's ► **Inn at Manitou**, considered one of the finest tennis resorts in North America. Tucked away on a small lake, a 30-minute drive east of Parry Sound, the inn has 13 tennis courts (one indoors) and 12 pros. Antiques from England, France, and Hong Kong, as well as skylights, fireplaces, and private saunas, make this an outstanding retreat, one that meets the rigorous standards of the Relais & Châteaux group. There's much more than tennis, handsome furnishings, and inspired cuisine here—horseback riding, mountain biking, fishing, and aerobics can also be arranged, and a full-service spa was recently added to the lineup. Guests usually take advantage of the three-, four-, or seven-day tennis or spa packages, with the minimum stay two nights. Open from mid-May to mid-October only.

North of Muskoka

The ▶ **Waltonian Inn** in Callander, on Lake Nipissing, an hour's drive north of Huntsville (via Highway 11), is worthy of note because of its specialty: ice fishing in comfort. Although the main lodge has a few rooms, most of the accommodations are spread among 22 housekeeping cottages. What they lack in deluxe amenities is more than compensated for (if ice fishing is your thing) by the inn's four heated and radio-equipped Bombardiers, each taking up to 12 guests to one of 35 ice huts (four to six people a hut). Lunch arrives at noon, and guests need bring only a jacket and boots.

The ▶ **Killarney Mountain Lodge**, in the village of Killarney on Georgian Bay's north shore, may not offer the luxury of the top Ontario resorts, but none can match its scenic wilderness locale. (The village dates to the arrival of a fur trader's family in 1820, but it wasn't until 1962 that a road—Highway 637—was cut through to Highway 69, the Trans-Canada.) Pink granite rock and forest greenery, especially near the shoreline, send artists scurrying for paint brushes, while the range of other activities includes good fishing, nature hikes, overnight camping, sailing, kayaking, and tennis. The lodge accommodates 96 guests, mainly in heated cabins or attached units, and meals are excellent. Open May to October.

Also notable is the ▶ **North Ridge Inn** in Sundridge, at the southern end of Lake Bernard, midway between Huntsville and North Bay. Its dining room alone is a lifesaver, as good ones in the area are hard to find (it's wise to phone ahead; Tel: 800/461-5551 in Ontario, or 705/384-5373). Stone fireplaces and lots of knotty pine lend the two-story inn a cozy look, and with only 20 rooms one can count on being pampered. VCRs in every room, Arctic char and venison on the dinner menu, and an outdoor Jacuzzi are just a few of the nicer touches here.

HURONIA

The lower end of Georgian Bay from Owen Sound to Barrie, properly but seldom called Huronia, is quite distinct from Muskoka. In fact, when Muskoka was entertaining its first guests in the 1880s, Huronia was nothing but a sparsely settled outback. Today it's a burgeoning year-round vacationland, with skiing in winter and beach life, water slides, golf, and the like in summer. An explosion of condominiums and town houses is now transforming parts of the area. In addition to attractive, sometimes even posh, living quarters, most resorts have every imaginable facility for the sports- and fitness-minded (all resorts mentioned below have a swimming pool, a whirlpool, and a sauna, for example). There is also a variety of good cafés and restaurants in the region, some with entertainment. Wasaga Beach, on the other hand, is Ontario's Coney Island.

Bruce Trail

The western portion of Huronia is popular with nature lovers who appreciate well-marked trails for hiking and cross-country skiing. The Bruce Trail, which begins at Queenston on the Niagara River and follows the Niagara Escarpment 425 miles to the tip of the Bruce Peninsula, makes a couple of loops here. The variety of scenery and challenging terrain make it one of the more memorable parts of the trail, as it hits the top of Blue Mountain, winds through wide valleys, crosses streams, and, at the top of Mount Baldy near Kimberley, skirts remarkable rock formations.

Blue Mountain

With 29 runs, 16 lifts (including a high-speed quad chair), and computerized snowmaking, Blue Mountain, near Collingwood, is the largest and most developed ski resort in the province. Cafés and bars abound—the newest is in the recently renovated Central Base Lodge. And with three slide rides (one alpine, two water) and the new 18-hole Monterra golf course (play out to the bay and back to the mountain), the resort is just as busy in summer.

Visitors can stay in the 103-room ▶ Blue Mountain Resort, or in one of the 100 two- and three-bedroom condominiums that their owners make available. The knotty pine and copper lamps of the inn (which is also a conference center) give it a friendly, rustic ambience. Fitness facilities and racket sports get wide play here, with five tennis courts in the new recreation center as well as three courts outdoors.

Closer to Collingwood on the same highway (Highway 26) is the ▶ Cranberry Village Resort, a more upscale operation with 80 rooms overlooking cedar woods. All rooms have pine furniture and big bathrooms. Also on the property are 725 condominiums, believed to be the largest cluster in Canada. In addition, the resort has eight tennis courts, a marina on Georgian Bay, and an 18-hole golf course open to the public. Horseback riding is available in summer, and in winter there's on-site cross-country skiing and ice skating; downhill skiing is ten minutes away.

The ▶ **Horseshoe Resort**, a longtime ski mecca located 16 km (10 miles) north of Barrie and an hour's drive north of Toronto via Highway 400 and County Road 22, is another developing area resort. Parlor rooms and loft suites in the 102-room inn feature queen- or king-size beds, cherrywood furniture, walk-in showers, and Jacuzzis. The eight loft suites, which have a second TV (much appreciated if you've brought the kids along) and a skylight in the bedroom, overlook the valley and the 18th hole of a golf course. The inn is an upscale operation, with fine dining overseen by an Austrian chef, a sports-and-leisure complex with a small gym and two squash courts, indoor and outdoor pools, and two outdoor tennis courts.

Huronia Heritage

The little neighboring towns of **Midland** and **Penetanguishene** (known as Penetang) are situated in the most historic area of the province. (From Barrie, use Highways 400 and 12.) Here, on the rim of Georgian Bay, Etienne Brûlé learned his Indian ways and, in 1649, the Iroquois murdered six Jesuit missionaries. **Sainte-Marie among the Hurons**, 5 km (3 miles) east of Midland on Highway 12, is a reconstructed mission where student guides, some in Jesuit garb, demonstrate the making of moccasins, square nails, and so on. A film of 17th-century pioneer life is also shown. The **Martyrs' Shrine**, on a hill on the north side of the highway, commemorates the slain Jesuits. Thousands of visitors and pilgrims flock to the site annually, one being Pope John Paul II in 1984.

On the opposite side of the road, the **Wye Marsh Wildlife Center** features a floating boardwalk, canoe excursions, guided nature walks, and, in winter, cross-country skiing and snowshoeing. It is open year-round, while the other attractions are open only from mid-May to mid-October.

In Midland proper you'll find the **Huronia Museum**, which includes a full-scale replica of a 16th-century Huron Indian village, off King Street in Little Lake Park. Open daily April through November, weekdays only the rest of the year. Ten kilometers (6 miles) to the west, in Penetang, is the **Historic Naval and Military Establishments**, established in 1814 to prevent Americans from disrupting a supply route to the upper lakes. The site has reconstructions of 15 buildings, impromptu play-acting by student guides, shops, a 120-seat restaurant, and three tall ships—one for boarding and inspection, and the other two offering three-hour sails ($25 to $35 per person) during which paying passengers help crew the boat.

On the Water

Elsewhere in Huronia, **Orillia Boat Cruises** operates daily and three times weekly at dinnertime from the town of **Orillia**, on Lake Simcoe. The same cruise line also offers an intriguing six-hour trip twice weekly on the 138-passenger *Lady Belle* out of **Port Stanton** on Sparrow Lake, a few miles north of Orillia. The cruise follows the Severn River west through a lock to Big Chute, where passengers can go ashore (bring your own picnic lunch) to see boats lowered 62 feet by marine railway to Georgian Bay. Reservations advised; Tel: (705) 325-2628.

HALIBURTON AND THE KAWARTHA LAKES

East of Highway 11 (which heads north out of Toronto) and Lake Simcoe are two smaller vacation areas: Haliburton and the Kawartha Lakes. These areas have many of the same features as Muskoka and Huronia—rocks and hills, lakes, rivers, deep snow, a profusion of spring flowers, and the unforgettably brilliant color of autumn leaves—but are separated from Muskoka and Huronia by an upland area that directs waters west into Georgian Bay and south into the Trent system—the latter emptying into Lake Ontario.

The Haliburton Highlands

The Haliburton Highlands, encompassing more than 600 small lakes, snuggles in the southwestern arms of Algonquin Park. With the exception of the 2,800 members of the Haliburton County Snowmobile Association, said to be the largest such club in the world, this area is little known as a year-round vacation destination. The association maintains close to 400 miles of groomed trails, a third of which are ten feet wide (others measure just six feet) and form a two-lane loop that runs through the two main villages of Minden and Haliburton.

STAYING IN THE HIGHLANDS

A few small, attractive inns have made their mark—none more so than the ▶ **Domain of Killien Resort**, on the scene since 1984. Here, in the middle of the Canadian wilderness, guests are treated to simple elegance, French cuisine, and hospitality at its finest. The lodge, which along with 10 cabins (all but two with a sunporch and sitting room) can accommodate 14 couples, sits beside Drag Lake near Haliburton, on the rim of 5,000 acres owned by a French count and his two stepsons. No hunting or motorized vehicles are allowed, but guests can walk or ski the trails as well as swim, fish, or go boating on its private lakes. Weekends often have special themes, including wine tasting and nature walks. One son manages the inn while the other heads a team of innovative—usually French—chefs. Rooms in the lodge, simply done in knotty pine, have dressing rooms and five-piece bathrooms; modern amenities are conspicuously absent. The Domain of Killien is open year-round, and air and limousine transportation to and from Toronto can be arranged.

The ▶ **Red Umbrella Inn**, on Twelve-Mile Lake near Minden, dates to the late 1920s. This family-oriented establishment accommodates up to 60 guests in 23 cabins (many with fireplaces) and a few in the lodge. Some antiques are spread around, quilts cover the beds, and the lounge could be someone's living room; meals are also home-style, with fresh bread and muffins daily. With table shuffleboard, a pinball machine, card tables, piano, and refreshment bar, the game room attracts all ages, and an outdoor Jacuzzi was added a few years ago. The inn is also one of three places near Minden that offers huts for ice fishing.

Among the better-known retreats in the area is ▶ **Sir Sam's Inn**, the one-time country estate of Sir Sam Hughes, Canada's minister of defense during World War I. Located on Eagle Lake, a few miles north of Haliburton, it is eagerly sought out by young and sports-minded couples who appreciate good food, contemporary surroundings, and privacy. In summer the inn offers water sports galore as well as tennis; in winter it has the only alpine skiing in the Highlands right out its back door (with a vertical drop of 425 feet)—and no lift lines.

With its meeting rooms, jogging track, health spa, art gallery, indoor and outdoor pools, cross country skiing, exercise equipment, golf, live entertainment—you name it—the ▶ **PineStone Resort and Conference Centre**, which opened in 1976 off Highway 121, 7 km (4½ miles) southwest of Haliburton, caters to businesspeople. Guests can stay in the inn, with 62 rooms, or opt for one of 20 suites (all with whirlpool baths) or 23 chalets and villas (all with whirlpool baths and fireplaces).

The ▶ **Wigamog Inn** on Lake Kashagawigamog (which means "land of the long and winding waters") is a casual, family-style vacation spot that can keep 135 guests happy, some in the inn (rustic, with down comforters), others in poolside suites (soothingly modern) and one- and two-bedroom chalets. The atmosphere is pleasant, the food good, and the activities endless any time of year.

Red Umbrella, PineStone, and Wigamog are three of the ten resorts in the area that in 1983 developed a 150-mile linked trail for cross-country skiers. All now offer lodge-to-lodge skiing in January and February; guests ski with a guide while the luggage follows in style. For further information contact Haliburton Nordic Trails, P.O. Box 670, Haliburton, Ontario K0M 1S0, Tel: (705) 457-1640; or the Haliburton Highlands Chamber of Commerce, Tel: (705) 286-1760 or (800) 461-7677.

Bancroft, outside the resort area proper, being considerably east of Haliburton (follow Highways 121 and 28), is a mecca for rock hounds seeking semi-precious stones and rare minerals. Its highly regarded five-day **Gemboree** is held every year in late July or early August.

The Kawarthas

Peterborough is the gateway to the Kawarthas, whose many lakes are part of the Trent–Severn system. This area was first explored by Champlain in 1615, and is now popular with boaters and fishing enthusiasts. The **Trent–Severn Waterway** extends from Trenton on Lake Ontario, northwest through island-dotted lakes, sluggish rivers, a few small towns, and 45 locks to Port Severn on Georgian Bay, a distance of some 240 miles.

Visitors come from as far away as Europe for the **Wildlife Art Festival**, held the third weekend in August in the village of **Buckhorn** (on Highway 507 north of Peterborough). More than 100 artists—printmakers, wood-carvers, painters—offer their work for sale, with a variety of other festivities preceding the final big sale, tickets for which are sold out weeks in advance.

The **Gallery on the Lake**, east of Buckhorn on 120 acres, is a hexagonal knotty-pine building in which the work of two dozen artists, potters, and sculptors is shown. Behind the scenes in the same building is the Buckhorn School of Fine Art, offering instruction in various media. The newly refurbished ▶ **Westwind Inn**, with 32 rooms and a large dining room overlooking Lower Buckhorn Lake, is a five-minute walk away. The inn is now fully air-conditioned, and canoes, rowboats, sailboats, and cross-country ski equipment are available to guests.

The ▶ **Viamede Resort**, with its long, sweeping ve-

randahs overlooking the north shore of Stony Lake, originally was a lodge for fishermen and lumbermen that became
a grand hotel in 1909. Careful restoration of the building has
added 20th-century comfort, a long patio deck, and a dining
room seating 150. Viamede is a bouncy place with endless
entertainment that appeals to young families and couples.
The resort is also the only licensed spot on the lake, so
cottagers flock here for nighttime fun. Except for group
bookings, the hotel is open Friday to Sunday only in winter,
when cross-country skiers and snowmobilers take over.

Just south of Peterborough in the vicinity of Keene, a 90-
minute drive from Toronto, is ▶ **Elmhirst's Resort**, a casual
family resort on Rice Lake offering cottage accommodations,
each with its own boat ramp. The resort also has an air strip,
its own air service that brings guests in from Toronto Island
Airport, and a fly-in (accessible only by air) fishing camp that
accommodates up to six people. Weekly bookings only in
summer.

On the Water

Cruises depart from several spots. In Peterborough, two-
hour cruises ($8 to $15 per person) depart from the marina
on George Street. From the oldest lock on the waterway
(dating to 1833), in downtown **Bobcaygeon**, the *Island Lass*
takes off for two-hour cruises of Pigeon Lake ($16 per
person). The *Skylark VIII,* based in **Lindsay**, goes out on
dinner and moonlight cruises ($27.50 and $30 per person),
as well as three-hour daytime cruises ($15). It departs from
the Wellington Street dock in downtown Lindsay. The season
for all these excursions is late May to early September.

Serpent Mounds Provincial Park and Petroglyphs
Provincial Park

Just west of Elmhirst's, also on Rice Lake, is Serpent Mounds
Provincial Park, a grouping of prehistoric mounds in the
shape of a gigantic serpent. The mounds are thought to date
to the second century A.D., but little else is known about
their origin.

Just a few miles up Highway 134, along the Indian River
just beyond the village of Warsaw, are some caves whose
walls contain fossils. Above ground are uncounted potholes
formed by boulders caught in river whirlpools.

Near the east end of Stony Lake, off a back road north of
Highway 7, is **Petroglyphs Provincial Park**, which harbors
remarkable rock carvings. Perhaps the most interesting of
these is a huge piece of white crystalline marble on which
are engraved 900 drawings of birds, beasts, and persons,

perhaps mythical, perhaps real. Called the **Peterborough Petroglyphs**, and today protected by a steel-and-glass structure, they are thought to have been carved by Ontario Algonkian Indians, probably between 900 and 1400 A.D. They are not the oldest engravings in Canada, but they do constitute the largest concentration of such drawings in the country.

ALGONQUIN PARK

Algonquin Park's 2,900 square miles of unspoiled forests and streams were a source of inspiration for landscape artist Tom Thomson in the early 1900s. Today Algonquin Park is the end of the rainbow for legions of canoeists. Civilization— in the form of campgrounds, picnic sites, wilderness outfitters, and a few lodges—has penetrated its southwest corner; otherwise, except for the effects of acid rain, the park has remained unchanged since it opened in 1893. Moose, bears, wolves, and birds still thrive here.

Canoe routes (more than 900 miles north) web the park. The place to start is **Canoe Lake**'s Portage Store, near Algonquin's western entrance on Highway 60, which cuts a 56-km (35-mile) swath through the southern portion of the park. Anything from food packs to complete outfitters' packages (with a choice of three types of canoe) is available at this beautiful site. (There's also an 85-seat restaurant and a well-stocked crafts and gift shop here.)

Backpackers can choose between the Highland and Western Uplands trails, both requiring overnight bivouacs. Less ambitious hikers will find a dozen shorter trails varying in length from 1.2 to 6.6 miles. Fall colors are usually at their best during the last week of September and the first few days of October (a week earlier than in Muskoka and the Haliburton Highlands).

STAYING IN THE PARK

For rustic yet luxurious accommodations and magnificent food, try ► **Arowhon Pines**, where the guests are as likely to be from Europe as North America. Arowhon offers lodging in stained-log cottages finished with peeled logs, pine paneling, and wallpaper, and furnished with Canadian antiques and contemporary pieces. Each cottage has its own lounge and stone fireplace. The focal point of the property is a hexagonal red-roofed dining room with wide verandahs overlooking Little Joe Lake. Inside, appetizers, salads, and desserts are served buffet-style around a massive stone fireplace that rises through the cathedral ceiling. The prix-fixe dinner costs about $40 per person (plus tax and tip), and the public is welcome. Note, however, that park regulations do not permit alcoholic beverages or wine to be sold; guests usually bring their own.

▶ **Killarney Lodge**, east of Arowhon off Highway 60 on Lake of Two Rivers, has 27 one- and two-bedroom cabins (each with its own canoe) that seem to be popular with couples and families, especially in August. It's a colorful spot with well-tended flower gardens and geranium-red trim on all the buildings.

Bed and Breakfasts

All over Ontario, but especially in tourist and resort areas, bed-and-breakfast homes have mushroomed in recent years. Preferred by many visitors as much for the ambience and experience as the price, they may be lovely Victorian homes full of antiques, or, as at ▶ **Pretty River Valley Farm** (just south of Collingwood near Norland, in the Huronia region), a log home with a valley view, whirlpool, pine-furnished rooms and suites, private baths, and fireplaces.

Ontario B&Bs tend to be modeled after those in Europe. Some hosts may have only two or three rooms or may welcome guests only part of the year, but others make it a year-round affair and may even manage a registry of other homes. Very rarely is an Ontario B&B a small inn with prices at hotel levels, as is common in the United States. In all cases, rooms will have been specially prepared and are inspected regularly. Generally, full breakfasts are served.

The handiest sources of information, updated every year, are Patricia Wilson's *Ontario Bed & Breakfast Book* and Gerda Pantel's *Canadian Bed & Breakfast Guide*. Along with specific homes, both list reservation services. Other sources of information, including the Muskoka Bed & Breakfast Association, can be tracked down through the local chamber of commerce or tourist office.

EASTERN ONTARIO

The drive from Toronto to Ottawa (via Highway 401 along Lake Ontario and the St. Lawrence River, then north just past

Prescott on Highway 16) usually takes much longer than the allotted six hours. That's because the journey itself is a scenic one, with some good spots to explore en route. Visitors can stop for a boat cruise through the beautiful **Thousand Islands** or opt for a meandering excursion along the winding roads of **Quinte's Isle**. Eastern Ontario is an area of farmland and dairies, of country roads and interconnecting yachting canals, of historic military forts and modern-day ferry rides.

This is where Lake Ontario becomes the St. Lawrence River and huge freighters travel down to the Atlantic Ocean, sailing between two countries before starting their ocean crossing. Some ships are so large that passengers can almost touch the province of Ontario on one side and New York State on the other. (The St. Lawrence River is a perfect place to view the world's longest undefended border between two countries.) Three bridges along the river connect Ontario with New York State: between Ivy Lea in Canada and Watertown, New York; Prescott and Ogdensburg; and Cornwall and Massena.

MAJOR INTEREST

Quinte's Isle
Old Fort Henry in Kingston
Boat cruises through the Thousand Islands
Boldt Castle
Upper Canada Village
Antiques shopping

Antiques and Collectibles

As you poke along the back roads of Eastern Ontario en route to Ottawa (just follow Highway 7 northeast from Peterborough), you'll get a taste of country living at its best. Here, too, in the little towns along the route—Marmora, Madoc, Tweed, Perth, and Smiths Falls—inveterate shoppers for "pre-loved" articles (including bona fide antiques, secondhand goods, and cute collectibles) will find various old, sometimes ramshackle buildings piled with countless goodies, from original turn-of-the-century oil lanterns to a Queen Elizabeth commemorative teaspoon. In antiques shopping one person's garbage is another's lifelong treasure. Every little community along this route has at least one such store; just ask any local for directions as you pass through his or her town.

For those who wish to go farther afield in their search, there are many shops along the county roads that follow the Ottawa River, which flows through the northern regions of

Eastern Ontario along the border with Quebec. In Pembroke alone (about 88 km/55 miles northwest of Ottawa) you'll find the **Quilter's Corner** (which sells not only quilts but fabric and instructions for do-it-yourselfers); **Heritage House** for fine crafts and stained glass; and **A and J Crafts**, with a stoneware pottery showroom that, according to their sign, is "open by chance or appointment."

The Trent–Severn System

Many Ontarians spend their summer vacations in this area taking yachts, canoes, cruisers, or rented houseboats through the Trent–Severn system of lakes and locks. "Houseboating on the Trent" has become an extremely popular vacation for couples or groups. You can rent houseboats in varying sizes from **Egan Marine Sunburst Houseboat Rentals** (Tel: 705/799-5745). Egan Marine's prices range from $800 for a week off-season to a high of $1,150 in July for a two-bedroom floating cottage complete with equipped galley, propane barbecue, and fresh-water shower.

Every year, thousands of pleasure boats travel the 384-km (238-mile) waterway from the initial lock at Port Severn on Georgian Bay southeast to the Trenton Lock near Trenton on Lake Ontario. Boaters can anchor their yachts for the evening and cook on board or paddle their canoe to shore, pitch a tent, and prepare a campfire for freshly caught fish. You'll pass through dozens of lakes—Couchiching, Simcoe, Scugog, Pigeon, and Buckhorn among them—and can even spend the night at dockside resorts. Accommodations range from the old-world charm of the ▶ **Old Bridge Inn Hotel** in Young's Point, to the more modern ▶ **Holiday Inn Peterborough** on Peterborough's waterfront, to the many inland campgrounds along the waterway itself.

In other words, this is a relaxing holiday cruise that can be done in a week or stretched to fill two. If, on the other hand, your time is limited, the scenic and varied drive from Toronto to Ottawa can be accomplished in as little as a day.

THE LAKE ONTARIO SHORE

Oshawa

Most visitors prefer to drive from Toronto east along Lake Ontario and the St. Lawrence River without detouring inland into Eastern Ontario. If you're seriously interested in your automobile (other than making sure it has enough gasoline and oil), your first stop after leaving Toronto should be the

Canadian Automotive Museum (open daily year-round) in Oshawa, a busy center of the Canadian automobile industry located some 25 km (16 miles) northeast of Toronto. (Take Highway 401 to exit 417; the museum is at 99 Simcoe Street.) With over 80 antique vehicles as well as related memorabilia dating from the beginning of the auto era, the museum is a tribute to Colonel R. S. ("Sam") McLaughlin, who founded an automotive plant here in 1907 that later became the foundation of General Motors Canada, in the process turning Oshawa into the country's first major industrial center.

Colonel Sam also built **Parkwood**, a 55-room mansion that contains priceless antiques, murals, and tapestries, along with a number of works by the famed Group of Seven. Tours of the house and property, located at 270 Simcoe Street North, are offered during the summer between 10:30 A.M. and 4:30 P.M.; closed Mondays. The colonel's impressive collection of works by modern and contemporary Canadian artists can be seen at the **R. S. McLaughlin Gallery**, downtown in the Civic Center. Open year-round; closed Mondays.

Port Hope and Cobourg

About 35 km (22 miles) farther north and east via Highway 401 are the neighboring towns of Port Hope and Cobourg. With their picturesque lakeside settings (many homeowners keep their boats moored at backyard docks), tree-lined sidewalks, 19th-century homes in pristine condition, and ornate stone churches, the two towns seem to exist in a century-old bubble of serenity.

Surprisingly for towns this size, there are some good little restaurants, especially in Port Hope, where **The Carlyle** (originally the Bank of Upper Canada; Tel: 905/885-8686) dates to 1857 and features Continental cuisine at reasonable prices. The ▶ **Greenwood Inn**, which dates to 1877, offers 48 guest rooms on wooded estate grounds.

Quinte's Isle

The beautiful beaches of **Prince Edward County**—or Quinte's Isle, as the locals call it—can be reached by three main bridges off either of the mainland highways (Highways 401 or 2): at Carrying Place (Highway 33), Belleville (Highway 14/62), or Tyendinaga (Highway 49). The surrounding area, settled by the Empire Loyalists after the American Revolution, is tinged with echoes of the pioneer past, and the many museums, historical sites, and antiques shops are interspersed with roadside stands selling fresh fruit and vegetables.

Picton, with a population of 5,000, is the largest town on

Quinte's Isle and the center for local tourist information. After a drive through the wooded island countryside, head for the south-shore **Sandbanks** and **North Beach provincial parks**, where sand dunes rise behind the shoreline, and picnicking, swimming, and camping are the favorite visitor pastimes. For a small fee you can explore the six-mile-long sandbar across the mouth of Athol Bay, created over the millennia by the action of the wind and waves. During the summer the beach is patrolled by lifeguards and rangers, although the water can be quite chilly.

If you don't feel like barbecuing your own hot dogs, stop at the stately graystone **Waring House Restaurant** (Tel: 613/476-7367), originally built in 1835 as a family home, and now a restaurant specializing in European cuisine and fresh, home-baked breads and pastries. In season, the restaurant offers afternoon tea with fresh scones and jams.

Quinte's Isle is dotted with little motels, resorts, and bed-and-breakfast spots. Check with the local tourism office in Picton, or try the ▶ **Isaiah Tubbs Resort** or the housekeeping cottages at the ▶ **Sandbanks Beach Resort**, both in the Picton area.

Kingston

The main city of the region is Kingston, situated at the northern end of Lake Ontario where it narrows and becomes the St. Lawrence River. **Old Fort Henry**, east of the downtown area, was built during the War of 1812 (and rebuilt in 1832) to repel the American invaders and protect the Rideau Canal system at its strategic juncture with Lake Ontario. Daily tours of the fort are conducted from mid-June through Labour Day, with the sunset ceremonial retreat, complete with precision military maneuvers, a fife and drum corp, and a fairly dramatic muzzle-loading cannon, staged every Monday, Wednesday, and Sunday. The specially trained Fort Henry Guard, who maintain the 19th-century routine of the fort, are summer students from Kingston's **Royal Military College** (Canada's version of West Point or Sandhurst). The campus museum is situated in Canada's largest Martello tower and emphasizes the history of the college and its graduates. The RMC is just east of the city off Highway 2.

Strategically located for defense, Kingston was established as a fur-trading station in 1673 and quickly became a military stronghold. From 1841 to 1843 it was the capital of a united Upper and Lower Canada, and was also the home of Sir John A. Macdonald, Canada's first prime minister. Today it retains its rich architectural and historical ties to the 19th century.

For a good overview of the city, daily summer tours leave on the hour from **Confederation Park** across from City Hall.

On the Water

Kingston is a water-oriented city, with many of the boat tours of the beautiful **Thousand Islands** region originating from its main pier. **Ivy Lea Thousand Islands Boat Tours** (Tel: 613/659-2293) features a replica of a double-decker paddle-wheeler, while the *Wentworth Lady* has the intimacy and style of a 1950s cruise ship. The **Kingston and Islands Boat Line Ltd.** (Tel: 613/549-5544) offers two different cruises on its triple-decker *Island Queen* or a replica St. Lawrence steamship, the *Island Belle*. Prices vary depending on the ship and cruise duration, but figure $5.00 to $14.95 per adult. To take a cruise just wander down to the bottom of Ontario Street and choose a ship.

Instead of a three-hour cruise, you can opt for five or six days aboard the MV *Canadian Empress,* which offers six different cruises, including downriver to Montreal and Quebec City. There are 32 staterooms on board, each with private washroom, as well as dining areas and a bar. Prices vary depending on the duration of the cruise, but the average cost is about $200 per day (including all meals). Contact **St. Lawrence Cruise Lines**; Tel: (800) 267-7868 from the United States; or, direct in Ontario, Tel: (613) 549-8091.

There are good accommodations in Kingston, ranging from hotels and motels to little guest houses, but your best option is to stay on the picturesque waterfront. Try the ▶ **Holiday Inn Kingston** on Princess Street or the ▶ **Howard Johnson Kingston Hotel** on Ontario Street, both good and both conveniently located to the cruise-ship operators, with all the amenities one expects in a deluxe hotel. (If you book in advance, be sure to request a lakefront view.) Or try the 26-room ▶ **Prince George Hotel** on Ontario Street, a gracious example of late-Victorian architecture and one of Kingston's oldest private residences. The Prince George also has a good dining room.

THE UPPER ST. LAWRENCE AREA

THE THOUSAND ISLANDS

For a bird's-eye view of the area, check out the **Thousand Islands Skydeck** on Hill Island northeast of Kingston (below the Thousand Islands International Bridge). This 400-foot-high observatory provides visibility up to 40 miles on a clear day. If you care to sightsee longer, there's also a restaurant here.

Yes, as legend has it, the famous Thousand Island salad dressing was named for these islands. George Boldt, at one time the owner of New York's Waldorf Astoria hotel, was cruising the area aboard his yacht when a steward served a new dressing with the salad. Boldt decided to use the dressing at his hotels and named it in honor of the beautiful area where it was first created.

Boldt Castle

If you take a Thousand Islands cruise, and you should, make certain to take one that stops at Boldt Castle, perched atop a hill on **Heart Island**. As a gift to his wife, the same George Boldt bought the island in 1899, had it reshaped in the form of a heart, and commenced to build a huge castle with materials from all over the world. Boldt had already invested more than $2 million in the project when his wife died suddenly a few years later. He immediately ordered work on the project stopped, and never had it resumed, leaving a shell that continues to intrigue and inspire tourists 95 years later.

Gananoque

A few miles farther downriver is the village of Gananoque (pronounced "gannon-ock-way," an Iroquois name that means something like "land sloping gently to the water"). Located in the center of the Thousand Islands region, this pretty little town has its own cruise-boat outfit; **Gananoque Boat Lines** (Tel: 613/382-2144) operates the world's largest aluminum vessels, carrying up to 500 passengers on a three-hour cruise. Lunch and dinner with bar facilities are available on board. Before boarding the boat, check out the bargains in sweaters and knitting yarns available at the **Gan Mill Outlet** in town.

If you'd rather dine on land than on a boat or skydeck, you'll find Gananoque blessed with two historic inn/restaurants, rare for such a small town: the ▶ **Gananoque Inn** (Tel: 613/382-2165) on Stone Street South and the rather oddly named ▶ **Blinkbonnie Motor Inn** (Tel: 613/382-7272) on Main Street. Both buildings are well over 100 years old, though thoroughly renovated, and both dining rooms serve good fresh fish and Continental cuisine. The tiny 120-year-old ▶ **Victoria Rose Inn** on King Street West is a good bed-and-breakfast in the area.

Something a little different for nautical fans—and the curious—is the nondenominational church service conducted every Sunday afternoon on nearby **Half Moon Bay**. The weekly sermon is delivered from a rock pulpit at the edge of a natural amphitheater as the congregation listens to the service from their boats.

Morrisburg

Many drivers continue northeast along Highway 401 through historic Brockville and Prescott before heading up Highway 16 to Ottawa. Even if this is your plan, continue past the Prescott turnoff another 42 km (26 miles) to the town of Morrisburg and the nearby **Crysler's Farm Battlefield Park**, where the attractions include an 18-hole golf course, riding corral, marina, theater playhouse, and a large recreational and swimming area—a strange fate for the site of one of the most decisive battles in the War of 1812. As every student of Canadian history knows, Canada's defeat of the American army here was a turning point in the United States' attempt to annex Canada. The actual battlefield site is now under the waters of the river, but when the shoreline was built up (so the story goes) the contractors used the topsoil from the site. For diehard nationalists this is the equivalent of Canadian "holy soil," although no one has yet bottled it for sale in tourist shops.

Upper Canada Village

To continue digging up those Canadian roots, visit nearby Upper Canada Village ($8 for adults, $6 for students), per- haps the country's most authentic re-creation of mid-19th- century pioneer life in what was then called Upper Canada. The "village" is a showplace of restored period homes, churches, and stores, with a working smithy and an old-style bakery that produces some of the freshest bread you'll ever eat. Rides are available in buggies or boats, both drawn by horses—the one through town and the other on the river. There's also a miniature train that chugs slowly through the village and around the Crysler's Farm battlefield. Open daily, May 15 to October 15, 9:30 A.M. to 5:00 P.M.; open weekends in winter for sleigh rides and cross-country skiing.

If you're a fan of old-fashioned cooking—and lots of it— be sure, before leaving the compound, to stop at **Willard's Hotel**, where you'll be served hearty soups, chunky stews, and slabs of roast beef in portions more suitable for a field- plowing farmhand of the 1800s than a modern traveller.

From Morrisburg you can either continue up Highway 401 to Cornwall, the easternmost city in Ontario, and then on to Montreal, or head north via Highway 31 to Ottawa, a two-hour drive to the nation's capital and its Parliament Buildings, the National Arts Centre, and the Canadian Museum of Civilization.

NORTHERN ONTARIO

While most Ontarians believe they are in the "northland" when they drive the 160 km (100 miles) from Toronto to their Muskoka cottages, in reality they haven't even begun to explore the North. The real North is a country of impenetrable forests, limitless rivers and rapids, lumbering brown bears and watchful majestic moose; the awesome scenery of Agawa Canyon and crashing whitecaps along the Lake Superior shoreline; or a remote fly-in fishing lake with no other human being in sight. Ontario's North begins *above* Algonquin Park—which for many Ontarians is the limit of their north—and extends hundreds of miles farther north to Hudson Bay and as far west as Minnesota in the United States.

This is the North painted by the **Group of Seven**, Canadian artists who, in the early years of the century, captured the flaming leaves of autumn and the blue stillness of winter in what were then still unpopulated northern areas. (The **McMichael Gallery Canadian Collection** of the Group of Seven in Kleinburg, just north of Toronto, will give the uninitiated a startling insight into the real "Great White North.")

The predominant geographic feature of the region is the Precambrian, or Canadian, Shield underlying it—one of the oldest and largest rock formations on the planet. The rugged landscape of trees, rocks, and rivers provides vast quantities of paper products, essential minerals, and hydropower. In fact, the region is crisscrossed by 68,500 square miles of rivers and lakes (up to half a million of the latter—too many to accurately count or name), accounting for fully one-quarter of the world's supply of fresh water.

The name Ontario itself stems from either an old Iroquois word meaning "shining water" or a Huron word meaning "beautiful lake." Or perhaps a word in the Iroquois dialect meaning "rocks that stand by the lake," referring to the Niagara Escarpment. In other words, no one quite knows

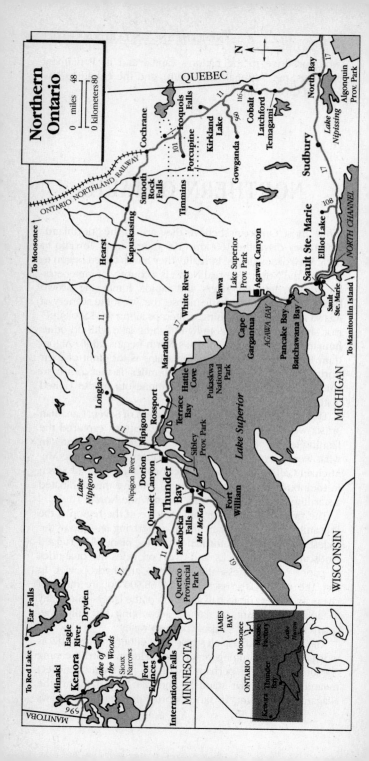

(although the smart money would bet on the Iroquois, since by 1649 they had completely wiped out the Huron tribe).

Northern Ontario is (to paraphrase a well-worn cliché) a great place to visit, but . . . not many people live there. Most of the province's nine million inhabitants cling resolutely to within a few hundred miles of the U.S. border. There are various reasons for this, from economics to weather. Residents of the region, on the other hand, will tell you it's a simple matter of gravity; everyone knows that cream rises to the top.

MAJOR INTEREST

Train tours of the interior, including the Polar Bear
    Express and Agawa Canyon Train
Indian pictographs
Visits to operating silver and gold mines
Amethyst mines
Fishing and hunting
Wilderness parks and camping
Northern wilderness scenery
Lodges and resorts

Unless you're a dedicated wilderness enthusiast who loves hiking and canoeing, to explore Northern Ontario you'll stick mostly to main auto routes like the Trans-Canada Highway, as well as to wilderness roads that literally take you to the end of the line. There are, however, some interesting rail alternatives.

NORTHERN ONTARIO
BY RAIL
VIA Passenger Rail

For many, this is the ideal method for seeing central and western Canada: sitting, chatting, reading, perhaps drowsing as the inhospitable cliffs of Lake Superior disappear during the night and become the flat prairies of wheat by morning, then the looming Rockies by twilight. For the three-day trip from Toronto to the West Coast you'll want to arrange sleeper accommodations (see the Getting Around section at the end of the chapter).

VIA offers specialized tours that include seal watching off Charlottetown, P.E.I., or walrus sightings in Repulse Bay at the top of the Northwest Territories. The newest offering is a two-day "**Rockies by Daylight**" excursion, including Edmonton and Jasper, that departs from Vancouver every Sunday morning. (Daylight—or lack of it—has always been the problem with a regular, complete trans-Canada train trip; owing to scheduling difficulties, the train approaches the magnificent Rocky Mountains at sunset, which means passengers pass through the most scenic part of the journey at night. The best you can do is pray for a full moon.)

VIA Rail also links up with smaller lines that will take you into Ontario's North—the only way to see certain isolated settlements where roads do not exist.

Moosonee

Every day (except Fridays), for $45 per person, the **Polar Bear Express** departs Cochrane, 380 km (236 miles) north of North Bay on Lake Nipissing, and chugs some 300 km (186 miles) into otherwise inaccessible wilderness before reaching the tiny native village of Moosonee on the shore of James Bay's Arctic tidewaters. (James Bay is the southernmost finger of mighty Hudson Bay.) Trans-Canada VIA Rail passengers transfer to the **Ontario Northland Railway** (ONR) in North Bay for the detour to Cochrane and beyond. Motorists can get to Cochrane by following Highway 11, the northern branch of the Trans-Canada.

Although the scenery on the way to Moosonee is impressive, the town isn't—the seemingly impenetrable forests thin out and completely disappear before you reach the tiny settlement. Instead, Moosonee's interest to the visitor lies in being able to observe how a native community functions in an isolated northern region; you can also see and purchase Indian crafts created in the James Bay Educational Centre. For various reasons, alcohol can be purchased through the government stores Monday through Thursday only; no booze is served after 8:00 P.M., even on the motels' special Saturday "pizza night."

While here you'll want to board one of the freighter canoes for the 15-minute trip to the island of **Moose Factory**, site of some of the oldest buildings in the province: Explorers from the Hudson's Bay Company established their first outpost on the island some 300 years ago. **St. Thomas Church**, a still-active museum piece here dating to 1860, displays such unique items as moose-hide altar cloths, silk embroidery on white deerhide, and prayer books in the Cree language.

In the fall, the James Bay Frontier Area is noted for some of the finest fowl hunting in Canada. The frontier region is for the most part unpopulated, definitely untamed, and basically inaccessible during the long winter months. But it is also a beautiful and wild part of the province for those who wish to experience the farthest reaches of the North. You'll have to plan ahead, however. The ▶ Hannah Bay Goose Camp, the most popular base for such activities in the area, is booked up to a year in advance for September and October, the only two months it operates.

You can also stay overnight in Moosonee at the cinder-block ▶ Moosonee Lodge, although people may wonder about you if you do. And you'll certainly be a curiosity among the locals. For most visitors, the five-hour stop before the train heads back to Cochrane should be enough.

The Agawa Canyon

The **Agawa Canyon Train**, like the Polar Bear Express, is the only way to see some of the most spectacular wilderness scenery in the world—and all from the comfort of a luxury passenger train. The one-day excursion on the Algoma Central Railway ($40 for adults, $20 for children under 12) starts in Sault Ste. Marie (see below) and winds 200 km (124 miles) through luxuriant forests and over vertigo-inspiring railway trestles to a two-hour picnic stop (you can purchase a box lunch on the train) at the photographer's paradise known as Agawa Canyon.

The canyon itself, designated a natural wilderness park, is maintained by the Algoma Central Railway and cannot be reached by any other means. During the stop you can explore the canyon along various hiking trails, fish for trout in a nearby stream, or just admire the fjordlike beauty in the middle of northern nowhere.

A first-time passenger will soon learn that the train often stops to pick up trappers, hikers, and the occasional group with canoes; the train is simply a rural version of an urban taxicab. People either flag it down or book a stop, arranging to meet it at a specific time.

The same excursion from December to March (weekends only) becomes the **Snow Train**, allowing passengers to experience the true winter wonderland found only in the Great White North—but from the warmth and comfort of a railroad car.

EXPLORING NORTHERN ONTARIO BY CAR

Just beyond Algonquin Park, the northernmost expanse of accessible wilderness for most Ontarians, the two branches of the Trans-Canada, Highways 11 and 17, come together momentarily in **North Bay** (on the northern shore of Lake Nipissing) before heading off again in different directions. From North Bay, Highway 11 heads due north through Temogami and Latchford, begins to veer west past the towns of Kirkland Lake and Iroquois Falls, and then turns sharply west at Cochrane, passing through Kapuskasing, Hearst, and Longlac before turning south just east of Lake Nipigon and rejoining Highway 17 in the town of Nipigon.

Highway 17, the more picturesque and popular route across Northern Ontario, heads due west from North Bay through the mining center of Sudbury before dropping down to follow Lake Huron's **North Channel** shoreline. At Sault Ste. Marie it turns sharply north and follows the eastern shore of Lake Superior through **Lake Superior Provincial Park** and past the town of Wawa, continues in a northerly direction through White River, hits the Lake Superior shoreline again outside of Marathon, and follows the latter to Nipigon (where it meets Highway 11) and the Nipigon River, one of the best fishing spots in the world for trout and walleye, before continuing in a southerly direction into the town of Thunder Bay. Although you could drive the 1,280 km (794 miles) of this route in two days, you'll want to do it more slowly in order to give yourself time to enjoy the scenery of the Canadian Shield region.

West of Thunder Bay, Highway 17 becomes the sole branch of the Trans-Canada, continuing in a northwesterly direction to Kenora and the Lake of the Woods region, and then on to Winnipeg, Manitoba. Highway 11 heads in a more westerly direction past the northern fringes of **Quetico Provincial Park** and on to the Minnesota border.

The vast region circumscribed by these two routes is not only an area of rivers and forests but also of a million roadside motels, fishing camps, rustic resorts, and the occasional fancier hotel. There is no shortage of accommodations in the area; we mention a very few of the best or more interesting. Most, however, are pleasant little mom-and-pop motels, so just pick one that strikes your fancy or get a copy of the Ontario government's accommodations guide before starting your trip. The government information is free; contact the Ministry of Tourism and Recreation, 77 Bloor Street, Toronto, Ont. M7A 2R9; Tel: (800) 668-2746. You can also stop by any of the roadside Ontario information centers.

The descriptions that follow assume you'll be travelling in season, not in winter or bordering months.

THE NORTHERN ROUTE
Mining Communities

Highway 11, the northern route, takes you into rougher, rockier terrain populated by miners and engineers, the land of prospectors and boom towns gone bust. Legend has it that the town of **Cobalt** was born in 1903 when Fred LaRose, a frustrated blacksmith, threw a hammer at an inquisitive fox that was spooking his horses. Apparently his anger affected his aim; LaRose's hammer missed the fox, chipped a rock, and in the process uncovered what would eventually prove to be the world's richest silver vein.

Fred's hammer also produced one of the greatest mining stampedes in history, which in turn led to the development of various other communities in the area, including Gowganda, Kirkland Lake, Iroquois Falls, and Porcupine. All of these towns have quieted down somewhat since their heady days of fast fortunes, although there are many old-timers around still panning for precious minerals and throwing hammers at rocks. Each community holds its own "Miners' Festival" at varying times throughout the summer months (check in advance for their dates, which change from year to year), and grizzled prospectors will gladly spin tales of the olden golden years of fortune.

Kirkland Lake
Kirkland Lake, one of these former boom towns, is the site of the elaborate **Sir Harry Oakes Château**, where there are displays about prospecting, geology, and mining, as well as material on the early prospectors who flocked into the region.

No one left such an indelible stamp on the mining communities as the château's former owner, Sir Harry Oakes, the epitome of the rough, bullheaded prospector. Oakes made his fortune in the North, moved briefly to Niagara Falls, then continued his southern migration to the Bahamas, where the often belligerent former miner was murdered by persons unknown in the 1940s. His son-in-law was accused of Oakes's murder, tried and acquitted, and then banished from the islands, leaving the infamous crime unsolved to this day. In fact, there is a statue of Sir Harry in downtown Nassau, and though the locals may tell you "he was a generous Canadian who came here to live and died," there is more to the story than that. Canadian writer Timothy Findlay's excellent novel *Famous Last Words* explores the mysterious circumstances surounding Sir Harry's death, including his friendship with the duke of Windsor and Wallis Simpson and rumors about their alleged Nazi sympathies.

Timmins

Farther north along the highway you'll see signs announcing your entry into Timmins, although it will be miles before you spot a settlement. Timmins, with a population of 45,000, actually has "city" boundaries that encompass 1,260 square miles, thus living up to its claim as the "largest city in Canada."

The many minerals prospected hereabouts at the turn of the century brought prosperity to the region, and the subsequent discovery of most of the world's supply of silver and zinc ensured its future. There are tours of the various mines in the area during the North's two summer months; in most, the fascinating "underworld" operations are explained while you are some 3,500 feet beneath the earth's surface. For further information, contact the Timmins Chamber of Commerce; Tel: (705) 360-1900. Those with lung or heart conditions are advised to remain in the gift shop; they can also visit the **Timmins Museum** (open year-round; Tel: 705/235-5066), where the local mining history is explained.

Farther on, the little town of Cochrane is the southern terminus of the **Polar Bear Express**, the northland railway route "down" to the Arctic watershed communities of Moosonee and Moose Factory (discussed above).

Paper Mills

Several logging towns in the area—Iroquois Falls, Smooth Rock Falls, Kapuskasing, and Hearst (mainly French-speaking) among them—offer public tours of their pulp and paper mills, the lifeblood industry of these northern communities. Typical of these is the **Abitibi-Price** company in Iroquois Falls, which arranges very popular plant tours during the summer months. Although it may sound otherwise, these tours offer a fascinating look at an assembly line where huge trees are cut, folded, spindled, mutilated, stomped, mashed, and pressed into the miles of spinning paper rolls that eventually end up with the daily news stamped on them.

For further information, contact the Iroquois Falls Chamber of Commerce; Tel: (705) 232-4656.

From here it is several hundred miles of straight highway to the tall cliffs of **Nipigon**, which mark the end of the northern trail. The dense forests flanking either side of this virtually unpopulated stretch of road are busy in summer with visiting rock hounds who come in search of the minerals, agate, fool's gold, and fossils scattered throughout the region. In Nipigon itself, the northern and southern routes (Highways 11 and 17) meet for their joint run into Thunder Bay, the capital city of the so-called lakehead area.

THE SOUTHERN ROUTE
Sudbury

The highway into Sudbury runs through a more populated area than the northern route and is a much more picturesque drive. Not that the city itself, the first significant population center west of North Bay, can be described as pretty (although it has been improving).

The area around Sudbury is the same lunar-like landscape that drew the Apollo astronauts here to train for their moon missions. The pitted surface is believed to have been caused by the impact of a meteorite (almost two billion years ago), which brought with it vast mineral wealth, including nickel, platinum, copper, gold, and cobalt. Sudbury is known, in fact, as the nickel capital of the world, a distinction noted with a 30-foot-high Canadian five-cent piece prominently displayed near the highway.

It is somewhat ironic that this wilderness town has pollution rivaling that of smoggy Los Angeles. Much of it is spewed into the air by the the smokestacks of continuously operating metal refineries, which produce colorful hues 24 hours a day. However, the city has been upgrading its image, one of the attempts being **Science North** (open daily year-round), a hands-on museum devoted to the natural wonders of physics and geology. The snowflake-shaped museum is a fascinating place to browse, and is worth an hour or two of your time. Here you can pet a porcupine, dig for fossils, and even create a mini-tornado. Perhaps the best reason to visit, however, is to experience the everyday working conditions of a miner in the Big Nickel Mine. Visitors to the museum are whisked by elevator to a quarter-mile-long mine shaft where they witness different types of mining operations— and, if they feel inspired, mail postcards to their friends back home from Canada's only underground post box. Tours of the various mining museums and mineral companies in town, including INCO and Falconbridge, are also available.

If you decide to stay overnight in the Sudbury area, the ▶ **Sheraton Caswell Inn** on Regent Street South offers comfortable rooms, an indoor pool and sauna, and a good dining room.

The Chi-Cheemaun Ferry

The bridge between Southwestern and Northern Ontario is actually a boat. Or, to be more precise, a car ferry. This is the famed *Chi-Cheemaun,* a 140-vehicle, 638-passenger ferry that sails from the little mainland port of **Tobermory** at the northern tip of the Bruce Peninsula to the dock at **South Baymouth** on Manitoulin Island. (Manitoulin lies off the coast of Northern Ontario halfway between Sudbury and Sault Ste. Marie.) The *Chi-Cheemaun* (Ojibwa for "big canoe") makes the 1-hour-and-45-minute trip twice daily (three times on Fridays) and, because it is one of the most popular summer excursions in Ontario, is usually packed both coming and going. (Tourists can always drive around Georgian Bay, but most would rather line up for the ferry.) The trip is so popular, in fact, that three summers ago Ontario Northland Marine Services (which has the ferry concession) decided to add another boat to the route. The *Nindawayma,* or "little sister," is a slightly smaller version of the original ferry and a welcome addition, allowing visitors to leave from either port every other hour instead of once every four hours, as used to be the case.

Both ferries have large cafeterias, a snack bar, and pleasant on-deck easy chairs. Rates range from $10 per person to $40 for a whole family (no maximum); car prices start at $25 and increase with the size of the vehicle. Bicycles are $5, while motor homes are $42. Reservations are available on early and late sailings only. Contact the Chi-Cheemaun Ferry Service, Owen Sound; Tel: (519) 596-2510.

Manitoulin Island

Manitoulin Island is one of the great undiscovered and undeveloped tourist areas of the province. Most visitors coming from the south simply leave the ferry at South Baymouth and drive straight across the island to the Little Current bridge linking Manitoulin to the Northern Ontario mainland. In doing so, they pass up the opportunity to dawdle and explore the quiet bays and inlets, sandy beaches, and tiny island villages of the world's largest freshwater island.

For the earliest inhabitants of the region Manitoulin was a sort of "middle earth," neither north nor south, as well as a place of dreams and legends. The Ojibwa saw it as the home of the "Great Spirit": Nature and all its forces were represented in the spirit world as "manitous," and superior to all was the Great Spirit, the "Gitchi Manitou." Since it is only fitting that this supreme being should live apart from others, what better place than a private island. Literally translated, Manitoulin means God's Island.

The 110-mile-long island has 1,000 miles of coastline and is dotted with sleepy villages ranging in size from Little Current (1,500 people) to South Baymouth (62). There are seven different Indian reserves on the island, and several specialty stores, including the **Perivale Gallery** in Spring Bay, which sell the magnificent handiwork of Manitoulin's native craftspeople.

Fishing charters and excellent yachting possibilities are the summertime norm in the protected waters of Lake Huron's **North Channel**, off the island's north shore. Scuba divers will find some fascinating old shipwrecks here in the waters around Meldrum Bay.

In terms of accommodations, Manitoulin is a very relaxed vacation retreat that, for the most part, offers little mom-and-pop motel operations, housekeeping cabins, and fishing camps. Of the few resort complexes and major hotels on the island the best are the ▶ **Manitowaning Lodge and Tennis Resort**, in the town of the same name, and the ▶ **Silver Birches Resort** in Little Current. Campers will do best to stay in the campgrounds behind the sand beach—Canada's longest—of Providence Bay.

The island's major attraction is the annual native pow-wow held over the long weekend in early August at the 30,000-acre **Wikwemikong Indian Reserve** on the island's easternmost peninsula. Native Americans come from across Canada and the U.S. for the four-day event, which features tribal folklore and customs, dancing, craft-making, and art. For further information, contact the Manitoulin Tourist Information Centre, P.O. Box 119, Little Current, Ont. P0P 1K0; Tel: (705) 368-3021.

Elliott Lake, on the mainland off Highway 17 near the end of Highway 68 (west of the bridge leading to Manitoulin), was known as the uranium capital of the world until 1960, when the mineral bubble burst. It is still a well-planned community of 20,000, and recent developments have led to the reopening of some mines. If wild northern hospitality is your cup of tea, you won't want to miss its annual **Uranium Festival** toward the end of June.

Sault Ste. Marie

Sault Ste. Marie, affectionately known as the "Soo," is the navigational gateway between Lake Superior and Lake Huron; the International Bridge across the St. Marys River connects the city to its Michigan sister of the same name. For a bustling port and industrial town, the city of 85,000 is surprisingly clean.

This is also the best place to watch huge lake freighters lumber through the **Soo Lock System**; better still, you can take a boat cruise through the system, a two-hour tour with frequent departures (May to October) from the Norgoma Dock next to the Holiday Inn.

Exhibits at Ermatinger House, 831 Queen Street East, and the Sault Ste. Marie Museum (open daily year-round), as well as aboard the floating M.S. *Norgoma* (next to the Holiday Inn on Foster Drive) detail the city's history, from its founding in 1669 by a Jesuit priest, to the wild fur-trading days of the Hudson's Bay Company, to the development of area industries in our own century.

Sault Ste. Marie is also the southern terminus for the Algoma Central Railway and the **Agawa Canyon Train** trip (see the Northern Ontario by Rail section above).

The recommended accommodation here is the moderately priced ▶ **Algoma's Water Tower Inn** on Great Northern Road. If you're booked for the Algoma Central, tell them you have to catch the 8:30 A.M. excursion and ask for a confirmed wake-up call.

Heading North

It may feel as though you're leaving civilization behind as you head north from Sault Ste. Marie along Lake Superior's shoreline. And no wonder. Until you reach Thunder Bay, some 800 km (500 miles) distant, all you'll encounter will be a handful of tiny towns (the largest, Wawa, has a population of 5,000), dense forests, and the loveliest deserted beaches you have ever seen—one of the many secrets of the North.

The little village of **Batchawana Bay**, about 80 km (50 miles) north of the Soo, is a pleasant place to explore the bays and beaches fringing the lake's shoreline. But here perhaps a word of caution about Lake Superior: It is cold and very unpredictable. Exercise caution when fishing or canoeing—even on a sunny day its calm waters can become turbulent whitecaps in a matter of minutes.

Pancake Bay

As you approach this tiny town situated some 96 km (60 miles) north of the Soo you'll see two stores located on the east side of the highway. Slow down, turn your steering wheel to the right, park, and spend some browsing and buying time at the **Agawa Indian Crafts** and the **Canadian Carver**. Formerly across the road from each other, the two are now side by side for the convenience of the customer.

Proprietors June and Gerald Demers, who own both shops, have amassed in each a collection of authentic native arts and crafts, including Iroquois pottery, Micmac basketry, and Ojibway leatherwork. Look in particular for the rough handcarved ceremonial masks, the visual interpretation of native deities.

Pancake Bay is hardly an Indian name, although its roots lie deep in Canadian folklore. It was here, legend has it, that early fur traders stopped on their way east from Fort Williams (now Thunder Bay) and used up their remaining flour to make pancakes, knowing they could reprovision the next day in Sault Ste. Marie. Today you can overnight at one of the 355 campsites in the provincial park here and fish for rainbow trout in the lake. The long sand beach is a good place to swim, sunbathe, and relax, and there are hot showers available (something the 16th-century voyageurs would have liked) on the grounds.

Should hunger pangs strike, keep an eye out for the **Black Forest Motel** and its simple, home-style restaurant. For more than 25 years the motel's German-born owner has been serving generous platters of food and the best homemade sausage this side of Bavaria—and Lake Superior is just across the road.

LAKE SUPERIOR PROVINCIAL PARK

Campers can stock up on supplies in **Montreal River Harbour,** one of the few inland deep-sea harbors in the world, before entering Lake Superior Provincial Park. Highway 17 winds some 90 km (56 miles) through the 580 square miles of this wilderness park, and entry is free; campers must pay a site fee for the main camping areas and also to camp along the interior hiking trails. If you have the time, follow the winding dirt road (it will be marked) off Highway 17 to the long sandy beach, picnic tables, and overnight facilities at lovely **Gargantua Bay**. It's a little-known spot that you just may have all to yourself.

Most campers gather at the **Agawa Bay** campground, with its hiking trails and canoe routes, guided nature walks, and evening events in the park's amphitheater. The beach here is littered with sparkling stones and gnarled pieces of drift-wood, which are taken as souvenirs to be tumbled and shined, sanded and lacquered, eventually to appear as objets d'art on countless mantelpieces.

Longfellow's Hiawatha

The centuries-old pictographs carved into **Agawa Rock**, a cliff face rising some 75 feet above Lake Superior, are the park's most fascinating feature. These 30 Indian rock paint-ings are the basis for Longfellow's saga of Hiawatha, a poem once taught in every North American public school. (Longfel-low himself never saw the pictographs but rather based his story on descriptions related by an explorer who had visited the region.) The prehistoric depiction of a migration by canoe through the Lake Superior region—sculpted into stone and darkened with rust-colored iron-ore pigments—can be seen by anyone who wishes to climb the cliff; the rocks can be wet and slippery, however, so wear good hiking shoes and exercise caution.

Wawa

Wawa, north of the park on Route 101, is "famous" for the gigantic statue of a goose (Wawa is Ojibway for "wild goose") housing a tourist information booth; spend some time at nearby **Old Woman Bay**, a bit of the Bahamas in Ontario, where shallow sandy waters ensure bathtub-like temperatures in normally chilly Lake Superior (assuming you're travelling in summertime, of course). For accommo-dations, try the ▶ **Wawa Motor Inn** on Mission Road. There are units out front, but ask for one of the cabins, which are hidden from the road. These are log structures with cathedral-like ceilings, kitchens, and fireplaces, all affording dazzling northern sunsets from your back porch.

Pukaskwa National Park

In Marathon, 200 km (124 miles) farther west, you have the option of turning south on Highway 627 to visit vast (714 square miles) Pukaskwa National Park. The park offers good wilderness walks and canoe routes, with some basic camp-ing sites along the coastal trail. Pukaskwa protects a large chunk of Canadian Shield wilderness and its boreal forest, and is also the southernmost range of a small woodland caribou herd; sit quietly by the shoreline at sunset and you may see one of these rare creatures. **Hattie Cove**, at the northern entrance to the park, has a small campground, a sandy beach, a few picnic areas, very cold water, and a boat launch.

Rossport

The drive along the north shore of Lake Superior provides some magnificent wild scenery broken up by picturesque lakeside towns and villages such as Terrace Bay, Rossport, and the fishing center of Nipigon. Perhaps the best one to explore is Rossport, a little fishing village with a natural harbor and an archipelago of islands offshore ideal for sailing and boating (you can charter a craft at the government dock).

For overnight accommodations or a meal, try the ▶ **Rossport Inn** on Bowman Street, a recently refurbished railway stopover built in 1884. There are six homey guest rooms here, and the dining room features the local catch of the day. The inn has retained its rustic railway roots, and offers friendly northern hospitality.

The **Forget Me Not Gift Shop** in town specializes in better-than-average souvenirs, everything from native pottery to hand-tooled leather goods. The shop also offers the best view of the town's picturesque harbor (so many people come to shop and stay for the view that owner Olav Sundland has a section of his yard marked "husbands' waiting area").

Nipigon to Thunder Bay

Nonfishermen may be content to pass through Nipigon— where Highway 11 rejoins Highway 17—but most travellers will be interested in **Ouimet Canyon Provincial Park**, farther south near the town of Dorion. Two miles long, more than 450 feet across, and 300 feet deep, the canyon was formed in prehistoric times by shifting glacial ice that ground out a huge depression in the rock. Rare arctic plants cover the canyon floor and cliffs, and snow lingers year-round in its most protected recesses. Much of the footpath around the canyon's rim is not protected by safety railing, however, so tread carefully.

There are several amethyst mines on the outskirts of Thunder Bay where you can hunt for rough specimens at open pit mines (paying by the pound as you leave); all have gift shops stocked with jewelry and polished stones as well. Two of the biggest are the **Ontario Gem Amethyst Mine** and the **Amethyst Mine Panorama**.

Just before you reach Thunder Bay you'll see a bronze statue of Terry Fox, the 21-year-old athlete who planned to run a "Marathon of Hope" across Canada on his artificial leg in order to raise money for cancer research. It was at this halfway mark that his doctors convinced him to stop before his malignancy spread any further; he was flown home to

Vancouver, where he died soon after. It was Terry Fox who inspired wheelchair athlete Rick Hanson to undertake his "Man in Motion" odyssey around the world. Vancouver's Hanson, now Canada's representative to Australia, raised millions of dollars of research money to assist the physically challenged in the course of his two-year quest.

Thunder Bay

Sleeping Giant, Thunder Bay's best-known natural landmark, rises from the waters of the bay; from the harbor, this piece of land some 25 km (16 miles) distant looks like a man, arms across his chest, floating on the water. Ojibway legend has it that the giant was once Nanibijou, or the Great Spirit, who lived on Mount McKay, which today is an Indian reserve. Nanibijou protected his tribe, but also warned that they would perish and he would be turned into stone if the white man ever discovered their silver mine. Alas, one of his tribesmen revealed the mine's location to the white men, and as the invading ships came within sight Nanibijou created a storm that sank them. The next morning, as prophesied, he was found in the bay turned to stone, and was left there to guard the mine.

Thunder Bay (or T-Bay, as it's called by locals), a sprawling amalgamation of two cities, Fort William and Port Arthur, is a bustling seaport of some 125,000 people that annually stores over one billion bushels of wheat for shipment to the Canadian east. Early French explorers were the first to settle the area and used Fort William as a gateway to the fur-trading routes of the Northwest.

Old Fort William

An authentic reconstruction (the largest of its kind in North America), Old Fort William shows what the original settlement looked like in the early 19th century. From May to September the fort is peopled by "residents" who carry on their daily business in period costume and speech. Visitors can watch the blacksmith shoe horses, help make tallow candles, or attend a meeting of the town council.

The best way to see Thunder Bay is either from the scenic lookout atop **Mount McKay** (one of the area's four winter ski resorts), or aboard the cruise ship *Welcome* (leaving daily from the North Marina dock at the foot of Red River Road), which navigates among the Great Lakes freighters in the harbor. After the cruise, take a short drive west of town to majestic **Kakabeka Falls**, the "Niagara of the North," for a picnic lunch beside the Kaministiquia River.

STAYING AND DINING IN THE AREA

The Thunder Bay area also has the largest Finnish population outside of Finland, supposedly because early Finnish settlers found that its rugged terrain reminded them of home. Try the **Hoito Restaurant** (hidden away in a church basement on Bay Street; Tel: 807/345-6323) for some authentic Finnish food, or the **Kangas Sauna** on Oliver Road for true Nordic steam.

You won't be disappointed by the lodging options if you decide to spend a few days in the area. Good accommodations and hotel dining can be found at the ▶ **Valhalla Inn**, the ▶ **Victoria Inn**, and the ▶ **Airlane Hotel**, all clustered near the junction of Highways 11 and 17 and Arthur Street West; the ▶ **Landmark Inn** on the other side of town is also good. All four are similar, although the Valhalla has the edge in style and amenities. The first three also have indoor pools and saunas, a godsend for the weary traveller, as well as a full range of dining and bar facilities, while the Victoria is the only one with evening entertainment and dancing. The Airlane gets the nod for the best dining. (The Victoria will be undergoing extensive renovation throughout 1994.) Another good bet is the ▶ **Best Western Norwester Resort Hotel**, which recently underwent major renovation and expansion, including the addition of fireplace- and Jacuzzi-suites. The hotel is located 8 km (5 miles) south of town on Highway 61.

Uncle Frank's Supper Club (Tel: 807/475-9141), also on Highway 61 heading south toward the ski hills, is a 1950s-style dining room of faded yet comfortable elegance, with a wonderful fieldstone fireplace and a menu featuring 20-ounce porterhouse steaks. The **Neebing Roadhouse** (Tel: 807/475-0792), farther down the highway, has a glassed-in dining room overlooking the ski slopes, and a casual country bar that has become the area's most popular après-ski gathering place. (As mentioned, Thunder Bay has four ski areas within a 15-minute drive of the downtown area. It also boasts "Big Thunder," the 90- and 70-meter ski jumps that annually play host to international competitions.)

One of the most popular spots in the area, day or night, is the **Brasserie and Brew Pub** (901 Red River Road; Tel: 807/767-4415), with a five-page menu that includes everything from burgers and chicken wings to prime rib and an exceptional shrimp-and-scallop tortellini dish. The restaurant's house beer, a rich, dark brew, is made on the premises, as is a lighter version known as "bambi beer"—named, according to local aficionados, for a former, rather elusive, T-Bay resident.

WEST OF THUNDER BAY

The region west of Thunder Bay is a land of summer resorts, sports lodges, and hundreds of fly-in fishing outposts tucked away on the shores of countless lakes. This time it's Highway 11 that takes the southern turn and runs along the northern fringes of **Quetico Provincial Park**, a designated wilderness park with hiking trails and canoe routes (best to avoid May and June, however, when the dreaded black flies may just carry you away).

Highway 11 eventually meanders through the border town of Fort Frances, a popular U.S. crossing for vacationers coming through International Falls, Minnesota, and then ends at Rainy River and the Minnesota border, where it becomes U.S. Route 11. The northern route, Highway 17, takes you past the moose-hunting center of Dryden before reaching the magnificent Lake of the Woods resort area.

Dryden

Dryden has a population of close to 6,000, most of whom owe their livelihood to Canadian Pacific Forest Products Ltd. (formerly Great Lakes Paper). The mill presides over everything in town, announcing its presence with a constant haze of billowing smoke and—depending on the winds that day—a strong assault on the olfactory senses. Business at the moment is booming, with a recent multimillion dollar addition and, in this age of factory layoffs, the hiring of an extra 150 workers. (During the summer, free tours—about an hour and a half in length—can be arranged by calling 807/223-9376, Monday through Friday.)

Its pungent aroma notwithstanding, Dryden is a pleasant little town, and is known for its hunting and fishing camps as much as for its famous paper products. For local information, look for the huge statue of "Max the Moose" located just outside the tourist bureau. Of particular interest for the uninitiated is the **MNR** (Ontario Ministry of Natural Resources) **Northwestern Regional Fire Management Centre**, which has the unenviable task of fighting forest fires in a vast region comprising almost half the province. A tour (daily from May to the end of August; Tel: 807/937-4402) of this fascinating facility will ensure, if nothing else, that your campfire is stone cold the next time you leave a wilderness area.

Kenora

Once in this pretty little town, set your watch back one hour; even though you're still in the province of Ontario you are now in a different time zone.

This is the **Lake of the Woods** area, a gorgeous landscape of lakes and wooded islands, rustic cottages and remote camps. It is also one of those regions of the globe that can justifiably vie for the title "God's Country." There are probably more good fishing and hunting lodges scattered around the region than anywhere else in the world, with literally hundreds of resorts offering fly-in fishing camps, native guides, and fall moose hunts. Among the better known are **Red Indian Lodge** and the **Rod and Reel Resort** in Sioux Narrows; **Lindmeier's North Shore Lodge** in Eagle River; the **Keyamawun Lodge** on Red Lake; **Long Legged Lake Resort** in Ear Falls; and the aptly named **Canadian Wilderness Camp** near Kenora. (For additional information on places to stay overnight, see the Accommodations Reference list at the end of this chapter.)

You can get a good overview of the area from the tenth-floor dining room of the ▶ **Best Western Lakeside Inn Hotel and Conference Centre**, a circular hotel overlooking the boat-filled lake where the view, thanks to a seemingly immutable Law of Travel, surpasses the cuisine. The hotel itself offers basic accommodations—nothing fancy, just clean and comfortable—and an indoor pool. (Be sure to request a room with a lake view.) The best method for exploring the region is to rent a houseboat and dawdle around the large, beautiful lake and its thousands of islands. For information and/or reservations, contact **Houseboat Adventures**; Tel: (807) 543-2911.

Kenora, not to be outdone by Wawa with its goose or Dryden with its moose, boasts its own 20-foot roadside mascot. "Husky the Muskie," a huge statue of a jumping fish (a giant muskellunge) overlooks the bay. Based on an informal survey, Husky is photographed by more tourists than the other two combined.

For the best steak ever (except for the one you cook on your own barbecue) visit the **Kenmore Hotel** at 15 Chipman Street. Don't let the rather seedy exterior—or interior, for that matter—fool you. Instead, concentrate on your meal and try to figure out whether it's the aging process or the seasoning that makes the Kenmore's steaks so superb.

As a reward for the long drive from North Bay and all the nights in little roadside motels en route, you should treat yourself to a night at the ▶ **Minaki Lodge Four Seasons Northland Resort**, in the little fishing village of Minaki, about 50 km (31 miles) north of Kenora via Highway 596. This magnificent timber-and-stone structure with its impressive cathedral ceiling was built as a midpoint lodge for travellers crossing the country by rail. Having been grandly refurbished by the Four Seasons chain, today it features hand-some guest rooms with a range of amenities; a good dining room; facilities for golf, tennis, and boating; and its own fly-in fishing.

West to Manitoba

As you backtrack to Highway 17 and continue west, the roadside scenery, which has been dominated by dense forests and rugged outcrops, becomes flatter and less thickly wooded. By the time you cross into Manitoba on the Trans-Canada Highway, 52 km (32 miles) west of Kenora and some 1,800 km (1,100 miles) west of Toronto, flat prairie dominates the landscape, as it will for the next 1,600 km (1,000 miles). In fact, the scenery changes so dramatically when you reach the Manitoba border that that western province seems to be declaring its own identity, rejecting the tangled wildness of Ontario's northland—filled with trees, rocks, and lakes—for the flat calm of golden prairie wheat.

GETTING AROUND

Muskoka and Ontario's Cottage Country

By Car. To reach their cottages or the resorts of the area, most people go by car, heading north up Highway 400 and then branching off on Highway 26 to Collingwood or Highway 11 to Muskoka. For the Kawarthas and Haliburton Highlands, the back roads are more scenic, but to save time go as far east as possible on Highway 401 before turning north. Most people use Highway 35. This is the best exit for the Trent–Severn Waterway as well, the major portion of which is in the Kawarthas. Information on the system from most parts of North America can be obtained by telephoning Ontario Travel Information at (800) 668-2746. Alternately, contact the Friends of Trent–Severn, Box 572, Peterborough, Ont. K9J 6Z6; Tel: (705) 742-2251.

Driving time is short. From the north end of Toronto it takes two and a half hours to reach Huntsville in northern Muskoka, and only one and a half hours to reach Collingwood in Huronia or Rice Lake in the lower Kawarthas. Haliburton is about a three-hour drive.

Other Options. One train a day (except Saturdays) leaves at noon out of Toronto's Union Station, stopping at Orillia, Gravenhurst, and Huntsville on its way to northern Ontario. Book through VIA Rail in Canada or Amtrak in the United States.

Buses offer frequent, sometimes express, service on all well-travelled routes, and serve all communities regularly.

Many resorts will arrange pickup and return by air, usually from Toronto's Island Airport.

Northern Ontario

By Rail. The trans-Canada VIA Rail may not be on a par with the famed Orient Express, but then neither is the price. The basic rate between Toronto and Vancouver is $925 per person for a roomette. The train is clean and comfortable, the roomettes tiny (two seats facing each other during the day, a small bed at night), and the food ranges from four-star to the snack-bar variety.

Most people board the train in Montreal or Toronto, although some start right on the East Coast (i.e., Halifax) for a full cross-country tour (switching trains in both Montreal and Toronto). You can even board Amtrak at Penn Station in New York City and connect with a VIA train at the border. (VIA Rail, Passenger Services, Union Station, 65 Front Street West, Toronto; M5J 1E7; Tel: 416/366-8411, or 800/561-3949 from the U.S.) U.S. visitors thinking about this option are better off checking with a travel agent, as Amtrak is not always known for its cooperative spirit.

U.K. visitors can contact VIA Rail's general sales agent: Leisurail, 3rd floor, Priest Gate House, 5–7 Priest Gate, Peterborough, U.K. PE1 1LE; Tel: 0733-517-80.

Central information sources in Canada are VIA Rail, 2 Place Ville Marie, Suite 400, Montreal, Que. H3B 2G6, Tel: (516) 871-6000; or VIA Rail, 55 York Street, Suite 1300, Toronto, Ont. M5J 1R7, Tel: (416) 868-7211. Although the government imposed massive cutbacks in 1990, VIA Rail service has been stabilized, with lines to remote areas the only part of the operation likely to suffer additional cuts. Still, travellers are advised to check their routing well in advance.

The Polar Bear Express

Book tickets through Ontario Northland Railway, 555 Oak Street, North Bay, Ont. P1B 8L3; Tel: (705) 472-4500, or Union Station in Toronto.

The Agawa Canyon Train

This train leaves from the ACR Mall station (Algoma Central Railway) on Bay Street in Sault Ste. Marie daily from June to October at 8:00 A.M. and returns by 5:00 P.M.; both cold and hot lunches are served; the fare is about $45 round trip per adult. Book well in advance, especially if you're planning to travel during the peak fall season in order to ogle the most brilliant autumn colors imaginable. Contact: Algoma Central

Railway, 129 Bay Street, Sault Ste. Marie, Ont. P6A 5P6; Tel: (705) 946-7330.

ACCOMMODATIONS REFERENCE

The rates given below are projections *for peak seasons during the 1994 calendar year; at other times of the year they* may *be considerably less. Unless otherwise indicated, rates are based on double rooms, double occupancy; provincial and federal taxes are included in all rates. As rates are subject to change, always double-check before booking. Those who wait to make last-minute reservations will do even better by checking the travel sections of the daily newspapers. In Ontario, the* Toronto Star *is the best source for such information.*

Southwestern Ontario

► **Albion Hotel.** Main Street, P.O. Box 114, **Bayfield**, Ont. N0M 1G0. Tel: (519) 565-2641. $62–$84.

► **Benjamin's Restaurant & Inn.** 17 King Street, **St. Jacobs**, Ont. N0B 2N0. Tel: (519) 664-3731; Fax: (519) 664-2218. $100–$115 (includes breakfast).

► **Benmiller Inn.** R.R. 4, **Goderich**, Ont. N7A 3Y1. Tel: (519) 524-2191; Fax: (519) 524-5150; in the U.S. and Canada, Tel: (800) 265-1711. $110–$165.

► **La Brassine.** R.R. 2, **Goderich**, Ont. N7A 3X8. Tel: (519) 524-6300. $56 (includes breakfast).

► **Chantry House Inn.** 118 High Street, **Southampton**, Ont. N0H 2L0. Tel: (519) 797-2646; Fax: (519) 797-5538. $106–140; suites $140–$168.

► **Days Inn.** Highway 77, **Leamington**, Ont. N8H 3V4. Tel: (519) 326-8647; Fax: (519) 326-5531; in Canada, Tel: (800) 265-5329. $72–$78.

► **Duffy's Motor Inn.** 306 Dalhousie Street, **Amherstburg**, Ont. N9V 1X3. Tel: (519) 736-2101; Fax: (519) 736-2103. $76–$110.

► **Dyconia Resort Hotel.** 381 Mosley Street, **Wasaga Beach**, Ont. L0L 2P0. Tel: (705) 429-2000; Fax: (705) 429-7193. $73–$140.

► **Elora Mill Inn.** 77 Mill Street West, **Elora**, Ont. N0B 1S0. Tel: (519) 846-5356; Fax: (519) 846-9180. $106–$224 (includes breakfast).

► **Erie Beach Hotel.** 19 Walker Street, **Port Dover**, Ont. N0A 1N0. Tel: (519) 583-1391; Fax: (519) 583-3250. $69.

► **Gate House Hotel.** 142 Queen Street, **Niagara-on-the-Lake**, Ont. L0S 1J0. Tel: (905) 468-3263; Fax: (905) 468-7400. $140–$162.

► **Heidelberg Brewery and Restaurant Motel.** P.O. Box

116, 2 King Street, **Heidelberg**, Ont. N0B 1Y0. Tel: (519) 699-4413. $45.

▶ **Hilton International Windsor**. 277 Riverside Drive West, **Windsor**, Ont. N9A 5K4. Tel: (519) 973-5555; Fax: (519) 973-1600; in the U.S. and Canada, Tel: (800) HILTONS. $114–$140.

▶ **Holiday Inn by the Falls**. 5339 Murray Street, **Niagara Falls**, Ont. L2G 2J3. Tel: (905) 356-1333; Fax: (905) 356-7128; in New York, Ohio, Pennsylvania, and Michigan, Tel: (800) 263-9393. $140.

▶ **Honeymoon City Motel**. 4943 Clifton Hill, **Niagara Falls**, Ont. L2G 3N5. Tel: (905) 357-4330; Fax: (905) 357-0423; in the U.S. and Canada, Tel: (800) 668-8840. $100.

▶ **Hotel Bedford**. 92 Courthouse Square, **Goderich**, Ont. N7A 1M7. Tel: (519) 524-7337; Fax: (519) 524-2913. $75.

▶ **Idlewyld Inn**. 36 Grand Avenue, **London**, Ont. N6C 1K8. Tel: (519) 433-2891; Fax: (519) 433-2891. $88–$173 (includes Continental breakfast).

▶ **Inn on the Bay**. 1800 Second Avenue East, **Owen Sound**, Ont. N4K 5P1. Tel: (519) 371-9200; Fax: (519) 371-6740. $106–$162.

▶ **Ivy Rose Motor Inn**. 2885 Howard Avenue, **Windsor**, Ont. N8X 3Y4. Tel: (519) 966-1700; Fax: (519) 966-1700, ext. 400; in the U.S. and Canada, Tel: (800) 265-7366. $60–$70.

▶ **Jakobstettel Guest House**. 16 Isabella Street, **St. Jacobs**, Ont. N0B 2N0. Tel: (519) 664-2208; Fax: (519) 664-1326. $106–$157 (includes breakfast).

▶ **Journey's End Leamington**. 279 Erie Street South, **Leamington**, Ont. N8H 3C4. Tel: (519) 326-9071; Fax: (519) 326-3445; in the U.S. and Canada, Tel: (800) 668-4200. $73.

▶ **Kettle Creek Inn**. P.O. Box 2001, 216 Joseph Street, **Port Stanley**, Ont. N5L 1C4. Tel: (519) 782-3388; Fax: (519) 782-4747. $100; $150–$174 (suites).

▶ **Little Inn of Bayfield**. Main Street, **Bayfield**, Ont. N0M 1G0. Tel: (519) 565-2611; Fax: (519) 565-5474. From $110.

▶ **Lock 7 Motel**. 24 Chapel Street South, **Thorold**, Ont. L2V 2C6. Tel: (905) 227-6177. $75.

▶ **Michael's Inn**. 5599 River Road, **Niagara Falls**, Ont. L2E 3H3. Tel: (416) 354-2727; Fax: (416) 374-7706. $155–188; $308 (theme rooms).

▶ **Moffat Inn**. 60 Picton Street, **Niagara-on-the-Lake**, Ont. L0S 1J0. Tel: (905) 468-4116; Fax: (905) 468-4747. $84–$117.

▶ **Oakwood Inn Resort**. P.O. Box 400, **Grand Bend**, Ont. N0M 1T0. Tel: (519) 238-2324; Fax: (519) 238-2377. $95–$252.

▶ **Oban Inn**. 160 Front Street, **Niagara-on-the-Lake**, Ont. L0S 1J0. Tel: (905) 468-2165; Fax: (905) 468-4165. $140–$173.

▶ **Old Stone Inn.** 425 Robinson Street, **Niagara Falls**, Ont. L2G 7L6. Tel: (905) 357-1234; Fax: (905) 357-9299. $95–$101.

▶ **Pelee Island Hotel.** P.O. Box F-8 West Dock, **Pelee Island**, Ont. N0R 1M0. Tel: (519) 724-2912. $61.

▶ **Pillar & Post Inn.** 48 John Street, **Niagara-on-the-Lake**, Ont. L0S 1J0. Tel: (905) 468-2123; Fax: (905) 468-3551. $154–$171.

▶ **Prince of Wales.** 6 Picton Street, **Niagara-on-the-Lake**, Ont. L0S 1J0. Tel: (905) 468-3246; Fax: (905) 468-5521. $112–$250.

▶ **Queen's Inn at Stratford.** 161 Ontario Street, **Stratford**, Ont. N5A 3H3. Tel: (519) 271-1400; Fax: (519) 271-7373. $95.

▶ **Royal Connaught Hotel.** 112 King Street East, **Hamilton**, Ont. L8N 1A8. Tel: (905) 546-8111; Fax: (905) 546-8144; in the U.S. and Canada, Tel: (800) 263-8558. $66–$93.

▶ **Sheraton Armouries.** 325 Dundas Street, **London**, Ont. N6B 1T9. Tel: (519) 679-6111; Fax: (519) 679-3957; in the U.S. and Canada, Tel: (800) 325-3535. $121–$146.

▶ **Sheraton Hamilton.** 116 King Street West, **Hamilton**, Ont. L8P 4V3. Tel: (905) 529-5515; Fax: (905) 529-8266; in the U.S. and Canada, Tel: (800) 325-3535. $164–$204.

▶ **Skyline Brock Hotel.** 5685 Falls Avenue, **Niagara Falls**, Ont. L2E 6W7. Tel: (905) 374-4444; Fax: (905) 357-4804; in the U.S. and Canada, Tel: (800) 263-7135. $116–$223.

▶ **Skyline Foxhead Hotel.** 5705 Falls Avenue, **Niagara Falls**, Ont. L2E 6W7. Tel: (905) 374-4444; Fax: (905) 357-4804; in the U.S. and Canada, Tel: (800) 263-7135. $147–$223.

▶ **Skyline Village Inn.** 4800 Bender Hill, **Niagara Falls**, Ont. L2G 3K1. Tel: (905) 374-4444; Fax: (905) 374-4804; in the U.S. and Canada, Tel: (800) 263-7135. $78.

▶ **South Landing Inn.** P.O. Box 269, 21 Front Street, **Queenston**, Ont. L0S 1L0 Tel: (905) 262-4634. $90.

▶ **Valhalla Inn.** 105 King Street East, **Kitchener**, Ont. N2G 2K8. Tel: (519) 744-4141; Fax: (519) 578-6889; in the U.S. and Canada, Tel: (800) 268-2500. $117–$129.

▶ **Walper Terrace Hotel.** 1 King Street West, **Kitchener**, Ont. N2G 1A1. Tel: (519) 745-4321; Fax: (519) 745-3625. $100–$111.

▶ **Waterlot Inn.** 17 Huron Street, **New Hamburg**, Ont. N0B 2G0. Tel: (519) 662-2020; Fax: (519) 662-2114. $65–$85 (includes breakfast).

▶ **Westover Inn.** P.O. Box 280, 300 Thomas Street, **St. Mary's**, Ont. N4X 1B1. Tel: (519) 284-2977; Fax: (519) 284-4043. $105–$218 (includes breakfast).

▶ **Westview Motel.** Pelee Island, Ont. N0R 1M0. Tel: (519) 724-2072. $65.

▶ **Woods Villa.** 62 John Street North, **Stratford**, Ont. N5A 6K7. Tel: (519) 271-4576. $75–$80 (includes breakfast).

Muskoka and Ontario's Cottage Country

▶ **Arowhon Pines. Algonquin Park**, Ont. P0A 1B0. Tel: (705) 633-5661 in summer; (416) 483-4393 in winter; Fax: (705) 633-5795 in summer; (416) 483-4429 in winter. $185 per person (includes breakfast, lunch, dinner, and gratuities).

▶ **Best Western Hidden Valley Resort Hotel.** R.R. 4, **Huntsville**, Ont. P0A 1K0. Tel: (705) 789-2301; Fax: (705) 789-6586; in the U.S., Tel: (800) 528-1234; in Canada, (800) 465-4171. $100–$112.

▶ **Blue Mountain Resort.** R.R. 3, **Collingwood**, Ont. L9Y 3Z2. Tel: (416) 869-3799 or (705) 445-0231; Fax: (705) 445-5619. $122; condominiums $223–$301.

▶ **Cranberry Village Resort.** P.O. Box 4100, **Collingwood**, Ont. L9Y 4T9. Tel: (705) 445-6600; Fax: (705) 445-6600; in Canada, Tel: (800) 465-9077. $95–$118.

▶ **Deerhurst Resort.** R.R. 4, **Huntsville**, Ont. P0A 1K0. Tel: (705) 789-6411; Fax: (705) 789-2431; in the U.S., Tel: (800) 828-7447; in Canada, (800) 461-4393. $110; sports villa $167–$189; two-bedroom suite $380.

▶ **Domain of Killien Resort.** P.O. Box 810, **Haliburton**, Ont. K0M 1S0. Tel: (705) 457-1100; Fax: (705) 457-3853. $166–$229 per person (includes breakfast and dinner).

▶ **Elmhirst's Resort.** R.R. 1, **Keene**, Ont. K0L 2G0. Tel: (705) 295-4591; Fax: (705) 295-4596; in the U.S. and Ontario, Tel: (800) 461-1940. $1,197 for two people per week; each additional person $119.

▶ **Grandview Inn.** R.R. 4, **Huntsville**, Ont. P0A 1K0. Tel: (705) 789-4417 or (416) 368-2423; Fax: (705) 789-6882; in Ontario, Tel: (800) 461-4454. $157; suites $258 (includes breakfast).

▶ **Gryffin Lodge.** P.O. Box 2308, **Huntsville**, Ont. P0A 1K0. Tel: (705) 789-7491 or, in Ontario, (800) 565-7491; Fax: (705) 789-9746. $88–$100 per person (includes breakfast and dinner).

▶ **Horseshoe Resort.** P.O. Box 10, Horseshoe Valley, R.R. 1, **Barrie**, Ont. L4M 4Y8. Tel: (705) 835-2790 or (416) 283-2988; Fax: (705) 835-6352; in Ontario, Tel: (800) 461-5627. $123–$185 per person (includes breakfast and dinner).

▶ **Inn at Manitou. McKellar**, Ont. P0G 1C0. Tel: (705) 389-2171 in summer, (416) 967-3466 in winter; Fax: (705) 389-3818 in summer, (416) 967-6434 in winter. $217–$355 per person (includes breakfast, lunch, and dinner).

▶ **Killarney Lodge. Algonquin Park**, Ont. P0A 1K0. Tel:

(705) 633-5551; in winter, (416) 482-5254; Fax: (705) 633-5667 (summer only). $145–$200 per person (includes breakfast, lunch, and dinner).

▶ **Killarney Mountain Lodge. Killarney**, Ont. P0M 2A0. Tel: (705) 287-2242; Fax: (705) 287-2691; in the U.S. and Ontario, (800) 461-1117. $95–$123 (includes breakfast, lunch, and dinner).

▶ **Muskoka Sands Resort.** R.R. 1, **Gravenhurst**, Ont. P1P 1R1. Tel: (705) 687-2233; Fax: (705) 687-7474; in Ontario, Tel: (800) 461-0236. $140–$190; one-bedroom suite $235; two-bedroom cottage $318.

▶ **North Ridge Inn.** P.O. Box 87, **Sundridge**, Ont. P0A 1Z0. Tel: (705) 384-5373; Fax: (705) 384-7224; in Ontario, Tel: (800) 461-5551. $140 (includes breakfast and dinner).

▶ **PineStone Resort and Conference Centre.** P.O. Box 809, R.R. 2, **Haliburton**, Ont. K0M 1S0. Tel: (705) 457-1800; Fax: (705) 457-1783; in the U.S. and Canada, Tel: (800) 461-0357. $133; deluxe two-bedroom villa $300.

▶ **Pretty River Valley Farm.** R.R. 1, **Nottawa**, Ont. L0M 1P0. Tel: (705) 445-7598. $72–$95 (includes breakfast).

▶ **Red Umbrella Inn.** R.R. 2, **Minden**, K0M 2K0. Tel: (705) 489-2462; Fax: (705) 489-4604; in Ontario, Tel: (800) 461-0316. $73–$95 per person (includes breakfast and dinner).

▶ **Sherwood Inn.** P.O. Box 400, **Port Carling**, Ont. P0B 1J0. Tel: (705) 765-3131; Fax: (705) 765-6668; in Ontario, Tel: (800) 461-4233. $155–$208 per person (includes breakfast and dinner).

▶ **Sir Sam's Inn.** Eagle Lake Post Office, **Eagle Lake**, Ont. K0M 1M0. Tel: (705) 754-2188; Fax: (705) 754-4262; in Ontario, Tel: (800) 361-2188. $128–$165 per person (includes breakfast and dinner).

▶ **Viamede Resort.** P.O. Box 413, **Peterborough**, Ont. K9J 6Z3. Tel: (705) 654-3344; Fax: (705) 654-4749; in Ontario, Tel: (800) 461-1946. $90–$160 per person (includes breakfast and dinner).

▶ **Waltonian Inn.** R.R.1, Waltonian Drive, **Callander**, Ont. P0H 1H0. Tel: (705) 752-2060; Fax: (705) 752-4260. $50.

▶ **Westwind Inn.** P.O. Box 91, **Buckhorn**, Ont. K0L 1J0. Tel: (705) 657-8095; Fax: (705) 657-8096; in Canada, Tel: (800) 387-8100. $90–$100 (includes breakfast and dinner).

▶ **Wigamog Inn.** R.R. 2, **Haliburton**, Ont. K0M 1S0. Tel: (705) 457-2000; Fax: (705) 457-1962; in Ontario, Tel: (800) 661-2010. $115 per person (includes breakfast and dinner).

▶ **Windermere House. Windermere**, Ont. P0B 1P0. Tel: (705) 769-3611; Fax: (705) 769-2168; in Ontario, Tel: (800) 461-4283. $73–$180 per person (includes breakfast and dinner); cottage $582.

Eastern Ontario

▶ **Blinkbonnie Motor Inn.** 50 Main Street, **Gananoque**, Ont. K7G 2L7. Tel: (613) 382-7272; Fax: (613) 382-4096. $73–$112.

▶ **Gananoque Inn.** 550 Stone Street South, **Gananoque**, Ont. K7G 2A8. Tel: (613) 382-2165; Fax: (613) 382-7912. $78–$112.

▶ **Greenwood Inn.** 162 Peter Street, **Port Hope**, Ont. L1A 3V9. Tel: (905) 885-0000; Fax: (905) 885-5052. $58.

▶ **Holiday Inn Kingston.** 1 Princess Street, **Kingston**, Ont. K7L 1A1. Tel: (613) 549-8400; Fax: (613) 549-3508; in the U.S. and Canada, Tel: (800) HOLIDAY. $150.

▶ **Holiday Inn Peterborough.** 150 George Street, **Peterborough**, Ont. K9J 3G5. Tel: (705) 743-1144; Fax: (705) 740-6557 or 6559; in the U.S. and Canada, Tel: (800) HOLIDAY. $105.

▶ **Howard Johnson Kingston Hotel.** 237 Ontario Street, **Kingston**, Ont. K7L 2Z4. Tel: (613) 549-6300; Fax: (613) 549-1508; in the U.S. and Canada, Tel: (800) 654-2000. $125.

▶ **Isaiah Tubbs Resort.** R.R. 1, West Lake Road, **Picton**, Ont. K0K 2T0. Tel: (613) 393-2090; Fax: (613) 393-1291; in the U.S. and Canada, Tel: (800) 267-0525. $140.

▶ **Old Bridge Inn Hotel.** Young's Point, Ont. K0L 3G0. Tel: (705) 652-8507. $75.

▶ **Prince George Hotel.** 200 Ontario Street, **Kingston**, Ont. K7L 2Y9. Tel. and Fax: (613) 549-5440. $73–$117; suites $145.

▶ **Sandbanks Beach Resort.** R.R. 1, **Picton**, Ont. K0K 2T0. Tel: (613) 393-3022; Fax: (613) 393-1167. $80–$145; $560–$840 per week.

▶ **Victoria Rose Inn.** 279 King Street West, **Gananoque**, Ont. K7G 2G7. Tel: (613) 382-3368. $84–$140 (includes Continental breakfast).

Northern Ontario

▶ **Airlane Hotel.** 698 West Arthur Street, **Thunder Bay**, Ont. P7E 5R8. Tel: (807) 577-1181; Fax: (807) 475-4852; in Ontario, Manitoba, and Saskatchewan, Tel: (800) 465-5003. $95.

▶ **Algoma's Water Tower Inn.** 360 Great Northern Road, **Sault Ste. Marie**, Ont. P6A 5N3. Tel: (705) 949-8111; Fax: (705) 949-1912; in Canada, Tel: (800) 461-0800. $96.

▶ **Best Western Lakeside Inn Hotel and Conference Centre.** 470 First Avenue South, **Kenora**, Ont. P9N 1W5. Tel: (807) 468-5521; Fax: (807) 468-4734; in the U.S. and Canada, Tel: (800) 465-1120. $100–$110.

▶ **Best Western Norwester Resort Hotel.** 2080 Highway 61, **Thunder Bay**, Ont. P7C 4Z2. Tel: (807) 473-9123; Fax: (807) 473-9600; in the U.S. and Canada, Tel: (800) 528-1234. $85.

▶ **Hannah Bay Goose Camp.** 555 Oak Street East, **North Bay**, Ont. P1B 8L3. Tel: (705) 472-4500; Fax: (705) 495-4745. $1,496 per person (five days, all-inclusive).

▶ **Landmark Inn.** 1010 Dawson Road, **Thunder Bay**, Ont. P7B 5J4. Tel: (807) 767-1681; Fax: (807) 767-1439; in Canada, Tel: (800) 465-3950. $80.

▶ **Manitowaning Lodge and Tennis Resort.** P.O. Box 160, **Manitowaning**, Ont. P0P 1N0. Tel: (705) 859-3136; Fax: (705) 859-3270. $235–$325 (includes breakfast and dinner).

▶ **Minaki Lodge Four Seasons Northland Resort. Minaki**, Ont. P0X 1J0. Tel: (807) 224-4000; Fax: (807) 224-4211; in the U.S., Tel: (800) 332-3442; in Canada, (800) 268-6282. $110 (cabin)–$415 (two-bedroom bi-level suite). Three meals, $50 per person.

▶ **Moosonee Lodge.** 65 Enterprise Road, **Rexdale**, Ont. M9W 1C4. Tel: (705) 336-2351 or (416) 244-1495; Fax: (416) 241-2022. $86.

▶ **Rossport Inn.** Bowman Street, **Rossport**, Ont. P0T 2R0. Tel: (807) 824-3213. $65–$82.

▶ **Sheraton Caswell Inn.** 1696 Regent Street South, **Sudbury**, Ont. P3E 3Z8. Tel: (705) 522-3000; Fax: (705) 522-8067; in the U.S. and Canada, Tel: (800) 325-3535. $88.

▶ **Silver Birches Resort.** R.R. 1, **Little Current**, Ont. P0P 1K0. Tel: (705) 368-2669. $65–$76.

▶ **Valhalla Inn.** 1 Valhalla Inn Road, **Thunder Bay**, Ont. P7E 6J1. Tel: (807) 577-1121; Fax: (807) 475-4723; in the U.S. and Canada, Tel: (800) 268-2500. $100.

▶ **Victoria Inn.** 555 Arthur Street West, **Thunder Bay**, Ont. P7E 5R5. Tel: (807) 577-8481; Fax: (807) 475-8961; in Canada, Tel: (800) 387-3331. $100.

▶ **Wawa Motor Inn.** 100 Mission Road, **Wawa**, Ont. P0S 1K0. Tel: (705) 856-2278; Fax: (705) 856-2171. $58; eight-person chalet $168.

Fishing Lodges & Camps

There are hundreds of facilities not included here. For a complete listing, write for a free copy of the Northern Ontario book (also fishing, hunting, and boating) from **Northern Ontario Tourist Outfitters Association** (NOTO), P.O. Box 1140, North Bay, Ont. P1B 8K4; Tel: (705) 472-5552.

There are also many cozy country inns scattered throughout the Ontario countryside for those who prefer quiet charm to resort-style luxury. For additional information, contact **Ontario Travel**, Tel: (416) 314-0987, or (800) 668-2746 in the U.S. and elsewhere in Canada, and ask for a copy of their *Ontario Country Inns Guide*.

MANITOBA

By Lee Schacter

Lee Schacter was born in Manitoba and has lived there—currently in Winnipeg—all her life. She has written articles and reviews for the Winnipeg Free Press, *as well as scripts and articles for various magazines.*

Canada's "keystone province" is viewed by the uninitiated as a stretch of flat prairie where there is nothing to do and nowhere to do it. They're totally wrong on both counts.

While much of southern Manitoba *is* black-earth prairie, broken here and there by clumps of trees, visitors who take the time to explore will also find parkland, forests, hills, and lakes so clear you can see to the bottom. Travel west from Winnipeg on the Trans-Canada Highway and the country gradually changes, becoming hilly, treed parkland by the time you get to Riding Mountain National Park near the Manitoba–Saskatchewan border. North of the park, in Duck Mountain Provincial Park, Baldy Mountain tops out at 2,727 feet, the province's highest point.

Whiteshell Provincial Park, in Manitoba's southeastern corner, is known for its clear lakes, rocky outcroppings, and huge boulders—remnants of the last ice age—strewn about as if by a giant hand. The Whiteshell is civilized and picturesque, nature's gift to flatlanders.

Winnipeg, Manitoba's capital, is a lively, cosmopolitan city, and boasts a cultural scene that is the envy of cities twice its size. The Winnipeg Symphony, the world-renowned Royal Winnipeg Ballet, the Manitoba Theatre Centre, and folk-dance ensembles like the Rusalka Dancers have infused the life of the city with an elan that energizes residents and visitors alike. Sixty miles to the north, wild and turbulent Lake Winnipeg is fringed in places by swatches of golden sand, a favorite warm-weather playground for Manitobans.

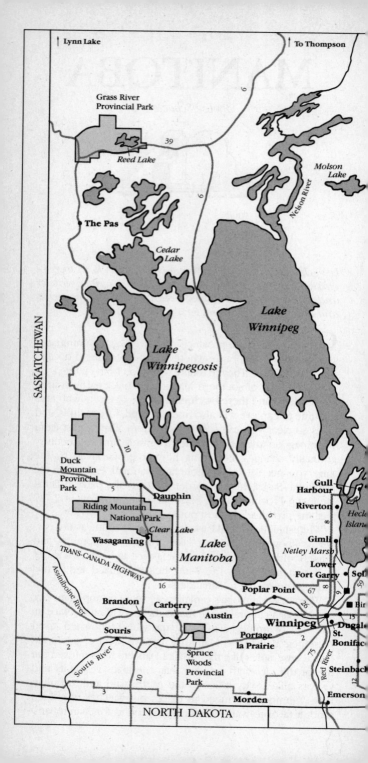

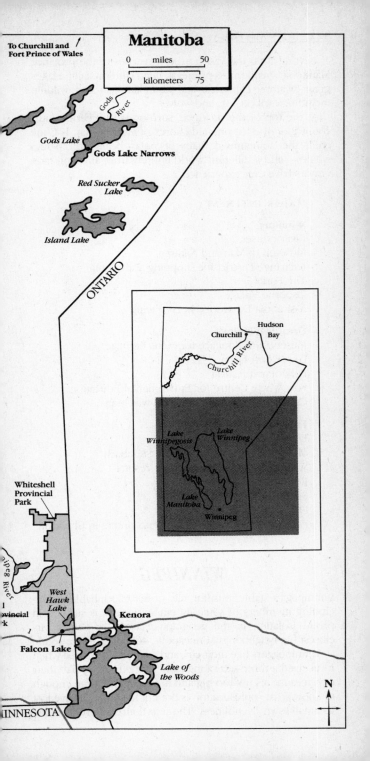

Beyond it, in the vast northern reaches of the province, Manitoba is wilderness primeval, filled with crystalline lakes, great swampy expanses, and abundant fish and wildlife, including caribou, elk, and wolves.

At the top of the province, surrounded by eerie tundra country on the ice-rimmed shores of Hudson Bay, is Churchill, the sometime-domain of polar bears and beluga whales—and a different world entirely from anything most visitors have ever experienced.

MAJOR INTEREST

Winnipeg
River cruises
Museum of Man and Nature
Exchange District for shopping and dining
The Forks
Osborne Village
Assiniboia Downs for horse racing

Greater Winnipeg
Musée Saint-Boniface for Métis heritage
Lower Fort Garry
Folklorama festival
Fort Whyte Centre for Enviromental Education
Oak Hammock Marsh for bird-watching

Elsewhere in Manitoba
Dauphin's Ukrainian Festival
Mennonite Heritage Village at Steinbach
Whiteshell and Gimli summer resorts
Rock hounding at Souris
Spirit Sands desert
Fishing and canoeing
Polar bear and beluga whale encounters in Churchill

WINNIPEG

Winnipeg, a stable, bustling city of 600,000 inhabitants, including members of some 40 ethnic groups, is situated in proud isolation in the geographic center of Canada. Its closest big neighbor is Minneapolis, 465 miles to the south.

Winnipeggers like their city, and were not surprised when it received a three-star rating from Michelin. They like their city because it's not too big and not too small, large enough to know what sophistication is but not too large to have lost its small-town friendliness. The arts flourish here, and the streets are quite safe in most areas. Compared to Toronto or Montreal, the pace of life is leisurely.

Winnipeggers don't sit at home, even on the coldest winter days. In fact, they're outside more often in winter than in summer. They also complain more about the heat than the cold—and there are no mosquitoes when it's cold.

Winnipeg's Rivers and Parks

The city is crisscrossed by rivers, the two greatest being the Red and the Assiniboine. The Assiniboine flows west to east, the Red south to north, and the two meet at The Forks, near Provencher and Water Street. Visitors can cruise these rivers on paddlewheel steamers. The *Paddlewheel Queen* and *Paddlewheel Princess* cruise the Red and the Assiniboine, passing through the city center. From May to mid-October, these are relaxing outings for tired sightseers, giving them a chance to see the city from a different perspective. Both sail from the foot of the Provencher Bridge at Water Street; for information and departure times, Tel: (204) 942-4500.

Winnipeg's city fathers saw to it that trees were planted everywhere, including some 163,000 elm trees. The elms form great leafy canopies over the city's boulevards, scrubbing the air of pollution and reducing temperatures in the heat of summer. The city is also dotted with parks, most of them a block or two of greenery. The biggest, at the end of Wellington Crescent west of the downtown core, is **Assiniboine Park**, 375 acres of rolling wooded lawns, picnic sites, a conservatory (a favorite place for weddings), and a zoo. The park even has cricket grounds, where every weekend polite white-clad cricketers indulge their passion for the game. The **Leo Mol sculpture garden** here gives visitors an opportunity to view the work of this internationally known artist amid charming natural surroundings. Assiniboine Park is very busy on weekends, but never rowdy or noisy; during the summer it's also the site of free ballet and symphony performances. To find the concert site, enter the park at the Tuxedo entrance and follow the crowds. Bring along a sweater or jacket if you don't want to sit on the grass—there are no chairs.

Assiniboine Forest, a 700-acre nature preserve across from the park, is home to rare wildflowers, a resident deer herd, and lots of waterfowl. The parking-lot entrance to the forest is between Grant Avenue and Chalfont Street. Guided tours of the preserve's Living Prairie Museum, open daily during the summer, are available upon request; Tel: (204) 832-0167.

At the north end of town is **Kildonan Park**, neither as manicured nor as staid as Assiniboine Park. In addition to some of Manitoba's oldest and largest trees, it has a creek and lovely flower gardens. It's also the home of **Rainbow Stage**, where musicals are presented in summer. To get there, follow Main Street north to the large sign at the park entrance (the park is at 2021 Main). Note, however, that parking is sometimes a problem, as almost everyone arrives by car.

History buffs on the way to or from Kildonan Park will want to take a look at **Ross House**, the first post office west of the Great Lakes, built in 1854 by William Ross. Located at 140 Meade Street, three blocks east of Main Street in Joe Zuken Heritage Park, the structure is one of the oldest examples of log-frame construction on the prairies.

Exploring Winnipeg

Winnipeg is a flat city, like the vast prairie surrounding it. The city's principal downtown thoroughfare, Portage Avenue, is bounded by Memorial Boulevard to the west and Main Street to the east. The **Museum of Man and Nature**, one of the finest interpretive museums in the country, stands at 555 Main Street; next door are **Centennial Centre** (Tel: 204/956-1360), the focus of Winnipeg's cultural life, and the **Planetarium**. The museum's seven galleries explore man's relationship to the environment through lifelike dioramas and reconstructions of things like an Indian encampment, a sod hut, and a street of shops from turn-of-the-century Winnipeg. But the pièce de résistance is a replica of the *Nonsuch,* the ketch that Grosseillers sailed into Hudson Bay in 1668, later returning to England with a cargo of furs that ultimately resulted in the founding of the Hudson's Bay Company. Visitors can board the ship and marvel at the temerity of the men who crossed the ocean in this tiny vessel, as well as speculate about their height—the bunks are less than five feet long. The hands-on science gallery, Touch the Universe, was designed for children but is equally fascinating for adults. Tickets can be purchased at the Concert Hall, and the price of admission entitles you to roam the entire complex. The museum is open daily from May through September; closed Sundays and holidays the rest of the year.

The Exchange District

The Exchange District, right across the street from the museum, was once the heart of Winnipeg's wholesale and manufacturing district. Today it's full of old buildings that have been restored and made over into fine stores and restaurants, with a park in the center. The name of the district derives from the Winnipeg Grain Exchange, which developed on the site from about 1881 to 1918. By the 1920s the Grain Exchange was the most important grain market in the world. The heirs of the men who made the big money are now among the city's elite, living in huge homes in the city's poshest residential area, Tuxedo. Walking tours of the Exchange District, offered free by the city's Parks and Recreation Department (July only), start at the Museum of Man and Nature and last about an hour. For further information, Tel: (204) 986-3131.

The Forks

The most recent urban renewal project in Winnipeg is The Forks, an ongoing development in the historic area at the juncture of the Red and Assiniboine rivers. First Indians, then European traders and missionaries who travelled here by foot, canoe, York boats, or whatever conveyance was available—people have been gathering for hundreds of years in this natural meeting place. The 19th century brought immigrants from Europe, with the community that grew up around The Forks eventually becoming the city of Winnipeg.

The Forks area is just east of the CN/VIA rail station on Main Street. Two large antique horse barns have been cleaned up, renovated, refurbished, and joined together to create a huge airy market filled with stalls selling vegetables, fruits, and handicrafts. There are three full-service restaurants, dozens of food kiosks (the place is filled every noon with office workers from the area), a six-story glass-enclosed tower for displays and exhibits, a skating rink, and an amphitheater. A lovely riverbank walkway under the jurisdiction of the Canadian Parks Services is constantly being lengthened, and a Parks Services program gives amateur archaeologists an opportunity to participate in the ongoing excavations (artifacts unearthed here show that the area has been the scene of human activity for at least 6,000 years). A park attendant is on duty at all times to answer visitors' questions.

The Forks is one of the loveliest public spaces in the city and a haven from the bustling crowds and traffic elsewhere in Winnipeg. Shuttle buses marked "The Forks" take visitors to the area. If you're driving, head down Main Street to Water Street, which funnels cars into the area. Parking is free on Sundays, holidays, and after 6:00 P.M. on weekdays.

Winnipeg Art Gallery

The Winnipeg Art Gallery, a spectacular prow-shaped building at 300 Memorial Boulevard, across from the Bay department store, contains the largest—and one of the best—collections of Inuit art in the world. Although exhibits are rotated on a regular basis, you can usually count on some part of the Inuit collection being on display. For information on gallery hours and exhibits, Tel: (204) 786-6641.

Legislative Building

Located at Broadway and Osborne south of the WAG, the Legislative Building is one of Winnipeg's glories. The magnificent Neoclassical structure was designed by British architect Frank Worthington Simon, and is constructed of Manitoba tyndall. Completed in 1919 and officially opened in 1920, the building is topped, 240 feet up, by the city's most familiar landmark, the 13½-foot, five-ton **Golden Boy**, who holds a torch in one hand and a sheaf of wheat in the other. Sculpted in France by Charles Gardet just prior to World War I, the statue was on its way to Canada when the war began. Almost immediately, the cargo ship it was stowed on was requisitioned as a troop carrier. As a result, the Golden Boy was forced to cross the Atlantic several times, not arriving at his final home until after the war.

Inside, the main lobby is graced by a grand staircase flanked by two life-size bronze bison—a favorite photo-op spot for visiting dignitaries. The building's long marble corridors are lined with statues and paintings, and lead to a variety of posh government offices as well as the legislative assembly chamber. Legislative sessions are open to the public, and tours of the building can be arranged. For information, Tel: (204) 945-5813.

Dalnavert

Winnipeg once boasted a prodigious number of wonderfully rococo Victorian homes. Today most have either been demolished or converted into rooming houses. One house rescued from exactly that fate is Dalnavert, built in 1895 for Sir Hugh John Macdonald, the only son of Canada's first prime minister, and himself premier of the province at the turn of the century. Restored to its gingerbread glory in the mid-1970s and designated a national historic site in 1991, Dalnavert re-creates the look of the era with elaborate wood paneling, overstuffed furniture, ornate drapes, and an abundance of Victorian gadgetry. The house, located at 61 Carlton Street, three blocks east of the Legislative Building, is open

Tuesday through Thursday and weekends from March 1 to December 31; in January and December it's open weekends only. For hours and further information, Tel: (204) 943-2835.

Osborne Village

One of the trendiest neighborhoods in the city is Osborne Village, five blocks of clever little shops, restaurants (some with outdoor dining), and art galleries centered around the intersection of River and Osborne streets, a ten-minute walk from the downtown core on the south side of the Assiniboine River. It took a great deal of courage for a few adventurous young entrepreneurs to open shops in this formerly tacky, run-down section of the city. But the idea caught on, much to the surprise of Winnipeggers, who had been programmed for generations to shop downtown. Soon more shops opened: a kitchen shop, dress shops, a health-food store, and several art galleries. Now it's a great area for browsing and noshing, not to mention the stomping ground of the city's young.

The **Tea Cozy**, 303-99 Osborne, is the place for afternoon tea and scones. Tel: (204) 475-1027. For heartier fare try the Mediterranean-style **Tap and Grill**, 137 Osborne Street (at the end of the block), where the waitresses actually smile, the portions are huge, and the prices are reasonable. Tel: (204) 284-7455.

Corydon Avenue

Farther south, Corydon Avenue, in staid River Heights, is the setting for more shops, most run by eager young business-people. Up until the early 1950s River Heights was the almost exclusive domain of the city's well-to-do, but the barriers started to come down when people who didn't know they weren't supposed to be there moved in, along with people from the country and those seeking well-kept homes in a quiet setting. Today River Heights is a multi-ethnic district, with excellent schools, neighbors who mingle, a colorful Italian area, and the highest voter turnout in the city. In summer, hanging baskets on lampposts and outdoor cafés enliven the avenue's east end, and there's a great street fair here in August.

A number of elegant shops have opened on Academy Road, which runs parallel to Corydon, in recent years. The merchandise is usually top drawer, and so are the prices. Among the best stores here are: the **Laughing Giraffe**, number 402, with a good selection of educational toys for well-to-do kids; the **Paper Gallery**, number 404, where you'll find every imaginable paper product; **A Touch of Class**, number 486, for gifts with style; and **Sofia's**, number 544, for expensive designer fashions.

Assiniboia Downs

From May to October, one of Winnipeg's most popular attractions is racing at Assiniboia Downs. The track and grandstand facilities offer some of the best horse racing in the West, pari-mutuel betting, and a terraced dining room. The track is located at 3975 Portage Avenue, west of the downtown core and Assiniboine Park; Tel: (204) 885-3330 for post times. Public transportation is available via any Portage Avenue bus: Take the bus to the Courts of St. James and transfer to the racetrack shuttle. For specific times and fares, consult the Transit Guide at the back of the Winnipeg phone book or call (204) 986-5700.

For people who have an irresistible urge to gamble, the prim Manitoba government, mirabile dictu, has introduced a European-style gambling casino on the seventh floor of the Hotel Fort Garry, 222 Broadway, called the **Crystal Casino**. There's a strict dress code (jackets and ties required for men, dress slacks, skirts, or dresses for women) and room for approximately 415 patrons at the various slot machines and tables. The casino is open noon to 2:00 A.M., Monday through Saturday, and 2:00 P.M. to 2:00 A.M. on Sundays. For further information, Tel: (204) 957-2600.

WINNIPEG THEATER

Winnipeg has one large regional theater and a number of smaller ones that tend to rise and fall according to government largesse. The **Manitoba Theatre Centre** (known across the country as the MTC), 174 Market Avenue in the Exchange District, is the city's most professional theater. It was started in 1958 by two stagestruck young men, Tom Hendry and John Hirsch. The brilliant Hirsch, who as a young refugee after World War II came to Canada and lived with a Winnipeg family, acted as director and soon established the MTC as one of the best regional theaters in Canada. Though he eventually left for more lucrative climes, both in the United States and eastern Canada, the MTC is still going strong. In 1970 the company, which had been operating out of rented premises, built its own theater. While the building isn't likely to win any design awards, it does have comfortable seats and excellent acoustics.

During the summer there are productions at **Rainbow Stage** (Tel: 204/942-2091), north of the downtown core in

Kildonan Park. This is an outdoor theater with a roof that can be closed in the event of rain. The offerings are musicals, always well done, and it's a wonderful way to spend a balmy summer evening.

The 232-seat **Gas Station Theatre** in Osborne Village offers productions by local as well as touring groups, and is the perfect size for shows that wouldn't fill larger halls. The program includes modern dance, excellent children's shows, some experimental works, and standard drama. Tickets are not difficult to obtain, but it's a good idea to check with the box office beforehand; Tel: (204) 284-2757.

The **Prairie Theatre Exchange**, located in Portage Place, a huge indoor mall on Portage Avenue, is big on plays that enlighten—that is, if you have the medium, send a message—but it does provide a forum for local playwrights; Tel: (204) 942-5483.

The best of the small theaters, as well as the most professional, is **The Warehouse**, 140 Rupert Avenue, right behind Centennial Centre. The Warehouse features alternative theater in a small house that seats 300 people on three sides of a floor-level stage, bringing the audience right into the play; Tel: (204) 942-6537.

In July there's the **Fringe Festival**, a binge of affordable theater, with touring companies from all over the globe playing in various parts of the city. For information, call the Warehouse box office.

STAYING IN WINNIPEG

(Taxes are included in all rates. The telephone area code for Winnipeg is 204.)

Winnipeg has many hotels and motels, but most of its better accommodations are located in the downtown area. The few neighborhood hotels tend to be mere excuses to run a pub, and often are noisy.

Close to the airport on the west side of town is the ▶ **Best Western International Inn**, a bustling place with a warm atmosphere and all the usual amenities, including indoor and outdoor pools, shuttle service to the airport, and a professional dinner show in its Hollow Mug restaurant. The one drawback is its distance from downtown, about a 20-minute drive.

106-1808 Wellington Avenue, R3H 0G3. Tel: 786-4801; Fax: 786-1329; in the U.S. and Canada, Tel: (800) 528-1234. $75.

Giving the International a run for its money is the ▶ **Radisson Suites Hotel**, also close to the airport. As its name suggests, this is an all-suite hotel, great for guests who want to entertain in something other than a bedroom. Recreational facilities, dining room, coffee shop, and shuttle service to the airport are also available.

1800 Wellington Avenue, R3H 1B3. Tel: 783-1700; Fax: 786-6588; in the U.S. and Canada, Tel: (800) 333-3333. $154–$170.

The ▶ Relax Inn downtown is your basic budget inn—clean and adequate.

360 Colony Street, R3B 2P3. Tel: 786-7011; Fax: 772-1443; in the U.S. and Canada, Tel: (800) 578-7878. $83.

For sheer posh, Winnipeg has the ▶ Westin and ▶ Sheraton, both downtown, both expensive, and both catering to guests who want to be pampered. In addition, the Westin offers two above-average restaurants: the moderately priced Chimes (breakfast and lunch only) and the expensive Velvet Glove.

Westin: 2 Lombard Place, R3B 0Y3. Tel: 957-1350; Fax: 956-1791; in the U.S. and Canada, Tel: (800) 228-3000. $155–$178.

Sheraton: 161 Donald Street, R3C 1M3. Tel: 942-5300; Fax: 943-7975; in the U.S. and Canada, Tel: (800) 325-3535. $85–$177.

The ▶ Delta Winnipeg, right downtown, has been totally revamped, and is now a pleasant, if unremarkable, place to stay, with all the usual amenities. The Delta is also connected by covered walkway to Portage Place and Eaton's department store.

288 Portage Avenue, R3C 0B8. Tel: 956-0410; Fax: 947-1129; in the U.S., Tel: (800) 877-1133; in Canada, (800) 268-1133. $176–$211.

The ▶ Hotel Fort Garry, the grande dame of Winnipeg hostelries, is in a class by itself. This regal hotel was built by the Canadian National Railway in the early part of the century and was for decades the epitome of elegance. When the railway could no longer carry the hotel, it fell on hard times, with the city and historical trust groups desperately trying to save it. It has since been named a heritage building, and by great good fortune bought by a gentleman who loves hotels. The Fort Garry has been repolished, refurbished, and updated without sacrificing any of its previous grandeur, so that once again it is a truly beautiful hotel.

222 Broadway, R3C 0R3. Tel: 942-8251; Fax: 956-2351; in the U.S. and Canada, Tel: (800) 665-8088. $90–$148.

With 389 rooms, the ▶ Holiday Inn Crowne Plaza, downtown next to the Convention Centre, is the city's largest and busiest hotel. As is true of this chain's hotels wherever you find them, guests know what to expect: clean rooms, efficient service, and a basically sterile atmosphere. An indoor pool, sauna, whirlpool, and restaurant round out its facilities. The ▶ **Holiday Inn South**, 1330 Pembina Highway, is a pretty place with an excellent all-day buffet and an indoor pool. It's also on Highway 75, the fastest route to the Manitoba–Minnesota border.

Holiday Inn Crowne Plaza: 350 St. Mary Avenue, R3C 3J2. Tel: 942-0551; Fax: 943-8702; in the U.S. and Canada, Tel: (800) 465-4329. $160.

Holiday Inn South: 1330 Pembina Highway, R3T 2B4. Tel: 452-4747; Fax: 284-2751; in the U.S. and Canada, Tel: (800) 465-4329. $130.

If you prefer the intimacy and warmth of a private home to the impersonality of a hotel, and don't mind sharing a bathroom, there are a number of lovely bed-and-breakfast accommodations in Winnipeg. A very nice place—for non-smokers only—is ▶ **Bannerman East**, a Georgian-style home close to the Red River and Kildonan Park. Evening tea is offered in addition to a very filling breakfast.

Bob and Arlene Jones, 99 Bannerman Avenue, R2W 0T1. Tel: 589-6449. $40.

▶ **West Gate Manor**, on a lovely treed street lined with huge old homes within walking distance of downtown, offers a number of air-conditioned bedrooms, each reflecting a different period and theme. Nonsmokers only.

John and Louise Clark, 71 West Gate Street, R3C 2C9. Tel: 772-9788; Fax: 943-8371. $45–$55.

For a complete list of bed and breakfasts in Manitoba contact **Bed-and-Breakfast Manitoba Ltd.**, 533 Sprague Street, Winnipeg, Man. R3G 2R9; Tel: (204) 783-9797.

DINING IN WINNIPEG

Winnipeg has more than 900 restaurants, ranging from the elegant and very expensive to family establishments. The latter are usually ethnic places, often small and inexpensive. (With a shortage of great scenery to look out on, visitors should know that Winnipeg restaurants tend to be closed in and dim.)

The telephone area code for Winnipeg is 204.

Winnipeggers will tell you their city has the best Chinese restaurants in Canada. (Montreal, Toronto, and Vancouver might argue the point, but a fact is a fact.) Of the 50-plus in the city, the best are **Sargent Mandarin**, 613 Sargent Street, and **Foon Hai**, 329 William Avenue. The Mandarin is owned by a Chinese scholar who emigrated from China to France, where he taught history before settling in Winnipeg. Try the hot-and-sour soup and the black bean and garlic shrimp.

Reservations are advised, as it's not a big place; Tel: 775-7819. Foon Hai, located in the middle of nothing of importance just outside the city's *schmatta* district, is a small, unobtrusive place run by one busy family. Favorites here include the mu shu, the sizzling shrimp with black bean sauce, and the ginger beef. Tel: 943-5032.

Sumhay, in Chinatown at 225 Logan, is a hole-in-the-wall mom-and-pop affair where the food is spicy, the portions huge, and the prices ridiculously low. The almond shrimp here is especially good, and a bowl of hot-and-sour soup is large enough to satisfy four. Those who know about this place have tried to keep it a secret, but the word is getting out. Tel: 957-5050.

At **India Gardens,** 764 McDermot (in the Exchange District; Tel: 783-0306), food is prepared as hot or as mild as you wish. **Taste of Sri Lanka,** 841 Ellice Avenue, is another family-run place, and serves delicious dishes from that Southeast Asian country. Try the superb fried eggplant with onions and tomatoes; the spring rolls; the breaded fried crepes stuffed with ground pork or beef; or *badum,* a Sri Lankan specialty made with your choice of shrimp, fish, beef, or pork. Closed Mondays. Tel: 775-7802.

Amici's, 326 Broadway, serves imaginative Italian food, heavy on the pastas and sauces. It is chic and expensive, and is patronized by the young and prosperous. Reservations are a good idea; closed Sundays. Tel: 943-4997. **Victor's** (Tel: 947-2751), located in the Marlborough Inn at 331 Smith Street, leans toward Continental cuisine, and is very elegant and expensive.

The Sandpiper, in The Forks market, has windows overlooking the water, spectacular food, and equally spectacular prices. Try the veal escalopes with smoked salmon and caper sauce, or the bife a Portugais. For those who believe the taste of chicken changes when different sauces surround it, the stuffed chicken Normandy should please. Along with Amici's (see above), the Sandpiper is rated one of the best restaurants in the city, although the service can be excruciatingly slow. Reservations for either lunch or dinner are a must; closed Sundays. Tel: 942-0918.

The longest established ethnic restaurants in Winnipeg are Jewish and Ukrainian. For these, however, the visitor must drive to the **North End,** which is not merely a geographic location but a national institution. This was the area where immigrants from Eastern Europe settled in the early part of the century. Intensely ambitious, they expected their children to succeed in life, and succeed they did, to an astonishing degree. Many of them, like Monty Hall, are internationally known; others have achieved outstanding positions in Canadian law, medicine, and education. Countless books, plays, and songs have been written about Winnipeg's North End, and wherever ex-Northenders wind up, they carry fond memories of that part of the city with them.

The Jews and Ukrainians have moved on, and a new wave of immigrants, mostly native people from Manitoba's reserves, now inhabit the North End. In fact, Winnipeg has the largest native population per capita of any North American city. (Los Angeles has the second largest.)

As for eateries in the North End, **Alycia's**, 559 Cathedral Avenue, is a modest, family-run Ukrainian restaurant where borscht, cabbage soup, holopchi, pirogies, and kolbassa dominate the menu. This is a very popular neighborhood place, with reasonable prices. Closed Sundays. Tel: 582-8789.

For deli food, there's a pair of great places—**Garry**, at 675 Jefferson (a second branch has opened among the underground shops of Winnipeg Square); and **Oscar's**, at 1204 Main. The two are in perpetual competition to see which can serve the best corned beef and pastrami. Fortunately, there doesn't seem to be a clear-cut winner, and businesspeople from around the city crowd them both at lunchtime.

True-blue Northenders (most of them in exile in the United States) have fond memories of a restaurant with a history dating back to the 1930s. **Kelekis**, 1100 Main Street, is owned by a Greek family that started out selling hot dogs and chips from a pushcart, then graduated to a hole-in-the-wall restaurant where the beautiful black-haired Kelekis daughters waited tables. Kelekis attracted all the locals, who insisted that its hot dogs and chips were the best in the city. Although it now occupies a slightly bigger building, Kelekis is still the first place former Northenders run to when visiting Winnipeg—not least, they insist, because it still has the best hot dogs and chips in the city. Tel: 582-1786.

Back downtown, **Rae and Jerry's**, 1405 Portage Avenue, is another Winnipeg institution. Conservative and quiet, with food that's consistently good (especially the steaks and roast beef), it's a busy, moderately expensive place with maternal waitresses who seem to have been here forever. Reservations advised; Tel: 783-6155.

The **Olive Garden**, 1544 Portage Avenue, is a franchise that serves surprisingly tasty food in generous portions. All the soup, salad, and hot garlic rolls you can eat, and at reasonable prices. No reservations, so there is often a wait, especially on Saturdays. Tel: 774-9725.

You'll find a bit of Olde England inside **Jim's Fish & Chips**, a plain café at 1656 Portage Avenue that serves the best halibut in town. There's no ambience to speak of here, just good food at reasonable prices. Jim's reputation has spread throughout the city, and he doesn't take reservations, so be prepared to wait. Tel: 774-4884.

Finally, **Between Friends**, south of the downtown area at 1480 Pembina Highway, is primarily a seafood place that serves a great cioppino (a thick fish stew), as well as roast duck in orange sauce. Expensive and elegant. Reservations recommended; Tel: 284-8402.

As for nightlife, the **Marble Club**, 65 Rorie, and **Night Moves**, a cabaret in the Windsor Park Inn, 1034 Elizabeth in St. Boniface, are extremely popular with young people. **Rumors Restaurant and Comedy Club**, 2025 Corydon, features standup comics. Again, reservations recommended; closed Sundays. Tel: 488-4520.

SHOPPING IN WINNIPEG

Favorite purchases for visitors to Winnipeg are Hudson's Bay blankets, still made, as they have been for the past 300 years, from thick pure wool; Indian and Inuit artifacts; bone china; and woollens. Go to **The Bay**, at the corner of Portage Avenue and Memorial Boulevard, for blankets and woollens, or **Birks**, an upscale jewelry store with two locations (the Portage Place Mall and the Polo Park Shopping Centre), for china. For Inuit carvings and prints, try the **Crafts Guild of Manitoba**, 183 Kennedy Street, an excellent shop run by volunteers, or the **Winnipeg Art Gallery**'s gift shop at 300 Memorial Boulevard (across from the Bay). Sheepskin coats and jackets are very popular because they're light and very warm. The best place to buy them is at **Lambskin Specialties**, 579 Selkirk Avenue in the North End (the store will even make them to order).

Winnipeg has many indoor shopping malls. The prettiest is **Polo Park** on Portage Avenue, completely renovated and now bright, airy, and lively. The best time to go is Saturday afternoon, when what appears to be half the population of Winnipeg, especially the young, gathers under its roof.

St. Boniface

To find St. Boniface, Winnipeg's French quarter and the largest French community in western Canada, follow Main Street south across the Norwood Bridge and Red River. When you cross into St. Boniface, a street becomes a *rue;* a road is a *chemin;* "hello" becomes *bonjour.* On Provencher, the main boulevard in St. Boniface, you can order croissants or frogs' legs, buy a French-Canadian novel, and try out your French. You may be answered in English, however, as only a quarter of the population of 43,000 still speaks French.

The community dates to 1738, when a small party led by the explorer Pierre Gaultier de la Vérendrye made it to the confluence of the Red and Assiniboine rivers, the first Europeans to do so. The party built Fort Rouge, now the site of **La Vérendrye Park**, before continuing west down the Assiniboine to Portage la Prairie, where they built a second encampment, known as Fort la Reine. In 1844 four members of the Sisters of Charity order (one of them Sarah Riel, sister of the Métis leader Louis Riel) made the 2,000-mile, 59-day journey from Montreal to the Red River settlement in birchbark canoes paddled by Hudson's Bay voyageurs.

In time, the nuns founded a four-bed hospital, which later became the St. Boniface Hospital, today renowned for its research and palliative care. The original convent that had housed the nuns eventually was converted into the **Musée de Saint-Boniface**. The building, the oldest in Winnipeg and the largest oak-log construction in North America, contains an extensive collection of Métis artifacts that vividly recalls the early days of the community.

In the first half of the 19th century, the colony was predominantly Métis (French and Indian). Then, in 1869, its leader, Louis Riel, led a rebellion resisting a takeover by Canada that came to an end when the territory agreed to enter the confederation. Riel fled to Saskatchewan, where he led an even bloodier rebellion before he was captured, tried, and hanged in 1885. His body was brought back from Saskatchewan and buried in the cemetery next to what is now the museum. In time Riel became a folk hero, with plays and songs written and sung about him. (His will turned up in July 1991, 106 years after his death. In it, he invoked his blessings on his children). Nearby is St. Boniface College, the French campus of the University of Manitoba.

The most exciting annual event in St. Boniface is the **Festival du Voyageur**, a fun-filled ten-day carnival held every February. The festival, Manitoba's grand winter get-together, pays homage to the legendary trappers and traders who did so much to open up the interior regions of the North American continent. In addition to lots of food and merriment, the festivities include the usual as well as not-so-usual winter-carnival activities, with the cold weather giving everything a wonderfully keen edge. For information regarding dates and a schedule of events, Tel: (204) 237-7692.

DINING IN ST. BONIFACE

St. Boniface has a number of excellent restaurants specializing in traditional French-Canadian fare. **La Vieille Gare**, 630 Des Meurons, occupies a converted, elegantly appointed railway station built in 1914, and serves such specialties as châteaubriand, *canard à l'orange,* sole meunière, or breast of capon in Champagne sauce. Tel: (204) 237-5015. **Le Lantern Rouge**, 302 Hamel Avenue, is a cozy little place whose specialties include coquilles St. Jacques and steak au poivre vert. Tel: (204) 233-4841. Located just a five-minute drive from downtown, **Le Beaujolais**, 131 Provencher Boulevard, is *haut ton,* expensive, and serves traditional as well as nouvelle cuisine. Tel: (204) 237-6276. **Le Couscous**, 135 Marion, is a bit of Africa transplanted to St. Boniface, and features excellent northern African food. Closed Sundays. Tel: (204) 237-3775. Reservations are advised at all these restaurants.

The Red River Basin

The Red River basin is rich in history. It was here, for example, that the Hudson's Bay and North West companies battled for supremacy in the fur trade in the early 19th century; Lord Selkirk arrived with Scottish and Irish homesteaders in 1812; and Governor Robert Semple and 20 settlers were massacred in 1816 by traders of the North West Company.

Highway 238 (off Highway 9), the River Road Heritage Parkway, follows the Red River north from Winnipeg. This lovely drive offers visitors plenty of scenic appeal in the form of overlooks, pretty homes, and the charming 19th-century **St. Andrew's Church**. The church, built in 1845, became the largest and most successful missionary society station in Manitoba during the second half of the 19th century. Services were held in Cree, and fruits, vegetables, wheat, and barley were grown on its grounds. St. Andrew's prospered until 1928, when it fell on hard times. In 1976 the rectory and grounds were bought and restored by the Canadian government. Today St. Andrew's is once again a thriving parish community, with the church still in use.

Kennedy House, across the way, was built in 1866 by Capt. William Kennedy, a Métis, and his English wife, Eleanor. (The captain and his wife are buried in the St. Andrew's churchyard.) Today three rooms of the house are furnished in 1870s style, much as they would have appeared in Captain Kennedy's day. After poking around the church and furnished rooms here, visitors are invited to have tea in a glassed-in tearoom overlooking English-style gardens. The house is open daily, May through September, 11:00 A.M. to 4:30 P.M.

Lower Fort Garry

Manitoba's fur-trading past is evoked a bit farther north at Lower Fort Garry, the only stone fur-trading fort still intact in North America. Built in the early 1830s by Hudson's Bay Company governor George Simpson, it stands on the banks of the Red River, 32 km (20 miles) north of Winnipeg. The fort, which was never used as a military garrison but instead served as the company's administrative headquarters, has been restored to its original state by Parks Canada. It's easy to spend a whole day in this fascinating place, and knowledgeable guides in period costume will be happy to answer your questions as well as lead you on a tour of the grounds. The grounds and buildings are open daily during the summer; the rest of the year only the grounds are open to inspection. Tel: (204) 785-6050 for hours and information on special events.

Festivals

From May to October Manitoba is *en fête,* with every town and hamlet doing its utmost to celebrate. It's good business, among other things. (When the town of Austin, population 400, draws 60,000 people to its four-day Threshermen's Reunion, that's good business.)

The best of these many festivals, **Folklorama**, takes place in August in Winnipeg itself. Put on by the city's 40 or more ethnic communities, it's a colorful and lively two-week celebration featuring the folk dances, music, arts, and food of each ethnic group.

Another big celebration is the **National Ukrainian Festival**, held near Dauphin, just north of Riding Mountain National Park, over the long first weekend of August. The festival draws thousands of people from across the United States and Canada, and is so popular that rooms in the area are reserved a year in advance. The festivities include stage shows with Cossack dancing and brilliant costumes at a 5,000-seat amphitheater on a hillside south of town, and, of course, authentic food and handicrafts. Dauphin, with an eye to its annual fiesta, has a number of motels. The one of choice is the ▶ **Rodeway Inn Motel**. Dauphin also has the small but charming **Fort Dauphin Museum** (open daily May through September), a replica of a North West Company trading post, with some ancient fossil remains that are the envy of large museums across the country.

The mid-July **Winnipeg Folk Festival**, held at Birds Hill Park on Highway 59, 25 km (16 miles) northeast of Winnipeg, is a four-day feast of country, bluegrass, gospel, jazz, old-time music, and prayers—for sun, not rain. Musicians from all over North America perform at the festival, which is billed as a "gentle" experience (no alcohol or drugs allowed). It's mainly attended by younger people, with a sprinkling of babies and older folks, and it's very respectable. Birds Hill is a provincial park where Winnipeggers go to picnic in summer and cross-country ski in winter.

Bird-Watching

Fort Whyte Centre for Environmental Education
Manitoba is a bird-watcher's paradise, with one of the best sites within metropolitan Winnipeg itself. The Fort Whyte Centre is just a 20-minute drive from the downtown area at 1961 McCreary Road. Here, 200 acres of land reclaimed from a cement company's excavations have been converted into one of the most diverse wildlife areas on the continent. The Waterfowl Gardens, which re-create eight different Manitoba wetland habitats, ranging from prairie potholes to the tundra of the far north, are populated by pinioned species of wild ducks indigenous to each type of environment. Elsewhere, self-guided trails lead over a marsh, and it's all so quiet and restful that it's hard to believe it lies within the limits of a big city.

Oak Hammock Marsh
Thirty-two kilometers (20 miles) north of Winnipeg, off Highway 67, is Oak Hammock Marsh, home to thousands of ducks, geese, and waterfowl. Fall, when the birds are migrating south, is the best time to visit, but summer is equally enjoyable. The serenity of the 8,646-acre marsh is soothing; there are dikes and a boardwalk to wander on; and you can drink the ice-cold artesian well water that flows into the marsh. Thousands of visitors, many of them highly experienced and travelled birders, visit Oak Hammock every year.

Although prime bird-watching spots are scattered throughout the province (**Churchill**—see below—is famous worldwide, with some 200 species, including the rare Ross's gull, passing through every year), the two spots mentioned above are the most accessible.

TOURING MANITOBA
Farm Vacations

More than 40 farms throughout the province open their homes to visitors, who can choose from any number of activities or just relax and do nothing at all. Some farms specialize in hunting or horseback riding; others cater to seniors, children, or families. They all offer full room and board, separate accommodation in cottages, or trailer and camping areas. Guests may eat all or some meals with the family, and are welcome to help out with the chores. A booklet with rates and information is available from the **Manitoba Country Vacations Association,** c/o Bob Frost, R.R. 1, Elm Creek, Man. R0G 0N0; Tel: (204) 436-2599.

Southern Manitoba

Whiteshell Provincial Park
Whiteshell Provincial Park, 144 km (90 miles) east of Winnipeg via the Trans-Canada Highway (Highway 1), is a good place to start your exploration of the province. The Precambrian Shield here, the oldest geologic formation in the world, is carpeted with pine and birch trees, ferns and wild roses, dozens of lakes (all cold), rivers, and rocky outcrops. The 1,000-square-mile park is green and still, and a woodsy smell hangs in the air. Just be sure to take along lots of mosquito repellent. At the southern end of the park, **Falcon Lake**, with a resort motel, marina, campgrounds, 18-hole golf course, and beaches, is one of the Whiteshell's most popular attractions. There are, in addition, more than two dozen lodges scattered throughout the park where you can fish, swim, and go boating. Among them are the ▶ **Big Buffalo Resort** and the ▶ **Penguin Resort and Marina,** both in the town of Falcon Lake. The Big Buffalo has well-maintained duplex cottages with light housekeeping and showers. The Penguin Resort is older, but it too has pretty log cabins with light housekeeping, television, and showers or tubs. Neither resort has telephones, but who wants a telephone on vacation anyway?

With its icy, crystal-clear waters and lovely surroundings, **West Hawk Lake**, just north of Falcon Lake via Highway 312, is a favorite with American visitors. The individual cabins at the ▶ **West Hawk Lake Resort** have four-piece baths, television, and carpeting. All are equipped with basic kitchen facilities, but again, no phones.

Where to eat in the Whiteshell presents a problem, as the restaurants cannot, in all honesty, be described as gourmet. The **Falcon Lake Golf Club** (Tel: 204/349-2554) has a licensed dining room and good service. Also in Falcon Lake is the **Falcon's Nest Café** (Tel: 204/349-2213) for sandwiches, hamburgers, and the like.

Steinbach

In the late 1800s many Mennonites fled persecution in Europe and settled in southern Manitoba. Steinbach, 56 km (34 miles) southeast of Winnipeg via Highways 1 and 12, was one of those early settlements. Today the **Mennonite Heritage Village** here, a collection of authentic buildings that includes a house-barn, a sod hut, a huge windmill, and a livery barn converted into a restaurant serving Mennonite specialties, gives visitors a glimpse into the lives of these hard-working, deeply religious people.

Morden

Morden, some 120 km (75 miles) southwest of Winnipeg, is one of southern Manitoba's prettiest and liveliest towns. The **Morden District Museum** offers the most comprehensive display of marine reptile fossils in Canada. Most of the fossils found in the area were laid down during the Upper Cretaceous period along the Manitoba Escarpment, the ancient shoreline of glacial Lake Agassiz, and are usually found in association with bentonite and shale.

Elsewhere in town, several unusual stone houses were built around the turn of the century by a master stonemason whose name, alas, no one seems to remember. The houses, according to their fortunate owners, are a marvel to look at but more than a little expensive to heat in the winter.

To get to Morden, follow Highway 75 south along the Red River to Highway 14, which becomes Highway 3 just east of town. The museum is located in the Morden Recreational Centre on Second Street North.

The Interlake Region

Gimli

Gimli, 100 km (60 miles) north of Winnipeg on the western shore of Lake Winnipeg (take either Highway 8 or Highway 9), was settled by Icelanders in the mid-19th century. (Gimli means "home of the gods.") Today it's a quiet, modest summer resort whose blond, beautiful Icelandic youth move to Winnipeg as soon as they can—while Winnipeggers flock to Gimli in droves. Nothing is elaborate here, including its

restaurants, which are pleasantly passable, nothing more.
The Bus Depot has good chips and hamburgers, the Falcon
Café decent sandwiches. Most cottage owners in Gimli eat at
home.

As with restaurants, so with motels. The best accommodation in town is the relatively new 77-room ▶ **Country Resort
Gimli** on Centre Street, which offers comfortable lodgings
but needs to work on its food.

While it may not offer great food or lodgings, Gimli does
have pure air, delicious drinking water, and a wonderful
peaceful feeling about it.

Hecla Island

The ▶ **Gull Harbour Resort and Conference Centre**, on
Hecla Island, another 80 km (50 miles) to the north, offers
solid luxury for which you pay commensurately. You'll need
a car (it's a straight shot up Highway 8), as bus service has
been discontinued. It's a lovely drive, however, especially
north of Gimli, with fields of fragrant sweet clover crowding
the road, stands of evergreens and poplars, and miles of
marshland and lakescape—wild, unspoiled Lake Winnipeg
country, in other words. Once here, many guests simply rest
and soak up the sun, but for the activity-prone there's golf on
a spectacular course, with several fairways laid out along the
shore of Lake Winnipeg, as well as tennis, sailing, windsurfing, and swimming.

There's also a picturesque bed and breakfast on Hecla
Island. The ▶ **Solmundson Gesta Hus** overlooks the lake
and offers golfing, hiking, and swimming, in addition to
delicious home-cooked meals and a friendly, informal atmosphere.

West of Winnipeg

For something a little different, head west from Winnipeg on
the Trans-Canada Highway past Headingley and the giant
statue of the white horse beside the road (ask a local
resident to tell you the Indian legend behind the statue; it
concerns a young maiden whose soul passed into the
horse's body). Turn north on Highway 26, drive past the
gladiolus farms, and continue on to Poplar Point, where
you'll find **St. Anne's Anglican Church**, one of the oldest log
churches still in use in western Canada.

Portage La Prairie

From Poplar Point, continue west to the **Fort la Reine Museum** (open daily, May through mid-September), on the

outskirts of Portage la Prairie. The original fort, built by Pierre Gaultier de la Vérendrye in 1738, was his headquarters while he explored the territory. The present complex includes a trading post, a blacksmith's shop, a log cabin, and the 1882-vintage rail car of William Van Horne, builder of the Canadian Pacific Railroad. **Wayne's Inn** (904 Saskatchewan Avenue East; Tel: 204/239-1174) has surprisingly good hamburgers, sandwiches, and pies. **Mary's Too** (Tel: 204/239-1063), in the Portage Mall, is another lunch and dinner stop popular with travellers and locals. For unusual accommodations, consider the ▶ **Red Roof House**, 102 First Street S.W., where the Pelechatys have converted an historic 17-room house into a bed and breakfast. Breakfast comes with Champagne, and the Pelechatys serve gourmet meals. Another glamorous note—Carole Lombard and Clark Gable once stayed here.

Spruce Woods Provincial Park

From Portage La Prairie, follow the Trans-Canada to Austin and the Manitoba Agricultural Museum, which is devoted to antique farm machinery. Past Austin is Carberry, where the topography begins to change as the flat prairie gives way to gently rolling hills. At Spruce Woods Provincial Park, 16 km (10 miles) south of Carberry via Highway 5, you'll find a desert, complete with sand dunes, reptiles (if you're lucky enough to spot one), and cacti unique to Manitoba. The dunes (known as Spirit Sands) are what's left of a huge sand delta piled up during the Ice Age. They are extremely fragile, and visitors are confined to a single self-guided trail. Walking the desert, which the Plains Indians knew as the Bald Head Hills, takes about two hours, and when it's hot in the rest of Manitoba, it's even hotter here. But it's worth seeing a desert right in the middle of Canada.

Brandon

If you decide to venture on, follow the Trans-Canada west to Brandon. With a population of 40,000, Brandon is Manitoba's second-largest city. It's a pretty place, with a small-town atmosphere leavened by considerable sophistication. It also has a good number of restaurants, a Sportsplex with an Olympic-size swimming pool, and the **B. J. Hales Museum**, with displays of mounted birds and mammals.

On the whole, restaurants outside Winnipeg leave a great deal to be desired, but Brandon has three good ones, for which the traveller should be grateful. They are the **Kokonas Restaurant and Lounge** (Tel: 204/727-4395) at 1011 Rosser Avenue, the **Colonial Inn** dining room (Tel:

204/728-8532) at 1944 Queens Avenue, and **Chicago Joe's** (Tel: 204/728-5775), in the Royal Oak Inn at 3130 Victoria Avenue. Kokonas is done up nicely with wood paneling, but, as with most Manitoba restaurants, tends to be dimly lighted. The steaks are good, however (Brandon is a center for the cattle industry), and they do nice things with sea-food. The Colonial Inn serves up good food and delicious pastry in its otherwise standard motel-style dining room. Chicago Joe's offers a rather ordinary menu, but does it well. You don't have to get all gussied up to eat in these restaurants, particularly in the motels—Brandonites cer-tainly don't expect it—and Kokonas is the only restaurant where you might be advised to make a reservation.

Brandon also has three decent hotels—the ▶ **Victoria Inn** and ▶ **Royal Oak Inn**, both on Victoria Avenue, and the ▶ **Trails West Motor Inn** on 18th Street North. All have adequate dining rooms, the Royal Oak's being the best. Elsewhere in town, the ▶ **Casa Maley** on Victoria Avenue is a top-rated bed and breakfast. The three-story Tudor house was built in 1912 and has an Old World look and feel, thanks in part to its beautiful antique furnishings and art objects. Two of the bedrooms have fireplaces. For breakfast, guests are offered a menu with half a dozen choices on it, and for an added fee the owners will arrange transportation, sight-seeing tours, even baby-sitting (but note: nonsmokers only).

Souris

The next day, drive on to Souris, 40 km (25 miles) southwest of Brandon on Highway 2. Souris is a delightful town with a core of Old English cottages (each with a name) and lawns dressed up in masses of flowers. Even the fire hydrants are painted brilliant colors. The Souris River runs through town and is crossed by the longest suspension foot bridge in Canada. True, it wobbles as you walk on it, but it hasn't yet collapsed under the weight of a human being. There's an-other reason for going to Souris: It's the site of an agate pit that contains the largest variety of semiprecious stones on the continent. For a small fee you can grub around in the pit as long as you want and take out whatever you find. (Pit permits are available in town at the Rock Shop on First Avenue.)

Riding Mountain National Park

From Souris, backtrack on Highway 2 to Highway 10 and follow the latter north about 145 km (90 miles) to Riding Mountain National Park, where you'll find 75 chilly lakes, dozens of nature trails, a resort town—**Wasagaming**—and unbelievably pure air. The park encompasses a chunk of the Manitoba Escarpment and is an oasis of evergreen woods in the middle of a sea of farflung prairie. Just beyond the entrance to the park is the ▶ **Elkhorn Resort and Conference Centre**, which offers luxury accommodations in a central lodge and several chalets, along with a lovely natural setting overlooking rolling grassland, forest, and the resort's nine-hole golf course.

WILDERNESS ADVENTURES IN MANITOBA

Fishing

Manitoba is a large province, and could easily accommodate North Dakota, Illinois, Iowa, and Wisconsin, with room left over for part of Rhode Island, within its borders. In all these thousands of square miles there are literally tens of thousands of lakes, making Manitoba an angler's paradise.

Fishing often means waiting patiently, so it's important that the location you choose will make the waiting game pleasant. The beautiful, unpolluted, tranquil lakes of Manitoba are one of its greatest resources, so it's no surprise that over the last few years more than 100 highly rated fishing lodges offering the maximum in comfort and relaxation have opened.

The ▶ **Knee Lake Resort**, northwest of Gods Lake in the east-central region of the province, has 13 cabins with showers, a dining room, a lounge with a fireplace, and a store that sells fishing tackle. This fly-in but wheelchair-accessible lodge is open from late May to September only.

On the other side of the province, ▶ **Big Sand Lake Lodge**, located on beautiful sand eskers northeast of the hamlet of Lynn Lake, has seven modern cabins with showers, a sauna, an excercise room, a licensed dining room, a store, outcamps on three other lakes in the area, and hunting for moose. Open June to September, Big Sand Lake Lodge is also a fly-in camp (out of Winnipeg only).

▶ **North Knife Lake Lodge**, north of centrally located Thompson, has a new lodge and three cabins, a dining room, boats, guides, and outcamps at North Knife River as well as other lakes in the area. Open June to September, this is another fly-in.

Northwest of Churchill and the 60th parallel—this is

really north—is the ▶ **Nejalini Lodge**. It has a dining room, store, fly-out service, sauna, guides, and outcamps at two lakes, and is open from mid-June to mid-September. Don't expect hot weather here, just comfortably warm.

The ▶ **Grass River Lodge** is a pleasant surprise—a top-rated lodge that can be reached by car. Situated on Reed Lake in the west-central portion of the province, it has 11 modern cabins with showers, four outcamps, a licensed dining room, and hunting for bear and moose. To get there, take Highway 6 from Winnipeg north 580 km (360 miles) to its intersection with Highway 39, head west for another 87 km (54 miles) to Grass River Provincial Park, and then follow the signs to Reed Lake.

It should be noted that lodges fill up very quickly in the summertime; it's advisable to write early in the spring for reservations. For more information, call Travel Manitoba at (800) 665-0040; Fax: (204) 945-2302. (You'll find booking information for the above-mentioned lodges in the Accommodations Reference list at the end of the chapter.)

Canoeing

With its thousands of pristine lakes and numberless rivers, Manitoba has more accessible canoeing terrain than virtually any other region of North America. The degree of skill and experience needed to explore this terrain varies from quiet creek paddling to slugging across big lakes to fighting through white-water rapids. You name it, Manitoba has it. One such route starts at Keewatin, Ontario, and follows the Winnipeg River—the principal route of the fur-trading era, with spectacular wilderness scenery to boot—to Lake Winnipeg, and from there up the Red River to Winnipeg.

Netley Marsh

With its aroma of decaying flora and multitude of water plants, Netley Marsh, situated at the southern end of Lake Winnipeg where the Red River flows into the lake, is the very essence of marsh. While the marsh, which comprises a maze of channels and shallow lakes that abound in wildlife, is a birder's paradise, it is also a great challenge for canoeists. Although the junctions are well marked, it's essential to have a good map of the area, as distances can be deceiving. To get there, take Highway 9 from Winnipeg north to Selkirk, and then follow Highway 320 to your destination. Allow about an hour and a half for the one-way trip.

Land of Little Sticks

In the far north, there's the Land of Little Sticks route, a 2,000-mile marathon (with exit by chartered plane) during the course of which the landscape changes from thick forest to almost treeless tundra. This route is recommended for experts only. Topographic maps, which are essential, are available at the Surveys and Mapping Branch, 1007 Century Street, Winnipeg, Man. R3H 0W4.

Another excellent source of books, maps, and general information on canoe/kayak routes and adventure travel in Manitoba is the Canadian Recreational Canoeing Association. Contact: CRCA, 1029 Hyde Park Road, Suite 5, Hyde Park, Ont. N0M 1Z0; Tel: (519) 473-2109; Fax: (519) 473-6560.

Churchill and Polar Bears

One of the last great wilderness adventures in the world is a trip to Churchill, the "polar bear capital of the world." It's also Canada's only inland seaport, as well as the feeding ground of beluga whales and the summer home for 200 species of migrating birds.

Twelve hundred intrepid people live in Churchill, which is situated on the shores of Hudson Bay, 1,600 km (1,000 miles) north of Winnipeg. They have to be intrepid to live so far from civilization. For nine months of the year this is a bleak and desolate area. For the other three months it's bearable. In the spring (late) and fall (early) the tundra is a blaze of color, covered with lichen and miniature shrubs and flowers; ships from around the world take on grain in the harbor.

It's a lonely existence, and the residents here are a special breed—tough, skillful, hardy, and very independent. They cope with cold, with isolation, and with polar bears. The bears, which gather on the outskirts of town while waiting for the Hudson Bay ice pack to solidify at the beginning of the long Arctic winter, occasionally wander into town. Those that do are tranquillized by the Canadian Wildlife Service, then relocated, three bears at a time, several hundred miles to the north in an operation known as Bearlift. All this fuss and expense is necessary: while the bears are truly handsome beasts, an impromptu encounter with a 1,200-pound behemoth is no joke.

The residents of Churchill have built themselves a complex that houses a high school, library, swimming pool, curling rink, and hockey arena. (You can't play hockey outdoors when it's 40° below.) They also have a museum filled with Inuit carvings and artifacts that are among the finest and oldest in the world.

The town is geared to tourists and to grain. Inuits who live in the region have seen their old way of life disappear under the onslaught of civilization, with very little to replace it, although some of them create sculptures and paintings that fetch very good prices in the south—that is, in Winnipeg. Inuit men also act as guides to tourists, who flock to Churchill by the thousands to see the polar bears and beluga whales.

The prime polar bear season is from early October to mid-November, when you can view the bears from the vantage point of a "tundra buggy," a buslike contraption on huge tractor tires. The sight of the world's biggest land-dwelling carnivore a dozen feet away is an awesome one. (Tours on these vehicles, which are the only way to reach the expanses outside of town where the bears roam, should be booked well in advance—up to a year's notice may be required.)

In summer the mouth of the Churchill River is the feeding ground for hundreds of white beluga whales. These friendly 12-foot relatives of the dolphin have never been known to harm man or boat, though they may swim right alongside. It's fascinating to listen to their high-pitched tones as they call to one another.

Churchill Outfitters

People who come to Churchill to see the polar bears or whales would be well advised to book with a tour. There are any number from Churchill, some for a day, some overnight camping trips, some up to five days. **The Great Canadian Travel Company** and **Frontiers North** are two Winnipeg outfits that will arrange custom-made packages. (See below for phone numbers and addresses.)

All the touring companies in Churchill offer both whale and polar bear excursions, and some do bird-watching as well. **Churchill Wilderness Encounter**, led by Bonnie Chartier, a well-known birder, does all three. **Invitational Tours** is led by Dan Guravich, a native Canadian transplanted to Mississippi who is famous for his work with, and photographs of, polar bears. (You've probably seen his photographs in books and magazines.) Guravich personally escorts all his tours. **Sea North Tours**, headed by Mike Macri, operates a 40-foot boat for whale sightings, and puts hydrophones into the sea to magnify the whales' songs. (In Churchill, belugas are called sea canaries.) **B&B Scuba**, with a complete scuba shop in Winnipeg, also recently began offering scuba tours in Churchill. You can rent equipment, including dry suits, in Winnipeg, with the air tanks available in Churchill. Although the operation is still in an experimental stage, it appears that the whales are not afraid of the rubber-clad newcomers to their ice-cold waters, and in fact often approach divers out of curiosity.

Dymond Lake Air Services offers aerial sightseeing tours that allow you to fly over polar bears, caribou, and other local wildlife. Canoeing, fishing, and other packages are also available. **Northern Expeditions Tours** offers whale-watching and birding expeditions in summer and polar bear safaris in the fall, and **North Star Tours** has tundra buggy and boat tours in season to view beluga whales and Fort Prince of Wales (see below).

Another excursion to the land of the Inuit is now available via Winnipeg or Churchill by air. Visitors are flown to Sila Lodge on Wager Bay in the Northwest Territories, located just 50 miles south of the Arctic circle on a virtually untouched 150-mile-long inlet where salt and fresh waters meet. The magnificent scenery ranges from 1,500-foot-high cliffs to lakes and cascading waterfalls. Here, you'll see polar bears and caribou in their summer habitat, and, if you're lucky, the rare peregrine falcon and gyrfalcon. Again, check with the outfitters listed below for availability and further information on this and other tours.

- **B&B Scuba.** c/o Bob Bartmanovich, #2-1333 Niakwa Road East, Winnipeg, Man. R2J 3T5. Tel: (204) 257-3696; Fax: (204) 254-4695.
- **Churchill Wilderness Encounter.** c/o Al and Bonnie Chartier, P.O. Box 9, Churchill, Man. R0B 0E0. Tel: (204) 675-2248; Fax: (204) 675-2045.
- **Dymond Lake Air Services.** c/o Doug and Helen Webber, P.O. Box 304, Churchill, Man. R0B 0E0. Tel: (204) 675-8875; Fax: (204) 675-2386.
- **Frontiers North.** c/o Lynda Gunter, 774 Bronx Avenue, Winnipeg, Man. R2K 4E9. Tel: (204) 663-1411; Fax: (204) 663-6375; in the U.S. and Canada, Tel: (800) 663-9832.
- **The Great Canadian Travel Company.** 273 Donald Street, Winnipeg, Man. R3C 1M9. Tel: (204) 949-0199; Fax: (204) 949-0188.
- **Invitational Tours.** c/o Dan Guravich, P.O. Box 891, Greenville, Mississippi, 38702. Tel: (601) 335-2444; Fax: (601) 332-9528.
- **Northern Expedition Tours.** c/o Louise Foubert,

P.O. Box 614, Churchill, Man. R0B 0E0. Tel: (204) 675-2793; Fax: (204) 675-2647.

- **North Star Tours.** c/o Mark Ingerbrigtson, P.O. Box 520, Churchill, Man. R0B 0E0. Tel: (204) 675-2629; Fax: (204) 675-2852; in the U.S. and Canada, Tel: (800) 665-0690.
- **Sea North Tours.** c/o Mike Macri, P.O. Box 222, 39 Franklin Street, Churchill, Man. R0B 0E0. Tel: (204) 675-2195; Fax: (204) 675-2198.

Across the river mouth from Churchill is **Fort Prince of Wales**, a huge stone fort built by the Hudson's Bay Company in the 1700s to defend its fur trade interests in the New World. A few miles upriver from the fort is Sloop's Cove, used by whalers and fur traders in the 18th century. Bird-watching is excellent throughout the region.

The only way to get to Churchill is by plane or train. For those with the luxury of time, VIA Rail's service to Churchill includes good food and comfortable sleeping quarters. Trains leave Winnipeg at 9:55 P.M. every Tuesday, Thursday, and Saturday, and arrive in Churchill a day and a half later at 8:20 A.M. (Upon arrival, passengers are treated to a guided bus tour of the community and its surroundings.) Another VIA Rail tour includes a day trip by air to Eskimo Point in the Northwest Territories (weather permitting). Air service to Churchill is handled by Air Canada and Canadian Airlines International, which fly over hundreds of miles of lakes, forest, and, finally, tundra en route to Churchill. Either way, this is truly *terra incognita.* The train (summer only) will set you back about $1,550, round trip; airfare runs about $1,395.

There are several nice places to stay in Churchill. After all, tourism is a big industry here. The ▶ **Seaport Hotel** and the ▶ **Tundra Inn** are both comfortable, clean, and have dining rooms. The ▶ **Polar Motel** will also do. All three have cable and satellite television, bathtubs or showers, and shuttle service to and from the airport. Reservations should be made well in advance.

At night the skies over Churchill can put on the most brilliant display of aurora borealis seen anywhere in the world. The lights literally dance across the sky, outstripping the most spectacular fireworks or laser show.

"Primitive liberty, I have regained thee at last," remarked Chateaubriand at the sight of the boundless North American wilderness. Churchill makes many a visitor feel the same way.

GETTING AROUND

From Winnipeg International Airport visitors can rent a car, take a taxi or the bus, or use the airport shuttles to get downtown. Five hotels—the International Inn, the Westin, the Charterhouse, the Sheraton, and the Radisson—offer airport-shuttle bus service. Travellers planning to spend a few days in Winnipeg should rent a car. Taking buses can be inconvenient, as the tourist sights are spread around the city. The exception is a bus tour offered by the Paddlewheel River Rouge company in red double-decker buses; Tel: (204) 947-6843 for tour descriptions and pick-up points.

With the exception of Churchill, touring Manitoba outside Winnipeg demands a car. For VIA Rail information, see the Getting Around section for Ontario Province (or, for flights, check with Air Canada or Canadian Airlines International).

A caution: Lyme disease, which is transmitted by the bite of an infected deer tick, has been widely reported in the United States. While still relatively rare here, people who spend time in the outdoors, and particularly in wooded areas, should be aware of the problem. For complete information, which includes a card with color photos of the tick and a measuring hole should one need to be identified, send a stamped, self-addressed long envelope to the Lyme Disease Information Center, P.O. Box 1523, Racine, WI 53403.

ACCOMMODATIONS REFERENCE

The rates given below are projections *for peak seasons during the 1994 calendar year; at other times of the year they* may *be considerably less. Unless otherwise indicated, rates are based on double rooms, double occupancy; provincial and federal taxes are included in all rates. As rates are subject to change, always double-check before booking. (See also accommodations in the Winnipeg section.)*

▶ **Big Buffalo Resort. Falcon Beach**, Man. R0E 0N0. Tel: (204) 349-2259. Rates upon request.

▶ **Big Sand Lake Lodge**. Contact: Rm. 1-1808 Wellington Avenue, Winnipeg, Man. R3H 0G3. Tel: (204) 774-6666; Fax: (204) 774-5500. $1,300–$1,800 (four days, all-inclusive).

▶ **Casa Maley**. 1605 Victoria Avenue, **Brandon**, Man. R7A 1C1. Tel: (204) 728-0812. $35–$45.

▶ **Country Resort Gimli**. 10 Centre Street, **Gimli**, Man. R0C 1B0. Tel: (204) 642-8565; Fax: (204) 642-4400; in the U.S. and Canada, Tel: (800) 456-4000; $62–$89.

▶ **Elkhorn Resort and Conference Centre**. P.O. Box 40,

Onanole, Man. R0J 1N0. Tel: (204) 848-2802; Fax: (204) 848-2109. $124–$136.

▶ **Grass River Lodge**. P.O. Box 1680, **La Pas**, Man. R9A 1L5. In summer, Tel: (204) 358-7171. In winter, contact: 12000 S. 195th E. Avenue, Broken Arrow, OK 74014; Tel: (918) 455-2324. Rates upon request.

▶ **Gull Harbour Resort and Conference Centre**. P.O. Box 1000, **Riverton**, Man. R0C 2R0. Tel: (204) 475-2354; Fax: (204) 279-2000. $103–$114.

▶ **Knee Lake Resort**. 1791 Dublin Avenue, Suite 3, **Winnipeg**, Man. R3H 1A9. Tel: (204) 632-6098; Fax: (204) 632-6204. $2,395–$2,520 (three days); $3,455 (seven days).

▶ **Nejalini Lodge**. P.O. Box 38, Group 347, R.R. 3, **Selkirk**, Man. R1A 2A8. Tel: (204) 284-6947 or 482-6884; Fax: (204) 482-8400. Rates upon request.

▶ **North Knife Lake Lodge**. P.O. Box 304, **Churchill**, Man. R0B 0E0. Tel: (204) 675-8875; Fax: (204) 675-2386. Rates upon request.

▶ **Penguin Resort and Marina**. Faloma Beach, **Falcon Lake**, Man. R0E 0N0. Tel: (204) 349-2218. $45–$115.

▶ **Polar Motel**. P.O. Box 1031, 15 Franklin Street, **Churchill**, Man. R0B 0E0. Tel: (204) 675-8878; Fax: (204) 675-2647. $87.

▶ **Red Roof House**. 102 First Street Southwest, **Portage La Prairie**, Man. R1N 1Y3. Tel: (204) 857-7109. $130.

▶ **Rodeway Inn Motel**. P.O. Box 602, Highway 10 South, **Dauphin**, Man. R7N 2V4. Tel: (204) 638-5102. $65.

▶ **Royal Oak Inn**. 3130 Victoria Avenue, **Brandon**, Man. R7B 0N2. Tel: (204) 728-5775; Fax: (204) 726-5828; in Manitoba, Tel: (800) 852-2709. $78–$88.

▶ **Seaport Hotel**. P.O. Box 339, 299 Kelsey Boulevard, **Churchill**, Man. R0B 0E0. Tel: (204) 675-8807; Fax: (204) 675-2795. $91.

▶ **Solmundson Gesta Hus**. P.O. Box 76, **Hecla**, Man. R0C 2R0. Tel: (204) 279-2088. $59–$74.

▶ **Trails West Motor Inn**. 210 18th Street North, **Brandon**, Man. R7A 6P3. Tel: (204) 727-3800; Fax: (204) 726-1116. $58.

▶ **Tundra Inn**. P.O. Box 999, 34 Franklin Street, **Churchill**, Man. R0B 0E0. Tel: (204) 675-8831; Fax: (204) 675-2764; in the U.S. and Canada, Tel: (800) 265-8563. $95.

▶ **Victoria Inn**. 3550 Victoria Avenue West, **Brandon**, Man. R7B 2R4. Tel: (204) 725-1532; Fax: (204) 727-8282; in Manitoba, Tel: (800) 852-2710. $70–$80.

▶ **West Hawk Lake Resort**. **West Hawk Lake**, Man. R0E 2H0. Tel: (204) 349-2244. Rates upon request. (Sunday-to-Sunday bookings only during July and August.)

SASKATCHEWAN

By David Starre

David Starre, a freelance journalist and writer based in Saskatchewan, is also an avid outdoorsman and canoeist. He has lived in both northern and southern Saskatchewan, where he has held a number of communications and public relations positions.

Saskatchewan has two distinct regions, each with its own treasures to offer visitors. The southern half of the province is predominantly level plain broken by scattered ridges and valleys. Here, seemingly endless fields of wheat stretch north before giving way to the mixed woods of the province's central parklands. History draws many visitors to this region; the story of how the land was transformed from buffalo grass to wheat is a fascinating one that is retold in the province's many museums.

The northern half of Saskatchewan is dominated by hummocky, lake-studded terrain typical of the Canadian Shield. Sparsely populated, it attracts sportsfishermen, canoeists, and campers, who come to enjoy secluded waterways that have changed little since the first days of settlement.

MAJOR INTEREST

Wilderness experiences
Fishing and canoeing

Regina
Museum of Natural History
Saskatchewan Science Centre
Buffalo Days exhibition
Royal Canadian Mounted Police Museum

Saskatoon

Saskatoon Western Development Museum

Wanuskewin Heritage Park

Mendel Art Gallery

Ukrainian Museum of Canada

Annual Folkfest and Saskatoon Exhibition celebrations

Shakespeare on the Saskatchewan

Saskatchewan Jazz Festival

Elsewhere in Saskatchewan

Moose Jaw, North Battleford, and Yorkton western development museums

National and provincial parks (especially Prince Albert National Park and Cypress Hills Provincial Park)

Big Valley Jamboree in Craven

Saskatchewan Handcraft Festival in Battleford

Community rodeos

Enter Saskatchewan along its east–west corridors, the Trans-Canada and Yellowhead highways, or venture out from the province's two major cities, Regina (Ree-JI-nah) and Saskatoon, and you very quickly discover that wheat is king here. Wheat fields are everywhere—dusty gray to a deep black at seeding time, rich green during the heat of summer, and ripe and golden in the fall.

The prairies these fields blanket are grand in their immensity. Far horizons are seldom broken, and when they are, it is usually by tall, brightly colored grain elevators. So it is understandable that a bread-basket image is what most visitors carry away. It's an image that Saskatchewan people are proud of. Still, the traveller should know that there is another, more subtle side to the province—as Robert Moon writes in *This Is Saskatchewan!*

No, do not judge Saskatchewan by its prairies alone. Go into the hills and at the top stand breathless from the climb and the magnificence of what you have seen. Dip down into the valleys and offer no struggle as you succumb to the enchantment you find there. Walk into its forests, climb over its northern rocks and late at night listen to the lap of the lake waters.... Talk to its people and learn how closely men are linked with this earth. Pause and listen to its lore and you will have as your reward as remarkable legends of strangeness and heroism as exists.

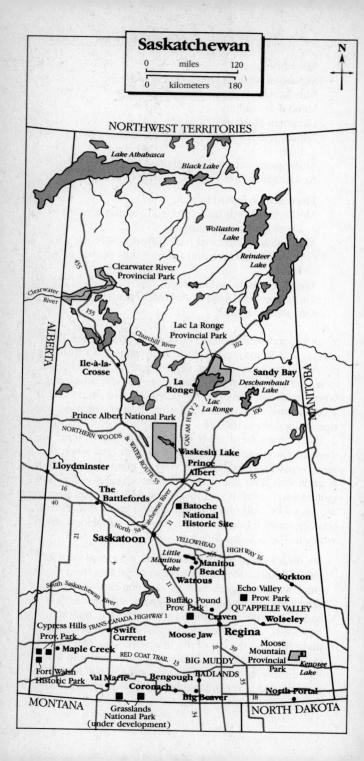

Moon's colorful words are sound advice on how to "do" Saskatchewan.

The Heritage

While little is known of Saskatchewan's inhabitants prior to historic times, there is evidence suggesting habitation more than 10,000 years ago. At the time of contact with early fur traders and explorers, Chipewyan Indians wintered in the northern fringes of Saskatchewan, moving out onto the tundra during the summer to hunt caribou. The Blackfoot and Assiniboine roamed the parklands and the plains, hunting the buffalo that provided both food and shelter. Later, migrant Cree pushed west, eventually becoming the dominant tribe. Some Cree adopted the ways of the Assiniboine and moved out onto the plains. Others moved north, deeper into the woods.

The first European to arrive on the prairies, in 1671, was Henry Kelsey, an employee of the Hudson's Bay Company sent inland to encourage distant Indians to make the long journey north for trade. What followed are stories of proud, noble Indians and their struggle to cope with change; of courageous voyageurs and the great rivalry between Bay men and the peddlers of the North West Company; of stouthearted Mounted Police red coats and the outlaws and whisky traders they were sent to tame; of rebellious Métis, under Louis Riel, and the army that marched west to defeat them; and of determined settlers who broke the sod and endured the drought and Depression of the 1930s.

The story of the Métis in Saskatchewan, a mixed culture of European and native Indian heritage, is told at **Batoche National Historic Park**, northeast of Saskatoon, and in the play *The Trial of Louis Riel,* performed in Regina at the **Norman Mackenzie Art Gallery** three times weekly during August.

Wanuskewin Heritage Park, on the banks of the South Saskatchewan River just north of Saskatoon, is dedicated to the cultural legacy of Canada's northern plains Indians. Archaeological studies at the park have uncovered 19 prehistoric and two historic sites, including a 1,500-year-old medicine wheel, ancient teepee rings, and a buffalo pound and jump.

Canada's acquisition of Hudson's Bay lands in 1870, the arrival of the railroad, and the signing of Indian treaties cleared a pathway for immigrants to head west. As recently as 1885 there were only slightly more than 32,000 people living in what is now Saskatchewan; most newcomers were

Canadians born in settled regions to the east. Today the province has approximately one million residents, with its ethnic population a mix of British, German, Ukrainian, Scandinavian, French, Native American, Dutch, Polish, Russian, and non-European cultures.

For early pioneers, starting out was a hard life at best, especially for those with little money. Yet nowhere else in Canada did so few people change a landscape so quickly as in Saskatchewan—mostly through a cooperative spirit that remains visible today in the friendly, helpful nature of the province's citizens.

The story of development in Saskatchewan is told through four branches of the **Western Development Museum**. Each branch of the museum has its own theme. The story of the province's people is told in **Yorkton**. In **Moose Jaw** the theme is transportation. Here, a quick look at the oxen-powered Red River cart, which brought settlers west at what can best be called a steady pace of 15 miles a day, leaves modern-day travellers thankful for progress. The museum's gem is its railway display. In **Saskatoon** visitors step out onto the streets of Boom Town 1910. Agriculture is the theme of the museum in **Battleford**, which boasts a living historical farm that grows and harvests its crops using methods and machinery of the early 20th century. All four branches stage special events during the summer.

TWIN CITIES

Saskatchewan's two largest cities, Saskatoon and Regina, serve as the most convenient starting points for travel in the province. Saskatoon only recently surpassed Regina in population; both are around the 180,000 mark.

Ever since their beginnings the two cities have been in friendly rivalry with each other. Each competed for the right to become capital; Regina was the victor. Each competed for the University of Saskatchewan; Saskatoon won out. Regina created a man-made lake; Saskatoon built a mountain.

Regina

The founders of Regina had few natural ornaments to work with. As Edward McCourt notes in his book *Saskatchewan,* the selection of a featureless creek crossing as capital of the Northwest, with the beautiful Qu'Appelle Valley only a short distance north, has been a puzzle to geographers and historians alike. In favor of the site was the fact that it was central to the southern plains and on the line surveyed for the Canadian Pacific Railroad. But, as McCourt suggests, the possibility of land holdings by certain influential individuals may have had more to do with it.

Originally called Pile O' Bones (after a pile of buffalo bones that lay along the banks of Wascana Creek), Regina was renamed by Princess Louise in 1882 in honor of her mother Queen Victoria. Ever since, Regina's citizens have worked hard to build a city worthy of its regal status. They dammed Wascana Creek to create a lake, and later 2,100 men enlarged the reservoir, dredging it with shovels and dump wagons. The dredgings were piled up to form islands in the enlarged waterbody. In 1908 workers started construction on Saskatchewan's Legislative Building, a grand center of government next to Wascana Park strongly reminiscent of the Palace of Versailles; today it is the city's most notable landmark.

WASCANA CENTRE

A walk through Wascana Centre is a good place to start a tour of Regina. Attractions include the Saskatchewan Legislative Building, the Museum of Natural History, the Saskatchewan Science Centre, and the Norman Mackenzie Art Gallery. See the **Museum of Natural History** as a prelude to touring the province if starting out from Regina. A recently opened Earth Sciences Gallery on the lower level tells the story of how Saskatchewan evolved from temperate seas through the age of dinosaurs to the arrival of man. The gallery and a new native peoples gallery are part of a three-phase, seven-year redevelopment of the museum.

The **Saskatchewan Science Centre**, the park's newest attraction, is housed in a wonderful old building that once operated as the city's main power station. Exhibits explore the human body, the living planet, astronomy, and geology. A new addition to the Science Centre itself is the Kramer IMAX Theatre. In typical IMAX style, the theater brings together a five-story screen with 11,000 watts of six-channel four-way sound. The results are eye- and ear-opening, to say the least.

The **Norman Mackenzie Art Gallery** in the T. C. Douglas Building has a collection that ranges from Chinese and Egyptian antiquities to contemporary works by Canadian, American, and international artists. Gift shops are located at the museum, the art gallery, and Wascana Place.

(For the Royal Canadian Mounted Police Museum in Regina, see the section on the southern part of the province.)

Regina has its own symphony orchestra and active theater groups. The **Saskatchewan Centre of the Arts**, located in Wascana Park, houses a 2,000-seat concert hall. Watch for performances at the Centre as well as annual events such as **Buffalo Days**, the city's summer fair and exhibition, held the first week in August. Buffalo Days celebrates Regina's "Old West" heritage with a variety of concerts and dances, as well as the usual midway attractions. For a detailed schedule of events in Saskatchewan, call or write Tourism Saskatchewan (1919 Saskatchewan Drive, Regina, Sask. S4P 3V7; Tel: 800/667-7191 or 306/787-2300) and ask for their summer events calendar.

STAYING AND DINING IN REGINA
The city's most luxurious hotels are located in its downtown core, with another cluster of easily accessible accommodations located south of downtown on Albert Street, Regina's main north–south corridor. The ▶ **Regina Travelodge** and the ▶ **Landmark Inn** on Albert Street are good quality, moderately priced hotels. The family-oriented Travelodge has a pool, hot tub, and 250-foot waterslide; suites feature king-size Jacuzzis. The Landmark also has a pool and small waterslide, and offers a bit more on the eating and drinking end of things.

Major hotels downtown include the ▶ **Delta Regina** and the ▶ **Regina Inn**, on Victoria Avenue, the city's main east–west corridor; the ▶ **Chelton Inn**, a heritage property on 11th Avenue, across from the Galleria Shopping Plaza; and the ▶ **Ramada Renaissance**, on Saskatchewan Drive adjacent to the Cornwall Centre, the city's largest shopping complex.

Also on Victoria Avenue, and overlooking Victoria Park, the historic ▶ **Hotel Saskatchewan**, Regina's grande dame, has emerged from a major renovation with its Old World elegance restored. All of the hotel's 217 rooms have been lavishly redecorated and now feature queen- and king-size beds. New additions elsewhere on the premises include a health club, parking facility, and complimentary limo service to the airport.

The aforementioned hotels are all good choices for dining. If a sophisticated ambience is important, your first pick should be the Hotel Saskatchewan, where the stunning chandeliers and brassy elegance of the lobby hint at what awaits diners in the **Ranch Room** (Tel: 306/522-7691). Along with the usual steak, prime rib, and lobster dishes, popular selections here include British Columbia salmon, breast of duckling "Marengo," and wiener schnitzel. The hotel also has a smaller specialty seafood restaurant and a fast-fare bistro-style café.

Recommended lunch spots downtown include **Alfredo's** (Tel: 306/522-3366), on the South Street Mall and known for its homemade pastas and a great seafood salad with house dressing. **Bartleby's Emporium** (Tel: 306/565-0040) on Broad Street across from the Regina Inn, has the best hamburgers in town and a recipe for caesars—a popular Canadian drink made with vodka, clam-flavored tomato juice, and spices—that other Regina watering holes have been trying to sniff out for years. **Mieka's** (Tel: 306/522-6700), in business on Smith Street (one block north of City Hall) for 14 years, offers a changing menu of gourmet sandwiches, soups, and salads..

Recommended evening spots include the **Neo Japonica Restaurant** (Tel: 306/359-7669) on Hamilton Street, a cozy establishment located in a renovated two-story home south of the downtown core. The **Edgewater** (Tel: 306/569-2233), adjoining the Saskatchewan Science Centre, offers superb French cuisine along with pleasant views of Wascana Lake. Closed Sundays. Two of the more popular steak houses in town are **Golf's** (Tel: 306/525-5808), at the corner of Hamilton and Victoria, and the **Lakeshore** (Tel: 306/584-3780), farther south at Hillsdale and 23rd Avenue.

For something a little different, visitors might want to try the **Applause Dinner Theatre** (open Wednesday through Sunday) in the Regina Inn, where patrons often become part of the two-act musical comedy. Diners can choose from four entrées and two desserts; for reservations, Tel: (306) 791-6868. Another (summertime only) option is the **Crown Room** at Queensbury Downs in Regina's Exhibition Park, which offers a popular evening buffet every Wednesday, Friday, and Saturday evening. Reservations advised; Tel: (306) 781-9270.

Wolseley

Many Reginans make the one-hour-plus drive via Highway 1 to **Le Parisien**, a classic European restaurant in the small town of Wolseley, east of the city. The fact that people from across southern Saskatchewan will drive this far for a meal says all that needs to be said about the wonderful French and Swiss cuisine served at this culinary oasis. Reservations advised; closed Mondays. Tel: (306) 698-2801.

Right next door to Le Parisien, and operated by the same management, is the ▶ **Banbury House Inn**, a turn-of-the-century prairie home restored to its former elegance during its transformation into an inn.

NIGHTLIFE IN REGINA

To top off an evening in Regina head out to a country-and-western bar: The **Pump** on Victoria Street East and the **Long Branch Saloon** in the warehouse district just north of downtown on McIntyre Street are the most popular with the locals. You'll find alternative music and a very different crowd at **Channel One**, in the warehouse district on Hamilton. Popular bars for the young at heart are **Lauderdale's** in the Regina Inn and the **Manhattan Club** in the warehouse district on Dewdney Avenue.

The Qu'Appelle Valley

The beautiful Qu'Appelle Valley, sandwiched beween the Yellowhead and Trans-Canada highways and running in the same general east–west direction almost two-thirds of the way across the province, is a short drive north of Regina. Once a glacial spillway, the steep-sided valley now strings together a number of scenic parks and lakes, providing a dramatic visual counterpoint to the flat tableland that stretches in all directions from its rim. No trip to Saskatchewan would be complete without a drive through it, and a couple of provincial parks within its boundaries—Buffalo Pound, north of Moose Jaw, and Echo Valley, northeast of Regina—are recommended stops for campers. Watch for route signs and be sure to bring a camera and plenty of film, especially when the valley is lit up with the colors of fall.

A country-and-western festival in the Qu'Appelle at Craven is establishing quite a name for itself as well. Held in July, the **Big Valley Jamboree** annually attracts some 40,000 country-and-western fans from across the Canadian and American Midwest who come to see some of the best performers in the business.

Visitors will find plenty of cowboys and cowgirls at the festival—most attendees own a Stetson or two that they dust off for the weekend. The event attracts a mixture of people, some who come to picnic and others who come to party. Despite their differences, the two groups get along. Most people bring a motor home or trailer, creating the biggest collection of campers on wheels to be seen anywhere. And for visitors without their own wheels, bus service is available from Regina hotels.

Big Valley is also the site of a major rodeo held annually in August. In other parts of the province keep an eye out for small-town rodeos; they can be as entertaining as some of the larger city rodeos, if not more so—provided you don't mind rolling up your shirt sleeves and mingling with the locals.

Moose Jaw

A short drive west of Regina is Moose Jaw, a city noted for its past as a hideaway for American gangsters. Rumor has it that Al Capone was among the shady visitors who once frequented the city. In addition to the branch of the Western Development Museum mentioned above, Moose Jaw is home to a native wild animal park and Canada's famous aerobatic team—the Snowbirds. The Canadian Forces Base at Moose Jaw is the Snowbirds' home, and they always put on a special performance for the hometown crowd at the Saskatchewan Air Show, held annually here in early July.

Art lovers should take time to view the growing number of murals being painted on the walls of many of the buildings in town—part of Moose Jaw's efforts to increase tourist traffic.

LITTLE MANITOU LAKE

Long known for the healing powers of its waters, Little Manitou Lake is located just south of Saskatoon and the Yellowhead Highway on Route 365. Fed by deep springs, the lake has a mineral content similar to the Carlsbad Spa in Europe and a density greater than that of the Dead Sea. A heated mineral pool complex in the resort village of Manitou Beach is the perfect prescription for tired, stiff travellers. The 60-room ▶ **Manitou Springs Hotel** here, with a dining room and lounge facilities, is your best bet for overnight accommodations.

Saskatoon

There's a story told about two travellers who had lost their way. Upon seeing a distant city, the driver stopped and asked a farmer working in his field where they were. "Saskatoon, Saskatchewan," the farmer replied. The slightly perturbed tourist went back to his car none the wiser. "I don't know where we are," he told his companion. "That farmer doesn't speak any English."

Both Saskatoon and Saskatchewan, like many place-names in the province, are Cree derivatives. Roughly translated, Saskatoon is what the Indians call a tasty purple berry found in abundance in Saskatchewan. (Try some Saskatoon pie if you get the chance.) Saskatchewan is Cree for "the river that flows swiftly."

Adorned by the South Saskatchewan River, Saskatoon came by its beauty much more easily than did Regina, and is one of the prettiest cities in western Canada. There can be little doubt that the city's founders, teetotaling temperance colonists, would be proud of the city as it stands today, despite the fact it's a far cry from what they had in mind. The elbows bend as much here as anywhere else in Saskatchewan—if not more. For evidence of that, check out the country-and-western bars or the city's discos. The **Bar-K Ranch House** on 22nd Street West and the **Texas T** on 8th Street East are popular country-and-western spots. Another lively night spot is the **Artful Dodger** on 4th Avenue South, an English-style pub with decor inspired by the writings of Charles Dickens.

It is the city's harmony with the South Saskatchewan River that gives Saskatoon its character. Overlooking the river is the Delta Bessborough, one of the great Canadian château-style hotels, and the city's most notable landmark. Also decorating the riverbanks are the graystone neo-Gothic buildings of the University of Saskatchewan, the Mendel Art Gallery, and the Ukrainian Museum of Canada.

Attractions on the campus of the **University of Saskatchewan** include several science and archaeological museums, as well as the Diefenbaker Centre. John Diefenbaker was Canada's prime minister from 1957 to 1963. His popularity in Saskatchewan is made obvious by the number of his former abodes now operated as tourist stops. These include his early homestead (which was moved to Regina's Wascana Park), his former law office in Wakaw, and the house he occupied while in Prince Albert (to the north of Saskatoon). Diefenbaker Centre doubles as a working archive and museum that documents the career of the "Chief."

Mendel Art Gallery and Civic Conservatory

The Mendel Gallery (open daily year-round) occupies one of the most picturesque spots in the city on the west bank of the South Saskatchewan River. Opened in 1964, the gallery was named in honor of the late Fred Mendel, a prominent Saskatoon businessman who helped with its funding and who donated many Canadian paintings to its permanent collection. An important part of that collection are paintings by members of the early-20th-century Group of Seven, donated by the Mendel family in 1965. The museum is also a good place to see contemporary Saskatchewan artworks.

Ukrainian Museum of Canada

The Ukrainian Museum showcases a culture that has contributed much to Canada's mosaic. The museum's focus is on immigration, settlement, and community life on the prairies.

Among its many artifacts is a collection of 1,000 decorated Easter eggs, some brought to Canada by early immigrants. Easter eggs can be purchased in the museum gift shop. Open daily June 1 to August 31; closed Saturdays the rest of the year.

Theatre and Festivals

Like Regina, Saskatoon has an active theater scene, its own symphony orchestra, and a 2,000-seat concert hall, the latter located in Centennial Auditorium. **Folkfest**, held annually over the third weekend in August, is a celebration of the province's rich cultural heritage. The increasingly popular **Shakespeare on the Saskatchewan** features a different production annually. The outdoor play is performed downtown on the banks of the river five nights a week, July through mid-August. International jazz stars can be heard at the week-long **Saskatchewan Jazz Festival**, a six-year-old event that continues to grow in popularity. The festival is held during the week of Canada Day (July 1).

The **Saskatoon Exhibition**, a highlight of Saskatoon's summer for more than a century, has retained its pioneer flavor over the years. The fair, held during the first week of July, is kicked off by the Louis Riel Relay, which combines canoeing, horseback riding, and running. Elsewhere, the Saskatoon branch of the Western Development Museum features activities such as butter and ice cream making, while at nearby Pioneer Circle vintage farm machinery is brought back to life. A midway, an entertainment grandstand, chuckwagon races, and agricultural displays are among the many other activities.

Wanuskewin Heritage Park

Wanuskewin, which encompasses a scenic valley five minutes north of the city limits on Warman Road, has been developed with the active participation of area tribal members to highlight the traditional culture and age-old presence of native peoples on the northern plains. Borrowing its name from a Cree word meaning "seeking peace of mind," Wanuskewin gives visitors an opportunity to follow meandering trails past habitation sites, a buffalo jump and pound, a medicine wheel, and a number of archaeological excavations. Audio-visual presentations in the interpretive center and live performances of traditional Indian dances and storytelling help bring the past to life.

Visitors can taste traditional Indian foods at a small cafeteria-style **restaurant** in the center. A gift shop here also sells native handicrafts and artwork. The park is open daily year-round. Call ahead to check on the times of special performances; Tel: (306) 931-6767. To get to the park, head north on Idylwyld Drive and follow the signs bearing the bison emblem to Highway 11.

STAYING AND DINING IN SASKATOON

The major hotels in Saskatoon are located downtown on or near the South Saskatchewan River, or near the airport in the northwest part of the city. Room rates and quality are comparable to what Regina has to offer.

Standing like a sentinel on the banks of the South Saskatchewan River since 1935, the 230-room château-style ▶ Delta Bessborough recently emerged from an extensive restoration project that successfully balanced the demands of modernization with the need to preserve the hotel's historic elegance. Despite its noble character and ornate details, the hotel's most endearing feature is its grand setting on five acres of riverfront gardens. Amenities include indoor and outdoor pools, an exercise room, and a steam room.

The ▶ Sheraton Cavalier, on Spadina Crescent East (as is the Delta Bessborough), offers a variety of rooms with river views in addition to the usual comfort and range of amenities travellers have come to expect from the Sheraton chain.

Downtown Saskatoon's largest and newest hotel is the 18-story 290-room ▶ Ramada Renaissance, on 20th Street East. Similar in style to its Regina counterpart, with bright, modern public spaces and large, comfortable rooms, the Ramada also has a recreation complex with two giant waterslides, a swimming pool, a whirlpool, and saunas.

The ▶ Holiday Inn Saskatoon, on 22nd Street East, is conveniently located close to Idylwyld Drive, the city's major north–south corridor and main commercial thoroughfare.

Hotels serving the airport include the full-service, 257-room ▶ Saskatoon Inn and the smaller, more economical ▶ Relax Inn. Both are located ten minutes northwest of the downtown core at the corner of Circle and Airport drives.

In addition to the downtown hotels, which all have good dining rooms, Saskatoon boasts a number of better-than-average restaurants beyond the limits of its downtown core. Station Place (Tel: 306/244-7777), adjacent to the city's former CP rail station on Idylwyld Drive, was built to honor the railroad's role in the history and development of the province. Two luxuriously appointed railcars have been incorporated into the building's side walls, with plenty of brass, stained glass, and wood detailing adding to the ambience. Finger foods are available in the lounge, while specialties served in the main dining room include pork, chicken, and lamb souvlaki, Greek ribs, and the station master's prime rib.

Grain elevators are a common sight on the Canadian prairie, serving as collection points and storage and distribution depots for wheat and other cereal crops grown on the region's countless farms. **The Granary** (Tel: 306/373-6655), on 8th Street East, proudly borrows its architecture and Western motifs from these prairie landmarks. Steak and Saskatchewan prime rib are the house specialties, of course, with seafood, chicken, and a bountiful salad bar rounding out the menu.

Lydia's (Tel: 306/652-8595), at the corner of Broadway and 11th Street, is known for its Ukrainian and Hungarian dishes, and has a casual dining area in addition to a more formal parlor.

Popular eateries back downtown include the intimate **Sardi's Ristorante Italiano** (Tel: 306/244-2226) and **St. Tropez Bistro** (Tel: 306/652-1250), both on 3rd Avenue South. Locally famous for its sumptuous eight-course gourmet dinner is **Cousin Nick's** (Tel: 306/374-2020), on Grosvenor Avenue across from the Grosvenor Park Shopping Centre.

The Battlefords

Separated from each other by the North Saskatchewan River, the city of North Battleford and the town of Battleford are located 137 km (85 miles) west of Saskatoon via the Yellowhead Highway.

Battleford is home to the **Saskatchewan Handcraft Festival**, a juried show and sale held annually in mid-July. The festival features many of Saskatchewan's better-known artists and craftspeople working in a variety of mediums, including wood, clay, stained glass, leather, and wheat. A surprising number of the festival's exhibitors in the past have won international recognition for their work, among them sculptors Joe Faffard and Victor Cicansky, potter Folmer Hanson, wood-carver William Hazzard, and painters David Thauberger and Allen Sapp.

Sapp's paintings can be seen at a North Battleford gallery dedicated to his works. Sapp is an internationally acclaimed Cree artist who was born on the Red Pheasant Reserve just south of the city; his gifted depictions of his people's history and culture have won him the Order of Canada. The gallery is located at 1091 100th Street, and is open daily, May to September, and Wednesday to Sunday the rest of the year. Don't miss it if your travels take you nearby.

Also located in the Battlefords and well worth the stop are a branch of the **Western Development Museum** and **Battleford National Historic Park**, an original North West Mounted Police post. The development museum is located in North Battleford at the junction of Highways 16 and 40. The NWMP post is southeast of Battleford on Central Avenue.

THE SOUTH

In July 1874 the first regiment of the North West Mounted Police began its historic march west to halt the whisky trade. Today two Saskatchewan Mountie posts are still maintained as national historic parks: Fort Battleford, northwest of Saskatoon, and Fort Walsh, in the southwest corner of the province.

Royal Canadian Mounted Police Museum

Regina is the home of the RCMP's modern-day training base and its official museum. One of the most visited museums in Canada, the Royal Canadian Mounted Police Museum (open mid-May to mid-September, 9:00 A.M. to 6:45 P.M.) documents the force from its beginnings to the present day. It also provides a history of the northwestern frontier. Among the exhibits are a beaded rifle case and tobacco pouch presented by Sitting Bull to Police Superintendent James Walsh. Like many of the force's founding commanders, Walsh was a master at using first impressions to gain respect and establish authority. And when Sitting Bull crossed the so-called "medicine line" in 1877, Walsh was there to meet him, backed only by a small contingent of Mounties.

You'll find the museum and training academy at the west-central edge of Regina; turn west onto 11th Avenue from the Lewvan Expressway. Museum visitors should time their arrival with either the Sergeant Major's Parade, regularly held on weekdays at 12:50 P.M., or the force's Sunset Ceremonies, usually held on Tuesdays during the summer at 6:45 P.M. Call the museum at (306) 780-5838 to confirm times.

Travellers can follow the Mounties' route west by taking the **Red Coat Trail** (Highway 13) from Winnipeg, Manitoba, to Fort Macleod, Alberta. Along the Saskatchewan portion of the route you'll pass a number of attractions, including Moose Mountain Provincial Park, the Big Muddy Badlands, Grasslands National Park, Fort Walsh National Historic Park, and Cypress Hills Provincial Park.

Moose Mountain Provincial Park

Moose Mountain, a poplar- and birch-covered plateau located in the southeast corner of the province, is a favorite with local residents and visitors alike. Attractions within the park include its natural environment trails for hiking and horseback riding, a great golf course (with greens fees a very reasonable $15 to $20), and the waters of **Kenosee Lake**.

Most visitors to Moose Mountain camp, although there are a number of accommodations in and adjacent to the park for those who prefer not to rough it. The 30-room ▶ **Kenosee Inn**, inside the park boundaries off Highway 9, offers a full range of amenities, including a dining room and lounge, an indoor pool, sauna, and whirlpool. The inn also rents out two-bedroom lodge-style units and cabins. For lunch or evening dining try the golf-course clubhouse, just a short distance away, or the **Moose Head Inn** in Kenosee, a small resort village just outside the main entrance to the park. The Moose Head has a restaurant on one level and a nightclub on its second level.

Big Muddy Badlands

Once a haven for outlaws, the weathered buttes of the Big Muddy Badlands are located approximately 192 km (120 miles) southwest of Moose Mountain near Bengough and the junction of Highways 13 and 34. Before the arrival of the North West Mounted Police in 1902, the Big Muddy served as station number one on Butch Cassidy's Outlaw Trail between Canada and Mexico. Caves in the area are also said to have provided hideaways for the likes of Sam Kelley and Dutch Henry, notorious horse thieves and cattle rustlers who marauded across the border, using Canada as a safe haven from U.S. lawmen.

The best way to see the area is to take the **Big Muddy Tour** offered out of Coronach on weekends during the summer. (Coronach is located approximately 48 km/30 miles south of the Red Coat Trail near the junction of Highways 36 and 18.) The tour lasts about five hours and costs $16 per person. For departure times and additional information, contact the Coronach Information Centre, Tel: (306) 267-3312. The annual trail ride through the Big Muddy (held in late July) is another fascinating way to explore the area—for people who can bring their own horses. Contact Donna Robinson, Tel: (306) 268-4420, for trail-ride information. For those who don't have the time or can't bring a horse, **Castle Butte**, one of the valley's best-known landmarks, can be viewed from Highway 34 between Big Beaver and Bengough.

Grasslands National Park

About two hours farther west, Grasslands National Park is being developed to preserve the grandness of the Great Plains as well as to protect such threatened plains inhabitants as the prairie falcon, the black-tailed prairie dog, and the prairie rattlesnake (perhaps the only resident of Saskatchewan that won't greet you with a friendly handshake). Eerie badlands, Indian tepee rings, and historic trails are some of the park's notable features, with the suggested starting point for exploring the endless acres of grass located in **Val Marie**, due south of Swift Current at the junction of Highways 4 and 18. The park's interpretive center is here as well, although facilities and services for visitors are still limited. Another option is to take the guided tour offered by longtime resident Lise Perrault, who has plenty of stories to tell and a small museum with bits and pieces of local history in her basement. Call the Parks Canada office at (306) 298-2257 or Lise Perrault at (306) 298-2241.

CYPRESS HILLS PROVINCIAL PARK

Cypress Hills, about 192 km (120 miles) northwest of Grasslands via Highways 18 and 21, is one of 31 provincial parks in Saskatchewan. The Indians call the hills hereabouts Mun-a-tuk-gaw, "the beautiful highlands." Left untouched by the last Ice Age, the hills boast a variety of flora and fauna not found elsewhere in the region, including the lodgepole pine that incorrectly gave them their name. Rich in wildlife, the region once was a popular Indian hunting ground, and remains one of the best places in the province to see elk.

▶ **Cypress Hills Four Seasons Resort**, a 36-unit hotel complex alongside Loch Leven on Highway 21 in the eastern portion of the park, has all the amenities essential for a comfortable stay. It also rents out condominiums and cabins, the only other non-campground accommodations in the park.

The western portion of the park is connected to the eastern portion by a narrow, winding, and sometimes dirt road known locally as the "gap." The **Conglomerate Cliffs** here offer a commanding view of the prairies below. Just beyond the southern boundary of the provincial park is **Fort Walsh National Historic Park**, where an early NWMP post and Farwell's Trading Post have been restored. Note, however, that during and just after a heavy rain the gap road is impassable, requiring a roundabout trip via Highways 21 and 271 through the town of Maple Creek to reach the overlook.

At Cypress, as at all the province's major parks, it is

essential to book ahead, especially during the summer months, when the parks become popular destinations for visitors and locals alike. Weekend stays in particular should be booked as far in advance as possible. In terms of setting and quality of accommodations, hotels in the parks are superior to those in nearby communities. On the average, expect to pay about $50 for one night's stay; cabins, on the other hand, vary greatly in price, depending on how modern they are.

Farm Vacations

Another option is to stay with one of the local farm families who have opened up their homes to visitors. Some operate like bed and breakfasts, offering visitors a chance to get a good old-fashioned farm-cooked meal. Others give their guests the opportunity to enjoy the peace and quiet of the countryside or to participate in activities such as horseback riding, hiking, and bird-watching. Both types offer visitors a chance to learn about the province's people and their way of life, as well as to experience rural hospitality at its finest. These farms are a great place to find out more about the things you've seen along the road and had questions about, and they also provide an opportunity to swap a story or two. Accommodations are usually shared with the home-owner and can be quite basic, with limited privacy. And, of course, arrangements must be made in advance. For a free guide to these farms, call Tourism Saskatchewan (see their phone number above) or write to Beatrice Magee, President, Saskatchewan Country Vacations and Bed and Breakfast Association, P.O. Box 654, Gull Lake, Sask., S0N 1A0; Tel: (306) 672-3970; Fax: (306) 672-3656. Although rates vary, most will run $35–$45 per night.

THE NORTH

Canoeing

The great rivalry among fur traders stimulated competitive exploration and the establishment of many fur-trading posts from the South Saskatchewan River north. Many of these posts survived to develop into modern-day communities. Others have vanished into the woods from which they came.

The early voyageur routes are still in use. Now, however, the canoeists who ply their waters come for a different reason: some for the adventure and excitement of white water and wilderness; others for the recreation and relaxation that northern Saskatchewan's tranquil beauty provides.

The province has documented more than 50 canoe routes, with several rivers ranking among Canada's best canoeing waters. These include the mighty Churchill River, which traces a meandering route from its headwaters at Peter Pond and Churchill lakes near the Alberta border across the province and into Manitoba, eventually emptying into Hudson Bay; and the Clearwater River, which flows from Lloyd Lake in the northwest to its confluence with the Mackenzie River in Alberta.

The **Churchill River**, as it crosses Saskatchewan, is actually a series of elongated lakes connected by powerful rapids and waterfalls. Its shoreline and island mazes are a juxtaposition of rock knobs and ridges, boreal forest and muskeg. The relatively inexperienced should stick to that portion of the river that passes through **Lac La Ronge Provincial Park**. The **Clearwater River**, a more typical river trip, is best left to seasoned canoeists with wilderness experience. Along both, prehistoric pictographs can be found on rock outcrops, offering a mute record of earlier travellers who used these same waterways. Travel on both routes is at your own risk—and there are no McDonald's along the way. A reputable canoe outfitter will be able to help with all your equipment needs as well as set you up with an experienced guide. (The two listed below also offer canoe clinics for beginners.) For further information, contact Cliff Speers at **Canoeski Discovery Company** (which also offers guided cross-country ski trips and instruction in winter), 1618 9th Avenue North, Saskatoon, Sask. S7K 3A1, Tel: (306) 653-5693; or Rick Driediger at **Horizons Unlimited/Churchill River Canoe Outfitters**, P.O. Box 1110, La Ronge, Sask. S0J 1L0, Tel: (306) 635-4420. Horizons Unlimited also offers guided tours, as well as trips for advanced canoeists and those who wish to try whitewater canoeing.

Fishing Lodges

While canoeing in the region offers spectacular scenery, challenging whitewater, and almost unimaginable solitude, freshwater fishing is northern Saskatchewan's premier attraction, with anglers from across North America heading here each summer to test their skills against trophy-size northern pike, walleye, lake trout, and Arctic grayling. There are close to 250 fly-in and drive-in camps catering to anglers (as well as moose and black-bear hunters) in Saskatchewan, with **La Ronge**, in the north-central region of the province, the most popular gateway to this lake-studded wilderness.

Accommodations run the gamut from luxurious (by wilderness standards) lodges to basic outpost cabins. For a stay of a week or more, most visitors will be happiest with a lodge that offers all the comforts of home, regardless of expense. Located on an island in Saskatchewan's far north, ► **Hatchet Lake Lodge** offers 20 modern, fully equipped cabins, a five-star reputation for quality service, and trophy-size northern pike and lake trout. The lodge also provides direct charter air service to and from Minneapolis, Minnesota, making for easy access from the States.

Like Hatchet Lake Lodge, ► **Camp Grayling**, on Black Lake, is one of a number of Saskatchewan lodges that provides its guests with the opportunity to pull off the "Canadian Grand Slam"—that is, successfully landing five species of game fish at one location. As its name suggests, Camp Grayling offers some of the best grayling fishing in the province. And you don't have to go far to find these majestic sailfish of the north: One of the best spots is barely 200 yards downstream from the camp on the Fond du Lac River, above Elizabeth Falls. The 11 modern cabin units at Grayling's base camp can accommodate up to 20 guests, and Grayling's also rents canoes and provides fly-out service for outdoors enthusiasts interested in canoeing the rugged Fond du Lac River.

The ► **Beyond La Ronge Lodge** on the Churchill River, just north of Lac La Ronge Provincial Park, offers ten modern cabins and a magnificent setting between Robertson Falls and Twin Falls. Here, below the rivers myriad rapids, tasty walleye are caught almost as fast as you can get your line in the water. Quiet bays on the river also yield sizable northern pike. It's the majestic scenery of this section of the Churchill, however, that is the lodge's prime attraction, with visitors quickly realizing that a northern fishing trip isn't just about fishing.

To the southeast, the ► **Northern Lights Lodge**, a drive-in lodge on the southeast arm of Deschambault Lake off Route 106, is one of the few lodges in the north country that is wheelchair-accessible. Blinded in a hunting accident, owner Ted Ohlsen has a first-hand appreciation for the special needs of the disabled: The six modern two-bedroom cabins can accommodate up to 36 people, and a full range of facilities opens up the world of sportsfishing to people who might otherwise never have given it a thought.

No matter where in the northern part of the province anglers end up, they will catch fish—especially when accompanied by an experienced native guide (provided at most lodges). At ease with the land, many of these guides still make their living hunting, fishing, and trapping, and most seem to have a sixth sense when it comes to finding the best fishing spots. (Either that or they tell one another where the fish are biting.) For information on lodges call the Saskatchewan Outfitters Association "Fishing Line" at (306) 763-5434, or write for Saskatchewan Tourism's *Outdoor Adventure Guide,* Tourism Saskatchewan, 1919 Saskatchewan Drive, Regina, Sask. S4P 3V7; Tel: (800) 667-7191.

PRINCE ALBERT NATIONAL PARK

The town of **Prince Albert,** about 144 km (90 miles) northeast of Saskatoon, is the gateway to the northern half of Saskatchewan. A short distance north of the city via the CanAm Highway (Highway 2) lies Prince Albert National Park, perhaps the province's prettiest preserve, located in an area of transition between parkland and boreal forest. Wildlife in the park reflects the changing vegetation. Moose, wolves, and caribou populate the northern forests; elk, deer, and badgers inhabit the aspen-dotted parkland; and bison roam freely in the park's southwest corner.

Waskesiu, a small resort town inside the eastern boundary of the park, offers a variety of recreational services along with plenty of quality accommodations to choose from. Semi-modern cabins, hotels and motels, and condominium-style suites are all available. The immediate area also boasts a popular beach (one of several in the park), a golf course, and fully serviced campsites. (More primitive campsites are available in outlying areas.)

▶ **Waskesiu Lake Lodge** and the ▶ **Hawood Inn** both offer comfortable one- and two-bedroom suites. The Hawood's suites have fireplaces, while those at the Lake Lodge have balconies and gas barbecues. For lunch or dinner, try the golf-course clubhouse or the dining room at the Hawood Inn.

Many visitors to Prince Albert National Park make the long hike in to a small log cabin deep in the backwoods on the shores of Ajawan Lake. It was here that **Grey Owl**—a trapper turned conservationist—lived, worked, wrote his popular books, and was finally buried. In the 1930s the colorful naturalist was heralded as Canada's, if not the world's, leading spokesman for wilderness preservation. His image was tarnished somewhat when, upon his death, it was discovered he was not the son of an Apache mother and Scots father who had served as a scout in the U.S. Indian wars, as he claimed, but rather Archibald Stansfield Belaney, a white man born in Hastings, England. Despite this revelation, Grey Owl remains a folk hero in the eyes of many and will long be remembered for his message: "Remember you belong to nature, not it to you."

GETTING AROUND

By Plane. Saskatchewan's two major airports are located in Saskatoon and Regina. Both cities are served by the country's two major domestic carriers, Canadian Airlines International and Air Canada, as well as a regional carrier, Time Air. In Canada, flights to Saskatchewan depart daily from Halifax, Ottawa, Montreal, Toronto, and Winnipeg to the east, and Vancouver, Calgary, and Edmonton to the west. In the United States, direct daily connections can be made through Minneapolis to Regina and Saskatoon as well as to provincial points north. A number of car-rental companies operate out of the province's major airports.

By Rail and Bus. VIA Rail operates between Winnipeg and Edmonton through Saskatoon. Greyhound Bus Lines operates routes along the Yellowhead (connecting Saskatoon with Winnipeg and Edmonton) and Trans-Canada (connecting Regina with Winnipeg and Calgary) highways.

By Car. The Trans-Canada Highway (Highway 1) and the Yellowhead (Highway 16) are the province's principal east–west corridors. Other, less direct routes offering a change of scenery include the Red Coat Trail (Highway 13) in the south and the Northern Woods and Water Route (Highway 55), which cuts across the center of the province. North–south travellers can follow the CanAm International Highway—alternately, from the North Dakota border, Highways 35, 39, 6, 3, 2, and 102—to La Ronge. When completed, this route will eventually connect with El Paso, Texas.

Provincial information centers are located along the Yellowhead and Trans-Canada highways at entry points into the province as well as at North Portal along the North Dakota/Saskatchewan border. The province also operates a toll-free travel inquiry service. Call Tourism Saskatchewan: from Regina, (306) 787-2300; from the U.S. and Canada, (800) 667-7191. The address is 1919 Saskatchewan Drive, Regina, Sask. S4P 3V7.

Most visitors to Saskatchewan come in June, July, and August, when temperatures typically are in the mid-70°s F. May and September can also be quite pleasant. The climate is quite dry in summer and winter and sunny skies generally prevail. Fishing season opens in late May and hunting seasons for waterfowl, upland game birds, and big game (with the exception of a spring bear season) run from September through December, depending on the species and zone. Fall colors generally appear in early September and winter snows first arrive in early November. Winters in Saskatchewan can get cold, with temperatures occasionally plunging to −40° F in January and February.

ACCOMMODATIONS REFERENCE

The rates given below are projections *for peak seasons during the 1994 calendar year; at other times of the year they* may *be considerably less. Unless otherwise indicated, rates are based on double rooms, double occupancy; provincial and federal taxes are included in all rates. As rates are subject to change, always double-check before booking.*

▶ **Banbury House Inn.** 104 Front Street, **Wolseley**, Sask. S0G 5H0. Tel: (306) 698-2239 or 2801. $58–$70.

▶ **Beyond La Ronge Lodge.** 270 A. E. Adams Crescent, Saskatoon, Sask. S7K 5M9. Tel: (306) 242-3294; in summer, (306) mobile operator JK3-2064 via La Ronge. $1,320 (four days, departure from La Ronge).

▶ **Camp Grayling.** General Delivery, **Stony Rapids**, Sask. S0J 2R0. Tel: (306) 249-2655; in summer, (306) 284-2178; Fax: (306) 439-2178. $1,995 (four days, departure from Stony Rapids).

▶ **Chelton Inn.** 1907 11th Avenue, **Regina**, Sask. S4P 0J2. Tel: (306) 569-4600; Fax: (306) 569-3531; in the U.S. and Canada, Tel: (800) 667-9922. $87–$109.

▶ **Cypress Hills Four Seasons Resort.** P.O. Box 1480, Cypress Hills Provincial Park, **Maple Creek**, Sask. S0N 1N0. Tel: (306) 662-4477; Fax: (306) 662-3238. $74 (hotel); $64–$77 (cabins); $97 (condos).

▶ **Delta Bessborough.** 601 Spadina Crescent East, **Saskatoon**, Sask. S7K 3G8. Tel: (306) 244-5521; Fax: (306) 665-7262; in the U.S. and Canada, Tel: (800) 268-1133. $174.

▶ **Delta Regina.** 1818 Victoria Avenue, **Regina**, Sask. S4P 0R1. Tel: (306) 569-1666; Fax: (306) 525-3550; in the U.S. and Canada, Tel: (800) 268-1133. $104; $225–$320 (suites).

▶ **Hatchet Lake Lodge.** P.O. Box 1852, **Maple Creek**, Sask. S0N 1N0. Tel: (306) 662-2535; in summer, (306) 633-2132; in the U.S., Tel: (800) 661-9183. $2,400 (four days, departure from Minneapolis).

▶ **Hawood Inn.** P.O. Box 188, **Waskesiu Lake**, Sask. S0J 2Y0. Tel: (306) 663-5911; Fax: (306) 663-5219. $102–$160.

▶ **Holiday Inn Saskatoon.** 90 22nd Street East, **Saskatoon**, Sask. S7K 3X6. Tel: (306) 244-2311; Fax: (306) 664-2234; in the U.S. and Canada, Tel: (800) 465-4329. $108–$126.

▶ **Hotel Saskatchewan.** 2125 Victoria Avenue, **Regina**, Sask. S4P 0S3. Tel: (306) 522-7691; Fax: (306) 522-8988; in the U.S. and Canada, Tel: (800) 667-5828. $157.

▶ **Kenosee Inn.** P.O. Box 70, Moose Mountain Provincial Park, **Kenosee Lake**, Sask. S0C 2S0. Tel: (306) 577-2099; Fax: (306) 577-2465. $80.

▶ **Landmark Inn.** 4150 Albert Street South, **Regina**, Sask.

S4S 3R8. Tel: (306) 586-5363; Fax: (306) 586-0901; in Saskatchewan, Tel: (800) 667-9811; elsewhere in Canada, (800) 667-8191. $68.

▶ **Manitou Springs Hotel.** P.O. Box 610, **Manitou Beach,** Sask. S0K 4T0. Tel: (306) 946-2233; Fax: (306) 946-2554. $66.

▶ **Northern Lights Lodge.** P.O. Box 471, **Weyburn,** Sask. S4H 2K3. Tel: (306) 842-1440; Fax: (306) 465-2883. $65; boat rentals, guides extra.

▶ **Ramada Renaissance.** 1919 Saskatchewan Drive, **Regina,** Sask. S4P 4H2. Tel: (306) 525-5255; Fax: (306) 781-7188; in the U.S., Tel: (800) 228-9898; in Canada, (800) 854-7854. $87–$122.

▶ **Ramada Renaissance.** 405 20th Street East, **Saskatoon,** Sask. S7K 6X6. Tel: (306) 665-3322; Fax: (306) 665-5531; in the U.S., Tel: (800) 228-9898; in Canada, (800) 854-7854. $111.

▶ **Regina Inn.** 1975 Broad Street (corner of Victoria Avenue), **Regina,** Sask. S4P 1Y2. Tel: (306) 525-6767; Fax: (306) 525-3630; in Canada, Tel: (800) 667-8162. $92–$139.

▶ **Regina Travelodge.** 4177 Albert Street, **Regina,** Sask. S4S 3R6. Tel: (306) 586-3443; Fax: (306) 586-9311; in the U.S. and Canada, Tel: (800) 255-3050. $67.

▶ **Relax Inn.** 106 Circle Drive West, **Saskatoon,** Sask. S7L 4L6. Tel: (306) 242-8881; Fax: (306) 665-7378; in the U.S. and Canada, Tel: (800) 667-3529. $57.

▶ **Saskatoon Inn.** 2002 Airport Drive, **Saskatoon,** Sask. S7L 6M4. Tel: (306) 242-1440; Fax: (306) 244-2779; in Canada, Tel: (800) 667-8789. $90.

▶ **Sheraton Cavalier.** 612 Spadina Crescent East, **Saskatoon,** Sask. S7K 3G9. Tel: (306) 652-6770; Fax: (306) 244-1739; in the U.S. and Canada, Tel: (800) 325-3535. $118–$130.

▶ **Waskesiu Lake Lodge.** P.O. Box 56, Prince Albert National Park, **Waskesiu Lake,** Sask. S0J 2Y0. Tel: (306) 663-5975; Fax: (306) 663-5900. $100.

ALBERTA

By Roberta Walker

Roberta Walker founded her own magazine for adventurous travellers, Real Travel. *During her 12 years as a resident of Alberta, she walked, fished, and skied in most parts of the province.*

Because Alberta is barely a century old, its history is meager and its cities new; the traditions of the frontier still flourish here. The Rocky Mountains and Calgary's annual rodeo—the Stampede—are the main attractions for visitors wanting to explore the province's abundant wilderness or relive its Wild West days.

The mountain parks provide easy access to an extraordinary expanse of uninhabited wilderness. Horse-packing trips, climbing, canoeing, and hiking draw visitors to the mountains in the summer, while winter snows lure the skiers. And though the mountains are far from civilized in the urban sense, they have been hosting tourists since the 1890s. Lodgings range from turn-of-the-century resorts that resemble castles more than hotels to rustic cabins.

Most visitors enter and leave by air from Calgary or Edmonton, Alberta's capital city. Because the province's main attractions are huddled in its southwest corner, Calgary, affectionately known as Cowtown, is the most convenient gateway for visitors from the U.S. Two attractions outside the city—the Tyrrell Museum of Palaeontology in Drumheller and the Head-Smashed-In Buffalo Jump near Fort Macleod—are worth separate day trips. Both recently joined Machu Picchu and the Parthenon, among others, as UNESCO World Heritage sites.

The northern half of the province, with Edmonton as its gateway, attracts hardy travellers to its two large wilderness

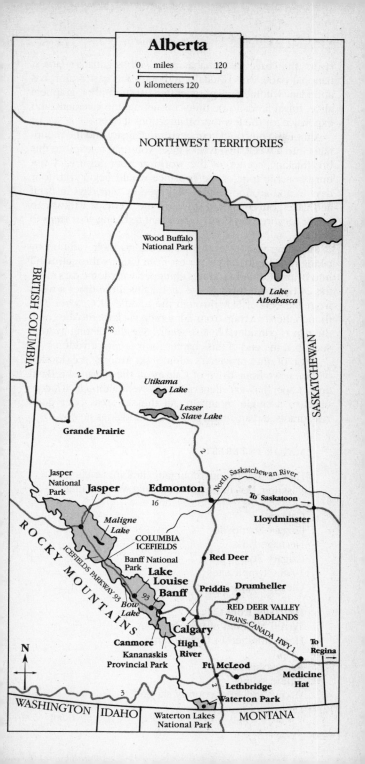

Alberta

0 miles 120

0 kilometers 120

NORTHWEST TERRITORIES

BRITISH COLUMBIA

SASKATCHEWAN

Wood Buffalo
National Park

*Lake
Athabasca*

35

2

*Utikama
Lake*

*Lesser
Slave Lake*

Grande Prairie

Jasper
National
Park

Jasper

2

Edmonton

North Saskatchewan River

To Saskatoon

16

Lloydminster

*Maligne
Lake*

COLUMBIA
ICEFIELDS

ROCKY MOUNTAINS

ICEFIELDS PARKWAY 93

Banff National
Park

Red Deer

**Lake
Louise**

93

Priddis

Drumheller

Banff

RED DEER VALLEY
BADLANDS

*Bow
Lake*

Calgary

TRANS-CANADA HWY 1

*To
Regina*

N

Canmore

Kananaskis
Provincial Park

**High
River**

Ft. McLeod

**Medicine
Hat**

3

2

Lethbridge

WASHINGTON   IDAHO

Waterton Park

Waterton Lakes
National Park

MONTANA

rivers, the Peace and Athabasca, as well as Canada's largest national park: Wood Buffalo. Although this vast region has abundant wildlife for sports enthusiasts and photographers alike, travel tends to be time-consuming, inconvenient, and expensive for the few tourist attractions it offers.

Although you could cram a visit to Calgary and the mountains into a week, two weeks gives you time to explore this breathtaking corner of the world at your leisure. A not unreasonable tour of the province would begin with four days in and around Calgary, followed by four days in Banff and Lake Louise, a day's drive up the Icefields Parkway to Jasper for three days, and a day spent retracing your steps to Calgary.

First-time visitors may want to extend their vacation by taking the scenic train trip west from Calgary through Banff into British Columbia. Trains equipped with dome cars make the 24-hour run through the mountains three times a week from the end of May through the middle of October. (Although there's a train from Edmonton via Jasper to the coast, the trip is considerably less scenic. See the Getting Around section at the end of this chapter for more information.)

Most of the province's alpine ski resorts are located within a two-hour drive of Calgary in the Kananaskis/Banff area. Jasper has excellent skiing as well, although it's confined to a single mountain. All the ski areas offer good restaurants and an ample selection of lodgings nearby.

MAJOR INTEREST

Hiking, trail riding, mountain climbing, cycling, skiing, hot-air ballooning, whitewater rafting

Calgary
Calgary Stampede
Heritage Park
Calgary Zoo
1988 Olympic sites
Glenbow Museum

Day Trips from Calgary
Tyrrell Museum of Palaeontology
Head-Smashed-In Buffalo Jump

Kananaskis Country
Alpine skiing
Hiking and cross-country ski trails
Helicopter tours

Banff
Cave and Basin Centennial Centre
Banff Springs Hotel
Sulphur Mountain Gondola
Museums and galleries

Lake Louise
Tea houses
Moraine Lake
Hiking

Jasper
Maligne Lake

Edmonton
Festivals
Historic homes and museums
Old Strathcona district
Muttart Conservatory
West Edmonton Mall

In Alberta some of the plainest scenery in the world presses against some of the most spectacular; very recent human history is neighbor to the ancient relics of the dinosaur age; and a modern city overlooks the stupendous wilderness of the Rocky Mountains. This combination of wild scenery, prehistoric remains, and solitude has drawn visitors since the infancy of modern tourism.

The province's uninhabited mountain wilderness, encompassing an area half the size of Denmark, isn't the least bit dented by the three million visitors a year who pass through it. And though the whole Rockies region is now prime bus-excursion territory for tourists from North America, Germany, and Japan, you can still hike for hours without seeing another soul.

Think of Alberta as an elongated rectangle trimmed by a spine of huge, rocky mountains along its southwestern quarter, the rest filled with grassland and a few people. By European standards, the population is sparse; Alberta could fit six Englands inside its provincial boundaries but accommodates barely one twenty-fifth England's population.

Despite having half a million inhabitants each, Calgary and Edmonton are uncongested cities with the flavor of big small towns—and culturally one-dimensional, with the exception of their Chinatowns. The Chinese provided much of the labor for the construction of the transcontinental railroad in the 1880s, then settled in the region. With 93 reserves and 41 bands accounting for almost 5 percent of the province's population, the other cultural group that distinguishes Alberta is its aboriginal people.

Two centuries ago the prairies in the southeastern quarter of the province were the domain of the buffalo, the Plains Indians, and the fur traders. A hundred years later the demise of the buffalo cleared the way for cattle ranching on a vast scale, while the Canadian Pacific Railway's transcontinental line opened Calgary as a shipping center and the Rocky Mountains as a vacation retreat for wealthy Europeans. Banff, located in the midst of the Rockies, became Canada's first national park in 1885; after the Canadian Pacific Railway (CPR) built the castle-like Banff Springs Hotel in 1887 and the Chateau Lake Louise in 1891, the mountains were open for business.

Without the corporate push of the CPR, tourism in the Rockies wouldn't have charm or history. In 1886 Canadian Pacific executives were searching for a way to pay for their recently completed railroad. Aware of the sudden popularity of "wilderness" trips to Switzerland, the CPR's general manager decided to capitalize on Alberta's mountain splendors by marketing them as a Swiss experience in the New World. Swiss guides were soon imported, and hotels were designed to civilize the wilds to European standards.

From the 1880s until the Roaring Twenties, dozens of new resorts throughout the region played host to the Victorian adventurers who spent good money to climb with Swiss guides, ride trails with cowboys, or simply soak up the mountain air. Things haven't changed much. The combination of comfort, accessibility, and rugged scenery that charmed the 19th-century visitor still draws people to Alberta today.

SOUTHERN ALBERTA

Although most visitors to the province come to see the mountains, there are a couple of equally outstanding attractions in Calgary and southern Alberta. The Calgary Stampede is one of the premier events on North America's rodeo circuit, while the dinosaur park and museum and buffalo jump are exceptional archaeological sites.

Calgary

Though Calgary pushes its cow-town image, visitors will see little of the ranch influence. Instead, they are met by an ultramodern skyline, good restaurants and theater, and a sophisticated oil business that left ranching in the dust as the region's top money-maker back in the 1950s.

Calgary got its name from the Gaelic word for "clear running water," which aptly described the site of Fort Calgary, Canada's first North West Mounted Police outpost, built on the banks of the Bow River in 1875. The only building extant from those days is **Deane House**, built in 1896 by Captain R.B. Deane, commanding officer of the North West Mounted Police, and today situated on the eastern outskirts of the city at the corner of 8th Avenue and 6th Street S.E. The building has been converted into a small museum and tea house serving lunch and high tea. The food is excellent, and in summer the salad greens are freshly picked from the garden on the grounds.

The city itself rises out of flat, bald prairie, with the river cutting through the downtown area the only relief from an otherwise dull landscape. The completion of the Canadian Pacific Railway's transcontinental line through Calgary in 1886 breathed new life into the frontier town. Early Calgary was so dominated by the CPR, in fact, that until 1904 the city streets bore the names of CPR executives. Good ranching and good transport later made Calgary the hub of the Canadian meat business. Alberta beef still arouses provincial pride, and to show it off local restaurants offer 550-gram steaks. **Hy's** restaurant (Tel: 403/263-2222) on 4th Avenue S.W. draws a business lunch crowd seeking the best steaks in town. Although the food is western, country music and jeans are frowned upon in this restaurant, which leans to candlelight and red velvet.

The Stampede

In 1912 a sag in the ranching business prompted four local cattlemen to finance promoter Guy Weadlick in his Wild West show, the Stampede. Today the **Calgary Stampede** draws a million spectators, reviving Calgary's Wild West traditions for ten days each July. Horses appear downtown, and western dress and square dancing take over city street corners. Every shop sports western decor, and the city's restaurants and bars are jammed with merrymakers. The throngs of people are part of the fun, but be forewarned: Hotels will be full, and you may have to wait for an hour or two to get into a bar with live country-and-western music.

Stampede Park, located a few blocks south of downtown, is the principal venue for festivities and the rodeo events. Tickets for each afternoon's rodeo (including bull riding, bucking bronc riding, and calf roping) may be purchased in advance, but you can usually pick up last-minute seats at the

Grand Stand box office located on the grounds. Even if you miss the rodeo, a trip to the grounds is an experience in itself: There are hundreds of displays, an amusement park, an Indian village with tepees and ceremonial dancing, and a shootout scene staged daily.

Corners of genuine cowboy culture persist beyond the Stampede; these include the **Riley & McCormick** western-wear shops in the 8th Avenue Mall and at the airport. Riley & McCormick have clothed cowboys since the turn of the century, and carry the essentials as well as items such as holster diaper pins for western babies.

Heritage Park and the Calgary Zoo

Located off 14th Street and Heritage Drive S.W., Heritage Park is an authentic re-creation of a pre-1915 prairie railroad town. More than 100 buildings, including the homes of famous Calgarians, have been moved to the park from sites throughout the province and then restored. These include furnished homes, a newspaper office, and a church; visitors can sample goodies from the bakery, eat at the Wainwright Hotel, or ride on the steam engine.

The Calgary Zoo, the second largest in the country, is located along the Bow River within the city limits. If you're up for a hike, you can get there in an hour by following a path along the river; otherwise, take the Light Rail Transit train east, heading for Whitehorn. The zoo contains a Prehistoric Park, where life-size replicas of the dinosaurs found in Alberta are displayed in their natural habitat.

Olympic Park

In the winter, **Canada Olympic Park** offers beginners downhill skiing within the city limits. Advanced skiers will be bored unless they take a ride on the bobsled run, which was built for the 1988 Winter Olympics. From top to bottom the run takes a minute and costs $100—an expensive minute, but survivors report the terror is worth it. The chicken start is lower and cheaper; only half the terror for half the price. Located on the western edge of town, the park was the site of the ski-jumping, bobsled, and luge events for the Olympics. Site tours are given; Tel: (403) 286-2632.

DOWNTOWN CALGARY

The ▶ **Palliser Hotel**, on 9th Avenue S.W., was Calgary's first skyscraper when it was completed in 1912, and remains the only hotel in the city with any character. Located in the heart of downtown, it is the lodging choice for the prime minister and the royal family, as well as the traditional haunt of the ranching elite. Named after Captain John Palliser, who mapped the province for the Royal Geographic Society, the Palliser was one of four hotels built by the CPR to break up the journey for rail passengers travelling to the Rockies. (As dining cars were not a feature of early rail travel, these hotels gave guests a place to rest and eat amid the trappings of the era.) The **Rimrock** dining room may be wallpapered with leather murals reflecting western life, but the atmosphere is elegant and the food first-rate. Menu favorites include the clam chowder and crusty French bread, made in the hotel's original ovens. The hotel's public areas recently have been restored to their turn-of-the-century grandeur, and many of the rooms have been refurbished. Try to get a room on the ninth or eleventh floor on the west side; for a slight difference in price you'll be treated to superb service and gorgeous rooms with a view of the mountains.

The ▶ **Westin Hotel Calgary**, a large, newly renovated establishment on 4th Avenue, offers the comfortable sameness of any modern first-class hotel. It is home to many visiting businesspeople and conventioneers, and contains the **Owl's Nest** (Tel: 403/267-2823), an outstanding formal dining room.

A short walk from the Westin, or from the Palliser for that matter, is the wonderful food of Chinatown (on Centre Street between 4th and 2nd avenues S.W.). If you go for brunch early on a Sunday morning at the **Silver Dragon** you might even think you're in China, owing to the scarcity of Westerners.

The **1886 Café**, a downtown breakfast spot popular with those who can find it (334 Riverfront Avenue S.W. at Third Street), is housed in a homely little wooden building with an old sign saying Eau Clair and Bow River Lumber Co. It is indeed the former home of that outfit, and was built in 1886. Don't expect to find croissants at this place; the menu is strictly eggs, juice, whole-wheat toast, and award-winning coffee, with a few oddities, including a peaches-and-cottage-cheese omelet. Decorated with an eclectic assortment of antiques, the building is a café upstairs and a museum of Calgary history downstairs. Open for breakfast and lunch only.

Right behind the café is Prince's Island Park, a popular location for many outdoor festivals and fairs. You can pick up the extensive Bow River bicycling and walking path nearby.

East of the Palliser is the Glenbow Museum, and in the next block is the Calgary Centre for the Performing Arts. The **Glenbow Museum** has an excellent permanent collection of western Canadian art and artifacts, as well as realistic displays tracing western Canadian life from the fur trade to the oil boom. The **Calgary Centre for the Performing Arts** has two theaters and a concert hall in which a variety of mainstream and offbeat musical and dramatic entertainment is staged.

Theater buffs should try the **Lunchbox Theatre**. Buried in the Bow Valley Square office tower on 5th Avenue and 1st Street S.W., this casual venue fills with businesspeople from 12:10 to 12:50. The Lunchbox, as the name implies, encourages you to eat during its abbreviated performances of light musicals, mysteries, and the like. Arrive early; there are no reservations, and the Lunchbox often sells out.

Devonian Gardens is an indoor subtropical garden with fountains and waterfalls. For downtown workers, it is also an oasis among the huge assortment of stores in the Toronto Dominion Square shopping plaza (about two blocks north of the Palliser). Farther down 8th Avenue, the Penny Lane shopping center offers a variety of unusual stores and lunch spots. The two-story **Canterbury's Bookstore** here is reminiscent of a private library in an English manor, with comfortable wing-back chairs, a cappuccino bar, and a backdrop of classical music inviting you to linger over the extensive selection of books. Across the way, Canterbury's sister store, the **French Horn**, specializes in classical, jazz, and New-Age music. Here, too, the atmosphere is part of the appeal, with a fireplace and comfortable antique chairs outfitted with headphones.

If you want to hear live jazz and blues, head for the **King Edward Hotel** in the evening, where the excellent entertainment more than compensates for its run-down decor and dubious location on 9th Avenue East.

For formal dining and some dancing, try **La Caille on the Bow** (Tel: 403/262-5554). The dining room, complete with a huge stone fireplace, resembles a room in an old French castle. Upstairs you can step back a hundred years or so in its lively dance bar (weekends only), which rivals **Orestes**, the neighboring Greek restaurant and lounge, as the most popular dance spot in town for the over-30 crowd.

The best neighborhoods for people-watching, boutique shopping, noshing, and designer coffee are **Kensington** and lower **Mount Royal**. The Kensington area, across the river from downtown in the neighborhood of 10th Street and Kensington Road N.W., is loaded with interesting shopping, from locally designed clothes to Canadian crafts. The **Galleria** on Kensington Road sells a huge variety of crafts by Alberta artisans. The centerpiece of the neighborhood, however, is the Plaza Theatre, featuring offbeat, foreign, and classic films.

One of the best French restaurants in town faces the Plaza Theatre. The small, intimate **Jacques Bistro** (Tel: 403/283-1343) is very much the creation of its owner, who infuses the place with a hospitable, partylike atmosphere. The many regular customers are treated to a lot of fanfare when they enter, the walls are decorated with hundreds of photos of restaurant parties, and the food is deliciously creative.

North on 10th Street is the **Roasterie Rio Gourmet Coffee**, a stand-up coffee bar so popular with locals that its business invariably spills out onto the street in summer. The ever-expanding selection of coffees at this place attracts a trendy clientele of writers, artists, and java aficionados all day long.

Farther west on Kensington Road is the **Kensington Delicafé** (Tel: 403/283-0771), tucked into the tiny Recreation Center mall. This café has a casual atmosphere and terrific home-cooked meals that end with delicious desserts. It's open all day and is visited by a steady flow of regulars. Folk and blues artists entertain here evenings after 9:00 P.M.

Seventeenth Avenue and 8th Street Southwest, just south of downtown, is Calgary's other fun neighborhood, with good restaurants and great shopping. The surrounding streets trim the Mount Royal area, the domain of old money in Calgary, with neighborhood shops catering to the carriage trade. **Mount Royal Village** is a small and exclusive shopping center with unusual gifts and high-quality clothes. Farther west on 17th Avenue is the tiny **Nellie's** (Tel: 403/228-3667), featuring good whole-earth kind of food and great soup.

A Touch of Ginger, 514 17th Avenue S.W. at 5th Street, is a small, elegant Vietnamese restaurant located in a renovated house. It adds gourmet touches to its excellent Vietnamese menu and makes some concessions to western tastes with chocolate fondue supplied by local chocolatier Bernard Callebaut. Tel: (403) 228-9884.

Day Trips from Calgary

The town of Drumheller, only an hour and a half northeast of Calgary, is home to the largest collection of dinosaur skeletons in the world. The **Royal Tyrrell Museum of Palae-ontology** opened in 1986, and contains 30 complete dinosaur skeletons, dozens of displays, and mini-theaters that lead visitors through the evolution of life on earth. Allow yourself a minimum of two hours' viewing time; the museum attracts hordes of visitors in the summer, so you may want to add an additional hour to your schedule then. Drumheller has little to offer after museum hours, so plan to return to Calgary in the evening.

The drive to Drumheller passes through the **Red Deer Valley Badlands**, the great graveyard of the dinosaur age and home of the Hoodoos—spires of rock saved from erosion by a hard sandstone cap. These strange hunks of landscape were feared by local Indians, who believed them to be petrified giants that came to life at night and hurled rocks at intruders.

Another worthwhile day trip takes you south over empty prairie, with inspiring mountain views to the west, to the largest and best-preserved buffalo jump in North America. Whenever possible, the Plains Indians got an edge on the buffalo by stampeding them over a cliff. The cliff, called a buffalo jump, was the centerpiece of the buffalo hunt.

Despite its unappetizing name, **Head-Smashed-In Buffalo Jump** was used for more than 5,600 years by Plains Indians, and was last used for the purpose less than a century ago. (The name describes the unfortunate fate of a young Piegan Blackfoot tribesman who was crushed to death while watching the spectacle some 150 years ago.) The jump is a marvel of hunt engineering. Lanes five miles long channeled buffalo toward a 30-foot cliff, while people stationed along the lanes waved buffalo hides to keep the herd moving. Once the buffalo rushed off the cliff, hunters down below finished them off with spears and arrows. An elaborate interpretive center, opened in 1987, presents a dramatic audiovisual reenactment of the hunt and contains displays of hunt artifacts.

GUEST RANCHES

Calgary's ranching tradition has spawned a number of trail-riding outfits and guest ranches—40, at last count—for people who want a more authentic western experience. ► **Rafter Six Guest Ranch**, located in Seebe on the way to Banff, accommodates guests in a rustic, but far from shabby, three-story log lodge and 11 cabins (four of which are housekeeping units).

Other guest ranches are located south of Calgary in the foothills country more commonly associated with ranching. One such ranch is the ► **Homeplace Guest Ranch** in Priddis, which was homesteaded in the early years of the century and today offers accommodations to just 12 guests in the main ranch house, year-round. Activities here include trail riding, pack trips, hiking, fishing, golfing, sleigh rides, and cross-country skiing in season.

THE ROCKY MOUNTAIN REGION

Winter or summer, the mountains are a playground for outdoor adventures and the pursuit of leisure. Within a two-hour drive of Calgary there are five major ski resorts; championship golf courses in Banff, Jasper, and Kananaskis Country; and hundreds of superb hiking trails that double as cross-country ski trails in winter. (The difficulty of choosing among them is eased by the numerous Travel Alberta information booths staffed by knowledgeable people.)

The wall of craggy peaks is visible as you leave Calgary's western city limits; by the time you reach the parks you're surrounded by rocky summits that enjoy only a couple of snow-free months a year. Every hotel or restaurant in the region is dedicated to the magnificent setting; even gas-station coffee shops are bestowed with great views.

In choosing a time to visit the Rockies, you should consider both the weather and the crowds. The summer months, when the sun sets at about 10:00 P.M., can be beautiful and warm but very crowded. Visiting in late spring or early fall may be a better choice, as the crowds have thinned but the daytime temperatures still feel summery. In winter the scenery is spectacular but many of the services and attractions are closed. Still, if you like snow, winter in the mountains is breathtaking.

WATERTON LAKES NATIONAL PARK

Waterton Lakes lies about three hours south of Calgary by car on the Montana border. (The protected wilderness area is split between the United States and Canada, with the U.S. portion called Glacier National Park.) It is a rugged, remote park offering terrific hiking and cross-country skiing opportunities, as well as a couple of decent accommodations. The name property here is the 82-room ▶ **Prince of Wales Hotel**, a rambling Victorian-style "cottage" plunked down on a bluff overlooking spectacular mountain-ringed Waterton Lake. Built in 1927 by the Great Northern Railroad, it looks from the outside like one of the great CPR hotels. Inside, however, it reveals itself to be a poor cousin of those more luxurious properties. Although the Prince of Wales has its own charm and commands its share of repeat business (especially bus-tour groups), the rooms have not been updated since the 1950s. Instead, you may want to stop by for tea, served every afternoon in the hotel's cavernous lobby (which was built without the benefit of a single nail), before settling in for the evening at the smaller, more rustic ▶ **Kilmorey Lodge**, in the townsite of Waterton, which has its own dining room and a licensed lounge.

KANANASKIS COUNTRY

Located south of the Trans-Canada Highway about an hour west of Calgary, Kananaskis Country encompasses a mixture of recreation areas and formally designated parks, including Peter Lougheed Provincial Park and Bow Valley Provincial Park. Though the least publicized of Alberta's mountain areas, Kananaskis benefited greatly in the early 1980s from the attention of former Premier Lougheed, who poured millions of provincial tax dollars into its recreational facilities. These include more than 140 miles of trails (for hiking and cross-country skiing, depending on the season); a network of paved trails and a specially designed wilderness lodge for the physically challenged; and two ski venues built for the 1988 Winter Olympics: **Nakiska**, the site of the alpine events, and **Canmore**, the venue for the Nordic events.

While there's no actual town in the region, Kananaskis Village, located 26 km (16 miles) south of the Trans-Canada Highway on Highway 40, offers lodgings ranging from the intimate and luxurious ▶ **Hotel Kananaskis** to the family-style ▶ **Kananaskis Inn Best Western**, as well as a number of bars and restaurants. Golfers can test their skills on either of the two 18-hole championship layouts nearby (both designed by Robert Trent Jones, Sr.), and then enjoy a drink or light meal on the clubhouse terrace, which is open to the nongolfing public as well. Even the campsites hereabouts are first class; the **Mount Kidd RV Park** takes reservations (Tel: 403/591-7700), and is equipped with tennis courts and a hot tub.

If you want to see the Rockies from a helicopter, Kananaskis Country is the place to do it—in the national parks choppers are only allowed to fly in for emergencies. Heli-hiking is a nice way to spend the afternoon in remote backcountry—provided you can afford it. Although such outings are not cheap, running anywhere from $75 to $160 per person, they usually deliver their fair share of thrills and incredible mountain scenery. For information and/or reservations, try Canmore Helicopters, Tel: (403) 678-4802; or Canadian Helicopters, Tel: (403) 678-2207.

Banff National Park

An easy hour-and-a-half drive west of Calgary, **Banff** is the only real town in the park and, though small, offers all the amenities of a city, including live theater, museums, numerous restaurants, hotels, and designer shops, all crammed into a five-block strip along Banff Avenue.

The town's location was determined by the discovery of hot sulfur springs in 1887, which led to the creation of a European-type spa. Restoration of the Cave and Basin Spa, now the **Cave and Basin Centennial Centre**, retained the design of the original outdoor pool but improved the facilities.

The ▶ **Banff Springs Hotel**, nestled among huge mountains, was the largest hotel in the world when the CPR opened its doors to the public in 1888. "The Springs," a castlelike structure that dominates the valley, has undergone numerous face-lifts aimed at preserving its somewhat faded elegance over the years. Still, the mezzanine lounge, lined with large picture windows framing the mountains, can entice anyone into having a drink here in the afternoon.

If you have any doubt about the hotel's age, the clanging pipes, irregular heat, and lack of air conditioning will remind you. The rates may be the highest in town and some rooms a bit seedy, but the Old World glamour of this dowager resort makes up for its deficiencies. Its fairy-tale appearance has even earned the hotel a spot on Japanese television as a backdrop for soap operas. The resulting publicity makes it the lodging of choice for the Japanese tour groups that flock to Banff each summer; you'll want to book six months in advance if you plan to visit then.

The Springs is the only true resort in town, with an internationally acclaimed 27-hole golf course, tennis courts, a swimming pool, stables, a variety of restaurants, and the lounge. Wildlife is also plentiful here—the elk have identified the golf course as a tasty grazing spot and can form quite a crowd at dusk. If you can, try the Sunday brunch, which is not only gigantic but superb: eggs Benedict perfectly cooked, smoked salmon, seafood salad, and fresh strawberry sorbet.

The mountains around Banff rank as one of the world's scenic treasures. Visitors who'd like to explore them but aren't up to a lot of strenuous hiking can opt instead for a gondola ride. The **Sulphur Mountain** gondola, located close to town on Mountain Avenue, carries passengers to the Summit Observation Deck and the highest restaurant in Canada. Tel: (403) 762-2523 for information and hours.

DINING IN BANFF

Just because rustic seems to be the prevailing motif in this neck of the woods does not mean Banff is without first-rate restaurants. Located upstairs at the corner of Buffalo Street and Banff Avenue, **Beaujolais** offers elegant French dining amid Banff's mountain majesties (two walls of the restaurant are lined with picutre windows). The menu is large and includes such specialties as fresh mussels, escargot, lobster soup, rack of lamb, and Dover sole, in addition to a well-chosen wine list. Beaujolais is the best restaurant in town, so be prepared to pay accordingly. Reservations advised; Tel: (403) 762-2712.

In recent years a couple of authentic Japanese restaurants have opened in response to the influx of Japanese tourists into the area. While the sushi bar at the Banff Springs Hotel is good, aficionados seem to favor **Suginoya** (Tel: 403/762-4773), downtown on the second floor of the Banff Avenue mall, with its more traditional atmosphere and private *ozashiki* rooms.

If you're looking for something more in keeping with the spirit of the surroundings, head for the **Grizzly House** (Tel: 403/762-4055) at 207 Banff Avenue. The stuffed animal heads and pelts on the walls will have you thinking you've wandered into a mountain guide's cabin; the western theme is carried over to the menu, which offers a couple of fondues in addition to its caribou, buffalo, and rattlesnake specialties.

The bustle of Banff Avenue during the busy summer season may not appeal to everyone. If you'd just as soon avoid it, head over to Tunnel Mountain Road (overlooking town) and the dining room at the ▶ **Buffalo Mountain Lodge** (Tel: 403/762-2400). The rustic wood-beamed decor and huge stone fireplace provide a lovely backdrop for the lodge's Continental menu, featuring hearty soups, homemade bread, and creative regional dishes like venison in a port wine sauce. The lodge's 86 bungalow and chalet units, many with fireplaces and some with kitchenettes or fully equipped kitchens, are also delightful.

SHOPPING AND NIGHTLIFE

Stores downtown sell everything from tee-shirts to fine jewelry and furs, with big-names designer labels like Ralph Lauren and Bree well represented. The **Quest Gallery**, 105 Banff Avenue, has a large and interesting selection of Canadian handicrafts, including sculpture, jewelry, ceramics, and fine-art prints. You'll find the best selection of native artifacts and handicrafts at the **Banff Trading Post**, housed in a turn-of-the-century log building at the corner of Birch Street and Cave Avenue. Worthwhile purchases here include West Coast Indian sweaters, porcupine quill baskets, peace pipes, hand-sewn moccasins, and a variety of bead-work items. For an unusual selection of hard-to-find books on Banff and the Rockies, visit the **Banff Book and Art Den**, 130 Banff Avenue.

There are, in addition, many bars and restaurants on Banff Avenue. The two most popular watering holes are the English pub–style **Rose and Crown** and the **Barbary Coast**. For dancing, **Silver City** is a popular country-and-western bar. The other two good night spots are located in the Banff

Springs Hotel—a large disco bar that's popular with all ages, and the **Rob Roy Dining Room**, which features dancing to big-band music during the summer months.

CULTURAL ACTIVITIES

Despite its outdoorsy bent, Banff has a spirited cultural life. The **Banff Centre** on St. Julien Road has been the focal point for much of it ever since its founding in 1933. Today musicians as well as dance and theater companies from around the world perform here during the summer-long **Banff Festival of the Arts**. For information on upcoming events, contact the box office at (403) 762-6300. In addition to its theaters, the Centre's **Walter Phillips Gallery** houses a permament collection of contemporary art, and is the venue for changing monthly exhibitions as well; Tel: (403) 762-6281 for a schedule of upcoming events. Open noon to 5:00 P.M., Tuesday through Sunday, year-round, and on Mondays and until 8:00 P.M. Fridays and Saturdays during the summer.

For a small town, Banff boasts a surprising number of good museums. The **Luxton Museum**, 1 Birch Avenue, is devoted to the arts and daily lives of the native peoples indigenous to the northern plains and Canadian Rockies. Open daily year-round, 9:00 A.M. to 5:00 P.M., and until 6:00 P.M. during the summer.

The **Banff Park Museum**, 93 Banff Avenue, was created in 1903 for the edification of Edwardian adventurers not particularly keen on exposing themselves to danger or discomfort. Today it's a designated historic site, and offers a fine collection of wildlife specimens and displays in old-style glass cases. Open daily 10:00 A.M. to 6:00 P.M.

The **Whyte Museum of the Canadian Rockies**, 111 Bear Street, houses three galleries, a heritage collection and archives, and six historic homes on its wooded grounds beside the Bow River. The art exhibitions change monthly, and afternoon tea is served every weekday between 2:30 and 4:30 P.M. Tours of Banff's heritage homes are given on weekends; for information, Tel: (403) 762-2291.

Lake Louise

Although Lake Louise, located a half-hour's drive north and west of Banff, has no town to speak of, it does offer more spectacular scenery and more interesting accommodations than Banff. A small shopping center and a handful of ordinary restaurants and hotels constitute the village of Lake Louise. The main attraction is the lake itself, originally named Emerald because of its brilliant color, but later re-named Louise after Queen Victoria's daughter.

STAYING IN LAKE LOUISE

The palatial ► **Chateau Lake Louise** sits at one end of the lake facing the impressive Victoria Glacier at the opposite end. The hotel, situated at an altitude of 4,000 feet, was built in 1913 and was completely renovated in 1989 with a Bavarian motif. Now bigger and better than ever, the hotel is characterized by beautiful rooms, magnificent public areas, and an elegant atmosphere throughout. With a couple of bars and six restaurants offering everything from coffee-shop fare to pricey Continental cuisine; a mini-mall with a dozen boutiques; and activities ranging from horseback riding to dog-sledding, the Chateau Lake Louise is a self-contained universe plunked down amidst some of the most gorgeous scenery on the planet.

Many of the hotels, camps, lodges, and tea houses in the area were built by the CPR and are still in use, albeit accessible primarily by foot, horseback, or on skis. Within a two-hour walk of the hotel are the tea houses built in 1923 at **Lake Agnes** and the **Plain of the Six Glaciers**. Hikers who make the short but steep walk to the former will be treated to bread, apple crisp, and tea, all made on wood-burning stoves. The log cabin on the shore of the lake starred in the winter scenes of the film version of *Dr. Zhivago*. Heartier guests can opt for the 14½-kilometer (9-mile) hike to ► **Skoki Lodge**, which offers wonderful goosedown quilts to snuggle under (book through the Chateau Lake Louise).

► **Deer Lodge**, located within sight of the Chateau Lake Louise, was built as a trading post in 1923. Renovations have preserved its rustic ambience and huge stone fire-places, while the rooms have been upgraded to resemble bedrooms in a home rather than a hotel. (Be sure to ask for one in the new section, as not all rooms have been upgraded; the difference in price is worth it.) The lodge's dining room (Tel: 403/522-2182) serves excellent Continental cuisine, and outdoes its neighbor, the Chateau, in both food and atmosphere.

Moraine Lake and the Valley of the Ten Peaks

One of the region's most photogenic spots, Moraine Lake and the Valley of the Ten Peaks, is located 11 km (7 miles) east of the Lake Louise access road. The tea house here was built in 1906, and today is called the ► **Moraine Lake Lodge**. Open June 1 to September 30, the lodge offers full meals in its dining room as well as basic accommodations (bed, hot water, flush toilet) in the main unit or in one of 24 rustic cabins (six of them deluxe). It's a bit primitive for the price, but then having your own private corner of such a spectacular piece of wilderness is more than enough for most nature lovers.

The lodge also is conveniently located to some of the most popular hikes in the Rockies. The 5½-km (3½-mile) **Eiffel Lake** trail climbs upward through spectacular subalpine meadows and scenery. Serious hikers can continue along the trail for 9½ km (6 miles) to **Wenkchemna Pass** and rugged Desolation Valley. The **Larch Valley** (2½ km/1½ miles) and **Sentinel Pass** (9½ km/6 miles) trails are popular with leaf peepers in early October, when the changing larches turn the entire valley to gold.

The Village

The village of Lake Louise itself offers a few nondescript motels and an anonymous strip mall with a good bakery, a bookstore, and a ski shop. The only lodging of note here is the ▶ **Post Hotel**, built in 1942 as a base for alpine enthusiasts who arrived in town by train. After undergoing a complete renovation in 1989, the only reminder of those rough-and-ready days is the hotel's **Outpost Bar**. Nowadays the hotel offers first-class accommodation and a fine dining room with a Continental menu featuring such standards as fresh salmon and rack of lamb. The hotel is owned by the people who own the Beaujolais restaurant in Banff, and the same style and quality service prevail throughout.

Icefields Parkway

Originally constructed as a make-work project during the Depression, the Icefields Parkway (Highway 93) winds through 230 km (143 miles) of rugged mountain scenery. Completed in 1960, the parkway connects Lake Louise and Jasper, and gets its name from the icefields looming above either side of the road. The glaciers are most visible at the Columbia Icefield, located 105 km (65 miles) southeast of Jasper. Here, the tongue of the Athabasca Glacier nearly touches the highway; you'll also find a hotel, an interpretive center, and guided tours to take you onto the surface of the glacier by Sno-Cat (summer only). It all makes for a truly spectacular drive any time of year, though it can be dangerous in winter. Avalanches are not uncommon, and the road may be closed for hours at a time. Check with the Royal Canadian Mounted Police (Tel: 403/762-1450) for a road and weather advisory before setting off, and be sure to bring along proper survival gear—warm blankets or sleeping bags, extra food, a snow shovel, tire chains, and flares. If you'd rather not drive yourself, Brewster Transportation in Banff (see the Getting Around section below) offers a weekly winter bus service to and from Jasper.

The only hotel on the parkway with any character (there are only three hotels in all, none of which stay open for the winter) is the ► **Num-Ti-Jah Lodge**, located 35 km (22 miles) north of Lake Louise. A small, wooden structure built on the shores of Bow Lake in 1939, the lodge was the setting for many Hollywood productions in the 1940s, most notably the Nelson Eddy Mountie movies. The rooms are comfortable, if somewhat basic, and the dining room serves only average food, but the old-fashioned atmosphere redeems the place.

The lodge's prime location at one of the highest points on the Icefields Parkway gives guests access to spectacular sub-alpine scenery with a minimum amount of climbing. The 4-km (2½-mile) trail leading past glacial fingers of the Columbia Icefield to **Bow Glacier Falls**, for example, runs right past the lodge, and is perfect for a morning or afternoon outing. There's another, more rigororus hike leading up a headwall to the foot of the glacier itself that can be done in a full day or as an overnight excursion.

Jasper National Park

Jasper National Park, adjoining Banff National Park's northern boundary, was established in 1907. Named after trapper Jasper Hawes, the park is located 362 km (224 miles) west of Edmonton and 426 km (264 miles) northwest of Calgary. (It's about a four-hour drive from the former and roughly five hours from the latter.) The Jasper townsite was determined by the logistics of the railroad business, not tourism, so it is less touristy than Banff, although there are a couple of great restaurants and hotels here.

STAYING IN JASPER

Many of the cabin accommodations, including ► **Becker's Roaring River Chalets** and the ► **Tekarra Lodge**, are closed during the winter but are terrific places to stay in summer. Private log cabins with stone fireplaces and indoor plumbing, riverside locations outside town, and excellent dining at both make Becker's and Tekarra popular with visitors to the area, so reserve well ahead.

Although the ► **Jasper Park Lodge** is a sister to the CPR's

Banff Springs and Chateau Lake Louise hotels, its summer camp–like atmosphere sets it apart from the other two. Individual cabins, complete with bedroom, verandah, and fireplace, are strung along beautiful Lac Beauvert alongside a couple of larger cabins that look like summer homes. (The Outlook Cabin, built in 1930, housed King George VI and Queen Elizabeth II on their royal visit in 1939.) You literally can get lost on some of the wooded walking trails that lace the grounds, and the privacy and character of the place appeal to many movie stars and rock musicians, who come here to hide away for weeks at a time in the summer. The lodge is the only resort in Jasper with golf, a swimming pool, tennis, horseback riding—in short, the works. And the French cuisine in the new **Edith Cavell Dining Room** has already it earned it four stars.

MALIGNE LAKE

Maligne Lake, an hour's drive southeast of Jasper (easy to find if you drive; otherwise book a bus tour and cruise at Maligne Tours in Jasper; Tel: 403/852-3370), is the second-largest glacial lake in Canada. The two-hour boat cruise on the mountain-rimmed lake is breathtaking, with Spirit Island, at the far end of the lake, the most photographed spot in the Rockies after Moraine Lake and Lake Louise.

Maligne Lake is also a good starting point for hikes along the Continental Divide. The most challenging is the **Skyline Trail**, which begins near the Maligne Lake ranger station and follows the ridges of the Maligne Range for 43 km (27 miles), with nearly half of that above timberline. If that sounds daunting, try the shorter (9½-km/6-mile) **Shovel Pass** section for a smaller dose of the same magnificent scenery. Though rather ordinary for much of its length, the 5-km (3-mile) **Bald Hills Lookout** trail delivers an extraordinary view of Maligne Lake and wildflower-blanketed meadows in late July and early August.

EDMONTON

Some wags still hold that Edmonton, Alberta's capital and by far the oldest city in the province, is simply a government town spiced up by the presence of the world's largest shopping center. The city owes its development to location: It is perched on top of the escarpment overlooking the North Saskatchewan River. The deep river valley divides the city and adds a hilly, scenic component to an otherwise flat landscape. Fort Edmonton was established in 1795 as a fur-trading post for the Hudson's Bay Company and later became a supply center for the Canadian North. Edmonton earned its reputation as the gateway to the North in 1898, when the Klondike gold rush sent thousands of gold seekers pouring through what was then a frontier outpost on their way to the Yukon. Edmonton still holds its **Klondike Days** festival in July, although a number of newer festivals seem to have eclipsed it in popularity.

In fact, summer, when the daylight hours stretch well into the evening and Edmonton becomes the Festival City, is the best time to visit. The celebrations begin July 1, with the two-week-long jazz festival drawing top musicians and appreciative audiences from across North America to the city's clubs and bars. Klondike Days happens over the last two weeks of July, followed by the **Heritage Festival** on the first weekend in August. The latter, featuring the traditional foods and dancing of numerous ethnic groups, draws a quarter of a million people annually.

The Edmonton **Folk Music Festival** takes place over the second weekend in August. With a nod to the 1960s, this outdoor festival features a variety of music not often heard on the radio. For ten days in mid-August, the **Fringe Theatre Event** occupies center stage in the Old Strathcona area. An outstanding alternative theater event, the Fringe launches some 150 new productions every year in the city's 14 theaters.

DOWNTOWN EDMONTON

Even without the Fringe festival, **Old Strathcona** is the city's most interesting browsing area. Located on Whyte Avenue (also called 82nd Avenue) between 101st and 106th streets, the neighborhood's active historical society has restored many of the buildings to their turn-of-the-century grandeur. Walking-tour brochures of the area are available from the Old Strathcona Foundation Office at 8331 104th Street. Guided tours are available upon request; Tel: (403) 433-5866.

The **Strathcona Hotel**, 10302 82nd Avenue, is popular with beer-drinking undergrads from the University of Alberta, Canada's second-largest English-speaking university. Nearby at 10501 82nd Avenue, **Strathcona Square**, a redevelopment project in the Old Post Office Building, is filled with boutiques, galleries, and restaurants. South on 103rd Street is the **Cook County Saloon**, a western dance hall featuring country bands and Texas two-step lessons on Tuesdays and Thursdays.

The ▶ **Hotel Macdonald**, another majestic CP Railroad hotel dating back to the years just before the outbreak of

World War I, reopened its doors in 1991 after eight long years. Before the hiatus, the stately château-style hotel was the social center of the city and the lodging of choice for visiting royalty and celebrities. Happy to report, the extensive face-lift has restored the hotel to its original grandeur. Even if you can't afford a night or three under its elegant roof, it's well worth a visit to admire the cameo ceilings in the Wedgewood Room or the elaborately painted ceiling in the Empire Ballroom.

The ► **Westin Hotel Edmonton,** another excellent establishment in the heart of the shopping and entertainment district, is within walking distance of the Citadel Theatre complex and the Edmonton Art Gallery. The Citadel and Shoctor theaters (located in the same complex) should not be overlooked, as both are venues for consistently fine work.

Cultural Attractions

A number of esoteric collections are housed in the city's smaller museums, which include the **Old Strathcona Model & Toy Museum,** 8603 104th Street (open Wednesday through Friday, 1:00 to 9:00 P.M., Saturdays from 10:00 A.M. to 6:00 P.M., and Sundays from 1:00 to 5:00 P.M.); the **Edmonton Police Museum,** in police headquarters at 9620 103-A Avenue (open Tuesday through Saturday, 10:00 A.M. to 3:00 P.M.); and the **Ukrainian Canadian Archives & Museum,** 9543 110th Avenue (open May 1 to September 30, Monday through Saturday, 1:00 to 4:00 P.M.; and Tuesday through Saturday, 1:00 to 4:00 P.M. the rest of the year). Ukrainians played a large role in the settlement of Edmonton, and are still its dominant ethnic group.

Four huge glass pyramids located in the river valley adjacent to downtown are among Edmonton's more prominent landmarks. Built in 1976, the **Muttart Conservatory** houses a wide variety of plants, with each of three pyramids representing a different climatic zone—tropical, temperate, arid—and the fourth reserved for unusual floral displays. For hours and information, Tel: (403) 496-8755.

The Mall

Edmonton gained a bit of notoriety as well as a place in the *Guinness Book of World Records* a few years back for the **West Edmonton Mall,** the largest shopping mall in the world. Don't let the crassness of this monster keep you away. In addition to its 800 stores, 110 restaurants, and 19 theaters, there is an NHL-size ice rink where the Edmonton Oilers practice, recording studios where you can cut your own record, an indoor amusement park, a five-acre water park with 22 waterslides, an indoor lake with trained dolphins, a submarine ride, and a replica of a Spanish galleon. (The indoor lake would be at home in Hollywood, but the amusement park is getting a bit tattered.) The West Edmonton Mall is as much entertainment center as shopping mall, and it is fun.

DINING IN EDMONTON

The Westin's award-winning **Carvery** dining room is elegant and expensive, and can get busy on Fridays and Saturdays; best to call ahead; Tel: (403) 426-3636. For people-watching in a colorful coffeehouse atmosphere, the **Bistro Praha**, 10168 100 A Street and 101st Avenue, is perfect. Popular with the onstage and after-theater crowds, the Bistro serves up an array of Central European dishes and superb desserts. The food is obviously a hit because the menu hasn't changed in nearly 20 years. Tel: (403) 424-4218.

Located in an elegant residential district east of the downtown core on 112th Avenue, ▶ **La Bohème** is a superb French restaurant and bed and breakfast occupying the Gibbard Block, the first apartment building in Edmonton with running hot water. The restaurant, on the main floor, sports lace curtains and a tin ceiling, while upstairs there are eight recently renovated antiques-filled guest rooms. On weekends, dinner reservations are a must; Tel: (403) 474-5693.

Packrat Louie, one block off White Avenue at 10335 83rd Avenue, moved from its old location on Jasper Avenue, but still serves Swiss Italian cuisine and specializes in homemade pizza cooked in a wood-burning oven. Tel: (403) 433-0123. If you're interested in Chinese food, don't be deterred by the tattered exterior of the **Blue Willow**, 11107 103rd Avenue at 111st Street. The National Hockey League players and other notorious appetites who frequent the place are a tribute to its great food. Tel: (403) 428-0584. The **Sidetrack Café** (Tel: 403/421-1326), located in a converted-warehouse setting near the railroad tracks at 10333 112th Street and 103rd Avenue, also serves good food but is best known for its international lineup of bands. The music here runs the gamut from blues to jazz to pop-rock, and whatever the style, the quality is consistently good.

GETTING AROUND

The Rockies region is packed with bus tours and tourists from June until September, so hotel reservations are a must.

Even the campgrounds fill up by early afternoon. The same holds true for the Christmas season, when Banff and Jasper hotels fill with skiers. The best time to visit is late September and early October, during Indian summer. The days are still warm and the towns less crowded, which gives you options when it comes to eating and sleeping. It's also cheaper then, with some of the hotel rooms discounted 30 to 40 percent. The only drawback may be snow if you decide to hike up to the higher elevations.

Choosing the right kind of clothing is tough even for the locals owing to the whimsical nature of the weather. Southern Alberta boasts chinooks, warm winds that within a matter of hours blow spring across the winter prairie. Temperatures may fluctuate by 20° C within a single day. In summer, Alberta generally has hot days and cool evenings that require slacks and a sweater. In the mountains it can snow at any time.

Buses will take you from the airport to the major downtown hotels in Calgary for one-third the price of a taxi, with many hotels offering complimentary shuttle-bus service.

Calgary's LRT train system will squire you around the city quickly and cheaply. Transit along the 7th Avenue strip downtown is free, but the "freebie" ends at City Hall Station heading south and 8th Street heading north. Calgary's relatively uncongested grid system makes the city easy to navigate. The Trans-Canada Highway (Highway 1), which doubles as 16th Avenue N.W. within the city limits, is the main thoroughfare to the mountains. North–south Highway 2 leads to the other attractions in the province, including Head-Smashed-In Buffalo Jump and Waterton Lakes National Park, but posted directions to the highway from the city center are nonexistent, so a city map is essential.

Edmonton's International Airport is located so far out of town that the price of a taxi to a downtown hotel ($16) is nearly equal to a day's car rental. Since the attractions are not clustered downtown, a car is useful anyway. If you don't rent a car, stick to taxis for transport, as the public transportation is spotty—with the exception of the shuttle service to the West Edmonton Mall offered by many hotels.

For booking and complete information on the train trips between Calgary and Vancouver or Jasper and Vancouver, call the Great Canadian Train Company, Tel: (604) 984-3315; Fax: (604) 984-2883; in the U.S. and Canada, Tel: (800) 665-7245. The trip is spectacular, but mountains do present some hazards, and train service can be interrupted by avalanches in the spring. Fall is a beautiful and less crowded time to take either trip. Although advance bookings are best—and some people book as much as a year in advance—a month or two in advance should suffice.

ACCOMMODATIONS REFERENCE

The rates given below are projections for peak seasons during the 1994 calendar year; at other times of the year they may be considerably less. Unless otherwise indicated, rates are based on double rooms, double occupancy; provincial and federal taxes are included in all rates. As rates are subject to change, always double-check before booking.

▶ **Banff Springs Hotel.** 405 Spray Avenue, **Banff**, Alta. T0L 0C0. Tel: (403) 762-2211; Fax: (403) 762-5755; in the U.S., Tel: (800) 828-7447; in Canada, (800) 268-9411. $173–$363.

▶ **Becker's Roaring River Chalets.** P.O. Box 579, **Jasper**, Alta. T0E 1E0. Tel: (403) 852-3779; Fax: (403) 852-7202. $87.

▶ **Buffalo Mountain Lodge.** P.O. Box 1326, **Banff**, Alta. T0L 0C0. Tel: (403) 762-2400; Fax: (403) 762-4495. $190–$213.

▶ **Chateau Lake Louise. Lake Louise,** Alta, T0L 1E0. Tel: (403) 522-3511; Fax: (403) 522-3834; in the U.S., Tel: (800) 828-7447; in Canada, (800) 268-9411. $180–$373.

▶ **Deer Lodge.** P.O. Box 100, **Lake Louise**, Alta. T0L 1E0. Tel: (403) 522-3747; Fax: (403) 522-3883; in the U.S. and Canada, Tel: (800) 661-1595. $123–$146.

▶ **Homeplace Guest Ranch.** P.O. Box 6, Site 2, R.R. 1, **Priddis**, Alta. T0L 1W0. Tel: (403) 931-3245; Fax: (403) 931-3245. $80–$128 (includes breakfast, lunch, and dinner).

▶ **Hotel Kananaskis.** P.O. Box 6666, **Kananaskis Village**, Alta. T0L 0C0. Tel: (403) 591-7711; Fax: (403) 591-7938; in the U.S., Tel: (800) 828-7447; in Canada, (800) 268-9411. $165–$275.

▶ **Hotel Macdonald.** 10065 100th Street, **Edmonton**, Alta. T5J 0N6. Tel: (403) 429-6481; Fax: (403) 424-8017; in the U.S., Tel: (800) 828-7447; in Canada, (800) 2680-9411. $151–$179.

▶ **Jasper Park Lodge.** P.O. Box 40, **Jasper**, Alta. T0E 1E0. Tel: (403) 852-3301; Fax: (403) 852-5107; in the U.S. and Canada, Tel: (800) 828-7447. $264–$460 (summer); $117–$252 (winter).

▶ **Kananaskis Inn Best Western.** P.O. Box 10, **Kananaskis Village**, Alta. T0L 2H0. Tel: (403) 591-7500; Fax: (403) 591-7633. $123.

▶ **Kilmorey Lodge.** P.O. Box 100, **Waterton Lakes National Park**, Alta. T0K 2M0. Tel: (403) 859-2334; Fax: (403) 859-2342. $78–$94.

▶ **La Bohème.** 6427 112th Avenue, **Edmonton**, Alta. T5W 0N9. Tel: (403) 474-5693; Fax: (403) 479-1871. $85.

▶ **Moraine Lake Lodge.** P.O. Box 70, **Lake Louise**, Alta. T0L 1E0. Tel: (403) 522-3733; Fax: (604) 985-7479. $207 (lodge); $218–$252 (cabins). Open June 1 to September 30.

▶ **Num-Ti-Jah Lodge.** P.O. Box 39, **Lake Louise**, Alta. T0L 1E0. Tel: (403) 522-2167; Fax: (403) 522-2425. $106.

▶ **Palliser Hotel.** 133 9th Avenue S.W., **Calgary**, Alta. T2P 2M3. Tel: (403) 262-1234; Fax: (403) 260-1260; in the U.S., Tel: (800) 828-7447; in Canada, (800) 268-9411. $263.

▶ **Prince of Wales Hotel. Waterton Lakes National Park**, Alta. T0K 2M0. Tel: (406) 226-5551 (May–September); (602) 207-6000 (September–May); Fax: (403) 859-2630 (summer only). $90–$120.

▶ **Post Hotel.** P.O. Box 69, **Lake Louise**, Alta. T0L 1E0. Tel: (403) 522-3989; Fax: (403) 522-3966; in the U.S. and Canada, Tel: (800) 661-1586. $157–$277.

▶ **Rafter Six Guest Ranch.** General Delivery, **Seebe**, Alta. T0L 1X0. Tel: (403) 673-3622; Fax: (403) 673-3961. $84–$168 (open May 1 to October 31).

▶ **Skoki Lodge.** Reserve through Chateau Lake Louise.

▶ **Tekarra Lodge.** P.O. Box 669, **Jasper**, Alta, T0E 1E0. Tel: (403) 852-3058; Fax: (403) 852-4636. $49–$115 (open May 15 to September 30).

▶ **Westin Hotel Calgary.** 320 4th Avenue S.W., **Calgary**, Alta. T2P 2S6. Tel: (403) 266-1611; Fax: (403) 233-7471; in the U.S. and Canada, Tel: (800) 228-3000. $178–$200.

▶ **Westin Hotel Edmonton.** 10135 100th Street, **Edmonton**, Alta. T5J 0N7. Tel: (403) 426-3636; Fax: (403) 428-1454; in the U.S. and Canada, Tel: (800) 228-3000. $133–$275.

VANCOUVER
AND VICTORIA

By Garry Marchant

Garry Marchant writes for the Asian Wall Street Journal
Weekly *and magazines in North America, Asia, and Europe.*

Few cities make such a powerful first impression on visitors as Vancouver. Lofty mountains, often blanketed by fresh snow, rise straight out of the ocean; blue inlets cut deep into the city center; and dense temperate rain forests edge against the intruding high-rises. The sea air fairly sparkles, and when the breezes are right the natural perfume of fresh-cut cedar from the Fraser River mills scents the city.

The dramatic meeting of mountains, forests, and sea—and the gentle climate warmed by the Japan Current—shape the local character, setting Vancouverites apart from other Canadians. No other major city lives so close to raw nature. From downtown high-rise towers of commerce, three-piece-uniformed stockbrokers and lawyers look out on tugboats hauling strings of barges loaded high with logs or wood chips and on floatplanes landing in the harbor, bringing lumberjacks, hunters, fishermen, and prospectors fresh from the bush.

On rugged Coast Range peaks, which are almost close enough to touch, eagles nest—and inexperienced city hikers often get lost overnight. Game wardens frequently have to chase bears away from suburban yards, and even in the crowded West End residential area raccoon families saunter single file across trimmed lawns and terrorize local cats.

Still, like other large Canadian cities, Vancouver has become increasingly sophisticated and cosmopolitan in recent decades. Increased prosperity and immigration from all over the world, particularly Asia, have turned it into a truly international city. For visitors, this means greater cultural attractions and a wide range of good restaurants.

Outside of Victoria, Vancouver has Canada's finest climate. It *does* rain frequently in this West Coast marine climate, but even then the showers only serve to freshen the coast air. And despite its soggy reputation, Vancouver has less rain in June, July, and August than Edmonton, Winnipeg, Toronto, or Montreal.

Vancouverites (a Vancouverite is anyone who has been here more than a few months) boast of being able to swim and ski on the same day, although no one actually does. You can also do much more; there are nine miles of public beach within the city limits, 18 public and seven private golf courses, 152 tennis courts, and miles of ocean, lakes, and rivers for canoeing, kayaking (ocean or white water), and waterskiing. Alpine and cross-country ski slopes begin 20 minutes from the city center.

MAJOR INTEREST

Beautiful setting
West Coast good-living atmosphere
Gastown (historic buildings, shops)
Granville Island (market, shops, theaters,
   restaurants)
Chinatown (restaurants, unusual shops)
Stanley Park
Grouse Mountain by tramway

Day trip to Victoria

Eastern Canadians consider Vancouver beautiful and fun-loving but somewhat frivolous. It is part of modern Canadian mythology that many young people yearn to escape the bitter winters and small-city life of the prairies. The ambitious career-oriented types go to Toronto or Ottawa to become lawyers, accountants, advertising executives, or solemn civil servants, while the romantics and poets head west, searching for the good life and surviving however they can. This young city nurtures not just hedonists but confirmed oddballs—Easterners like to say that they tilted the country, and all the loose nuts rolled down to Vancouver. During the daft decade of the 1960s, the city had an official town fool, complete with court-jester cap-and-bells outfit. All forms of aberrant and extreme behavior in Canada, both social and

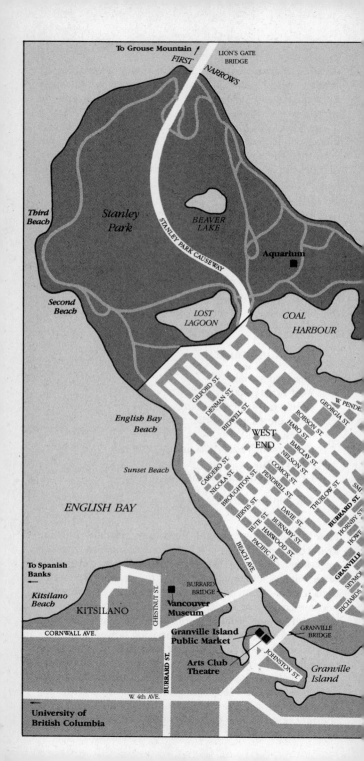

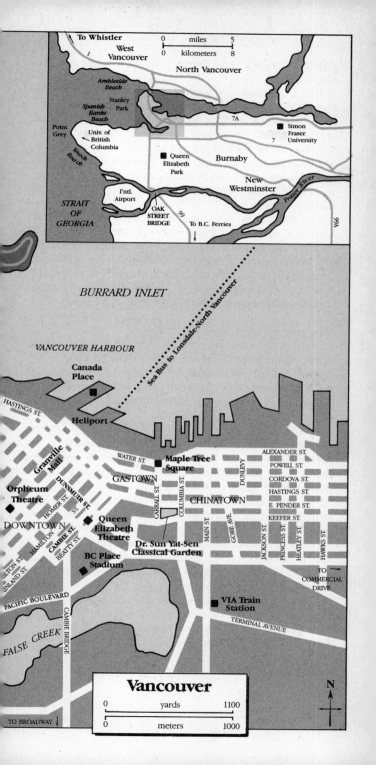

political, start here, take deeper root in the fertile soil, and last longer.

It is a Canadian New Year's Day tradition for the rest of Canada to snuggle sensibly before fireplaces and TV sets and gaze in wonder as thousands of Vancouver loonies, still steeped in the glow of New Year's Eve parties and clad in costumes or formal wear, plunge into chilly English Bay.

On sunny summer days, **Wreck Beach**, Canada's largest, most famous nudist beach, attracts more than 5,000 people in search of the seamless tan. This, too, is part of the Vancouver mystique.

The Polar Bear Swim and events like the Fraser River Outhouse Race and the International Bathtub Race from Nanaimo across the Strait of Georgia confirm the image the rest of Canada has of Vancouver: that this is a city of flakes, a Lotus Land insufficiently imbued with the stern work ethic of Toronto, Ottawa, Hamilton, or Halifax. All this, of course, makes Vancouver entertaining for visitors as well.

Vancouver's Heritage

Vancouver was just a big port and lumber town in the years following World War II. Its rapid growth has ben a phenomenon of the past few decades, so it is rare to meet a native-born Vancouverite in this community of newcomers. Most residents are refugees from the harsh winters of the rest of Canada, or immigrants from abroad.

As a result, the city, supported by the mining and lumber industries, retains a certain pioneer air, enhanced by its proximity to sea and forest. Aside from natural resources, there is some manufacturing (high-tech electronics and computer software) and, of course, tourism.

Vancouver is more than just a pretty setting, though. Recent years have seen a resurgence of interest in traditional Native American arts and crafts. West Coast Indians were North America's greatest native artists, crafting totem poles, elaborate longhouses, carved dishes, ceremonial masks, drums, rattles, and household items. New totem poles have been raised in several parks and other public places in Vancouver and Victoria, and art shops stock masks, carvings, silver jewelry, and prints bought directly from native artists. Totem-pole carvers can be seen working at a number of places, including the Capilano Suspension Bridge and Park in North Vancouver.

Around in Vancouver

Canada's third-largest city, at 1.5 million people, is merely middle-sized by American or European standards. The "city" part is concentrated in the West End and downtown area, bordered by False Creek/English Bay to the south and Burrard Inlet to the north. Many attractions are free, or inexpensive, and most are easy to reach.

GASTOWN

Vancouver can boast no noble beginnings, no Romulus and Remus mythology. On a Sunday in 1876, a garrulous river-boat captain named "Gassy Jack" Deighton paddled a dugout canoe laden with his wife, mother-in-law, yellow dog, two hens, $6, and a barrel of whisky away from the town of New Westminster. He landed at a spot the Indians called Lucky Lucky, cracked the keg, and passed the cup around to workers from the nearby Hastings Mill. Appreciative mill workers built him a shack/saloon, and Vancouver was on its way.

When the Canadian Pacific Railway chose the spot as the terminus of the new transcontinental railway, the town's future was ensured. After the original shantytown burned down in 1886, new brick, stone, and cast-iron buildings rose in its place.

Gastown, as the town's original core area was called, degenerated by the middle of this century as the city center moved steadily west, spurring a move to tear it down. Instead, in the late 1970s the city restored the 19th-century buildings, laid brick sidewalks and streets, planted trees, and installed decorative streetlights. The resulting heritage area has won a number of international design awards, and Gastown is now a popular area of restaurants, bars, and shops ranging from the chic to the tacky and selling everything from antiques and totem poles to urban cowboy gear and "Made in Hong Kong" moose-head ashtrays. On summer evenings, it's also a popular nightlife area.

A statue of Gassy Jack atop a barrel now stands before the site of his first saloon, the Globe, on Maple Tree Square at the east end of Water Street. At the other end, the world's only steam-powered clock, built to cover a steam vent, cheerfully toots the Westminster Chimes on the hour. Place-names such as Blood Alley and Gaoler's Mews remind us of rowdier, more colorful times.

GRANVILLE ISLAND

Like Gastown, False Creek's Granville Island, under the Granville Bridge, was a grubby industrial area of factories, foundries, warehouses, shipyards, and railway sidings. In the 1970s, a time of awakening appreciation for the city's heritage, a major redevelopment began. Today the rejuvenated island is a favorite recreation center that includes a houseboat community, theaters, the Emily Carr School of Art, art galleries, craft shops, bookstores, and equipment stores and chandlers for all the yachts moored nearby.

The Granville Island Public Market, housed in a massive converted warehouse with a rough-edged decor of exposed pipes, beams, and tin sheeting, isn't the cheapest place to shop. But its cheese merchants and butchers, its fresh seafood, pasta, and pâté sellers, and its craft shops provide such ambience and diversity of goodies that no one seems to mind the slightly higher prices. Granville Island even has its own micro brewery, which produces beer according to ancient Bavarian regulations.

Granville Island is a short taxi trip or, better still, a rowboat-size ferry ride from the West End dock under the Burrard Street Bridge. (Parking on the island is difficult, especially on weekends.) The island is a perfect spot for an informal lunch, with a wide range of takeout-food outlets (deli, Greek, fish and chips). Sit on the dock outside watching the fishing boats and yachts go by, or rent a rowboat, kayak, or sailboat and lunch on the water.

THE WEST END

The heart of Vancouver is a peninsula surrounded by English Bay, First Narrows, and Burrard Inlet. Stanley Park, with Lions Gate Bridge crossing to the North Shore, occupies the northern half of the peninsula. (Getting your bearings in Vancouver is easy—provided visibility is good. Find the mountains and you are facing north.)

Extending south and east from Stanley Park, the West End is one of Canada's most densely packed yet desirable residential areas. Here are many of the better hotels, restaurants, parks, and beaches, as well as fashionable **Robson Street**. This once-interesting ethnic strip, known also as Robsonstrasse, has been transformed into a row of expensive boutiques and cute restaurants.

DOWNTOWN AND THE ETHNIC NEIGHBORHOODS

Abutting the West End, the downtown core extends from **Burrard Street** ten blocks east to Beatty Street, an area filled with office towers, hotels, theaters, many (though certainly not all) of the best restaurants, and the city's nightlife.

Gastown, the original Vancouver, and Chinatown are just east of downtown. Granville Island is south across False Creek under the Granville Bridge.

To the north of this peninsula are the North Shore mountains and suburbs, including the Grouse Mountain recreational area (see Elsewhere in Vancouver, below). South, across the Burrard, Granville, and Cambie bridges, are residential areas, the university, several museums, and more beaches and parks. To the east, a variety of ethnic neighborhoods give way to suburbs like Burnaby and New Westminster, which stretch out into Fraser Valley farming communities.

Ethnic neighborhoods are scattered loosely throughout the city, with the Greeks on West Broadway (toward the university), the Italians in East Vancouver, the East Indian community highly visible on south Main (toward the airport), and the Japanese (now mainly dispersed, except for food stores and restaurants) east of Gastown along Powell Street. The borders are by no means fixed, and these areas are frequently filled with ethnic specialty shops and restaurants rather than residences.

Chinatown

Vancouver is the terminus of both Canadian transcontinental railways, and is the largest port in North America after New York City, shipping coal, grain, and forest products to the Far East. Turned resolutely toward the Pacific, this is perhaps the continent's most Asian city, and its large Chinatown is probably North America's most authentic, thanks to the influx of Hong Kong and Southeast Asian Chinese immigrants in the past decade.

Its broader, cleaner streets aside, Chinatown, centered around Pender and Main streets, is remarkably like districts of Kowloon, Hong Kong; its stores overflow with Asian bric-a-brac and curios, and wailing Cantonese pop music and Peking opera pours out of record shops. Chinese social clubs, movies, and newspapers abound, and the sidewalks are crowded with noisy shoppers. Fat, shiny-brown ducks hang from butcher-shop windows, and boxes of such exotic vegetables as *bok choy* and *gai lan* clutter sidewalks.

The Eastern-influenced buildings with their moon doors and upturned tile roofs, the neon Chinese signs, and the pagoda-like telephone booths help to reinforce the feeling of exoticness. According to *Ripley's Believe It or Not,* the world's narrowest building stands on 8 West Pender. It is two stories high, 96 feet long, and only 5 feet 10 inches wide. Of interest here is the **Dr. Sun Yat-Sen Classical Garden,** the only one of its kind outside China. Artisans from the People's Republic modeled the classical garden at Pender and Carrall streets after the Ming dynasty–era garden in the city of Suzhou. The tools and techniques used were almost the same as those employed to build the original, and most of the material, including hand-fired roof tiles, carved wood-and-lattice windows, and limestone rocks, were shipped from China. The peaceful garden includes pavilions, covered walkways, terraces, lookout platforms, and reflecting pools.

Little India

Vancouver has the largest overseas community of South Asians (from India, Pakistan, and Sri Lanka—many by way of Uganda or Fiji) outside of London, and the largest Sikh community outside of India. Turbans and beards are commonplace in Little India, which occupies four blocks of South Main between 48th and 51st streets, an area powerfully evocative of the Indian subcontinent. In these few blocks you'll find incense-scented sari shops, video stores advertising epic Indian movies, and restaurants serving India's Sovereign beer (brewed in Bangalore and sporting a likeness of Queen Victoria). Bolts of silver- or gold-threaded silk for saris are stacked high next to displays of Indian costume jewelry: bangles, baubles, nose pins, five-finger rings, armlets, ankle bracelets with little tinkling bells, and toe rings. Food markets, fragrant with spices, sell subcontinental produce and such fruits as mangoes, jackfruit, and durians, along with papadums, jars of sauces, pickles, chutneys, henna, and anything else you might find in a well-stocked shop in India.

Other Ethnic Neighborhoods

Other ethnic neighborhoods scattered throughout the city are sought out by visitors seeking novel sensations. The Japanese have been on East Powell Street since early in the century, and though forcibly evicted during World War II, many have returned. In these two short blocks are a number of Japanese restaurants, shops selling exquisite pottery and crafts, and fishmongers supplying the city's many sushi shops.

Greeks settled on Broadway, across English Bay from downtown, and Italians on Commercial Drive, in the East End several miles from the city center; both areas are worth seeking out for their grocery stores, coffee shops, and fine, inexpensive restaurants.

East Hastings, an older area of shops, small department

stores, and seafood cafés, separates Gastown and Chinatown. It is ethnic, working-class Canada at its most colorful, populated by husky, hairy loggers in red-plaid shirts and nail boots, fishermen and deckhands in bulky sweaters, and railway workers in denims. East Hastings, with its low-cost department stores, pawnshops, cheap hotels, beer joints, war-surplus stores, and greasy spoons, is another reminder of how recently removed the city is from its frontier origins.

VANCOUVER'S BEACHES

Vancouver's beaches are popular and crowded in summer, more for sunbathing, games (Frisbee, volleyball, windsurfing), and people-watching than swimming. The water is too cold even for locals, except for New Year's Day, when thousands traditionally join in the Polar Bear Swim. **Sunset** and **Second beaches**, stretching along the south shore of the city center peninsula to Stanley Park, are popular with urbanized West End residents and visitors from the downtown hotels.

Kitsilano Beach, across English Bay from the West End, is crowded with young adults from that popular neighborhood. Farther west, near the university, **Spanish Banks**, with some of the best beaches, draws families, picnickers, and barbecuers. Farther west still, and the hardest to get to (snug under the cliffs of the university), **Wreck Beach** is Canada's most famous public nudist assemblage, complete with unclothed beer and piña colada hawkers. By contrast, West Vancouver's **Ambleside Beach** is the domain of fashionable matrons, their well-dressed progeny, and designer-accoutered joggers.

STANLEY PARK

Stanley Park, one of North America's largest urban parks, is a vital playground for outdoorsy Vancouverites, who often lose themselves on the 22 miles of hiking trails and bicycle paths winding through the more than 1,000 acres of thick, broody rain forest here.

The area of the park bordering downtown has beaches, bowling greens, cricket pitches, and tennis courts within walking distance of most major hotels. There is also a zoo with polar bears, a miniature train that even adults can ride, totem poles, a Japanese monument, summertime cricket games, and outdoor theater. The seven-mile seawall is almost always crowded with joggers, roller skaters, and bicyclists.

The **Stanley Park Aquarium**, Canada's largest, with more than 8,000 aquatic creatures, is also one of the largest in the world. It concentrates on marine and freshwater aquatic life of the North American West Coast, and is best known for the dolphin and killer whale displays of grace and power at the

Max Bell Marine Centre, as well as for its comprehensive viewing galleries with large picture windows. Other popular displays show world-famous Pacific salmon sports fish, Arctic grayling, and several species of trout in their natural habitat. Depending on the season, the sharks, sawfish, and giant sea bass are fed on Wednesdays and Saturdays at about 1:00 P.M.; the sea otters and harbor seals are fed throughout the day.

Stanley is only one of 157 parks scattered throughout the city. Residents claim that there are actually thousands of parks, for, as a New York writer once commented, Vancouverites are such ardent gardeners that the city looks like a seed catalogue.

Elsewhere in Vancouver

GROUSE MOUNTAIN

For the best panorama of the city, take Canada's largest, most modern tramway 3,700 feet up Grouse Mountain to a restaurant, coffee shop, and, of course, ski slopes and hiking trails. For the Grouse Mountain Skyride, drive west on Georgia Street through Stanley Park and across Lion's Gate Bridge, turn right onto Marine Drive, then left onto Capilano Road. Follow the road to the base of the mountain, where there is parking.

EXHIBITION PARK

Gamblers can head east about 7 km (4 miles) on Hastings to Exhibition Park (thoroughbreds), the local track, where, along with the many losers, there is a winner in every race. For information regarding starting times, call the B.C. Jockey Club at (604) 254-1631.

UNIVERSITY OF BRITISH COLUMBIA

The University of British Columbia campus, 1,000 acres of virtually untouched forest on the tip of Point Grey at the western end of the city, is a popular hiking spot. (From Granville Street downtown, the number 10 bus goes directly to the university—but avoid the morning rush hour, when the buses are packed with students.) The university welcomes visitors; information booths at all entrances provide maps and brochures. The main attractions, aside from the Museum of Anthropology, discussed next, are the **Nitobe Memorial Gardens**, a traditional Japanese garden with a ceremonial tea house; an extensive rose garden; and the campus itself. The new University Endowment Lands Park, 1,700 acres of wilderness, is now officially protected from developers.

Museum of Anthropology

The university's Museum of Anthropology, a stylized version of an Indian longhouse set on cliffs overlooking the Pacific at the western end of the city, brings home the powerful feel of the West Coast Indians' highly developed art. The huge concrete-and-glass building stores and displays some 20,000 artifacts, the majority from the British Columbia coast. This is one of the world's most comprehensive collections of West Coast art—art that has been compared favorably with that of ancient Greece and Rome. The 46-foot-high windows in the Great Hall illuminate some of the grandest native pieces in existence, including towering totem poles, giant carved house-front figures, and feast dishes that resemble tub-size bowls on wheels. The museum is open Wednesday through Sunday, 11:00 A.M. to 5:00 P.M., and Tuesdays from 11:00 A.M. to 9:00 P.M. Next door is a full-scale Indian longhouse and a group of contemporary totem poles.

THE CULTURAL AND SPORTING SCENE

Despite its reputation, Vancouver has a rich cultural life. You'll find a dozen professional theater companies scattered throughout the city, two major universities (the other being Simon Fraser in nearby Burnaby, worth a look for its distinctive architecture), and the Vancouver Symphony Orchestra. The refurbished **Orpheum** on Granville Street, home to the VSO, is worth visiting for its elegant architecture alone, especially in a town that is sadly lacking in fine old buildings. Most musical performances in the city, from classical guitar to old-time jazz or grand musicals, are held in this ornately decorated theater, or else in the larger, more modern Queen Elizabeth Theatre on Robson Street near the bus depot.

The **Arts Club Theatre**, with two locations on Granville Island, features fine contemporary productions, musical revues, and home-grown plays—a few of which make it to New York and London. Performing-arts patrons can dine at a Granville Island restaurant first, then enjoy the performance and drinks at the theater. Same-day half-price tickets for most performances are available at Front Row Centre, 1025 Robson Street (cash only). Tel: (604) 687-1644 for tickets and information.

Eastern Canadians complain that it is pointless to make a business call to Vancouver after lunch on Friday, as the lazy hedonists already will be gone for the weekend. True enough. On winter weekends most cars sprout rooftop ski racks and join the stream heading out of the city to the slopes. And on warm Friday afternoons a parade of sailboats, cruisers, fishing boats, kayaks, and canoes heads out to sea past the sunbathers on English Bay Beach.

For four days in mid-July, the **Vancouver Sea Festival** celebrates the city's maritime heritage, with visits from U.S. Navy ships, a parade, salmon barbecues, and fireworks. Coinciding with the festival, some 125 zany international competitors navigate the turbulent Strait of Georgia from Nanaimo on Vancouver Island to Vancouver City in the **Great International Bathtub Race.**

At **Lonsdale Quay,** North Vancouver, where the Seabus docks, there are a number of modern but unattractive commercial and residential buildings. The seaside walk to Sailor's Point Park is pleasant, however, with scenic views of the city across the harbor. The busy quay is one of the city's most successful new Art Deco markets, with a variety of food stalls as well as produce, bakery goods, seafood, and handicrafts for sale.

There are, in addition, some good restaurants on this side of the water (see below), though not much nightlife.

GETTING AROUND

By Plane. More than a dozen international carriers connect Vancouver International Airport to cities in the United States, Europe, and Asia, with the number growing every year. The major domestic carriers are Air Canada and Canadian Airlines International, which between them provide service to the U.S., Europe, South America, Asia, and the Pacific. Delta, United, Continental, and Alaska Airlines fly to Vancouver from the United States, with Seattle, San Francisco, Los Angeles, Honolulu, and Chicago the major U.S. gateways to the city. British Airways, Lufthansa, and KLM fly to Vancouver from Europe, while Air New Zealand, Cathay Pacific, Japan Air Lines, Singapore Air Lines, Korean Airlines, and Qantas cross the Pacific.

A number of small commuter airlines operate within B.C., with some utilizing floatplanes only. AirBC offers daily service from Coal Harbour downtown to Victoria's Inner Harbour. San Juan Airlines connects Vancouver and Victoria with Seattle and other waypoints. Time Air also operates within the province. Small aircraft can be chartered for more remote areas. Those flying private aircraft should contact the

B.C. Aviation Council for information on the 374 land and water airports in the province, as well as for practical trip-planning information. Write B.C. Aviation Council, Esso Avitat Building, #303-5360 Airport Road South, Richmond, B.C. V7B 1B4. Tel: (604) 278-9330.

By Rail and Car. Not everyone arrives by air. VIA Rail, an excellent option for anyone eager to get the feel of this vast province, arrives from the east, and major highways lead into the city from the east and south. Vancouver is a 3½-hour drive from Seattle, and except on summer and holiday weekends, when there are long lines, border crossings are a simple affair.

On the Water. Vancouver is the major departure point for cruise ships to Alaska. More than ten major lines, including Princess, Holland America, Hapag-Lloyd Pacific, Sitmar, Costa, Cunard, Royal, Exploration, Admiral, and World Explorer, depart from the impressive Canada Place cruise-ship terminal at the north end of Burrard Street. Many tourists visit Vancouver for the first time while joining one of these cruises.

The 400-passenger **Seabus** crosses from downtown to the North Shore suburbs, providing an inexpensive sea view of the city in the process. Tickets are $1.35 during off-peak hours, and you can transfer onto buses at either end. The catamaran-hulled ferries leave the old Canadian Pacific Railway station in downtown Vancouver every 15 minutes for the 12-minute ride across Burrard Inlet to the North Shore.

The occasional few who start their Canadian journey in Victoria can cross to Vancouver by **B.C. Ferries** (1 hour and 40 minutes of stunning scenery through the Gulf Islands), fly city center to city center by AirBC floatplane, or take a helicopter. (See the Victoria Getting Around section below for more details.) Any way you go, the scenic rewards are great.

On the Ground. From Vancouver's airport it's about a 25-minute taxi or bus ride to downtown hotels. A taxi costs about $25; the Airport Express bus is $10. Most attractions, including Gastown and Stanley Park, are within walking distance of or a short taxi ride from most major hotels.

AAA Horse & Carriage Ltd. offers a variety of rides year-round. In addition to their popular Stanley Park tours, they run Grouse Mountain sleigh rides during the winter months. Private carriages are available for hire throughout Vancouver. For information, Tel: (604) 681-5115.

Early Motion Tours Ltd. offers limousine service and sight-seeing tours of the city in a restored 1930 Model A Ford Phaeton convertible. Tel: (604) 687-5088.

For most of its length, the Skytrain, Vancouver's rapid

transit system, operates above ground; the half-hour trip between Vancouver and New Westminster, the old end of the line, is worth making for the interesting perspectives of the city as well as to see the major redevelopment occurring at the old Expo grounds near False Creek and Chinatown. New Westminster, the former provincial capital on the banks of the Fraser River, has an interesting and active public market and a pleasant riverside bar and restaurant called the **Paddlewheeler** (810 Quayside Street; Tel: 604/524-1894). Vancouverites insist they built the system (which now crosses the Fraser River as far as the suburb of Surrey) above ground not just because it was cheaper but because they did not want to deprive riders of the view.

Owing to their mild climate, Vancouver and Victoria have a longer tourist season than the rest of Canada. Generally, you can expect mild weather from April to October, although, especially in Vancouver, it can rain at any time. In the past few years American and Japanese skiers have discovered B.C.'s slopes, with a resulting increase in winter tourism.

ACCOMMODATIONS

Vancouver boasts many of the country's finest hotels. Of only five Canadian hotels awarded the American Automobile Association's coveted Five Diamond Award, three are in this city—the Four Seasons, Le Meridien, and the Pan Pacific. Although the real bargains of post-Expo years, when hotels were running at low occupancies, are no longer so readily available, prices are still reasonable for a major city, and there is a wide choice, especially of first-class hotels. All the top hotels are located within a few blocks of each other—another indication of how compact this city really is.

Hotel reservations can be made through Vancouver Travel InfoCenter, Tel: (604) 683-2000; or, in the U.S. and Canada, through the Tourism Vancouver hotel reservation desk, Tel: (800) 888-8835.

The telephone area code for Vancouver and the rest of British Columbia is 604.

The stately ► **Hotel Vancouver**, the city's oldest quality hotel, is a less elaborate version of the great Canadian Railways château hostelries (including Quebec City's Le Château Frontenac and Victoria's Empress Hotel). Built in a modified 16th-century French Renaissance style, the hotel, with its steep verdigris copper roof, decorative gargoyles, and stone exterior (the same stone used for the provincial legislative building in Victoria), stands out in a city not known for its architecture. Still one of the city's best accommodations, particularly on the Entree Silver and Deluxe

Entree Gold floors, the hotel offers comfortable, high-ceilinged rooms in a variety of styles and sizes. Marble imported from Europe and the lavish use of exotic wood paneling (the hotel's new owners, C.P. Hotels, recently completed major renovations) lend the public areas a palatial air, and the lobby bar is an exceptionally good spot for midday people-watching.

900 West Georgia Street, V6C 2W6. Tel: 684-3131; Fax: 662-1929; in the U.S. and Canada, Tel: (800) 828-7447. $146–$270.

The ▶ **Four Seasons**, part of the deluxe Canadian chain, is the best of the city's pre–building boom hotels. Large rooms, including a number of luxurious suites, offer grand views from the higher floors, and the service throughout is excellent. The spacious, airy **Garden Lounge**, a haven of tropical plants and splashing waterfalls, is one of the city's most popular hotel bars, and the **Chartwell Restaurant** has reaped a number of culinary awards. In addition, shoppers have direct access to the hundreds of shops, department stores, and restaurants of the Pacific Centre Mall.

791 West Georgia Street, V6C 2T4. Tel: 689-9333; Fax: 684-4555; in the U.S., Tel: (800) 332-3442; in Canada, (800) 268-6282. $263–$350.

The ▶ **Wedgewood** is unique among the city's fine hostelries in that it's the only major Vancouver hotel not part of a chain. The owner imbues this small hotel (94 rooms, including 29 suites and four penthouses; no pool) with her personal touch (each room has a distinctive look), and the dedication shows. The Wedgewood has that intimate, friendly, old-European feel; here, the helpful staff quickly gets to know the guests. In the lobby and public rooms antiques and original artwork accent gleaming brass, glass, marble, and polished woods, while elsewhere the bright, gardenlike **Bistro**'s tall Palladian windows look out on the glass and waterfalls of the courthouse complex across the street, making it an excellent spot for lunch.

845 Hornby Street, V6Z 1V1. Tel: 689-7777; Fax: 689-3074; in the U.S. and Canada, Tel: (800) 663-0666. $187–$328.

▶ **Le Meridien** established itself as one of Vancouver's top hotels within a few years of its opening in 1986. As one expects of a property owned and operated by the luxe Air France chain, the hotel's public areas are lavishly decorated with antiques and marble throughout. The comfortable bar is typical: Rich wood paneling, leather-button wing chairs, and mounted stag horns create the atmosphere of a genteel British men's club. Rooms, many with good views of the mountains to the north or the lights of the city to the south, are large and tastefully decorated, while the hotel's **Le Club** restaurant rates as one of Vancouver's finest.

845 Burrard Street, V6Z 2K6. Tel: 682-5511; Fax: 682-5513; in the U.S. and Canada, Tel: (800) 543-4300. $146–$187.

The ► **Pan Pacific**, another successful newcomer, is dramatically situated on the water overlooking the North Shore mountains. Along with the billowing "sails" of the adjacent Canada Palace convention center and cruise-ship terminal, the great glass structure ranks as one of the most recognizable symbols of the city. The hotel's atrium-style entrance, with the lobby two floors above, furthers the feeling of West Coast glamour—an illusion that is soon dispelled. Although it boasts one of the best equipped health clubs in town, the hotel caters to convention and cruise ship business, and is better known for its scenic views than for its rooms or the quality of its service.

999 Canada Place, V6C 3B5. Tel: 662-8111; Fax: 685-8690; in the U.S. and Canada, Tel: (800) 663-1515. $345–$380.

The luxury 34-story ► **Hyatt Regency**, the city's largest hotel, is conveniently located a short block from what might be considered the center of the city (the intersection of Georgia and Burrard streets). Rooms, all recently redecorated, are large and offer balconies and excellent views. The Hyatt also has a good bar and multiple restaurants.

655 Burrard Street, V6C 2R7. Tel: 683-1234; Fax: 689-3707; in the U.S. and Canada, Tel: (800) 233-1234. $214–$243.

The CP's ► **Waterfront Centre Hotel**, the newest accommodation downtown, opened in 1991 across the street from the Convention Centre (and is linked to the latter by an enclosed walkway). The spacious rooms here offer harbor and mountain views, while special business-class floors include terraces, a private breakfast lounge, and concierge service. Among the hotel's first-rate facilities are a heated outdoor pool, a fitness center, a whirlpool, and steam rooms.

Waterfront Centre, 900 Canada Place Way, V6C 3L5. Tel: 691-1991; Fax: 691-1828; in the U.S. and Canada, Tel: (800) 828-7447. $280–$310.

In addition to these, Vancouver has many smaller, though very good, hotels. The old red-brick ivy-covered ► **Sylvia Hotel**, on English Bay adjacent to Stanley Park, is popular for both its location and atmosphere of days gone by. The rooms in its original wing are large and have high ceilings, while those facing the beach are among the city's best accommodation bargains. And watching the sunset over the freighters moored in the bay from the **Sylvia Bar** has long rated as one of the city's finest experiences. Unfortunately, the bar recently was cut in half in order to put in a forgettable restaurant.

1154 Gilford Street, V6G 2P6. Tel: 681-9321; Fax: 682-3551. $76–$94.

The ▶ **Pacific Palisades**, in the heart of the West End's chic shopping area and what is left of the old Robson-strasse (Robson Street) commercial strip, is a favorite with long-term visitors. A former apartment block, the all-suites Palisades is popular with Hollywood types—directors, technicians, cameramen, actors—filming here, which makes it a likely spot for discreet star-gazing. The Hong Kong–based luxury chain Shangrila International, which purchased the hotel in 1989, has not made any major changes.

1277 Robson Street, V6E 1C4. Tel: 688-0461; Fax: 688-4374; in the U.S. and Canada, Tel: (800) 663-1815. $193–$252.

In the same area, a number of once small, slightly worn West End hotels have been renovated in recent years and now provide comfortable lodging at moderate prices. Of these, the three-story ▶ **Barclay Hotel** is conveniently located and pleasantly remodeled, with a congenial bar in the lounge. Prices are particularly attractive off season (October 1 to April 30).

1348 Robson Street, V6E 1C5. Tel: 688-8850; Fax: 688-2534. $77–$111.

A few hotels outside the city center are also worth considering. The ▶ **Granville Island Hotel**, a refurbished former warehouse south of downtown on what was an industrial island beneath the Granville Bridge, has a fine view of the cityscape across the water. Rooms here are bright, modern, and individually configured rather than assembly-line identical.

1253 Johnston Street, V6H 3R9. Tel: 683-7373; Fax: 683-3061; in the U.S. and Canada, Tel: (800) 663-1840. $205–$293.

The ▶ **Park Royal**, across Lion's Gate Bridge, which connects the rest of the city with quaint and quiet West Vancouver, is suitable only for those with cars or a healthy budget for taxis. The ivy-covered Tudor building (just 30 rooms) resembles a country inn in a park setting. With well-tended English-style gardens on the Capilano River, a few minutes' walk from Ambleside Beach, one of Vancouver's finer suburbs, this is a pleasant retreat from the nearby city.

540 Clyde Avenue, West Vancouver V7T 2J7. Tel: 926-5511; Fax: 926-6082. $193.

DINING

Longtime Vancouver residents recall the days, just a few short decades ago, when dining out was limited to steak and baked potato (with wine in a brown bag) or the number-seven special with egg rolls and fortune cookies in Chinatown. Although this is an exaggeration, the city's dining possibilities have developed remarkably in recent years, so much so that—in terms of variety at least—it leads the country, with due respect to Toronto.

This culinary range has been sparked by a combination of large-scale immigration and Vancouverites' determination to savor all of life's pleasures. A recent trend has been for many good restaurants to move away from the city center. While visitors can certainly eat and drink in style within walking distance of their downtown hotel, some of the city's most interesting places now require a drive or taxi ride.

Vancouver is also part of the worldwide trend toward quality restaurants attached to hotels. Le Meridien Hotel's **Le Club** (Tel: 682-5511), though a relative newcomer, is already established as one of the city's top restaurants. The elegant salmon-hued room seats 72 and is decorated with original artwork and classical European furnishings. Continental-style entrées prepared by the restaurant's French chef include braised shelled lobster on buttered linguini with a saffron sauce, broiled filet of coho salmon with sun-dried tomato coulis, and open-flame rack of lamb with an herb and garlic emulsion. Closed Sundays.

The Hyatt's **Fish & Co.** (Tel: 682-3663), downtown on Burrard Street, is one of Vancouver's top seafood restaurants and a good choice for lunch or dinner. Its Sunday brunch, with a buffet stocked with up to 25 items, is perhaps this port city's finest presentation of fresh fish and seafood.

Vancouver's newest hotel, the Waterfront Centre across from Canada Place, combines the visual with the culinary arts in a unique Sunday Brunch Art Tour offered by its **Prow** restaurant. Following the midmorning meal, a guide takes interested patrons around the hotel to view its collection of more than 45 original West Coast paintings and sculptures. For reservations, Tel: 684-1339.

Dining with a View

In a city so formed by its setting (and so chauvinistically loyal to it), dining with a view is important. The **Salmon House on the Hill**, 2229 Folkestone Way, West Vancouver, some distance from downtown, is dramatically situated on a mountainside facing the city to the south. The dining room is spacious and open, with a West Coast cedar decor. It is especially pleasant to sit outside here on a sunny summer day while savoring a lunch of salmon grilled over alder wood. The main complaint about this place (aside from its somewhat out-of-the-way location) is its popularity with tourists. Better reserve; Tel: 926-3212.

Bridges, on Granville Island overlooking the city across False Creek, is more conveniently located. Though somewhat trendy, it is nevertheless a place to which locals take visitors to show off their city; the view is especially good from the top deck. The food, which comes from the sea, is also good. If you want the views without the food, there's a pub downstairs. In summer tables appear on the dock, and diners laze away sunny afternoons in a setting filled with fishing boats, sea gulls, and passing yachts. Tel: 687-4400.

Native American and West Coast

Quilicum, 1724 Davie Street, near the Sylvia Hotel and Stanley Park, is the only authentic West Coast Native American restaurant in existence. Cedar-plank walkways along a floor of smooth, round stones pass between elevated eating platforms with sunken areas for patrons' legs. The original artwork gracing the walls (masks, carvings, prints) is for sale, and the food, cooked over a fire at the end of the longhouse, includes such indigenous dishes as alder-wood-grilled salmon, caribou stew, grilled goat, rabbit, and *oolichan* (a small local fish). The place is run by Native Americans, and the service is relaxed. Diners are guaranteed an unusual meal, a distinctive experience, and the opportunity to purchase some interesting artwork. Tel: 681-7044.

Making its debut in 1989, the **Raintree Restaurant** (1630 Alberni Street, downtown) has become one of Vancouver's most popular restaurants. This bright, airy, and ultra-trendy eatery celebrates the West Coast lifestyle in its food, wine, and decor. Tel: 688-5570.

French

The city has many wonderful French restaurants besides Le Club (in the Meridien) from which to chose. Although they vary in style, service, and decor, in terms of quality the differences are picayune; all are excellent.

La Côte d'Azur, 1216 Robson Street, is housed in the only extant wood-frame structure on this flashy commercial strip, and has a dining room with tables arranged around a wood-burning fireplace. In summer you can dine out on the verandah among potted geraniums and roses while overlooking the passing show of power shoppers, punk rockers, perambulators, and dressed-to-be-seen West Enders. Closed Sundays. Tel: 685-2629.

Its worldly patrons (and there are many) say the **Café de Paris**, 751 Denman Street in the West End, is as authentic a bistro as you'll find on the continent, with worn wooden floors, serviceable marble-topped tables, and black-clad

French waiters in long white aprons. But it's the fine cuisine more than the atmosphere that attracts the Francophiles. If you cannot stomach the *tripe à la Parisienne,* veal kidneys in porto sauce, or sweetbreads in heavy cream and calvados, there is simpler fare: pepper steaks, veal sautéed in Dijon mustard, rabbit, mussels, and several imaginative fish dishes. Tel: 687-1418.

The name of **Le Crocodile**, 909 Burrard Street, comes from the owner/chef's favorite restaurant in his hometown of Strasbourg. A romantic, elegant establishment with mustard-colored walls, wooden floors, and mahogany trim, Le Crocodile is the perfect place for an intimate dinner. In addition to regional specialties like Alsatian onion pie, the menu lists a full range of Gallic offerings, from duck pâté or smoked breasts of goose in a port sauce to pepper steaks, roast lamb with a mustard sauce, and, for dessert, pears poached in red wine. Closed Sundays. Tel: 669-4298.

Italian

For the best—although not cheap—Italian food, head for the two restaurants side by side on Hornby Street, about ten blocks south of the Vancouver Art Gallery and Hotel Vancouver. Owned by restaurateur Umberto Menghi, each has its own specialty: **Umberto's** (Tel: 687-6316), the original, for game; and **Il Giardino** (Tel: 669-2422), with an especially nice garden, for gourmet Italian cuisine, from simple grilled mushrooms and excellent pastas to grilled veal, roasted rabbit, and pan-fried seafood. Closed Sundays.

Not as toney as Umberto's places, **Il Corsaro**, 920 Commercial Drive, is out in Little Italy in the East End. The decor in this sprawling place tends to the gaudy—plaster arches and paintings-of-Venice style—but the food is authentic and moderately priced, and the atmosphere cheerful, unpretentious, and friendly. Tel: 255-1422.

Not too many years ago, **Yaletown**, a few blocks of red-brick industrial buildings just east of the city center, was a work-worn warehouse district. Then artistic types—graphic designers, photographers, architects—started to move into the renovated warehouses, and Yaletown became a fashionable area for those in the know. While of no particular interest for sightseeing, the neighborhood has a few restaurants worth visiting. The oldest is the **Chicago Pizza Works**, 996 Homer, which complements its deep-dish pizza with a relaxed and informal atmosphere. Of more recent vintage is **Il Barino**, 1116 Mainland Street, where tiled floors and leafy potted plants are meant to conjure up sunny Italy. Here, seeing and being seen is as important as the menu's northern Italian specialties. Tel: 687-1116.

Budget with Character

Vancouver has a number of budget restaurants that serve good food, often in interesting settings. You'll probably have to line up for the delicious servings of noodles, *gyoza* (Chinese dumplings), and rice dishes Tokyo style at **Sapporo Ramen Shogun**, 518 Hornby Street, a short walk from Canada Place. Bamboo wall mats, traditional prints, and scurrying waitresses give this establishment the feel of an authentic, efficient, Japanese businessman's café. It is also one of downtown Vancouver's great bargains. Tel: 689-2922.

The **Only Fish and Oyster Café** (20 East Hastings, on the edge of the East End) has been a Vancouver landmark since 1912 (which is almost forever in this relatively new city). It has no toilets, no liquor license, no class. Aside from a painting of the restaurant, the only decoration is a giant red fire extinguisher. You'll have to line up, though, even for the counter. The place is frequented by lawyers and stockbrokers, laborers and the literati—and for good reason. The clam chowders, served out of pots as big as Douglas fir stumps; steamed clams; salmon, sole, halibut, and cod; and jumbo shrimps in batter and oyster pepper stew are all excellent. It's a terrific lunch spot but a bit too basic for dinner—and some visitors might not choose to be in the area after dark.

The **Old Spaghetti Factory**, 53 Water Street, has been serving up pasta and fun in Gastown for more than 20 years. The centerpiece of this sprawling building, formerly a coffee and tea factory, is a real Vancouver streetcar, now a dining car within the restaurant. A good budget bet, especially for the young. Tel: 684-1288.

East Asian

Vancouver excels in East Asian–style restaurants, although the scene is as volatile as a Chinese chef's moods. Just a few years ago food lovers grumbled that the city had every kind of Asian cuisine except Thai. In not much more than a year, a dozen Thai places surfaced, most of them good. The **Thai House** (Tel: 683-3383), on the second floor of a building at 1116 Robson Street, is the most convenient for visitors staying downtown. It is also quite authentic, with samples of Thai artwork on the walls. The service can be a little slow, however. The **Nakorn Thai Restaurant**, 1157 Davie Street, is also centrally located, and noted for its excellent Thursday and Friday buffets, a good introduction to this fiery cuisine. Tel: 683-6621.

Chauvinistic Vancouver gourmets claim, flatly, that their city has the finest Chinese food this side of the Pacific. Visitors from San Francisco or New York will likely disagree, but, arguments aside, you can dine well on almost any of the Middle Kingdom's cuisines here. Not long ago, most restaurants were the garden-variety Cantonese, with a smattering of Mandarin. Now you can find everything from Shanghainese to Szechuan and Chiu Chau; the only thing missing is a good, hearty snake-food place.

For seafood (expensive), the downtown **Tsui Hang Village**, 1193 Granville Street, serves excellent lobster in a black bean or butter sauce as well as a whole range of finny dishes. With fish tanks all around, the atmosphere is quasi-aquarium; the place fills up on weekends, and it gets noisy—just the way the Chinese like it. Tel: 683-6868.

For Szechuan food, the bright, airy **Grand View** at 60 West Broadway, about a ten-minute drive from downtown, offers some of the city's finest. It is especially popular with the local Chinese, who go for the excellent noodle dishes and great variety of highly spiced dishes. Tel: 879-8885.

Vancouver has long had a smattering of good Japanese restaurants. But in recent years an influx of Japanese businessmen yearning for the familiar has resulted in the opening of numerous new establishments, most very good. The ever-popular **Kamei Sushi**, on the second floor at 811 Thurlow Street, is conveniently located just off Robson Street. Excellent lunch specials are the rule, and you can sit at the counter and watch the sushi chef at work or get a private table behind the sliding paper screen. Prices are reasonable, and reservations are advised. Tel: 684-4823.

Greek and Spanish

Of the many fine restaurants in the Greek district—Broadway south of the city center across the Burrard Bridge—**Orestes**, 3116 West Broadway, stands out, not just for its food (which is superb) but for its party atmosphere. This was one of the first Greek restaurants in Vancouver, and it remains popular with University of British Columbia students (the campus is nearby), who keep coming back after graduation. Food aside, Orestes is a lively place, especially on Thursdays; nooks and crannies spread over two floors and several rooms, and even open out onto the sidewalk on dry summer days. And Orestes, Vancouver's only Greek singles' restaurant, is certainly friendly, especially later in the evening after the ouzo and retsina begin to flow. Tel: 732-1461.

La Bodega, 1277 Howe Street (a 10- to 15-minute walk south of most city-center hotels), is a deservedly popular tapas bar that draws stockbrokers and New Agers, Spanish language students, the theater set, and anyone who has ever discovered the place and made it a regular hangout. It's not just the crispy, deep-fried calamari, the garlicky *patatas bravas,* the tender pork loin, or even the sizzling prawns in garlic that keep them coming back. Nor is it the lovingly made sangria or the baleful black bull staring from the wall. Most patrons claim, instead, that it's the authentic Iberian atmosphere which makes this delightful, informal, and inexpensive bar/café one of the best in town. Closed Sundays. Tel: 684-8815.

Pubs

Beer lovers eventually discover one of the three **Fogg n' Suds,** which, despite the corny name, are great places for a beer and burger-type lunch or dinner. Fogg claims to stock over 200 brands of beer and ale, Canada's largest selection, and takes the drinking of the amber nectar so seriously that it offers "passports" to the persistently experimental who want to keep records. The most accessible and pleasant Fogg is in an old West End brothel just off English Bay at 1215 Bidwell Street, with tables out on the sidewalk in summer.

For a pint and a pie (steak and kidney, sausage, Melton Mowbray) in an atmosphere that reasonably simulates an authentic British pub, the best places are the **Elephant and Castle,** 701 West Georgia Street; the **Rose and Thorn,** 757 Richards Street; and **Ten Sixty-Six,** at 1066 West Hastings Street. All are located within a few blocks of the city center.

NIGHTLIFE

Despite its fun-loving nature, Vancouver did not become a great late-night town until relatively recently. It seemed as if all those skiers and pleasure sailors needed a good night's rest and an early start to their play day. Evenings were lively enough, especially in the many fine restaurants, but the city closed too early for night owls. In the past decade or so that has changed, with a large number of nightclubs and dance spots opening (and some of them closing). Today Vancouver by night is well served with coffee shops and music halls, comedy clubs, bars, and discos—as well as theater, opera, and symphony for the serious minded.

The city is also North America's leading center for one popular form of dance: Its strippers have been celebrated internationally in film and song. Attractive young women perform at dozens of bars where there is no cover charge and drinks are served at standard prices. The most notable downtown venues are the Marble Arch on Richards and the Cecil, Austin, and Champagne Charlie's on Granville.

Dancing

Revelers can wine, dine, and dance in style at the **Roof Restaurant and Lounge** atop the grand old Hotel Vancouver (900 West Georgia Street). In its previous incarnation as the Panorama Roof this was a longtime favorite spot with Vancouverites, and today locals are again celebrating special occasions here. It's the only place of its kind in Vancouver— somewhat dressy, pricey, and perfect for over-40s and a sophisticated younger set—with live music (including bigband jazz) just right for dancing, views of the city (now slightly hemmed in by encroaching high-rises), and an elegant restaurant. You can spend your whole evening here, or move on to more frenetic disco action after working out a few of the kinks.

Most of Vancouver's good dance clubs are located in a compact downtown area bordered by Smithe, Seymour, Pacific, and Beatty streets, which means dedicated dancers can hit nearly a dozen of the city's most popular spots without ever having to get in a car or hail a taxi.

For several years **Richard's on Richards** (1036 Richards Street) has been the most popular club for the mid-20s, 30s, and still-kicking 40s set. You can spot it by the lines spilling out the front door. It is upscale and noisy, with live Top-40 bands, music videos, and a crowded dance floor. If you're lucky, you may get a seat in the mezzanine balcony from which to watch the action below.

Graceland (1250 Richards Street, entrance in an alley) is a newer alternative to Dick's on Dicks (see above). West Coasters call this a "New York–style" club: warehouse-size, with a large stage, some seats, lots of floor space, and murky lighting. It is definitely for the young—new wavers and ravers—with something always going on, from taped music to concerts featuring local or touring bands and even fashion shows.

Vancouver's dining and dancing spots are few but interesting. The **Soft Rock Café**, in Kitsilano at 1925 North 4th Avenue, has something for just about everyone: dinner theater on Tuesdays, live jazz on Sundays, and Top-40 bands weeknights, when the place is especially packed with the under-35 set. **Mulvaneys**, on Granville Island, is a bit unusual even for eclectic Vancouver. Named for a British Major Mulvaney, it leans toward a New Orleans theme, with late 19th-century decor and Louisana fare: jambalaya, blackened redfish, Cajun lamb, gumbo soup, and grills. There is dancing on weekends, when the disc jockey plays Top-40 music or tailors his selections to suit the crowd.

Music

A former strip club turned beer-and-blues joint, the **Yale Pub**, 1300 Granville Street, is a lively, down-home place where patrons come as they are, draft beer is the drink of choice, and old-time blues greats are frequently booked. There's a cover charge on weekends and when special acts are playing. A little more upscale (with a fairly hefty cover charge on weekends) is the Sheraton Landmark's **Prime Time** (1400 Robson Street), which offers Top-40 music in a mellow atmosphere.

Comedy

As in the rest of North America, comedy clubs have taken hold in Vancouver. Those who like to laugh, even if the humor is at times both off-color and off the mark, can spend a few happy hours in **Punchlines Comedy Club** (Tel: 684-3015), 21 Water Street in Gastown. This is the city's most established humor and improv haven, complete with movie-poster decor, scattered tables, and a stage with stool and microphone where would-be Woody Allens will break you up or bomb out. The place is inexpensive and fun, even when the amateur comedians flop. **Yuk Yuk's**, at Pacific Boulevard on the old Expo site (Tel: 687-LAFF), also offers a wide range of standup humor, from giggles to belly laughs. Closed Sundays.

The Celtic School

The **Unicorn**, an "Irish singing pub" owned by the Rovers folk group, was such a huge hit at Expo 86—with long lines from midday to midnight—that it stayed on. Despite its inconvenient location at 770 Pacific (past the domed BC Place Stadium), it still draws crowds who love its lively, loud, get-into-the-act brand of Irish folk music, good basic menu, and reasonable prices. Take a cab and be prepared to squeeze around a table with other guests and sing along with the group.

The Blarney Stone Inn, 216 Carrall Street, in the heart of Gastown, is an old-time favorite restaurant/cabaret for those who don't seem to care what the latest musical trend is. There's a small cover charge unless you have dinner, and the menu offers standard meat-and-potato fare with some bows to the Gaelic (cock-a-leekie soup, Irish lamb stew, and salmon St. Patrick). After dinner this big, open place settles in for foot-stomping Irish music, sweet folk songs (alternating with standard rock and Top-40), and dancing. Some bands provide Canadian content as well, with "Farewell to Nova Scotia" and all 53 stanzas of "I'se the Boy That Built the Boat" regularly featured.

The look at **O'Ryan's Cabaret**, around the corner on the second floor of an old brick building on Powell Street, is warehouse-chic, with bare walls, exposed beams, and wooden tables and bar stools. Twin pianos sit before huge mirrors on an elevated stage, and requests written on soggy beer coasters are passed on to the musicians, who display remarkable versatility in covering rock, schlock, ragtime, and blues favorites.

Quieter and more low-key, the **George V Pub**, in the high-ceilinged basement of the old Hotel Georgia downtown at 801 West Georgia Street, gets lively at night when a kilt-clad singer belts out Scottish and Canadian folk songs. This relaxed beer-drinkers' hangout, with standard British pub fare such as steak and kidney pie and bangers and mash, is also popular for lunch.

Gambling

While Vancouver's casinos lack the flair and sparkle of those in Las Vegas (no floor shows and no alcohol), they provide the gambler with a full range of games of chance, including blackjack, roulette, and several Chinese varieties. The dozen or so casinos in town are open seven days a week from 6:00 P.M. to 2:00 A.M. (ask at your hotel for names and addresses).

Views

In a city that lives off its looks, a suitable end to any Vancouver evening is a nightcap in a bar with a view. There are several in downtown hotels, all worth a drink for the lofty sight of the city lights. Visitors will find especially good views of the ocean, Stanley Park, and the houses climbing the North Shore mountains from **Windows on the Bay**, on the 35th floor of the Coast Plaza, 1733 Comox Street. The Sheraton Landmark's 42nd-floor revolving restaurant lounge, aptly named **Cloud Nine**, is the highest spot in town. Nurse a drink in this adult carousel and you will eventually see the entire city and its environs slip by (including Mount Baker in Washington State by day).

For a ground-level view earlier in the evening, try for a window table at the bar of the **Sylvia Hotel**, one of old-time Vancouver's favorite haunts, on English Bay. A twilight drink while the sun slips behind freighters moored in the bay, the seawall joggers head home for a shower, and the popcorn men pack up their red and orange carts is one of this fortunate city's finest experiences.

SHOPS AND SHOPPING

Vancouver shopping is more than an excursion—it's an experience. The scope has stretched beyond the doldrums of dependable department stores that characterized city shopping several decades ago and now includes internationally acclaimed designer boutiques, lively public markets, ethnic areas, and fine art galleries filled with works by Canadian and international artists as well as much-sought-after native Indian artworks.

Omiyage

The Japanese have a term for special souvenirs that typify countries visited: *omiyage*. Local *omiyage* here include such quality items as Northwest Coast Indian and Inuit art and carved B.C. jade.

In cobblestoned Gastown, Vancouver's historic birthplace, **Hill's Indian Crafts'** (165 Water Street) collection of coastal native art includes the famous handspun Cowichan sweaters, vests, mittens, and socks made by that Vancouver Island tribe. In the adjacent alleyway, totem-pole carvers can sometimes be seen carving great cedar poles with small hand tools and a piece of equipment their forefathers never knew: the chain saw. The nearby **Inuit Gallery**, in a Gastown heritage building at 345 Water Street, has one of Canada's finest collections of Inuit and Northwest Coast Indian artwork. The gallery features carvings and silkscreens by prominent Haida artist Robert Davidson, as well as soapstone sculptures by Kaka Ashoona of Cape Dorset.

Among the numerous other native art shops, three stand out. **Leona Lattimer**, in a cedar "longhouse" at 1590 West 2nd Avenue, adjacent to Granville Island, specializes in quality Northwest Coast Indian art. Native artisans often can be seen carving in the adjacent lot. The University of British Columbia's **Museum of Anthropology Shop** features silver jewelry, carved cedar masks, intricate woven baskets, and silkscreen prints. Although the museum is 20 minutes by car or bus from downtown, it is well worth the trip to see the award-winning architecture and exquisite native artworks here.

A noteworthy newcomer to the Indian art scene is the **Gallery of Tribal Art**, 2329 Granville Street, which features the best of two ancient cultures: British Columbia's coastal natives and the tribes of Papua New Guinea.

B.C. has the world's largest-known jade deposits, ranging in color from the most common forest-green to pale green and black. The gem is used to make exquisite jewelry, ornaments, and decorative tiles. Locally designed and crafted jade is available at **Lyle Sopel's Studios Inc.**, 332 East Esplanade in North Vancouver. Sopel, one of Canada's top jade sculptors, sells commissioned pieces, not souvenir trinkets. At **Jade World**, 1696 West 1st Avenue, near bustling Granville Island, you can see master carvers transform the raw product into finished art. The shop sells everything from small keepsakes to collectors' items.

Vancouver's proximity to the Pacific results in an abundance of fresh seafood, notably salmon, some of which is packed for travel. Recommended "seafood couriers" include the **Salmon Village** at 779 Thurlow Street, **Jet Set Sam** at the airport, the **Lobster Man** at 1807 Mast Tower on Granville Island, and the **Salmon Shop**, located at three public markets: Granville Island, Robson Street, and Lonsdale Quay.

With some 70 galleries displaying and selling everything from fringe works by up-and-coming local talents to the best contemporary work, the city at times resembles a sprawling artists' colony. Those interested in contemporary paintings by renowned Canadian and international artists should visit **Buschlen/Mowatt Fine Arts**, downtown at 111-1445 West Georgia Street. The **Diane Farris Gallery** at 1565 West 7th Avenue is internationally acclaimed for its quality contemporary and folk art, and represents a talented group of Vancouver artists, including Attila Richard Lukacs. The **Federation of Canadian Artists** gallery (952 Richards Street, downtown) rotates works by leading local talents in every medium.

Those who like glasswork are certain to find two studios of interest. At the **Robert Held Studios**, 2130 Pine Street, and **David New-Small & Sterling Studio Glass**, 1440 Bridge Street on Granville Island, visitors can watch master glassblowers create exquisite works of art out of great gobs of molten glass. Both shops also have showrooms in which everything from delicate Christmas ornaments to large vases and sculptures are sold.

South Granville Street, between Broadway and about 15th Avenue, is Vancouver's unofficial Antique Row. Shops like **Uno Langmann Antiques & Art** (2117 Granville) sell estate jewelry, silverware, and gorgeous period furnishings and paintings. On the city's West Side along 4th and 10th avenues, near the university, eclectic specialty shops sell everything from Southeast Asian artifacts to fitness togs and brass and oak furnishings.

Eaton's department store downtown (Georgia and Granville streets) carries an amalgam of Canadiana: canned salmon in attractive cedar gift boxes, native carvings, jade trinkets, maple syrup, Cowichan Indian knits, and other collectibles.

Fashion

In recent years, several top Vancouver fashion designers have achieved international status. **Zonda Nellis**, 2203 Granville Street, is known for her exquisite handwoven and dyed creations for women. Martha Sturdy's oversize, avant-garde jewelry regularly appears in *Vogue* and *Harper's Bazaar*. Her boutique, **Martha Sturdy Originals**, is located at 3065 Granville Street. **Peter Fox Shoes**, 303 West Cordova, is where many Hollywood actresses shop for footwear when they're in town. The look is funky, yet stylish, with retro-seventies, Victorian, and other influences evident in these exclusive Italian-made designs.

To climb British Columbia's lofty peaks and ford its rushing rivers you need rugged outdoor gear. Two of the most reputable outfitters in town are **Taiga**, 390 West 8th Street in Kitsilano, and **Coast Mountain Sports**, 1828 West 4th Avenue. One of the better places to purchase ski clothing and equipment is **Skyline Sports**, 5395 West Boulevard.

The usual designer boutiques (Canada's Alfred Sung, Gianni Versace, and Rodier Paris) are found mainly downtown on trendy Robson Street, in the **Pacific Centre** (at the corner of West Georgia and Granville streets), and in the historic, arched-ceiling restorations of **The Landing** (375 Water Street) and the **Sinclair Centre** (757 West Hastings). Filled with specialty boutiques and food stalls, **City Square**, 555 West 12th Street, occupies two heritage school buildings refitted and combined under a skylight roof.

Robson Street, which once housed small European bakeries and delis, has recently seen the decline of the deli and the rise of Art Deco designer shops, transforming Old World Continental into New World yuppie. Although the old ambience has vanished, Robson, with its cappuccino bars, al fresco dining, and sidewalk flower stands, is still a pleasant place to stroll and people-watch.

Among Vancouver's numerous noteworthy furriers, **Pappas Furs**, 449 Hamilton Street, is Canada's largest, with an impressive pedigree spanning three generations.

British Imports

Vancouver's ties with "old Blighty" are evident in tea vendors like **Murchie's Tea & Coffee Ltd.** (970 Robson Street) as well as numerous downtown tartan outlets—notably **House of McLaren** (125–131 Water Street), the **Edinburgh Tartan Shop** (375 Water Street), and **The Scotch Shop** (674 Seymour

Street). **Miller & Coe**, on Hastings Street downtown, has one of the city's best selections of English bone china and crystal. To satisfy any yearnings for "the old country," **Marks & Spencer** department stores (downtown in the Pacific Centre and other shopping malls) offer a good selection of St. Michael's clothing and such specialty foods as English-style bacon, kippers, toad-in-the-hole, and shortbreads.

Public Markets

Within the past decade, city planning has transformed acres of prime waterfront from unsightly industrial wasteland into attractive public markets like **Granville Island**. The informal atmosphere here appeals to locals as well as tourists. While the covered market overflows with fresh produce and local crafts, the scene outside includes lively street entertainers, cawing gulls, and myriad watercraft, from barges to kayaks.

The Granville Island Public Market is accessible by car or harbor ferries from downtown; **Lonsdale Quay** in North Vancouver by car or Seabus from downtown; and **Westminster Quay** by car or Skytrain from the city center.

Richmond's attractive new **Bridgepoint Market**, 8811 River Road, is easily accessible by bus or car. Head south over the Oak Street Bridge and turn right at the Richmond exit. At Number 3 Road turn right again and continue to the end.

Ethnic Shopping

Vancouver's **Chinatown** is the second largest in North America after San Francisco's. The lively shops east of downtown along Pender Street, between Carrall and Gore, sell wicker products, china, celadon porcelain, teas, and exotic remedies from Kirin deer antlers to Korean red ginseng. **Ming Wo**, 23 East Pender Street, has one of the city's best selections of cookware. The **Ten Ren Tea & Ginseng Company**, 550 Main Street, will serve you complimentary teas as you choose from among hundreds of exotic flavors.

Tailors and dressmakers delight in **Little India**, centered 20 minutes south of downtown at 49th Avenue and Main Street. Among the large sari shops here is the **Guru Bazaar**, 6529 Main Street, a fantasyland of bright bolts of silks and synthetics from India and Japan.

Little Italy, on Commercial Drive north of Broadway in East Vancouver, is a gastronome's delight. For more than 30 years, **Olivieri's**, 1900 Commercial Drive, has supplied the city's restaurants and supermarkets with its homemade tortellini, ravioli, lasagna, linguine, and savory sauces. Down the street at number 1810, **Falcone Bros. Meat Market** attracts customers from as far as Washington and Oregon with its superb veal, lamb, Genoa salami, and homemade sausages.

The **Renato Pastry Shop** at number 1795 tempts sweets lovers with a range of delectables, including Santa Loren cream puff cake, supe (a sponge cake-and-liqueur concoction), and rulli (a sponge cake, liqueur, and chocolate concoction). **Joe's**, at number 1824, serves soup bowl–size cups of cappuccino topped off with a soufflé-like froth of milk.

Although most Italian couture is found in the upmarket shopping plazas of downtown Vancouver, **Renzo**, at 1684 Commercial Drive, is a respected tailor, while **Kalena**, at number 1526, sells fine imported Italian shoes.

—*Marnie Mitchell*

DAY TRIP TO VICTORIA

To the rest of Canada, Victoria lies somewhere "behind the tweed curtain." British Columbia's small (about 290,000 inhabitants) capital is certainly very British, and proud of it. Flower baskets hang from lampposts, shops sell Harris tweed and Irish linen, and citizens play cricket and croquet. This charming island city has a different feel from Vancouver, one that is slower paced, more relaxed. (Although in summer, especially on weekends, hordes of tourists shatter the city's otherwise bucolic serenity; it's the price Victoria pays for its popularity.) With its pleasant pubs, inns, and bed-and-breakfast places; its lack of high-rises, traffic, and crowds; and its quiet, open spaces and numerous parks, Victoria remains decidedly Victorian.

Whether you arrive by air or by sea, from Vancouver or direct from the U.S., you will find a charming city with a distinctive character quite different from that of the mainland. Despite its Union Jack image, Victoria is a curious mixture of British gentility and logger/frontier ruggedness, of high tea and draft beer. Here, *Town and Country* meets *Field and Stream*. This city of prim elderly ladies and dapper gentlemen living close to forests and the sea is also a community of plaid-clad youth.

The city is worth much more than a day trip, but a day trip *is* possible from Vancouver via B.C. Ferries, the city center–

to–city center AirBC floatplane, or by Helijet Airways helicopter. (See Getting Around at the end of this section for details.)

MAJOR INTEREST

Bastion Square Area (historic buildings)
British ambience with frontier flavor
Parliament Buildings
Royal British Columbia Museum
Butchart Gardens

Though much older than Vancouver, the capital of British Columbia remains a pleasant oasis of gentility. Established in 1843 as Fort Victoria, a Hudson's Bay fur-trading post, it was the first European settlement on the island. The natural harbor at **Esquimalt**, west of town, was the British Royal Navy's Pacific base for a time, and the city later thrived on lumbering, farming, and fishing. Today its industries include government and the armed forces (the Royal Roads Military College and a Canadian Navy and Army base). Its equable climate, the country's balmiest, draws retirees from across Canada, giving Victoria its dichotomous genteel-among-the-great-outdoors aspect.

An outburst of creative energy and a striving to emulate the European masters resulted in Victoria's physical makeup. In just 35 years (1890 to 1925), the Parliament Buildings, the Empress Hotel, Craigdarroch Castle, Hatley Park Castle (now the Royal Roads Military College), and Crystal Garden were built. During the same period, Victoria developed its own distinctive style of architecture, as seen in the many stately residences that still stand.

The city is situated on the **Saanich Peninsula**, which extends out from the southeastern part of Vancouver Island (below the 49th parallel). It is an almost-rural area of rocky bays and inlets, forested parks, small lakes, and a few low-lying hills.

Exploring Victoria

Red double-decker buses and horse-drawn carriages allow you to see Victoria in style, although most of the city's attractions can easily be seen on foot. The historic downtown area is filled with brick sidewalks, arcades, squares, and alleys. Street names such as Bastion Square, Trounce Alley, and Market Square serve as reminders that this was truly a

Victorian colony. The old downtown area is a few square blocks that runs from the Inner Harbour east to Douglas Street. Places of historical interest extend from the Parliament Buildings north to Chinatown, Centennial Square, and City Hall.

The heart of Victoria is the Inner Harbour, busy with ferries from B.C. and Washington State, seaplanes from Vancouver, Seattle, and outlying bush communities, and yachts from all over the world.

DOWNTOWN VICTORIA

Empress Hotel

The stately, castle-like Empress Hotel, one of the great Canadian Pacific Railways château-style hotels, overlooks the Parliament Buildings and the waterfront. The ivy-covered Empress, with its pinnacles, turrets, and verdigris roofs, fairly reeks of the British Empire. Rudyard Kipling, the old imperial apologist himself, stayed here and must have felt at home among the columned grand lobby, the plush, richly appointed lounges, the clublike Bengal Room, and the former **Library Bar** (now a native art gallery), with its distinctively ornate ceiling. Perhaps it was the Empress that inspired Kipling's turn-of-the-century comment that Victoria had all the best of Bournemouth arranged around the Bay of Naples.

Tea in the lobby, complete with scones, crumpets, clotted cream, cakes, and Empress Blend, is a must for visitors, even if it is somewhat contrived. The hotel was starting to show its age, but a recent and extensive refurbishing has restored it to the condition of its glory days.

Parliament Buildings

The proud, neo-Gothic Parliament Buildings across the harbor were built of native granite and wood, and completed in 1897. The stately structures sit on expansive grounds dotted with statues of writers, philosophers, pioneers, and, of course, Queen Victoria. When the house is not sitting there are tours of the interiors, with their mosaic tile floors, intricate stained-glass windows, and "golden gates" leading to the marble-paneled legislative chambers.

During sessions, visitors can listen in on the debates—in B.C. known more for acrimony than for subtle parliamentary repartee. At night the buildings blaze like a fairyland castle with thousands of light bulbs. (The first illumination of the exterior was on June 21, 1897, to commemorate Queen Victoria's Diamond Jubilee.)

Royal British Columbia Museum

The impressive Royal British Columbia Museum, between the Empress and the Parliament Buildings, gives visitors a good sense of B.C.'s pioneer days. Exhibits include re-creations of a frontier town, a coal mine shaft, a fish cannery, a Peace River farm, and Captain Cook's private cabin aboard his ship *Discovery*. Elsewhere on the premises, the third-floor gallery incorporates a complete Kwakiutl longhouse filled with a full range of traditional housewares.

The forest of totem poles in **Thunderbird Park**, outside the museum, is one of the world's finest collections. The authentic hand-hewn Haida Indian longhouse here, the tradi-tional coast Indian dwelling, includes a studio. Inside, native artists carve full-scale totem poles, many of them commis-sioned by heads of state, corporations, and municipal gov-ernments around the world.

Emily Carr

Many Eastern Canadians know British Columbia through the work of Emily Carr, who lived among the Coast Indians and filled her canvasses with depictions of totem poles, Indian villages, and dark, brooding forests. The house where she was raised, and later retired, still stands at 207 Government Street, a few blocks from the Parliament build-ings. The **Emily Carr Gallery**, with much original artwork, manuscripts, and film presentations about the artist's life and work, is at 1107 Wharf Street, and is open Tuesday through Saturday, 10:00 A.M. to 4:00 P.M.

BUTCHART GARDENS

Butchart Gardens, located 20 km (12 miles) north of Victoria on the road from the airport and the Swartz Bay ferry terminal, is best reached by car (although there is frequent bus service from downtown). In 1904 Jennie Butchart, an avid gardener, began to transform the limestone quarry on her estate into something wonderful. Topsoil from local farms was delivered by horse and cart to the site and the first flowers planted. From these humble beginnings Mrs. Butch-art's project grew into the elaborate sunken gardens cover-ing some 50 acres that more than half a million visitors now visit annually. Open daily year-round, 9:00 A.M. to 5:00 P.M.; admission is $4. For information about the special events and fireworks displays staged on many a summer evening, Tel: (604) 652-5256.

SHOPPING IN VICTORIA

Shopping is a popular Victoria pastime and a very British experience. The **English Sweet Shop** on Yates Street sells English toffee, teas, biscuits, souvenirs, and china. **Celtic Casuals** on Harbor Square has fine Welsh tapestries, woollen clothing, and crafts items. For quality native handicrafts, Cowichan sweaters, jewelry, wood carvings, jade, and totem poles visit the **Indian Craft Shoppe** or **Sasquatch Trading**, both on Government Street. The **Gallery of the Arctic**, 611 Fort Street, is good for Canadiana, with limited-edition collector-quality Arctic prints, as well as art and artifacts of the North, including Inuit sculpture in stone and whalebone and stone-cut prints. In addition to Canadian handicrafts, pottery, prints, jade, and carved soapstone, **The Quest**, 1023 Government Street, features exhibitions by contemporary Canadian artists.

STAYING IN VICTORIA

Most of the city's good hotels and inns are located within the fairly limited downtown area. The ► **Holland House Inn**, just two blocks from the Inner Harbour at 595 Michigan Street, is a pleasant old street-corner building typical of Victoria. The distinctive rooms in this small inn have balconies, fireplaces, and four-poster beds.

Even closer to the harbor, the ► **Captain's Palace**, 309 Belleville Street, provides accommodation in a three-story 17-room Victorian mansion complete with crystal chandeliers, tapestries, stained-glass windows and doors, and rooms furnished with antiques. Its restaurant of the same name offers a good view of the harbor.

The 11-room antiques-filled ► **Beaconsfield Inn**, in an English mansion on a quiet street near Beacon Hill Park, has a guest library, a conservatory/sunroom, gracious rooms with fireplaces and canopy beds, and a full breakfast every morning. By contrast, the ► **Laurel Point Inn** near the Parliament Buildings is modern and features indoor/outdoor pools, a sauna, a whirlpool, and tennis courts. In addition, all rooms have balconies with a harbor view.

The ► **Victoria Regent Hotel**, another modern establishment, is located on Wharf Street in the central waterfront area and offers standard rooms with city views as well as apartment-style one- and two-bedroom suites, some with Jacuzzis and fireplaces.

The ▶ **Chateau Victoria Hotel**, on Burdett Street down-town, is one of the city's top luxury hotels and offers recently renovated, pleasantly furnished rooms with views of the city or harbor. The rooftop restaurant on the 18th floor likewise provides a bird's-eye vista of Victoria.

The old ▶ **Oak Bay Beach Hotel**, located on the sea in a pleasant residential area south of the city center, resembles an English Tudor country inn. The recently renovated rooms are large, and many overlook the Haro Strait, with the U.S.–Canadian border running mid-channel. The inn's 41-foot yacht, the *Mesouda,* makes lunch and sunset cruises around the harbor, while the M.V. *Pride of Victoria* (also operated by the hotel) takes passengers on lunch and dinner cruises of the harbor, the strait, and the coast north of Victoria. In summer, both dock at the bottom of the garden. For hotel guests, cruise patrons, and those wishing high tea, the hotel provides complimentary shuttle bus service. Tel: (604) 598-4556.

And then there is the ▶ **Empress Hotel**, in a class by itself. A Victoria landmark anchoring one end of the country (with Quebec City's Le Château Frontenac at the other), this ornate palace has been completely refurbished and now boasts large, modern rooms with perfect plumbing. More than a hotel, the Empress is one of the city's major tourist attractions.

DINING AND ENTERTAINMENT IN VICTORIA

While big-sister Vancouver wasn't looking, Victoria grew into a lively, sophisticated town. For the convenience of its many tourists and well-heeled politicians, Victoria is unusually well served by good restaurants and nightlife.

Pagliacci's, or Pag's, open for lunch and dinner, is among the most popular dining spots in town, with consistently good food matched by a loud atmosphere, colorful decor, and prompt service. It is centrally located at 1011 Broad Street, within shouting distance of the Eaton Centre. You'll likely have to stand in line—and this is no place for an intimate candlelit evening. Tel: (604) 386-1662.

The **Herald Street Caffé**, 546 Herald Street, is also very popular with both young and old, formal and denim clad. Its atmosphere is bright and cheerful and the decor is Art Nouveau, with contemporary paintings hanging on the walls. Lunch and dinner is served, and the Herald stays open late. Tel: (604) 381-1441.

The **Parrot House**, atop the Chateau Victoria Hotel, offers outstanding panoramic views of this scenic seaside city. The music is classical, the cuisine Continental (French, Swiss,

Italian, Hungarian). Try to book a harbor-view table; Tel: (604) 382-9258.

The **Spinnakers' Brew Pub** (Tel: 604/384-6613), across the Johnson Bridge from the city center, is well worth the few minutes' drive. (Once you cross the bridge, turn left on Catherine Street. The pub is in a large waterfront building at the end of the road.) Spinnakers' started a trend in Canada by brewing its own beer and ale. Most of their brews are flat and dull, British-style, but there are some lively European-type lagers on tap. The fish and chips are unique—made with a halibut filet coated with brewer's yeast and whipped egg-white batter—even if the fries are too thick. There's no reserved seating, however, so you have to hustle for a table by the window, and the kitchen runs out of specials early.

With its dark wood wainscoting, hand-hewn beams, and leaded windows overlooking the sea, **The Snug**, in the Oak Bay Beach Hotel (see above), is an excellent choice for lunch even if you're not planning on staying the night. The lobby has a good, solid Edwardian ambience, with stuffed furniture, 19th-century antiques, and a fine hundred-year-old piano that the resident pianist still plays. Tel: (604) 598-4556.

There's more to do here than you might expect from a staid government town. Victoria is particularly well served by lively pubs, among them the **Sticky Wicket** in the Strathcona Hotel, 919 Douglas Street, and, somewhat re-moved from the city center, the **Barley Mow** at 2581 Penrhyn Street and the **Monkey Tree** at 4025 Borden Street.

Harpo's Cabaret, 15 Bastion Square at Wharf Street, is a jumping spot featuring everything from reggae and Afro-pop to rock and rhythm and blues. **Sweetwaters**, 27–560 Johnson Street, serves up jazz to a younger set.

GETTING TO VICTORIA

By Ferry. The cheapest way to get to Victoria from Vancouver is via Pacific Coach Lines from the downtown Vancouver bus depot at Beatty and Dunsmuir streets ($21.25 one way; $38.25 round trip). Buses board the ferry at Tsawwassen (ta-WAH-sen), south of Vancouver, and continue to downtown Victoria. The ferry crossing takes 1 hour and 35 minutes, the whole trip about 3½ hours. During peak summer hours (7:00 A.M. to 10:00 P.M.) there are 16 scheduled crossings daily. Buses leave the station 70 minutes prior to the ferry departure; Tel: (604) 662-8074 in Vancouver.

You can also drive—although in peak seasons, especially during long weekends, there may be a several-hour wait for a place on the ferry. Best to check conditions ahead of time;

B.C. ferry schedule information is available 24 hours a day by phoning (604) 277-0277 in Vancouver and (604) 656-0757 in Victoria. The fee for car and driver is $25.50 each way, and $5.50 for each additional passenger.

To reach the Victoria ferries from Vancouver, follow Oak Street south onto Highway 99 and turn right soon after the George Massey Tunnel. The turnoff is well marked.

The Swartz Bay Terminal on Vancouver Island is 32 km (20 miles) northwest of Victoria via Highway 17. A new ferry route from mainland Tsawwassen to Nanaimo takes U.S. travellers to northern Vancouver Island more directly by avoiding downtown Vancouver.

By Plane. Harbor-to-harbor AirBC floatplanes do the trip in 35 scenic minutes. In Vancouver, they depart from the Coal Harbor Terminal near the Pan Pacific Hotel (close to Stanley Park), and land in Victoria's Inner Harbour. Basic fares as low as $126 are available. For reservations, Tel: (604) 685-5515 in Vancouver, (604) 360-9074 in Victoria; in the Pacific U.S., Tel: (800) 663-8868; elsewhere in the U.S., (800) 776-3000; in B.C., (800) 663-3721.

Helijet Airways flies jet helicopters from the heliport near the Seabus Terminal or the international airport in Vancouver to Ogden Point in downtown Victoria, a 30-minute trip. The normal fare is $122 one way, with a weekend round-trip special of $160. Tel: (604) 273-1414.

From the States. Clipper Navigation's 300-passenger Victoria Clippers make the run between Victoria and Seattle in about 2½ hours. Fares start at $49 one way and $74 round trip, and vary according to the season. Tel: (206) 448-5000 or (604) 382-8100; in the U.S., Tel: (800) 888-2535.

Blackball Transport offers four sailings daily aboard the M.V. *Coho* between Victoria and Port Angeles, Washington. Sailing time is 1 hour and 30 minutes; the cost is U.S.$25 for car and driver one way, U.S.$6.25 per passenger. Tel: (206) 457-4491 or (604) 386-2202.

ACCOMMODATIONS REFERENCE FOR VICTORIA

The rates given below are projections for peak seasons during the 1994 calendar year; at other times of the year they may be considerably less. Unless otherwise indicated, rates are based on double rooms, double occupancy; provincial and federal taxes are included in all rates. As rates are subject to change, always double-check before booking.

▶ **Beaconsfield Inn.** 998 Humboldt Street, **Victoria**, B.C. V8V 2Z8. Tel: (604) 384-4044; Fax: (604) 721-2442. $129–$275.

▶ **Captain's Palace.** 309 Belleville Street, **Victoria**, B.C. V8V 1X2. Tel: (604) 388-9191; Fax: (604) 388-7606. $111–$246 (includes full breakfast).

▶ **Chateau Victoria Hotel.** 740 Burdett Street, **Victoria**, B.C. V8W 1B2. Tel: (604) 382-4221; Fax: (604) 380-1950; in the U.S. and Canada, Tel: (800) 663-5891. $119–$228.

▶ **Empress Hotel.** 721 Government Street, **Victoria**, B.C. V8W 1W5. Tel: (604) 384-8111; Fax: (604) 381-4334; in the U.S. and Canada, Tel: (800) 828-7447; in Ontario and Quebec, (800) 268-9420; elsewhere in Canada, (800) 268-9411. $270–$304.

▶ **Holland House Inn.** 595 Michigan Street, **Victoria**, B.C. V8V 1S7. Tel: (604) 384-6117; Fax: (604) 384-6117. $135–$246 (includes full breakfast).

▶ **Laurel Point Inn.** 680 Montreal Street, **Victoria**, B.C. V8V 1Z8. Tel: (604) 386-8721; Fax: (604) 386-9547; in the U.S. and Canada, Tel: (800) 663-7667. $146–$234.

▶ **Oak Bay Beach Hotel.** 1175 Beach Drive, **Victoria**, B.C. V8S 2N2. Tel: (604) 598-4556; Fax: (604) 598-4556; in the U.S., Tel: (800) 668-7758. $99–$468 (includes breakfast).

▶ **Victoria Regent Hotel.** 1234 Wharf Street, **Victoria**, B.C. V8W 3H9. Tel: (604) 386-2211; Fax: (604) 386-2622; in the U.S., British Columbia, and Alberta, (800) 663-7472. $146–$427 (includes breakfast).

BRITISH COLUMBIA

By Marnie Mitchell

Marnie Mitchell, a Vancouver native, has worked in tourism both in British Columbia and abroad. She specializes in travel writing, contributing to Canadian and international publications.

While Canada's eastern provinces were busy forming the Dominion of Canada in 1867, British Columbia, the rugged renegade "out west," was busy with other affairs. The newly colonized province was in the throes of a gold rush. In fact, two of its towns were then the largest ones north of San Francisco and west of Chicago.

Eventually the first transcontinental railroad linked the last frontier to the rest of Canada, and British Columbia (B.C.), somewhat reluctantly, joined the confederation in 1871. But her stubborn pioneer spirit remains. The Rocky Mountains, between B.C. and Alberta, are perhaps as much a psychological divider as a geographic one, but whatever the cause, B.C. is a strong-minded independent.

Easterners have long sought to make the agreeable province their home, particularly the mild Pacific port of Vancouver, which they enviably call "Lotus Land." As a result, the city is so inundated with newcomers that it is unusual to ferret out a native Vancouverite.

Most of the province's roughly three million people live in its southwestern corner, in and around Vancouver and Victoria, the provincial capital on Vancouver Island. Victoria is decidedly British, all tea and crumpets, brollies and double-decker buses. Vancouver, the province's largest city, is a vibrant, cosmopolitan metropolis, yet retains the air of a pioneer town. Indeed, the wilds are right on Vancouver's front doorstep—in several suburbs bears still wander into backyards and squirrels scamper into some West End condos.

B.C. looks more to the south than the east, and considers itself the California of Canada, both for its ideas and attitudes. This notion has been strengthened by the influx of movie moguls, who have dubbed Vancouver "Hollywood North." In recent years Asian influences have also increased through immigration and trade, making B.C. an important part of the Pacific Rim region.

Most visitors enter B.C. through Vancouver, the provincial gateway. After spending several days touring the city, the more adventurous head to Vancouver Island, the Southwest, the Cariboo, or the Okanagan. These regions require several days each to tour adequately. Return visitors, or those with more time, head to the wilds of the north and then beyond to the Yukon and Alaska. Those arriving by car from Alberta can explore the Rockies on their way. Many first-timers and even repeat visitors take the comfortable trains: B.C. Rail and VIA Rail pass through some of the world's most spectacular scenery.

British Columbia's weather varies greatly because the province encompasses so many geographic zones. Generally, the coast is temperate, while the central Okanagan, High Country, and Cariboo areas are warm and dry in summer, cold and clear in winter. Weather throughout the province is usually pleasant from May through October. Ski season in the Rockies and the Cariboo usually runs from December through April (June at Whistler).

MAJOR INTEREST

Rugged mountain scenery
Hiking, canoeing, and salmon fishing
Skiing Whistler, the Okanagan, and the Rockies
Cariboo Highway area for rodeos and dude ranches
Barkerville (authentic gold rush–era heritage park)
Okanagan vineyards
Kootenay hot springs
'Ksan Historical Indian Village

We cover the province starting from Vancouver (see the separate chapter on the city and a day trip to Victoria), with Vancouver Island to its west, the Sunshine Coast to its immediate north, and the Fraser Valley to its immediate east (the latter two included in "Southwest British Columbia"). Then we move north of the Fraser Valley and explore the Cariboo Highway past Hope.

After that, we double back to the High Country ("South-Central B.C."), and from there move east to the Okanagan; the Kootenays; and the Rockies and Alberta border (with Banff, Jasper, and Calgary on the other side).

Finally, we head to the far north (the "Northwest")—from Prince George west to the town of Prince Rupert on the Pacific coast, and ending with the nearby Queen Charlotte Islands.

VANCOUVER ISLAND

Coddled at its southern end by Washington's Olympic Peninsula across the Strait of Juan de Fuca, Vancouver Island resembles a great ship at berth, a 12,000-square-mile landmass characterized by craggy mountains, evergreen forests, and rolling farms inland. The island charms visitors with a laid-back cordiality reflecting its logging, fishing, and mining heritages.

While Victoria, the provincial capital at the island's southern tip, is decidedly British, numerous communities elsewhere have Indian names and cultural distinctions reflecting their heritage. Coastal villages and towns hug the eastern shore, while the mountainous west coast, with its vast, wind-shaped Pacific Rim National Park, is largely unpopulated.

Long before Captain Cook arrived, the Kwakiutl, Nootka, and Coast Salish Indians shared the rich land and marine wealth of the largest and most diverse of North America's West Coast islands. Cook's arrival at Nootka Island in 1778 prompted further British, then Spanish, explorations.

Eventually Spain ceded her interests, and the British Hudson's Bay Company established Fort Victoria in 1843. Some 15 years later gold was discovered on the mainland along the Fraser River. Victoria, across the Strait of Georgia, became the supply hub and provincial capital—the latter a position it retained when British Columbia joined Canada in 1871.

Island Coach Lines (Tel: 604/385-4411) serves all the major communities, from Victoria north to Port Hardy, but a private vehicle is needed to visit more remote areas.

BOTANICAL BEACH

Allow a full day to visit this cluster of natural aquariums frequented by marine biologists, southwest of Victoria along Highway 14 past Sooke and Port Renfrew. Because access involves a strenuous hike, visitors should be reasonably fit; phone ahead to the Sooke Travel Information Center at (604) 642-6351 for tide conditions.

En route, the ▶ **Sooke Harbour House**, one of the finest country inns in B.C., overlooks the Strait of Juan de Fuca, where it accommodates overnight guests in interesting sea-view rooms (some with Jacuzzis) outfitted with pottery sinks, fireplaces, and patios or balconies. Dining here is as much visual as culinary art: Its restaurateur-owners grow herbs, cultivate 150 edible flowers, and dive for their seafood.

THE GULF ISLANDS

From Victoria, B.C. Ferries provides service to seven Gulf Islands in the Strait of Georgia between Vancouver Island and the mainland. Artists and naturalists favor these temperate islets cloaked with Douglas firs and twisted arbutus trees. Because transportation is limited, it's recommended that you bring your own vehicle. Saltspring Island's elegant ▶ **Hastings House** hotel (open mid-March to the last weekend of November) is fashioned after an English Tudor manor, with mullioned windows facing farm or sea views, classical background music, and exceptional meals. On Sundays locals join the guests for the substantial brunch.

The Gulf Islands also have good lodgings more moderately priced than Hastings House. The unpretentious ▶ **Beach House**, a delightful post-and-beam lodging on the western side of Saltspring Island, overlooks Sansum Narrows and a passing parade of log barges, tugboats, otters, sea lions, geese, cormorants, and other waterfowl. North Pender Island's ▶ **Cliffside Inn On-the-Sea** offers tranquil sea views, fireside dining, and eiderdown quilts. Guests can book a private hour in the Jacuzzi and enjoy such breakfast fare as Okanagan baked apples.

The ▶ **Woodstone Country Inn** on Galiano Island has a forest setting and rooms named for flowers like the trillium and wild rose. The inn is bright and airy, and rooms, some with fireplaces, have forest or valley views. One of the owners is a chef, and prepares a number of creative dishes, including roast game hen baked in grape leaves and mahi mahi with mango sauce.

NORTH OF VICTORIA

Back on Vancouver Island: Highway 1 climbs to the Malahat summit for dramatic views of the Saanich Peninsula and Washington's Mount Baker. Perched at the top here is ▶ **The Aerie**, with 13 luxury units, private hot tubs, fireplaces, and balconies affording breathtaking views. The inn is also

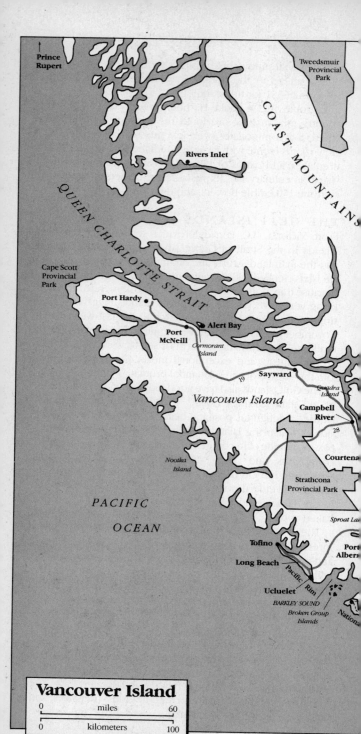

Prince
Rupert

Tweedsmuir
Provincial
Park

COAST MOUNTAINS

Rivers Inlet

QUEEN CHARLOTTE STRAIT

Cape Scott
Provincial
Park

Port Hardy

**Port
McNeill**

Alert Bay

*Cormorant
Island*

19 **Sayward**

*Quadra
Island*

Vancouver Island

**Campbell
River**

28

*Nootka
Island*

Courtena

Strathcona
Provincial
Park

PACIFIC

OCEAN

Sproat La

Tofino

4

**Port
Alber**

Long Beach

Pacific Rim

Ucluelet

BARKLEY SOUND

*Broken Group
Islands*

Nationa

Vancouver Island

| 0 | miles | 60 |
| 0 | kilometers | 100 |

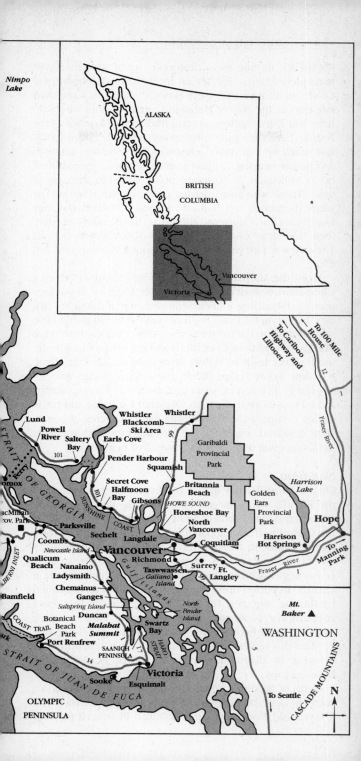

known for its fine meals featuring coastal specialties and hand-picked herbs. Farther on in the town of Duncan, the Cowichan Indians sell their famous heavy-knit **Cowichan sweaters** at the **Native Heritage Centre**. Visitors who stop here will learn the legends and traditions of Canada's First People, have the opportunity to try authentic native foods, and watch or join native artisans at work carving, knitting, and basket weaving. Duncan's native heritage is exemplified by its collection of 60 totem poles, scattered throughout town. Those who aren't driving can travel this route on the scenic Esquimalt and Nanaimo Railway's **Malahat Dayliner** from Victoria to Courtenay, halfway up the island's east coast. (See Courtenay under The Island's North section below.) The one-way fare from Victoria is about $35, the round trip $70.

From the Malahat Summit, Highway 1 winds north past **Chemainus**, a small coastal community noted for its outdoor murals chronicling a fascinating shipping and logging history. In summer artisans from around the world gather here to contribute to the town's alfresco artwork at the **Festival of Murals**. Just north of Chemainus and the town of Ladysmith, the highway leads to Yellow Point Road and, farther along, ▶ **Yellow Point Lodge**. When the original lodge was destroyed by fire several years ago, dedicated former patrons rallied to restore it. The reconstructed log lodge and rustic cabins occupy a rocky peninsula with 180 acres of oceanfront parkland, excellent for bird-watching and romantic strolls on quiet trails along wave-washed beachfront.

Nanaimo

On the fourth Sunday in July, Nanaimo, a deep-sea port and the island's second-largest city, sends daring "tubbers" 30 miles across the turbulent Strait of Georgia to Vancouver in the Great International Bathtub Race—although most commuters prefer to take the ferry. Nanaimo's 1852 Hudson's Bay Company Bastion is among the Canadian West's oldest remaining structures. During the summer months, "Bastion Guards" in period dress fire the noon cannon accompanied by skirling bagpipes. Ferries for passengers on foot leave regularly for **Newcastle Island Provincial Park**, a nature sanctuary with hiking trails, sandy beaches, and a heritage pavilion that serves barbecued salmon. The mayor promotes his town by distributing chocolatey Nanaimo bars during business trips.

North of Nanaimo, Route 4 spurs west to Port Alberni. En route, in Coombs, goats graze on the marketplace roof. The 800-year-old Douglas firs in **MacMillan Provincial Park** resemble a vaulted cathedral and provide a tranquil respite from urban life. Farther on at Sproat Lake visitors can see the World War II Martin Mars water bombers used to fight forest fires throughout the province.

Port Alberni

In Port Alberni, noted for its exceptional salmon and steelhead fishing (as is Campbell River; see below), Alberni Pacific Charters (Tel: 604/724-3112) plies the local rivers in a unique flat-bottomed boat. The annual Salmon Festival, when even amateur anglers are guaranteed a sizable catch, is held over the Labour Day weekend. In summer, the historic freighter M.V. *Lady Rose* transports mail, cargo, kayakers, and other passengers from Port Alberni through the Broken Group Islands in Barkley Sound to Ucluelet on the Pacific Ocean ($40 per person; Tel: 604/723-8313 or, from April through September, 800/663-7192). The scenic, leisurely journey up the narrow 24-mile-long fiord is like a condensed Alaska cruise without the glitzy trappings or nightlife. The ship sails past forested mountainsides cut by waterfalls and around rugged, uninhabited islands. It is, as well, the principal means of communication with the outside world for dozens of logging camps and mills, fly-in fishing lodges and fish hatcheries, floating holiday homes and moss-covered cabins belonging to tree planters, oyster pickers, and coastal hermits.

Year-round, the *Lady Rose* also takes passengers through Alberni Inlet to Bamfield (south of Ucluelet; $35 per person), the northern end of the renowned **West Coast Trail**. This pre-1915 lifesaving trail was constructed to help shipwreck survivors along the island's west coast make their way back to civilization. From May 15 to September 30, stalwart souls hike the 77 km (48 miles) from Port Renfrew on the island's southwestern edge north to Bamfield, one of the west coast's few remaining hamlets, where a coastal boardwalk serves as the main street. In March and April, whale-watching excursions depart from Bamfield and other coastal communities.

Pacific Rim National Park

Highway 4 continues west to Long Beach, part of Pacific Rim National Park, where frequent torrents create hard sand beaches and cedar-scented rain forests. Here, naturalists study teeming tide pools, seals, sea lions, myriad birds, and gray whales, often sighted on their spring and fall migrations. Whale watching is an especially popular pastime hereabouts. From mid-March to mid-April, the towns of Tofino and Ucluelet act as hosts for the **Pacific Rim Whale Festival**, which celebrates the gray whales' annual migration to their summer home in Alaskan waters. The schedule of activities includes hikes to view the whales, films, lectures, and an arts-and-crafts show, as well as a whale "chase" and a gray whale race. For festival information, Tel: (604) 726-4641 in Ucluelet, or (604) 725-3414 in Tofino.

Ucluelet's Wickaninnish Nature Centre (summer only) illustrates the ocean's indelible effect on the environment through interpretive graphics, photos, and text. The historic *Canadian Princess* steamship, which once plied the Inside Passage to Alaska, is now permanently moored in Ucluelet and operates as the ▶ **Canadian Princess Resort** from March through September. The hotel offers single as well as multiple-berth staterooms, a dining room and various lounges, and whale-watching and fishing packages.

Guests of the ▶ **Pacific Sands Beach Resort** near **Tofino** can watch seasonal storms and spectacular sunsets from cozy housekeeping units or visit Tofino's waterfront **Blue Heron Inn Marine Pub**, with its post-and-beam interior and steaming local crab and clam platters. Nearby, the **Eagle Aerie Gallery**, in a converted longhouse, displays the paintings of native artist Roy Henry Vickers, whose reverence for nature and the coast results in a powerful blend of contemporary and traditional imagery.

THE ISLAND'S NORTH

Back on the east coast: Highway 19 links the pleasant seaside towns of Parksville and Qualicum Beach, both popular for beachcombing and water sports. The cottages of Parksville's ▶ **Tigh-Na-Mara Resort Hotel**, nestled in the woods by the sea, have a typical West Coast ambience. In town, **Spinnaker's** (Tel: 604/248-5532) makes good fish and chips. In Courtenay, 73 kilometers (45 miles) to the north, the **Native Sons Hall** is well worth a visit. Courtenay's **Old House Restaurant** (Tel: 604/338-5406), a timbered structure built in 1938, serves house-smoked seafood, chutneys, wild berries, and home-baked goods.

Campbell River and Quadra Island

Campbell River, north of Courtenay via Highway 19, vies with Port Alberni for the prestigious Salmon Fishing Capital of the World title, drawing anglers from every corner of the globe. The Campbell River Salmon Festival is held the first weekend in July.

From Campbell River a ten-minute ferry ride takes you to Quadra Island and the legendary ▶ **April Point Lodge**

and Fishing Resort. From April to November this luxurious anglers' mecca on a secluded cove arranges guides and equipment, as well as the freezing, smoking, or canning of your catch. The island's newest deluxe accommodation, the ▶ **Tsa-Kwa-Luten Lodge**, is situated on forested acreage high above Discovery Passage and is run by native people from the area. Most rooms have sea views and fireplaces, and the regional cuisine served in the dining room includes smoked salmon and alder-smoked pork ribs. The lodge also offers fishing packages and frequently hosts ceremonial dancers from the Kwagiulth tribe. The island's Kwagiulth Indian Museum, with its potlatch regalia and Cape Mudge petroglyphs, is likewise well worth a visit.

Strathcona Provincial Park

Strathcona Provincial Park, British Columbia's oldest, is reached via Highway 28 heading west out of Campbell River, and has an abundance of waterfalls, rivers, wilderness trails, alpine flowers, tarns, and wildlife. The ▶ **Strathcona Park Lodge**, with its lakefront chalets, teaches wilderness skills and arranges adventure packages centered around canoeing, kayaking, hiking, rock climbing, and fishing. Winter guests can cross-country ski and snowshoe.

Back on Highway 19, the **Cable House Restaurant** (Tel: 604/282-5532), a local oddity north of Strathcona in Sayward, is built almost entirely out of logging cables, 26 tons of them in fact. The restaurant serves down-home burgers and pies.

North of Campbell River

Few visitors will get as far as the northern community of **Alert Bay**, a living museum of Kwagiulth Indian culture accessible via Highway 19 from Campbell River to Port McNeill and then by ferry to Cormorant Island. Those who do will find the U'Mista Cultural Centre and the world's tallest totem pole.

At **Port Hardy**, about as far up-island as you can go, a chef in a kilt and tam prepares chicken and steaks over an open alder-wood fire at a restaurant called **Snuggles** (Tel: 604/949-7271). Port Hardy is also the departure point for the scenic Inside Passage vehicular ferry to Prince Rupert on the northern mainland. Serious hikers with good maps and wilderness skills may wish to spend a few days exploring nearby **Cape Scott Provincial Park**.

Finally, in secluded Rivers Inlet, northeast of Port Hardy on the mainland, the ▶ **Big Spring Sports Fishing Resort** arranges all-inclusive fly-in fishing packages (four, five, and eight days) from June to September. Guests who have packed little more than a toothbrush and checkbook are treated to a spectacular two-hour flight from Vancouver over coastal wilderness. The resort is both a welcome retreat for busy executives as well as a secluded hideaway for world travellers.

SOUTHWEST BRITISH COLUMBIA

Beyond Greater Vancouver, southwestern B.C. changes like a kaleidoscope. The Pacific Ocean has created a jagged coastline of coves, bays, and occasional beaches, home to shorebirds and soaring bald eagles. As you head inland, the Coast Mountains and rain forests give way to verdant farmlands in the Fraser Valley. It is scenery that impresses even native British Columbians.

Howe Sound

On summer days the historic *Royal Hudson* steam train leaves the district of North Vancouver for the Howe Sound fjords and **Squamish**, north of Vancouver. Sightseers can travel round trip by train, or take the M.V. *Britannia* one way and return by rail. Reservations can be made through Harbour Ferries (Tel: 604/687-9558). Those driving to Squamish take scenic Highway 99. En route is Britannia Beach, which once boasted the British Empire's largest copper mine. These days, from mid-May to mid-October, the **B.C. Museum of Mining** offers unique underground train trips and a historic village walking tour; Tel: (604) 688-8735.

The mountains surrounding Squamish are excellent for outdoor recreation, particularly hiking and rock climbing. The experienced scale the great granite Stawamus Chief or hike Diamond Head and Black Tusk in **Garibaldi Provincial Park**. In summer, and on a limited basis in winter, Alpine Adventure Tours (Tel: 604/683-0209) offers exhilarating glacier flights. B.C. Rail and Maverick Coach Lines provide regular year-round service to Britannia, Squamish, and Whistler. A speedy and scenic alternative to the train is the 40-minute helicopter ride from downtown Vancouver or the airport to Whistler. Expect the cost for four people to run about $900. For further information, call Canadian Helicopter at (604) 278-5502.

Whistler/Blackcomb

Some 122 km (75 miles) north of Vancouver past Squamish on Highway 99 is Whistler/Blackcomb, recently rated one of North America's top two ski resorts by *Ski Magazine*.

Whistler/Blackcomb has the longest lift-serviced vertical drop in North America, with the two mountains combined offering 180 runs, groomed cross-country trails, snowmobile tours, even heli-skiing. But this is truly a four-season resort. In summer, when lodging rates are drastically reduced, visitors can heli-hike, canoe, raft, horseback ride, or golf on courses designed by Arnold Palmer and Robert Trent Jones, Jr.

The resort's center, trendy **Whistler Village**, is a place to see and be seen. Although generally expensive, it is also pleasant and social, with bars, bistros, and boutiques clustered together. Street minstrels entertain the crowds on summer weekends, and the village has several fine restaurants, notably **Trattoria di Umbertos** (Tel: 604/932-5858) for traditional Italian fare; **Sushi Village** (Tel: 604/932-3330) for Japanese delicacies; and **Chez Joel** (Tel: 604/932-2112) for classic French cuisine and fondues.

The newest addition to Canadian Pacific Hotels' prestigious line of château-style lodgings is its 343-room ▶ **Chateau Whistler Resort**, a year-round facility offering ski, golf, and tennis packages. Adjacent to the hotel are high-speed chair lifts to Blackcomb for summer glacier skiing and a new gondola to Whistler's 6,000-foot peak. A long-standing favorite, the modern ▶ **Delta Mountain Inn** has indoor tennis, some in-room Jacuzzis, and exercise equipment. Guests appreciate the extra touches here, including morning newspapers, oversize terry robes, suites with fireplaces or kitchenettes, and nonsmoking floors. ▶ **Le Chamois**, a condominium-hotel, opened in 1990 at Blackcomb. Some of the suites have microwaves and private Jacuzzis, and all are just minutes from the lifts. For additional information about accommodations in the area, call Whistler Central Reservations toll-free from Vancouver at (604) 685-3650, or, in the U.S., (800) 944-7853.

The Sunshine Coast

The Sunshine Coast, with its quiet coves, bays, cedar and fir forests, and windblown arbutus trees, is a 90-mile stretch of coast lying northwest of Vancouver across Howe Sound. The gentle, unhurried lifestyle here lures fishermen, retirees, logger poets, and others seeking a peaceful rural atmosphere. Visitors can spend one to several days touring by car, or take Maverick Coach Lines from Vancouver. B.C. Ferries has 40-minute sailings, year-round, from West Vancouver's Horseshoe Bay to Langdale, the ferry terminal near Gibsons. From there, the Pacific Coast Highway (Highway 101) winds north to Earls Cove, where another ferry crosses to Saltery

Bay. This crossing allows motorists to continue up the highway to **Powell River** (where ferries depart for Comox on Vancouver Island) and, farther on, Lund, an isolated fishing village and the terminus of the Pacific Coast Highway.

In Gibsons, near Langdale, visitors and locals appreciate the dramatic view of mountains and sea from **Gramma's Marine Pub**. Gramma's also runs a beer-and-wine store and sells tongue-searing Portuguese sausage. Tiny shops elsewhere in town sell local pottery and handwoven items.

Sechelt, with a fine, sandy beach, is noted for its progressive Indian community, the first in Canada to attain self-government. The impressive **House of Hewhiwus** (House of Chiefs) cultural center here, with its massive sloping roof, cedar pillars, and jumping-salmon motif, houses a museum, theater, and gift shop. The ▶ **Driftwood Inn**, a pleasant waterfront hostelry with "pecan-finished" suites, some with sea views, also offers fine dining. Its **Pebbles Restaurant**, which overlooks the water, serves up a variety of homemade soups and fresh local seafood. Or try the tiny **Sechelt Fish Market** for succulent local salmon and other seafood.

The ▶ **Wakefield Inn**, a favored watering hole just north of Sechelt, provides basic but clean accommodation in antiques-furnished rooms above the pub. (Light sleepers may want to bring ear plugs.)

Elsewhere along the highway, buccaneerish names hint at a colorful past. There is Smuggler's Cove Marine Park at Secret Cove, for example, and the comfortable ▶ **Lord Jim's Resort Hotel**, right on the water 1 km (½ mile) north of Secret Cove. Lord Jim's offers fine views of twisted arbutus trees as well as salmon-fishing charters year-round. In scenic Halfmoon Bay is the ▶ **Jolly Roger Inn**, with wood-frame town houses set amid trees overlooking the sea. Boat rentals and fishing charters are available as well.

Although moderate rainfall keeps it green, the Sunshine Coast is blessed with 14 more sunny days a year than temperate Victoria. The area's numerous marine parks attract boaters, fishermen, beachcombers, and divers. Scuba diving in the clear, protected waters south of **Pender Harbour** (rated among the world's best dive sites) and around Powell River reveals sea caves, enormous octopuses, reefs, and shipwrecks. ▶ **Lowe's Resort Motel and Campground** in nearby Madeira Park rents cottages, boats, and air tanks for divers.

The Lower Fraser River Valley

East of Vancouver, Highway 7 meanders past tumbledown barns, grazing livestock, sawmills, tugs, log booms, and the lower Fraser River, which runs east to west here. Some 48 km (30 miles) inland is **Fort Langley National Historic Park**, where the Crown Colony of British Columbia was established in 1858. Daily year-round, this authentic reconstructed Hudson's Bay depot employs park historians in period costume to regale visitors with tales of days gone by.

Harrison Hot Springs
Farther east, Harrison Hot Springs, a small lakeside resort situated amid lofty mountains, is noted for its therapeutic mineral pools. Locals regularly take the waters alongside visitors, either at the public pools or in the waterfront ▶ **Harrison Hot Springs Hotel**, which was expanded a few years ago and refurbished with local Harrison brick. The neighboring Bavarian-themed **Black Forest Restaurant** (Tel: 604/796-9343) serves up hearty German fare as well as steaks and seafood. Cascade Bus Lines serves the resort from Vancouver.

Manning Park
Longtime Vancouverites remember cross-country skiing in Manning Park as children. Today this year-round recreation area is as popular as ever, with Nordic and alpine skiing, hiking and bird-watching in lodgepole pine forests, and comfortable chalet-style lodgings and cabins at the ▶ **Manning Park Resort**. The park is located past Harrison on the Crowsnest Highway (Highway 3), some 230 km (143 miles) east of Vancouver.

THE CARIBOO HIGHWAY

In the mid-1800s, determined prospectors travelled from the Pacific Coast up the relentless Fraser River to Lillooet (the river flows southward past Lillooet, turning west at about the latitude of Vancouver), then north to the Barkerville gold mines. The province's original Gold Rush Trail was once described as "utterly impassable for any animal but a man, goat, or dog."

Today's paved Cariboo Highway (Highway 97), with its Gold Rush Trail signposts, passes historic mile-house communities where guest ranches and deluxe resorts have replaced prospectors' roadhouses. In the Cariboo, horses outnumber people on sprawling, sun-bleached ranchlands, and television-satellite dishes stand incongruously beside chicken coops and beehive barns. To the west of the turbulent Fraser, the landscape is high alpine with evergreen forests.

Visitors should allow several days to tour the area adequately. From North Vancouver, B.C. Rail's *Cariboo Dayliner* follows this scenic route on its run to Prince George, the gateway to the province's vast North. Motorists can drive past Whistler, then take the spectacular Duffey Lake Road to Lillooet, where it connects to Highway 12 and, eventually, the Cariboo Highway, or take the Trans-Canada Highway to Lytton and, from there, follow Highway 12 north to Lillooet.

Lillooet and Vicinity

In 1863, Lillooet was Mile Zero on the Cariboo Highway, the second-largest town (after Barkerville) north of San Francisco and west of Chicago. Today that past is revisited at the **Lillooet Museum** (open daily during the summer).

Some 100 km (62 miles) west of Lillooet on Tyaughton Lake, ▶ **Tyax Mountain Lake Resort**, the largest log structure on the West Coast, is noted for its cross-country and heli-skiing in winter, horseback riding and heli-hiking in summer. Although you can drive to Tyaughton Lake, the road is rough and unpaved. It's easier, instead, to take B.C. Rail to Lillooet, where the resort provides pick-up service. Eighty kilometers (50 miles) northeast of Lillooet, the small, adult-oriented ▶ **Cariboo Rose Guest Ranch** in Clinton offers private cabins, hearty home cooking, riding clinics, and plenty of old-fashioned western ambience from May to October.

100 Mile House

In winter the south Cariboo area is dusted with light powder snow, ideal for Nordic skiing through stands of birch and aspen. In February, the 30-mile Cariboo Marathon, the largest cross-country ski event in western Canada, attracts some 1,500 international competitors to B.C.'s major cross-country ski center, the town of 100 Mile House. The 120 miles of machine-groomed trails here are concentrated around the Hills resort and the nearby ▶ **Best Western 108 Resort**. Guests of the 108 stay in an attractive wood-frame lodge overlooking a par-72, P.G.A.-approved golf course. Other summer activities include tennis, riding, and fishing.

The nearby ▶ **108 Hills Health and Guest Ranch** cleverly combines laid-back western hospitality with the elitist fitness craze. The spa features individual physical assessments and weight-loss programs year-round, and horseback riding, fishing, sleigh rides, and cross-country skiing seasonally. Summer guests also enjoy hayrides and singalongs. Accommodations are in the ranch or six-person chalets. B.C. Rail arranges rail and accommodation packages, or guests can book through the resort; Tel: (604) 791-5225 for details.

Often, nothing disturbs the region's still lakes in summer except a solitary boat or a flickering fish tail. North of 100 Mile House, Lac La Hache and Quesnel Lake are noted for kokanee salmon and rainbow trout, respectively. Outdoors enthusiasts gravitate toward the region's many wilderness fly-in resorts, like the remote ▶ Stewart's Lodge and Camps on Nimpo Lake. From May to October guests here stay in waterfront cabins and enjoy fly fishing and casting for rainbow trout in local lakes and streams. Guests can drive the partially paved Highway 20, which winds west to Nimpo Lake from the town of Williams Lake, or fly in. Air transportation to the lodge can be arranged through Tweedsmuir Air Services; Tel: (604) 742-3388.

Another popular fishing lodge hereabouts, and the only one with a licensed lounge, is the ▶ Anahim Lake Resort, situated some 320 km (200 miles) west of the Cariboo Highway via Highway 20. The remote high-country region surrounding both places is characterized by magnificent vistas of the Coast Mountains and the grand waterfalls of Tweedsmuir Provincial Park. It's also a mecca for anglers, who find its hundreds of lonely lakes and rivers irresistible.

Williams Lake to Barkerville

The dusty, sprawling cowboy country around Williams Lake (north of 100 Mile House on the Cariboo Highway) breeds top rodeo athletes who compete with other Canadian and U.S. professionals in the acclaimed **Williams Lake Stampede**. The four-day event, held the first weekend in July, is Canada's second-largest rodeo (after the Calgary Stampede).

Farther north along the Cariboo, Quesnel's **Billy Barker Days**, held each third weekend in July, is billed as more fun than the actual gold rush. Locals don period costumes for the gala parade, which is followed by gold panning, fireworks, and B.C.'s largest amateur rodeo.

Located 97 km (60 miles) east of Quesnel and the Cariboo Highway via Highway 26, **Barkerville** became "the largest town west of Chicago and north of San Francisco" in 1862 when Billy Barker, a wily Cornish prospector, hit the prospecting jackpot. In Barkerville's heyday, the mines outside town yielded some $50 million in gold. In 1958 the government declared the town a provincial historic park and restored the many heritage buildings that had survived. Today it's one of the finest and most extensive restorations in the

West, with more than 40 19th-century buildings still standing. In summer, lively costumed entertainers portray notorious citizens such as Hanging Judge Begbie, while elsewhere in town the Theatre Royal presents bawdy musicals.

Bowron Lake Provincial Park

Just east of Barkerville, Bowron Lake Provincial Park's 73-mile canoe circuit, once travelled by Indians and trappers, now lures canoeists from around the world. The entire route takes six to ten days, revealing unspoiled vistas and seldom-seen wildlife such as moose, bear, beaver, and ospreys. The circuit has become so popular, in fact, that advance reservations through local outfitters are required. From June to September, ▶ **Becker's Lodge** (see the Accommodations Reference list at the end of the chapter), 117 km (73 miles) east of Quesnel on Bowron Lake, provides canoes, camping gear, fishing equipment, tent sites, and log cabins. **Pathways Canada Tours** provides guided canoe packages from June through September; for information and reservations, Tel: (604) 257-2040 or, in B.C., (800) 663-3364. Non-motorists can take B.C. Rail or Greyhound bus to Quesnel, where transportation to and from the lakes region can be arranged.

SOUTH-CENTRAL BRITISH COLUMBIA
The High Country

The country east of the Fraser Valley is a vast jumble of sprawling cattle ranches, fingerlike lakes, wilderness parks, and immense mountain ranges like the Monashees.

The best way to explore the region is by car, allowing several days to see the sights at a leisurely pace. Heading east out of Vancouver, the Trans-Canada Highway leads past Hope to the Hell's Gate Airtram, an exhilarating six-minute ride across the Fraser Canyon that operates from March through October. To the northeast lie sun-parched grasslands and "a lake a day as long as you stay," as the regional tourism board likes to boast. Tattoos and western gear constitute the dress code at the **Coldwater Hotel** in Merritt, where pub patrons gustily chorus cowboy laments.

The 86-year-old ▶ **Quilchena Hotel** on nearby Nicola Lake started as a gold-rush packing company, then became a luxury retreat for the wealthy. Today it's a somewhat worn but charming lodging with gurgling hot-water heaters, tiny floral-papered rooms, and a bullet-scarred saloon bar. The hotel welcomes guests from April to October.

Sagebrush scents the air and covers the hills at the ▶ **Sundance Guest Ranch**, one of B.C.'s largest guest ranches, located 8 km (5 miles) south of Ashcroft. (From Nicola Lake, return to Merrit and follow Highway 97C approximately 100 km/60 miles northwest to the ranch.) Here, authentic cowboys round up horses in spring and fall, and meat from the buffalo herd is sometimes featured on the excellent menu. The reasonable rates include lodging, hefty meals, two daily horseback rides, and, in summer, tennis and swimming. Docile and spirited horses are matched with similarly disposed riders.

The **Ashcroft Manor Tea House**, a refurbished 1860s gold-rush lodge with century-old elm trees, is now a restaurant serving a traditional tea from March to mid-November. Guests can shop for local jade and other art amid the roadhouse relics. The excellent **Ashcroft Historic Museum** (summer only) displays several restored turn-of-the-century buildings.

Kamloops

Some 95 km (56 miles) east of Ashcroft, the town of Kamloops ("meeting of the waters" in the local Indian dialect) is named for the area's many lakes and rivers, all of them popular with trout fishermen. For the excursion-minded, the paddlewheeler *Wanda Sue* plies the South Thompson River from Kamloops on summer days.

Shuswap Lake District

Another 108 km (67 miles) east of Kamloops on the Trans-Canada Highway is **Shuswap Lake**, a squiggly, H-shaped body of water with almost 600 navigable miles, making it ideal for canoeing, kayaking, and houseboating. In **Sicamous**, Canada's self-proclaimed "Houseboat Capital," several companies rent the floating homes, among them: **Three Buoys Houseboat Vacations**, Tel: (604) 836-2403 (in B.C. and Alberta, Tel: 800/663-2333); and **Waterway Houseboats**, Tel: (604) 836-2505 (in B.C., Tel: 800/663-4022).

Amateur naturalists, nature lovers, and photographers know the area for another reason: In 1994, thousands of brilliant-red sockeye salmon will surge through the nearby Adams River en route to their spawning grounds. This is the culmination of a four-year cycle, with crowds lining the riverbanks in late September and October to watch the extraordinary and emotional event. (In off years, a smaller run takes place in October.)

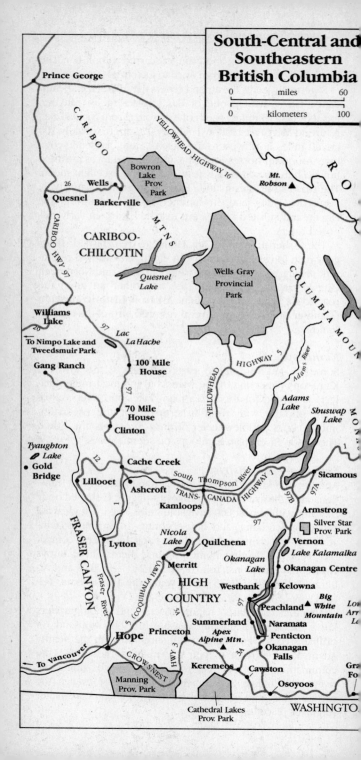

South-Central and Southeastern British Columbia

| 0 | miles | 60 |
| 0 | kilometers | 100 |

Prince George

CARIBOO

YELLOWHEAD HIGHWAY 16

Mt. Robson ▲

RO

26 Wells

Quesnel

Barkerville

Bowron Lake Prov. Park

MTNS

CARIBOO-CHILCOTIN

Quesnel Lake

Wells Gray Provincial Park

COLUMBIA MOUN

CARIBOO HWY 97

Williams Lake

To Nimpo Lake and Tweedsmuir Park

97

Lac La Hache

Gang Ranch

100 Mile House

YELLOWHEAD

HIGHWAY 5

Adams River

97

70 Mile House

Clinton

Adams Lake

Shuswap Lake

M O

Tyaughton Lake

Gold Bridge

12

Cache Creek

South Thompson River

Sicamous

Ashcroft

TRANS-CANADA HIGHWAY 1

97A

Lillooet

Kamloops

97B

Armstrong

1

Lytton

Nicola Lake

Quilchena

97

Silver Star Prov. Park

Vernon

Lake Kalamalka

Okanagan Lake

Merritt

Okanagan Centre

FRASER CANYON

(COQUIHALLA HWY)

HIGH COUNTRY

5A

Westbank

Kelowna

97

Big White Mountain ▲

Lo Arr Lo

Fraser River

Peachland

Naramata

Summerland

Apex Alpine Mtn. ▲

Penticton

Princeton

3A

Okanagan Falls

Hope

CROWSNEST

HWY 3

Keremeos

Cawston

Gra Fo

To Vancouver

Manning Prov. Park

Cathedral Lakes Prov. Park

Osoyoos

WASHINGTO

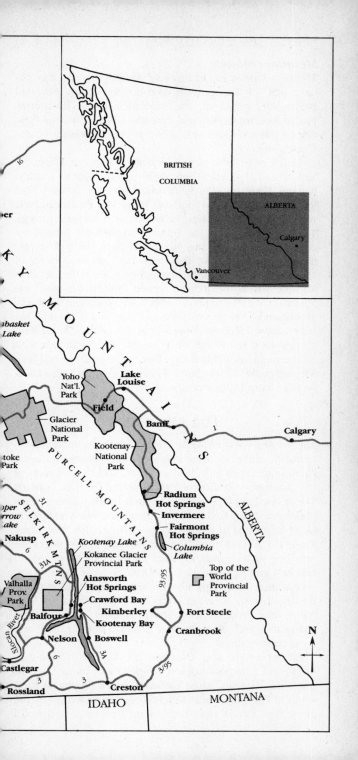

Mountain Majesty

To the northeast mountains rise abruptly beyond the "banana belt" of the Shuswap Lake district. Craggy, glaciated peaks, lofty meadows, and wilderness trails characterize **Mount Revelstoke National Park** and **Glacier National Park**, among the most dramatic scenery found along the Trans-Canada Highway.

To the north, the view is equally impressive. Here, the Yellowhead Highway (Highway 5) and the Great Canadian Railtour Company's *Rocky Mountaineer* (Tel: 800/665-7245 in the U.S. and Canada) wind past **Wells Gray Provincial Park**, with its extinct volcanos, lava beds, and mineral springs. Travellers can follow the Yellowhead Highway (which becomes Highway 16) into Alberta or, from the end of May through October, take the train. Both provide views of 13,000-foot **Mount Robson**, the highest point in the Canadian Rockies, which the Indians named "Yuh-hai-has-hun," the Mountain of the Spiral Road. After just four seasons the *Rocky Mountaineer* has proven a great success, and is listed by *The International Railway Travellers* as one of the 20 best train excursions in the world. It's a two-day, all-daylight tour, with an overnight stay in Kamloops. During the peak season (June 5 to September 22) the fare is $499 per person; a Calgary add-on is an extra $49 per person.

The Okanagan

Anyone who has seen *My American Cousin,* an impressionistic movie about innocent summer love, will recognize the rolling sagebrush hills, lush orchards, and slender lakes of the Okanagan–Similkameen area south of the High Country. This sunny land lures young, summer beach partiers, oenophiles gravitating to B.C.'s wine region, and sun-worshippers of all ages tired of being bludgeoned by rainy West Coast winters. The sun shines 2,000 hours a year in this part of the province—which makes it ideal for lounging on one of 30 beaches, golfing from March to October, most water sports, even skiing. Under typically fair skies, bronzed skiers tackle the dry, crisp snow on Kelowna's Big White, Penticton's Apex Alpine, and Vernon's Silver Star mountains. Non-skiers can spend the cold, clear days ice skating, sleigh riding, and cross-country skiing.

Farther south, arid **Osoyoos**, on the B.C.–Washington State border, harbors a desert complete with horned lizards, owls, and cactuses, while **Cathedral Lakes Provincial Park**, south of Highway 3 near Keremeos, is characterized by the awesome Cascade Mountains, alpine-type lakes, and weird rock formations sculpted by the elements over millions of years.

From Vancouver, Greyhound offers regular bus service to the region's major population centers: **Penticton, Kelowna,** and **Vernon.** Motorists should follow the Trans-Canada Highway east to Hope. Here you have a choice: Either Highway 3 (the Crowsnest) through Manning Park to Princeton and beyond, or Highway 5 (the Coquihalla), a toll road ($10), to Merrit and Highway 97C. Allow a full day on the bus, and about five hours if driving.

Fruit and Vines

Abundant sunshine nurtures terraced vineyards and orchards dripping with fruit. Visitors can pick the produce themselves or purchase it at roadside stands. One of these, the **Mariposa Fruit Stand** in Keremeos, on Highway 3, sells delicious blueberry and cherry pancake syrup as well as fresh fruit and juices. On summer days visitors head back to the coast loaded down with Okanagan produce. Kelowna's **Orchard Industry Museum** (closed Sundays in summer; Sundays and Mondays in winter) traces the development of the industry from 19th-century backyard fruit stands to modern symmetric orchards. The **Pioneer Country Market**, on Benvoulinn Road in Kelowna, sells locally made antipasto, herbs, chutneys, and wine jelly.

In this produce-rich region, two restaurants are worth a special mention. In Penticton, **Granny Bogner's**, 302 Eckhardt Avenue West, serves up French cuisine as well as halibut, prawns, lobster, salmon, and fresh fruit desserts in an old house with antique oak furnishings and a wrap-around verandah. Call ahead to reserve; Tel: (604) 493-2711. Intimate, fireside dining is what you'll find at the somewhat grandiose **Country Squire** (north of Penticton in Naramata), where the proprietor assists guests with their selections from an ever-changing menu featuring such items as venison cassis, osso bucco, roast rack of lamb, and tiger prawns. To help digest such extravagance, diners often take long walks between courses. Again, reservations a must; Tel: (604) 496-5416.

Grapes have been grown in British Columbia since 1899, when resident botanist G. W. Henry tended the first vines. Local wines have placed prominently in national and international competitions since the 1960s. Hilltop and lakeside vineyards from the central Okanagan to Osoyoos, on the Washington State border, offer tasting rooms, wine stores, and tours year-round. At the **Sumac Ridge Estate Winery,** near Summerland, visitors can play golf on the adjacent nine-hole course, then imbibe at the tenth hole. For those with a fondness for the grape, the **Okanagan Wine Festival** is held at the end of September and the beginning of October. Visitors to the region at that time are treated to guided vineyard tours, copious samplings, and much spirited competition among the attending wineries, which include **Hainle Vineyards**, B.C.'s first estate winery, located near Peachland.

Among the approximately 80 bed-and-breakfast establishments in the area, only one, the ► **Windmill House**, 13 km (9 miles) east of Vernon in the Coldstream Valley, has rooms in an actual mill and serves homemade "windmill waffles" and preserves. The sprawling ► **Lake Okanagan Resort**, 18 km (11 miles) north of Kelowna on the west side of the lake, features tennis instruction on championship courts, a hilly par-3 golf course, horseback riding, a full-service marina, and heated outdoor pools. Ask for one of the chalets, which are more modern and attractive than the main building.

On the Water

In addition to enjoying its fruits and wines, visitors to the region can take part in plenty of recreational pursuits. Extensive waterways are ideal for most aquatic sports, particularly fishing. South of Vernon, **Lake Kalamalka** (Lake of Many Colors) yields plump kokanee salmon and trout. Trophy rainbow trout are the winter catch in **Okanagan Lake** itself, while smaller trout, whitefish, and burbot are hooked year-round. Although never proved, a Disneyesque serpent, Ogopogo, is said to live in these waters as well. Local visitor bureaus dispense a history of its sightings, which date back to the 1800s, and at least one provincial official has suggested protecting it as an endangered species.

Houseboating is a pleasant way to see the lake and Canada's longest floating bridge, which links Kelowna and Westbank. Kelowna's **Bridge Bay Marina** (Tel: 604/769-4411) rents out luxurious, fully equipped Pleasurecrafts and "a complete selection of water toys." You can catch the paddlewheeler M.V. *Fintry Queen,* which leaves for excursions of the lake on summer afternoons and evenings, at the town marina.

SOUTHEAST BRITISH COLUMBIA
The Kootenays

Southeastern B.C.'s Kootenays (east of the Okanagan area), where long, slender lakes flank the dramatic Selkirk Mountains, are an outdoor playland for mountain sports, golfing, and year-round bathing in natural hot springs. The region's beauty and generally amiable residents compensate for the occasional display of small-town provincialism.

In the late 19th and early 20th centuries the region flourished thanks to gold and silver mining. Today silent ghost towns are eerie reminders of those lucrative times. Among the Kootenays' curiosities are wild whistling swans and the world's longest free ferry ride.

The easiest way to explore the area is by car, allowing a very full day for the drive from Vancouver via Hope and the Crowsnest Highway (Highway 3). Remnants of early 20th-century Russian immigrant life are scattered throughout the farmlands surrounding Grand Forks, on the B.C.–Washington State border, as well as at Castlegar's **Historic Doukhobor Village** on the banks of the Columbia River. Try the *galooptsi* (cabbage rolls) and borscht at the **Doukhobor Village Restaurant** in Castelgar.

In nearby **Rossland**, turn-of-the-century mines produced 50 percent of British Columbia's gold. From May to October visitors to this mountain town can tour the Rossland Historical Museum and former Le Roi Gold Mine—the province's only hard-rock mine open for tours.

Nelson

Nelson, 80 km (50 miles) northeast of Rossland via Highways 3 and 6, is an architectural treasure trove of historic buildings situated on the west arm of Kootenay Lake. It was here that Hollywood star Steve Martin perched on the roofs and swung from the rafters of several exquisite Victorian homes in the film *Roxanne*. Self-guided walking tours lead visitors past some 350 provincially designated heritage buildings, with complimentary maps available at businesses throughout town. Nelson's newest attraction is its authentic turn-of-the-century streetcar, which operates along two miles of scenic Lakeside Park.

Kootenay Provincial Parks and Hot Springs

Motorists heading west on Highway 3A, then north on Highway 6 into the Slocan Valley, pass the Valhalla Mountains and Slocan Lake. **Valhalla Provincial Park** offers mountaineering, hiking, and remote beach camping. Alpine flowers here are at their best in August. The nearby ghost town of **Sandon**, once a silver miner's El Dorado, now has little more to offer than a half dozen restored buildings, a small museum, and an even smaller café. Farther north via Highway 6, the **Nakusp Hot Springs**, outside the beautifully situated town of Nakusp, burble among substantial cedars and lacy ferns, offering visitors a soaking pool naturally heated to 112° F, and a swimming pool heated to a comfortable 105°.

Southeast of the hot springs via Highway 6 and 31A is **Kokanee Glacier Provincial Park,** from which the B.C.-brewed Kokanee beer derives its name. The park is noted for excellent hiking, ski touring, and trout and salmon fishing. Tucked under the mountains near the park are more effervescent mineral pools. Guests of the ► **Ainsworth Hot Springs Resort** on Highway 31 can steam out their frustrations while soaking in outdoor mineral pools overlooking Kootenay Lake. Water temperatures soar to a sauna-like 110° F in the back of the Horseshoe Cave and hover around 90° F in the main pool. There is also a cold plunge.

The ferry that crosses Kootenay Lake from Balfour to Kootenay Bay is the world's longest free ride, and takes about 40 minutes, depending on which side you start from. On the Kootenay Bay side, golfers at the ► **Kokanee Springs Golf Resort** are afforded spectacular views of nearby glaciers; open mid-April to mid-October.

The Kootenay Skyway, the country's highest major thoroughfare, soars above Creston south of the lake, where wild whistling swans nest in the protected **Creston Valley Wildlife Center.** Amateur naturalists can canoe or join meadow walks and "marsh crawls."

The Rockies

In the province's southeastern corner, the Purcell and Rocky mountains command the landscape as if demanding recognition. The Rockies, constituting the Great Divide between B.C. and Alberta, are showcased in two national parks on either side of the provincial border. In B.C. these are **Kootenay** and **Yoho.** (Opposite them in Alberta are Banff, and, farther north, Jasper National Park.) Superlative scenery aside, the region has all the recreational advantages of high alpine terrain: wilderness treks, downhill and heli-skiing, rafting, and abundant wildlife. (B.C. claims 700 vertebrate species, 60 percent of the world's mountain goats, and 25 percent of its grizzly bears. For information and suggestions on wildlife viewing, call the Wildlife Watch Coordinator at 604/387-9767.) In addition to the four-legged beasts, craggy mountain men live here year-round, ardent skiers flock from the coast and the prairies at the first negotiable snowfall, and camera-toting tourists come to see the Rockies whenever they can.

The Trans-Canada Highway (Highway 1) and the *Rocky Mountaineer* penetrate the region from either side of the rocky divide. It takes some ten hours to drive from Vancouver, and three hours from Calgary. Greyhound buses stop at major centers.

This vast, rugged land was virtually impenetrable until the late 1800s, when the Canadian Pacific Railroad was pushed through the mountains, completing the last link in the country's transcontinental railway. Unfortunately, *The Canadian,* the southern rail link through B.C. to Calgary, was canceled in 1990 because of federal budget constraints. The railway museum in **Cranbrook** houses the *Trans-Canada Limited,* a vintage 1920s train once operated by the Canadian Pacific.

Fort Steele

Fort Steele Heritage Town, north of Cranbrook on Highway 93/95, is dwarfed by the Rockies. The site of B.C.'s first North West Mounted Police post, Fort Steele has some 40 restorations gathered from around the province, including the original officers' quarters and a water tower. The park is open daily from May through October, with summer steam-train trips, vaudeville shows, and lively staged street dramas.

The new ▶ **Three Bars Cattle and Guest Ranch**, 21 km (13 miles) north of Cranbrook, houses guests in handcrafted duplex log cabins set amidst the splendor of the Rockies. Activities on this working cattle ranch include horseback riding, fly fishing, river rafting, cookouts, and cross-country skiing in winter. Among the facilities are an indoor heated pool, an outdoor Jacuzzi, a tennis court, and a childrens' play center.

Kimberley

Kimberley, one of Canada's highest cities at 3,652 feet, is perched in the Purcell Mountains on Highway 95A. With its giant cuckoo clock, a square called Der Platzl (people place), cozy restaurants serving up strudel and schnitzel, and its quota of *lederhosen,* it has been called the most Bavarian village outside the Alps. Pizza joints and taco stands confirm that this is not Bavaria, however.

Just east of Kimberley, ▶ **Top of the World Guest Ranch**, near the provincial park of the same name, is a back-to-basics working cattle ranch where teaching guests to ride is the main objective. Summer guests stay in snug log cabins, while the main lodge with its peeled-pine furnishings is open year-round. (Riding instruction is provided from April to November; in winter the lodge is open to groups only.) The ranch offers chuckwagon cookouts and glimpses of wildlife and Canada geese nesting in local lakes. Don't expect late-night hootenannies at this quiet cowboy retreat. (Pickup service from nearby towns is provided for guests without cars.)

Commercial Hot Springs

Coddled by the mountains, Fairmont and Radium (the latter in Kootenay National Park) have year-round public hot springs. At the northern tip of Columbia Lake (source of the mighty Columbia River), the ▶ **Fairmont Hot Springs Resort**, an attractive complex with a cedar-sided lodge and woodland villas, has been attracting guests since 1922. Four odorless mineral pools range in temperature from 95° to 112° F. Guests are attracted to this mountain retreat for its two 18-hole golf courses, horseback riding, skiing, and a 6,000-foot runway minutes away. In Invermere, 16 km (10 miles) north of Fairmont, you'll find **Strand's Old House Restaurant**. This culinary hideaway in a historic 1912 building specializes in pepper steaks, New Zealand spring lamb, and venison smothered in savory homemade sauces. Reservations are recommended in summer; Tel: (604) 342-6344.

Farther north, **Radium Hot Springs** bubbles away just beyond the western entrance to **Kootenay National Park**. The park stretches some 65 miles along both sides of the Banff–Windermere Highway (Highway 93). Here glacial icefields have carved out deep valleys and chasms. Some 125 miles of hiking trails ascend the slopes and afford jaw-dropping panoramas. Autumn, when bighorn sheep, grizzlies, elk, wolves, coyotes, and the occasional moose can be seen, provides some of the best wildlife viewing.

With more than 30 sawtooth peaks exceeding 9,000 feet, **Yoho National Park** (Yoho is the Cree word for "how wonderful") gives new meaning to the word *pristine*. The ▶ **Emerald Lake Lodge**, near the town of Field, was first opened in 1902 to serve wayfarers venturing into the Canadian Rockies. After extensive restoration, the exclusive resort reopened in 1986. To preserve the natural setting, vehicles are not allowed on the property—guests drive to a parking lot, where a chauffeur transports them to the lodge. The original hand-hewn lodge remains the dining and social center (with its Kicking Horse bar), while guests are lodged in modern wood-frame chalets with green corrugated roofs and lake and mountain views set among the trees. It is wonderful.

NORTHWEST BRITISH COLUMBIA

In the early 1900s, British Columbian artist Emily Carr painted powerful, haunting landscapes of the province's northwest rain forests and remote Indian villages. Her works constitute a telling portrait of the vast, sparsely populated region that is perhaps best known as Canada's gateway to the Yukon and Alaska. Although the few towns that dot the map have grown substantially since Carr's time, they still thrive on forestry, mining, agriculture, and fishing—as well as the railroad that unites them.

Prince George

To reach the central hub of Prince George on the upper Fraser River, visitors can take B.C. Rail's spectacular 13-hour *Cariboo Dayliner* from Vancouver, or follow the Cariboo Highway (Highway 97) north from its junction with the Trans-Canada Highway at Cache Creek. From Prince George, VIA Rail hugs the Yellowhead Highway (Highway 16) as it heads west to the coastal port of Prince Rupert.

Lacy aspens, sturdy spruce trees, and pulp incinerators resembling huge inverted badminton birds characterize the countryside surrounding Prince George, a fur-trading fort in 1807, and now a rugged mill and railroad center. In summer the new Railway Museum (open weekdays) and the Northwood Pulp and Timber facility (which conducts three-hour tours) honor these industries.

In downtown Prince George, Sergeant O'Flaherty's Irish New York Pub in the ► **Coast Inn of the North** serves its own tasty, dark brew. The inn is comfortable and clean, with an indoor pool, sauna, and, of all things, a fine Japanese steakhouse named **Shogun** (Tel: 604/563-0121). Ten kilometers (6 miles) east on alternate Highway 16A (Giscome Road), the German proprietor of the celebrated **Log House Restaurant** (Tel: 604/963-9515) displays his taxidermic trophies. Recommended big-game hunting and fishing outfitters in the Prince George area include Rocky Mountain Outfitters, Tel: (604) 964-9186; and Bear Lake Guide Outfitters, Tel: (604) 971-2220.

Some 97 km (60 miles) west of Prince George is the ► **Tachick Lake Fishing Resort**, on Kenney Dam Road south of Vanderhoof. From May to October guests can stay in cottages with kitchen facilities and fish for rainbow trout. But the big treat here is the excellent restaurant (open weekends only), which serves local game prepared by a German chef.

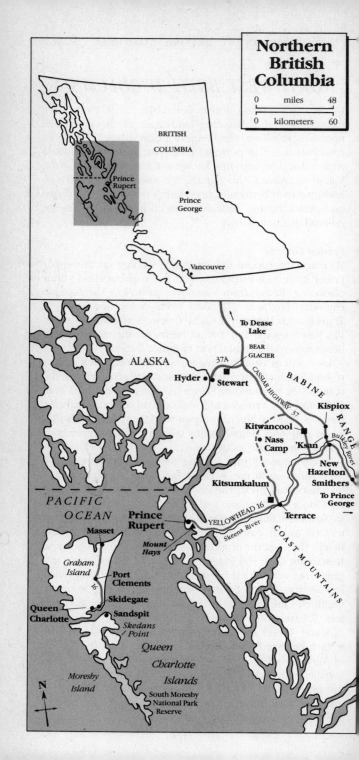

Northern British Columbia

| 0 | miles | 48 |
| 0 | kilometers | 60 |

BRITISH COLUMBIA

Prince Rupert

Prince George

Vancouver

To Dease Lake

BEAR GLACIER

ALASKA

37A

Hyder • Stewart

CASSIAR HIGHWAY 37

BABINE RANGE

Kispiox

Kitwancool

Nass Camp

'Ksan

Bulkley River

New Hazelton

Smithers

Kitsumkalum

To Prince George

PACIFIC OCEAN

YELLOWHEAD 16

Terrace

Skeena River

Prince Rupert

Mount Hays

COAST MOUNTAINS

Masset

Graham Island

16

Port Clements

Skidegate

Queen Charlotte

Sandspit

Skedans Point

Queen Charlotte Islands

Moresby Island

N

South Moresby National Park Reserve

WEST TO PRINCE RUPERT
AND THE COAST

In 1912 the Grand Trunk Pacific, the last leg of Canada's newest transcontinental railway, was pushed across the Great Divide, thereby linking northern B.C. to the rest of Canada. Today VIA Rail's *Skeena* (River of the Clouds) *Liner* winds west almost 725 km (450 miles) from Prince George to Prince Rupert. Pole-straight aspens, mirror-calm lakes, and pulp mills gradually yield to sturdy cedar and spruce forests. The train leaves just before midnight (at 11:59 P.M.) and arrives in Rupert the following afternoon at 1:00 P.M. En route, it makes a 6:25 A.M. stop at **Smithers** for 25 minutes, enough time for early risers to take pictures of the glorious mountains and to stretch their legs. A dining car serves tasty sit-down meals, or you can purchase light snacks.

The town of Smithers, with its pseudo-Bavarian architecture, is noted for cross-country and alpine skiing. The cozy ▶ Hudson Bay Lodge here has an indoor whirlpool, a sauna, and a fireside lounge. The ▶ Driftwood Lodge offers clean, basic accommodations, along with skiing, fishing, and hiking packages. The historic 'Ksan and Kispiox Indian villages, frequently painted by Emily Carr, are nearby.

Although VIA Rail and Greyhound serve the town of New Hazelton, visitors will need a car to see **'Ksan**, set amid the rushing Bulkley River and the sawtoothed Babine Range— "The home of the quiet people"—8 km (5 miles) to the north. Seven tribal houses guarded by cracked, graying totems, some more than a hundred years old, preserve the Indian legacy. In the House of Wood Carving, on-site artists using saws and tools their forefathers never had infuse the air with a chopped-cedar scent. The 'Ksan Village House of Arts and Crafts is open daily during the summer and closed Tuesdays and Wednesdays in winter.

The Cassiar Highway

Slightly south and west of 'Ksan, the Cassiar Highway (Highway 37) branches north to **Kitwancool**, a small Gitksan village with the world's oldest standing totem, called Hole-in-the-Ice. Some 160 km (100 miles) farther on is the glaciated, mountain-rimmed river port of **Stewart**, which has appeared in several Hollywood movies, including *The Thing, Ice Man, Bear Island,* and *Never Cry Wolf.* The road is paved, although lonely and not well lit. En route, wispy deciduous trees give way to substantial evergreens, and, nearing Stewart, the enormous Bear Glacier extends its icy blue paw.

In July and August Seaport Limousine offers four-hour tours to the nearby Salmon Glacier, giving visitors an opportunity to see real prospectors, alpine wildflowers, and the occasional bear or eagle. For information and reservations, Tel: (604) 636-2622.

Neighboring **Hyder**, Alaska, is accessible by land only from Stewart. Even with the highest bar-per-capita ratio in the United States, the hamlet somehow manages without law enforcement, local taxes, and customs officials. In the raucous **Glacier Inn**, imbibers "get Hyderized" drinking Everclear, a 190-proof straight-grain Kentucky alcohol, with a water chaser. September visitors may see chum spawning in the nearby Salmon River, while gulls and grizzly bears enjoy the spoils.

Lodging in this remote region is limited to the **Stewart Lions Campground and RV Park**, open May to the end of September. To reserve a spot, Tel: (604) 636-2537.

Keen adventurers can continue north on the Cassier Highway to **Dease Lake**—self-proclaimed "Jade Capital of the World"—and beyond to the Yukon and Alaska. From Dease Lake it's another 234 km (145 miles) on partly unpaved road to the Yukon border. The scenery along this stretch is striking, with glaciers, narrow canyons, wildflower meadows, and extinct volcanoes. At Jade City, about halfway to the border, there are unserviced RV sites; otherwise, services along this stretch of road are scarce.

Others will want to backtrack toward Terrace on Highway 37 or the rough but rewarding Nass logging road, which runs past the 220-year-old Tseax Lava Flow, an eerie moonscape of lichen-covered rocks. Kermodei, North America's rarest species of white bear, are only found roaming the salmon streams and mountains surrounding Terrace.

Terrace

Terrace's Heritage Park, open in summer, displays several architecturally diverse log homes. Nearby, the **Northern Light Studio** sells quality native art, alder and yellow-cedar carvings, and B.C. jade. In an area synonymous with hunting, the **Bavarian Inn** restaurant (Tel: 604/635-9161) here features gourmet buffalo dishes and schnitzel, as well as a Hunters' Den filled with stuffed wildlife. The towering cedar poles outside the Kitsumkalum Indian reserve at Terrace are the first to have been raised here in 150 years. Tribal members also sell native artwork. For information, Tel: (604) 638-1629.

From Terrace to Prince Rupert on the coast (147 km/91 miles), the Yellowhead Highway and VIA Rail wind west along the Skeena River through the mist-shrouded and rain-soaked Coast Mountains.

PRINCE RUPERT

In Prince Rupert, where the Skeena empties into the Pacific, few views can match those from the elegant ► **Crest Motor Hotel**. The Prince Charles Lounge here, with its warm brass accents, wood paneling, and Scottish tartans, overlooks the Coast Mountains and tiny tugs pulling log booms a hundred times their size. Whales migrate this way in spring, while seals and sea lions are common sights year-round.

A Cannery Row of weathered pilings and clustered fishing boats supports several good, uncommercialized seafood restaurants, including **Boulet's** (Tel: 604/624-9309) and **Smiles Seafood Café** (Tel: 604/624-3072). With its low ceiling, polished-wood interior, and historic fishing photos, Smiles looks as if it has hardly changed since it opened in 1934. Gargantuan portions of Boston clam chowder and halibut are popular items.

Prince Rupert's **Museum of Northern British Columbia** has a superb ethnographic collection of area artifacts. Outside, visitors may catch native artists at work in the carving shed. Nearby, the **North Pacific Cannery Village and Fishing Museum**, a national historic site, is probably the last remaining accessible cannery in North America. Machine shops, net lofts, canning lines, and hoists have been refurbished along the waterfront. The site is open from mid-May to Labour Day. Those who are so inclined can rent rods and angle right from the dock.

B.C. Ferries' scenic 15-hour sailings back down to Vancouver Island are best during the extended daylight hours of June and July. The vehicular ferries make fewer trips in the off-season. There is also year-round B.C. Ferries service (six times a week) to the neighboring Queen Charlotte Islands. On summer days and on weekends the rest of the year, a gondola climbs 1,850 feet from Prince Rupert to Mount Hays, which overlooks the harbor, the Alaska Panhandle, and the Charlottes.

The Queen Charlotte Islands

These misty, time-warped islands (six hours from Prince Rupert by B.C. Ferries) lure adventurous naturalists who seek the water-logged rain forests and ancient Haida totems eulogized by Emily Carr. The fallen totems of Ninstints on Anthony Island, declared a World Heritage site by UNESCO, are now protected in the Gwaii Haanas **South Moresby National Park Reserve**.

The islands, often referred to as Canada's Galapagos, are a treasured wilderness rich in Haida Indian culture, spectacu-

lar wildlife (including some species unique to the area), and
pockets of old growth among the "managed" forest. The
Charlottes are also an active logging area. Proud locals (the
Haida are politically and economically active) will gladly
share a pint of good B.C. beer and tell a tale or two to those
inclined to listen. While July and August are the warmest
months here, April and May, when gray whales feed along
the coast and thousands of shorebirds dive for herring, are
the most exciting.

In summer, B.C. Ferries makes six runs weekly from
Prince Rupert to Skidegate on Graham Island. There are
fewer sailings the rest of the year. Time Air flies daily into
Sandspit, a short ferry ride south of Skidegate, on Moresby
Island. Rental cars (a must) are available in Queen Charlotte
City as well as at the Sandspit airport. (Graham Island has
paved roads, and both Graham and Moresby islands have a
network of logging roads.) You can also tour the islands by
float plane, sailboat, power cruiser, or kayak. In addition,
Vancouver Island Helicopters (Tel: 604/637-5344) offers aerial tours of ancient Haida settlements such as Skedans, on
Louise Island east of Moresby Island.

Lodgings on the island are clean and offer typical Charlottes charm. One hostelry worth a mention is the ► **Spruce
Point Lodging**, an attractive waterfront bed and breakfast in
Queen Charlotte City. The cedar building has Scandinavian-
style pine furnishings and is attached to a pottery studio; they
also offer kayak rentals. In Sandspit, the ► **Moresby Island
Guest House** provides Continental breakfasts and can arrange hunting and fishing expeditions. A pleasant local hangout in Port Clements on Graham Island is the waterfront
Yakoun Inn (Tel: 604/557-4440), which serves burgers and
other standard grilled fare in a cozy setting. The **Café Gallery**
(Tel: 604/626-3672), at the northern end of the island in
Masset, is more upscale, with a menu featuring steaks and
local seafood.

With its 19th-century totems salvaged from Tanu, Skedans,
and other ancient Haida villages, the **Queen Charlotte Islands Museum** in Skidegate is a must. Skidegate's council
office, overlooking the bay and designed in the traditional
longhouse style, is presided over by a great totem pole
created by the renowned master carver Bill Reid. The *Loo
Tass,* the famous expedition canoe designed by Reid, is also
on view beside the Haida Gwaii office.

If you're planning on visiting the Queen Charlottes, be
sure to bring plenty of cash; although credit cards are
becoming more widely accepted, there are no banks. In
Queen Charlotte City, Kallahin Expeditions and Travel Ser-

vices is a one-stop-booking shop that can arrange accommodations, car rentals, and adventure travel year-round. Tel: (604) 559-8455.

GETTING AROUND
For details on getting to Vancouver, the area's main gateway, see the preceding chapter on the city. From Vancouver, you can drive or take a variety of trains, buses, and small planes to the outlying B.C. regions. Information is given throughout the text of this chapter.

For information on B.C. Ferries from Vancouver Island (Victoria and Nanaimo) to the mainland, see the Getting Around section at the end of the Vancouver chapter.

ACCOMMODATIONS REFERENCE
The rates given below are projections *for peak seasons during the 1994 calendar year; at other times of the year they* may *be considerably less. Unless otherwise indicated, rates are based on double rooms, double occupancy; provincial and federal taxes are included in all rates. As rates are subject to change, always double-check before booking.*

▶ **The Aerie.** P.O. Box 108, **Malahat**, B.C. V0R 2L0. Tel: (604) 743-7115 or 4055; Fax: (604) 743-4766. $173–$184; suites $230–$391 (includes breakfast).

▶ **Ainsworth Hot Springs Resort.** P.O. Box 1268, **Ainsworth Hot Springs**, B.C. V0G 1A0. Tel: (604) 229-4212; Fax: (604) 229-5600. $78–$138.

▶ **Anahim Lake Resort.** P.O. Box 3400, **Anahim Lake**, B.C. V0L 1C0. Tel. and Fax: (604) 742-3242; in the U.S., Tel: (800) 667-7212. $58.

▶ **April Point Lodge and Fishing Resort.** P.O. Box 1, Campbell River, **Quadra Island**, B.C. V9W 4Z9. Tel: (604) 285-2222; Fax: (604) 285-2411. $160–$263.

▶ **Beach House.** P.O. Box 472, 930 Sunset Drive, **Saltspring Island**, B.C. V0S 1E0. Tel: (604) 537-2879; Fax: (604) 537-4747. $178–$218 (includes breakfast).

▶ **Becker's Lodge. Wells,** c/o P.O. Box 129, Bowron Lake, B.C. V0K 2R0. For reservations only, 1-259 McLean Street, Quesnel, B.C. V2J 2N8. Tel: (604) 992-8864; Fax: (604) 992-3886. $58 (two people)–$172 (five to six people).

▶ **Best Western 108 Resort.** Box 2, **108 Mile Ranch**, B.C. V0K 2Z0. Tel: (604) 791-5211; Fax: (604) 791-6537; in the U.S. and Canada, Tel: (800) 528-1234 or (800) 667-5233. $132–$140.

▶ **Big Spring Sports Fishing Resort. Rivers Inlet**, B.C. Reservations: Suite 101, 4680 Cowley Crescent, Richmond, B.C. V7B 1C1. Tel: (604) 273-1433; Fax: (604) 273-3171; in the U.S. and Canada, Tel: (800) 663-4400. $1,260–$2,000 (five-day, all-inclusive).

▶ **Canadian Princess Resort.** P.O. Box 939, Peninsula Road, **Ucluelet,** B.C. V0R 3A0. Tel: (604) 726-7771; Fax: (604) 726-7121; in the U.S. and Canada, Tel: (800) 663-7090. $45–$144.

▶ **Cariboo Rose Guest Ranch.** P.O. Box 160, **Clinton,** B.C. V0K 1K0. Tel. and Fax: (604) 459-2255. $1,083 per week (per person, all-inclusive).

▶ **Le Chamois.** P.O. Box 1044, 4557 Blackcomb Way, **Whistler,** B.C. V0N 1B0. Tel: (604) 932-8700; Fax: (604) 938-1888; in the U.S. and Canada, Tel: (800) 777-0185. $287 (studio).

▶ **Chateau Whistler Resort.** 4599 Chateau Boulevard, **Whistler,** B.C. V0N 1B0. Tel: (604) 938-8000; Fax: (604) 938-2020; in the U.S. and Canada, Tel: (800) 441-1414. $345.

▶ **Cliffside Inn On-the-Sea.** 4230 Armadale Road, **North Pender Island,** B.C. V0N 2M0. Tel: (604) 629-6691. $182–$257 (per person, including breakfast and dinner).

▶ **Coast Inn of the North.** 770 Brunswick Street, **Prince George,** B.C. V2L 2C2. Tel: (604) 563-0121; Fax: (604) 563-1948; in the U.S. and Canada, Tel: (800) 663-1144. $131.

▶ **Crest Motor Hotel.** P.O. Box 277, 222 1st Avenue West, **Prince Rupert,** B.C. V8J 3P6. Tel: (604) 624-6771; Fax: (604) 627-7666; in the U.S. and Canada, Tel: (800) 663-8150. $111–$140.

▶ **Delta Mountain Inn.** P.O. Box 550, 4050 Whistler Way, **Whistler,** B.C. V0N 1B0. Tel: (604) 932-1982; Fax: (604) 932-7332. $268; executive suite, $443.

▶ **Driftwood Inn.** P.O. Box 829, 5454 Trail Avenue, **Sechelt,** B.C. V0N 3A0. Tel: (604) 885-5811; Fax: (604) 885-5836. $74–$102.

▶ **Driftwood Lodge.** Babine Lake Road, R.R. 2, Site 53, Comp. 11, **Smithers,** B.C. V0J 2N0. Tel: (604) 847-5016. $98 (bed-and-breakfast double).

▶ **Emerald Lake Lodge.** P.O. Box 10, **Field,** B.C. V0A 1G0. Tel: (604) 343-6321; Fax: (604) 343-6724; in the U.S. and Canada, Tel: (800) 663-6336. $253–$425.

▶ **Fairmont Hot Springs Resort.** P.O. Box 10, **Fairmont Hot Springs,** B.C. V0B 1L0. Tel: (604) 345-6311; Fax: (604) 345-6616; in the U.S. and Canada, (800) 663-4979. $150; six-person loft with kitchen, $195.

▶ **Harrison Hot Springs Hotel.** 100 Esplanade Avenue, **Harrison Hot Springs,** B.C. V0M 1K0. Tel: (604) 796-2244; Fax: (604) 796-9374; in the western U.S. and British Columbia, Tel: (800) 663-2266. $104–$195.

▶ **Hastings House.** P.O. Box 1110, 160 Upper Ganges,

Ganges, B.C. V0S 1E0. Tel: (604) 537-2362; Fax: (604) 537-5333. $310–$483 (includes breakfast and tea).

▶ **Hudson Bay Lodge.** P.O. Box 3636, 3251 East Highway 16, **Smithers**, B.C. V0J 2N0. Tel: (604) 847-4581; Fax: (604) 847-4878; in British Columbia and Alberta, Tel: (800) 663-5040. $90.

▶ **Jolly Roger Inn.** Highway 101, R.R. 1, **Halfmoon Bay**, B.C. V0N 1Y0. Tel: (604) 885-7184 or, in Canada, (800) 663-0180; Fax: (604) 885-7564. One-bedroom, $132; two-bedroom, $127–$161.

▶ **Kokanee Springs Golf Resort.** P.O. Box 96, **Crawford Bay**, B.C. V0B 1E0. Tel: (604) 227-9226; Fax: (604) 227-9220. $98 (golf packages available).

▶ **Lake Okanagan Resort.** 2751 Westside Road, **Kelowna**, B.C. V1Y 8B2. Tel: (604) 769-3511; Fax: (604) 769-6665; in the U.S. and Canada, Tel: (800) 663-3273. One-bedroom suite, $207; Jacuzzi suite, $288; three-bedroom condo or chalet, $345.

▶ **Lord Jim's Resort Hotel.** Ole's Cove Road, R.R. 1, **Halfmoon Bay**, B.C. V0N 1Y0. Tel: (604) 885-7038; Fax: (604) 885-7036; in Vancouver, Tel: (604) 681-6168. $98; suite, $158.

▶ **Lowe's Resort Motel and Campground. Pender Harbour**, P.O. Box 153, Lagoon Road, Madeira Park, B.C. V0N 2H0. Tel: (604) 883-2456. One-bedroom cottage, $75.

▶ **Manning Park Resort. Manning Park**, B.C. V0X 1R0. Tel: (604) 840-8822; Fax: (604) 840-8848. $72–$100.

▶ **Moresby Island Guest House.** P.O. Box 485, 385 Alliford Bay Road, **Sandspit**, B.C. V0T 1T0. Tel: (604) 637-5300; Fax: (604) 637-2355. $58–$70 (includes breakfast).

▶ **108 Hills Health and Guest Ranch. 108 Mile House**, c/o 108 Ranch, Comp. 26, 100 Mile House, B.C. V0K 2E0. Tel: (604) 791-5225; Fax: (604) 791-6384. Ranch house, $58–$63 (per person, breakfast included); chalets, $127–$137 (six people).

▶ **Pacific Sands Beach Resort.** P.O. Box 237, 1421 Pacific Rim Highway, **Tofino**, B.C. V0R 2Z0. Tel: (604) 725-3322; Fax: (604) 725-3155. $109–$210.

▶ **Quilchena Hotel. Quilchena**, B.C. V0E 2R0. Tel: (604) 378-2611; Fax: (604) 378-6091. $66–$77.

▶ **Sooke Harbour House.** 1528 Whiffen Spit Road, R.R. 4, **Sooke**, B.C. V0S IN0. Tel: (604) 642-3421; Fax: (604) 642-6988. $224–$316 (includes breakfast and lunch).

▶ **Spruce Point Lodging.** P.O. Box 735, 609 6th Avenue, **Queen Charlotte City**, B.C. V0T 1S0. Tel: (604) 559-8234. $70 (includes breakfast).

▶ **Stewart's Lodge and Camps.** General Delivery, **Nimpo Lake**, B.C. V0L 1R0. Tel: (604) 742-3388. $63–$75.

▶ **Strathcona Park Lodge**. P.O. Box 2160, **Campbell River**, B.C. V9W 5C9. Tel: (604) 286-8206; Fax: (604) 286-8208. $75–$127.

▶ **Sundance Guest Ranch**. P.O. Box 489, Highland Valley Road, **Ashcroft**, B.C., V0K 1A0. Tel: (604) 453-2422; Fax: (604) 453-9356. $145 (per person, all-inclusive).

▶ **Tachick Lake Fishing Resort**. Tachick Lake, P.O. Box 1112, Vanderhoof, B.C. V0J 3A0. Tel: (604) 567-4929. $40–$67.

▶ **Three Bars Cattle and Guest Ranch**. Site 19–62, **Cranbrook**, B.C. V1C 6H3. Tel: (604) 426-5230; Fax: (604) 426-8240. $163 per person (minimum stay of four nights in July and August; weekly rates available).

▶ **Tigh-Na-Mara Resort Hotel**. 1095 East Island Highway, **Parksville**, B.C. V9P 2E5. Tel: (604) 248-2072; Fax: (604) 248-4140; in the U.S. and Canada, Tel: (800) 663-7373. $95–$167 (three-night minimum stay in summer).

▶ **Top of the World Guest Ranch**. P.O. Box 29, **Fort Steele**, B.C. V0B 1N0. Tel: (604) 426-6306. $805 per week (per person, all-inclusive).

▶ **Tsa-Kwa-Luten Lodge**. P.O. Box 460, Quathiaski Cove, **Quadra Island**, B.C. V0P 1N0. Tel: (604) 285-2042; Fax: (604) 285-2532; in the U.S. and western Canada, Tel: (800) 665-7745. $132–$260; $529 (guest house).

▶ **Tyax Mountain Lake Resort**. Tyaughton Lake Road, **Gold Bridge**, B.C., V0K 1P0. Tel: (604) 238-2221; Fax: (604) 238-2528. $110.

▶ **Wakefield Inn**. R.R. 1, Wakefield Site, Comp. 59, **Sechelt**, B.C. V0N 3A0. Tel: (604) 885-7666. $40–$63.

▶ **Windmill House**. 5672 Learmouth Road, R.R. 1, Site 19A, Comp. 2, **Vernon**, B.C. V1T 6L4. Tel: (604) 549-2804. $45–$60.

▶ **Woodstone Country Inn**. Georgeson Bay Road, R.R. 1, **Galiano Island**, B.C. V0N 1P0. Tel: (604) 539-2022. $95–$150 (includes breakfast and tea).

▶ **Yellow Point Lodge**. 3700 Yellow Point Road, R.R. 3, **Ladysmith**, B.C. V0R 2E0. Tel: (604) 245-7422. $110–$185 (includes breakfast, lunch, and dinner).

THE NORTHWEST TERRITORIES AND THE YUKON

By John Goddard

John Goddard has travelled throughout Canada's North as a reporter and photographer for the Canadian Press news agency, and is the author of Last Stand of the Lubicon Cree, *a land-rights saga set in northern Alberta. Currently based in Montreal, he is at work on a new book,* Cargo Cult, *chronicling a recent trip through Indonesia.*

THE NORTHWEST TERRITORIES

The Northwest Territories attract outdoors people who like to climb, fish, canoe, spot birds, track wild animals, or sit alone on a rock nurturing a sense of well-being. The place is unimaginably huge, accounting for almost a third of Canada's landmass. Nobody tries to see it all in one trip. A

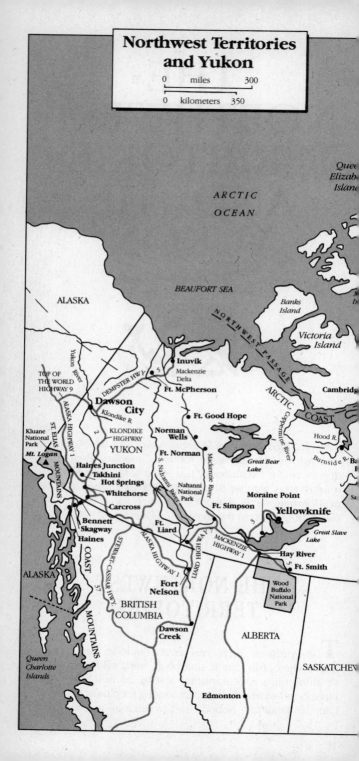

Northwest Territories and Yukon

0 — miles — 300

0 — kilometers — 350

ARCTIC OCEAN

Que Elizab Island

BEAUFORT SEA

NORTHWEST PASSAGE

ALASKA

Banks Island

Victoria Island

M Is

TOP OF THE WORLD HIGHWAY 9

DEMPSTER HWY

Inuvik

Mackenzie Delta

Ft. McPherson

Cambridg

ARCTIC

COAST

Yukon River

ALASKA HIGHWAY 1

Dawson City

Klondike R.

Ft. Good Hope

Coppermine River

Kluane National Park

ST. ELIAS MOUNTAINS

Mt. Logan

KLONDIKE HIGHWAY

YUKON

Norman Wells

Ft. Norman

Hood R.

Burnside R.

Ba I

Haines Junction

Takhini Hot Springs

Whitehorse

Carcross

S. Nahanni River

Nahanni National Park

Mackenzie River

Great Bear Lake

Moraine Point

Ft. Simpson

Yellowknife

Sa

Bennett

Skagway

Haines

COAST

STEWART-CASSIAR HWY.

37

Ft. Liard

ALASKA HIGHWAY 1

LIARD HIGHWAY

MACKENZIE HIGHWAY 1

Great Slave Lake

Hay River

Ft. Smith

ALASKA

MOUNTAINS

BRITISH COLUMBIA

Fort Nelson

Wood Buffalo National Park

Queen Charlotte Islands

Dawson Creek

ALBERTA

SASKATCHEW

Edmonton

good approach, instead, is to focus on a single objective: an activity or a geographical area.

It helps to know that there are two distinct geographic regions, defined by the tree line, which runs on a diagonal from the Mackenzie Delta in the extreme northwest to Hudson Bay at Churchill, Manitoba, in the southeast. Everything above the line is treeless Arctic—the traditional domain of the Inuit, formerly called Eskimos. Everything below the line is treed sub-Arctic—the traditional domain of the Dene (DUH-neh), also called northern Athapaskan Indians.

It also helps to know that transportation routes tend to be north-south, connecting Baffin Island to Montreal, for example, and the Mackenzie Valley to Edmonton, Alberta. For travel planning, the territories comprise five areas: Baffin Island, the High Arctic, Keewatin, the Arctic Coast, and the Mackenzie Valley.

MAJOR INTEREST

Baffin Island
Cape Dorset artist cooperative
Kekerton historic whaling station
Auyuittuq glaciated wilderness park
Inuit camping at the floe edge
Nanisivik marathon run

The High Arctic
Ellesmere Island wilderness park
Lake Hazen thermal oasis
Fort Conger historic camp
Polar Bear Pass naturalist site

The Keewatin
Baker Lake art
Inuit camp
Thelon game sanctuary
Outings to view caribou, walrus, and whales
Wilderness canoeing

The Arctic Coast
Bathurst Inlet naturalist lodge
Flora and wildlife
Wilderness canoeing

Yellowknife and the Mackenzie Valley
Yellowknife and environs
Prince of Wales Northern Heritage Centre
Moraine Point Lodge
Nahanni National Park Reserve

Visiting the Northwest Territories

Almost all parts of the Northwest Territories have become accessible to visitors in recent years through the efforts of the territorial government. Standards for accommodations and meals in most settlements have risen by leaps and bounds, and services are offered almost everywhere to help you make the most of a trip. Prices are much higher than in southern Canada: up to $200 per person, per night, for room and board in an Arctic hostel. The best time to go is between mid-March, when the long days of sunlight begin and travelling conditions over ice and snow are still good, and late August, when summer wanes. The weather is highly changeable, demanding flexible schedules. Two pairs of sunglasses, warm clothing, and rugged footwear are essential for trips almost anywhere in the region. Credit cards and traveller's checks are not accepted in some outlying settlements, and cash is especially useful for buying items such as mukluks direct from a craftsperson. Maps and brochures, including the annual *Explorers' Guide,* can be requested from Travel Arctic, Government of N.W.T., Yellowknife, N.W.T. X1A 2L9; Tel: (800) 661-0788.

The People

Northerners tend to like visitors and to view tourism as a pollution-free, renewable resource that creates jobs like guiding and outfitting—jobs that utilize skills learned on the land and are compatible with native ways of living.

Adapting traditional skills to a modern context is a broad-based, ongoing program in the territories, where nearly 60 percent of the people are native. Of the 52,000 people resident in the territories, 18,500 are Inuit, 11,500 Dene and Métis (mixed racial heritage), and 22,000 are grouped as "other." Representatives of all racial groups and geographic regions have been meeting for several years to develop new government structures for the territories, which, if adopted, would revolutionize the present colonial structure controlled by the federal powers in Ottawa. The proposal that has been accepted in principle would divide the territories in half for more efficient administration: **Nunavut** in the east; **Denendeh** in the west. Draft constitutions for both territories would guarantee native representation in the legislatures and would give native peoples power over areas of special concern, such as culture and wildlife protection. A remarkable aspect of the discussions has been the support of the white minority in promoting the native character of the territories, part of a general attitude the astute visitor is bound to notice: Despite a plethora of ethnic and regional differences, racism in the territories is minimal.

Archaeologists believe the Arctic regions were populated by a succession of migrating Inuit peoples from Asia over the past 4,000 years, each wave either dying out or being absorbed by the one that followed. The earliest groups— called Independence I, pre-Dorset, Independence II, and Dorset—collectively are known as the Arctic Small Tool tradition because of their common affinity for small stone scrapers, blades, and awls. Next came the Thule people, who many scholars believe to be the direct ancestors of the modern Inuit, and who are probably best known for their whalebone houses. Archaeological awareness is high in northern communities, thanks mostly to the programs that hire students from the region to work as junior archaeologists every summer in the High Arctic Islands.

The first known Europeans to become interested in the Arctic were British navigators looking for a northwest trading route to the Far East. Martin Frobisher arrived in 1576, followed by Henry Hudson, Robert Bylot, and William Baffin in the early 1600s. Not until 1905 was the Northwest Passage navigated successfully—by Roald Amundsen, a Norwegian— by which time the route held no commercial interest. During most of this century, many coastal Inuit were in contact with whaling vessels, whose crews exposed native people to fatal diseases but also introduced such innovations as tea, firearms, and iron cookware.

In the western sub-Arctic, where the great river valleys stayed relatively ice free during successive ice ages, early peoples are believed to have occupied the Mackenzie Valley for at least 10,000 years. They lived as small groups of nomadic hunters surviving on caribou, moose, beaver, rabbit, and fish. The five main groups of northern Dene today are the Loucheux (or Kutchin) in the extreme northwest, the Hare of Fort Good Hope, the large Slavey (or Slave) group south and west of Fort Norman, the Dogrib of Great Slave Lake, and the Chipewyans east of Great Slave Lake.

Fur traders from the rival Hudson's Bay and North West companies began penetrating the Mackenzie Valley overland in the late 1700s, setting up posts and engaging native peoples in the fur trade. The Hudson's Bay Company expanded to engage coastal Inuit groups in the early part of this century. Life gradually came to revolve around these posts, and to a large extent northern natives came to depend on fur sales for their livelihood. Profound changes in this status quo have occurred only recently. When fur prices fell in the 1950s, federal-government personnel arrived to distribute welfare funds, establish schools, and build houses. For the first time, native people moved into settlements on a large scale.

Although a few families continue to live full time on the land, settlements now characterize life in the territories. There are about 60 of them, widely dispersed. They differ in size, setting, and atmosphere, but they are all alike in the way they function. The typical house is a prefabricated, pastel bungalow (although log houses are beginning to reappear in some Dene communities). Running water is uncommon; a water truck makes the rounds once or twice a week to fill a barrel or tank in each home. Small industries such as log milling and commercial char (trout) fishing have developed in some settlements, but most places have no economic base. The settlements are heavily subsidized, and almost all families take part of their living from the land. Even the most casual visitor is struck by the paraphernalia outside almost every home: snowmobiles, hide stretchers, animal-fur clothing, gasoline jugs, sleds, ropes, traps, and axes.

There are towns, too, in the Northwest Territories, the most important ones being Iqaluit on Baffin Island in the east, Inuvik near the Mackenzie River mouth in the northwest, and Yellowknife, the capital, on Great Slave Lake in the southwest.

THE BAFFIN REGION

The Viking adventurer Eric the Red, who is generally credited as the first European to visit it, late in the tenth century, did not leave a lasting impression on Baffin Island, at the farthest northeastern reach of Canada. The first well-documented visit was made in 1576 by English explorer Martin Frobisher, who had been looking for a northwest route to Cathay until rocks resembling gold quartz distracted him. He regrouped in England and returned to Baffin in 1578 with 15 ships full of settlers and supplies, intent on establishing a mining colony. The venture failed when the ore turned out to be iron pyrite.

South Baffin

IQALUIT
Today a town of 3,000 people, Iqaluit, the capital of the Baffin region, stands near where Frobisher started to mine. It was founded as Frobisher Bay in 1914 by the Hudson's Bay

Company, and renamed Iqaluit ("fish camp"), the Inuit word for the spot, in 1987.

Few travellers make Iqaluit a primary destination, but it can be a worthwhile stopover before going on to places of greater interest. Its importance as a regional center dates from 1942, when the United States Air Force built an air base here. The base was turned over to the Canadian armed forces after World War II. Following the addition of a hospital and a regional Mountie headquarters, the community achieved town status in 1980. But the townsfolk had little to be proud of. Frobisher Bay had a reputation as an Arctic slum, a bad clash of southern and northern cultures. The subsequent growth of social services and a general maturing of the town now make it a comfortable and pleasant place to visit.

The ► **Navigator Inn**, the ► **Discovery Lodge Hotel**, and the ► **Frobisher Inn** all meet southern Canadian standards of comfort and efficiency (the Frobisher Inn is not quite as new as the other two), and include Arctic char, caribou, and Greenland shrimp on their dinner menus, as does the popular igloo-shaped **Komotiq** restaurant (Tel: 819/979-5937). Although accommodations in Iqaluit are plentiful, reservations are advisable, and are virtually a must in outlying settlements during the busy spring and summer seasons. The newest attraction in the area is the **Unikkaarvik Visitors' Centre and Library**, with a panoramic view of Frobisher Bay and information about the entire Baffin region. Records and tapes of northern musicians such as Charlie Panigoniak and William Tagoona are available from the Hudson's Bay Company store in town. The hunters and trappers association runs an outlet at the airport, selling travel-packaged frozen char for departing visitors.

Whalebone homes built by the Thule people as much as 1,000 years ago can be visited by boat 20 minutes away at the **Qaummaarviit Historic Park**. Also of interest is the **Baffin Arts and Crafts Centre**, a crafts store that doubles as an experimental workshop for native carvers, who are running out of their famous Baffin Island soapstone. Stones like Keewatin alabaster and Cape Dorset marble are being carved for the first time, with the help of diamond-edged power saws and air-driven hammers.

CAPE DORSET

There are scheduled flights twice weekly (three times a week in summer) from Iqaluit to this settlement at the foot of the Kingnait mountain range on the southwestern extremity of Baffin Island. Cape Dorset is known for its gifted artists, foremost among them the carver and printmaker Kenojuak.

In 1953, after the market for white-fox fur had collapsed, Canadian artist James Houston arrived under government auspices to develop Eskimo carving as a commercial enterprise, an initiative that met with an overwhelmingly positive response in southern Canada and Europe. A number of Cape Dorset artists subsequently founded the West Baffin Eskimo Co-Operative, and by 1959 it was turning out high-quality prints using techniques Houston had studied in Japan (techniques that have since spread to other communities). The co-op, which welcomes visitors, continues to be Cape Dorset's largest employer.

Dogsled trips and boat rides can be taken to the nesting grounds of the blue goose in the **Dewy Soper Bird Sanctuary**, as well as to important archaeological sites. It was at Cape Dorset in 1925 that the archaeologist Diamond Jenness discovered the remains of an ancient Inuit people who inhabited the Arctic between 1000 B.C. and A.D. 1100. He later called this the "Dorset culture," after Cape Dorset. The ► **Kingnait Inn** accommodates up to 50 people in 25 rooms, eight of which offer private bath. As in most northern hostels, the rooms here are furnished with a bed and side table, meals are served in a small dining room, and there's a common room for reading and watching television.

PANGNIRTUNG

Scheduled flights from Iqaluit stop in Pangnirtung (population 1,000) three times a week, sometimes more often in summer. The settlement stands at the base of glaciated mountains north-northeast of Iqaluit in a fjord off Cumberland Sound, which once teemed with bowhead whales. From the 1840s until about 1910 the area was chiefly a whaling center—at its peak, the most important one in the Arctic. White fox became valuable by 1921, when the Hudson's Bay Company built its trading post at Pangnirtung. Today marine mammals and furbearers remain important to the subsistence of local residents. In addition, a thriving artists' cooperative produces carvings, prints, tapestries, and parkas. The **Angmarlik Visitors' Centre and Library**, with much information about Pangnirtung and its whaling past, also serves skiers and hikers bound for Auyuittuq National Park and places like Kekerton. The newly renovated ► **Auyuittuq Lodge** here accommodates 50 people in 25 rooms, and features a sitting room with giant windows affording a spectacular view of fjord-like Cumberland Sound.

KEKERTON

Kekerton, on an island 49 km (30 miles) south of Pangnirtung, opened in 1988 as the first historic park in the
Northwest Territories. British whaler William Penny erected
a station house on the site in 1857, quickly establishing it as
the principal Arctic destination for British and American
whalers. Their target was the magnificent bowhead whale,
larger and heavier than a Greyhound bus. One bowhead
could yield 150 barrels of oil, a major source of lighting and
lubrication in those pre-petroleum days, as well as a ton of
whalebone, which found countless uses in products requiring the flexibility now provided by plastics. Between 1820
and 1920 more than 18,000 bowheads were slain in the
eastern Arctic; today only a few hundred remain. Kekerton is
a monument to the majesty of the bowhead, the hardiness of
the whalers, and the mingling of two starkly different whaling cultures—white and Inuit. It was also at Kekerton in
1883 that the pioneering German anthropologist Franz Boas
formed his perspective on the equality of mankind. "I often
ask myself," he wrote, "what advantages our 'good society'
possesses over that of the 'savages,' and find, the more I see
of their customs, that we have no right to look down upon
them."

A boardwalk through Kekerton leads the visitor past whale-
spotting lookouts, blubber-stripping sites, oil-rendering pots,
Inuit houses, graveyards, and station-house foundations. To
get there, visitors can hire a licensed Inuit guide through the
Pangnirtung visitors' center; allow 12 hours for a round trip
(by snowmobile in spring, by boat in summer).

AUYUITTUQ

Auyuittuq (oh-you-EE-too) **National Park,** north of Pangnirtung, boasts superlative ski touring and ski mountaineering.
Downhill skiing is better in western Canada, but Auyuittuq,
which protects a portion of the Penny Ice Cap, offers the
more thrilling, all-around wilderness experience. Skiers are
completely isolated and must be self-sufficient. The best
snow conditions are in April and May, but temperatures are
usually more comfortable in summer. Spectacular **Pangnirtung Pass**, a popular though cruelly windy hiking route,
winds through the park between Pangnirtung and **Broughton Island,** a settlement of 440 people that offers accommodations with private in-room baths and meal service at the
▶ Tulugak Co-operative Hotel. Broughton Island is also
served by scheduled flights from Pangnirtung and Iqaluit
two or three times a week, depending on the season.

North Baffin

A unique and unforgettable northern experience is travelling in springtime to the floe edge, where land-fast ice meets open water. Groups of Inuit journey to this transitional zone to camp, hunt seals, and enjoy the almost 24 hours of sunlight. At Pond Inlet and Igloolik, both north of the Arctic Circle, some outfitters and families are equipped to take visitors with them. The best time to go is usually late May and early June.

POND INLET

Pond Inlet (population 800), a sheltered, scenic spot near the entrance to the Northwest Passage, has a sweeping view of the glaciated mountains of Bylot Island. It is also an area rich in marine and bird life. Nearby, British whalers opened the Arctic whaling industry in 1820, killing bowheads by the hundreds for two decades before moving down to Cumberland Sound. A few whales are still around, and schools of single-tusk narwhals swim past in June or July—a phenomenon unique to north Baffin.

The ▶ **Sauniq Hotel**, a modern 16-room inn with a dining room, opened in 1986; its management helps visitors hire outfitters for dog-team and snowmobile excursions to the floe edge, to char-fishing camps, and to the **Bylot Island** bird sanctuary. The best way to get there is a flight on First Air up the east coast from Iqaluit, rather than via Nanisivik, on the Borden Peninsula, which is often fogged in.

IGLOOLIK

The island of Igloolik (population 850), often praised for the strength and cohesiveness of its people, has produced a number of political leaders, including Rhoda Inukshuk, past president of the Inuit political organization Inuit Taparitsat. It was also home during most of the 1970s to an eccentric American-born woman known simply as Georgia, who wrote pithy, lyric newspaper columns about Igloolik life, and later a book called *An Arctic Diary.*

The area around Igloolik, which is off the north end of the Melville Peninsula west of Baffin Island, became one of the first areas of human settlement in the Arctic after the last ice age, roughly 10,000 years ago. Archaeological evidence indicates that it has been occupied more or less continuously for the last 4,000 years. Besides looking at ancient campsites, visitors can become part of a living one. Outfitters are available for dogsled outings that can include camping in igloos and viewing walrus, seals, caribou, and polar bears. Regular flights reach Igloolik from Iqaluit and Resolute Bay. You can stay at the ▶ **Tujormivik Hotel** here, which accommodates up to 15 people in eight basic rooms.

NANISIVIK

Nanisivik (near the northern tip of Baffin Island), a lead/zinc mining settlement created in the mid-1970s, is where, at the height of the Arctic summer—the first weekend in July—the **Midnight Sun Marathon** is held. A chartered jet full of runners arrives from Montreal two days early, weather permitting. The resident miners open their homes and communal dining hall to the visitors as part of the annual town celebration. Short-distance races are held the day before the marathon. The major race starts at the neighboring Inuit settlement of Arctic Bay (population 475), which is also accessible by taxi. Runners wishing to enter the race can call (416) 869-0772.

THE HIGH ARCTIC

RESOLUTE BAY

Resolute Bay (population 200), on Cornwallis Island facing the Northwest Passage, is the staging site for trips to the North Pole and High Arctic Islands. It is named after the H.M.S. *Resolute,* which engaged in the search for the lost expedition of Sir John Franklin in 1850; later, wood from this ship was used to make a desk for U.S. President John F. Kennedy. The settlement began as an air base and weather station in 1947. An Inuit community was established in 1955, when the Canadian government moved several families from northern Quebec and Baffin Island to new hunting grounds here.

In a recent survey, Resolute Bay's weather ranked as the worst in the country for severity, discomfort, and gloominess, but a facility here for tourists ranks at the top for warmth, conviviality, and value for the money, drawing an adventurous, international clientele. Rates are less than $100 a day for room and board, the cheapest in the Arctic. Known officially as **High Arctic International Explorer Services Ltd.** (P.O. Box 200, Resolute Bay, N.W.T. X0A 0V0; Tel: 819/252-3875), the combination tourist base and outfitting service is run by Bezal Jesudason, a former engineer from Madras, India, and his wife, Terry, a former kindergarten teacher from Trail, British Columbia. (See the Accommodations Reference for booking details for the ▶ **International Explorer's Home**, and for another comfortable Resolute Bay lodge, the 48-room ▶ **Narwhal Arctic Services**.)

Anyone wishing to conquer the North Pole—whether by foot, motorcycle, dog team, or plane—talks to the Jesudasons first. Custom outings with Inuit guides, snowmobiles, and boats can be arranged, as can scheduled group outings of one to 11 days (minimum six guests for package tours). Day trips cost from $60 to $600 per person, per day, depending on the type of transportation and number of people participating, while longer tours range in price from $900 to $9,887, all-inclusive. The latter price is for the International North Pole Explorer tour, a seven-day trip from Resolute Bay to the Magnetic North Pole via northern Ellesmere island, then on to the Geographic North Pole; an Inuit community on northwestern Greenland; **Grise Fiord**, North America's northernmost Inuit community, on the south coast of Ellesmere Island (accommodations are in the ▶ **Grise Fiord Lodge**, with nine basic but newly renovated rooms); **Beechey Island**, a small island east of Resolute near Devon Island where you can see the graves of three sailors from Sir John Franklin's last expedition; and back to Resolute Bay. (No credit cards accepted.)

Northern **Ellesmere Island** itself, declared a national park reserve in 1986, is distinguished by its glaciated mountains. What scientists call a **thermal oasis**, an oddly warm (for this part of the world), relatively lush valley, is located around Lake Hazen, the largest lake north of the Arctic Circle. **Fort Conger**, the historic camp on northeast Ellesmere from which U.S. Admiral Robert Peary launched his drive for the pole in 1909, is still largely intact and accessible by chartered plane from Resolute Bay. **Polar Bear Pass**, on Bathurst Island, due west of Cornwallis Island and Resolute Bay, is particularly rich in Arctic vegetation, birds, and wildlife.

Resolute Bay is accessible from Montreal and Iqaluit in the east and from Edmonton and Yellowknife in the west, with flights three times a week in each direction.

THE KEEWATIN

Early fur-company explorers in the area west of Hudson Bay dubbed this area the Barren Lands because of its lack of trees. Stories from the first half of this century link the name to starvation. John Hornby and two companions exploring the Thelon River by canoe in 1926 were unable to find Beverly caribou—there were none there—and slowly starved to death over the winter. A similar tragedy occurred in the 1940s and 1950s, when the caribou bypassed the area again, bringing starvation to the Inuit. Their plight was later described by Canadian writer Farley Mowat in *People of the Deer* and *The Desperate People*—two books still popular though not always accurate.

RANKIN INLET

The Inuit survived and now populate seven settlements in the Keewatin, the largest of them being Rankin Inlet (population 1,400), established in 1955 on the west shore of Hudson Bay as a nickel mine. The mine closed after seven years, and Rankin Inlet was forced to endure trying times. Today, however, it thrives as an administrative and servicing center. Attractions for visitors include the well-equipped ▶ **Siniktarvik Hotel**, the more modest ▶ **Keewatin Guest Lodge**, and a craft shop featuring *ulus* (Inuit knives), *kamiks* (Inuit boots), and ivory jewelry. A newish visitors' center highlights historical and cultural aspects of the region. Visitors are also welcome at the Inuit Cultural Institute, a research center with a good library. Char-fishing trips by plane and freighter canoe and outings to the Marble Island whaling camps of the 1860s can be arranged at the hotel.

BAKER LAKE

One of the central attractions of the Keewatin is Baker Lake (population 1,000), a vibrant community northwest of Rankin Inlet known in art circles for its carvings and prints depicting the life and heritage of the caribou-hunting Inuit. In canoeing circles it is known as the terminus of wilderness trips down the Thelon, Dubawnt, and Kazan rivers, all considered challenging for their remoteness and harsh, changeable weather. In legal circles, Baker Lake is known as the hamlet that took a mining company to court and got a judgment in 1979 that reaffirmed the concept of aboriginal rights in Canadian law. The community is also known as the home of throat singers Emily Alerk and Lucy Kownak, masters of the art of manipulating the larynx to produce haunting, rhythmic sounds based on noises like the snap of a tent rope in the wind.

Daily flights to Baker Lake are available from Rankin Inlet. Good accommodations and dining are available at the ▶ **Iglu Hotel**, while more modest facilities can be found at the ▶ **Baker Lake Lodge.** Day trips to fishing spots, archaeological sites, and a model Inuit camp showing how life was once lived on the barrenlands can also be arranged in town. The **Thelon Game Sanctuary**, accessible by small plane from

Baker Lake, is a huge preserve for wide-ranging musk-oxen, caribou, and the Barren Ground grizzly. It is also popular with experienced canoeists, who arrange to be flown into the sanctuary and then paddle out. One outfitter that serves the sanctuary is **Great Canadian Ecoventures**, P.O. Box 25181, Winnipeg, Man. R2V 4C8; Tel: (204) 586-4584 or, in the U.S., Tel: (800) 667-WILD.

CORAL HARBOUR

Although expensive to reach because of its remote location on Southampton Island at the mouth of Hudson Bay, Coral Harbour (population 475) offers the chance to see beluga whales and walrus colonies. Highlights include the archaeological remains some 97 km (60 miles) distant (by boat) at **Native Point**, a sweeping ridge dotted with whalebone houses and stone graves that once was home to perhaps a thousand Sallirmiut Inuit, most of whom were wiped out by disease brought by European whalers in 1899. The village can be reached by plane or boat from Rankin Inlet. Accommodations are available at the clean, comfortable, and homey ► **Leonie's Place**, which can accommodate up to 12 people in six rooms.

THE ARCTIC COAST

The mainland Arctic Coast was one of the last regions of the Northwest Territories to be explored, and is still not heavily travelled. Botanists have recorded more than 1,100 varieties of plants in the region, and ornithologists have sighted 180 bird species, many of which nest in the expansive **Queen Maud Bird Sanctuary**. Canoeists know the area for its four challenging wilderness rivers: the Back, Burnside, Coppermine, and Hood. Tour operators offer flying excursions of the region, lasting a weekend to a week, as well as hunting trips for polar bears and musk-oxen. Caribou hunts can be arranged through local hunters and trappers associations.

CAMBRIDGE BAY

Cambridge Bay (population 1,000), on Victoria Island due north of Regina, Saskatchewan, is the regional capital, and is well known locally for a co-op fish plant that processes 110,000 pounds of Arctic char annually. Lying half-sunken in the harbor is the *Maud,* once used by Roald Amundsen and later sold to the Hudson's Bay Company. The settlement, which is served by scheduled flights from Edmonton and Yellowknife, acts as gateway to the six other settlements of the region. The ► **Ikaluktutiak Cambridge Bay Hotel** here accommodates up to 44 people in 22 rooms.

BATHURST INLET

A settlement of particular interest in the region is Bathurst Inlet, which has been occupied by successive Inuit cultures for thousands of years. The small community (population 60), one of the few in which Inuit carry on much as they did before contact with whites, has served as a trading post and mineral-exploration camp but has never developed into an established settlement. In 1969 the abandoned Hudson's Bay Company store and several other buildings were renovated by Glenn and Trish Warner of Yellowknife; the resulting ► **Bathurst Inlet Lodge** quickly acquired a reputation as a naturalists' haven, and today features Inuit help and a visiting scientist-in-residence. The lodge accommodates groups of visitors one week at a time for six weeks, from the end of June to mid-August. Sights include the local church, insulated with 300 caribou skins, and thundering **Wilberforce Falls**, the highest waterfall north of the Arctic Circle.

YELLOWKNIFE AND THE MACKENZIE VALLEY
Yellowknife

Yellowknife, due north of Edmonton, Alberta, on the northern shore of Great Slave Lake, is a city of 12,000 people, two struggling gold mines, and three thriving governments—municipal, territorial, and federal—all paying generous travel and housing subsidies, as well as salaries that are generally higher than in southern Canada. And while the pioneering past is still evident in the pace of life here, Yellowknife is a growing city, and is gradually replacing Edmonton as the gateway to the north. Hand-me-down shacks without running water fill the nooks and crannies of Old Town, while high-rise office and apartment buildings shape the skyline. The local population is a mix of old prospectors, dog mushers, miners, bush pilots, small-business people, architects, politicians, civil servants, and lawyers. The city possesses contrast, color, and a slightly invigorating tension in what might otherwise seem a dreary spot on the Precambrian shield. Yellowknife is also the main crossroads for people from around the territories, including representatives on the Northwest Territories legislative council, whose 24 elected members debate in nine simultaneously interpreted languages. The council usually meets for two to four weeks in February and October at chambers in downtown Yellowknife.

The city got its name from a local Indian group, the Yellowknives, now extinct and so named because they were using utensils of yellowish metal when explorer Samuel Hearne encountered them in 1770. The metal was copper, but the name seemed oddly prescient after gold quartz was discovered in 1896. Prospectors passed it up for the more accessible placer gold on the Klondike River in the Yukon, but they returned to erect a tent-and-shack city in the 1930s, where they established mines and a respectable little town. A three-hour bus tour arranged through the visitors' center near City Hall covers most of the historic landmarks, including the stone monument honoring early bush pilots. A two-hour historical walking tour of the Old Town is outlined in the locally available pamphlet "Footloose in Yellowknife."

The territorial museum, the **Prince of Wales Northern Heritage Centre** (open daily except Mondays year-round), stands at the edge of Frame Lake in a modern building designed by Vancouver architect Arthur Erickson. The exhibits, easily covered in half a day, document Yellowknife's beginnings and strongly emphasize the native culture and achievements of the region. One of the most striking exhibits is a moose-skin boat, built a few years ago under the museum's auspices by old-timers from the Dene settlement of Fort Norman, on the banks of the Mackenzie River. The mountain Dene of the area habitually built such boats in springtime to transport their winter fur catch to the trading post, and museum curators wanted one made before the knowledge of how to do so was lost. The construction was fully documented in the video and still photographs that accompany the display. Lunch can be purchased in summer in a large skylit room upstairs.

A social highlight of the year is the **Folk on the Rocks** music festival at nearby Long Lake in July. Native crafts from throughout the territories are available at **Northern Images** in the Yellowknife Mall, and Dene products at **Treeline Trappings** on Franklin Avenue. The **Book Cellar**, in the prominent new Panda Two mall, carries a wide selection of titles of local and regional interest.

STAYING AND DINING IN YELLOWKNIFE

The three main downtown hotels—the ▶ **Discovery Inn**, the ▶ **Explorer Hotel**, and the ▶ **Yellowknife Inn**—are busy, well equipped, and centrally located. They and the city's major restaurants regularly feature northern specialties, including Arctic char and whitefish—and sometimes musk-ox and caribou. For more conventional cuisine try the seafood crêpes at **Our Place Lounge and Restaurant** (50th Avenue and 50th Street; Tel: 403/920-2265) or the pasta at **Giorgio's Bistro** (5022 47th Street; Tel: 403/920-2754). In summer the refurbished log-built **Wildcat Café**, on Wyley Road in Old Town, is a must for its home-style cooking and friendly, frontier ambience.

In keeping with northern tradition, Yellowknife also has an active bar culture. No visit to Yellowknife is complete without a beer at the low-slung **Gold Range Hotel Bar**, with its crowded tables and country-rock bands.

EXCURSIONS FROM YELLOWKNIFE

Although the scenery on any of the roads leading out of Yellowknife is generally confined to stubby trees and rock outcroppings, there are a variety of worthwhile activities to choose from, from a daytime excursion and hike to Cameron Falls for a swim and picnic to an evening drive along the Ingraham Trail for a meal at the **Prelude Lake Lodge** (also a good fishing and camping spot, with motorboats and cabins available for overnight or extended stays). Float planes are available for hire to outlying lakes (of which there are hundreds) and lodges, while boat excursions on **Great Slave Lake**, one of the largest, deepest lakes in the world, are offered by a variety of outfitters. The best-equipped boat is the M.V. *Norweta,* a 103-foot cruise vessel offering deluxe accommodations for up to 20 people on five-day excursions to the lake's scenic East Arm, as well as weekend and evening cruises. For reservations, call the N.W.T. Marine Group, Tel: (403) 873-4686. For information on area outfitters, contact the Northwest Territories tourism office at (800) 661-0788.

Mackenzie Valley

The Dene settlements in the Mackenzie River Valley are not well equipped to receive vacationers, with the exception of **Fort Simpson** (population 1,000), west of Yellowknife, which has good accommodations (including the ▶ Nahanni Inn) and dining facilities, and to a lesser extent Fort Liard. Both are on the Liard Highway. The mighty Mackenzie River itself runs north from Great Slave Lake, past Fort Simpson, and eventually empties into the Beaufort Sea. The **Liard Highway**, one of three routes entering the western territories, branches off from the Alaska Highway at Fort Nelson in northern British Columbia and runs north through the Dene settlement of **Fort Liard** (population 400), known for its birch-bark baskets, past the eastern end of the Nahanni National Park Reserve, and through Blackstone Park campgrounds to Fort Simpson, where the pope held Mass for Canada's native peoples in 1987. From there you can drive east along the **Mackenzie Highway** to Yellowknife. You can also drive to Yellowknife from Edmonton, Alberta, passing the town of Hay River (population 3,000). Both routes are cut twice a year during freezing and breakup at the Mackenzie River crossing opposite Fort Providence. The third motor route into the territories is the **Dempster Highway** to Inuvik (covered in the Yukon section, below).

The Mackenzie region is great fishing country, and most of its lodges attract fishermen. The ▶ **Moraine Point Lodge** on Great Slave Lake, accessible from Yellowknife and Hay River, offers the kind of wilderness experience many travellers go to the High Arctic for. One of its owners is Yellowknife biologist Bill Carpenter, who during the 1970s was almost solely responsible for reintroducing purebred Canadian Eskimo dogs to Inuit communities. The lodge's peak season is February to mid-April, and activities include dog mushing, cross-country skiing, ice fishing, and the stalking of moose, caribou, wolves, and wood bison. Summer activities include kayaking, swimming, hiking, and bird-watching.

The Mackenzie region also attracts wilderness canoeists. The most popular river is the South Nahanni, which runs through the **Nahanni National Park Reserve**, recognized by UNESCO as a World Heritage site. The park is memorable for tumultuous Virginia Falls, narrow canyons, and stories of headless corpses, said to be those of prospectors seeking a lost gold mine. For further information, contact the park superintendent, Tel: (403) 695-3151. Further information on canoeing the South Nahanni and other rivers in the region can be obtained by calling the Nahanni–Ram Tourism Association at (403) 695-3178 or 3555.

THE YUKON

Tourism based on its majestic mountain wilderness and a fascination with the 1898 Klondike gold rush is the Yukon's number-one industry.

Unlike the Northwest Territories, the Yukon has roads—breathtakingly scenic roads—and is an ideal destination for

owners of recreational vehicles. Motorists can reach the
territory over Highway 37, the **Stewart-Cassiar Highway**,
which cuts through northwestern British Columbia, or over
the more popular, better-serviced **Alaska Highway**, which
officially begins at Dawson Creek, British Columbia, halfway
up its eastern border with Alberta. Once in the Yukon,
ambitious motorists can continue north all the way to the
Mackenzie River mouth in the northwest corner of the
Northwest Territories on the **Dempster Highway**. They can
also drive to Alaska, either along the foot of the St. Elias
Mountains from Whitehorse through Haines Junction on the
Alaska Highway, or west along the **Top of the World Highway** from Dawson City in west-central Yukon. The excellent
commercial guidebook *Milepost,* available in the travel sections of most good bookstores, gives a mile-by-mile description of all Yukon highways, including roads leading into the
territory from British Columbia, Alberta, and the Northwest
Territories, and is an invaluable source of information for
anyone planning to tour the Yukon by car or RV.

Scheduled ferries carrying passengers and vehicles con-
nect Seattle, Vancouver, and Prince Rupert (on the coast of
British Columbia) with the Alaskan ports of Haines and
Skagway, both gateways to the Yukon. For airline passengers,
there is daily jet service to Whitehorse from Vancouver and
Edmonton.

Yukon visitors are well served between mid-May and mid-
September by reception centers in the six main communities. Yukon Gold, a visitor radio station at 96.1 FM, broadcasts
historical programs and news of special events from 9:00 A.M.
to 9:00 P.M. daily. Free vacation catalogues and maps are
available from Yukon Tourism, P.O. Box 2703, Whitehorse,
Yukon, Y1A 2C6; Tel: (403) 667-5340; Fax: (403) 667-2634.

MAJOR INTEREST

White Pass & Yukon Railroad
Chilkoot Trail
Historic Skagway, Alaska
Whitehorse and environs
Cruises on the Yukon River
Carcross on the Tagish Loop
Historic Dawson City
Dempster Highway to Inuvik in the far north
Kluane National Park and St. Elias Mountains

A dour and determined Scot named Robert Campbell opened
the Yukon to the British fur trade in the early 1840s, exploring

the Liard, Pelly, and Yukon rivers for the Hudson's Bay Company, which had been anxious about encroaching traders from what was then Russian-controlled Alaska.

It was gold that put the Yukon on the map, however. An Indian prospector from Carcross named Skookum Jim made the greatest gold strike in history on August 17, 1896, when he knelt for a drink of water in Rabbit Creek, a tributary of the Klondike River near the site of what is today Dawson City. Jim ran to tell his partners, Tagish Charlie and George Carmack, that he had seen slabs of gold in the creek bed. "Then, as near as I can remember," Carmack, a white man originally from California, later recalled, "three full-grown men tried to see how big damn fools they could make of themselves. We did a dance ... composed of a Scotch hornpipe, Indian fox-trot, syncopated Irish jig, and a sort of a Siwash hula-hula." They renamed the creek Bonanza and set off to tell the world.

Tens of thousands of people headed north, most of them by steamer up the British Columbia coast to Skagway, Alaska, and then over the rugged Coast Mountains by foot and mule through either White Pass or the even tougher **Chilkoot Pass**. Long lines of humanity stretched from horizon to horizon, bent double under their supplies, as they negotiated the mountains. Once safely over, they floated down a series of rivers and lakes to the mud flats where Dawson was fast expanding at the confluence of the Klondike and Yukon rivers. One of the most outstanding personages of the day was Sam Steele, superintendent of the North West Mounted Police. He and a hundred men imposed safety regulations and civil law, staking the territory for Canada and ensuring a certain orderliness amid the chaos.

The next group to stampede into the area was the U.S. Army, in 1942. Fearing invasion by the Japanese army via Alaska, the American military built a highway (today called the Alaska Highway) from Dawson Creek, British Columbia, through the southern Yukon to Fairbanks, Alaska, in just nine months. "The Road to Tokyo," as the soldiers called it, was 1,500 miles of track through virgin sub-Arctic wilderness. Whitehorse, along the route, was transformed almost overnight from a town of 500 people to a construction hub for 30,000 workers. The Japanese never came.

By 1982 all of the Yukon's major mines had closed because of low prices for zinc, lead, silver, and copper (some of the mines have since reopened, and the economy has stabilized). The main challenge to Yukoners now is to create a social system that achieves the difficult balance of economic growth, wilderness preservation, and the rebuilding of the native community after the disruptions of the gold rush and the highway boom. Of the 27,000 people resident in the territory, about 6,000 are native. The Council for Yukon Indians has negotiated a land-rights agreement with the federal and Yukon governments that, if ratified by the region's 14 individual bands, will give Yukon natives $232 million in compensation and partial control over 16,000 square miles of land, a deal that is expected to bring economic benefits to the entire Yukon.

The White Pass & Yukon Railroad

The train through historic White Pass from Skagway, Alaska, is a spectacular way to enter the Yukon, and offers an almost mandatory side trip for visitors arriving from other directions. Passengers ride in luxurious old parlor cars along a narrow-gauge line built between 1898 and 1900 to ease travel over one of the most treacherous segments of the route to the gold fields.

The trip begins in Skagway, climbing past panoramic vistas, Bridal Falls, and over Deadhorse Gulch, where 3,000 packhorses and mules died under the ruthless ambitions of gold stampeders. The train continues to White Pass Summit, 2,865 feet above sea level near the Canada–U.S. border, then descends the other side to Fraser, British Columbia. From there, passengers have a choice. They can ride the train back to Skagway, or continue by bus to Carcross and Whitehorse, the Yukon capital. The Skagway round trip takes three hours, and runs twice daily between the third week of May and the third week of September. The trip between Skagway and Whitehorse takes six and a half hours, and is offered once daily from either direction.

The railway also serves hikers of the popular **Chilkoot Trail**, which begins near Skagway and rises over the Chilkoot Pass to Bennett, British Columbia. The spectacular trail was carved out by gold stampeders before the railway was finished and takes about four days to cover. People of all ages do the trail every year. Backpacking experience is not important, although fitness is essential. From Lake Bennett, the train takes hikers to Fraser to board the train back to Skagway or the bus to Whitehorse.

Skagway, Alaska

Skagway, the northernmost port on Alaska's Inside Passage, evolved from a camp with a single log cabin in 1897 to a staging center for thousands of gold seekers one year later.

Soon known as the toughest town in America, it came under the control of a bland, smiling hooligan named Soapy Smith, who prospered through gambling, prostitution, hijacking, theft, and murder before finally being gunned down on the Skagway docks. Today Skagway's carefully renovated buildings and boardwalks give travellers a flavor of those gold-rush days.

Skagway is also a starting point for the White Pass & Yukon Railroad and the **Golden Circle Route**, one of the north's most scenic and historic drives. Covering 576 km (357 miles), it runs north through Carcross to Whitehorse, west to Haines Junction, then south to Haines, Alaska, where a ferry picks up motorists for the final leg back to Skagway. Among the attractions are the White Pass summit and Deadhorse Gulch.

Whitehorse

Whitehorse, in the south-central Yukon north of Skagway, began as a staging ground for gold seekers emerging through White Pass and intent on descending the Yukon River to the Klondike. With a population of 19,000, it is the largest urban center in the Canadian North, as well as the Yukon's capital and a crossroads for travellers between Alaska, British Columbia, historic Dawson City, and Inuvik, in the Northwest Territories at the mouth of the Mackenzie. Although hotel accommodations are generally plentiful in the Yukon, advance bookings are recommended in summer, especially in July. In Whitehorse, the best are the ▶ **Edgewater Hotel** and the ▶ **Best Western Gold Rush Inn** on Main Street, and the ▶ **Westmark Whitehorse Hotel** on Wood Street.

From early June to mid-September nightly performances of the Frantic Follies featuring skits and cancan dancing are staged at the Westmark Whitehorse. A two-hour boat cruise can be taken through the once-dangerous rapids of **Miles Canyon**; cruises are offered twice daily from June 15 to August 15 and once a day from June 1 to June 15 on the M.V. *Schwatka,* which holds up to 40 passengers and can be booked by calling (403) 668-4716.

The stern-wheeler S.S. *Klondike,* launched in 1937, is on display downtown and creates a focus for Yukon River history. The Yukon Historical and Museums Association offers free guided walking tours of downtown Whitehorse; guided bus tours are also available, and the Yukon Conservation Society provides guided nature walks in the area. The **Mac-Bride Museum**, at First Avenue and Wood Street downtown, is worth visiting for its gold-rush collection and stuffed Yukon animals.

Outside town there are opportunities to pan for gold, ride horses, and eat fresh barbecued salmon while listening to the works of Robert Service, a figure whose legacy is difficult to avoid here. Service is celebrated as the Bard of the Klondike for entertaining, if not particularly literary, poems such as "The Law of the Yukon," "The Shooting of Dan McGrew," and "The Cremation of Sam McGee." **Takhini Hot Springs**, often crowded on long weekends but easily accessible most other times, is a 20-minute car ride to the north. To get there, take the Alaska Highway out of town, bear right on the Klondike Highway heading north, and continue on for 8 km (5 miles) until you see the turnoff for the springs.

Full details on how to enjoy Whitehorse and its surroundings are available at the **Whitehorse Visitor Reception Centre**, 302 Steele Street, one block north of Main Street (Tel: 403/667-7545). The center is open from 8:00 A.M. to 8:00 P.M., mid-May to mid-September, and provides information on shopping, accommodations, restaurants, and local events. (See also the Accommodations Reference list at the end of the chapter.)

CARCROSS

An easy side trip from Whitehorse is the **Tagish Loop**: south on the Klondike Highway to Carcross, east along the Atlin Road, and back to Whitehorse along the Alaska Highway. The 160-km (100-mile) trip takes you through the scenic lake district of southern Yukon, and is easily covered in an afternoon. **Carcross** (population 150) is home to the **Matthew Watson General Store**, established in 1911, and the ▶ **Caribou Hotel**, a year-round full-service hotel in operation since 1910. An old steamboat and tiny locomotive are also on display, but of greater historical significance are the graves in the overgrown cemetery of Skookum Jim, Tagish Charlie, and George Carmack— discoverers of the Klondike goldfields.

Dawson City

Re-creating for visitors some idea of the place as it existed in gold-rush days, the Canadian parks system has done much to restore the luster of Dawson City (population 1,500) that was lost to time and shifting permafrost. Local characters colorfully play out personal myths in prospector hats and dungarees. Commemorative stamps can be purchased at a post office dating from 1901; the **Gaslight Follies revue** is staged nightly at the reconstructed Palace Grand Theatre; gambling is legal at **Diamond Tooth Gertie's Gambling Hall**; period fashions are on sale at the historic Madame Tremblay's Store; and readings from his works are held at Robert Service's old cabin. A cabin that was once home to American writer Jack London is also open to visitors, but, oddly, another historic building has been overlooked by Parks Canada. It stands near the Service cabin—paint peeling, boardwalk overgrown, the only hint of its significance a sign saying "Berton home." It is the boyhood home of author and broadcaster Pierre Berton, one of Canada's most prolific writers and the son of an 1898 stampeder. Berton's mother, Laura, wrote the book *I Married the Klondike*—based mostly on her years in this house. Local arts groups are raising money to buy and renovate the house with a view to renting it free of charge to an annually chosen writer-in-residence.

Among the annual special events in Dawson City is the **Commissioner's Ball** in June, a dance at the Palace Grand Theatre thrown by the head of the Yukon government to which revellers come in period dress. **Discovery Days** in mid-August marks Skookum Jim's historic find with a parade, canoe races, and dances. The Great Klondike Outhouse Race through town in early September features a bizarre competition of outhouses on wheels.

Hotels are varied and plentiful. The four main ones are the ► **Downtown Hotel**, the ► **Eldorado Hotel**, the ► **Midnight Sun Hotel**, and the ► **Westmark Klondike**. (See the Accommodations Reference list at the end of the chapter for room rates and booking information.)

DEMPSTER HIGHWAY

Beginning near Dawson City, the all-weather, gravel-surfaced Dempster Highway runs 717 km (445 miles) north through sub-Arctic bush and over Arctic tundra to Inuvik, in the Northwest Territories. The wide-open scenery along the way is spectacular, but it is not a road for amateurs or the unprepared: There is only one service stop in the 300 miles between Dawson City and the Dene settlement of Fort McPherson (population 700) in the Northwest Territories.

Inuvik

Inuvik (population 3,200), built in 1954 as a regional government center, was developed during the 1970s into a supply base for oil exploration in the Beaufort Sea. Development of offshore reserves is on hold pending a change in world oil prices, but Inuvik nevertheless remains a lively town—especially in the 24-hour daylight of midsummer—filled with trappers, pilots, scientists, and entrepreneurs. Good accommodations and dining are available, as are outfitters who will take you to explore the sprawling, labyrinthine Mackenzie River delta. The best hotels are the high-rise ▶ **Eskimo Inn** downtown and the more elegant ▶ **Finto Motor Inn** on the outskirts of town.

Kluane National Park

Kluane is a wilderness park embracing the St. Elias Mountains as well as Canada's highest peak, Mount Logan (19,850 feet). Moose, grizzly bears, mountain goats, Dall sheep, and caribou roam here unthreatened by hunters, and 150 species of birds have been recorded, including the rare peregrine falcon. Conditions and regulations for serious adventurers are rigorous, but casual visitors have easy access to day trails, one of the most memorable being the hike up Sheep Mountain near Haines Junction, where hikers can approach to within a few yards of docile big-horned Dall sheep. Kluane has been recognized as a United Nations World Heritage site, and access to it is strictly controlled from park headquarters in Haines Junction, 154 km (95 miles) west of Whitehorse. Information about overnight stays in the park and other regulations can be obtained by calling park headquarters at (403) 634-2251; Fax (403) 634-2686.

GETTING AROUND

Visitors to the Northwest Territories are wise to prepare for unexpected changes in weather. Visitors to the Yukon can usually rely on semi-arid summer weather and average temperatures around 57° F (14° C).

Transportation routes to the Northwest Territories and Yukon tend to run north–south. Montreal and Ottawa are the air gateways to the **Baffin region**, with direct flights to Iqaluit. Flights from Ottawa serve the west coast of Baffin Island, while flights from Montreal serve Resolute Bay, sometimes with stops at Hall Beach on the Melville Peninsula, or Nanisivik at the western end of Baffin Island. All settlements in the region can be reached by regularly scheduled flights, the main jump-off points being Iqaluit and Resolute Bay.

Direct flights from Winnipeg serve Rankin Inlet, capital of the **Keewatin**, and regularly scheduled flights from Rankin Inlet serve the other Keewatin communities. In an exception to the north-south rule, Rankin Inlet can also be reached directly from Iqaluit to the east and Yellowknife to the west.

Edmonton is the air gateway to the **Mackenzie River Valley** and **western Arctic**, with direct flights to Yellowknife.

Passengers from Edmonton can also reach Fort Smith, Hay River, Fort Simpson, Norman Wells, Inuvik, Cambridge Bay, and Resolute Bay without changing planes. The regional centers are: Yellowknife, serving the Great Slave area, the Mackenzie River, and Arctic Coast; Norman Wells, serving nearby Mackenzie River communities; Inuvik, serving the western Arctic; and Cambridge Bay, local jump-off to the Arctic Coast communities.

Edmonton and Vancouver are the air gateways to Whitehorse, in the **Yukon,** with some flights connecting to Dawson City as well as to Inuvik in the Mackenzie Delta.

In addition, dozens of package tours originate from Montreal, Ottawa, Toronto, Winnipeg, Edmonton, Vancouver, Seattle, and all northern regional centers. Some of them cover giant swaths of territory, others are locally oriented. A complete list of tour operators and outfitters for the Northwest Territories is available from: TravelArctic, Government of the Northwest Territories, Yellowknife, N.W.T., X1A 2L9; Tel: (800) 661-0788. For similar information on the Yukon, contact: Yukon Tourism, P.O. Box 2703, Whitehorse, Yukon, Y1A 2C6; Tel: (403) 667-5340; Fax: (403) 667-2634.

ACCOMMODATIONS REFERENCE

Accommodation standards in the North have changed dramatically for the better in recent years. You will find all—or almost all—the comforts of home in Iqaluit, Yellowknife, Fort Smith, Hay River, Inuvik, Whitehorse, and Dawson City. Visitors are also well served in intermediate-size centers such as Pangnirtung, Cape Dorset, Pond Inlet, Resolute Bay, Rankin Inlet, Baker Lake, and Fort Simpson. In outlying settlements, services generally diminish along with the size of the population. Visitors can be asked to double up, and the cuisine tends to be basic—circumstances that can generate camaraderie and enhance a visit. Rates are in flux at the moment, down in some areas and subject to change almost everywhere as hoteliers respond to the recession. The rates given below are projections *for the summer 1994 season; at other times of the year they may be considerably less. Federal taxes (there is no provincial tax in the northern territories) are included in all rates.*

▶ **Auyuittuq Lodge.** P.O. Box 53, **Pangnirtung,** N.W.T. X0A 0R0. Tel: (819) 473-8955; Fax: (819) 473-8611. $95 per person.

▶ **Baker Lake Lodge.** Baker Lake, N.W.T. X0C 0A0. Tel: (819) 793-2905; Fax: (819) 793-2965. $100.

▶ **Bathurst Inlet Lodge.** P.O. Box 820, 3618 McAvoy, **Yel-**

lowknife, N.W.T. X1A 2N6. Tel: (403) 873-2595; Fax: (403) 920-4263. $3,146 weekly (per person, including three meals and flight to and from Yellowknife).

▶ **Best Western Gold Rush Inn**. 411 Main Street, **Whitehorse**, Yukon Y1A 2B6. Tel: (403) 668-4500 or (800) 528-1234; Fax: (403) 668-7432. $106.

▶ **Caribou Hotel**. P.O. Box 136, **Carcross**, Yukon Y0B 1B0. Tel: (403) 821-4501. $32.

▶ **Discovery Inn**. P.O. Box 784, **Yellowknife**, N.W.T. X1A 2N6. Tel: (403) 873-4151; Fax: (403) 920-7948. $127.

▶ **Discovery Lodge Hotel**. P.O. Box 387, **Iqaluit**, N.W.T. X0A 0H0. Tel: (819) 979-4433; Fax: (819) 979-6591. $198.

▶ **Downtown Hotel**. P.O. Box 780, **Dawson City**, Yukon Y0B 1G0. Tel: (403) 993-5346; Fax: (403) 993-5076. $127.

▶ **Edgewater Hotel**. 101 Main Street, **Whitehorse**, Yukon Y1A 2A7. Tel: (403) 667-2572; Fax: (403) 668-3014. $106–$129; $259 (suites).

▶ **Eldorado Hotel**. P.O. Box 338, **Dawson City**, Yukon Y0B 1G0. Tel: (403) 993-5451; Fax: (403) 993-5256. $123.

▶ **Eskimo Inn**. P.O. Box 1740, **Inuvik**, N.W.T. X0E 0T0. Tel: (403) 979-2801; Fax: (403) 979-3234. $139.

▶ **Explorer Hotel**. Postal Service 7000, **Yellowknife**, N.W.T. X1A 2R3. Tel: (403) 873-3531; Fax: (403) 873-2789. $163.

▶ **Finto Motor Inn**. P.O. Box 1925, **Inuvik**, N.W.T. X0E 0T0. Tel: (403) 979-2647; Fax: (403) 979-3442. $134.

▶ **Frobisher Inn**. P.O. Box 610, **Iqaluit**, N.W.T. X0A 0H0. Tel: (819) 979-2222; Fax: (819) 979-0427. $160.

▶ **Grise Fiord Lodge**. **Grise Fiord**, N.W.T. X0A 0J0. Tel: (819) 980-9913. $177 (per person, all-inclusive).

▶ **Iglu Hotel**. Box 179, **Baker Lake**, N.W.T. X0C 0A0. Tel: (819) 793-2801; Fax: (819) 793-2711. $134 (per person).

▶ **Ikaluktutiak Cambridge Bay Hotel**. P.O. Box 38, **Cambridge Bay**, N.W.T. X0E 0C0. Tel: (403) 983-2215 or 2201; Fax: (403) 983-2215. $150.

▶ **International Explorer's Home**. P.O. Box 200, **Resolute Bay**, N.W.T. X0A 0V0. Tel: (819) 252-3875; Fax: (819) 252-3766. $140 (per person, including accommodations, meals, and airport transportation).

▶ **Keewatin Guest Lodge**. P.O. Box 190, **Rankin Inlet**, N.W.T. X0C 0G0. Tel: (819) 645-2807; Fax: (819) 645-2999. $107 (per person).

▶ **Kingnait Inn**. P.O. Box 89, **Cape Dorset**, N.W.T. X0A 0C0. Tel: (819) 897-8924; Fax: (819) 897-8907. $203 (includes breakfast, lunch, and dinner).

▶ **Leonie's Place**. P.O. Box 29, **Coral Harbour**, N.W.T. X0C 0C0. Tel: (819) 925-9751 or 8810; Fax: (819) 925-8606. $165 (per person, all-inclusive).

► **Midnight Sun Hotel.** P.O. Box 840, **Dawson City**, Yukon Y0B 1G0. Tel: (403) 993-5495; Fax: (604) 993-6425; in winter, Tel. and Fax: (604) 291-2652. $100.

► **Moraine Point Lodge.** P.O. Box 2882, **Yellowknife**, N.W.T. X1A 2R2. Tel: (403) 920-4542 or 873-8249; Fax: (403) 873-4790. $150 (per person, all-inclusive).

► **Nahanni Inn.** P.O. Box 248, **Fort Simpson**, N.W.T. X0E 0N0. Tel: (403) 695-2201; Fax: (403) 695-3000. $123.

► **Narwhal Arctic Services.** P.O. Box 88, **Resolute Bay**, N.W.T. X0A 0V0. Tel: (819) 252-3968; Fax: (819) 252-3960. $195 (per person, all-inclusive).

► **Navigator Inn.** P.O. Box 158, **Iqaluit**, N.W.T. X0A 0H0. Tel: (819) 979-6201; Fax: (819) 979-4296. $165.

► **Sauniq Hotel.** Toonoonik Sahoonik Co-op, **Pond Inlet**, N.W.T. X0A 0S0. Tel: (819) 899-8928; Fax: (819) 899-8770. $183 (per person, all-inclusive).

► **Siniktarvik Hotel.** P.O. Box 190, **Rankin Inlet**, N.W.T. X0C 0G0. Tel: (819) 645-2807; Fax: (819) 645-2999. $141 (per person).

► **Tujormivik Hotel.** Igloolik, N.W.T. X0A 0L0. Tel: (819) 934-8814; Fax: (819) 934-8816. $145 (per person, all-inclusive).

► **Tulugak Co-operative Hotel.** General Delivery, **Broughton Island**, N.W.T. X0A 0B0. Tel: (819) 927-8874; Fax: (819) 927-8124. $200 (per person, all-inclusive).

► **Westmark Klondike.** P.O. Box 420, **Dawson City**, Yukon Y0B 1G0. Tel: (403) 993-5542; Fax: (403) 993-5623. $132–$144.

► **Westmark Whitehorse Hotel.** 201 Wood Street, **Whitehorse**, Yukon Y1A 2E4. Tel: (403) 668-4700; Fax: (403) 668-2789. $95–$158.

► **Yellowknife Inn.** P.O. Box 490, **Yellowknife**, N.W.T. X1A 2N4. Tel: (403) 873-2601; Fax: (403) 873-2602. $170.

CHRONOLOGY OF THE HISTORY OF CANADA

- **A.D. 986**: Bjarni Herjolfsson, sailing from Iceland, misses Greenland and sights the Canadian coast.
- **1000**: Leif Ericsson heads an expedition to Vinland and establishes a settlement at what is now L'Anse aux Meadows, Newfoundland.

France and England in the New World

- **1497**: John Cabot, sailing for England's Henry VII, discovers Canada's east coast—along with its rich fishing grounds.
- **1504**: St. John's, Newfoundland, is established as a base for English fisheries.
- **1534**: Jacques Cartier lands at Gaspé, in Quebec, and claims it for France.
- **1535**: Cartier sails up the St. Lawrence to Hochelaga, now Móntreal, and names the vast territory he has discovered Canada, from the Iroquoian word "kanata," meaning settlement.
- **1577**: Martin Frobisher reaches what is now called the Hudson Strait.
- **1583**: Humphrey Gilbert claims Newfoundland for England, even though fishing vessels from France, Spain, and Portugal are a common sight in the waters around it.
- **1605**: Port Royal (Annapolis, Nova Scotia) is established by the Sieur de Monts and Samuel de Champlain.
- **1608**: Champlain founds the settlement of Quebec and begins his sporadic eight-year exploration of the interior of this vast new country, reaching Georgian Bay.

- **1610**: Etienne Brulé is sent to a Huron village on Georgian Bay in exchange for an Indian who is sent to France.

   Henry Hudson discovers Hudson Bay.

- **1616**: Indian schools are established at Tadoussac and Trois Rivières.

- **1617**: The first Quebec colonist—apothecary Louis Hébert—arrives from Nova Scotia.

- **1639**: The Hôtel Dieu, Canada's first hospital, is established in Quebec.

- **1642**: Ville Marie, later Montreal, is founded by the Sieur de Maisonneuve.

- **1649**: The Jesuit missionaries Jean de Brébeuf and Gabriel Lalemant are burned at the stake by the Iroquois, and their mission among the Hurons on Georgian Bay destroyed.

   The Sieur des Groseilliers and his young brother-in-law, Pierre Radisson, reach Lake Superior and return with 60 canoes full of beaver pelts.

- **1666**: Jean Talon, the colony's first business manager, arrives in Quebec and conducts a census: 3,215 Europeans, including two married couples under the age of 15.

- **1668**: Groseilliers leaves England for Hudson Bay, returning in 1669 with pelts worth £19,000.

- **1670**: With the success of Groseilliers' most recent expedition, the Hudson's Bay Company is founded by Prince Rupert and given title over the vast Hudson Bay watershed.

- **1672**: The Comte de Frontenac is appointed governor of New France, and orders the construction of Fort Frontenac on the site of present-day Kingston, Ontario.

- **1678**: Niagara Falls receives its first white visitor, Father Jean-Louis Hennepin.

- **1713**: France surrenders to Britain any claim to the Hudson Bay region, Newfoundland, and Acadia (including parts of present-day Nova Scotia, New Brunswick, Prince Edward Island, southeastern Quebec, and eastern Maine).

- **1714**: In order to protect what is left of New France, Louis XIV orders the construction of Louisbourg fortress.

- **1734**: The first road between Quebec and Montreal is opened.

- **1749**: Fort Rouillé (later Toronto) is built at the head of the Toronto Trail, the main east–west route to the fur-rich lands bordering Georgian Bay.

Edward Cornwallis, the new governor of Nova Scotia, arrives with 2,000 colonists and founds Halifax. St. Paul's Anglican Church, built the same year, still stands.

- **1755**: Nova Scotia expels all Acadians (settlers of French descent) not swearing allegiance to Britain.
- **1758**: Louisbourg falls to the British.
- **1759**: General Wolfe defeats the Marquis de Montcalm on the Plains of Abraham outside Quebec City, effectively ending France's role as a New World power.
- **1763**: France and Spain cede to Britain all territory east of the Mississippi River except the islands of St. Pierre and Miquelon.

Building a Nation

- **1774**: The Quebec Act establishes nonrepresentative government and makes provisions for freedom of worship in what was formerly New France. At the same time, the act's extension of Quebec's borders into the Ohio region angers New England colonists (who covet the region themselves) and pushes the colonies closer to a break with England.
- **1775**: Outbreak of the American Revolution. American colonists, concerned the British might use it as a base of operations, lay siege to Quebec.
- **1778**: Captain Cook lands on Vancouver Island and claims the Pacific coast north of the 48th parallel for Britain.
- **1783–1784**: Following Britain's defeat, some 40,000 to 60,000 United Empire Loyalists emigrate to Canada. Most settle in what is now New Brunswick, although 5,000 or so make their homes along the St. Lawrence, Lake Ontario's Bay of Quinte, and the Niagara and Detroit rivers.
- **1789**: Sir Alexander Mackenzie reaches the Beaufort Sea by following the river that will later bear his name.
- **1793**: The importation of slaves into Upper Canada is outlawed.
- **1803**: The first paper mill is established near Lachute, Quebec.
- **1807**: David Thompson, noted mapmaker, crosses the Rockies; Simon Fraser travels 800 miles from the source of the Fraser River to the Pacific.

- **1811**: In eastern Ontario John McIntosh finds and transplants an apple tree from which his son Allan later develops the McIntosh apple.

  The Red River settlement, western Canada's first, is founded near present-day Winnipeg by Lord Selkirk and 12,000 Irish and Scottish pioneers.
- **1812**: The newly confederated United States of America declares war against Britain and is defeated at Detroit and Niagara by troops led by Sir Isaac Brock.
- **1813**: To warn of another American attack at Niagara, Laura Secord walks 19 miles through dense bush with her cow.
- **1824**: The first medical school in Canada opens in Montreal, and later becomes part of McGill University.
- **1829**: The Welland (linking lakes Ontario and Erie) and Lachine (bypassing the St. Lawrence River near Montreal) canals open.
- **1832**: The Rideau Canal linking Lake Ontario and the Ottawa River is opened.
- **1837**: Rebellions in Lower and Upper Canada against the ruling establishments. Lord Durham leaves England to act as governor.
- **1839**: Durham's report to the Colonial Office criticizes the ruling cliques and recommends self-government and the union of the two Canadas.
- **1841**: Canada's first Parliament convenes in Kingston.
- **1844**: In Nova Scotia, Charles Fenerty discovers how to make paper from ground wood pulp. George Brown, age 26, publishes the first issue of the *Toronto Globe* as a weekly Liberal paper; it goes daily in 1853.
- **1846**: Irish-born and U.S.-bred Reverend William King establishes the Elgin Settlement for escaped slaves on the shores of Lake St. Clair, opposite Detroit.
- **1847**: Lord Elgin arrives as governor-general, with instructions to give responsible government a fair trial.
- **1857**: Queen Victoria chooses Bytown (later Ottawa) as the capital of Canada.
- **1858**: Gold is found in the Fraser River Valley (British Columbia).
- **1859**: Tariffs are established to help manufacturers compete in their home market.
- **1864**: The "Fathers of Confederation" meet at Charlottetown, Prince Edward Island, October 10–27, and

in London, December 4, to pass resolutions for the British North America Act.

- **1866–1867:** Fenian raids (militant Irish-Americans angry with Britain).
- **1867:** On July 1, Nova Scotia, New Brunswick, Quebec, and Ontario unite to become the Dominion of Canada, with Sir John A. Macdonald the first prime minister. Toronto schoolteacher Alexander Muir writes "The Maple Leaf Forever" for his pupils and, for $30, has 1,000 copies printed. It is soon pirated by a music publisher.

  The age-old Indian game of field lacrosse becomes Canada's national game by law. It still is.
- **1869:** Outbreak of the Red River Rebellion, an uprising of the Métis (Canadians of mixed French and Indian descent) out west under the leadership of Louis Riel. After a second rebellion in 1885, Riel is executed. (See the Manitoba and Saskatchewan chapters.)
- **1875:** The Canadian Supreme Court is established.
- **1885:** Last spike driven for Canadian Pacific's transcontinental railway at Craigellachie, British Columbia.
- **1896:** Gold is discovered in the Klondike, touching off the last of the great gold rushes.
- **1900:** The economy of Canada booms; thousands of Europeans accept the government's offer of free land out West.
- **1901:** Marconi receives the first transatlantic wireless message at St. John's, Newfoundland.
- **1903:** Fred LaRose, blacksmith, accidentally discovers the world's richest silver deposit in Cobalt, Ontario, and starts a mining stampede.
- **1909:** J.A.D. McCurdy's Silver Dart completes Canada's first flight of a self-propelled heavier-than-air machine.
- **1914:** Oil is discovered at Turner Valley, near Calgary.

On the World Stage

- **1914–1918:** Canada, with a population of eight million, joins Great Britain and other members of the British Empire in declaring war on Germany. By war's end, fatalities total 62,224; casualties, 174,623. During the same period, the national debt increases by $2 billion, requiring the temporary imposition of an income tax. The income tax stays, but many other aspects of Canadian life change: The economy expands and becomes more diversified; the country's prestige is enhanced and national spirit strengthened; relations between the French- and English-speaking populations are damaged.

- **1917**: Women get the vote in federal elections.

  The collision of munitions and supply ships in Halifax harbor results in an explosion that kills 2,000 and injures 9,000 people.

- **1923**: The world's first hockey broadcast is made by Foster Hewitt from a telephone booth in Toronto.

- **1926**: At the Imperial Conference in London, Prime Minister Mackenzie King asks for Canadian independence, and the Balfour Declaration recognizes the autonomy of all members of the Commonwealth. This status for Canada is codified in 1931 with the passing of the Statute of Westminster. Among other changes, the governor-general becomes a representative of the sovereign rather than a mere appointee of the Colonial Office.

- **1934**: The Dionne quintuplets, the first quintuplets to survive more than a few hours, are born near Callander, Ontario.

- **1938**: In Kingston, Ontario, Prime Minister King greets Franklin Roosevelt, the first U.S. president to visit Canada.

- **1939–1946**: Canada declares war on Germany in September of 1939, and by December has landed troops in Great Britain. More than one million men and women enlist in the three services, of whom 42,042 are killed and 54,414 wounded, considerably fewer than in World War I. The financial cost, on the other hand, is an astronomical $21.8 billion. By war's end, Canada's status as an independent country is unassailable.

- **1947**: Oil is discovered at Leduc, Alberta.

- **1949**: Newfoundland and Labrador becomes the tenth province of Canada.

- **1961**: A national program for health insurance goes into effect.

- **1965**: The red maple leaf becomes the official flag.

- **1967**: On July 7, French President Charles de Gaulle visits Montreal and declares, "Vive le Québec libre!" The remark so offends the prime minister and federal government that de Gaulle is compelled to return home without having visited Ottawa.

- **1969**: Parliament decides that Canada should adopt the metric system of weights and measures.

- **1970**: The FLQ (Front de Libération Québecois)

kidnaps Pierre Laporte, Quebec minister of labor, and leaves his body in the trunk of a car; the War Measures Act is declared and 500 people eventually arrested.

- **1976**: Montreal hosts the summer Olympic games, Canada's first.

  Led by René Lévesque, the Parti Québecois, which advocates independence for Quebec, wins a majority in the National Assembly. In the 1980 referendum, 60 percent of Quebeckers vote to remain in Canada.

- **1978**: Spanish galleons dating to the 16th century are discovered in the icy waters off Red Bay, Labrador.

- **1982**: Canada gains a new Constitution, the Charter of Rights and Freedoms.

- **1986**: Expo 86 in Vancouver, British Columbia, attracts 22 million visitors.

- **1988**: The Winter Olympics are held in Calgary, Alberta.

- **1989**: On January 1, a Free Trade Agreement with the United States, signed in 1988, becomes law. By 1998 all tariffs between the two countries are to be phased out.

- **1990**: The Meech Lake constitutional accord fails to gain approval from all ten provinces, leaving Quebec a non-signatory to the Canadian constitution. To keep the country intact, discussions aimed at the redistribution of powers between federal and provincial governments continue.

- **1991**: The Canadian government announces an agreement, in principle, creating a new political territory out of the eastern two-thirds of the Northwest Territories. The new territory, to be known as Nunavut, an Inuit term meaning "our land," would, when approved, grant land rights and political control over the region to its 17,500 Inuit inhabitants.

- **1992**: In October, a referendum on a new constitutional arrangement granting "special status" to Quebec and increased autonomy for Canada's native peoples is soundly defeated.

- **1993**: Having all necessary approval for creation of Nunavut, Parliament passes necessary legislation. The new territory will not appear on a map until 1999, the time needed by the Inuit for preparation to run the new government. In June, Kim Campbell becomes the first woman prime minister as well as the first from British Columbia.

—Jean Danard

INDEX

*H*ere's what others say...

"As a longtime reader of *Passport*, I trust it as a source of intelligence and ideas on independent travel."

Alan Deutschman
Associate Editor
Fortune Magazine

"The best little newsletter in America."
Crain's Chicago Business

"*Passport* has been appearing for more than 20 years with a brisk, colorful roundup of travel information. Substance prevails over style."
National Geographic Traveler

"In *Passport*, I consistently find the kind of information I want from a travel newsletter—sophisticated, concise and straightforward, without a lot of ego to get in the way."
Travel Editor
Town and Country Magazine

"*T*he first and unquestionably the best luxury travel newsletter."
Alan Tucker, General Editor
Berlitz Travellers Guides
"

*S*ince 1965, *Passport*, the monthly letter for discriminating travelers, has revealed hard-to-find information about the world's best destinations. Return this card for a free issue or call 800-542-6670. Available worldwide!

Please send a free issue of *Passport* to:

Name _____

Address _____

City _____ State _____ Zip _____

"*This* is the granddaddy of travel letters... *Passport* emphasizes culture, comfort, and quality...it can glow with praise, or bite with disapproval."

Condé Nast Traveler